# SECRETS OF THE

# Dead Sea Scrolls

## Dr. Randall Price

Harvest House Publishers
Eugene, Oregon 97402

Cover by Terry Dugan Design, Minneapolis, Minnesota.

For a catalog of other works by Dr. Randall Price, to schedule him for a conference or speaking engagement, or to join one of his annual tours to the Bible Lands, please contact:

**World of the Bible Ministries, Inc.**
110 Easy Street
San Marcos, Texas 78666-7336

(512) 396-3799    FAX (512) 396-1012
E-mail: wmbrandl@itouch.net

**SECRETS OF THE DEAD SEA SCROLLS**

Copyright © 1996 by World of the Bible Ministries, Inc.
Published by Harvest House Publishers
Eugene, Oregon 97402

Library of Congress Cataloging-in-Publication Data

Price, Randall
    Secrets of the Dead Sea scrolls / Randall Price.
        p.   cm.
    Includes bibliographical references.
    ISBN 1–56507–454–8
    1. Dead Sea scrolls—Criticism, interpretation, etc.   I. Title.
BM487.P85  1996
296.1'55—dc20                                                                                    96-10719
                                                                                                              CIP

**Printed in the United States of America.**

96    97    98    99    00    01    02    /    BF    /    10    9    8    7    6    5    4    3    2

In memory of

**Jonas C. Greenfield**

Dead Sea scholar,
professor, and friend
*One of his last acts
of kindness was
for me.*

To

**Edvin & Mamie Rollack**

and

**Paul & Tracy Streber**

*who gave of their
substance and themselves
to help our family
and give fortitude to our faith*
(2 Corinthians 8:5,9).
*They are forever friends.*

"From the God of knowledge comes all that is and shall be.
Before ever they existed He established their whole design,
and when as ordained for them, they come into being, it is in
accord with His glorious design that they accomplish their
task without change. The laws of all things are in His hand
and He provides them with all their needs."

*Manual of Discipline* 3.15-17

# FOREWORD

The breadth of topics collected and discussed by Randall Price in *Secrets of the Dead Sea Scrolls* is unavailable elsewhere in one volume. For this reason alone, the book makes a significant contribution to the study of the Scrolls.

Dr. Price's account of the discoveries of the Scrolls is fresh, and his publication of interviews with Muhammed edh-Dhib will assist in the quest to know more exactly when, where, how, and by whom the first Scrolls came to light, all questions not as yet settled to everyone's satisfaction.

The description of the "scandal" of the scrolls is fair and gracious, if, necessarily secondhand. Finally, someone has spoken to the right people and come to the right conclusions.

Everywhere, the author tries to be evenhanded: he is primarily out to inform, not polemicize. His own theological background naturally informs his approach to the relationship between the Hebrew Bible and the Scrolls, and likewise, their relationship to the New Testament and Christianity. Yet he has also studied Judaism and lived in Israel, and is both sympathetic to and knowledgeable of other, specifically Jewish, approaches to texts which, after all, were written by Jews for Jews.

Readers may not agree entirely with every opinion and proposition of the book, but they will not be able to escape the general impression that the author made the effort to talk to and use the best sources available, and is himself conversant with the wide scope of literature encompassed by the Scrolls.

Dr. Price has presented the fruits of his research in a way that lay readers will feel welcomely invited into the sometimes arcane world of Scrolls scholarship, and perhaps even become just as addicted to and fascinated by the Scrolls as are many of us who have been involved in their research and publication at the scholarly level.

I am happy to recommend the *Secrets of the Dead Sea Scrolls*, for I suspect that it is destined to earn a place as one of the primary sources for education of the present generation of Christians in the vast field of research surrounding the Dead Sea Scrolls, the most important archaeological discovery of our time.

Weston W. Fields, Th.D., Ph.D.
Executive Director, *The Dead Seal Scrolls Foundation*
Jerusalem

# JAMES E. REDDEN

# Contents

## Maps, Charts, and Illustrations

# Abbreviations (SIGLA) for the Dead Sea Scrolls Texts Cited

Numerical prefix = number of the cave in which the document was found; numerical suffix = designated sequence; subscript = particular copy of manuscript; Q = Qumran; letter abbreviations following numerical + Q = ascribed title (in English or Hebrew), p = *Pesher* (commentary) + name of book. Columns and lines in Scroll references are usually separated by a colon, but sometimes by a comma (except where several fragments of a text must be numbered separately, e.g., *1Q27 1 2 25* = text 27 from Cave 1, fragment 1, column 2, line 25). Raised lowercase letters attached to Scroll abbreviations = copy of manuscript.

| | |
|---|---|
| *CD* | *Damascus Document/Rule* (first or second copy [A–B] from the Cairo Genizah [primary copy], also called *Damascus Covenant* and *Zadokite Fragments* Qumran copies signified as *4Q266-273, 5Q12, 6Q15*) |
| *1Q20* | *Genesis Apocryphon* (in Aramaic); also *1QapGen* |
| *1QH* | *Thanksgiving Hymns* (or *Hodayot*) |
| *1QIsa*[a,b] | First or second copy of *Great* (or *Large*) *Isaiah Scroll* [primary copy] (other copies *4Q55-69*) |
| *1QM/1Q33* | *War Scroll* (*Meggillat ha-Milkhamah*) [primary copy], possible lost addition— *4Q285*; also copies *4Q491-496* and possibly *4Q471*; texts connected with *War Scroll 4Q259, 4Q285, 4Q471, 11Q14* |
| *1QpHab* | *Pesher on Habakkuk* or *Habakkuk Commentary* |
| *1QS* | *Rules of the Community* or *Manual of Discipline* (*Serek hay-yahad*); also copies *4Q255-264* and possibly copy *5Q11* |
| *1QS*[a]/*1Q28*[a] | *Rule of the Congregation* or *Messianic Rule* (Appendix A to *1QS*) |
| *1QS*[b] | *Rule of Benediction* or *Blessings* (Appendix B to *1QS*:) |
| *1Q71-72* | Fragmentary copies of the book of Daniel; also copy *6Q7* |
| *3Q15* | *Copper Scroll* |

| | |
|---|---|
| *4QpIs<sup>a</sup>* | *Pesher* on Isaiah |
| *4Q394-399* | (also *4QMMT*)—*Miqsat Ma'aseh Ha-Torah* ("Some Rulings Pertaining to the Torah," also as *Halakhic Letter*) |
| *4Q11,22* | Copies of portions of Genesis and Exodus (in palaeo-Hebrew) |
| *4Q51* | Fragmentary copy of the book of Samuel (considered oldest Qumran manuscript) |
| *4Q157* | *Leviticus Targum* (Aramaic) |
| *4Q169* | *Pesher Nahum* (also, *4QpNah)* |
| *4Q174* | *Florilegium* (or *Eschatalogical Midrashim)* |
| *4Q175* | [*Messianic*] *Testimonia* |
| *4Q177* | *Catena A* (commentary employing eschatological exegesis); also signified as *4QCatena<sup>a</sup>*; second copy *4Q182* (*4QCatena<sup>b</sup>*) |
| *4Q180-181* | *Ages of Creation* (pseudepigraphal text) |
| *4Q243-245* | *Pseudo-Daniel* texts |
| *4Q246* | *Aramaic Apocalypse* or *Son of God* |
| *4Q247* | *Apocalypse of Weeks* (apocryphal Books of Enoch) |
| *4Q252* | *Pesher on Genesis* (also known as *Patriarchal Blessings* [*4QPBless*], and *Genesis Florilegium*) |
| *4Q285* | *Serekh Milhamah* (also known as *Dying* or *Pierced Messiah*) |
| *4Q286-287* | *The Chariots of Glory* |
| *4Q385-388* | *Pseudo-Ezekiel* texts; possibly also *4Q391* |
| *4Q390* | *Angels of Mastemoth and the Rule of Belial* |
| *4Q394-398* | *Halakhic Letter*—popularly signified as *4QMMT<sup>(a-f)</sup>* |
| *4Q448* | *Prayer for King Jonathan* |
| *4Q485* | *War Rule* |
| *4Q521* | *Messianic Apocalypse* |
| *4Q525* | *Beatitudes* |
| *4Q534* | *Elect of God* (or *Messianic Aramaic*) |
| *4Q541* | *4QAaron A* |
| *4Q552-553* | [*Vision of the*] *Four Kingdoms* |

| | |
|---|---|
| *4Q554-555* | *New Jerusalem* (Aramaic); also copies *1Q32, 2Q24; 4Q232, 5Q15,* and *11Q18* |
| *7Q3-19* | Unclassified Greek fragments from Cave 7 (identified by some as portions of the New Testament) |
| *11Q1* | *Leviticus Scroll* (in palaeo-Hebrew); also copy *1Q3* |
| *11Q4* | *Ezekiel Scroll* (partial Hebrew) |
| *11Q12* | Copy of the apocryphal Book of Jubilees |
| *11Q13* | *Melchizedek* (Eschatological *Midrash* of Leviticus 28) |
| *11Q14* | *Blessings* |
| *11Q19* | *Temple Scroll* (*Megillat ham-miqdash*) primary copy [also signified as *11QTemple$^a$* or *11QT*]; second copy *11Q20* (*11QTemple$^b$*) |
| *11QtgJob* | *Targum to Job* (in Aramaic) |

## OTHER ABBREVIATIONS

| | |
|---|---|
| [   ] | square brackets indicate letters supplied for a lacuna or broken text |
| (   ) | parenthesis indicate words enclosed have been added to complete English translation |
| TB/BT/b. | *Babylonian Talmud* (followed by name of the tractate referenced) |
| TJ | *Jerusalem Talmud* (followed by name of the tractate referenced) |
| *Ant.* | Flavius Josephus, *Antiquities of the Jews* |
| *Wars* | Flavius Josephus, *Wars of the Jews* or *Jewish Wars* |
| trans. | translated by (followed by name of translator) |
| ed. | edited by (followed by name of editor) |
| LXX | Septuagint (Greek translation of Hebrew Bible, c. 250 B.C.) |
| MT | Masoretic Text (Authorized version of the Hebrew Bible, c. A.D. 500) |
| B.C.E./C.E. | Jewish equivalent of the Christian reckoning B.C./A.D. |

# PREFACE

The title of this book—*Secrets of the Dead Sea Scrolls*—was chosen for a specific purpose. All the world loves a mystery, and there is something about the announcement of a secret that attracts instant attention. However, by use of the word *secrets* there is no intention to tease an audience into believing that the Dead Sea Scrolls are mysterious documents, that they contain hidden facts about Judaism or Christianity, or that they have been suppressed and sequestered by scholars. There are books that promote these kinds of "secrets," but this is not one of them. The term *secrets* was selected for two reasons.

First, the idea is prominent in the Dead Sea Scrolls themselves. In a real sense it was their "secrets" that defined the Qumran community, who both produced and preserved the Scrolls. They believed that the prophecies of the Bible (for them, the Old Testament) were mysteries or secrets. They also believed that these secrets were to be understood uniquely by them through their divinely inspired Teacher of Righteousness. Further, they believed that the fulfillment of these mysteries was to be expected in their own day, which they thought was at the end of the age. In their doctrine and their daily life, the Dead Sea Sect sought to guard their secret understanding—an understanding which, since the discovery of the Scrolls, is largely a secret no more.

The second reason for the term *secrets* is a practical one. For almost 50 years the Dead Sea Scrolls have been a part of the public vocabulary. Perhaps more books and articles have been written about them than on any other subject touching the Bible. Nevertheless, for most people (and especially most Christians) the subject of the Scrolls remains a mystery, or if you will, a secret. My purpose in writing this book is to help remove the popular mystique that has surrounded the Scrolls and, in as nontechnical a way as possible, reveal their significance for us today. If this has been achieved, it will hopefully serve to awaken a new generation to Scroll study and prepare them for new discoveries and the greater secrets the Scrolls may reveal in days to come.

# Introduction

When the Scrolls made their debut in America in 1955 (almost a decade after their discovery), *The New Yorker* was the first magazine to publish a full report.[1] No one at *The New Yorker* or any other publishing entity could have anticipated the response that was to come. The public demand for the article on the Scrolls was so great that within a few days every issue of the magazine had completely sold out! Still, America's immediate love affair with the Scrolls was not to be quenched; when Oxford University Press soon afterward brought out the article in book form,[2] it quickly made the bestsellers list and remained there for many months. This following continued to gain momentum through the years by the announcement of new discoveries in the Judean desert. More books, both scholarly and sensational, took their turns as bestsellers, and unprecedented audiences turned out for lectures on the Scrolls.

Then, as discoveries waned and the familiar story became old news, the Dead Sea Scrolls, once a household term, was abandoned to the *genizah* of worn-out words. For some time thereafter, interest in the Scrolls remained largely within scholastic circles.

That, however, changed in 1989, when the public was made privy to an in-house controversy among scholars over the delay in Scroll publication. The news media exposed the fact that in over 40 years only a small number of the Scrolls had actually seen print, while hundreds more had never been read by anyone other than the select coterie of scholars to whom they had been assigned. A new generation of people, seasoned by Watergates and savings and loan scandals, took notice at once and cries of a cover-up (with Vatican or Israeli connections) propelled the subject of the Scrolls again to center stage. When the Huntington College Library released complete photographic sets of the Scrolls the following year, an instant audience had been created to consume whatever revelations were forthcoming. The Scrolls were back big time! With increased interest came renewed excavations and news that more Scrolls were out there. As a result, a new wave of books and films about the Scrolls have been and continue to be released, each in its own way seeking to reveal the secrets of the Scrolls.

## My Seasons with the Scrolls

I remember well my first acquaintance with the Dead Sea Scrolls. It was 1979, and I was a graduate student in Semitic languages and archaeology at the Hebrew University in Jerusalem. But despite my professional interest, I was *not* looking for Scrolls but for a job to provide extra income. My wife was expecting our second child, and domestic obligations had to outweigh scholarly ambitions or else the added expense would drain our savings and end my studies altogether.

The needed job came through a Yeminite-Israeli neighbor who was working in sales for the American-Israeli Television Association and wanted to let go of some hours. God often has a way of both supplying our needs and satisfying our desires, and as it turned out, this job would provide both. It would have me working at, of all places, the Shrine of the Book, Israel's Museum of the Dead Sea Scrolls. I was to rent to tourists Professor Yigael Yadin's audio self-guide for the Dead Sea museum exhibitions and sell slide sets about the Scrolls themselves.

So it was that I found myself positioned every day (and some nights) within the corridor of the Shrine of the Book, surrounded by these ancient Scrolls. In that job I not only had to learn all I could about the Scrolls, but I also had to listen to every tour guide in Israel give his version of their discovery and importance! In my position, I also was situated (at the only entrance to the museum!) to meet many of the archaeologists and scholars involved with the history and decipherment of the Scrolls. And when the tourist season slowed down, I had many quiet hours available to wander through the museum and ponder the amazing treasures that had become so familiar a part of my working world.

In 1989 I was again involved in graduate studies when the Scrolls returned to public prominence. In the summer of 1990 when the Scroll controversy was at its height (and before there was any idea they would be released just three months later), I journeyed to Jerusalem to attend the Second International Congress on Biblical Archaeology. There, on an evening when the Scrolls session convened, most of the known universe of Scroll scholarship was present. Many of my former professors at the Hebrew University were now part of an Israeli contingent within the formerly non-Israeli International Team of Scroll translators. At the end of the session, senior scholar Harry Orlinsky, whose own role in the drama of the Scrolls is legendary (see pp. 48-49), gave the closing remarks and made a statement about the Scrolls that I had not expected. He said,

As I look back on the three or four decades of research on the Scrolls since they began to be published, it is my judgment that it is not only additional research that is needed . . . but basic research, that is we need to go back to the sources . . . rather than relying on and repeating what many, if not most scholars have been saying for years.[3]

His words surprised me because, as I knew from my own research, entire volumes of bibliography on the Scrolls already existed. How could more research be needed? Yet the research Professor Orlinsky admonished was of a primary kind: going back to the original texts of the Bible and the extrabiblical literature (including the Scrolls themselves) to chart a new course independent of established consensus.

So it was with this encouragement that I, among other doctoral students whose dissertations required the newly accessible Cave 4 documents, sought access to these unpublished texts from the Huntington College Library and became part of the continuing drama of the Scrolls. In addition, my own work on the subject of the Jerusalem Temple has forced me into closer contact with the world of the Scrolls. These studies have not only confirmed Professor Orlinsky's judgment, but also renewed my appreciation for these treasures of time, which began almost two decades ago in Jerusalem when I worked as a "salesman of the Scrolls."

## What This Book Is All About

When the first wave of American enthusiasm for the Scrolls was evidenced in the 1950s, some individuals wondered why so many people were so interested in these ancient writings. Professor Millar Burrows of Yale University Divinity School, who wrote and lectured extensively for a popular audience, gave this answer:

> . . . the chief factor in this extraordinary public interest in the Scrolls was religious. People wanted to know what these documents would mean for traditional beliefs. Some were anxious lest the foundations of their faith might be weakened; some welcomed what they thought might justify their own rejection of the faith of their fathers.[4]

Burrows' insight reveals why the story of the Scrolls still continues to enthrall readers—because it touches upon that greatest story of all, the

Bible. *Secrets of the Dead Sea Scrolls* joins a host of other books that have sought to tell this story in their own way. However, my purpose in telling the story anew is to offer previously untold information and address subjects of interest that have often been neglected. Also, as I write, I have in mind evangelical readers whose concerns are often different than the concerns of the nonevangelical or critical scholar. For evangelicals, issues such as how this material helps support the historical accuracy of the Bible or illuminate the biblical text is paramount because they hold the Bible to be divinely inspired. Most nonevangelical scholars also share this concern, but for them the integrity of the biblical text as a matter of faith is not an integral issue.

Evangelicals are also very much interested in Bible prophecy, the defense of doctrinal positions against the teachings of the cults and New Age movement, and the work of scholarly revisionists whose biblical interpretations challenge what Christians have traditionally believed concerning Jesus and the origin of Christianity. In this book I have attempted to address these special concerns as they pertain to the Dead Sea Scrolls.

As has been my practice in my other books, I have included much firsthand material taken from personal interviews with leading scholars in the field. I have also sought to provide information about the latest archaeological excavations and discoveries related to the Scrolls. In a field where a limited number of scholars are working with restrictive budgets and even more restrictive schedules, the valuable information they are gleaning from their research and study may have to wait many years to see publication elsewhere. The inclusion of my interviews with these scholars will offer an immediate glimpse into their discoveries while hopefully increasing the demand for their finished work.

Finally, my encouragement to you is the same as that offered by Professor Orlinsky: to go back to sources to substantiate your beliefs. If we become solid students of the Scriptures we will find a valuable ally in the Dead Sea Scrolls, whose secrets reveal that in both positive and negative ways the Lord will look "to him who is humble and contrite of spirit, and who trembles at My word" (Isaiah 66:2).

# PART I

The Discovery Heard
Around the World

# 1

# THE DRAMA OF THE SCROLLS

*From the discoveries of archaeology we have learned that civilizations and cultures never die or are forgotten in the strictest sense. The more we unearth, the more we see how ancient civilizations have had a subtle but unmistakable impress and bearing upon our lives today.*[1]

—Dr. Paul Ilton

Without a doubt, the Dead Sea Scrolls comprise the greatest literary discovery of all time. Those who were the ancient keepers of the Scrolls hid their treasures with intent, trusting that the God of which they spoke would guard them throughout time. One writer described the actions of these keepers in this way:

> They simply inserted hundreds of Scrolls—both sacred and mundane—into clay storage jars and cast them into futurity like messages in bottles. Just how far into futurity those bottles

would sail, the preservers of Qumran could scarcely have dreamed.[2]

Indeed, some 2,000 years into the future, above the shores of the southern end of the Dead Sea, a young Bedouin shepherd stumbled onto one of the caves containing these storage jars and brought out the "messages in bottles." His excited shout of discovery has since been heard around the world. And today, some 50 years later, they are still the talk of our times.

Yet the years of research and study on the Scrolls have not yet clarified the most basic questions: Who sent these messages into our time, and how do they affect our traditional interpretation of their times? After a half century of work, scholars now have even more theories than when they began. Nevertheless, the secrets of the Scrolls are being revealed in our days, and in the years to come there is promise of even greater insight into days gone by.

The traditional approach taken by many authors is to begin with the story of the Scrolls and then describe their contents and explain their significance. This, of course, is a necessary path, and we shall walk it together. However, there are also important questions about the Scrolls that deserve to be explored. Therefore, two preliminary questions to focus on are: Why were these Scrolls found at such a place as the Dead Sea? And, why did they appear on the present scene when they did, after an absence of nearly 2,000 years?

The answers to those questions introduce us to the drama of the Scrolls—a drama that began in antiquity but has reached across the millennia to correspond with events in our days and capture the curious minds of a world seeking evidence of something greater than itself.

## A Unique Region

When we look at a detailed map of the Judean region, we can quickly observe that the geography of the area is unique. Jerusalem sits upon one of a series of mountains at a height of some 2,600 feet above sea level. Twenty miles to the southwest lies the Dead Sea at a record 1,300 feet *below* sea level (a diver could swim yet another 1,300 feet to the bottom at the northern end of the Dead Sea for a total of 2,600 feet below sea level). So between Jerusalem and the Dead Sea there is a drop of almost 4,000 feet, with about 2,000 feet of that descent occurring within a short distance of less than one mile!

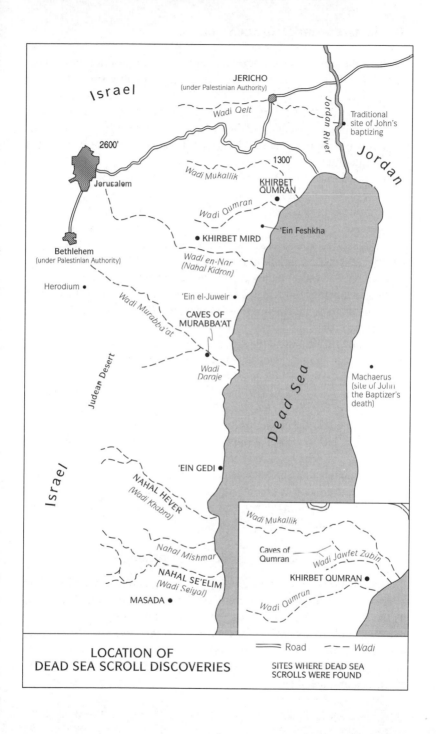

LOCATION OF
DEAD SEA SCROLL DISCOVERIES

Road --- Wadi

SITES WHERE DEAD SEA
SCROLLS WERE FOUND

This topographical phenomenon serves as an introduction to what visitors testify is one of the planet's most inhospitable spots. Coming down from the bleak, rugged limestone cliffs east of Jerusalem we quickly meet the sun-parched desert. Though this desert receives less than two inches of rainfall a year, during the rainy season terrible floods can occur without warning. Even those who know the area well have been killed by such natural disasters.[3]

When we reach the Dead Sea itself we find a shimmering body of water 45 miles long and nine miles wide. The clear blue water is deceptively alluring, giving the appearance of a freshwater lake, but the sea is actually a concentrated chemical stew of 26 percent solid matter in the form of dissolved salts. The sea is so dense with these minerals that objects placed in the water remain at the surface. It is recorded that when the Romans were in the area they used to tease newcomers in their ranks by binding and throwing them into the deepest part of the sea. Instead of drowning as they imagined, the victims would float on the surface as if by magic!

The hot, arid air around the Dead Sea is mixed with a tinge of salt and sulfur, and can sting the eyes or make a person nauseous. In former times it is reported that thick masses of black tar (bitumen) would float on the surface, thus giving the waters one of their many names: Lake Asphaltitis (cf. Josephus, *The Jewish War* 4.480). Just being alongside the Dead Sea can give a person the impression that he or she has reached the netherworld itself. No wonder a Jordanian nightclub that once straddled the water's edge advertised to travelers: "The Last Place on Earth."

Although this body of water is never identified as the Dead Sea in the Bible, its designations as "the Salt Sea," "the Sea of Sodom," and "the Sea of the Plain" give evidence of the part this region played in the spiritual history of the Bible.

## A Place of Spiritual Refinement

When we view the community of Qumran we encounter a people living an aesthetically simple and austere lifestyle in extremely difficult environs by the Dead Sea. They survived only because of a nearby spring of water they were able to channel to their retreat, and they lived in this desolate region with utmost dedication to God. What was it that caused some 200 men, along with their families, to leave the protection of the city and congregate in this desert region?

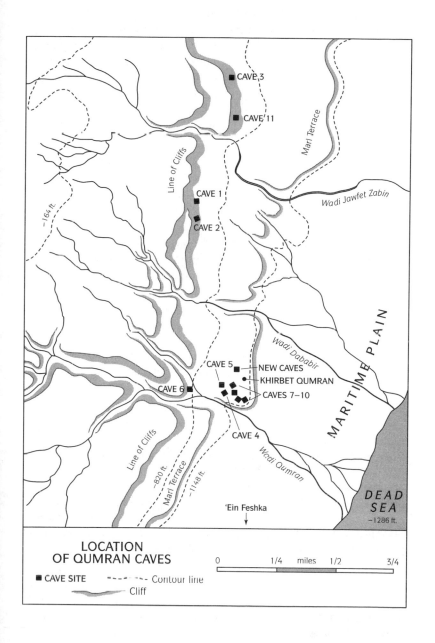

CAVE 3

CAVE 11

Marl Terrace

Line of Cliffs

CAVE 1

CAVE 2

Wadi Jawfet Zabin

−164 ft.

MARITIME PLAIN

Wadi Dababir

CAVE 5     NEW CAVES
                • KHIRBET QUMRAN
CAVE 6          CAVES 7–10

CAVE 4

Line of Cliffs

−820 ft.

Marl Terrace

−1148 ft.

Wadi Qumran

'Ein Feshka

DEAD
SEA
−1286 ft.

## LOCATION
## OF QUMRAN CAVES

0          1/4     miles   1/2          3/4

■ CAVE SITE    - - - - - - Contour line

〜〜〜 Cliff

The desert has always played a major role in the Bible—not because it was a place of solitude or escape, but because by its barren nature it served as an instrument to refine faith. The New Testament summarizes the historical verdict of the Old Testament when it declares: "Without faith it is impossible to please Him [God]" (Hebrews 11:6). Throughout biblical history, whenever God sought to refine a man for His purposes, He led him into the wilderness. Such a fierce and foreboding region robs a person of his natural strength, thereby stripping away the veneer of a superficial faith. With no place to hide in a realm of absolute exposure, the human options are reduced to trusting God or perishing in futile persistence. The harsh conditions of the desert reveal the natural barrenness of our lives; there is nothing quite like experiencing these conditions. The desert is where God forced many of His chosen vessels to develop their faith.

So it is that we see some of the greatest spiritual examples of Scripture—Abraham, Isaac, Jacob, Joseph, Moses, Aaron, Joshua, Samson, David, Elijah, Elisha, John the Baptizer, Jesus, and Paul—all spend their season of testing in the desert. It is interesting how many of these same people are in the hall of heroes in Hebrews chapter 11, which offers the divine assessment of faith in relation to this region when it concludes with these words: "men of whom the world was not worthy, wandering in *deserts* and *mountains* and *caves* and holes in the ground. And all these, having gained approval through their *faith*" (Hebrews 11:38-39, emphasis added).

As one of the great deserts of the Bible, and that closest to the Bible's central city—Jerusalem—the Judean desert has played its part in the biblical drama. During patriarchal times, in Abraham's battle against the Mesopotamian kings, the kings of Sodom and Gomorrah fell into tar pits that once were plentiful in the Dead Sea region (Genesis 14:10). At this same time one of the great "refining" events of history took place near the Dead Sea's southern shores as the five cities of the plains (including Sodom and Gomorrah) were destroyed in a great heaven-sent conflagration (Genesis 19:24-25). In the centuries that followed, some of the aforementioned men (Joshua, David, Elijah, Elisha, John, and Jesus) demonstrated their faith in the region that, by New Testament times, was called "the wilderness of Judea."

Moving to the time of the Qumran settlement, we find that the Judean desert is mentioned in the literature as a place to which the especially pious were apt to flee. At the outset of the Antiochean persecution (the hellenizing institutions of the Syrian-Greek ruler Antiochus Epiphanes IV) in 167 B.C., some priests physically withdrew to the Judean desert seeking "righteousness and justice" (1 Maccabees 2:29ff). Literary analysis has demonstrated that these priests cannot be connected with the Essenes (as some have tried to do by equating them with one of the groups of the *Hasidim* described in 1 Maccabees 2:42). Rather, they were a group of the Hasmonean movement described in 1 Maccabees 2:39-48. These priests show the precedent set by those who viewed the Judean desert as a place spiritually suited to their ends.

## Choosing an Ideal Site

The community that selected the site of Qumran did so with a clear understanding of its history and were convinced that they were inhabiting an ideal site for those who had made a renewed covenant as the true Israel (*CD* 6:19; 20:12). The site of Qumran appears in the biblical record, going back to the City of Salt (Joshua 15:61-62), one of six walled cities that together formed the district of the "wilderness."[4] Another of these cities, Secacah, has also been identified by some people with Qumran;[5] however, others contend that its ruins are located about four miles to the southwest.[6]

The site has also been suggested as one of the locations for "the sons of prophets," or prophetic groups that served alongside the prophets Elijah and Elisha (1 Kings 20:35; 2 Kings 2:3). Although these groups appeared to live ascetically and in partial seclusion in the desert at Jericho (2 Kings 2:18; 6:1-2), there is no biblical evidence that they occupied the area at Qumran. A more possible biblical reference to Qumran during the period of Israel's monarchy is the mention of Uzziah's "towers in the wilderness" (2 Chronicles 26:10).

Some people have also proposed that Qumran is the site referred to in one of the Scrolls (the *Copper Scroll*) by the name *Wadi Ha Kippa*.[7] They argue that the name *Qimron* (from *kamoor*, the Aramaic synonym for the Hebrew *kippa*) must have been at least the first-century designation for the present Wadi Qumran. Because *kippa* indicates a "covering" (such as a hat), some people have seen a connection to the natural topography of the marl cliffs, especially at the end of the Wadi, which resembles a dome (*see photo section*). It appears, then, that the Sect that occupied Qumran around the second half of the second century B.C. went to a site that had prior biblical significance.

## The New Exodus at Qumran

Although the site of Qumran had a biblical history, the Dead Sea Sect chose it primarily for theological reasons. They thought of themselves as repeating the wilderness experience of the Israelites who came out of Egypt during the exodus. They affirmed this identification by calling themselves "the exiles of the wilderness" *(1QM* 1:2-3). This region was ideally suited, both in geography and in connection with the generation that came out of Egypt during the exodus to Canaan. The historic sojourn of Israel in the wilderness influenced their own decision to retreat to the desert as well as the proper time to do so.

Using this model, the Qumran Sect determined that just as Israel had to endure the desert for 40 years, so also would their time of testing at Qumran last for 40 years (generally the lifespan of one generation; *CD* 20:13-15). The members of the Sect divided into tribes following the arrangement Israel had in the desert *(1QS* 2:21-23; cf. Exodus 18:25; Deuteronomy 1:15), living in the same camplike formation (*CD* 7:6; 10:2; 14:3; 20:26; cf. Numbers 2:1–5:4) and regulated by the same biblical statutes *(1QM* 7:3-7; cf. Numbers 5:1-4). While the pattern set by the exodus may not be the sole key for understanding the Dead Sea community, it, combined with the Sect's eschatological view, may explain what led them into the wilderness.[8]

The eschatological (or, end times) view held by the Sect led the people to identify themselves with the spiritual call of Isaiah 40:3—a call to withdraw to the wilderness and prepare for the Day of the Lord.[9] Thus, in the *Rule of the Community* we read:

> When these things shall come to pass in the Community of Israel, according to these rules, they shall withdraw from the city of the men of iniquity [i.e., Jerusalem] to go into the wilderness to clear the way of the Lord as it is written: In the wilderness clear the way of the Lord, make level in the desert a highway for our God *(1QS* 8:12-16; cf. 9:19).

Through the retreat into the wilderness, the Qumran community identified with biblical Israel in its sin (*CD* 5:17-20). It was in this place that the nation had once before been punished for disobedience because of unbelief (Numbers 14:27-37; cf. Psalm 106:7,13-39).[10] For this reason the prophet Isaiah saw the site as a place of spiritual preparation, the first stage of which was repentance. Therefore the Sect referred to itself as "the penitents of the wilderness" *(4QpPs^a* 3:1; cf. John the Baptizer,

Matthew 3:1-3). As a second stage, during their stay in the desert, the group saw itself preparing the way for the end metaphorically through a study of the Law *(4QS^e; 1QS* 9:20). In this connection, the Sect saw themselves as an eschatological fulfillment of the historical exodus, which had as its ultimate conquests Jerusalem and the land of Israel (Joshua 11:16–12:24).

The desert community, then, awaited the completion of the new exodus, which began in the Babylonian exile, was now in a transition period awaiting the end-time war, which would be climaxed with the retaking of the land as part of the final redemption.[11] It was from the desert alongside the Dead Sea that the blessings expected from the redemption would first be seen. The prophets predicted that when restoration came to Jerusalem and the new Temple of the Lord was established, living waters would flow to the Dead Sea ("western sea") from beneath the Temple's Holy of Holies and make the sea's waters fresh (Zechariah 14:8; cf. Ezekiel 47:1-2,12). Ezekiel may have had in mind the site of Qumran when he refers to a place called Eneglaim ("the spring of Eglaim") next to Ein-Gedi, where the restored Dead Sea will host a bounty of fish rivaling the Mediterranean Sea itself (Ezekiel 47:10). No doubt the people at Qumran, who saw themselves as the vanguard for this new era, were aware of these prophecies concerning the desert and chose the Qumran site in the belief that they were to enjoy the fulfillment of these biblical predictions.

## The Scrolls and the State of Israel

One of the theological distinctives of the Dead Sea Sect was their emphasis on predestination. They believed that from creation all people and events were predetermined, and that there existed a divine order which was progressively unfolding in the history of Israel. Those who wrote the Scrolls felt they had been chosen to live in the last days as that remnant of Israel who would inherit the promised blessings of the coming age. They thought that their fidelity to the Torah and understanding of the divine order were evidence of God's preservation of a people who would survive the tribulation of the end time *(see* Daniel 12:1-2).

It is an interesting coincidence that the Scrolls, as a record of Israel's hope of restoration, were found on the eve of Israel's rebirth as a nation. This coincidence has not escaped the notice of Israel's Scroll scholars. It was of particular significance to Major General Yigael Yadin (whose story we will tell shortly), who, as a scholar and soldier, was intimately connected with Israel's politics and the preservation of the Scrolls. He wrote:

> I cannot avoid the feeling that there is something symbolic
> in the discovery of the Scrolls and their acquisition at the moment
> of the creation of the State of Israel. It is as if these manuscripts
> had been waiting in caves for two thousand years, ever since the
> destruction of Israel's independence, until the people of Israel
> had returned to their home and regained their freedom. This sym-
> bolism is heightened by the fact that the first three Scrolls were
> bought by my father for Israel on 29th November, 1947, the very
> day on which the United nations voted for the re-creation of the
> Jewish state in Israel after two thousand years.[12]

We cannot minimize the importance of this historic symbolism for an Israeli. Able to read the Scrolls in a Hebrew not far removed from that which he reads in his newspaper, he is able to connect with his ancestors in a way unparalleled by any other society. Consider this connection for a moment: The writers of the Scrolls thought of themselves as Israel's last hope in a world that was set on the destruction of the Jewish people. They embraced the messianic promises and were zealous for the Jews in the Diaspora (outside the Land) to return to Israel and restore it to the independent glory it had enjoyed during the biblical period. The Zionist movement, which in one sense began with the expulsion of Jews in Roman times, found its earliest expression in messianic movements that stressed a return of all Jews to the "Land of the Fathers." Its modern birth came as a result of the many centuries of attempts to force Jews in the Diaspora to assimilate to the prevailing culture, usually through oppressive means. The climax of these attempts was the Holocaust and the decimation of the European Jewish community by the loss of six million lives. In the face of such worldwide anti-Semitism, a majority of nations in the United Nations voted favorably for the formation of the Jewish state. In the Zionist speeches at the time of this national rebirth we can hear echoes of the apocalyptic language of those who wrote the Scrolls. For example, Israel's first Prime Minister, David Ben Gurion, declared:

> In our sight and in our days the scattered people is homing
> from every corner of the globe and every point of the compass,
> out of all the nations among which it was cast away, and is
> coursing over its land, over Israel redeemed. . . . Through gen-
> erations untold we, and no other people, believed in the vision

of the last days.... Our first concern must be to build up the Land, to foster its economy, its security and international status. But these are the whereby not the end. The end is a State fulfilling prophecy, bringing salvation, to be guide and exemplar to all men.[13]

With such a continuity in history expected between Israel's past and present it is understandable the impact the discovery of the Scrolls would have on the average Israeli. Professor Yadin may have summarized this connection best:

> They [the Scrolls] constitute a vital link—long lost and now regained—between those ancient times, so rich in civilized thought, and the present day. And just as a Christian reader must be moved by the knowledge that here he has a manuscript of a Sect whom the early Christians may have known and by whom they were influenced, so an Israeli and a Jew can find nothing more deeply moving than the study of manuscripts written by the People of the Book in the Land of the Book more than two thousand years ago.[14]

## Intriguing Parallels

Some people have observed details in the Scrolls that offer parallels between the Scrolls and the modern State of Israel. For instance, the Dead Sea Sect expected to wage a war to liberate Israel from its occupying enemies. The *War Scroll* records that this war would be against "the company of Edom and of Moab and the sons of Ammon and the com[pany of ... and of] Philistia, and against the companies of the Kittim of Ashur...." (*1QM* 1:1-2). When modern Israel fought its War of Independence in 1948, some of these same ancient enemies were involved (Jordanians, Syrians, Lebanese, and indirectly, the Europeans [Kittim=Romans]). Even most of the archaeological finds in Cave 1 could be thought to relate symbolically: the *Isaiah Scroll* (prophesying the rebirth and restoration of Israel), the *War Scroll* (predicting the war of Israel with her enemies), the *Rule of the Congregation* (describing the ideal Jewish community), and the *Commentary on Habakkuk* (revealing the Zionistic and messianic aims). While such an observation may not impress a historical purist, we cannot help but detect a sense of "symbolism," as Yadin noted.

It is also noteworthy that one of the most important Scrolls for understanding the practice of Judaism in the Second Temple period (522 B.C.–A.D. 70), the *Temple Scroll*, was recovered by Israel on the very day that Jerusalem was captured and reunited as Israel's capital (June 6, 1967). Here was a treasure that, when read, brought to the religious Jew a sense of continuity with the writer, who had actually seen the Temple and beheld its ritual. Moreover, with Jerusalem in Jewish hands for the first time since the destruction of the Temple 2,000 years ago, aspirations for the rebuilding of the Temple were awakened.[15] Some orthodox Jews in the present-day Temple movement in Israel believe that the *Temple Scroll's* emergence at this time is a sign that the Temple will be rebuilt by this generation. Just as the *Temple Scroll* may have served as a blueprint for the Dead Sea Sect's conception of a future Temple, so also has it served the researchers and architects today who have prepared their own blueprints for the expected Third Temple.

There are, too, modern religious Israelis who see the prophetic end-time aspirations of the ancient Sect being experienced today. They, like the Dead Sea community, sense that they are the last generation before the coming of Messiah, the Battle of Gog and Magog, and the advent of the Age of Redemption. They adopt the same eschatological scenario proposed by the Sect, only their interpretation would flow more from the stream that connected the biblical prophets with the rabbinic sages.

Clearly, then, for an Israeli, the Scrolls are much more than another archaeological relic from their past. In one sense, they are documents that bridge their past with their present, and in another sense, also their future. They are priceless treasures, "won" in the midst of wars, to which are connected not only their national pride but also their prophetic destiny.

And, as in a drama, the audience is also a part, and so the Scrolls may in a mysterious manner link us together with a history that has ever been moving according to an often-unseen divine agenda. In the next chapter we will begin to explore the various scenes in this drama that made the majority of these Scrolls again a part of history and Israel's heritage.

# 2

# THE STORY OF THE SCROLLS

*I have discovered one important fact: much less is actually known about the circumstances of the discovery of the various caves and Scrolls than the published accounts would lead one to believe.*[1]

—Weston Fields, Executive Director,
The Dead Sea Scrolls Foundation

The story of the Scrolls has been told and retold countless times. However, there is always room for another retelling, especially if in the telling one can add something never told before. In this chapter I want to take you through the adventure of the first discovery and introduce you to the obscure characters who were made famous as the Scrolls gained international attention. Along the way, we'll take a look beyond the old story to new revelations that may help unlock some of the secrets of the Scrolls.

## The Discovery at the Dead Sea

The seven ancient Scrolls that the American Dean of Biblical Archaeology, William Foxwell Albright, hailed as "the greatest manuscript discovery of modern times" were first discovered by semi-nomadic shepherds of the Ta'amireh Bedouin tribe. The Ta'amireh, who had settled between Bethlehem and the Dead Sea, had for generations kept their flocks and herds in the Judean desert, which is honeycombed with ancient caves. According to the well-told story, one of these shepherds, a yet-unmarried man by the name of Muhammed edh-Dhib ("Muhammed the wolf" because he killed wolves which attacked the flocks), was responsible for the original discovery of the Scrolls.[2] As he and friends were tending their goat herds, he left the group to go in search of one of his stray goats. After roaming far from his companions, he came upon a cave with a small opening at its top. Supposing the goat to have fallen inside, he threw stones into the opening. Instead of hearing the sound of a startled goat, he heard the shatter of breaking pottery. Believing that treasure might be inside, he lowered himself into the cave and found ancient clay jars. Inside one jar was intact leather Scrolls, which he hoped could be used for sandal straps. He took these Scrolls back to share with his friends, and then he hanged them in his tent. Later he sold them to a merchant in Bethlehem, who in turn sold them to those who made their presence known to the world.

When the Scrolls came to light, a desperate search began for the Bedouin who found them and the cave in which they were found. Some of these searches included tactics found in the best of spy novels; in one case, the searchers even hired Ta'amireh Bedouin to covertly pry the coveted information from their fellow tribesmen. Yet despite these attempts at espionage, the secret could not be cracked. Not until 1949, after British archaeologist Lankester Harding compelled the Jordanian Arab Legion (an elite military unit) to search various caves at the suspected site, was the original cave found. Even then, the story of the cave's discovery still remained somewhat of a mystery. As a result, over the years, many different stories have emerged or were formulated about the Scrolls' discovery, ranging from a fraudulent conspiracy theory in the forties[3] and a murder in the late thirties[4] to a looted synagogue in the twenties.[5] Harding did attempt to get the real story, which was included in the first of the *Discoveries in the Judean Desert* (*DJD*) series (1955), but his account still contains estimations and assumptions.[6]

Most scholars who have dealt directly with the Dead Sea texts have never met the Bedouin and merchants originally responsible for securing the Scrolls they study.[7] Among the reasons for that are the ongoing tensions in the Middle East; the significant social, religious, and political differences that prevail; and the proven distrust that exists between archaeologists and the Bedouin, who obtain part of their subsistence by illegally plundering archaeological sites. Thus the personal testimonies of the major players in the Dead Sea Scrolls drama have rarely been sought, giving rise to the many variations of the account.

## An Early Interview with Muhammed edh-Dhib

On October 23, 1956, a serious attempt was made to find out the truth about the discovery of the Scrolls. This was done by setting up the first "official" interview with the Bedouin discoverer Muhammed edh-Dhib. The interview had been arranged by Michail Awad, an employee of the Latin Patriarchate, and took place in the company of two Arab Bethlehem businessmen: Mr. Najib S. Khoury and Hanna Jackaman. Muhammed edh-Dhib was asked to give his complete account of the Cave 1 discovery and, after hearing his own story played back on a tape recorder, the interviewers had him swear on the Koran and asked him to sign an affidavit verifying the truthfulness of his account.[8] This testimony was then published the following year in the prestigious *Journal of Near Eastern Studies*.[9] Unfortunately, the testimony was still at variance: Muhammed reported the finding of *ten* jars in *1945*—three jars *more* and two years *less* than was stated in the report as it had been understood since 1948 by those who had first obtained the Scrolls. So few scholars trusted the interview as being any more reliable than the previous account.

The time difference between the two accounts can be explained by Muhammed's claim that he kept the Scrolls hanging in his tent for more than two years before giving them to his uncle, who showed them to an antiquities dealer. However, Muhammed later gave even *more* jars and *earlier* dates for the same event. In light of this it is well to keep in mind the words of a veteran scholar of the modern Middle East concerning the Bedouin's accuracy with numbers:

> Anyone who is dealing with Arab boys knows that they haven't the vaguest notion of how many years have passed. If you ask them how old they are, they say maybe 15, maybe 19—

> I don't know really. It is hardly likely that he [Muhammed] would
> have any serious idea of how many years ago it was.[10]

If the *Journal of Near Eastern Studies* interview did not resolve all the
questions surrounding the discovery, it at least provoked another interview. This came in the fall of 1961 through the efforts of Anton Kiraz
with the help of Bethlehem mayor 'Ayub Musallam.[11] They conducted a
lengthy tape-recorded interview with Muhammed edh-Dhib and his cousin
Jum'a Muhammed, who had shared in the discovery. The substance of
the interview was 63 carefully worded questions to the men. As a result,
the date now given for the discovery was November 1946, the location
was Qumran, the entrance hole to the cave was from above, and the jars
were ten in number—all with three handles each. They also said they
found "red earth" in some of the jars. In addition, they reported that they
hadn't gone back to investigate the cave until after three days, and then
they left the Scrolls and jars in the cave for eight more days. These and
other significant discrepancies in the account are so remarkable that this
may rather be Muhammed and Jum'a's story of their later discovery at
Cave 4 rather than Muhammed's earlier discovery at Cave 1—a fact
unknown at the time of the interview.[12]

## A New Interview with Muhammed edh-Dhib

As one who had heard the story of the discovery of the Scrolls numerous
times in the Shrine of the Book, and had told it an equal number of times
on tours to Qumran, I would never have dreamed that one day I would
have the opportunity to relive that drama with the most famous member
of its original cast!

It happened one November evening (1995) in Jerusalem as I sat and
talked with Dr. Weston Fields, Executive Director of the Dead Sea Scrolls
Foundation. As we talked about a Scroll that was for sale and had been
offered to him, he told me that he had met Muhammed edh-Dhib. This
unexpected bit of information hit me like an exploding bombshell. I
responded with a volley of questions: You mean he's still alive? Are you
sure he's the real one? Where is he? Can *I* meet him?" Weston wasn't
sure if it was possible, but he said he would take me that very night to
meet the Old City antiquities dealer who had first introduced him to
Muhammed two years earlier. So we made the journey to the Jewish
Quarter to the antiquities shop known as The Ancient Coin.

When we arrived, David Bar Levav, the shop owner and our contact, was busily inspecting a batch of ancient clay votive figurines that he had just purchased from one of his many clandestine Arab contacts. David, an orthodox Jew, is one of Israel's most knowledgeable dealers, speaking 12 languages and capable of any level of discussion on the Bible, history, ancient languages, and more. For many years he has known Muhammed edh-Dhib, who has brought him artifacts he has found in the desert and in Arab villages. After the usual courtesies, David said that our timing was perfect! Muhammed would be coming to his shop at 1:00 P.M. the next day. If I wanted to meet with him, he would arrange it. I got home late that night and couldn't sleep because of the anticipation of the next day. Was I really going to meet the man who so long ago had set in motion the whole revolution brought about by the Dead Sea Scrolls?

The next day, Paul Streber (my photographer and filmmaker) and I had morning meetings scheduled with Jerusalem's mayor, Ehud Olmert, and archaeologist Hannan Eshel, who was about to begin excavating four newly discovered caves at Qumran (see chapter 20). As much as I enjoyed these meetings, I was anxious to meet with the famous Muhammed edh-Dhib. We arrived early at David's shop, and there he was, sitting in the corner of the small shop looking quite in place amid the cramped collections of ancient artifacts. Rising to meet me with outstretched hand, I saw that he was every inch a Bedouin, the epitome of a son of the desert. His skin was brown and weathered from a lifetime of exposure to the sun. His small frame was covered by a suit jacket over the traditional *jalabia* (robe), and framing his head and face was a red-and-white checkered *kafieh* (head covering) (*see photo section*). After exchanging the customary formalities, I learned that, following a Bedouin custom, his name had been changed after the birth of his first son (David). In order to reflect his new family status, Muhammed edh-Dhib (whose real name had been Muhammed Ahmed edh-Hamed) was now known as Abu-Dahoud ("David's father").[13] This name change had taken place in 1960, and was perhaps one of the reasons why so few students of the Scrolls had ever met this living legend.[14] Yet I could not help but ask myself: Could this *really* be the Bedouin shepherd who first found the Scrolls? (After an investigation into his identity the next day, I became convinced, even though there were the expected variations in his telling and retelling of the story,[15] that this was in all probability the real Muhammed edh-Dhib.[16])

After an hour of questioning Abu-Dahoud (with David serving as trans-lator) about unexplained details of his discovery, I decided to present the proposal that had preoccupied my mind during my restless night: "Would you come with me to the Dead Sea caves tomorrow and show me where and how you found the Scrolls?" It was a business proposition, and Abu-Dahoud quickly accepted, adding an offer to bring me as many old oil lamps as I wanted to buy!

The next morning we met early and drove to the Dead Sea caves to do what, as far as we knew, had never before been done—to recreate on film the original events of the Scroll discoveries.[17] We drove first to Kibbutz Almog, where an exhibit of replica Scrolls and jars is on permanent exhibit. Here we wanted to see how acquainted Abu-Dahoud was with the Scrolls, and if it was possible for him to remember from viewing the replicas which Scrolls he had found. He could not identify any specific Scroll, but thought his find was like the "big ones" (the *Isaiah* and *Temple Scrolls*). He also observed that his jars were like the jars on display, only many were larger.

We next drove to the Wadi Jawfet Zaben and started out with our equip-ment toward Cave 1. We let Abu-Dahoud guide us, and it became clear he wanted to take us to Cave 11. We insisted on going straight to Cave 1. When we got near to Cave 1, he seemed confused and protested that we were not going in the right direction. He had also made a similar protest to Dr. Fields when they visited the region two years earlier. Nevertheless, when he stood in front of the entrance to the cave he became excited and started describing how the larger entrance was not there when he first came to the site (a correct fact, for archaeologists had widened the entrance). He then began demonstrating how he had thrown stones in the smaller opening above to scare out his lost goat (*see photo section*). We went inside the cave, and he showed us how he had lowered himself into the cave from the small opening, where he had found the jars, and their number and contents. He repeated similar demonstrations in Cave 11 and Cave 4, from which he also claimed to have removed manuscripts.

Our filming complete, I decided to take advantage of our return trip from the Dead Sea to Abu-Dahoud's house in Bethlehem by asking him additional questions about his history with the Scrolls. Drawing upon this interview and my previous one in Jerusalem, I have attempted to offer some new information to the well-told story. I have also incorpo-rated some material from Dr. Field's unpublished notes[18] of his inter-views with Abu-Dahoud in order to balance the account. Disregarding the discrepancies in dates and numbers of jars, if the new information is accurate, it may prove useful in answering some unresolved questions about the chronological history of the Dead Sea Scrolls discoveries.

## Details of the New Account

In his latest account, Muhammed edh-Dhib said that when he lowered himself through the entrance hole and dropped into the cave he saw 47 jars. Because he was smoking a pipe at the time, he had both matches and candles in his pocket and thus was able to investigate the jars. The first of the jars were broken, and putting his hand into others he found mostly debris—the remains of Scrolls destroyed by insects. He was joined that day by five other shepherd friends: Juma'a Abu-Hashaba (his older cousin), Ahmed Muhammed, Khalil Musa, Aziza Muhammed, and Mahmoud;[19] however, he alone was the first to go into the cave. He then called his friends to the cave and they began to go through the jars. As Abu-Dahoud tells the story, only one jar contained intact Scrolls, and all five of them were somehow stuffed into the jar. There was in another jar one Scroll that was so brittle it broke into pieces as they picked it up. They thought the Scroll was damaged and therefore worthless, so they simply threw it outside the cave. All the Scrolls were leather, and some were wrapped in linen cloth. The boys thought that these rolls of leather might be good for sandal straps, so they took them back to their tents. They agreed not to remove the jars, but left them in the cave for at least another month. Later, Muhammed edh-Dhib returned to the cave with British archaeologist Lankester Harding. He did not tell him about the Scrolls, and Harding acted only mildly interested in the empty jars. Abu-Dahoud believes he took them to the Palestinian Archaeological Museum (which, in 1967, was renamed the Rockefeller Museum). However, most of these jars are no longer part of the museum inventory, and it is now evident that some were sold or went other places.[20]

For more than a year the Scrolls were left lying around his tent. (According to his 1957 report he said that "he took his share of the leather home and hung it in a skin bag in a corner.") There the bag remained "for more than two years." He said that because no one seemed interested in the old leather rolls, the kids in his tribe played with one like a toy until it broke into pieces. Some of the pieces were blown away by the wind, and the rest they threw in the garbage!

The Scrolls were then taken by his uncle to the house of a friend in the village of Irtas, near Bethlehem, where they remained for three months.

Next they went to a Dahoud Ansalam in Bethlehem for four months. Finally, they went to two antiquities dealers in Bethlehem: a cobbler who doubled as an antiquities dealer by the name of Jalil Iskander Shahin Kando and another man named Feidi Salahi (who received them only after another transaction went sour). Kando was the main operator; he paid for the Scrolls and became the sole representative for the Bedouin in all future dealings. According to Abu-Dahoud, Kando paid only £16 (Jordanian) for the first four Scrolls.

After the Scrolls were found to have brought a price, the whole Ta'amireh tribe became excited about looking for more Scrolls. Abu-Dahoud and his friends went back to Cave 1 to try and find the Scroll they had thrown outside the cave entrance, but after two years of wind and rainwater washing down the cliffs, it had completely disappeared. Then they began searching in other caves. Abu-Dahoud says that they found one Scroll in Cave 11, another in Cave 4 at Khirbet Qumran, and another in a cave he could not describe.[21] Although he claims that the date for these discoveries was 1938, as our discussion progressed, he said that he sold these Scrolls to Kando in 1948. He remembers this date clearly because they asked (and received) the price of $5,500 after hearing on the radio a news broadcast telling about Bedouin finding very valuable ancient Scrolls (from Cave 1) in the desert. Based on this confirmation of their value they were able to demand a higher price than they received for the previous four Scrolls.

Abu-Dahoud says that his chief occupation between 1935–1950 was searching for and selling Scrolls. After his fellow tribesmen learned of the amount Kando made on the first seven Scrolls, more than 50 men in his tribe also began looking for Scrolls. It is a matter of fact that more Scrolls have been found by these Bedouin than by professional archaeologists. Among these discoveries were finds of Scrolls and coins at the high caves of Wadi edh-Daliyeh. These objects, according to Muhammed edh-Dhib's memory, were simply lying on the floor of the caves and required little effort to remove. He says he also found an intact Scroll at Wadi Murabba'at in 1940, which he sold to Kando for J-D 1,500 (Jordanian dinars), and hundreds of Scroll fragments at Endera (near Ein-Gedi) in 1941, which he sold mostly to "a French priest named [Père Roland] de Vaux, and some to Kando."

### An Uncertainty About Dates

I was startled by these dates, because the conventional dates for the discovery of the first Scrolls are between 1946–1947, some eight to nine years later. If Abu-Dahoud was correct in his dates, then where were the Scrolls during those "missing years" after the Bedouin recovered them from the cave? More importantly, when were the Scrolls actually first discovered? The conventional dates of winter 1946 or sometime in 1947 were based on when the existence of the Scrolls was first made known through the efforts of those trying to sell them or buyers trying to gain information about them.

The conventional date of 1947 was apparently given by Muhammed edh-Dhib or his friends when they later became known and were questioned. Yet even at that time there was some confusion because the authorities at St. Mark's Monastery, who originally made the discovery known, attempted to conceal the date. For some time they told their consultants, including the American School of Oriental Research, that the Scrolls had been in their monastery library for 40 years. Even when the school learned that the Scrolls had been purchased during the previous year (1946) and issued a press release announcing the discovery, the article in the papers reported the Scrolls "had been preserved for *centuries*" in St. Mark's!

Matters were not clarified by later interviews with Muhammed edh-Dhib. In 1957 he issued an affidavit revising the discovery date to 1945. I also found these inconsistencies in dates when I pressed him several times during the two days we talked. However, we must keep in mind that Bedouin do not keep track of time as we do, but like the ancients, they keep time in connection with other events. By this form of reckoning Abu-Dahoud placed his discovery of the Scrolls "before Harding came to the country, and before I was married" (Bedouin do not continue to shepherd animals after they have taken a wife). British archaeologist G. Lankester Harding was already excavating at Lachish in the early thirties, and Abu-Dahoud said he married his first wife 57 years ago at age 20 (he is now 77). That would put his marriage in 1938 and set the date for the Scroll discovery sometime around 1936. As we discussed dates based on these events, he came to insist that he visited Cave 1 in 1935 or 1936.

When I asked if Kando still had the first four Scrolls in his possession at the time Abu-Dahoud and his friends sold the next three,[22] he recalled asking Kando what had happened to the first four Scrolls shortly after their transaction with him, and he was told that they had been sold. This presents an interesting but irreconcilable piece to the Scroll chronology puzzle. Although Kando served as an agent for the seven Scrolls in 1948, they were then sold to two different buyers: four to one group and three to another. If Abu-Dahoud is correct that the first four Scrolls and next three Scrolls were discovered and sold at different times, it could shed new light on these separate transactions. However, Abu-Dahoud still cannot account for the missing years between his selling the first four Scrolls in 1938 and the second three Scrolls in 1948. His latest account also raises another problem: It has always been thought that all seven Scrolls came from Cave 1 (just as it was originally assumed that all had been discovered at the same time). It would certainly make a difference to many scholars' theories regarding the provenance of the Scrolls if these latter three Scrolls came from different caves as Abu-Dahoud claims.

Nevertheless, as Abu-Dahoud continued to talk about his Scroll discoveries and the people to whom he sold Scrolls, I began to think that if a person added ten years to most of his dates they would probably be more accurate. I am not suggesting that anyone revise the accepted dates based on Abu-Dahoud's testimony, but since firsthand testimony is becoming increasingly impossible to retrieve (both Kando and Metropolitan Samuel are now deceased), his statements should be considered at least for historical reasons.

## From Muhammed to the Metropolitan

As interesting as Abu-Dahoud's (Muhammed edh-Dhib) testimony may be, his story is only the beginning. Once Muhammed's uncle and friends decided to see if the Scrolls would sell, they began looking for the right customer. The Bedouin settled on taking their seven Scrolls to an antiquities dealer because they had been told the strange writing on the parchment might be Syriac (a form of Aramaic and a cousin to Hebrew and Arabic). They knew Syriac was one of the holy languages used by the Christians, and they also knew that nearby Bethlehem was an Arab Christian town where Syrian Christians lived. There they would find those who knew the value of their finds and might wish to buy them. Perhaps to increase his chances on getting something for the Scrolls, Muhammed's uncle sought out Kando, a local cobbler (and main supplier of goods to the tribe) who also dabbled in antiquities. He may have figured that if the writing on the leather was not worth anything, perhaps he could sell the leather itself for scraps! Fortunately, Kando recognized the writing was ancient and bought the Scrolls for their antiquity value rather than for shoe repair. We cannot be sure how much time lapsed before Kando contacted George Isha'ya, a member of the Syrian Orthodox Church in Jerusalem, but he assisted him in resolving the mystery of the Scroll's script. We do know that when George took the Scrolls to his archbishop at the Monastery of St. Mark's, the Metropolitan Mar Athanasius Yeshue Samuel, the date was April of 1947.

According to the Metropolitan Samuel, once he revealed to Kando that the Scrolls were written in Hebrew rather than his language of Syriac, Kando thought he had lost a sale. That may be the reason the Metropolitan was able to obtain the Scrolls for a rather paltry sum (the equivalent of $250), although Mar Samuel claimed it represented every penny of his hard-earned savings.[23] Every manuscript expert and archaeologist that he consulted—including a representative from the Jordanian Department of Antiquities—told him that the Scrolls were either medieval copies or clever forgeries. No one had ever found manuscripts as old as these were purported to be, and they were certain that no manuscripts so old could have survived in such perfect condition. Conventional archaeological opinion was that the humid climate of the region was unsuitable for the preservation of organic matter, including the material used for manuscripts. As Edward Cook said, "The idea of finding such a manuscript was just too good to be true, and therefore probably wasn't."[24]

When I visited St. Mark's the story of the famous purchase by Mar Samuel was still fondly remembered. It was recounted to me by the Rev. Shemun Can while standing beside their venerated hand-written Syriac Bible inside the monastery's chapel.[25] He remembers best how Mar Samuel almost lost the opportunity to purchase the Scrolls. As he tells it, Mar Samuel had asked for the Scrolls to be brought to the monastery, where, after examination, he promised to buy them. Kando and George Isha'ya came to the monastery one afternoon, bearing both the seven Scrolls and the Bedouin, who were hoping for further income from the sale. But upon their arrival they got into a fierce argument with the gatekeeper over admittance, and were finally sent away in a rude manner. When Mar Samuel learned about the incident he immediately sent apologies to Kando and begged that he might have another opportunity to buy the Scrolls. But a Bedouin's honor is not to be trifled with, and by the time Mar Samuel had reached Kando three of the Scrolls had already been sold to another Bethlehem antiquities dealer, Feidi Salahi.[26]

I can painfully identify with the feelings of Mar Samuel. I once had a similar encounter with a Ta'amireh Bedouin whose honor I unwittingly had violated. I had employed him and a younger man to assist me in the Dead Sea area, and in separate negotiations made at different times, I had paid each for their labors. Unfortunately I made the mistake of paying the younger man more money than the older—a thing not to be done with Bedouin. After they got together to discuss their respective payments, reports came to me of the older Bedouin's rage, supposedly the worst his friends had ever seen! It cost me a great deal more money to restore his honor and hopefully our relationship. Yet, Mar Samuel's loss actually became a great gain—for the state of Israel. This turn of events introduces us to yet another of the famous players in the Scroll drama: Professor Eleazar Sukenik of the Hebrew University.

## Some Scrolls Come Home

Just as Kando through George Isha'ya had sought out an expert in Mar Samuel to authenticate the Scrolls, so also did Feidi Salahi make arrangements to show his three newly acquired Scrolls to Eleazar Sukenik through an Armenian friend, Anton Kiraz. This was not an easy matter at the time. Jerusalem was still under British control, but this control was rapidly crumbling in the wake of increasing Arab-Israeli conflict. It was the closing months of 1947, and the British had attempted to secure Jerusalem against attacks carried out by Jewish underground resistance groups by dividing the city and restricting movement between zones. When Sukenik met with Kiraz it was on the opposite sides of a barbed-wire fence dividing one of these zones. Kiraz had brought a sample of one of the Scrolls, and at last the Scrolls were brought to the attention of the one man in all the country who could positively authenticate them as a genuine treasure. Sukenik had been prepared for this moment from his excavation of Jewish ossuaries (burial boxes) and a study of their inscriptions. As a paleographer Sukenik had identified Hebrew scripts on these ossuaries, which dated from the late second century B.C. to the first century A.D. When he saw his first glimpse of a Dead Sea Scroll through the barbed wire, he knew the script was like those he had seen carved in stone and he wanted to see more!

Sukenik immediately made plans to go to Bethlehem, view the other Scrolls, and, if he could, buy them for the university. But he had not anticipated the events about to unfold all around him. On the day he planned to go to Bethlehem, then in Jordanian territory, the United Nations was about to vote for the re-creation of the Jewish State. The fear and disorder in the city had turned to panic and chaos because the people were certain that the Arabs would go to war against Israel immediately after the vote, which would make it unsafe for a Jew to go there. Postponing his trip but desperate for a decision as to what to do next, Sukenik went to his son Yigael Yadin, who was also an archaeologist *and* the head of the underground army, the Haganah. If anyone would understand the enormous value of the Scrolls and could advise him on his chances of going to Bethlehem it was his son. Yadin writes of the moment his father asked for his counsel:

> What was I to tell him? As a student of archaeology myself, I felt that an opportunity of acquiring such priceless documents could not be missed. On the other hand, as Chief of Operations of Haganah, I knew perfectly well the dangers my father would be risking in traveling to Arab Bethlehem. And as a son I was torn between both feelings. I tried to hedge, but before leaving, son and soldier won and I told him not to go.[27]

No doubt Sukenik thought long and hard about the advice of his son, which had been previously asserted by his wife. But in the end, the role of archaeologist and preserver of Israel's heritage won out over that of father and husband. Sukenik went to Bethlehem on the very day the United Nations resolution was to be passed. But in the hours before the event, Sukenik was able to secure the Scrolls and return home safely. At the hour (a little past midnight) when the vote was announced on the radio, Sukenik was engrossed in a study of the Scrolls. Later he said, "This great event in Jewish history was thus combined in my home in Jerusalem with another event, no less historic, the one political, the other cultural."[28] The war indeed broke out, but fortunately Sukenik already had the Scrolls. He had earlier risked his life to see them, and then he had risked his financial future by mortgaging his own home for a bank loan to buy them.

A short time later, Sukenik learned about the Scrolls in the possession of the Syrian Monastery and was given the chance to examine them personally. Following a clandestine meeting with Kiraz at the Y.M.C.A. library, a building used for meetings by Arab leaders, he returned with the additional Scrolls and even the prospect of purchasing them. Unfortunately, circumstances at the time did not permit this. He was refused an additional loan, and by the time monies were finally approved by the Jewish Agency, the Metropolitan had decided not to sell. Sukenik died in 1953 believing that the four Scrolls he had briefly handled were lost to the Jewish people forever. The reasons for his belief—and the ironic circumstances that were to fulfill his dream of acquiring them for Israel— are the next episode in our drama.

## On to the United States

After the meeting with Sukenik, the Metropolitan was convinced of his Scrolls' antiquity. He now wanted to get more information about their contents and sought a means to obtain what he felt was a fair market value. Sukenik had offered $2,025. That was more than the archbishop had paid, but not what he felt they were worth on the open market. It is also possible, based on what we know about the archbishop's later actions, that he was unwilling to sell his Scrolls to the Jewish State. Because the present turmoil in the Middle East had cut him off from the marketplace he sought, he decided to go to the American School of Oriental Research (A.S.O.R.), which is now the Albright Institute, to seek foreign advice. So on a cold day in mid-February of 1948, Father Butrus Sowmy, an associate of the Metropolitan, contacted a young scholar studying the flora and fauna of Palestine—Dr. John C. Trevor. Trevor was serving as interim director of the school while Director Millar Burrows was away in Baghdad, and made the decision to view the Scrolls in the director's absence. Upon seeing the Scrolls, especially the *Great Isaiah Scroll,* he knew the script was comparable to the then-oldest-known Hebrew text, the Nash papyrus. He made a handwritten copy of part of the text, and discovered later that evening that he had been reading a portion of Isaiah chapter 65. Reflecting later on the text he had copied, Trevor wrote:

> Events moved so rapidly after my first view of the Scrolls that it was several months before I noticed the meaning of the whole passage which led to the identification of the Isaiah Scroll. Thumbing through a Gideon Bible one evening in a hotel room, I turned to Isaiah 65:1 and was startled to read the ironic words: "I am sought of them that asked not for me; I am found of them that sought me not...."[29]

The next day Trevor went to the monastery and asked for permission to photograph the Scrolls in view of the uncertain conditions that were worsening daily in the city. At first he was refused, but finally he persuaded the Metropolitan that photographing and publishing the Scrolls would increase their market value, just as had been the case with the famous New Testament manuscript, the Codex Siniaticus, recovered by Constantine Tischendorf. Thus, in the midst of a cold rain, Trevor carried the Scrolls back to A.S.O.R., and with both outdated film and inferior facilities, he hurriedly but carefully photographed each section of the Scrolls. He sent a print of the *Great Isaiah Scroll* to the renown William

Foxwell Albright of John Hopkins University, who immediately confirmed the discovery as the greatest of the century. About this same time Director Millar Burrows returned and convinced the Metropolitan to allow A.S.O.R. to inform the press about the discovery and to publish the photographs abroad.

It was now March of 1948, and bombings and attacks were killing hundreds of people throughout the region. As the end of the British Mandate approached and Jewish independence dawned (May 15), full-scale war in Jerusalem was imminent. All Americans were being told to leave the city, and the Scrolls, too, were in danger while they remained. A.S.O.R. did not want to lose access to the Scrolls, and Burrows' own anti-Zionist position would not allow the Scrolls to be claimed by Sukenik for the Jewish State.[30] Therefore, he and Trevor successfully appealed to the Metropolitan to take the Scrolls to the United States, where a greater market would be available, an idea for which the Metropolitan needed little convincing. On March 25, the Scrolls were taken by the Metropolitan and Father Sowmy to Beirut, and from there to the United States. With good reason, then, Sukenik could write that he thought the Scrolls were lost to Israel forever.

Yet shortly after Sukenik's death, ironic circumstances were about to be played out which would lead to the Scrolls' return.

## The Rest of the Scrolls Come Home

For several years the Scrolls went on tour with Mar Samuel throughout the United States. He had to walk a political tightrope over the question of who owned the Scrolls, because by this time (1951) both the new state of Israel and the Hashemite Kingdom of Jordan claimed rights to the Scrolls. The Metropolitan's rumored price of one million dollars (actually half a million) had frightened off institutions and other investors, especially in light of continued assertions—some in prestigious journals by recognized scholars—that the Scrolls were utter frauds. In addition, the publication of the Scrolls had in fact decreased, rather than increased, their market value, since copies of the texts were now readily available to scholars and libraries. Furthermore, Mar Samuel could not return home because the Jordanian government had branded him a smuggler and traitor. Even Anton Kiraz had reappeared, seeking his cut from the expected sale.

By 1954, Mar Samuel, frustrated by these difficulties and desperate to secure a buyer, decided to take a gamble. On June 1 he advertised the

Scrolls in the ad section of the *Wall Street Journal!* There, next to other ads for steel tanks and summer rentals, the world's greatest historical treasure was listed. The ad simply read, "Biblical manuscripts dating back to at least 200 B.C. are for sale. This would be an ideal gift to an educational or religious institution by an individual or group."

It was at this point that the irony—or what Yadin called destiny—now began. It just so happened that Yadin, Sukenik's son, was visiting in New York on a lecture tour about the Dead Sea Scrolls. The day that the *Journal* advertised the Scrolls, a fellow Israeli named Monty Jacobs who was on a journalistic assignment in America alerted Yadin to the ad. Yadin knew exactly what was being offered, and in fact had already made up his mind to try and purchase the Scrolls for the Hebrew University if he could locate Mar Samuel. Yet he knew his next steps would have to be taken carefully. Because of the conflict with Jordan, not to mention the archbishop's own anti-Semitic sentiments, Yadin realized he could not reveal Israel as the buyer. From his work in army intelligence he knew that the only way to obtain the Scrolls was to use an intermediary loyal to his cause yet convincing to the Metropolitan.

Also, the go-between had to be a scholar who would not arouse the archbishop's suspicions and who could positively confirm the authenticity of the documents for sale. To serve this purpose, Yadin called the esteemed Masoretic expert and professor at Hebrew Union College in Cincinnati, Ohio—Dr. Harry Orlinsky. As providence would have it, the professor was just getting in his car to leave on vacation when he heard the phone ring. Yadin would not divulge to him the whole reason for coming to New York; he only said that it was imperative that he come immediately. Upon arriving in New York, Professor Orlinsky was briefed in much the same manner as a spy being given a directive for an undercover mission—which this was! Yadin later called it "a cloak-and-dagger business."[31] As Dr. Orlinsky himself explained:

> I was to assume the name Mr. Green, an expert on behalf of the client. I was to take a taxi to the Lexington Avenue entrance of the Waldorf-Astoria Hotel, where the Chemical Bank and Trust Co. had a branch. I was to make sure that I was not followed. A Mr. Sydney M. Estridge would be waiting there for me; we had not been told how to identify one another. He would go with me downstairs to the vault of the bank. There we would find a representative of the Metropolitan, with the Scrolls ready for examination. I was to say as little as possible, and to admit

to no identification beyond being Mr. Green. . . . After leaving the vault, I phoned an unlisted number and spoke the word *lechayim*, meaning the Scrolls were genuine.[32]

Over the days of negotiation and on the day of purchase, Yadin had wired messages to Teddy Kollek, then director-general of the prime minister's office in Jerusalem (and later the city's first and, for two decades, only mayor). These, in part, read:

> An unexpected miracle has happened. The four Dead Sea Scrolls, including Isaiah, brought to US by the Syrian Metropolitan . . . can be bought at once . . . expect a positive reply.

The reply came, and once the payment of $250,000 was received by Mar Samuel, the Scrolls were in Yadin's possession, and he wired the follow-up message:

> . . . For the difficulties that are now facing you, find consolation! The treasures of the past are in our hands as of this morning at 10:30. Will send them to Jerusalem next week.[33]

Yadin had now completed the circle of what his father had begun. The Scrolls again belonged to Israel and were going home. The financing had come, in part, from New York philanthropist D.S. Gottesman, and his heirs later sponsored the construction of a permanent home for the Scrolls, known as *Hechal ha-Sefer* (the Shrine of the Book) and located in Jerusalem's Israel Museum (*see photo section*). Today the Scrolls, along other equally valuable treasures discovered in the Judean wilderness, are on display for all the world to see.

## Aftermath of the Purchase

Once the news of the sale in the United States reached the Bedouin, they launched a full-scale search through the desert caves for additional manuscripts. They found more Scrolls as well as large sections of Scrolls, and reasoned that they could get more money by tearing them into smaller pieces. The more pieces, the more money! In order to discourage this practice, a standard price for Scroll material was worked out by Kando. Whatever the condition of the Scroll material, the price was the same: one British pound per square centimeter of parchment. According to Professor Hartmut Stegemann, this calculation was based upon the size of the *Great Isaiah Scroll (1QIsaᵃ)* divided by one-fourth of the purchase price of the four Scrolls previously in the possession of the Metropolitan Samuel, or $250,000. During my interview with Abu-Dahoud, he said that when he learned about the sale of the St. Mark's Scrolls in America, he went to Kando and demanded more money. In the style of Bedouin justice, he took out a knife and tried to cut Kando's throat, but Kando grabbed the knife and ended up only with an injury to his hand. A Jordanian officer interceded, and for a settlement of 250 Jordanian dinars, Abu-Dahoud released Kando of any further claim.

The Jordanian government also reacted to the sale. They protested and threatened to sue, but could not complete their threat since to do so would force them to legally acknowledge the State of Israel—a move they were unwilling to take at that time. Ironically, unknown to the Jordanians, there were more Scrolls in Jordan, and Israel was again to have providence smile on her desire to unite these long-lost bequests from her ancestors.

## One More Scroll

One of the most intriguing stories about discovering the Scrolls has nothing to do with digging in Dead Sea caves but rather with the human drama surrounding the marketing of the Scrolls. When Cave 11 was first discovered by the Bedouin, they removed some Scrolls and sold them to Kando. These Scrolls were not immediately offered by Kando for sale. However, late in the summer of 1960 the existence of one of these Cave 11 Scrolls was surreptitiously revealed to Yadin by a man serving as Kando's intermediary, known then only as "Mr. Z" (an identity Yadin kept secret until the day of his death on June 28, 1984).[34] As it would turn out, this Scroll would be the largest and, by many scholars' assessment, the most important of all the Dead Sea Scrolls ever discovered. It came to be called the *Temple Scroll (11Q19* or *11QTempleᵃ)* because its contents included plans to construct a Third Temple in Jerusalem. The details of this Scroll have been highly significant for the study of Second Temple Judaism as well as early Christianity (see chapter 11). Its connection with Cave 11 was confirmed by the finding of an additional 38 fragments of another copy of the text in Cave 11 (now known as *11Q20* or *11QTempleᵇ*).[35]

The story of The Temple Scroll begins with a Virginia minister's tour of the Holy Land.[36] The minister was the Rev. Joseph Uhrig, who in the early 1950s, when television was still coming of age, had one of the first and most successful evangelistic broadcasts (later continued by Dr. Jerry Falwell as the Old Time Gospel Hour). During a 1955 trip to the lands of the Bible, Rev. Uhrig was given as a guide an Arab Christian by the name of Marcos Hazou. The next year Hazou wanted to immigrate with his family to the United States and asked Rev. Uhrig to sponsor him. The minister agreed to do so and even rented Hazou a house, bought furniture for his family, and gave him a job in his ministry's mailroom. One day in 1960, Hazou told Rev. Uhrig that his brother in Bethlehem had a friend named Kando, who had many ancient manuscripts in his possession. Using his connections through Hazou, Rev. Uhrig went to Bethlehem to meet Kando, was shown Scroll fragments, and offered to find proper buyers in Israel (where Uhrig believed they belonged). Thus, Rev. Uhrig became the mysterious "Mr. Z."

Returning to the United States, Uhrig contacted Yadin about one particularly large Scroll Kando kept in hiding. Kando's asking price was one million dollars, which both Uhrig and Yadin thought was absurd. Yadin, of course, refused, countering that he would make an offer only in the price range established by the Metropolitan Athanasius Samuel. Uhrig later said that Kando "had illusions that there would be some multimillionaire in the United States [who would eventually pay his price]."[37] Abu-Dahoud added the observation that the reason Kando held on to these Scrolls despite lucrative offers was because he had already become reasonably wealthy from previous deals and was not desperate for the money. He could afford to wait. Abu-Dahoud said that while Kando was a good man, he was a better businessman: "For something worth $1,000 he would buy it for $2-3!" But the asking price was not Yadin's only concern. By this time the Dead Sea Scrolls had become well known and forgeries abounded on the black market. Too, Yadin could not be certain of Uhrig's source. He needed more proof. This proof was about to come in an unexpected way.

Uhrig made another trip to Bethlehem and this time was shown the large Scroll, which was tightly wrapped and stored in a shoe box. He decided to buy from Kando the fragment he had been shown on his first trip (which later became known as the *Psalm Scroll*). Having had to bring him the news of Yadin's refusal, he wanted to convince Kando he was a serious buyer so that he could continue to negotiate for the large Scroll. When he got back home, he took the Psalm fragment, wrapped it in a paper napkin, and mailed it to Yadin in Israel in a manila envelope!

When Yadin saw the fragment he knew that it was a missing piece from a Scroll the Rockefeller Museum had obtained from Kando.

Yadin now decided to make an offer to Kando of $130,000—$10,000 in a cash deposit and $120,000 on deposit in the Chase Manhattan Bank. Uhrig went back to Kando with Yadin's $10,000 in his sock and tried to persuade Kando to let him take the large Scroll back to the States with him. Kando instead raised the asking price to $200,000. Yadin again refused, with the result that he retained the fragment and Uhrig the $10,000 deposit. This was in 1962, and after one final communication with "Mr. Z," Yadin lost contact and the dream of Israel's owning another Scroll began to fade as the years moved forward. However, in the Middle East, situations often change quickly, and Yadin was to finally get the Scroll but in a way he never would have imagined.

Five years had passed since Yadin last received a letter from Uhrig. He would from time to time check the listings from Jordan to see if there was any news about the Scroll having been purchased by their Antiquities Department, but no trace of it appeared. Then, on June 5, 1967, Jordan, along with other Arab countries bordering Israel, declared war on Israel. I was only a student in junior high school at the time, but I remember watching the coverage of the battle each night on our black-and-white television. I knew that it was a crucial time for Israel, but I had no idea it was also a turning point in the struggle for the *Temple Scroll*. The battle would not last long, and its brevity would be remembered in history through its name—the Six-Day War. Yadin was at this time serving as an advisor to the prime minister. When on June 7 the Israeli Defense Forces captured the Old City of Jerusalem and Bethlehem, Yadin thought that the Scroll might still be hidden at Kando's residence. Since Bethlehem was now within Israeli jurisdiction and Yadin had the power of command, he immediately instituted a search-and-seizure operation. Yadin well remembered the events that followed:

> With the approval of the prime minister, the General Staff placed a lieutenant colonel of the Military Intelligence at my disposal. All the information necessary to conduct a search for the Scroll was given to him, including a description of the exact nature and shape of the fragment in my possession. The dealer was traced and, after brief negotiations . . . he took the officer to his home where, from a primitive cache under the flooring tiles, he unearthed a BATA shoe box wrapped in a paper. . . . Inside it was the Scroll, wrapped in a sheet of cellophane and a towel. . . .

He had, in addition, a cigar box with many damaged, crumbled and macerated fragments that had become detached from the Scroll.[38]

The next day, as Israel's revered first prime minister David Ben Gurion was being shown the long-denied sights of the newly won *Temple Mount*, the *Temple Scroll* was on its way to Yadin. By 8:00 P.M. the Scroll was at last in his hands. Shortly thereafter Kando produced additional fragments of the Scroll, which he had hidden behind family pictures in his brother's home. Although the Scroll was lawfully confiscated by the military government in accordance with Jordan's own law of antiquities (Kando had illegally concealed the Scroll from the Jordanian authorities), the Israeli authorities eventually paid Kando $105,000. If for no other reason, the payment was made to encourage other dealers who might be holding Scrolls to bring them out of hiding.

The *Temple Scroll* then joined its family at the Shrine of the Book. Lost in a time of war when Israel suffered defeat and Jerusalem fell, it had now been found again in a time of war when by Israel's victory Jerusalem was regained. After a 2,000-year separation, one more Scroll had come home.

## Unsung Heroes in the Story

Before moving forward in our study of the Dead Sea Scrolls, we should make sure we don't overlook the unsung heroics of those who acted to bring the Scrolls to the world. Mar Samuel and Rev. Joseph Uhrig have both been criticized for their part in the selling or attempted selling of the Scrolls. Nevertheless, any seemingly negative actions on their part are outweighed by the positive action they took to help preserve the Scrolls. Mar Samuel took on a great financial risk when he purchased the four Scrolls from Kando. He had been told by almost all the experts he contacted that they were medieval forgeries or something worse, yet against these learned judgments he gambled on their being genuine. Had he not done so it is possible that Kando might have plied his cobbler trade and turned the Scrolls into sandal straps or shoe linings! And had Mar Samuel not later sold the Scrolls in America for a high figure, it is unlikely that the Bedouin would have been motivated to comb the caves and retrieve the additional Scrolls and the hundreds of fragments they alone produced.

As for Rev. Uhrig, had he not pursued at his own expense the rumor that Kando still had some Scrolls, the *Temple Scroll* might never have been revealed. Even though Uhrig's unsuccessful negotiations with Yadin were motivated in part by his own needs to fund his ministry and church, he nevertheless left Yadin with a description of the Scroll and its whereabouts. In the end, Uhrig's information enabled the Israelis to secure the Scroll, just as Uhrig had wished.

There are lesser heroes, too, such as Monty Jacobs, who called Yadin to tell him about the *Wall Street Journal* advertisement for the Scrolls. Had Monty not followed through on his convictions and pursued the matter, Yadin may have well missed his destiny. We must also commend John Trevor, for during times of cold and personal discomfort, often against the urging of his friends and amidst the dangerous days of 1947–1948, he pursued his passion to make the Scrolls available to the world. His dedication in doing so stands in marked contrast to the next 40 years, during which so very few of the Scrolls were revealed to scholars (other than those to whom they were assigned) and the public alike. Ultimately, all these men were driven by a desire to know the unknown, preserve the past, and tell the story of the Scrolls. Thanks to them, that story has been told.

# 3

# THE SCANDAL OF
# THE SCROLLS

*There is virtually unanimous agreement among all the con-
cerned parties—apart, of course, from the International Team
themselves and the École Biblique—that the history of Dead Sea
Scroll scholarship does constitute a "scandal."*[1]

—Michael Baigent and
Richard Leigh

When ancient artifacts like the Dead Sea Scrolls are discovered, the
scholarly community as well as the informed public eagerly await their
publication. The publication of the first discovered Scrolls from Cave 1,
as well as those from caves 2-3, 5-10 and Wadi Murabba'at, was in keeping
with this expectation. However, a massive assortment of fragments, mostly
from Cave 4, remained unpublished and generally inaccessible to scholars
outside the International Team from 1952–1992.[2] Even though this material represents only 20 percent of the total texts, the fact that it was held

in private domain for 40 years opened a Pandora's box of libelous accusations and charges of conspiracy.

Although legitimate concerns were voiced by responsible publishers in the field (such as Hershel Shanks of the *Biblical Archaeology Review*), sensationalistic authors were quick to capitalize on the controversy. Demonizing members of the International Team, they claimed that Catholic scholars were working under orders from the Vatican to suppress Scroll secrets that would destroy traditional Christianity, or that Israeli scholars were hiding evidence that would confirm Christianity against traditional Judaism. While photographs of all the unpublished material were released in 1992 and unofficial translations of selected texts have appeared recently, the bulk of this material still remains unpublished in the official *Discoveries in the Judean Desert* (*DJD*) series. As a result, the public continues to wonder if some type of scandal is going on.

## Getting the Scrolls Published

Strange as it may seem, the first publication effort related to the Dead Sea Scrolls came barely two centuries after they were hidden away. The early church father Origen found ancient Hebrew and Greek manuscripts in jars in the region of Jericho. In proper scholarly fashion, he endeavored to get these Scrolls published. He did this by incorporating the Greek text of one of the Scrolls (Psalms) into his critical edition of the Bible, which was finished about A.D. 245 and is known today as the *Hexapla*.[3] This was the first time in history that the information in the Dead Sea Scrolls was made accessible to scholars in any form. The original work of 15 volumes (more than 6,500 pages) was lost in the seventh-century fire that destroyed the Library at Alexandria; however, incomplete copies were preserved.[4]

Today, more than 1,700 years later, modern scholars have had the opportunity to follow Origen's example. After the first seven Scrolls came to light, the first complete English edition of two of the Scrolls (*Great Isaiah Scroll A, Pesher Habakkuk*) appeared in 1950, just two years after they were obtained by scholars. Another (*Manual of Discipline*) followed the next year, with three more (*Great Isaiah B, War Scroll, Thanksgiving Hymns*) in 1955, and the rest (*Genesis Apocryphon,* Cave 1 fragments) by 1956. While publication was in progress on the texts from Cave 1, caves 2-11 (with the exception of Cave 4) and Wadi Murabba'at were discovered (1952, 1955–56) and brought forth new Scrolls. Most of these were also promptly published in 1960–62, with the Cave 11 material being published at various dates in the 1960s and 1970s. Even the Cave 11 *Temple Scroll*, recovered in 1967, saw publication in Hebrew by 1977 (the English version was released in 1983). Therefore, including the *Temple Scroll*, approximately 80 percent of all the Dead Sea Scrolls have been available in English since 1983, and one popular English translation has been available since 1956 with new manuscript material added to each subsequent edition (1964, 1976).[5]

The remaining 20 percent of the texts, which are still unpublished, came mostly from Cave 4 (with a few items from Cave 11) and presented special problems for their decipherment. By contrast, the texts from Cave 1 had been relatively easy to translate and publish. The Scrolls had been in good condition, the text was legible, and most of the material was or included biblical texts, which, resembling the well-known Masoretic Text, allowed translation to proceed quickly. Although the texts from the other locations were often fragmentary, they could still be assembled and read in reasonable time.

The Cave 4 fragments, however, were a wholly different matter, which we will consider shortly. While the Cave 1 documents were all published by American and Israeli scholars who had no official affiliation with one another as Scroll editors, the Cave 4 material demanded the organization of a select Scroll Team. It is this team and this material that has received the accusations of scandal.[6] However, it should be noted that several team members published preliminary transcriptions of their texts apart from the *DJD* series, and team member John Allegro published all his Cave 4 assignments by 1965.[7] We need to remember as well that no accusations of scandal arose prior to the discovery of the fragmentary texts. Certain factors affected the publication of these texts, and we must consider them as we survey the theories for the long delays.

## The Dead Sea Scrolls Deception?

In 1991 a book was published in the United States by sensationalist journalists Michael Baigent and Richard Leigh with the forthright title *The Dead Sea Scrolls Deception*. Sensing that a bestseller could come out of the then much-publicized controversy over the delay in Scroll publication, these authors, with assistance from (and as propagandists for) revisionist historian Robert Eisenman (see chapter 17), produced a detective-type story of intrigue, conspiracy, and the collapse of traditional

Christianity. The authors were right in one respect: The book did become a bestseller (well over a million copies were sold in the United States, half a million were sold in Germany, and countless more worldwide. The book garnished media attention and generated a spate of academic and popular lectures and discussions on university campuses and in churches and religious organizations of all denominations.

The book's basic premise was that the Vatican, with help from the Scroll Team, was behind a conspiracy to conceal unorthodox revelations in the Scrolls that threatened to undermine the foundations of the Christian faith. One chapter, entitled "The Dilemma for Christian Orthodoxy," focused especially on this accusation. Yet only four members of the original Scroll Team were Catholic, a predominance dictated by the role that the Dominican Catholic institution, the École Biblique, played in the drama of the Scrolls. The other four members were Protestant: Lutheran, Presbyterian, and an ex-Methodist turned agnostic.

However, the Catholic Church was not alone targeted for destruction. In the conclusion of Baigent and Leigh's book, it is "Christian fundamentalism," not Catholicism, which the audience is warned against. Here, a diatribe is made against Christian, Jewish, and Muslim fundamentalism without distinguishing their obvious differences. Together they are labeled as being "chronically prone" to "bigotry, intolerance, and fanaticism."[8] In support of this the authors claimed to "disclose" information about these concealed texts and "the revolutionary" and "explosive material that has been suppressed" and what it reveals "about the earliest Christians hitherto unknown." One of their sources for "uncovering" these secrets were the papers of the late John Allegro, an agnostic member of the Scroll Team who embarrassed his fellow editors and himself by making the unsupportable allegation that he saw statements in the unpublished Scrolls that refuted Christianity. He had to issue a retraction when the rest of the Scroll Team publicly denied his claims.

Other sources used by the authors included interviews with Dead Sea Scroll scholars but most of the input came from Robert Eisenman. Despite their tantalizing promises, the authors revealed no new texts. This was because, as they noted, the unpublished texts were so secret that they never saw them! In addition, they admitted that they could not even persuade the scholars who had knowledge of the unpublished texts to divulge it in any form. This means they based their radical revision of the history and theology of Christianity on texts they had not seen and contents of which they could not learn! They had claimed that these "unseen and unknown" documents represented "seventy-five percent of the around 800 manuscripts written in Old Hebrew and Aramaic [that] are being withheld from the public."[9] Was there any truth, then, to their amazing charges?

## The Deception in
## *The Dead Sea Scrolls Deception*

We have already seen that at the time Baigent and Leigh published their book that the percentage figures for the published and unpublished Scrolls were actually the reverse of what they claim (80 percent published, 20 percent unpublished). Furthermore, there was no conspiracy to suppress the 80 percent that was previously published—material that was largely controlled by the Catholic scholar Roland de Vaux, whom Baigent and Leigh claim was at the time under secret orders of the Vatican to suppress the Scrolls. The consensus concerning the 80 percent of published texts was that they were no threat to the Christian faith. However, if, as Baigent and Leigh argue, the unpublished 20 percent was, then it can be countered that it was upon the 80 percent that Eisenman (whom they followed) developed his radical theories about Christianity at Qumran (since most of the unpublished texts were not accessible to him). But even with the publication of the photographs of the remaining 20 percent and their subsequent study by independent scholars, Baigent and Leigh's accusations of "spiritual dynamite" that might "demolish the entire edifice of Christian teaching and belief"[10] have been disproven. None of the photographs of the unpublished texts have revealed any of the kind of startling revelations claimed by Eisenman. The supposed "cover-up" by scholars came as a result of Eisenman's release to the press of his early interpretive translations of texts that purported to give evidence of a crucified and divine Messiah. These interpretations, often headlined sensationally by the media, were presented to the public as "official translations." Therefore, scholars who knew quite well that the texts in question were difficult and that any reconstruction would be subject to dispute were accused of conspiring to cover up the facts when they either disagreed or were reluctant to comment on such translations.

In 1992 Eisenman and Michael Wise produced a book with 50 translations of previously unpublished texts, entitled *The Dead Sea Scrolls Uncovered*. In the book they offered their interpretations with the purpose of buttressing Eisenman's unorthodox historical views.[11] For this reason, as well as the charge of unprofessional documentation, the late

Hebrew University professor and Scroll Team member Jonas Greenfield stated that "deception is afoot throughout the book."[12] Diminishing further the supposedly objective nature of the book's scholarship was the dust jacket's enthusiastic endorsement by Baigent and Leigh. Since the release of *The Dead Sea Scrolls Uncovered*, almost all the Scroll scholars have criticized the hasty reconstruction and interpretation of texts by Eisenman and Wise. What's ironic is that had these proved to be accurate interpretations, they would have been a boon, not a bust, for Christianity.

Contrary to Eisenman's fanciful historical reconstructions, no text discovered among the Scrolls ever mentioned a single figure that could be related to early Christianity. Neither has there been any evidence to suggest a connection between the Qumran Sect and Christianity. Thus Baigent, Leigh, and Eisenman's whole hypothesis falls apart completely, for without such connections there would be no reason for the Vatican to suppress the material.

What do those who are closest to the Scrolls say about this matter? Professor Emanuel Tov, the present head of the International Team of the Dead Sea Scroll Committee, emphatically disavows any Vatican connection. When I posed the conspiracy question to him, he replied:

> I would completely brush aside any accusations of suppressing material. There is no evidence whatsoever for this having been done by any Catholic source. What they would gain by it? This is all nonsense. [Yet] this accusation is to be heard until today, [even though] now all of the photographs are available and people can see that there is no fragment which could have even instigated the Vatican to consider such a suppression. We [the International Team] don't really give any serious thought to it.[13]

In like manner, Joseph A. Fitzmyer, a Catholic scholar and also a member of the International Team, states:

> The whole idea of a Vatican conspiracy to suppress the Scrolls that it [Baigent and Leigh's book] portrays is ludicrous nonsense. The only involvement that the Vatican ever had with the Dead Sea Scrolls . . . was not an effort to suppress the Scrolls, but to acquire them from the Bedouin at a time when foreign funds were needed. The Vatican sought to acquire some of the Cave 4 fragments for its library, a perfectly understandable move on its part, given the quality of its library and museum.[14]

I asked long-time Scroll scholar and retired University of Tübingen Professor Otto Betz, who published a book entitled *Jesus, Qumran and the Vatican*, to summarize the alleged Vatican connection and counter the assertions of Baigent and Leigh:

> The Vatican had nothing to do with the publication of the Scrolls. The [first seven] Scrolls were published by the Americans and the Israelis. Afterwards the order that had to be published was about 20,000 fragments from Cave 4. For this a team was established for which the most important figures were the Dominicans, but there were also Protestant scholars on the team, for example [Claus-Hunno] Hunsinger from Germany [Lutheran] and [Frank] Cross from America [Presbyterian], and also [the agnostic John] Allegro from England [ex-Methodist]. The Vatican did not influence them in any of the publications of these fragments. On the contrary the Vatican wanted them to finish it as soon as possible. That the Dominican [de Vaux] in this committee was the most prominent figure was only because he was the Oblate in Jerusalem to which these houses belonged [École Biblique], and they were the most capable ones for deciphering and bringing together these many thousands of fragments and publishing them. So there can be no doubt that the Vatican did *not* want to influence the publication of these fragments because it was afraid that it would do damage to the Christian faith. There was no explosive material in these fragments as was claimed by Eisenman—this is simply an invention of [Eisenman and] these journalists in order to make the publication of the Scrolls more exciting for the public.

## The Scandal of the Scrolls

Despite the fact that the claims of conspiracy and deception are unfounded, the handling of the Cave 4 Scrolls by the members of the original Scroll Team are still to be considered by many scholars as scandalous. In fact, the famous Oxford Qumran scholar Geza Vermes ranked it as "the academic scandal par excellence of the twentieth century."[15] According to German author Klaus Berger, Professor of New Testament at the University of Heidelberg, the nature of this scandal can be understood in several ways.[16] First, the arrogant attitude of the scholars entrusted with the texts—texts they could not hope to publish in their entirety within their lifetimes—constituted a scandal. Despite their obvious qualifications, most of these scholars were known to have personal problems and some had clearly abandoned the task for other duties without releasing their assignments to others. Thus these scholars appeared to be sitting upon their privileged information without regard to other scholars and the public, who were anxiously awaiting access. As a result, the Scroll Team came to be viewed as an "inner circle," "keepers of the grail," as a Scroll "cartel," "coterie," and "monopoly." In fact, their lack of disclosure invited the fanciful theories of suppression invented by Baigent and Leigh.

Second, members of the Scroll Team both teased scholars and excited the public by claiming that many of the unpublished texts had parallels to Judaism and Christianity that were so important as to cause a major revision of history and the interpretation of it. This may have been more the case for Christianity than for Judaism, yet claims of "crucified Messiah" texts certainly would affect both groups! Yet in the end no real information was ever released, and interested parties were left with only the word of the assigned scholars.

Third, because of the lack of accurate information, cults and sensationalists were able to use the Scrolls to undermine the faith of many people and instill doubts in others who might have considered a faith position. Because competent scholars were left unable to give answers to these groups' errant publications (because of a lack of information), there was a weakening of both the synagogue and the church.

Why did the Scroll Team act in such an apparently unprofessional and irresponsible manner? If Baigent and Leigh are incorrect about their reasons for the delay in publication of the Scrolls, then what are the real reasons?

## The Real Reasons for the Delay

The reasons for the delays in publishing the Scroll fragments can be explained apart from any collusion on the part of the team or some unseen hierarchy that wants to conceal publication of most of the unpublished texts. These explanations are not meant as excuses for what almost all scholars admit was excessive delay. Rather, they are given to help the nonscholarly public understand what is involved in the process of publishing the Scrolls. The factors we'll look at include the condition and accessibility of the Scroll fragments, the political situation, the scholastic responsibilities of the editors, the nature of the text assignments, and the financial and human problems imposed by the editors.

## Condition of the Texts

Even when Scroll fragments are easily legible for someone with a good knowledge of Hebrew and Aramaic, their interpretation still demands unique training and expertise. As we already know, many of the Cave 4 fragments were not clearly legible due to fragmentary letters or unclear script, and some could not be read at all for decades until technology provided the means. Even the fragments that could be read were often filled with *lacunae* (gaps or omissions), requiring conjectural reconstructions based on a vast knowledge of the language and comparative texts. Developing the skills to accomplish such a task takes years of specialized study. To make matters worse, most of the Cave 4 fragments were in extremely fragile condition and in an advanced state of decay (a deterioration accelerated by being stored at the scrollery). Frank Cross described their condition upon arrival at the museum as "brittle, warped, crinkled, shrunken, encrusted with soil chemicals, and blackened by moisture and age." Moreover, many thousands of the fragments are not much larger than a thumbnail. Those who have attempted to assemble a formidable jigsaw puzzle know the painstaking and frustrating work involved in bringing the pieces together. But imagine attempting such a project with puzzle pieces so delicate that they cannot be touched or even breathed upon, and written upon in ancient languages that can barely be read!

While assembly of the many pieces accounts for some of the delay, it cannot account for the majority of it, since most of that work was completed in 1960. Revisions in reconstruction and improvements being made thereafter were merely an expected part of the ongoing process of interpretation, even after publication. However, it was the problem of interpretation that had a significant part (combined with the human elements) in the delay. To give an idea of how difficult it can be to interpret a text, even after reconstruction and translation, consider the following example of just two fragments combined by F. Garcia Martinez, the editor of the recently published text known as *The New Jerusalem (11QNJ):*

1. The grape when separated from the palm [ . . . ] loosed yet for them, which is [ . . . ]

2. from the radiance in them, and the fi[fth] crown [ . . . ] and all which have finished his seven [ . . . ]
3. interior of the cover, and the sixth crown [ . . . ] his brothers entered in their place, four hundred [ . . . and the]
4. seventh [crown], according to the radiance and the [ . . . ], . . . And he said to me: to the twenty six [ . . . ]
5. [and the High Priest was clothed [ . . . ]
6. the holy of holies
7. [ . . . they] entered [ . . . ]

To arrive at the above translation, the editor may have combined two unrelated fragments which, in his opinion, could have been related in the intact text. Remember that everything in brackets [ . . . ] indicates words or lines missing from the surviving text, and that translation work included within the brackets is reconstruction based on the editor's opinion. Despite the obvious lack of clarity, the editor must propose an interpretation of the text. If the editor has incorrectly combined the two texts and used words from one to interpret the other, his entire interpretation may be flawed. In the case of this particular reconstruction, other scholars have challenged the combination of the two fragments and proposed alternate interpretations.[17]

The special aptitude and experience that is necessary for this kind of work is possessed by a limited number of men in the world. Although today we have computers that can help in the job of assembly and reconstruction, yet the task of interpretation is still all too human. With so many fragments and so few qualified scholars, it has taken a long time to interpret the texts.

### Accessibility of the Materials

The original Scroll fragments, in most cases, remain within the scrollery at the Rockefeller Museum in Jerusalem and are not immediately accessible to the scholars assigned to them. These scholars, even in Jerusalem, must work exclusively from photographs, cutting and pasting together these captured images as if they were real texts. If the photographs are unclear, or a letter is disputed, they must wait until they can return to the scrollery and make comparisons with the original text. Often this cannot take place until a summer recess from school or a sabbatical. In addition, these scholars are constantly hampered by inadequate resources, lack of assistance, and lack of necessary equipment. Often they must depend on archives, libraries, or laboratories that are at distant destinations and require a considerable waiting period for access. Fortunately, the advent of computer scanning of texts and Internet access have greatly aided scholarly access to needed materials.

### The Political Situation

When the original Scroll Team was assembled it was made up of a multinational and religiously diverse group of scholars. However, as pluralistic and ecumenical as the group may have seemed, there was one group excluded from representation: Jewish scholars. The condition of non-Jewish involvement was stipulated by the Jordanians, who then controlled the scrollery and both officially denied the existence of the state of Israel and continued in a state of war with her. This political cloud over the work of the Scrolls was unfortunate, since it would have been natural to include Jewish and especially Israeli scholarship among the members. The heritage of the Scrolls belonged to the Israelis. Because Hebrew is their native language and they have long been involved in study of the biblical texts, they were best prepared for work with the Scrolls. Also, it was Israelis who possessed the larger collection of the Scrolls, all housed within the same city. And it was Israelis who could most affordably access the fragments. Yet even though Jews were excluded, the Jewish philanthropist and financier John Nelson Rockefeller went ahead and sponsored the Scroll scholars in their work at the scrollery during the 1950s.

Interestingly, when the city of Jerusalem changed hands and the Israeli Department of Antiquities (as it was then called) took possession of the scrollery, Roland de Vaux, the head of the Team, continued the former policy of ostracizing Jews from the Scroll Team.[18] Professor Emanuel Tov explains:

> When the political situation changed in 1967 and Israel had control, the editorial situation was not changed. This was a result of conversations between a certain official person in Israel and the editor-in-chief of the International Team. Israel did not step in at that time and for many years thereafter in order to avoid a situation. I would say personally that it was a right decision because there were enough troubles with the Dead Sea Scrolls that it would have been unwise to mix these with political issues. Israel would have been accused of many things. When criticism demanded that Israel step in it was rather late, around 1989–1990.

In retrospect it could have been done a little earlier, a few years earlier. However, 1967 would have been too early.[19]

Professor Tov speaks practically as a scholar who accepts the reality of the constantly changing political climate in the Middle East. His point about Israel being "accused of many things" is well taken. After Israel captured East Jerusalem and with it the Palestine Archaeological Museum, Jordan raised an international protest that every Israeli excavation thereafter was a Zionist attempt to steal Jordanian antiquities. The Jordanian protest secured UNESCO's condemnation of Israel for Professor Mazar's excavations at the southern end of the Temple Mount (which began in 1968). The greatest protests were voiced over Yigael Yadin's seizure of the *Temple Scroll* from Kando's house in Bethlehem (formerly Jordanian territory, thus supposedly a Jordanian artifact!). Arab authorities have continued to complain whenever Israeli excavations have taken place in sensitive areas of Jerusalem; in 1995, these complaints provoked a year-long European boycott of Jewish celebrations that had been planned for Jerusalem's 3,000th anniversary up to ten years previous.

Political affinities were also an impediment to scholarly progress on the Scrolls. Most members of the original Scroll Team (de Vaux, Skehan, Starcky, Milik, Allegro) had anti-Semitic sentiments and openly aligned themselves with the Arab cause even after the 1967 Six-Day War.[20] Examples of this anti-Semitism include Patrick Skehan's refusal to publish his completed volume in the *DJD* series under Israeli auspices and Roland de Vaux's decision to discontinue his work at the École Biblique in protest of "Israeli occupation." At the time these attitudes temporarily shut down work on the Scrolls. Even though de Vaux later (1971) did become involved in archaeological excavation in Israel, he also died in the same year. Later, John Strugnell, who succeeded Père Benoit as editor-in-chief in 1987, was removed from his post because of his brazen anti-Semitic statements to the Israeli press (1990).

In my opinion, the Antiquities Authority should have made an issue of the Scroll Team's anti-Semitism and used it as justification for including balance on the Team by including Israeli scholars despite the political sensitivities. Had Israelis been involved in the process from the beginning, it is possible that the Scroll material would have been published much more quickly. While the Antiquities Authority did not impose Jewish scholars on de Vaux's team, it did request that the work be speeded up so that the world could see the texts. Fortunately, now that the work is proceeding under Israeli direction, better progress is being made.

## The Nature of the Text Assignments

From the very beginning of the translation process it was obvious that too much material had been assigned to too few scholars. It may be argued that the Team of seven to eight men were the best that could be found, but they were still not enough. Some 574 manuscripts had been identified by the Team from the Cave 4 fragments, and the work involved in publishing just one text fragment could occupy a full year. Thus the task of publishing hundreds of fragments was an impractical assignment for a group of this size.

Another problem was that the allotments assigned to these editors were unevenly distributed. For instance, all of the biblical material, about one-third of the whole collection, was divided between Frank Cross and Patrick Skehan. John Strugnell was given over 100 texts, while Joseph Milik received 197. Jean Starcky received a mere 30 texts, but managed to publish only one before his death in 1988.

Complicating this already gargantuan task was the Team members' growing tendency to abandon simple transcriptions of the texts with minimal notes and instead write extensive commentaries. This imposed an even greater burden on the editors and made impossible any hope of meeting the publication schedule (which was largely ignored anyway). Eventually many of the editors had to give up their assignments to other scholars due to other responsibilities, health, or death. Further delays were incurred as these new editors started afresh with previously unseen texts that their predecessors had already studied for years.

## Scholastic Responsibilities

The Scroll Team members, for the most part, had and presently have full-time careers, usually in the academic realm. So in addition to fulfilling their Scroll assignments, they also have many other obligations. As Dr. Weston Fields notes:

> The scholars who have been assigned the translation duties are almost without exception all university professors who have other full-time responsibilities in teaching, departmental and field research, journal and other writing in their respective areas of specialization, faculty committees, outside ministries, and of course—a personal life.[21]

Professor Tov, who himself teaches at a university, understands this as perhaps the single most significant factor affecting the publication process:

> The people involved in the publication of the Dead Sea Scrolls were and are university professors. They get no specific help [with their assignments] and must fulfill their [classroom] teaching [responsibilities]. Even though a person may be a great scholar, he still needs time. That is the sole reason for the delay.[22]

This reason was confirmed by University of Michigan Professor David Noel Freedman, who was assigned the *Leviticus Scroll* and finally published it in 1985. Although he was not a member of the official Team, and he did not deal with the Cave 4 material, he still spoke as a Scroll editor when in 1977 he confessed:

> I write as a guilty party, since I was assigned responsibility for the *Leviticus Scroll* from Cave 11 about ten years ago. There have been some diplomatic and other complications, but basically, the reason this document has not been published is that I was overloaded with other obligations and commitments which claimed my time. . . . Many if not most scholars harbor optimistic delusions about what they can and will do in the way of productive writing, and even after observing many colleagues fall into the pit, I have followed the same primrose path.[23]

As an author and editor who is also a pastor, professor, and president of a Christian organization, I well understand this problem. I struggle constantly with the burden of having assumed more literary assignments than can be reasonably fulfilled. However, I am also bound by strict publishing schedules that force me to produce or forfeit my assignment.

Until recently, the members of the Scroll Team were not kept under pressure to produce. Yet one problem they continue to face is that of finances. So even with increased pressure, there is still the need to maintain some kind of income through other means.

### Financial Problems

Just as money was a problem for the initial acquisition of the Scrolls, so it has continued to be a problem for those who have attempted to work with them thereafter. Dr. Weston Fields says that "the biggest single reason for the delay in publication of the remainder of the Scrolls, as well as the slow pace of conservation, is insufficient funding."[24]

Since the funds used to support the work of these scholars come through donations, many of them must wait until there is sufficient funding to continue or complete their work. This was made all too clear when, after six years of support, the Rockefeller Foundation withdrew its financing for work on the fragments in the scrollery. When the money ran out, most of the scholars simply packed up and went home—causing more delays.

## Human Problems

Professor Tov gives human problems as one of the significant causes for the Scroll scandal:

> Why did it take so long for our team to reach this stage that volumes actually start rolling from the press, and is there any truth to all those rumors and accusations that there was an official suppressing of publications by us, or by the director, or by anybody on the Jewish side? We believe that this is not the case. [In explanation of the delay] I sometimes use the word "looseness," because only human reasons determined the slow speed of publication of the volumes.[25]

One of these "human reasons" is the scholars' training and professional expectation of doing good work. Every scholar is judged by his colleagues and the entire academic community based on what he publishes. In some cases, the reviews of his work may determine an advancement or a standstill in his academic career. For example, when Allegro's texts were published as *Discoveries in the Judean Desert V* in 1965, there was widespread criticism that he had worked too quickly to get published and as a result the editing had been done carelessly. One German New Testament scholar, Karlheinz Müller, wrote in his review of Allegro's work, "In general, *DJD V* is the worst and most unreliable Qumran edition to be foisted on the reader since the beginning of the discoveries."[26] This criticism no doubt cautioned other scholars on the team to take the necessary time to assure they would not be similarly criticized.

This problem of "scholastic perfectionism" is not limited to the realm of the Scrolls—it is prevalent in archaeological circles as well. The excavation work at Qumran, which was necessary for better understanding the Scrolls, was carried out in five successive campaigns from 1951–1956 by

Fr. Roland de Vaux. I have had the opportunity to view the original note-books containing de Vaux's handwritten notes (which are in French), yet to this day the report of his work has not been published in English.[27] Dr. Dan Bahat, the former District Archaeologist for Jerusalem, comments on this problem:

> One of the most serious problems concerning the archaeology of Jerusalem is the problem of publication. The Dead Sea Scrolls have the same problem. Scholars forget that the enemy of the good is the very good. If you try to accomplish the very good you don't do the good. And this is the case with the publication of excavations. Everyone believes that their way of excavation must be [in keeping with] a good philosophy or science of archaeology or whatever it is, [rather than] just publish work they have found. [It is better] to do it as quickly and concisely as possible: what was found and where it was found and the circumstances [of the find]—this will do. This is what the late [Benjamin] Mazar has done with his publication of pictures and plans, which I think is worth more than waiting for the more typical analysis of pottery and other things.[28]

Another human problem is the scholarly incentive to publish based on the expectation that proper recognition (and even financial remuneration) will be accorded authors who have labored for years on these difficult texts. This concern was explained by Dr. Frank Cross, one of the original Scroll Team members, as the reason for the exclusive control exerted by the Scroll editors:

> It is material that people have put 10 to 20 years of their lives into and hence simply don't want to give it away to other scholars to publish and take the credit for. They're somewhat jealous of their work. . . . On the one hand, I would say that the team has been slow. On the other hand, I think one must understand the human desire to have some credit for work done, and that is the situation here.[29]

The human problems that have arisen can sometimes be far too human, and that has been the case for a number of the individuals on the original Scroll Team. The men who made up the Team were considered either exceptional leaders in their field or geniuses in the specific tasks set before them. Yet they were also susceptible to the "normal" pressures and predicaments of life. Two suffered as alcoholics, one had a nervous breakdown, and another renounced his priestly vows and got married.

John Allegro, the agnostic, spent the rest of his life trying to find ways to subvert the Christian faith. He lived out his obsession; among his activities were the writing of a play based on his Christianity-in-the-Scrolls hypothesis, excavations in search of the treasures listed in the *Copper Scroll,* an attempted dig on the Temple Mount that was thwarted by Jordanian soldiers, and finally, the writing of books that sought to prove that Christianity was a myth and the product of a sacred mushroom cult.[30]

Even though some of the Scroll scholars were inhibited by human obstacles of their own making, still, they accomplished an amazing feat in assembling the Cave 4 material. Their publications in the *DJD* series have made outstanding contributions to many fields of scholarship and study. As Professor Tov observed, "The initial team was a great team. There were problems around it, but that doesn't diminish their scholarly value. They were great scholars."[31]

With the many problems we've considered, we can see why there were delays in getting the fragmentary Scroll materials published. Ultimately, these delays incited protests that called for changes to be made.

## A Tiresome Wait

When I returned to graduate school in 1989 the protests over what had become a 40-year delay had been mounting for several years. It had taken form in 1985 with Hershel Shanks, editor of the *Biblical Archaeology Review,* who had provided through his magazine a popular forum for scholars who questioned the handling and publication schedule of the Cave 4 texts. While most scholars had not liked the slow pace of progress, they had grown to accept it and were content to wait out the inevitable. However, there were some scholars who had become impatient in waiting for the publication of these texts upon which their own research desperately depended.

In 1985 this impatience was set to action when John Strugnell and Elisha Qimron stated publicly that their unpublished text known as *Misqat Ma'aseh Torah (4QMMT)* contained important information for understanding the history and nature of the Qumran Sect. After this, some of these anxious scholars made repeated yet unsuccessful appeals to their colleagues who held these unpublished texts. Denied even limited access, they began to go public with their complaints of a "Scroll monopoly."

One of the scholars who had been bluntly refused access (in this case by John Strugnell) was California State University Long Beach Professor Robert Eisenman. Not one to be treated in such a cavalier manner and given to antiestablishment crusades, he immediately launched an attack on the Scroll Team through the news media.

By 1990, when I attended the meeting of Scroll scholars and the Scroll Team at the Second Congress on Biblical Archaeology in Jerusalem, the criticisms in the press had made most of the "inner circle" defensive rather than conciliatory. The Israeli Antiquities Authority announced their desire to see the Scrolls move toward publication, but according to their own timetable, not the demands of outsiders. Many of us, who were graduate students working on dissertations that would have benefited from the availability of the new material, were disappointed by this news. One of my fellow students was writing a dissertation on early *halakha* in the Dead Sea Scrolls and needed privileged access to *4QMMT.* Another was researching the peculiarities of the paleo-Hebrew script of the Scrolls, which required access to the full spectrum of texts containing this scribal custom. I was working on a dissertation on Temple motifs, including those from the Second Temple period, and likewise needed access to several unpublished texts that had been rumored to contain information that could greatly affect my final conclusions. Fortunately, help came the very next year with the unexpected end of the Scroll monopoly.

## The Scroll Monopoly Ends

Several clandestine events that were in competition with one another served as the catalysts that helped to make the Scrolls become public. The first of these began when Eisenman openly accused the Scroll scholars of being incompetent, greedy, and unwilling to share the Scrolls with other scholars for the benefit of mankind. The public responded, and by October 1989, unsolicited photographs of unpublished texts began arriving in his mail from a sympathizer in Jerusalem. By November of 1990 Eisenman had 1,700 photographs of almost all of the unpublished texts! Securing the assistance of James Robison, a California scholar, and Michael Wise of the University of Chicago, they began reading and editing the texts while Eisenman sought financial investors for their publication.

Meanwhile, a second group was privately preparing to release the same information by different means. Hebrew Union College Scroll scholar Ben Zion Wacholder and his then-graduate student Martin Abegg had gained access to a restricted Scroll Team concordance, which in the 1950s had been compiled for use by the scholars doing the translation work. This concordance listed all the words (with sentence contexts) from each document from Caves 2-10. Supposedly Scroll Team members were the only ones who possessed the concordance, but Wacholder and Abegg discovered that Strugnell had permitted copies to be distributed to the institutions where the scholars were working, and they found out that a copy resided right at their own school! Abegg believed that from this concordance he could, by computer, reconstitute the original transcription of the texts. Hershel Shanks of the *Biblical Archaeology Review* willingly committed to publishing the finished text.

While this was transpiring, Eisenman and Robison also turned to Shanks for help in publishing their photographs. They had previously arranged for the scholarly Dutch publisher E.J. Brill (who had published Eisenman's dissertation) to take on the project. However, when *The Qumran Chronicle*, a Polish journal, was threatened with a lawsuit over publication of a bootleg copy of the *4QMMT* text, E.J. Brill withdrew. Shanks might have done well to back out as well, but in the end he published Abegg's computer-generated reconstructions and was immediately slapped with a lawsuit by one of *4QMMT*'s assigned scholars, Elisha Qimron. In view of the impending case (which was finally decided against Shanks), the court ordered Shanks to stop all sales of the book.

Unknown to everyone fighting for access to the Scrolls, two complete microfilm sets of photographs of all the Scrolls were on deposit in two locations in Southern California, Eisenman's home grounds! Philanthropist Elizabeth Hays Bechtel had financed the photography project for the Ancient Biblical Manuscript Center in Claremont, California. However, following a disagreement with the center, she had a complete set of the photographs made for herself. This she bequeathed to the Huntington Library, known for its rare books collection, before her death in 1987. When Shanks first announced through the press the forthcoming publication of the computer texts, Huntington Library director William Moffett decided to join the ranks and make public their microfilm "in the spirit of intellectual freedom" and in order "not to impose further barriers to scholarship."[32] So, on September 22, 1991, the Huntington Library surprised the world by announcing that it would release its photos to all interested scholars. The Israel Antiquities Authority initially gave a hostile response to this news (they threatened a lawsuit), but eventually came to accept what could not be changed and granted unrestricted access to all official photos of the Scrolls. At last, the monopoly was ended.

## Moving Forward

Now that the Scroll photographs are accessible and the rate of publication has been accelerated, the "Scroll scandal" is a matter of the past. The revised Scroll Team has also gained a new respectability, as explained by Team head Emanuel Tov:

> The team had been very small from the beginning. It was by the organization of my predecessor, Professor Strugnell, that the team was somewhat expanded from the original eight or nine scholars to some twenty, which is when I joined the team. But that was not enough, and when I took over in 1990–1991, we reorganized the team under the guidance of the Oversight or Advisory Committee. [Then] under the Israel Antiquities Authority the number rose to about sixty and these are the same people today, except for a few who are completing their assignments. [Our method of selection was to choose] the best in the field regardless of sex or religion or country. These included both senior scholars and younger scholars who had just completed their dissertation and even a few who had not yet completed their dissertation.
>
> The work is proceeding well and, if I may say so, my team is well organized. We have improved staff both in Jerusalem and at Notre Dame University. I think this [method] worked because in the meantime publications have been flowing steadily from the presses.[33]

In the past 40 years very few volumes were published; however, in recent years the International Team has greatly advanced the timetable for publication and has greatly multiplied the number of Scroll volumes available. According to Professor Tov, one reason for this dramatic increase in productivity is superior technology and its availability to the Scroll Team:

> While in the past it often took seven years for one volume to appear, in the last calendar year (1994) we published no less than three volumes of the *DJD* series. This year, 1995, we have published two and have several volumes in varying draft stages of preparation. In the next year (1996) we expect to have four or

five volumes to be completely ready. Today we do this [more quickly] by actually producing the camera-ready volumes ourselves. We have our own laser printers here [at the Jerusalem office] and in the United States. These are presented to the press, whose main task is mainly to take care of the plates, the photographs.[34]

There are still about 20 volumes that must be published to complete the *DJD* series, and the Team is confident that it will reach its goal by the year 2000. Professor Tov shares the reasons for this success:

Why did we succeed? First, I think we have a devoted number of colleagues on several continents. You might say our team is equally divided between the United States, Europe, and Israel. Second, scholars realize that they have to get it done. It's now or never! Third, we have a good production team in Jerusalem and in the United States (Notre Dame). And last, but not least, we have some money. [Although] the money cash flow is low right now, we hope to get some income beyond what we have. However, the money we have takes care of the actual production. Scholars who need assistance can get some money from us to hire people to help them with preparation of their volumes. This kind of assistance was not as available in the past, but now makes all the difference.[35]

## The Dead Sea Scrolls Foundation

To assure the continued publication of the Scrolls, a foundation has been established to raise the needed finances for scholars who are involved in Scroll research, translation, editing, and publication. Executive Director Dr. Weston Fields says this about the organization:

The Dead Sea Scrolls Foundation was formed in 1990 by Dead Sea Scroll scholars to speed up the production of the official translation, transcription, and publication of the Dead Sea Scrolls from Oxford University Press as *Discoveries in the Judean Desert* (or *DJD*). All of the Scrolls will be published and made available to the public through the efforts of The Dead Sea Scroll Foundation, which is now supporting these efforts. The total set is envisioned now as comprising 35 volumes, and these 35 volumes are being produced by about 65 scholars around the world. The Dead Sea Scrolls Foundation helps to support these scholars and their assistants, buys equipment, coordinates the activities, and is in a unique position to do this since the chairman of The Dead Sea Scrolls Foundation is also the editor-in-chief of the publication project in Jerusalem. We have professors from around the world—all of the most well-known Dead Sea Scroll scholars—on our Boards of Advisors and Directors. We also help to coordinate various projects such as the concordance project, which will come out on CD-ROM, and some of the new imaging projects, as well as the new project to look for caves and Scrolls on both sides of the Dead Sea.[36]

With the breaking of the Scroll monopoly, the reorganization of the Scroll Team, and the creation of the Dead Sea Scrolls Foundation, the future appears favorable indeed for the Scrolls. On the positive side, the controversy over access to the unpublished Scrolls heightened public awareness and excitement over the Scrolls and led to both increased funding for research and more rapid publication of the Scrolls. Scholars are now using this newly released material in significant studies that are making major contributions in their fields of study. And in the future, as excavations uncover more Scrolls, we can expect that the significance of new finds will become known to us much more quickly than ever before.

It is time now to leave the history of the Scrolls and consider the Scrolls themselves. In the next chapter we will begin to gain an understanding of these priceless treasures through a survey of their characteristics and contents. Come join me for a trip to a library like none other you have visited before—the library of Qumran.

# PART II

---

Deciphering the Secrets
of Ages Past

# 4

# A Survey of the Scrolls

*Just as a Christian reader must be excited by the manuscript of a Sect who may have known and influenced early Christians, so a Jew finds nothing more deeply moving than manuscripts written by the People of the Book, in the Land of the Book, more than 2,000 years ago.*

—Yigael Yadin, purchaser
of the Scrolls for Israel

As a lover of rare books I have spent many hours searching through musty shops in hopes of discovering some lost literary treasure. One of my most memorable adventures took place when I was invited to search the attic storeroom of an old seminary library. The feeling upon entering this room cloaked in perpetual twilight was like that of secreting into a sanctuary. Shelf upon shelf emerged from the darkness crammed with books that I was told had escaped a fire over a century ago. These volumes had long ago been removed to the upper realms and then forgotten as newer acquisitions multiplied. My excitement mounted as I perused leather-bound sets of Greek and Hebrew grammars, Bible dictionaries, seventeenth-century volumes of Josephus' works, and rows upon rows of theological commentaries. Even though the purpose of my visit was to purchase books for a fledgling Bible college library, the sensation was as though I was plundering one of the tombs of the ancients. If we can appreciate the suspense and satisfaction of uncovering a century-old library, then we can begin to imagine the incomparable discovery of an immense "library" hidden away over 2,000 years ago!

In this chapter we're going to look at what this library contains, how and where it was written, how it was preserved over the millennia, and where it was found. While we may not think of a trip to a library as an adventure, this is different, for we're about to visit a "library" that is like none other. This "library," now numbering in excess of 800 volumes (represented by intact Scrolls plus 100,000 fragments), is known as the Dead Sea Scrolls.

## What Are the Dead Sea Scrolls?

The Dead Sea Scrolls were written in Hebrew (predominately), Aramaic, and Greek. Most of the writings are on leather parchment (made from goat or sheep skins) and papyrus (an early form of paper), but a Scroll written on pure copper has also been unearthed. Some 223 or more of the total manuscripts discovered are copies of biblical books. So far a representative of every book of the Old Testament has been found with the exception of Esther, although it is apparent that Esther was known to the writers of the Scrolls.[1] The remaining manuscripts include non-biblical books (apocrypha and pseudepigrapha), sectarian documents, apocalyptic works, and to a lesser degree, commercial documents. There are an additional 300 manuscript portions either too obscure to identify or too fragmentary to translate.

It may not be entirely proper to refer to the Scrolls as a "library" because there is no indication that these writings were collected for that purpose or that any kind of classification or cataloging procedure was ever performed.[2] However, many Scroll scholars have pointed out that a variety of sectarian texts were found with the Scrolls—texts that did not originate within the Qumran community. These "imported texts," though collected by the Sect, do not reflect their beliefs or practices, but represent the common heritage of Second Temple Judaism.[3]

In addition, we need to understand that a great many other finds called "Dead Sea materials" were discovered in areas not near the Dead Sea (such as caves near Jericho and the fortress of Masada). Yet because the majority of the Scrolls were found in caves close to the Dead Sea, for general purposes, the entire body of ancient manuscripts have been designated as the Dead Sea Scrolls.

The manuscripts that comprise the Dead Sea Scrolls have survived mostly in fragmentary form. The initial discoveries from Cave 1 were intact Scrolls, and Cave 11 also yielded intact Scrolls. Nevertheless, the majority of materials have come from Cave 4, where no Scrolls, as such, were recovered. While other designations such as "Dead Sea Literature," "Qumran Manuscripts," and "Texts from the Judean Desert" have been used, the popular usage of "Dead Sea Scrolls" has made it the preferred designation.

The Dead Sea Scrolls were both the property and the products of those who were part of the Jewish community that lived at the site of Khirbet (Arabic for "ruins") Qumran during the Second Temple period. When people joined this community they brought with them their own personal copies of the Scriptures and other treasured writings. These Scrolls, which would have had their own antiquity and provenance, became a part of the community's common literary resources and in time were accompanied by copies made by the community as well as other kinds of original documents.

When the Scrolls were first revealed, Professor Eleazar Sukenik of the Hebrew University called them *Megillot ha-Genuzot* (Hebrew for "Hidden Scrolls"). This description reflected his belief that the Scrolls had been deposited in a *geniza*—a storage area for sacred writings that have become worn out or damaged. While that may have been true for the Scrolls in Cave 4 at Qumran, which contained 15,000 fragments that made up more than 500 books, it does not explain the apparently deliberate concealment of certain Scrolls in Caves 1, 2, 3, and 11, which are a mile and a half to the north of the Qumran community at the site of the Wadi Jawfet Zaben.

## Where Were the Scrolls Found?

As of this writing, the Dead Sea Scrolls have come from 11 caves in the 'Ein Feshkha and Khirbet Qumran regions and also from additional caves in Jericho, Ein-Gedi, Masada, Murabba'at, Nahal Hever, Nahal

Se'elim, Nahal Mishmar, and Khirbet Mird (the places and dates of most of the discoveries are listed in the Dead Sea Scrolls Chronology at the end of this book). These caves have been assigned a number that reveals the order of their discovery.

The Qumran caves that yielded intact Scrolls were limestone caves located in high ridges above the desert floor. Some of these limestone caves (especially those south of Qumran) can be reached only by lowering rope ladders hundreds of feet down the cliff walls. Other such caves have collapsed from the earthquakes that frequent the area and have had to be completely excavated before entrance was even possible.

Most of the fragmentary finds came from Caves 4-10, which are part of the marl terrace formation at the Wadi Qumran. The caves in this loose, chalky limestone eroded easily and were not as suitable for the storage of Scrolls as the limestone cliff caves. Scrolls found in these chalky limestone caves were often buried beneath layers of erosion and large accumulations of bat guana. In some cases, Scrolls were even found buried beneath the footpath in front of the cave, where they had been swept out at some point by previous inhabitants (see chapter 20). Only Qumran Caves 1 and 11 contained intact jars with scrolls or scroll remains. However, evidence of broken jars was found in some of the other caves. The *Copper Scroll,* the most unique of the Scrolls (if it can be classified as a scroll) was found on an incised stone shelf in Cave 3 (see chapter 12). Unfortunately, in most cases we cannot know for certain the original arrangement of the finds because the Bedouin reached the caves first. Oftentimes when archaeologists finally arrived at the caves they were met with scant Scroll remains but fine collections of cigarette butts! Consequently, the majority of the Scrolls were obtained through the antiquities market or by direct purchases from the Bedouin. Yet in more recent years, since Israel extended its jurisdiction to the Qumran region, the Bedouin's activities have been curtailed and archaeologists have made significant discoveries of their own (see chapter 20).

## When Were the Scrolls Found?

Scrolls have been found in the Dead Sea region since ancient times. About A.D. 217 the Christian scholar Origen discovered jars containing scrolls written in both Hebrew and Greek in caves somewhere near Jericho. He provides no record of the contents of the Hebrew manuscripts, but among the Greek manuscripts he found a version of the book of Psalms.

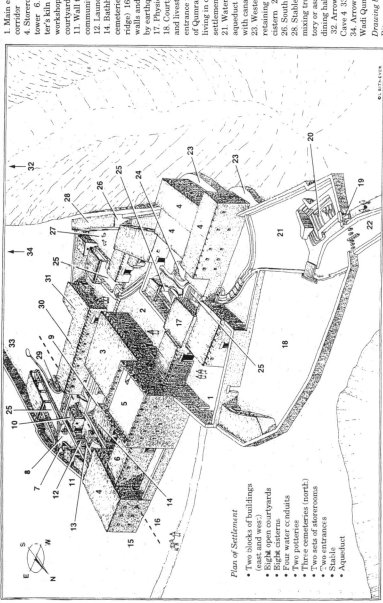

**Artistic Reconstruction of the Qumran Community (135 B.C.–A.D. 68)**

1. Main entrance  2. Central corridor  3. Scriptorium  4. Storerooms  5. Watchtower  6. Kitchen  7. Potter's kiln  8. Two potter's workshops  9. Inner courtyard  10. Dye shop  11. Wall to separate community from cemeteries  12. Laundry  13. Toilets  14. Bathhouse  15. Qumran cemeteries (along eastern ridge)  16. Fault line in walls and floors (caused by earthquake in 31 B.C.)  17. Physician's room  18. Courtyard for travelers and livestock  19. Private entrance for members of Qumran community living in caves or nearby settlements  20. Ritual bath  21. Water  22. Outlet of aqueduct and junction with canals of settlement  23. Western edge of plateau retaining wall  24. Round cistern  25. Large cistern(s)  26. South gate  27. Court  28. Stable  29. Potter's mixing trough  30. Refectory or assembly room and dining hall  31. Pantry  32. Arrow points toward Cave 4  33. Qumran plateau  34. Arrow points toward Wadi Qumran (east/west)

*Drawing by Dr. Leen Ritmeyer*

*Plan of Settlement*

- Two blocks of buildings (east and west)
- Eight open courtyards
- Eight cisterns
- Four water conduits
- Two potteries
- Three cemeteries (north)
- Two sets of storerooms
- Two entrances
- Stable
- Aqueduct

(This book of Psalms differed from what appeared in the Septuagint, a popular pre-Christian version of the Jewish Scriptures.) Origen incorporated this "Dead Sea Scroll" into his critical edition of the Bible known as the *Hexapla.*

Moving ahead in history, we have hints from the early eighth through the tenth centuries that Scrolls were discovered by both Christians and Karaites (a Jewish sect that elevated the Written Torah and rejected the Oral Torah of the rabbis). Around A.D. 800 a chance discovery of Hebrew Scrolls containing copies of Old Testament books and other Hebrew writings was reported in a letter by Timotheus, Patriarch of the Nestorian Christians, to Sergius, Metropolitan Bishop of Elam. In A.D. 937, Al Kirqisani the Karaite mentioned manuscripts that were found in caves in the Judean desert, but he identified these as belonging to the literature of the Magharians, a pre-Christian sect. In his account of Jewish sects he references earlier writers such as David Ibn-Merwan and Al-Biruni (seventh through ninth centuries), who in turn cited even earlier writers concerning the "Cave Sect." Kirqisani appears to date this sect in the era between the Sadducees (second century B.C.) and the followers of Christ (first century A.D.). The writer Shahrastani (A.D. 1090) records that the "Cave Sect" flourished 400 years before the Alexandrian presbyter Arius (who died in A.D. 336), which would place the sect in the first century B.C.

## When Were the Scrolls Written?

The study of the Dead Sea Scrolls is long past the earlier controversies that questioned their antiquity. For some time after the initial modern-day discoveries, Dr. Solomon Zeitlin of Dropsie College in Philadelphia and like-minded scholars contended that the Scrolls were simply medieval writings of a heretical Jewish sect known as the Karaites. Others, depending on their particular theory of who wrote the Scrolls, dated them to the late first century. If the Scrolls were interpreted as Zealot documents, then they were ascribed to the time of the first Jewish revolt (A.D. 66–70). If the Scrolls were believed to be early Jewish-Christian writings, then the accepted dates assigned to them ranged from the middle to the end of the first century. However, as the Scrolls were considered paleographically (dated by the style of their script) and they and their wrappings were subjected to scientific methods of dating (such as carbon 14), older dates began to appear. In addition, datable artifacts found in the caves or at the settlement of Qumran (such as coins and oil lamps) supported the dates arrived at through paleography and scientific testing.

In dating the Scrolls, we must distinguish between the Scrolls from the Qumran region and those found in caves in other places. The Scrolls from Qumran have yielded dates from 225 B.C. to A.D. 68. Most scholars believe they were composed during the Hasmonean period (152–63 B.C.) or the Early Roman period (63 B.C.–A.D. 68), although they recognize that some Scrolls were older manuscripts brought in from outside the community. The finds from other caves are either much older (Wadi el-Daliyeh, 352 B.C.) or much later (Wadi Murabba‘at, A.D. 69–136 and Khirbet Mird, A.D. 44).

### An Important Era

We can better appreciate the Dead Sea Scrolls when we understand the post-exilic (post-Babylonian captivity) or Second Temple period, since it was during this time that the Qumran community developed. Following is a brief overview of the highlights of this era combined with the major events connected with the Qumran Sect. This overview reveals the religious and political conditions that contributed to the development of the Qumran group as well as other sects. (For a historical survey of the Qumran community, see chapter 9, "The Historical Origin of the Sect" on pages 197-202, and the historical overview of the Second Temple period on pages 444-445.)

### The History of the Second Temple Period

The oldest of the Scrolls (those from Wadi el-Daliyeh) are dated about 352 B.C. It is possible, based on new evidence going back to the Persian period (see chapter 20), that a priestly Jewish group, as precursors of the Dead Sea Sect, settled at Qumran. Less than 20 years later Alexander the Great began his campaigns in Asia. Eventually Greek rule spread to Israel and Greek culture (Hellenism) was imposed on the Jewish people. In 250 B.C., because the Greek language was so widespread, Jewish scholars in Alexandria, Egypt, decided to translate the Old Testament into Greek (this work became known as the Septuagint, designated as LXX).

Half a century later (about 197–196 B.C.), Judea became a province of the Seleucid Empire and the Jewish Yahad (as the Dead Sea Sect is known in the Scrolls) began their initial period of settlement. Over the next 30 years religious and political upheavals occurred in Jerusalem. The Zadokite high priest Onias III was replaced by a hellenized Jew, then murdered. After that, forced hellenization took place, culminating in the plundering and polluting of the Temple by Antiochus IV Epiphanes (circa 169 B.C.).

Within three years a Jewish resistance movement (the Maccabean Revolt) retook Jerusalem, cleansed the Temple, and appointed a new high priesthood.

During this same period, the Jewish Yahad left Qumran, found its Teacher of Righteousness, and again returned. Shortly thereafter, the Samaritan temple on Mount Gerazim was destroyed by the Jewish high priest John Hyrcanus (128 B.C.). During his reign the sects known as the Sadducees and Pharisees became prominent. Over the next 50 years these sects were continually at odds with each other, and it is possible that a group of the Pharisees (who were not priests) joined the priestly membership of the Qumran community. Within the next 50 years Jewish independence ended with the Roman invasion led by Pompey (63 B.C.). The Jewish high priest was executed, and Herod the Great began his rule over Judea (circa 37 B.C.). Around the same time, either an invasion by the Parthians (40 B.C.) or an earthquake (31 B.C.) caused the Dead Sea Sect to leave Qumran for a brief period. Within another 65 years, Jesus was born (4–5 B.C.) and had carried out His earthly ministry (A.D. 27–30). Then over the following 40 years, significant changes took place in the Jewish nation. Paul's missionary outreach to the Gentiles reached many cities in the Roman world, much of the New Testament was written, the first Jewish rebellion against Rome was crushed, the Scrolls were hidden, the settlement at Qumran was destroyed (A.D. 68), the Temple in Jerusalem was destroyed (A.D. 70), and the final Jewish resistance at Masada was quenched (A.D. 73).

During the span of time we just reviewed, many major events took place (see the historical overview of the Second Temple period on pages 444-445.) This helps us to see that a Jewish sect in that era would inevitably have undergone significant changes. Though we cannot be sure about the time period that the Dead Sea sect actually existed in one form or another, we can be certain that this group changed with time. The Scrolls themselves reflect such changes to some degree.

### The Literature of the Second Temple Period

In past generations it was not easy to survey the literature of this era. Today, however, more than in any previous century since the time of Christ, we have an increasingly abundant supply of documents attesting to this period available for our study. Too often these primary-source materials about the Second Temple period have been neglected by evangelical

Christians. The reasons for this neglect range from simple unconcern or unfamiliarity with the content to prejudice against the use of non-canonical writings, to the fear of being aligned with critical scholars who have used these documents to buttress their attacks against evangelical doctrines.

However, when we fail to consider the original historical and cultural context of the text, our exegesis is susceptible to eisegesis—that is, interpretation according to our own historical and cultural context or controlled (even unintentionally) by our own subjective concerns, relational goals, or philosophical presuppositions. By disregarding these extrabiblical texts that permit us to properly view the context in which the authors lived, evangelicals may modernize the biblical text in a way not dissimilar to critical interpreters who reject the divine intent.

## Where Were the Scrolls Written?

The traditional view has been that a significant majority of the Scrolls were written at Khirbet Qumran. There, archaeologists excavated a two-story building with plaster and odd pieces of furniture that resembled tables (16' long × 1.3' wide × 1.6' high). These were reconstructed as workbenches for scribal activity. Also in this room were found several inkwells. The conclusion was that this was the community's Scriptorium—the room where the Qumran scribes copied or composed the Dead Sea Scrolls. While it is true that the jars in which the Scrolls were stored were made at Qumran (analysis of the clay links it with the settlement's pottery shop), there is no longer a scholarly consensus that all, or even some, of the Scrolls were produced there. This position is put forth by none other than Dr. Emanuel Tov, editor-in-chief of the Dead Sea Scrolls Translation and Publication Team:

> It is misleading to say that all of the Scrolls were written by the Qumran group, i.e., the Essenes. We now believe that many, maybe most, of the Scrolls found in Qumran were actually not written by the people who dwelt at Qumran. Some scholars even believe that all of the Scrolls were written outside of Qumran without any connection to the Qumran community. We are not [presently] able to pinpoint which Scrolls were written inside or outside of the community; however, I myself have developed a hypothesis whereby I believe that in certain cases I can pinpoint where the text was written.[4]

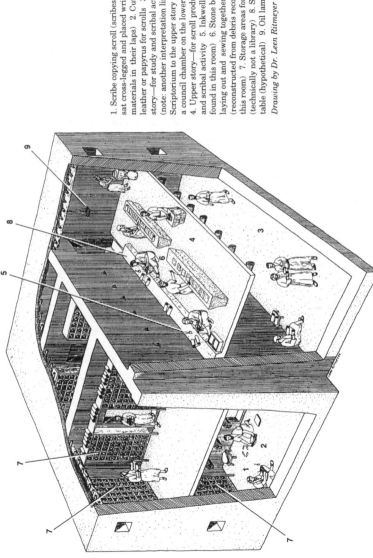

1. Scribe copying scroll (scribes always sat cross-legged and placed writing materials in their laps)  2. Cutting leather or papyrus for scrolls  3. Lower story—for study and scribal activity (note: another interpretation limits the Scriptorium to the upper story and has a council chamber on the lower story)  4. Upper story—for scroll production and scribal activity  5. Inkwell (several found in this room)  6. Stone benches for laying out and sewing together scrolls (reconstructed from debris recovered in this room)  7. Storage areas for scrolls (technically not a library)  8. Scribal table (hypothetical)  9. Oil lamp

*Drawing by Dr. Leen Ritmeyer*

*Artistic Interpretation of the Scriptorium Showing the Process of Making the Dead Sea Scrolls*

While the identification of a Scriptorium is now controversial, we must keep in mind that the Qumran area was occupied for a span of three centuries.[5] In such a time span biblical manuscripts would have worn out and needed to be replaced. Even if most of the original Scrolls had been brought from outside the community (and some are represented in the present collection), there would still have been a need to produce new copies. Given the special script insisted upon by the Sect, these copies could have been most easily produced within the community. Also, as in any Jewish community (e.g., the Bar Kokhba letters), personal correspondence, commercial documents, marriage contracts, and the like were also produced. These would require some place for their composition. Finally, we must not forget how many changes can take place within a community during this span of time, which, in part, could account for some of the variety in scribal styles (and locations) observed by Dr. Tov.

Another objection scholars have raised is that scribes in the ancient world wrote in a squatting position with their Scrolls in their laps, not working at tables. Accepting this, the workbenches could have been used for laying out the Scroll sections to dry and for stitching them together (see illustration). For these reasons, it is still quite possible that a type of Scriptorium existed at Qumran.

## How Were the Scrolls Preserved?

By their design and deposition within caves, the Scrolls were intended to be preserved against the ravages of time. This preservation was attained by a combination of factors.[6] First and foremost is the hot and arid climate of the Dead Sea region. The temperature often reaches 125 Fahrenheit, and there is almost no humidity (less than two to four inches of rainfall per year). Such conditions are ideal for material preservation, as evidenced by the similar "miraculous preservations" of normally perishable objects and papyrii in the tombs at Luxor, Egypt. The dry climate and stable temperature range in the Dead Sea region prevented the growth of bacteria that would have decomposed the Scrolls. Under these conditions the Scrolls gradually dehydrated until they reached a perfect state of equilibrium with the environment, which surrounded and protected them.

Another factor was the manner in which the Scrolls were stored. The clay jars in which the Scrolls were stored provided a second barrier of protection, keeping out the damaging rays of the sun and sometimes insects. In addition, caves in which the jars and Scrolls were hidden have almost no air flow. Also, the parchment on which the Scrolls were written was untanned sheepskin (tanning materials often contribute to the deterioration of parchment over long periods of time). And the choice of ink used for most of the Scrolls was a carbon ink made from soot or lampblack with gum arabic added as a stabilizer. Unlike many modern inks that fade after a relatively short time, lampblack is an inert and extremely durable substance, and as the Scrolls reveal, can last for more than 2,000 years. Unfortunately, once the Scrolls were removed from these ideal conditions, they began to deteriorate rapidly.[7] For this reason the *Great Isaiah Scroll* was removed from its center case under the rotunda in the Shrine of the Book and a replica put in its place. The Scroll fragments in the Scrollery of the Rockefeller Museum today are in an advanced state of deterioration. When these fragments were first collected and assembled, they were sandwiched between plates of glass for protection from dust and the oil of human skin. These glass-covered fragments were then laid out on large tables in direct sunlight for study. The sunlight shining through the glass created a greenhouse effect and accelerated the decay process by creating a thermal layer between the plates of glass. This, in turn, allowed moisture and bacteria to reach the parchments, which are now stored in drawers under controlled conditions.

## What Do the Scrolls Contain?

It will not be possible within this chapter to survey the more than 800 manuscripts represented by the Scrolls; there are many more technical works available for that purpose. For us it should be sufficient to consider a sampling of the texts that have been studied for the last 40 years, including most of the older works on which the Scrolls were based and the recently published texts from Cave 4. These texts can be grouped in categories: biblical texts, biblical commentaries, sectarian texts, apocryphal and pseudepigraphical texts, apocalyptic texts, and mystical or ritualistic texts.

### Biblical Texts

Copies of books of the Bible comprise some of the greatest finds among the Dead Sea Scrolls. Between 223-233 copies of biblical manuscripts have been found, a figure representing about one-fourth of the total manuscript collection. The following list shows the books of the Bible that were discovered and how many multiple copies (if any) were represented.

## Qumran Manuscripts of Books of the Old Testament

| Canonical Division (According to the Hebrew Bible) | Old Testament Book (According to Order in Hebrew Bible) | Number of Qumran Manuscripts (?=possible fragment) |
|---|---|---|
| Pentateuch (Torah) | Genesis | 18+3? |
| | Exodus | 18 |
| | Leviticus | 17 |
| | Numbers | 12 |
| | Deuteronomy | 31+3? |
| Prophets (Nevi'im) *Former Prophets* | Joshua | 2 |
| | Judges | 3 |
| | 1-2 Samuel | 4 |
| | 1-2 Kings | 3 |
| *Latter Prophets* | Isaiah | 22 |
| | Jeremiah | 6 |
| | Ezekiel | 7 |
| | Twelve (Minor) Prophets | 10+1? |
| Writings (Ketubim) | Psalms | 39+2? |
| | Proverbs | 2 |
| | Job | 4 |
| The Five Scrolls | Song of Songs | 4 |
| | Ruth | 4 |
| | Lamentations | 4 |
| | Ecclesiastes | 3 |
| | Esther | 0* |
| | Daniel | 8+1? |
| | Ezra-Nehemiah | 1 |
| | 1-2 Chronicles | 1 |
| | | Total 223 (233) |

* parallel expressions in other Dead Sea Scrolls indicate Sect's familiarity with Esther

**FACT:** The number of OT manuscripts at Qumran is more than double the number of Greek papyri of the New Testament (96) and these manuscripts are 1,000 years older than the Hebrew Bible manuscripts extant before their discovery.

| Distribution of the Biblical Manuscripts in the Qumran Caves | | Alignment of Biblical Manuscripts Found at Qumran with Other Biblical Versions | |
|---|---|---|---|
| Cave 1 | 17 | Proto-Masoretic Texts | 60% |
| Cave 2 | 18 | | |
| Cave 3 | 3 | Qumran-Style Texts | 20% |
| Cave 4 | 137 | | |
| Cave 5 | 7 | Non-Aligned Texts | 10% |
| Cave 6 | 7 | | |
| Cave 7 | 1 | Septuagintal-Type Texts | 5% |
| Cave 8 | 2 | | |
| Cave 9 | 0 | Proto-Samaritan | |
| Cave 10 | 0 | (Pentateuch) Texts | 5% |
| Cave 11 | 10 | | |

From the list we can see that certain books were more frequently represented than others. This implies that these were the most frequently used books of the community, and they fit our expectations for a strictly legalistic and apocalyptic group: Psalms (39), Deuteronomy (31), Isaiah (22), Exodus (18), Genesis (15), and Leviticus (13). These books, however, were also works that the Jewish community at large considered foundational for understanding God's program for Israel and the coming of the Messiah. For these same reasons the three books at the top of this list (Psalms, Deuteronomy, Isaiah) were also the ones most frequently quoted by the New Testament authors.

It should be noted that the book of Nehemiah does not appear by itself ]on the list. It is assumed that Nehemiah was included as one book with Ezra, which is listed. The book of Esther was not found either, but does appear in citations or allusions in the sectarian documents and one apocryphal Aramaic work related to it, entitled *Proto-Esther*. Most likely its absence is simply because it has not yet been found. After all, only one copy of a fragment of Ezra-Nehemiah and the Chronicles were discovered. Also of interest is the *Psalm Scroll* from Cave 11, which included a number of apocryphal psalms not found in the Bible.[8]

In addition to actual copies of books of the Bible, the Scrolls also contained samples of the biblical text in other forms. Three of these are the Targums, tefillin, and mezuzot. The Targums are translations of the Hebrew Bible into Aramaic. Their purpose was to give an understanding of the original text to contemporary readers who were no longer familiar with the older biblical Hebrew. In much the same way that the Roman Catholic Church came to abandon the use of Latin during mass because few parishioners could understand the services, so also did Jews in the synagogue orally translate the Hebrew text into the common vernacular of Aramaic.

The Targumim (plural for Targum) were born when these oral translations were written down and collected as manuscript documents. Among the Scrolls are the *Targums of Leviticus* and *Job*. Fragments of both have been found in Cave 4, but from Cave 11 came a complete *Targum of Job*; in fact, it was one of the best-preserved texts of all the Scrolls. The dates for these works range from the second century to the last half of the first century B.C. Their discovery and date have proved that the Targumim were not late productions, as some scholars formerly thought, but were well established in Judaistic circles before the rise of Christianity.

Tefillin and mezuzot are small, tightly rolled Scrolls that contain biblical passages from Exodus and Deuteronomy.[9] The tefillin (or phylacteries) were placed in boxes tied to the head or left arm. The mezuzot were placed in ornamental cases that were attached to the doorpost of a house. The tefillin and mezuzot were intended to fulfill (in a mystical manner) the biblical command in Deuteronomy: "You shall bind them [God's commandments] as a sign on your hand and they shall be as frontals [emblems] on your forehead. And you shall write them on the doorposts of your house and on your gates" (Deuteronomy 6:8-9).

Some of these documents (from Cave 5) were rolled so tightly that they have never been able to be opened. Those that could (21 documents from Cave 4 and one from Cave 1) revealed a Hebrew text that departed from the Masoretic Text and sometimes agreed with other ancient versions of the Old Testament. The writing on these is so minute that in most cases they must be read under a magnifying glass. Thus they are unique testimonies to the masterful skill of the Jewish scribes.

### Biblical Commentaries

The Dead Sea Scrolls brought to light for the first time a special kind of commentary on the biblical text called *pesher* ("commentary").[10] Prior to the discovery of the Scrolls our evidence of how Jewish commentators handled the biblical text was based on the rabbinic writings of the Mishnah, the Talmud, and the midrashim. However, these comments were not the rabbis' own interpretations of the biblical text, but of an oral tradition that had been passed down from sage to sage. The great difference in the Qumran *pesharim* (plural for *pesher*) is that they represent an actual exegesis of the Old Testament itself. The method was to quote the Old Testament verse by verse, then provide commentary. The writers' comments were separated from their citations by a word or phrase such as "the interpretation of it [or 'the word'] is about. . . ."[11] What made the commentary unique was the way the interpretation was made. Rather than simply give the literal meaning of the text, the writers related the text to their own historical situation and theological viewpoint.

These commentators believed that the gift of prophecy had been continued in their "Teacher of Righteousness," who was divinely inspired to discern the proper interpretation of prophetic passages. While none of the Scrolls directly credit the Teacher as author, most scholars believe that his commentary is directly or indirectly preserved in documents like the *Pesher Habakkuk*. As a result, these biblical expositions are specific to the Qumran community and provide us with an unusually vivid presentation of their sectarian theology. Yet University of Haifa professor and Scroll apocalyptic expert Devorah Dimant observes that "Qumranic *pesher* is not a unique phenomenon, but must be placed within the wider framework of Jewish exegesis of the Second Temple period."[12] In addition, because these commentaries contain excerpts of biblical text, they serve as a source of better understanding the transmission of the Scriptures.

These commentaries are of several forms,[13] each sharing a common structure (with slight modifications): a biblical quotation followed by an exposition introduced by the term *pesher*. These forms include: 1) *Continuous Pesharim*—running commentaries that go through single books of the Bible section by section and verse by verse. They all reference in similar ways the community, its history, and its leadership and opponents. 2) *Thematic Pesharim*—expositions made up of verses collected from various passages in different books (or separate parts of the same book) that relate to a common theme or themes. These are similar to the two kinds of sermons typically presented by preachers today: expository and topical. 3) *Isolated Pesharim*—expositions of one or two verses within works that were not intended primarily as commentary (e.g., *Cairo Damascus Document, Community Rule*). These expositions function as "proof-texts" for the community's historical events and doctrinal tenets, and are prophetic in nature (e.g., Isaiah 40:3 in *1QS* 8:13-16; cf. 9:20; Isaiah 24:17 in *CD* 4:13-15).

Among the *Continuous Pesharim*, the four commentaries that are the most prominent are those on Habakkuk, Nahum, Isaiah (see chapter 11), and the Psalms. Let's briefly survey some of these important documents.

## The Commentary on Habakkuk

The longest, best preserved, and first *pesher* to be published was the *Pesher Habakkuk (1QHab)*. This commentary expounds the first two chapters of Habakkuk verse by verse, reading contemporary events into the prophecies and making reference to three main figures in the Sect's history. These figures are described only by their epithets as "the Teacher of Righteousness" (based on Hosea 10:12; Joel 2:23), the prophetic leader of the community *(1QpHab* 2.7-10, 5.11-12, 7.4-5), "the Man of Lies" (based on Micah 2:11), a renegade student of the Teacher who formed his own group (possibly Pharisaical, cf. *4QpNah* 3-4 ii 2) in opposition to the Sect *(1QpHab* 2:1-3; 5:9-14; 10:9-13), and the "Wicked Priest," a priestly and political adversary of the Teacher *(1QpHab* 1:12-15; 11:4-8) who corrupted his office (8:8-13; 9:8-12; 11:12-16; 12:10), defiled the Temple (12:2-10), and persecuted the Teacher (11:5-7). The events surrounding the Teacher were taken to presage the eschatological era and the End of Days *(1QpHab* 7:7-14). The commentary reveals that the Sect believed that the wicked followers of "the Man of Lies" and "the Wicked Priest" would be imminently judged and their own members duly rewarded *(1QpHab* 8:2; 10:3; 12:14; 13:3). In their present-day interpretation of the ruthless Babylonian invaders of Habakkuk 1:6-10, who were sent by God as a punishment for Israel's departure from the Torah, they apparently saw the Roman army as the final rod of God's wrath against their enemies *(1QpHab* 6:1-12; cf. *4QpNah* 3-4 1.3). These, whom they called the Kittim, like their counterparts in Habakkuk, would also be destroyed for their arrogance against God's people (Habakkuk 1:11).

## The Commentary on Nahum

The *Pesher Nahum (4QpNah)* is a commentary on the biblical book of Nahum. It takes Nahum's oracle against the Assyrian capital of Nineveh as its basis for directing its own vindictives against a group (based on Isaiah 30:10) that is cryptically and literally referred to as "the seekers of smooth things" *(4QpNah* 3-4 1.7). This group has been thought to be identified with the Pharisees, whom the Qumran Sect regarded as traitors to the true Israel by "leading Ephraim astray with false teaching" *(4QpNah* 3-4 2.8). This commentary also has the distinction of being the first to record historical names, such as "Demetrius King of Greece" (that is, the Seleucid ruler Demetrius III Eukerus—*4QpHab* 3-4 1.2), who recruited thousands of Jews (especially Pharisees) against the Hasmonean ruler Alexander Jannaeus in Jerusalem. Like the *Pesher Habukkuk*, it also mentions the

Kittim, who are set in a historical context following Demetrius, Antiochus IV Epiphanes, and the kings of Greece *(4QpNah* 3-4 1.1-4). This supplies additional verification that the Qumranites identified the Kittim as the Romans, since the Roman Empire followed the Seleucid Empire in their domination of Jerusalem and Israel.

## The Commentary on the Psalms

This commentary is designated as the *Psalms Pesher (4QpPs^a;* also *4Q171, 173)* because the fragments that comprise it deal especially (though not exclusively) with Psalm 37. In the Psalms, the general themes of the righteous versus the wicked were taken as code words and given a *pesher* interpretation as "the Teacher of Righteousness" (here called "the Priest") and the Qumran community versus their opponents: "the Wicked Priest," "the Man of Lies," and their followers *(4QpPs^a* 1-10 1.26-27; ii 18; 3.15; 4.8). The commentary supplies details about the sharp division between the Teacher and the Wicked Priest, a contrast that is ultimately seen as part of the greater cosmic battle between the forces of good (God and His Messiah) and evil (Belial and his wicked spirits) *(4QpPs^a* 1-10 2.7-11).

Alongside the *Continuous Pesharim* are also the *Thematic Pesharim.* These are all apocalyptic in nature and include *The Florilegium, The Melchizedek Text, The Commentary on Genesis,* and *Messianic Testimonia* (see chapter 12). Let's look at the first three of these documents.

## The Florilegium

This *pesher* is comprised of eschatological midrashim (designated *4Q174)* and is organized around passages quoted from various biblical texts (Exodus 15:17-18; 2 Samuel 7:10-14; 1 Chronicles 17:9-13; Psalm 1:1; 2:1; Isaiah 8:11; Ezekiel 37:23; Amos 9:11). The primary texts in this collection are 2 Samuel 7, which concerns the Davidic Covenant, and Psalms 1 and 2, which deal with the contrast between the righteous and the Messianic War at the end of days. The Exodus 15:17-18 passage is used by the Qumranic commentator to clarify the ambiguous statement in 2 Samuel 7:10 that God would establish a place for His people to dwell securely. This place is the Jerusalem Temple, which the text describes in three separate historical phases (see chapter 11). The primary focus, however, is the eschatological last days, during which a permanent and undefiled sanctuary will be rebuilt under a restored Davidic dynasty *(4Q174* 1.1-13). The text also provides details about the eschatological enemies of Israel (Belial and company), and the Interpreter of the Law who would accompany another leader of the community (probably the Davidic Messiah, *CD* 6:7; 7:18).

## The Melchizedek Text

This *pesher* (designated *11QMelch*) was apparently originally designed to comment on ten jubilees (1 Enoch 93:1-10; 90:12-17); the only surviving section of this manuscript talks about a tenth and eschatological jubilee. As with other thematic *pesharim*, this text combines many Bible passages around the mysterious biblical figure of Melchizedek, King of Salem, who blessed Abram after the Battle of the Kings (Genesis 14:17-20) and who figures prominently in an eschatological judgment psalm (Psalm 110). Melchizedek is here pictured as a supernatural being who will be present at the final judgment as a liberator (i.e., one who will forgive the sins) of the Sons of Light, as a judge of the "holy ones of God" (probably "angels") according to Psalm 82:1, and as an agent of God's judgments, who with the elect angels will attend to the destruction of Satan *(11QMelch* 2.4-14). From this text we can see that Melchizedek held a prominent place in their interpretation of the end time. That may imply that Melchizedek was considered a central figure in other Jewish circles. This reveals that the New Testament author of Hebrews was compatible with the Jewish thinking of his time when he used Melchizedek as an illustration of an eternal priestly order to which Christ belonged (Hebrews 7:1–8:13; cf. Psalm 110:4).

## The Commentary on Genesis

In this recently published text variously termed *Pesher on Genesis*, the *Patriarchal Blessings*, and the *Genesis Florilegium* (designated *4Q252),* the author cites passages exclusively from Genesis, moving from a lengthy description of the Flood (Genesis 6-8), to the punishment of Ham's son Canaan (Genesis 9:20-29), the early days of Abraham (Genesis 11-17), Sodom and Gomorrah (Genesis 18-19), Reuben's offense (Genesis 37), and Jacob's blessing of his 12 sons (Genesis 49). The composition does not follow the established thematic *pesher* pattern of collected texts with commentary until it comes to the final section dealing with Jacob's blessing, which is interpreted in *pesher* style. This last section contains some interesting and explicit messianic statements connecting the "Messiah of Righteousness" with the Davidic dynasty ("the Branch of David") and especially the mysterious term "Shiloh" found in Genesis 49:10 (for more on this, see chapter 13).[14]

## Apocryphal Texts

Works from the *Apocrypha* (i.e., the collection of books considered non-inspired, hence non-canonical by orthodox Jews and Protestant Christians) have also been found among the Dead Sea Scrolls. Their presence and variety has suggested to scholars that the Qumran community may not have accepted the notion of a fixed canon of Scripture. That some of these parabiblical books seem to have also been considered authoritative has led some scholars to further conclude that the Scrolls may represent a transitional stage of canonicity. Dr. Shemaryahu Talmon explains:

> The possibility that other books [apocryphal] had a similar standing [with the biblical corpus] should be weighed very carefully. There is not one biblical book that is totally Aramaic, so I would be rather reticent in believing Enoch [in Aramaic] was considered [authoritative]. Jubilees is different because it is in Hebrew. It is put almost on an equal rank with the book of Moses because its calendar was decisive [for the community]. There is another book that may have had similar authority and that is the book quoted as *Sefer ha-Hage*. They attached tremendous importance to it and it must have been one their foundation documents. There is [therefore] the possibility that the collection of what we call the books of the Hebrew Bible were not yet finalized. This also explains the [later] necessity of the rabbis to decide what belongs and what doesn't belong. Qumran was sort of on the borderline.[15]

Three of the apocryphal texts have been identified as Tobit, Ben Sira (Ecclesiasticus), and Baruch (only chapter 6: "The Letter of Jeremiah"). Since these works have a known history, we will not comment on their contents.[16] However, one additional apocryphal work was found, a psalm included within the *Psalms Scroll (11QPs$^a$)*. Since it appears at the conclusion of the Qumran Psalter it is referred to as Psalm 151. All of these apocryphal works (including the extra psalm) were part of the Septuagint, which, as a popular version of the Bible (especially during the hellenized Second Temple period), would have been a part of the Qumranite collection.

## Pseudepigraphal Texts

The Pseudepigrapha is a collection of texts in which the authorship is ascribed to some important figure of history or literature who did not write them but who may appear as a figure in the work or whose name simply secures a readership. The pseudepigrapha of the Dead Sea Scrolls is represented by several texts well-known from their versions in other languages and other texts that were previously unknown. The first group contains the *Book of Jubilees (4Q176, 216, 219-221, 11Q12, 3Q5, 1Q18, 2Q20)*, the *Book of Enoch (4Q201-202, 204-207, 212)*, and the *Testament of the Twelve Patriarchs (4Q213-215, 537-548, 3Q7, 1Q21)*. A second group of previously unknown texts include the *Words of Moses (1Q22)*, *Pseudo-Moses (1Q29; 4Q374-376; 4Q387-390)*, *Pseudo-Samuel (4Q160; 6Q9)*, *Pseudo-Jeremiah (4Q385ᵇ, 387ᵇ)*, *Pseudo-Ezekiel (4Q385)*, *Pseudo-Daniel (4Q243-245)*, the *Prayer of Nabonidus (4Q242)*, *Pseudo-Jubilees (4Q227)*, *Apocryphon of Joseph (4Q372-373)*, *Apocryphon of David (2Q22)*, *The Book of Giants (4Q532)*, the *Testament of Amram (4Q534, 545-548)*, the *Testament of Kohath (4Q542)*, the *Testament of Naphtali (4Q215)*, *Apocryphon of Joshua (4Q522)*, *Hur and Miriam (4Q549)*, *The Book of Noah (1Q19)*, *The Birth of Noah (4Q534-536)*, and the *Book of Mysteries (1Q27; 4Q299-301)*. These strange titles by familiar names are indicative of the keen interest in and study of biblical texts during the early part of the Second Temple period, which was when these compositions were created. They reflect the messianic and eschatological developments of Judaism(s) at this time, and those selected by the Qumran community may assist us in understanding their own views more precisely. Several of the texts in each group require more extensive consideration because of their influence on the Sect or uniqueness in content.

## The Book of Jubilees

The *Book of Jubilees* (also known as *The Little Genesis*) presents itself as an account to Moses during the 40 days spent on Mount Sinai. It comes as a revelation from God mediated through the Angel of the Presence. A total of 16 copies of the book were found in several different caves (Caves 2, 3, 11), but mostly in Cave 4. Compared with the number of biblical manuscripts discovered, it ranks as one of the most popular books of the Sect; its popularity within the Qumran community is seen in its citation as a legal authority in the *Damascus Document*. It had a unique influence on the Sect through its promotion of a solar calendar and its exhortations, based on the lives of the patriarchs, for a disciplined lifestyle and proper ritual practice.

As a book with apocalyptic content (similar to the biblical book of Daniel and pseudepigraphical *Book of Enoch*), the *Book of Jubilees* also influenced the eschatological beliefs of the community. Its special division of time into jubilees and their weeks is reflected in the Sect's chronological and eschatological reckoning. Of great importance to scholars in this field was the fact that all of these copies were in Hebrew. It had been conjectured that the original version of Jubilees was in Hebrew, based upon the 1896 discovery of the *Cairo Damascus Document* (cf. *CD* 16.2-4). However, up until the time that the Scrolls were discovered, only copies in Greek, Syriac, Latin, and Ethiopic were known to have survived.

## The Book of Enoch

Enoch was of great interest to the Qumran Sect because he, like Melchizedek, carried an air of mystery and was a man so holy he was taken to heaven without dying (Genesis 5:24). Like the *Book of Jubilees*, the *Book of Enoch* was represented by a significant number of copies (11) at Qumran (again, in Cave 4). However, unlike Jubilees, which was written in Hebrew, these Enoch fragments were in Aramaic. The complete text of Enoch is comprised of five separate divisions, or books, with a total of 108 chapters, but this text is preserved only in the Ethiopic version. Most of the texts found at Qumran are merely of parts of three of these divisions (chapters 83–107), and several others are of parts of a division called *The Astronomical Book* (chapters 72–82). Missing entirely from this collection of Enoch fragments is any trace of a division known as the Similitudes of Enoch (chapters 37–71), which describe a supernatural figure called "the son of man" who would participate in the last judgment. Critical New Testament scholars had long believed that the Gospel writers borrowed their concept for Jesus as the "son of man" from the Similitudes. But this view was seriously challenged by the absence of this material in Qumran Enoch (while all the other parts were present). The implication is that the Similitudes was a later composition, beyond the time of the Gospel writers, and therefore, not an influence for them (unless, as some scholars counter, it came from a different strand of Judaism than Qumran).

What is equally significant in Qumran Enoch is that another division entitled *The Book of Giants,* a work widely read in the Roman Empire and not present in other versions of Enoch, had a special influence on the Sect. The contents of this work focused on the account in Genesis 6 of the union of fallen angels (called "Nephilim" and "Watchers") with human women ("the daughters of Eve")—a union that resulted in a race of giants. In addition, 1 Enoch also advocates a solar calendar and has significant apocalyptic material.

## Testament of the Twelve Patriarchs

The title of this work is taken from its account of the 12 sons of Jacob, who, like their father (Genesis 49) blessed each of their sons on their deathbed. While the complete work appears in Greek, Armenian, Slavonic, Aramaic, and Hebrew, only source document fragments have been found at Qumran. These are claimed as the *Testament of Naphtali (4Q215),* the *Testament of Judah (3Q7; 4Q484, 538),* the *Testament of Joseph (4Q539),* and the *Testament of Levi (1Q21; 4Q213–14).* If these sources contained much of the same material as the completed work, they bear witness to both an ethical/legal and cosmological/eschatological influence on the Sect. Both Levi and Judah were central figures in the eschatology of the Testaments, with Judah as king and Levi as anointed priest and Judah's superior. The rebuilding of the Temple in the end times is also a theme of these books, with the agent of redemption coming from both "Levi" and "Judah." These books also stressed obedience to the Law, but rarely did so with reference to legal statutes from the Torah. The *Testament of Naphtali,* too, had a strong cosmological emphasis, stressing that the natural order (law) was equivalent to the Law of God.

The presence of these books of the Testament, even in source form, attest to the existence of this work as essentially Jewish. The reason I say "essentially" is because for a long time scholars had believed that many of the passages in the Testament appeared to be Christian in origin. The supposition was that the work was a Jewish-Christian one, or that it had been amended (added to) by Christians. The Qumran discovery, however, has revealed that the sources for the work are clearly pre-Christian (third century B.C.).

## Sectarian Documents

While many or most of the works considered up to this point were not original products of the Qumran Sect, other primary or foundational documents have been found that are thought, in many cases, to be unique to the Sect. The best known of these works include legal texts: *The Damascus Document, The Community Rule* (or *Manual of Discipline*), *Miqsat Ma'aseh ha-Torah* ("Some Works of the Torah"), poetic worship texts: *Hodayot*

("Thanksgiving Hymns"), and eschatological texts such as *The War Scroll*. Among this latter group are also included the *Temple Scroll* and the *Copper Scroll*, since one or both may have been products of the Sect, as we'll soon see. Let's first consider several of the foundational documents.

## The Damascus Document

*The Damascus Document* (designated *CD* = *C*airo *D*amascus, for the Cairo copy, and by the sigla *4Q266-273, 5Q12, 6Q15* for the Qumran copies), is also referred to as the *Damascus Covenant* and the *Zadokite Fragments*. The first copy of this text did not come from the caves at Qumran, but from an old room of the Ezra Synagogue, where discarded manuscripts were stored in Cairo, Egypt. The discovery was well before any Bedouin entered a cave—1896—and the discoverer of the document was a Jewish scholar, Dr. Solomon Schechter (later president of the Jewish Theological Seminary).

No one knew exactly where this text originated, although many scholars suspected a Karaite source. The *Damascus Document* itself seems to imply that it may have been written for the Sect before it arrived at Qumran, when it was living in towns and villages where they would encounter non-Jews. The mention of Damascus in the document, if taken literally, may mean the document was intended for the Sect when it went into exile in this Syrian city, or if taken figuratively, of the exile to Qumran. While some of the legal statements made in the document are at variance with other sectarian legal texts, it is evident that it was a primary source of legal guidance, especially in laws governing the Sabbath (the largest section), the purity of priests, entry into the community, and communal organization (in these last two areas there are significant variants).

## The Manual of Discipline

*The Manual of Discipline* (or *Community Rule*), designated *1QS*, is considered perhaps the most important of the foundational documents (in a sense, a constitutional document) for an understanding of the communal practices of the Qumran Sect. As one of the first seven Scrolls found in Cave 1, it was published early and has had a long history of interpretation. Many scholars believe that the Teacher of Righteousness was responsible for the teaching recorded in the text, which primarily involves entrance into the community and regulations for community life and assembly (including penalties for violations). Two additional compositions found at Qumran serve as appendices to the complete text *(1QS)* and are distinguished as *The Rule of the Congregation (1QS^a)* and *The Rule of Blessings (1QS^b)*. These provide instructions for the "Latter Days" and the great "Messianic Banquet" scheduled for that period as well as blessings upon the Sect's leadership.

## Some Works of the Law

This work is most commonly referred to by its early siglum *4QMMT* (for the Hebrew *Misqat Ma'aseh ha-Torah*, but it is also called the *Halakhic Letter* and is now designated *4Q394-399* (for its six copies). A lot of speculation arose in the scholarly world because of its delay in publication and the controversy engendered by lawsuits over privately published copies (see chapter 4). Since its full publication by Professor Elisha Qimron, it has continued to cause excitement among scholars, especially those with rabbinical legal training, such as Dr. Lawrence Schiffman. Because the text deals with the legal (religious) differences between the Sect and its opponents, including "the Wicked Priest," it may provide new insights into the origin and makeup of the Qumran Sect. Already, on the basis of this text, Dr. Schiffman has proposed that the Sect represents a Sadducean movement (see chapter 5).

## The War Scroll

Another of the original seven Scrolls from Cave 1 was the *War Scroll (1QM),* and an additional six copies have been recovered from Cave 4 *(4Q491-497).* It is an eschatological text that deals, as the name implies, with the 40-year war between the "Sons of Light" and the "Sons of Darkness." Most of what is popularly known about the eschatology of the Sect has been drawn from a study of this document, which is rich in eschatological figures, a theological survey of the cosmic war between good ("Sons of Light") and evil ("Sons of Darkness") throughout human history, and victorious hymns of praise. We will learn more about this Scroll in chapters 9 and 10.

## Temple-Related Texts

Several sectarian documents deal directly or indirectly with the Temple. While these texts will be described in detail later (chapters 11–12), they will be listed here as part of our survey. These texts include the *Temple Scroll (11Q19),* the largest of all the Scrolls, which contains a description of a future Temple to be built in Jerusalem; the *Copper Scroll (3Q15),* made up of copper sheets that list [Temple] treasures buried in various places, and *The New Jerusalem (4Q554-555; 5Q15)*, a recently published apocalyptic text based on Ezekiel's vision of the Temple of the last days (Ezekiel 40–48). There are additional texts related to the Temple, such as *The Laws of the Red Heifer (4Q276-277)*, *The Messianic Leader (4Q285)*, *The Angels of Mastemoth and the Rule of Belial (4Q290)*, and the *Joshua Apocryphon (4Q522)*, which include scattered statements or allusions to the Temple.

## Messianic Texts

Among the sectarian Scrolls there are numerous fragments that mention a messianic figure and are therefore referred to as messianic texts (see chapters 10 and 11). Older published documents such as the *Community Rule (Manual of Discipline)*, the *War Scroll*, the *Pesher Habakkuk, Melchizedek*, and others contain messianic references and have served as principal sources for reconstructing the messianic concepts of the community. The newly released texts of Cave 4 have yielded a significant number of messianic texts, a listing of which would include: *The Messianic Apocalypse (4Q521)*, *The Son of God (4Q246)*, *Serekh Milhamah ("The Rule of War")* or *The Messianic Leader (4Q285)*, *The Servants of Darkness (4Q471)*, *The Birth of Noah (4Q534-536)*, *The Words of Michael (4Q529)*, *The New Jerusalem (4Q554)*, *A Genesis Florilegium (4Q252)*, and *The Tree of Evil (4Q458)*.

## Calendrical Texts

One of the most unique features of the Dead Sea Scroll Sect was their use of a calendar different from what was used by the rest of Judaism. Among the Scrolls are fragmentary calendrical texts that describe the intricate method of the Sect's ritual calculations. The foremost expert on the calendrical text is Dr. Shemaryahu Talmon, who describes the nature and importance of these special texts:

> We have now remnants of at least ten or more calendrical documents. This in itself is important because in comparison with the number of copies we have of other books, this represents a significant usage by the community. It shows immediately that we are dealing with an important issue. When we consider any of the foundation Scrolls, such as the *Zadokite Fragments*, the *Rule of the Congregation*, the *Temple Scroll*, and

so on, every single one will deal with the calendar. [The Qumran calendar] has tremendous advantages compared with the Jewish calendar of 364 days. [This is because in the Jewish calendar] the 364 days are divided equally into four quarters of 91 days. Each one divides easily into 13 weeks. Therefore, the first day of the first, fourth, seventh, and tenth months all fall within the same day of the week. [By contrast] in their calendar [of 354 days] the first of the year is always a Wednesday, the fourth day of the week. This is very clever because on that day God created the two luminaries. Without them there's no [day and night, therefore no] calendar. As one year is completed, the next year begins again on a Wednesday. Every quarter begins on a Wednesday of the next year. If that is the case, then every fifteenth of the month is a Wednesday. Now major Jewish festivals are on the fifteenth of the month. For this reason they are all on a Wednesday and they don't have the [same] problem Jews have today with having to figure out on which day of the week Passover will fall. Because they had no problem with this, a good deal of the biblical literature dealing with calendrical questions, as well as Jewish concerns, such as the observation of the new moon, are obsolete for them.[17]

The most recently published calendrical texts include 18 fragments *(4Q319-330, 337)*. Some of the more fragmentary and complex texts from Cave 4 are presently being assembled and prepared for translation and publication by Professor Talmon (see photo section).

This survey has given us an idea of the extensive nature and variety of the Dead Sea Scrolls. Such an awareness prepares us to appreciate the demands on the scholars who have labored and are laboring to make these texts available to the world.

Having surveyed these documents from the Dead Sea region, some readers may wonder whether they have any relevance to their more familiar world of the Bible. In the next two chapters, we'll see if these "unknown" texts relate to the well-known text of Scripture. And before we do so, we'll look at the origin of these writings and consider the debate that has erupted over their authorship.

# 5

# THE SCRIBES OF THE SCROLLS

*We are working too often with misleading views and I hope, and I trust, that in the years to come we will refine our criteria at all levels in order to be able to come closer to the truth with regard to the background of these texts.*[1]

—Emanuel Tov, Editor-in-Chief, Dead Sea Scrolls Editorial Team

The story of the Dead Sea Scrolls often reads like a mystery, and now that we've had the opport122unity to survey the Scrolls, we may feel they are more mysterious than we ever expected. And the mystery only deepens when we attempt to find out who wrote these texts. As Professor Shemaryahu Talmon observes, "After 45 years of research, and in spite of the tremendous new discoveries, the basic problems haven't changed and the basic answers haven't changed."[2]

While the answers have not changed, they have proliferated, and today we are faced with more conflicting theories than ever before. We might ask, "If the scholars can't figure out or agree on who wrote them, why should I bother?" Yet we face the same problem when we come to an election year. Candidates who vie for the same political position all speak with conflicting opinions about the most basic issues. We listen to their arguments, which are often moderated by political analysts or constitutional scholars who have just as many contrary views. In the end we may shake our head and say, "Why bother?" as some people, unfortunately, choose to do. But if we're eager to do what is best, despite our lack of certainty or understanding of a candidate and his position on the issues, we will go out and vote. Of course, when we discuss the authorship of the Scrolls there is no need to cast a vote, but merely to study the candidates (the various theories). In doing so we will have educated ourselves on the issues and will at least be in a position to appreciate the debate. Before we move on, however, there are two preliminary questions that we must address. First, what Scrolls are under debate? And second, what are sects, one of which is said to have been responsible for writing the Scrolls?

## The Debate Over Authorship

The Dead Sea Scrolls represent several types of texts: those that were copies of the Old Testament, those that were copies of previously known extrabiblical books (apocryphal and pseudepigraphal), and those that were previously unknown books. It is this last category of texts that are in the debate over authorship. While the Old Testament and previously known extrabiblical texts may have been copied by the scribes at Qumran, their origin lies outside the community, and in many cases these texts were most likely imported to it. By contrast, the previously unknown extrabiblical texts are, for the most part, texts that are believed to have been produced within the community and by the Sect. That's why they are known as "sectarian" texts. Since this term will be used to refer to both the Dead Sea community and other religious groups of that day, let's take a moment to understand its meaning and usage.

## The Dead Sea Sect

As we consider the authorship of the Scrolls we will be referring to various groups as "sects." We have already used this word in reference to the Qumran or Dead Sea Sect, but it is a term equally applicable to any and all of the groups that existed in that time period. Religious sociologists have often found it difficult to give a definitive definition of a sect because the dissidence of a group could also classify it as a movement, a school, a party, or a faction. However, certain separatist groups do have a characteristic that can help us to identify them uniquely as a "sect." According to Second Temple period historian Joseph Blenkinsopp this is a minority status that not only opposes the norms accepted by the parent-body but also exclusively claims its status or position. In addition, most sects have at some point in their formative development the entrance of a charismatic leader (usually at a time of political, cultural, or social disorientation) who wields a directional influence at an opportune moment.[3] In religious studies the term *sect* can have negative connotations when used to speak of a group that has left a mainstream religion. For many Christians the term is used interchangeably with *cult*. However, in historical studies, and particularly studies of the Second Temple period, all groups or parties, regardless of size or importance, are referred to as sects (including Christians). This is because (as we'll see in chapter 6) there was no normative, but only a transitional, Judaism during this period.

### The Essene Theory

The majority theory today, generally accepted as proven fact by most scholars since the publication of the Cave 1 Scrolls (1955), is the Essene Theory. Dr. Magen Broshi exemplifies most Qumran scholars when he emphatically states as his convictions:

> There is hardly anything in the 800 manuscripts which agrees with their rivals or enemies of the period. Nothing Pharisee. Absolutely nothing. Nothing Sadducee. Absolutely nothing. [On the other hand] there is nothing that does not agree with the spirit of the Essenes.[4]

So firmly entrenched is this theory in most modern discussions of the Scrolls that for many writers the Sect is automatically spoken of as the "Qumran Essenes" and the Scrolls as "Essenic literature."

According to the classical writers Josephus and Pliny, and perhaps Philo,[5] the Essenes were a group that exhibited unique piety and a distinctive theological perspective. However, despite the fact that scholarly consensus identifies the Qumranites as the Essenes, we do not know who the Essenes were. The meaning of their Greek name *Essenoi* or *Essaioi* is still uncertain, although a recent theory argues that they borrowed their name from a sect in Asia Minor that was devoted to the cult of Artemis and whose appearance and practices were similar to their own. Philo describes a group called the Therapeutae ("healers"), but it's not clear if they should be identified with Josephus' and Pliny's "Essenes" or if they constitute a similar group. Still, some people believe that the weight of evidence best supports this theory.

### Support for the Essene Theory

The strongest argument for the identification of the Qumran community with the Essenes is that of geographical location. Pliny, in his *Natural History* (5.15 § 70-73), describes the Jordan River and the Dead Sea, and then locates the Essenes on its western shore with Ein-Gedi to the south of them and then Masada. Geographically, the site of Qumran is about 8 miles south of Jericho, Ein-Gedi is about 20 miles south of Qumran, and Masada is about 11 miles south of Ein-Gedi.

Pliny also observed that the Essenes lived among palm trees, which best fits the area of Jericho, or given the other geographical factors, the area between the site of Qumran and 'Ein Feshkha, the major spring just south of the settlement's farm area. Dio Chrysostom (circa A.D. 40–112) is reported to have given a similar geographical location. Synesius of Cyrene (circa A.D. 400) wrote in his biography, "Also somewhere he praises the Essenes, who form an entire and prosperous city near the Dead Sea, in the center of Palestine, not far from Sodom." On the map, Sodom, which is traditionally located at the southern end of the Dead Sea's Lisan Peninsula, is south of Masada and quite a distance from Qumran. However, to an ancient cartographer this may have been "not far." Since archaeological surveys have not been able to offer an alternative site for this ancient location for the Essenes, it appears that Qumran still remains the only possible match.

We are told by classical sources that there were more than 4,000 Essenes scattered in communities throughout the Land of Israel. Father Bargil Pixner believes one large Essene community resided in the southern district of Jerusalem (in the area of modern Mount Zion), although some evidence shows that they generally avoided large cities. It is possible, then, that an Essene community could have existed in the Dead Sea region near to but not identical with the site of Qumran. However, as Dr. Frank Cross has pointed out, in order to argue against what the ancient sources say, "the scholar must suppose that one community carefully described by classical authors disappeared without leaving building remains or even potsherds behind; while the other community, systematically ignored by the classical sources, left extensive ruins and even a great library."[6]

Since the classical sources described the Essenes and their community, all that was needed was to harmonize the details of the Scrolls with the ancient sources in order to complete the historical picture. This was done by Dr. Todd Beall in his dissertation entitled *Josephus' Description of the Essenes Illustrated by the Dead Sea Scrolls*. This work was originally prepared for the Catholic University of America and subsequently published as a monograph in the prestigious Society for New Testament Studies.[7] In his work, Dr. Beall draws 26 parallels between the descriptions of the Essene community by Josephus and statements made in the sectarian documents concerning the beliefs and practices of the Sect.[8] Let's look at three of the more important of these.

First, Josephus noted that "the Essenes . . . are also extraordinarily interested in ancient writings" (*Antiquities* 18.1). The existence of the Scrolls is evidence of that. However, had Josephus told us what *kind* of ancient writings he was talking about, we could have more certainly identified the group. There would be great differences between a group that was interested in Greek literature and one that was interested in the Hebrew Scriptures.

Second, beliefs unique to the Essenes are reflected in the Scrolls. One prominent example is the belief in predestination. The Sadducees rejected the concept entirely. The Pharisees accepted some things as predestined, but others as wholly determined by the human will. Apparently only the Essenes and the Qumran Sect held the doctrine consistently among known groups in Judaism. Since the classical sources do not mention any other groups that believed in predestination, then the Essenes and the Qumran Sect must be either the same group or so closely related as to have been indistinguishable.

Third, there are minute similarities in practice that would not be expected unless the two groups were one. Examples of what appear to be shared communal or ritual practices included wearing white linen tunics, not replacing clothing or sandals, purificatory washings, a common meal, and maintenance of silence in the assembly. Even more detailed is their shared prohibition against "spitting in an assembly" (cf. *Jewish Wars* 2 § 147/*1QS* 7:13).

## Problems with the Essene Theory

Despite these interesting parallels, there are significant problems to the Essene theory.[9] First, the term *Essene* (in any form) does not appear in any of the Scrolls. The Qumran group called themselves the *Yahad,* the "Community of the Renewed Covenant," "the Elect," and "the Remnant," but never the Essenes. Some scholars have proposed that's what is meant by the Hebrew term *'esa*, which in the Scrolls is sometimes used to mean "council" or "party," however, the linguistic derivation is problematic and *yahad* ("community") means essentially the same thing.[10] It has yet to be explained why they deliberately avoided using the term *'esa* of themselves yet used it for others.

Also, the most significant distinction of the Qumran community, one that affected its sectarian life and its relations with other Jews, was the use of a 364-day luni-solar calendar (as opposed to a strictly 354-day lunar calendar). It is remarkable that none of the ancient sources detailing the unique Essene practices mentioned this important distinction. Likewise, the Qumran belief in two Messiahs is not known to be an Essene position—unless the Qumran view has been misunderstood and a single Messiah was meant. Professor Shemaryahu Talmon believes that these differences make the Essene theory untenable:

> I consider it methodologically wrong to begin identifying a new movement by making comparisons. I think that we should have started, as I did from the beginning, by basing my ideas on what they tell us about themselves. There are a fair number of similarities, including the fact that according to Josephus one of the main Essene settlements was near Masada or Ein-Gedi, which is not too far from Qumran. In spite of that I think we have to take into account that analogies should be expected from the very outset. For this reason [the authors of] the Scrolls have been identified with Christianity, the Ebionites, the Zadokites, and the Hassidians, et. al. The explanation for this is that all these groups draw on the same heritage, namely the Hebrew Bible. Other similarities can be explained to some degree by a similarity in societal structure. In this respect a group built on a simple figure like the *Moreh Ha-Sedeq* ("the Teacher of Righteousness" or better, "Legitimate Teacher") resembles Christianity built on Jesus Christ. However, in my opinion what is decisive are not the similarities but the differences. The differences are obvious and clear. Our three sources about the Essenes: Josephus Flavius, Pliny the Elder, and Philo of Alexandria never mention that they had a leader, a central figure, like "the Legitimate Teacher." They never mention a type like the Wicked Priest, who persecutes them. There is no reference to a difference in calendar between the Essenes and the other Jews. They do not tell us that the

Essenes consider themselves as the first post-exilic generation
and so the new Biblical Israel that arose in their time. We have
no reference to any type of inspired interpretation of Biblical
prophecy. So [in summary] I believe the similarities can be
explained by all these groups, including the Essenes drawing
upon the heritage of the Hebrew Bible, and that the differences outweigh the similarities.[11]

Another problem is that Dr. Beall's 26 parallels deal mostly with virtues
that were emulated by all religious Jews or that might have been practiced in any Jewish assembly at the time (a fact Beall notes). In my opinion,
all but a few parallels could fit many groups, and even these (such as spitting in public) could have been more universal prohibitions. If we thus
reduce the number of significant parallels, the number of discrepancies
between the accounts of the Essenes and the Scrolls become more pronounced. Dr. Beall listed six such discrepancies, and these are more specific in nature than were his parallels. For instance, when a new member
joined the Essene community, he had to give up his personal property to
the group (a socialized system akin to Israel's modern Kibbutzim).
Although a similar sharing of property is seen in one Dead Sea Scroll
(the *Manual of Discipline*), the act is contradicted by another, the
*Damascus Document*, which supports private ownership. In fact, four of
Beall's six discrepancies are with the *Damascus Document*. This has suggested to some that the *Damascus Document* may be describing a different order of Essenes than those at Qumran.

There are other discrepancies with the *Manual of Discipline* that are
equally striking. In Josephus, the Essene initiation oath is sworn at the
*end* of the probation period and is connected with sectarian tenets. In *1QS*,
the oath is at the *beginning* and is concerned with the Mosaic Law. Also,
in Josephus, a novice must wait two years to touch a meal, while *1QS*
indicates only a one-year wait.

Finally, the newly published Dead Sea text called the *Halakhic Letter
(4QMMT)*, reveals a substratum of Sadducean legal views. Because the
Sadducees differed from the Essenes in various areas of belief and practice, it is unlikely that they could be identified with the Qumran community. However, if both the Essenes and the Sadducees had the same
priestly origins—that is, from the line of Zadok—they might still exhibit
many areas of agreement on legal matters while remaining separate groups.
Alternately, it could be possible that neither belonged to the line of Zadok

but simply called themselves Zadokites as a term for and a claim to priestly legitimacy.

## The Sadducean Theory

The publication of the Cave 4 document known as *Misqat Ma'aseh Ha-Torah* ("*Some Works of the Torah*") and the *Halakhic Letter*, or popularly known as *4QMMT (4Q394-398)*, opened the door for a new interpretation of the Dead Sea Sect as Sadducean either at its inception, through influences, or simply in its legal viewpoint.

Our knowledge of the Sadducees is sparse; there is little information that helps to define this major group in Second Temple Judaism. Their earliest appearance historically is in connection with events in the time of John Hyrcanus (135–104 B.C.). Modern scholarship has connected their Greek name *Saddoukaioi* with the name Zadok (Hebrew, *sadoq*, from *saddiq*, "righteous"), the high priest at the time of David and Solomon (1 Samuel 8:17; 15:24; 1 Kings 1:34; 1 Chronicles 12:29). Zadok is also the high priest with whom the nucleus of priests who formed the Qumran community are said to be related *(1QS* 5:2, 9; *1QSa* 1:2, 24; 2:3; *1QSb* 3:22). It is believed that the Zadokite priesthood was dominant through the Persian period until the Maccabean revolt,[12] and that in time the name came to refer to all of the aristocratic circles connected with the high priests by marriage or other social relations.[13] It was these Hasmonean priests, called in the Scrolls "the last priests of Jerusalem," whom the Qumran Sect bitterly opposed and of whom they said that the Kittim (Romans) would punish *(1QpHab* 9:4-7; cf. *4QpNah* 1:11).

One problem with the study of the Sadducean sect is that all of our information about them comes only from sources who were hostile to them (the New Testament, Josephus, and the rabbinic writings). Based on these sources we learn that the beliefs that separated the Sadducees from other groups were their denial of immortality, determinism, and their adherence to the Oral Law. The rabbinic writings appear to affirm that the greatest differences between the Sadducees and the Pharisees were the laws and practices of ritual purity. Because information is so limited, however, one writer tells us that "we cannot draw a clear picture of the political, theological, nationalistic views or history of the Sadducees ... [even] the actual connection with the Sadducees and the priests is unclear."[14] For this reason, if the Dead Sea community was in some way related to the Sadducees, its writings would shed the light of a primary source on the Sect for the first time.

The chief advocate of a Sadducean connection is New York University professor of Judaic Studies Dr. Lawrence Schiffman. I first met Dr. Schiffman in 1990 at an archaeological congress in Jerusalem and had the opportunity to appreciate his command of Jewish *halakhic* (legal) literature as we talked together on our flight back to New York. There have always been supporters of the Sadducean hypothesis because the Qumran Scrolls mention their leaders as the *bene sadoq,* "sons of Zadok" (*CD* 4:4-5; 5:2). Schiffman, however, has based his arguments largely on *4QMMT,* which he believes comes from the earliest stage of the development of the Sect,[15] and in which he finds similarities between the legal disputes recorded there and those included in the Mishnah. But unlike previous advocates of this position, Schiffman does not see a sectarian Oral Law at Qumran that was related to that of the sages. Rather, his view is that the concept of Oral Law as seen in rabbinic literature was not introduced until the reorganization of Judaism after the destruction of the Temple (the Yavnean period). Thus, both the Qumran Sect and the later Mishnaic sages may have had a common body of *halakhic* material that they consulted. This provides for Schiffman a reason that the Sect developed their *halakha* directly from the biblical text and why these laws were then recorded.[16] This also explains why many Qumran texts (such as the *Community Rule*) differ so much from later rabbinic literature. Schiffman sees the Sect as having Sadducean origins and coming into being after the Hasmoneans took control of the high priesthood (circa 152 B.C.). It was the group's leader, the Teacher of Righteousness, that led them to their apocalyptic views and to beliefs that departed from Sadducean thought.[17]

The question now is whether the early *halakot* (laws) seen in the Scrolls is evidence of the existence of a pre-rabbinic Oral Law (before the redaction of the Mishnah). Dr. Kenneth Hanson has attempted to identify reflections of such *halakot* in the *Damascus Rule* and has developed procedures for evaluating it as such.[18] On the other hand, the Scrolls reveal that the Sect saw their laws as being derived from their unique spiritual enablement to interpret (actually, recover the lost interpretation) of the Torah. This amounted to something like new revelation rather than an ancient tradition of supplementary revelation handed down from Mount Sinai. It should not be any more surprising to find points of agreement as well as disagreement between the Qumran Sect and the Sadducees as with other sects within the Judaism of the time. This would be especially true, as mentioned above, if any of these sects also shared or claimed a common priestly heritage from Zadok.

This comparison of the *halakhic* material in *4QMMT* with preserved Sadducean arguments is impressive but not identical in every instance, and leaves, in my opinion, enough differences to see something other than shared origins. It seems to me that if two groups each attempted to formulate *halakha* from the same legal texts of the Torah they would achieve nearly the same degree of correspondences and contradictions. Also, another criticism of the Sadducean view is this: How could the Qumran Sect, if they were originally Sadducees, develop the radically anti-Sadducean doctrines of predestination and bodily resurrection as well as a complex angelology? Could the Teacher of Righteousness (a Zadokite priest himself) have taught such things and still been accepted as a divine interpreter by the Qumran Sect if it was Sadducean? This question is intensified by the identification of the Wicked Priest, who opposed and persecuted the Teacher *(1QpHab* 8:8; 9:9; 11:4). If, as most scholars suppose, this was a high priest in Jerusalem, then he must have been a Sadducee as well (see Acts 5:17). Yet as mentioned previously, the Sect rejected the Hasmonean/Sadducean high priesthood in Jerusalem.

Schiffman gets around this by contending that the Sadducees revealed in the sources with these doctrines are not the same type of Sadducee that formed the Qumran community, but rather a sort of breakaway group that was discontent with the in-house bickering, aristocratic behavior, and petrified legalism of the Sect. This could be, and it would resolve our question of priestly origin. But at the present time there still seems to be too little evidence for the Sadducean theory to overthrow the dominant Essene theory.

### *The Pharisaical Theory*

The Pharisees were considered by Josephus the major party among the four principal sects of the Jews. The later rabbinic sages were said to have been the successors of the first-century Pharisees; however, there are significant differences between them, and it is unwarranted in many cases to interpret the former by the latter (as a whole history of Christian interpreters have done, see chapter 6). There is no question that many aspects of religious regulation (particularly those for the Sabbath) accord well with later rabbinic *halakha*. It is known that one division of the Pharisees had very strict rules concerning membership and ceremonial purification, much like the Qumran Sect. Therefore, it has been proposed that the Qumran Sect was Pharisaical.

It is possible that at some point in the history of the Sect a Pharisaic element was present at Qumran, for the members appear to have come from the more common rank of people, with which the Pharisees identified. However, to make the Pharisees the core leaders is another matter, for it seems that Qumran was always led by priests. Those who wrote the Scrolls appear to have been as opposed to the Pharisees in Jerusalem as the Sadducees, calling the Pharisees by the derogatory name *dorese halaqot*, "seekers of smooth things" *(4QpNah* 1:2, 7; *1QH* 2[15], 32). This name is a pun on the Pharisees' obsession (i.e., "seeking") with laws, indicating their practice of adapting the Law to their own interpretation. The Qumran Sect felt the Pharisees tended toward laxness in the Law and considered themselves much stricter. The same problem with legalism continues today between religious groups whose denominations place less or greater stress on certain ordinances or social issues. If we add to these problems a different calendar for religious observance, the nonpriestly status of the Pharisees, and a variety of differences in customs (such as the Qumran requirement that people share communal property), we find that the Pharisaical theory has perhaps the least support of all views.

### The Zealot Theory

Another theory, with perhaps better support, is the Zealot theory. It was held by one of the original Scroll Team members, J.T. Milik,[19] and was defended on a historical basis by Christian Old Testament scholar G.R. Driver[20] and Jewish Oxford University professor Cecil Roth.[21] The Zealots were one of the sects mentioned by Josephus in his description of the major divisions or "philosophies" of the Jews in the first century (*Jewish Antiquities* 18.1.6; *Jewish War* 2.8.1). We may also have some mention of them in the New Testament (Acts 21:38), where the term *Sicarii* is used of a band of rebels led by an Egyptian messianic pretender. The rabbinic sources use this designation for the rebels at Jerusalem during the final siege (*Makshirin* 1:6). The second-century church father Hippolytus wrote that they were one of four divisions of the Essenes, calling them equally both Zealots and Sicarii (*Refutatio omnium haeresium* 9.26).

As to the nature and beliefs of the Zealots, Josephus paints their portrait with a wide brush, noting only that they were unlike the other sects and that they accepted no ruler but God. However, Hippolytus notes on this latter trait that their extremeness and violent manner was considered a departure from the strict life of the Essenes—so much so that members of the other Essenic parties would have no relations with them. This violent characterization is supported by the historical role the Zealots took in instigating the Jewish Rebellion against Rome in A.D. 63. This revolt eventually led to the destruction of the Qumran community, Jerusalem, and the Temple (A.D. 68–70). It was the Zealots who made the final stand against the Romans and died in a mass suicide at Masada in A.D. 73.

The connection made between the Zealots and the Qumran Sect stems in part from the destruction of the Qumran community by the Romans. Would the Romans have attacked if they had been a pacifistic sect? That the Qumran Sect might have been comprised of Zealots seems possible from their hatred of the Romans (revealed in the Scrolls) and their separation from all other sects. In addition, their extremism in matters of purity and practice and their apocalyptic perspective appear to make them Zealots. After all, did they not write a *War Scroll* detailing a future battle against the Romans? Another support for the Zealot theory comes from the excavations of the Qumran settlement, which revealed evidence of a fierce battle. Proponents of this theory believe that an elevated tower on the northern wall of the community was a defensive structure and that the whole settlement was in fact a Zealot outpost or fort. This, they say, is the reason the Romans attacked it. Other confirmation appears to come from Masada, where Scroll fragments of the Qumranic *Songs for the Sabbath Sacrifice* were discovered along with the unique-style Scroll jars that were determined to have come from the kilns at Qumran.

Yet the problems with the Zealot theory are many. There is no evidence that the Qumran Sect was at variance with the rest of Jerusalem or that other sects in Judaism refused contact with them (it was usually the other way around). Hatred for the Romans was common among many sects, but in the Qumran Sect it was on par with hatred for other Jewish sects. So their hatred was not like that of the Zealots. They didn't consider rejection of or separation from Gentiles to mean active opposition to them, as the New Testament depicts (John 18:28; 19:12,15).

There is also no evidence that hatred for any group was acted upon in an aggressive or violent manner. Just because a group is considered apocalyptic and expects an end-time battle to take place does not mean that it is militaristic or has violent tendencies. The same misunderstanding exists today in Israel between secularists and religious Jews. When I was in Jerusalem attending the state funeral of assassinated Prime Minister Yitzhak Rabin, I heard and read statements warning against orthodox Jews who believed in a literal advent of the Messiah. People reasoned that since the Messiah was expected to come in a great war and establish his own government, the Jews who are "messianists" must be seeking to overthrow the government by force and are no different than terrorists. This same misunderstanding has even caused some scholars to think Jesus was a Zealot![22]

However, a messianic hope was shared by almost all of the Jewish sects of the Second Temple period. For most sects the position was not one of intervention, but rather of working within the system while waiting for God to act in His own time.

A similar misunderstanding is made regarding the Romans' attack against the Jews. In a time of national revolt the Roman army did not limit its attacks to specific groups. The Roman Empire, when it came against Israel, was out to teach the Jews a lesson and all Jewish settlements were subject to attack, regardless of how harmless they may have seemed. Also, we cannot assume that the tower at Qumran was a defensive structure and hence the settlement was a fort. The walls of the structure are too thin and its height is insufficient for it to have served military purposes. Also, no ramparts or trenches have been found, which are common for military settlements. Too, there should have been some weapons recovered from graves at the site,[23] or the remains of a Roman bath (for non-Jewish mercenaries). Instead, many of the graves yielded women, which is out of character for a military fortress. And the other structures at the site, such as the Scriptorium, indicate a more peaceful society, not a renegade regiment. (Although those who believe Qumran served military purposes feel the Scriptorium may have had a different use.) Yigael Yadin, who was both a military expert (a general in the Israeli army) and an expert on the archaeology of the settlement, never thought of Qumran as anything other than a communal center.

That members of the Qumran community should end up at Masada is not surprising, either. With their own settlement destroyed and Jerusalem in flames, the only safe refuge in the area was the stronghold at Masada. It is also possible that after the Romans destroyed the community some of the Sect became more militant in their attitude and joined with Jews who were Zealots. Dr. Dan Bahat says,

> I was involved in the excavation of Masada, and one thing which we were interested in was what connection Masada had to the Essenes. We knew from Josephus' writings that the Essenes tried to be as separate as possible from the problems of the Second Temple period. But [when the Romans invaded] they saw that the entire future of the Jewish people was in the balance and decided to take part in it [the Jewish Revolt]. In other words, there

was a presence of the Zealots, or the Essenes with the Zealots in Masada, but to what extent is difficult to say.[24]

The presence of members from the Qumran community (be they Essene or of other origin) with the Zealots at Masada does not mean that the Qumranites were also Zealots. But could the Sect have adopted Zealot sympathies and remained members of their Sect? If they interpreted the Roman attack on their community as the beginning of the great 40-year war that had been predicted by the Teacher, then they could have thought it time to discontinue waiting and take action, even though the arrival of the messiah(s) of Aaron and Israel had not yet occurred. Yet it is difficult to believe that the Sect would have had a warlike attitude in view of a text like *4Q460:*

> Let not warriors boast themselves [in their strength . . . ] in
> their might, nor kings in the power of their strength, nor princes
> [ . . . ] in their weapons of war or in their strong cities.[25]

If some members of the Sect did join with the Zealots as warriors, then they would have no longer been considered a part of the other Sect. For this and other reasons, most scholars feel that the Zealot theory is not adequately supportable.

### The Jerusalem Theory

Among those who argue that the Qumran community was actually a Herodian fortress is Professor Norman Golb of the University of Chicago.[26] He believes the Scrolls could not have been produced or collected by a military regiment, and thus the Scrolls found in the Dead Sea region were not from the Qumran community, but rather were part of the Temple library in Jerusalem. He feels that the Scrolls were deposited in the Dead Sea caves by Jews who were evacuating the Holy City before the Roman siege of A.D. 70. His theory offers some solutions for the problems in other views by stating that the Scrolls were not the product of a single sect. In other words, if the *Community Rule* seems to contain Essene teachings, if *4QMMT* has Sadducean *halakha*, and if the *War Scroll* appears to reflect Zealot ideology, then it is probably because they do! There is no contradiction here because for Golb, all of the Scrolls came from different sects and places, just like books in a modern library come from many different sources.

Golb gives a number of arguments in support of his view. First, he points to the differences in the sectarian texts (as just mentioned) and finds this as proof that the documents represent a collection of sectarian views, not the compositions of a single sect. But we can respond to Golb by saying that just because some of the Scrolls are imported texts doesn't indicate that all of them are imported. In fact, the common elements in the Scrolls, elements distinct to the Sect, argue that they have to be related. We do not know of any other groups who followed a solar calendar and had a figure called the Teacher of Righteousness, and the sectarian documents have both of these elements in common. Also, even though there is a general unity in the Sect's documents, the group had a long enough history to allow for the development of new or different views. The fact that slightly different versions of the *Community Rule* and the *Damascus Document* were found in Cave 4 may support this point. Golb endeavors to support his view by stating that none of the sectarian documents are autographs (original copies). While it can be shown that some were not (through the presence of scribal errors and the like), no one can say some might not be originals. For instance, some of the *pesharim* could be original, since none of these were found in multiple copies. And if these texts were produced by the Teacher, as implied, autographs would most certainly have been preserved.

A second reason that Golb believes the Scrolls were not the product of only one sect is because Scrolls were found in other places, such as near Jericho. If the people of Jericho hid their Scrolls in caves, then so could the people of Jerusalem. This, Golb would say, makes a Scroll-writing community in the desert unnecessary. This, however, is a weak argument. Every home probably had a Scroll with a portion of Scripture, and certainly would have had Scrolls with marriage or commercial contracts. The mere fact that Scrolls would have come from elsewhere doesn't mean that the Qumran community could not have also produced many of their own Scrolls. Furthermore, hiding personal or community valuables in the desert during times of distress was a common practice. It was for this very reason that the Sect at Qumran hid their Scrolls where they did.

Third, and one of Golb's strongest points, is the *Copper Scroll's* testimony about a community that possessed amazing wealth. This Scroll records the hiding of treasures, supposedly from the Temple in Jerusalem, in 64 secret locations. Did not those mentioned in the sectarian documents give up their treasures when they joined the Sect? And did they not hate the Hasmonean priests, who greedily accumulated wealth and so corrupted themselves? How can this treasure have belonged to such a group? All scholars admit that the *Copper Scroll* is unique, being the only Scroll written on metal, written in a different Hebrew dialect, and stored in a different manner (on a shelf in the cave). Even if this particular Scroll were found to have no connection with the Qumran community and the treasure originated within the Temple at Jerusalem, why would this eliminate the rest of the Scrolls from being collected, composed, copied, and hidden by one sect? Well-worn trails leading from Khirbet Qumran to the caves in the region where the *Copper Scroll* was found *do* indicate a connection (see chapter 12).

We must keep in mind that the treasure bequeathed by new members (especially former priests from Jerusalem) over a period of several hundred years had to go somewhere. The community would most likely have been saving this wealth for the Temple they wanted to build in Jerusalem. Also, the diverse number of places where these treasures were hidden (the desert, Jericho, Jerusalem, the Galilee) and the depths at which some large quantities of treasure were buried imply that this was a carefully orchestrated plan. These treasures weren't buried in haste in the wake of the Roman invasion.

Golb's objections, for the most part, do not necessarily exclude the existence of the Qumran Sect, although they do argue against the Sect being the sole producer of the Scrolls. This, however, is universally conceded by scholars, as Professor Talmon and Magen Broshi point out:

> The collection of books at Qumran in the caves is surprisingly varigated. Not all books that are presented there are specific to that community, but represent the common heritage of all Israel. It is quite probable that a good bit of general Jewish literature of that time got into the collection (Talmon).[27]

> I don't think anybody has ever claimed that all the Scrolls are products of the same community. The Old Testament constitutes about one-quarter to one-third of the manuscripts, which are certainly not [the products of the Dead Sea Sect] (Broshi).[28]

While the diversity of the Scrolls argues against a common origin, it doesn't exclude the possibility that one sect possessed them and subsequently copied and preserved them in the caves. Yet common elements in many of the sectarian texts do argue for their unity, although one could counter that such a unified collection could have been represented in the

Jerusalem library and then stored together in the caves. To claim this alternative, however, Golb must prove that no connection exists between the Scrolls and the Qumran community. But archaeologist Hanan Eshel has now demonstrated that there was in fact a path leading between Caves 1 and 11 and the settlement (see chapter 17). This archaeological confirmation of the literary link between Qumran and the Scrolls makes Golb's theory less plausible.

## The Separatist Theory

If none of the arguments for the origin of the community are without problems, then perhaps none of the answers sought thus far are suitable. That is the premise of a theory that seeks to accept the Sect on its own terms and not match it to a previously known historical group. I call this view the separatist theory because it separates the Qumran Sect from all other sects, stressing the Sect's own claims to uniqueness. Professor Talmon explains this position:

> There is hardly a group, I think there's not one group, which we know from our classical sources in ancient Judaism with whom they have not been identified including the Samaritans. I believe that we should conceive of this group—until convincing evidence turns up which will teach us differently—as a phenomenon *sui generis*.[29]

Professor Talmon arrives at his conclusion after 45 years of study as a leading scholar of the Scrolls. His criticism with many of the present theories is that they are not developed based on the principal sources of the Sect but rather on fragmentary texts that were probably peripheral and likely had little or no authoritative influence on the Sect:

> Many pieces and compositions have nothing in them that could be called sectarian. Therefore when I come to consider the world view of this group I go to what I call the "foundation" documents. I take only these to build my interpretation of that community. Other pieces may be important but I'm never sure that they are part and parcel of what I would call the specific writings of that community. The foundation documents do not change, and in them we find the main principles of the group.[30]

Using these foundation documents, Professor Talmon has isolated the distinct beliefs and practices of the Sect, which he believes effectively separated it from Second Temple Judaism. In addition, he allows the Sect to define itself, using its own terms and theological claims:

> In one of my earliest papers (around 1951), I drew attention to what I considered to be a decisive reason for the separation of the community from mainstream Judaism. Mainly that they had adopted or lived a life according to a different calendar. Judaism lived by a lunar calendar of 354 days a year. [The Qumran Covenanters] arranged their lives by a cultic calendar, a solar calendar, of 364 days of year. Now sociologists will tell you that there's hardly anything more divisive in a society than a different pace of life. [Even today] in Judaism if someone attempts to make his own Sabbath, he is automatically excluded from the community. [Furthermore] this group considered itself as the first post-exilic generation of Israel. That is how the writer of the Zadokite Fragment opens his work. He says 390 years after destruction of the Temple God had mercy on His people and with us. I fall back on the names they give themselves. They speak about themselves as *habrit hahadashah* or *'asher ba'u habrit hahadashah*, i.e., those people who joined the community of the renewed covenant. I stress *renewed* and not new because I have found no correlative text [upon which they draw] in the Hebrew Bible. They were these with whom God re-established the covenant He had made with His people at the beginning of this [Persian] period. I believe this is the way we should treat them. Once we have more information about them we might fall back on the intent to compare them.[31]

Professor Talmon's observations comprise not a theory but a presentation of the Qumran group's internal testimony concerning itself. Because he has avoided comparison with any known group, he has avoided having to theorize about the group's origin. Talmon is not making a judgment about the accuracy or applicability of the Sect's claims about itself; rather, he is saying that if we want to understand them we must first come to them on their terms. However, if they are accepted as the first post-exilic generation, then this invites a historical comparison to other post-exilic communities. The idea of a renewed covenantal community especially calls for comparison with the "separated people and priests" (Nehemiah 10:28) who renewed the covenant upon entrance into the Land (Nehemiah 8:1–10:39). Professor Talmon has indeed followed this lead, and in these writings the concept of theory may be more prominent.[32] The only objection to his view is that it does not make enough of comparisons with other sources—an objection that concerns his methodology rather than his interpretation of the material.

## Other Theories

A new theory has recently been advanced in a 1995 dissertation by Dr. Raymond Edge.[33] His "Historical Tetragrammaton Hypotheses" proposes a different date for the origin of Qumran and a changing development for the community's two centuries of settlement. According to his theory, Qumran was originally founded by a Jerusalem group of conservative priests, led by the Teacher of Righteousness—a possible claimant to the high priesthood. They withdrew to the Judean Desert as a reaction to the persecutions of ancient Israel by Antiochus IV Ephiphanes. Based on an analysis of *4QMMT*, this conservative priestly movement attracted Pharisees, who joined the ranks as new members. The influx of this non-priestly element shifted the balance of power in the community to a laity-based leadership with strict regulations for membership. Ultimately, the movement became identified with the Essenes; however, toward the end of its settlement at Qumran, it became more reactionary to the Romans, although not in such a way as to identify it with the Zealots. The support for Edge's theory is based on his analysis of the community's use of two separate palaeo-Hebrew scribal traditions and their implications for understanding the history of the community.[34]

## My Opinion

I have deliberately avoided identifying the writers of the Scrolls with any particular theory. One reason is that although the Essene theory probably continues to have the strongest support, the debate is still raging over the supposedly Essenic character of some of the key documents. For instance, Dr. Hartmut Stegemann, professor of New Testament Science at the University of Göttingen and director of the Qumran Research Center (Göttingen), contends that the *Temple Scroll* could not be an Essene product. This is because, in his opinion, the uniqueness of language and subject matter in the *Temple Scroll* bears little resemblance to the other Scrolls he believes *are* Essene.[35] Other scholars add that the original composition date of the *Temple Scroll* was possibly before the Sect itself originated. These details don't necessarily exclude the *Temple Scroll* from being an Essene composition; they may point to a different type of Essene than that seen in the historical sources. This, of course, leads to the problem of circular evidences: using the classical sources concerning the Essenes to understand the people of the Scrolls, and then using the Scrolls to understand the Essenes of the classical sources. Perhaps the case for the Essene theory is good, but I will wait until there are additional convincing proofs before committing myself to the theory.

## Unraveling the Mystery

One of my former professors, Dr. Harold Liebowitz, loved to tell the story of a rabbi who was caught in the middle of a dispute between two members of his congregation. When asked by the first member for his judgment, the rabbi replied, "You're right!" Later, when the second member came along and asked for the rabbi's opinion, he replied, "You're right!" The rabbi's wife, who had heard his reply to both members, then asked him, "When the one came to you, you said he was right. And when the other came to you, you said he was right. How can both be right?" To which the rabbi replied, "You're also right!"

Perhaps at our present stage of knowledge about the Qumran Sect a little compromise is necessary. After all, when we try to categorize the Qumran Sect we do not find a comfortable fit with any one known group. If they were Essenes, they seem to have been a different sort of Essene than what Josephus and Pliny knew. If they were Sadducees, they must have been a breakaway Sadducee group. If they were Pharisees, they must have been a branch of Pharisees that rejected Oral Tradition. Thus, the Sect might have been Essenoid, or quasi-Sadducean, or Pharisee-like, or have had Zealotic tendencies, but apparently the group was not fully identical with any of these groups. Or, focusing on the many traits they shared, they could be seen as an Essenic/Pharisaic/Sadducean/Zealotic Sect.

My preference for now is to leave them as the *Yahad*—a unique but developing movement that was influenced to varying degrees and at various times, either by attraction or in reaction to the views of other groups present in the religious, social, and political context of Second Temple Judaism. Whatever form this took over their 300-year history is what we now call the Qumran Sect. Hopefully, it will not take scholars as long to finally unravel the mystery of the Sect's origin and to come to a consensus among themselves.

# 6

# THE SIGNIFICANCE OF THE SCROLLS

---

*The contribution of recent archaeological finds in the wilderness of Judaea has proved to be invaluable, indeed. The discovered materials have shed light on hitherto unknown or ambiguous areas of [a great many] subjects.*[1]

—Neil S. Fujita

---

We live in a practical age where we insist that everything must be relevant to be right. Because the Dead Sea Scrolls were written at a time far removed from our age, we may feel compelled to do what we can to make them mean something to us. Yet when we consider the Scrolls, we are not dealing simply with ancient artifacts, but with long-lost witnesses to the living Word. In touching their world we transport ourselves within reach of those whose words the Word records. And perhaps, in some Scrolls, find ourselves much closer to the context of sacred truth than we are able through any other non-biblical means.

The Dead Sea Scrolls are significant; they impact almost every area of biblical study and in many cases open new vistas of understanding or present new problems to be solved. In this chapter we will take a broad look at this significance before narrowing our focus to the Scrolls' relevance to the Old and New Testaments.

## A Significant Time Span

The Old and New Testaments are separated by a span of about 400 years.[2] With so much history having elapsed between them, some people might wonder how they could be related. Indeed, many Christians fail to recognize the connection between them. However, the distance that separates the testaments is not a chronological chasm to be jumped over but rather a historical bridge that connects them. These years were not "silent years" or "dark years" as some people have thought. More than 78 Old Testament apocryphal and pseudepigraphal works, as well as many letters and archaeological inscriptions, link together the testaments and shine light on their historical connection. To this list we must add the most significant of all intertestamental documents, the Dead Sea Scrolls, of which some 170 Scrolls establish a clear relationship between these times. Because the Scrolls have opened a window into the times before and after the birth of Jesus, we are able to see more clearly how He, His disciples, and the New Testament writers related to the Old Testament. As James Charlesworth has observed:

> They did not read them in a vacuum or in light of modern, usually German insights . . . [but] Jesus and the authors of the New Testament read what we call the Old Testament in the context of Early Judaism, which was vibrantly alive and attuned to the continuing power of God's word recorded in Torah.[3]

Today, more than in any previous century since the time of Christ, we have an increasingly abundant supply of intertestamental documents to assist our study of the New Testament. Too often, these primary-source materials from the Second Temple period have been neglected by religious conservatives.[4] However, as we read earlier (and it is worth repeating here): "Without due regard to the original historical and cultural context, every exegete is susceptible to eisegesis, interpreting according to his own historical, cultural context, or controlled (even unintentionally) by his own subjective concerns, relational goals, or philosophical presuppositions.[5]

One significant contribution of the Dead Sea Scrolls to the field of intertestamental literature is that they have actually improved our use of these documents. Many of these Jewish non-canonical books were formerly known to scholars only through ancient translations written in Greek, Syriac, or Coptic. But with the discovery of the Dead Sea Scrolls, scholars for the first time were able to read these works in their original Hebrew or Aramaic forms. This very advantage, however, originally presented somewhat of a difficulty to those who first worked with the Scrolls. Professor Hanan Eshel of the Hebrew University explains the nature of this problem:

> People who used to deal with the [subject of the] Second Temple never had to study Hebrew or Semitic languages because all the sources were in Greek. The New Testament was in Greek, Josephus was in Greek, the books of Maccabees were in Greek, and if you were dealing with Second Temple history you never learned Hebrew. There was no reason to learn it. Suddenly, we found texts in Qumran from the Second Temple period that shed light on these historical events. The people who were sent here to work on the Scrolls were not specialists in the Second Temple period, but biblical scholars, because they were the only ones who knew Hebrew. This is why biblical text scholars like [W.F.] Albright were originally consulted, and why scholars such as Father [Patrick] Skehan and Professor [Frank Moore] Cross were made part of the team. They did a wonderful job with the text, but they had to learn the history of the Second Temple period while dealing with the Scrolls.[6]

Today, with the help of this early work and a second and third generation of Israeli Second Temple scholars whose first language is Hebrew, we have uncovered much new information we can use to interpret the history and beliefs of those who lived between the Old and New Testaments. This new information can help us to better analyze and understand the biblical text.

## New Understanding Gained from the Scrolls

As more and more pieces of the intertestamental puzzle have begun to be brought together, we are coming to see the important role the Scrolls have in providing us with a clearer portrait of this period. There are many areas in which the Scrolls have had a pronounced influence, but the following four represent the most significant of these.

## Confirming the Accuracy of the Old Testament Text

Every person with a cursory knowledge of the Dead Sea Scrolls has been told that they are significant because they confirm for us the accuracy of the Old Testament text. This is true, and it was one of the more obvious benefits derived from discovering the Scrolls. Before the Dead Sea Scrolls were found, the biblical text of the Old Testament was known only from a text dating to the Middle Ages. The earliest known complete Hebrew manuscript of the Old Testament was the Ben Asher Codex in the Public Library of Leningrad. This was our oldest copy of the Bible, dating to about A.D. 1008; still it was more than 1,000 years removed from the last book composed by an Old Testament writer (circa 325 B.C.) Yet it was the best we had, so it became the basis for the scholarly standard edition of the Hebrew Bible, Kittel's *Biblia Hebraica*. Because of the vast amount of time that passed between the writing of the originals and the tenth-century copy, it was assumed that generations of scribes had entered mistakes of transmission into the Bible text. Yet in order for concerned scholars (textual critics) to discern these errors and suggest a more correct reading, they had to use copies of a Greek translation (the Septuagint) and a Latin translation (the Vulgate), the latter of which was written more than 600 years later than the Ben Asher Codex. As helpful as these texts were, nagging questions continued about the integrity and reliability of the traditional text of the Old Testament (the Masoretic Text).

These doubts were settled forever with one of the first Scrolls discovered, which was a copy of the entire book of Isaiah (later fragments representing another 21 copies were found). This text, originally part of the St. Mark's collection and dubbed the *Great Isaiah Scroll (1QIsaᵃ)*, was from about 100 B.C., or 1,000 years *earlier* than the Ben Asher Codex. Here was a copy that might have been in use at the very time Jesus opened and read from the Isaiah Scroll in the synagogue in Capernaum! Furthermore, since it was a *copy*, it may have reflected a text that went back to within only a generation or so of the prophet Isaiah himself![7] Dr. Weston Fields, executive director of the Dead Sea Scrolls Foundation, explains:

> With the discovery of the Dead Sea Scrolls, we are brought
> back almost within a generation of the writing of the last book

of the Bible. If the oldest Scroll is conservatively dated at 250 B.C., and some would date the oldest ones as early as 300 B.C., there is probably only 25 years or less between the time the last book was written and our earliest copies of the Hebrew Old Testament. This gives us a great deal more confidence about the text and the way it was passed along because we are able to compare what has been passed to us, which are later copies, but represent a very early text, with what we have in the Scrolls, however fragmentary it may be.[8]

Once a comparison was made between the text of the *Isaiah Scroll* and the Masoretic Text, it was evident that, except for minor details (such as spelling) that do not affect the meaning of the text, the two were almost identical.[9] Even though the Qumran text was more than six centuries older than the text of the Masoretes (the scribes of Tiberias responsible for the received version of the text), it confirmed the accuracy with which the scribes had carefully preserved and transmitted the biblical text through time. The Masoretes had sought to preserve the original understanding of the text, which had been written without vowels. The correct vocalization of this text had previously been transmitted orally, and by memory, from generation to generation. After six centuries in the Diaspora, a fear arose that the memory of the original Judean dialect was fading. Therefore, the Masoretes inserted markers in the text to indicate the original understanding of the vowels. The problem was that our Masoretic Text assumed that the memory of these Masoretes was correct. However, the scribes who wrote the Scrolls faced a similar problem and included consonants within the text, which served as vowels. This enabled scholars to see how incredibly accurate the transmission of the text had been, even by memory.

With the Dead Sea Scrolls, the scholarly world was suddenly faced with not one but hundreds of copies of the biblical text that predated even the translation of the Septuagint. Dr. Halvor Ronning, a member of the Jerusalem School for Synoptic Research, reflects on the positive change this revelation had in the academic community:

> This incredible faithfulness of the Jewish scribes in honoring that written text and preserving it for us has led in the scholarly world to an increased respect for that Hebrew text. This was especially the case in the Christian world where there had been an almost exclusive interest in the Septuagint text of the Bible.[10]

This careful preservation of the text reveals that the Jews of Qumran regarded the biblical text as authoritative—especially the Torah, which they took special pains to preserve in the old paleo-Hebrew script (more on that in a moment). While they also collected apocryphal and pseudepigraphal works, their allegiance to the biblical text appears firm. Upon it they wrote interpretive commentaries (mostly eschatological), and from it they amassed messianic proof texts or *Testimonia (4Q175)*. These efforts indicate that they also accepted the divine inspiration of the text, expecting it to have accurately predicted not only their days but the time of the end as well.

## Transmission of the Hebrew Text

The Dead Sea Scrolls have also helped us to understand how the Hebrew Bible was written, how it was transmitted, and how the books that are presently a part of its canon came to be included. Questions about these processes were formerly more difficult to answer because of the immense span of time separating our oldest copies of the Hebrew Bible from the original texts of the Hebrew Bible. Even though the proto-Masoretic text type was predominant, the Scrolls have revealed that in earlier periods a number of different text types circulated concurrently and within the same community. Dr. Emanuel Tov, editor-in-chief of the Dead Sea Scrolls Team and an expert in the textual criticism of the Bible, explains the importance of discovering these different text types:

> In Cave 4, fragments of the text of Jeremiah (designated A, B, C, and D) were discovered right alongside some other representations of Jeremiah. These fragments represent a type of text which more resembles the text of the Septuagint than that of the Masoretic Text (the Septuagint being about 15 percent shorter than the Masoretic Text). This was quite a surprise to scholars. For hundreds of years they had considered the text of the Septuagint inferior because they had no idea what Hebrew text it represented. The Scrolls have revealed for the first time evidence of a Hebrew text type represented by the Septuagint. Circulating in that time (third-first century B.C.), it was probably used by a large part of the Jewish communities just as other text types were. This helps us to understand that the final text of a book developed over a period of time and that God used a number of different writers or editors (whatever you want to call them) to bring a book to its present or to several final forms.[11]

Some scholars also believe that the Scrolls may imply that the list of books which were accepted as part of the Bible at Qumran differed from those that were established in Judaism as the official canon of the Hebrew Bible. The reason for this supposition is that many copies of the books that orthodox Jews and Protestant Christians consider apocryphal or pseudepigraphal were not only found at Qumran but also figured prominently in the Sect's literature. For example, several different copies of Ben Sira, or the Book of Ecclesiasticus (which is one of the 15 deuterocanonical books appearing in Roman Catholic Bibles and Greek Orthodox Bibles) were found at Qumran and Masada. Among them was the first known copy in Hebrew (all previous known copies were in Greek). Other apocryphal books, like *Enoch* and *Jubilees,* both highly apocalyptic works, also were found in multiple copies and exerted an authoritative influence on the calendrical and eschatological reckoning of the Sect. It is also possible, as Yigael Yadin thought, that such works as the *Temple Scroll* were regarded as canonical.

Based on this evidence, some scholars now feel that the Old Testament canon was not as fixed as had been previously believed. Rather, the constructing of the canon was a process that occurred gradually over time and involved many more people than envisioned before the Scrolls were discovered. They also believe that the canonical process was never viewed with complete unanimity among the various sects of Second Temple Judaism, even as it has not in Christendom until today. If this were so, it might explain why the New Testament mentions some of these books— for example, the allusion to Enoch in the epistle of Jude (verse 14). However, it does not follow that such allusions were considered by the biblical authors as inspired, and therefore this wouldn't reflect their view of canonicity. (For this reason, some people believe this implies that the inspiration and authority of Scripture "worked along the path of formation of these texts"[12]) Also, not all who hold this view see the immediate inspiration of a prophet or biblical writer as negated in the process of editing or canonizing their inspired work.

Though we are still uncertain of how nonbiblical literature was viewed by the Sect, the Scrolls make it certain that the three divisions of the Hebrew Bible were held as authoritative (the Torah, the Prophets, and the Writings). That the biblical commentaries and sectarian writings at Qumran profusely cite these three divisions as Scripture is evidence of this fact (see chapter 4). Whether the Qumran community (or at least some of it) held apocryphal and pseudepigraphal books as equally authoritative is not yet certain; I prefer the judgment of the late Rylands professor of Biblical Criticism and Exegesis (University of Manchester, England), F.F. Bruce:

> It is probable, indeed, that by the beginning of the Christian era the Essenes (including the Qumran community) were in substantial agreement with the Pharisees and the Sadducees about the limits of Hebrew scripture. There may have been some differences of opinion and practice with regard to one or two of the "Writings," but the inter-party disagreement remembered in Jewish tradition have very little to do with the limits of the canon.[13]

This means that it is not necessary to assume that an author of the Scrolls, or the author of the New Testament book of Jude, cited *Enoch* because his Hebrew Bible had a more flexible canon that included *Enoch.* He may have simply alluded to *Enoch* as a recognized and influential pseudepigraphal work. If these works had authority in the Qumran community, it may have been a *limited* authority that supported their sectarian doctrines and practices, but not determining them as would Scripture.

The Scrolls have also clarified for us some of the methods by which Scripture was referenced. In the Old and New Testaments, biblical writers cited other passages considered scriptural both with and without introductory formulas (for example, "as it is written . . ."). They also made allusion to texts through key words, phrases, or ideas.[14] In addition, they would paraphrase or loosely quote some texts. Scholars previously believed that such paraphrases were drawn exclusively from the writer's memory because he did not have access to the text at hand. But the Scrolls have now shown that paraphrase was a normal practice that helped to convert older and potentially misunderstood idioms into the common vernacular as well as allow the writers to compose their thoughts scripturally. The use of paraphrases does not seem to reveal any attempt to diminish the inspiration or authority of Scripture. As Dr. Emanuel Tov, an expert on Qumran scribal practices, observes:

> People approached the text of the Bible quite freely. We think about the scribes of the Bible as pious men who copied every word precisely and didn't allow for any changes. But that was in a different period. The farther back in time one goes the more freedom the scribe appears to have had, and the closer one comes to our times the less we find such differences. Yet, even when those major and minor differences were inserted in the biblical

text, the scribes approached the text with reverence and considered it to be sacred. However, their view of sacredness did not imply that changes could not take place. The biblical Scrolls from Qumran reveal many interesting features [changes, insertions] which we might call scribal.[15]

Not only did the biblical manuscripts of the Dead Sea Scrolls verify a long and diligent control over the transmission of the Hebrew text, but they also testified to a continued use and maintenance of the Hebrew language.

## Clarification of the Use of Jewish Languages

The Dead Sea Scrolls not only revealed the original language of many intertestamental texts but also opened a window through which we could hear the language of the peoples of the first century. The community at the Dead Sea, like most Jews in the Land during the middle-second century B.C. through the first century A.D., was multilingual.[16] According to the Jerusalem Talmud (TJ), "four languages are of value: Greek for song, Latin for war, Aramaic for dirges, and Hebrew for speaking" (TJ *Sotah* 7). Greek and Aramaic were well attested in other historical sources, so the discovery of Scrolls using these languages was expected. However, the discovery of Hebrew Scrolls has significantly improved and even altered the conventional concept of the evolution of the Hebrew language. Latin, which was the newest language acquired under the Roman conquerors (see John 19:20), does not appear in the Scrolls for the simple reason that it was rejected as the language of those predestined for destruction.[17] It is possible that some people at Qumran might have understood Latin, but it would have been unthinkable for them to use the language with one another.

### The Use of Greek

Greek was the *lingua franca* (universal or international language) of the day, much like English is today. A knowledge of Greek was necessary if a person wanted to contact government officials (Acts 21:37), conduct trade, or communicate with any Jews from Greek-speaking Asia Minor and Egypt as well as from parts of Israel where Greek was dominant, such as Caesarea, where it may have been used for prayers. Most of the scribes who wrote the Scrolls would have known Greek, although its use would have been restricted because of their resistance to the influences of Hellenistic culture and their preference for a stricter Hebraic lifestyle. Even then, the Qumran "Overseer of the Camp" was required to know Greek, and Cave 7 at Qumran yielded a unique collection of Greek manuscript fragments (mostly of the Septuagint). In addition, a personal seal bearing the owner's name in Greek ("Josephus") was found among the ruins at the Qumran settlement. Because their seals were used for commercial transactions, a seal in the language of commerce, rather than in Hebrew or Aramaic, would have been expected. It was once thought that the Jewish people's use of Greek was regional (limited to the Greek cities of the Decapolis and the area of the Galilee). The letters from the Bar Kokhba Revolt, found in several caves, reveal that Bar Kokhba gave orders to his military commanders in Greek. These documents alone were convincing proof that Greek was widely spoken by Jews during the Hasmonean and Herodian (New Testament) periods.[18]

## The Use of Aramaic

Aramaic was the older international language, derived originally from the Mesopotamian region. During the First Temple period, Imperial Aramaic was spoken between Israeli, Assyrian, and Babylonian court officials in their negotiations (2 Kings 18:26). It was popularly used by the beginning of the Second Temple period (Ezra 4:7), owing to the Jewish experience in exile, where it was learned by necessity (Daniel 2:4) and became a first language for the generation born there.

Many of the documents at Qumran were written in Aramaic. These texts are generally not sectarian, but apocryphal or targumic (*Genesis Apocryphon*, *Books of Enoch*, *Tobit*, *Testament of Levi*, *Targum of Job*, and so on), although sectarian works are included (for example, *4Q Amram*). They have provided scholars the first actual examples of western dialects of Aramaic which had only formerly been hypothesized to explain later developments in the language), and the first historical evidence that literary composition in Judea had continued between the Aramaic writings of the Bible (Ezra 4:11-22; 5:7-17; 6:2-12; Daniel 2:4–7:28) and the Aramaic texts of the later rabbinic tradition (circa A.D. 100).

The Aramaic text of the Scrolls has also supported conservative scholars who contend that the book of Daniel was written during the Persian period rather than the later Maccabean period. Before the Scrolls were discovered, critical scholars argued that the Aramaic found in Daniel was from a time not earlier than 167 B.C. However, the Aramaic text of the Dead Sea Scrolls, which comes from about the time of the Maccabean period, is considerably different than that found in the book of Daniel. This suggests what the commentator J.A. Montgomery noted even before the discovery of the Scrolls: that Daniel's Aramaic is linguistically closer to the fifth or fourth century B.C. than to the second or first (see pages 157-163). In addition, since parts of the New Testament have their historical origin in an Aramaic-speaking context, the Aramaic texts from Qumran can provide helpful insights into other areas of New Testament research.

### The Use of Hebrew

Though Greek and Aramaic were known and used by the Dead Sea Sect, the Scrolls reveal that the scribes had a linguistic loyalty to Hebrew. This loyalty was demonstrated foremost in their attempt to preserve the form of Hebrew in which the Bible had been written from earliest times through the First Temple period. This script, written in letters derived from the Phoenician alphabet, was first used by Moses in his autographs of the Torah, which were placed inside the Ark of the Covenant beside the tablets of the Ten Commandments (Deuteronomy 31:24-25). These sacred Scrolls then accompanied the new Israelite nation throughout their 40 years in the wilderness. A change in script form occurred when the Jews went into exile (722–528 B.C.). While in exile they adopted the Aramaic language and at some point began using the Aramaic script (square characters) when they made new copies of the Bible. (However, some Jews continued to use the older form of Hebrew in this later period.) The name given to this script in its revived usage is *paleo*-Hebrew.[19] The Scrolls at Qumran represent the first literary evidence of this post-exilic usage. There, copies of the five books of the Torah, as well as part of Joshua and the book of Job, were found written in this script.

Several reasons may be possible for the Dead Sea Sect's use of paleo-Hebrew. First, the desert community of Qumran wanted to demonstrate a historical and spiritual connection between the desert community of Sinai and their own 40-year period of establishment under their Teacher. Second, paleo-Hebrew had been the national script during the First Temple period, and the Sect's ongoing use of the script may indicate they saw themselves as the living continuation of this biblical/prophetic period. Third, this older script connected their priestly writers with the original Zadokite priesthood of the First Temple. This was evidenced by their preservation of the four-letter name of God (the *Tetragrammaton*) in the paleo-Hebrew script. It appears in their sectarian writings, and this style of text was even used in the Greek text of the *Twelve Prophets Scroll* found at Nahal Hever. And fourth, it has also been suggested that this might have possibly been used to identify writings ascribed to the Sect's Teacher, who as a priest was able to pronounce the sacred and ineffable name of God (YHWH).[20]

Not only did the Sect write sacred documents in paleo-Hebrew, they also used a form of Late Biblical Hebrew for many of their sectarian documents (such as the rule books, prayer-books, and Thanksgiving psalms). From a study of this script, which has been designated *Jewish script*, it was also learned that the Sect spoke Hebrew as a living language. Frequently, when they attempted to write in Late Biblical Hebrew, corruptions appeared in grammar and syntax. These "colloquialisms" betrayed their own Hebrew (closer to Mishnaic Hebrew), which they used in everyday affairs.[21]

This evidence from the Scrolls forced a change in the theory of how the Hebrew language developed during the Second Temple period. Scholars once believed that Aramaic had largely replaced Hebrew among the Jewish people (except in religious use). So established was this view that even though Luke's witness in the New Testament was that Paul addressed a general Jewish audience in Jerusalem in "the Hebrew dialect" (Acts 21:40–22:2), most modern Bible versions translated the Greek word *Hebraidi* ("Hebrew") as "Aramaic." Today, however, it is conceded by almost all scholars that the average Jew in the first century used Hebrew at least as much as Aramaic.[22] In fact, Israeli linguist Chaim Rabin has suggested that the only reason the community wrote Aramaic works was to accommodate Jews of the eastern Diaspora, who were unable to maintain a sufficient proficiency in literary Hebrew.[23] In addition, the variety of Hebrew scripts represented in the Dead Sea Scrolls has resulted in new classifications for the Hebrew language variations of this period: Archaic or Proto-Jewish (circa 250–150 B.C.), Hasmonean (circa 150–30 B.C.), and Herodian (circa 30 B.C.–A.D. 70).[24]

Thus, the Scrolls have confirmed theories of language use and enlightened our understanding of first-century communication. Beyond this, they have dramatically enriched our understanding of the Judaism of the Second Temple period and especially around the turn of the era—a time during which Jewish sects were proliferating and the two most enduring movements in Judaism (Christianity and rabbinic Judaism) were being formed.

## Correction of the History
## of Early Judaism

Prior to the discovery of the Dead Sea Scrolls, our knowledge about the Jewish people during the Second Temple period (536 B.C.–A.D. 70), and particularly during the formative political and religious period (167 B.C.–A.D. 70) came solely from Jewish works such as those by Flavius Josephus (circa A.D. 37–100), apocryphal historical books such as Maccabees (circa 125–63 B.C.), Philo of Alexandria (died A.D. 45), and especially from rabbinic literature. This latter source, including the Babylonian and Jerusalem Talmuds, though purporting to cite the oral tradition passed down by the Pharisees, and the Mishnah, which it contains, was not compiled and edited until A.D. 200. The Gemara (Commentary on the Mishnah) was not completed until A.D. 400–500. Also, this source represented only one sect in Judaism, yet its material was generally accepted as normative for all. Josephus identified four Jewish sects (Pharisees, Sadducees, Essenes, Zealots),[25] and even though he may have chosen the tradition of the Pharisees and perhaps once lived with the Essenes, his work and the other works were merely secondary sources about these sects' beliefs and practices. Primary documents from the sects themselves (unless we include the New Testament) were simply nonexistent prior to the Dead Sea Scroll finds.

Before the availability of the Dead Sea Scrolls, then, the standard reference books for this period, such as Emil Schürer's *A History of the Jewish People in the Time of Jesus Christ*[26] and George Foot Moore's *Judaism in the First Centuries of the Christian Era*,[27] were entirely dependent upon these limited sources and thus presented a distorted picture. Unfortunately this is also the case for most of the classic books dealing with Judaism and its institutions, which are still in print and used by pastors—books such as those by the Jewish-Christian scholar Alfred Edersheim.[28] My realization of this shortcoming in Second Temple scholarship occurred when I took a graduate course at the Hebrew University in 1979. Even then, the primary text assigned for the course in Second Temple Judaism by Professor Isaiah Gafni was the book by Emil Schürer (unrevised). No greater testimony could have been had to this paucity of published sources than for an orthodox Jewish professor in a modern, post-Holocaust Israeli university to have nothing better to offer his students than a century-old text by a German Protestant Christian![29] Another problem is that the primary aim of most of the aforementioned works was not to study early Judaism, but to use information about early Judaism to clarify Christianity.[30]

With the discovery (and ongoing publication) of the Dead Sea Scrolls, historians of this period now have for the first time the actual documents written by one of the sects of that era. And one of the most significant effects the Scrolls have had on the thinking of scholars was, in the words of John Collins, a specialist in Second Temple apocalyptic literature, to "dispel the mirage of normative Judaism in this period."[31] We now know there was a great variety in Second Temple Judaism and that no one kind of Judaism can necessarily be assumed as "normative" for the rest. In other words, the diverse elements that characterized intertestamental Judaism will not permit us to lump together the beliefs of all the Jewish people into a convenient Jewish theology. Second Temple Judaism was an heir of biblical Judaism, but was no more identical to it than to later rabbinic Judaism.

This enhanced understanding of Judaism was initially resisted by some scholars. Professor Hanan Eshel, who works with the Scrolls both as an archaeologist and as a scholar of Second Temple Judaism, explains one reason for this:

> There was always a great need to be able to connect history and archaeology. For the first time we had Semitic sources from Second Temple period, and [as a result] we had to change our whole approach. Professor [Patrick W.] Skehan was [among those who were] sure that the Scrolls were fake. He did so because he had just finished writing a book on the Second Temple period based on Greek sources, and he knew that if the Scrolls were really from Second Temple period, [especially] from the community that was living in Judea at the end of the first century, then he would have to change his book. This he was not willing to do because he had just finished it. So it was easier to say that the Scrolls could not be real than to try and re-think the Second Temple period. This is part of the main problem as I see it: that until now political history was not studied from the Dead Sea Scrolls because the scholars were more interested in other things—like the biblical text or like theological problems.[32]

However, a new generation of scholars have come to slowly embrace the Scrolls and have begun to modify their interpretations of the times accordingly.[33] This has led to a new consensus in the study of the development of Second Temple Judaism with less dependence upon rabbinic sources and more reliance upon intertestamental literature, especially the Dead Sea Scrolls.

## Second Temple Period Judaism

The Second Temple period was a transitional time in Judaism during which dynamic changes were taking place in response to complex conditions. Jews were challenged—perhaps more than at any other time in their previous history—to hold fast to their social and religious heritage based on the Bible, while being forced to adapt to the changing political and cultural realities of their day. The new portrait of Second Temple Judaism reveals a much more complex Judaism than the simple four-sect division of Josephus. There were diverse sects, sects within sects, and breakaway sects. Even the so-called mainline sects do not evidence an uninterrupted continuation between earlier and later parts of this period. Despite this plethora of ideas and aspirations, it seems that the average Jewish person belonged to none of these groups, but quietly maintained a nationalistic hope within a dominantly Gentile society. While certain basic beliefs characterized this Judaism, such as a messianic expectation, it was religious practice rather than a theological system that united Jews in their national or sectarian allegiance.

While the various Jewish sects arose in reaction to certain social and religio-political factors within the land of Israel, it is no longer possible to simply view Hebraic Judaism as uniquely Israeli and Hellenistic Judaism as the culture of Diaspora Jews. As Dr. Lawrence Schiffman notes:

> Second Temple Judaism can now be seen as a transition period in which the sectarianism and apocalypticism of the period gradually gave way to rabbinic Judaism, on the one hand, and Christianity, on the other. Indeed, it is now clear that the Second Temple period was a kind of sorting out process.[34]

Part of this new understanding of Second Temple Judaism has included additional and, in some cases, our only information about already-known Jewish sects. The Pharisees, known previously only from Josephus, the New Testament, and Talmudic literature, are referred to as "Ephraim" in the Scrolls and addressed in a polemical manner. They are called *doreshe halaqot* or "expounders of false laws"—literally, "seekers after smooth things" (*1QH* 2:15, 32; *4QpNah* 3-4 i. 2, 7; ii. 3, 7; *CD* 1:18), and "builders of the wall" (that is, those who erect fences around the biblical laws [*CD* 4:19; 8:12; 19:25, 31]). These terms reflect the Pharisaic practice of deriving new and more restrictive laws from scriptural laws in order to safeguard against the possibility of violating the latter.

In addition, in the uniquely legal text *4QMMT,* the author opposes laws that the Talmudic literature ascribes to the Pharisees. From this we can see that what became known as rabbinic rulings about the practice of the law—*halakhot*—were already a characteristic of this sect. The Scrolls support the view of both the New Testament and the Talmud that the Pharisees and their practices were well established during the Second Temple era, or well before this period, rather than as a development of post-destruction Judaism (after A.D. 70).

The Sadducees, who disappeared after their power base (the Temple) was destroyed in A.D. 70, are also described in the Scrolls. They, too, were given code names, such as "Manasseh" and the "opponents of Ephraim," and were pictured as members of the aristocratic priestly class. Their laws, which required a scriptural legal base and therefore permitted no "unbiblical" laws (such as the new laws of the Pharisees) are also reflected in *4QMMT* and possibly underlie the *Temple Scroll.* Based on this data, some scholars, such as Lawrence Schiffman, have contended that an offshoot Sadducean group must have played a major role in the formation of the Dead Sea Sect.[35] And if we accept that the Qumran community is to be identified with the Essenes, then the Scrolls also furnish us with the most extensive description of this sect to date, which was previously known only from Josephus, Pliny, and Philo.

Other corrections to the history of Second Temple Judaism were also brought about by the Scrolls. For one, evidence from textual affinities between the Scrolls and the Samaritan Pentateuch tells us that the "Samaritan schism" with Judaism took place much later than the time of Ezra as formerly supposed. For another, the differences between the Hebrew of the Scrolls and the Hebrew of earlier documents (such as Ben Sira, circa 180 B.C.) may indicate that the changeover from Late Biblical Hebrew to Mishnaic Hebrew (rabbinic Hebrew) was precipitated by religious and political factors. Yet another correction was made known to us through the different religious calendar used by Qumran. The Qumran community followed a solar (364-day) calendar rather than the lunar (354-day) calendar of rabbinic Judaism. The Sect believed that this was the correct calendar and that the priests in Jerusalem were employing a wrong calendar and thus defiling the religious observance of the ordained festivals. There is now reason to believe that this was not simply a sectarian calendar but one that may have been used in structuring portions of the Old Testament itself, especially in the late priestly literature.[36]

## Second Temple Period Topography

The Scrolls have not only given us new historical information about the Second Temple period, they have also contributed to our knowledge of Jerusalem's topography during that time. An example of their significance in this respect is given by Dr. Dan Bahat, former district archaeologist for Jerusalem and editor of Carta's *Illustrated Atlas of Jerusalem*:

> Our topographical sources are primarily eschatological texts such as the *Copper Scroll*, the *Temple Scroll*, and the description of *New Jerusalem*. Although all of these speak of a Jerusalem that will be in the future, their conception of that new Jerusalem could not have been made without reference to their present. As an example let us take Josephus' reference to the Essenes Gate and to a place which was called "Bethsoa." The precise meaning and location of "Bethsoa" was a complete mystery. Then a study of the *Temple Scroll* revealed that it referred to an area outside the Essenes Gate. [This also helped us understand the significance of the Essenes Gate.] At first it was believed that the Essenes Gate directed people from the residential section of the Essenes in Jerusalem into the Judean desert. Now we know the reference intended by the Essenes was for something completely different. It was the place where they used to go to meet their physical needs, especially on the Sabbath [when travel was restricted]. So the Bethsoa was the place of the latrine. This is important because it helps us establish the confines of the city and the southmost alignment of the city wall. It has also allowed us to fix, with more or less precision, the location of the Essenes Gate and the Essenes quarter in Jerusalem.[37]

As the New Testament continues to be read in light of this improved picture of its historical context, a better understanding of the origin and relationship between Christianity and Judaism is emerging.

## Revealing the Context for Early Christianity

Ever since the Scrolls were discovered, Christian scholars and sensationalists have searched them for parallels to the New Testament. Scholarly activity has largely focused on textual affinities, while sensationalists have sought direct references to New Testament figures. There *are* significant textual parallels between the Scrolls and the New Testament (see next chapter); however, the most important role the Scrolls have played for New Testament research is their revelation of another contemporaneous Jewish Sect whose approaches to Scripture, eschatological perspective, and religious conflicts were similar to those of the early Jewish-Christian church. Dr. Stephan Pfann, director of the Center for the Study of Early Christianity in Jerusalem, has been a significant contributor to Dead Sea Scroll research and publication. He offers several observations about the role the Dead Sea Scrolls have as a witness to the development of Christianity:

> The site of Qumran is a phenomenon. It is the only place we have in all of the land that comes from the time of the New Testament. It is the only place that has given us a primary liter-ature, not just copies of it from many generations later, but their actual writings. We also have [Old Testament] scriptures from that period by which we can confirm readings or check readings that we have in our Bible against the actual biblical text they held in their hands. We also have the archaeological record—the actual site where they lived. All of the different items that were found in that site also relate to the [biblical] text. When we speak about the people, about their life and habits, this is something that we can't compare with any other group during that time. We don't have the [original] books of the Bible that the first Christians held in their hands. But these [Scrolls] are contemporary [with early Christianity], and they are the best parallel we have to check our historical record of Christianity during that period.[38]

The Dead Sea Scrolls have returned Jesus, John the Baptizer, the writers, and the world of the New Testament to their Jewish context. It can no longer be successfully argued that the events and beliefs described in the New Testament were a product of Christian theologians centuries later. The intimate details of culture, language, sectarian controversies, and the like could not have been reproduced with such accuracy after the destruction of Jerusalem. The Scrolls have established the essential Jewishness of the New Testament and that the theological struggles of Jesus and the early church were not out of character with those of other Jewish groups existing at the same time.

None of this minimizes the uniqueness of the New Testament revela-tion; rather, it affirms that its revelation came within a verifiable context of history. For instance, the Scrolls reveal that terms used only once in the New Testament were not the inventions of later Christians, but were actually part of the Jewish vocabulary of the period. Unusual New Testament names such as Enoch, Melchizedek, Belial, Beelzebub, and "the man of sin" also appeared in the Scrolls. These Qumran counterparts have allowed scholars to understand the use of these figures outside the New Testament and within the larger context of Judaism. Seeing the New Testament in its proper Jewish context not only provides us with a more accurate interpretation of New Testament Hebraic idioms but also of the theology that arose in relation to and in conflict with other religious groups of the day.

In addition, the Scrolls have revealed that mysticism was active at Qumran. The mystical documents among the Scrolls have shed invaluable light on a trend in Jewish tradition during the pre-Christian period—a trend that seems to have influenced the development of Gnosticism, a heresy that dominated and threatened Christianity from the middle-second century to the fourth century A.D. Formerly, Persian (Zoroastrianism) or Greek (Orphism/Platonism) mysticism was thought responsible for the birth of Gnosticism, but the Scrolls have forced scholars to examine Judaism for Gnosticism's more important roots. The knowledge of Qumran mysticism is important for comparison with the so-called "incipient Gnosticism" countered by both Paul and John in their New Testament epistles.

## A Whole New Perspective

We have seen that the Dead Sea Scrolls have opened new windows on the ancient world during one of the most formative and transitional periods in Jewish history. They have provided us with actual documents that allow us to study a religious movement within a known time and context. Many of these documents have given us copies of the Bible older than ever believed possible and have enabled us to confirm the accuracy of the scribes upon whose work our modern versions are based. Finally, the Scrolls have shown us that the New Testament is true to its context and history and that Christianity was indeed a Jewish movement. And these are merely foundational aspects of the new perspective given to us by the Scrolls. In the next chapters, we will look at the specifics of how the Scrolls have expanded our knowledge of the Old and New Testaments.

# 7

# THE SCRIPTURES AND THE SCROLLS:
## The Old Testament

*The Dead Sea Scrolls' impact upon the study of the Old Testament . . . has been phenomenal.*[1]

—J. Julius Scott, Jr.

In the previous chapter we painted the significance of the Scrolls with broad brush strokes. In this and the next chapter we'll add detail to our canvas of significance with particular highlights about the relationship between the Scrolls and the Scriptures. We'll look at the Old Testament in this chapter, and the New Testament in the next. As we consider the Old Testament we'll examine Scriptures that were used in the Scrolls, and as we survey the New Testament we'll focus on points of correspondence between sometime contemporaneous movements. However, before we explore the relationship that exists between the Scrolls and the Scriptures, we need to affirm that the Bible's unique claim to special revelation is in no way affected by such a comparison.

## The Scrolls and Special Revelation

Back in 1956 William Sanford LaSor addressed fundamentalists and evangelicals about the tension they felt over the discovery of manuscripts that seemed to compete with the Bible and possibly undermine its unique claim to special revelation:

> A question that will continue to disturb many Christians is, What does all this have to do with revelation? On the one hand, if the Scriptures of the Old Testament are, as we believe they are, the Word of God, why should we care what the Qumran writings say? On the other hand, if we admit the interrelationship of the Qumran writings and the New Testament, does this not deny the revealed nature of the New Testament? To ask such questions, in my opinion, is to stop short of understanding what is meant by revelation, and to stop short of understanding God's work in history. Revelation is not only history . . . but revelation is in history. God entered into the history of the human race on this planet, whether it was by holy men of old, or later by His Son. The events of the Bible are history, and through historical events God gave His revelation. . . . It is here that the Qumran material, like all other pertinent historical material, is of value to the man of faith. Through historical materials we come to understand the revealed word better. The more similarities we find (if they are indeed true similarities), the better we understand the Scriptures.[2]

Indeed, we find many factors that make possible affinities between the Scrolls and the Scriptures, especially the New Testament. First, the Qumran Sect was more consistently rooted in the Old Testament Scriptures and better understood the implications of the divine program—especially eschatologically—than many of their contemporaries. It should not surprise us, then, that their views reflect those of the Old Testament prophets, nor that their thoughts and vocabulary paralleled those of the New Testament writers. Second, there is a shared stance against other sects, such as the Pharisees and Sadducees. Third, the existence of prior concepts and verbal parallels may offer an apologetic for evangelical purposes, but their use must be balanced with a proper regard for contextual and revelatory uniquenesses. Fourth, even though there are parallels in vocabulary, the meaning of the concepts expressed and their applications may be very different and sometimes only rhetorical. Because the New Testament authors wrote through divine inspiration, they could impart new meanings to older terms in light of their understanding of fulfilled prophecy.[3] Fifth, with the Scrolls, we are ushered into a context that verifies the New Testament against the accusation that it is merely the creation of later theologians. As James Charlesworth observes:

> These Scrolls transport us to the scribes who wrote upon, and even helped prepare, the leather and papyrus for writing. We are not left sequestered, either in the academic halls of the early church councils or in the communities—or schools—that shaped the canonical Gospels.[4]

## The Scrolls and Scriptural Preservation

Another problem for some Christians is the textual variations found in the traditional Hebrew text of the Bible (Masoretic Text), which underlies the English translation of our Old Testament. The concern here is for the integrity of our present Bibles. To properly understand this concern, we must distinguish between *inspiration* and *preservation*. *Inspiration* refers to the original autographs of the Bible as given by God through men, while *preservation* has to do with copies that have been passed down through the ages by human agency alone. Some people confuse preservation with inspiration and contend that the copies that have come down to us cannot have been altered in any way from the autograph, such as in an English translation like the King James Version.[5] This erroneous view must be rejected as both unbiblical and unfactual. Nothing in biblical statements such as "All Scripture is inspired by God" (2 Timothy 3:16), "Until heaven and earth pass away, not the smallest letter or stroke shall pass away from the Law, until all is accomplished" (Matthew 5:18), or "Heaven and earth will pass away, but My words will not pass away" (Mark 13:31) requires that every inspired word must likewise be preserved *outside* of the autographs. Yet we *can* say—and say with greater confidence than ever based on the witness of the Scrolls—that our present text is accurate and reliable, and that nothing affecting the doctrine of the original has been compromised or changed in any way in the manuscript copies.[6] The Scrolls have affirmed that the Masoretic Text behind our English translations *was* carefully preserved. As James VanderKam said, "It is a carefully annotated product of a centuries-long tradition throughout which the sacred words were meticulously guarded, copied, and checked by Jewish experts."[7] Furthermore, the very preservation and recovery of the biblical Scrolls, added to a colorful history of preservation of other copies of the Scriptures, testifies to the providential element in their safe-keeping. Rather than detracting from the proper understanding of scriptural preservation, the Scrolls have added new support to this truth.

## The Scrolls and the Old Testament

The number of Old Testament manuscripts discovered among the Dead Sea Scrolls (about 223-233) is more than twice the number of New Testament Greek papyri (96).[8] However, despite this abundance of ancient witnesses to the text of the Bible, few English translations of the Old Testament have been affected.[9] The reason is that generally the biblical Qumran texts are so close to the Hebrew text behind the Masoretic Text that they lend support to, rather than emend, those versions that rely upon the Received Text. Those who expected the Scrolls to produce a radical revision of the Bible have been disappointed, for these texts have only verified the reliability and stability of the Old Testament as it appears in our modern translations. However, the biblical Qumran texts have also lent support to both the Septuagint and Samaritan Pentateuch versions, confirming the antiquity of the latter and affirming the authority of the former. Many of the variants that support these versions in departure from the Masoretic Text are quite interesting, and may in certain cases offer significant clarifications and insights for our traditional translations.[10]

### Shedding Light on Textual Problems

#### Comparing Various Hebrew Texts

The understanding of the original composition of the Hebrew in the Old Testament is often illuminated by comparison with both the biblical and nonbiblical Qumran texts. These comparisons reveal that there is agreement with the Masoretic Text 80 percent of the time,[11] with the remaining 20 percent divided between agreement with the Septuagint (5 percent), the Samaritan Pentateuch (5 percent), and mixed texts from several traditions (10 percent). Scroll Team director Emanuel Tov described for us the nature of these divergences from the standard text:

If we compare our knowledge prior to the finding of the Qumran Scrolls, that is of the Masoretic text, to the Qumran Scrolls we find hundreds of thousands of differences and these differences are in small details and in large details. Small details will pertain to a letter here or a letter there, irregular spellings. The large differences could involve a singular word, a whole phrase, a sentence or sometimes even a paragraph.[12]

The textual diversity that appears in the Scrolls may reflect the geographical diversity of the sectarians themselves, their local text types (Egyptian, Babylonian, Palestinian), or perhaps indicate that they considered the biblical text still open to scribal activity rather than being closed (as occurred when the Bible was canonized). Whatever theory is accepted, the Scrolls have revealed different versions of the Hebrew text upon which the Septuagint, Samaritan Pentateuch, and the Masoretic Text all depended. It is the variations between these that are most interesting and have shed light on some textual problems that long concerned scholars.

Some of these variants are major, and some are minor. One major example is the Qumran biblical text of Jeremiah. Six copies of Jeremiah recovered from the caves have the longer form of the text in agreement with the Masoretic Text, but two *4QJer*[b,d] have the shorter in agreement with the Septuagint (LXX).[13] They also lack words, names, and sentences and exhibit a different sequence in some places. Before the discovery of these texts there was no evidence for the existence of a shorter Hebrew variant other than the LXX. Some minor examples include the Qumran biblical text of Deuteronomy 32:8 *(4QDeut*[j]*)*, which agrees with the LXX ("sons of Israel"), but not the Masoretic Text ("sons of God"). Similarly, the Qumran biblical text of Exodus 1:5 *(4QExod*[a]*)* records "75 descendants of Jacob" (with the LXX; cf. Acts 7:14) against the Masoretic Text's "70 descendants."

Also, the discovery of paleo-Hebrew texts of the Torah evidences the use of paleo-Hebrew after the adoption of the square Aramaic script that is used in the Samaritan Pentateuch. In particular, the *Paleo-Exodus Scroll (4Q22)* shows expansions of the text like that in the Samaritan Pentateuch, giving testimony to the latter's antiquity. So that we can gain a more detailed perspective, let us consider one of these textual variants as an example of how the variants have contributed to the Old Testament text as we know it.

## An Addition to the Book of First Samuel

One of the earliest biblical manuscripts in the Qumran collection is the *Samuel A Scroll* (designated *Samuel A–C, 4QSam$^{a-c}$,* or *4Q51-53*), which has been dated to the last quarter of the third century B.C. (a time that most scholars believe is well before the Qumran community was founded). The *Samuel A Scroll* is especially interesting because it contains textual variants that appear to support many of the Septuagint's deviations from the Masoretic Text (MT). This was important because it at last provided scholars with an example of the kind of Hebrew version that was behind the Septuagint. But this Scroll also has another exceptional feature: It contains a passage that was completely missing from the Masoretic Text but was apparently known and used by Flavius Josephus in his *Jewish Antiquities* (6.68-71). This text mentions Nahash the Ammonite, whose story is given in the Bible in 1 Samuel 11:1-6. There, we read that after Saul's first (and establishing) act as king (that is, the defeat of the Ammonites), Nahash proposed gouging out the right eyes of the men of Jabesh-gilead as part of a peace treaty requested by the inhabitants of the city after Nahash had besieged it. Scholars have long wondered why Nahash would have imposed this unprecedented punishment on the Israelites. The *Samuel A Scroll* provided the answer with a passage that occurred just prior to 1 Samuel 11:1 in our present text:

> [And Nahash, king of the children of Ammon, sorely oppressed the children of Gad and the children of Reuben; and he gouged out a[ll] their right eyes and struck ter[ror and dread] in Israel. There was no one left among the children of Israel bey[ond the Jordan who]se right eye was no[t go]uged out by Naha[sh king] of the children of Ammon; except (for) seven thousand men (who had) [fled from] the children of Ammon and entered [J]abesh-gilead. About a month later . . .

Since the events in this Qumran text contain historical references that are so closely aligned to the context and do not derive from any other biblical source, it has been suggested that this is an original passage lost from all copies of the biblical text that have come down to us previously. This text reveals why Nahash wanted to mutilate the men of Jabesh-gilead: because this had been his usual practice with the inhabitants of Jewish cities east of the Jordan, and now he wanted to do the same to the people who lived west of the Jordan, beginning with Jabesh-gilead (about three miles north of Jerusalem). If this passage was omitted from the original text by a careless scribe, it may have been because the scribe confused the last words of 1 Samuel 10:27 ("but he kept silent") with the opening words of 1 Samuel 11:1 (as contained in some LXX copies: "about a month later"). These two phrases look much the same in Hebrew and might have caused the scribe to skip from the end of the first phrase to the end of the second, omitting the *4QSam^a* paragraph in between.[14] Emanuel Tov notes that this conclusion has divided scholars, yet many of them have accepted the inclusion as genuine:

> Is this part of the original text or is it a result of later exegesis? This disagreement may never be resolved because there is always room for different views, however, many scholars believe, and I'm among them, that this may well be part of the original book of Samuel.[15]

Based on this explanation, one of our modern English versions of the Bible, the New Revised Standard Version (NRSV), has included the passage as an unnumbered paragraph serving as a prologue to 1 Samuel 11.

However, it is also possible that this inclusion was simply an explanatory addition and not intended to be part of the original text of Samuel. This is consistent with all other Qumran text additions, which can be explained as the result of biblical interpretation by the scribes. Otherwise, *4QSam^a* stands alone as the single example of a missing piece of original biblical composition. As an example of explanatory additions, albeit in reverse, Emanuel Tov offers the case of proto-Judges:

> In proto-Judges, a portion from chapter 6 [of the biblical Judges] is missing—a whole paragraph. It is in our present Hebrew Bible, and also in English translations, but it is a paragraph which had puzzled scholars for centuries because it seems to be out of place. Suddenly we found this fragment at Qumran, in which there is a text of Judges that doesn't have this paragraph. The text reads better without it. It helps us understand that at some point in the transmission of the text this paragraph was added, but the book was already circulating in another form before it was.[16]

In like manner, the paragraph in *4QSam^a* may have been an explanatory addition in a text of Samuel circulating either prior to the time of canonization or, as Schiffman notes, in "part of the Book of Samuel used by some Jews in Second Temple times."[17] Its addition by ancient interpreters was meant to clarify the eye-gouging mentioned in Nahash's treaty.

Josephus' use of this passage does not necessarily prove that he was familiar with such a text. His information could have come from historical records preserved in the Temple archives or from some other source now lost to us. If we examine Josephus' account we find other additional information not found in the *4QSam$^a$* text, such as an invasion by "a large and warlike army," the reduction of cities to "servitude," and Nahash's "cunning and ingenuity" in weakening those captured in war by gouging out the right eye "since the left eye was covered by the buckler—to render them utterly unserviceable." These appear to be interpretive explanations by Josephus, and as such could have even been derived from the shorter version in our present text. If *4QSam$^a$* was indeed an explanatory addition to a Samuel text circulating either before or during Josephus' time, and recognized as such by careful scribes, that would explain its omission from our three primary versions (MT, LXX, Samaritan Pentateuch), which attempt to present a canonical text.

In light of this example, as well as the others we've surveyed, Emanuel Tov concludes with this admonition about the use of the Scrolls in biblical exegesis:

> When we collect data of this kind we realize that the Scrolls do make a difference and they should be taken into consideration, not only in the study of textual criticism but also in the [area of] exegesis, [for] in that area there too the knowledge of the Scrolls is an absolute requirement for anyone studying the Bible critically.[18]

### Biblical Exegesis Reflected in the Scrolls

Some of the biblical Qumran texts also reveal attempts to rework or rephrase the biblical texts or to add exegetical commentary to them. Professor Tov has cautioned against speaking about "biblical exegesis at Qumran," since, in his opinion, relatively few of the examples of such compositions were actually written by members of the Qumran Sect.[19] With this proviso, we are confronted with various forms of biblical interpretation in the Scrolls, which reflect exegetical technique. Some of the Torah Scrolls at Qumran reveal expansions of the biblical text, such as the *Rewritten Pentateuch (4Q364-367)*. Others represent a retelling of a biblical account, such as the *Genesis Apocryphon* retelling of Abram and Sarai in Genesis 12:10-13 (*1Q20* 19:14-20),[20] or the story of the flood in *4Q252*.[21] In other cases biblical exegesis is seen as a harmonization of the biblical text, interpreting an unclear text in light of a similar one so that they say the same thing (for example, the *Temple Scroll's* harmonization of Deuteronomy 17:1 from 15:21).

Two other forms of biblical interpretation are *halakhic* Midrash and Targums. In the first, which is rather rare, a number of passages are harmonized to yield a unique sectarian legal interpretation (for example, *CD* 9:2-8; 10:20-21). In the second, Aramaic paraphrases of the Hebrew text often reveal the interpretations of their translators. Some of the more important are the *Leviticus Targum (4Q157)* and the *Job Targum (11Q10; 4Q157)*.

Finally, the most prominent form of biblical exegesis is the plain sense commentary, or *pesher*. A variation on this is seen in the Bible's book of Daniel and the influence this book had on the interpretive technique of the Sect.

### Daniel and the Dead Sea Scrolls

Noel David Freedman has stated, "From Daniel it is a relatively short distance to Qumran. Not only was the book admired or at least copied and preserved in the Essene community . . . but there may be a historical link between the book and the community."[22] The Aramaic cognate of *pesher* appears 31 times in Daniel (along with *raz*, "mystery") in reference to Daniel's "interpretation" of dreams.[23] Indeed, the Qumran community appears to have believed that Daniel's visions, which had not been completely fulfilled in the horrible events surrounding the persecutions of Antiochus IV Epiphanes, were to be fulfilled in their own day. They saw themselves as the embodiment of the *maskilim* ("discerning teachers") and of Daniel's *qedoshim* ("holy ones"), who sat on high and watched over Israel, announcing and interpreting the events of the end times.[24]

In keeping with Daniel, in the Qumran *pesher* literature, both *pesher* and *raz* are given by divine revelation. However, *raz* is the first stage of the revelation (that imparted to the biblical writer), which remained "hidden" until the second stage, *pesher*, was imparted by the Teacher of Righteousness. One of the clearest explanations of this appears in the Qumran *pesher* on Habakkuk 2:1-2 (cf. Daniel 9:20), which says:

> And God told Habakkuk to write down the things that will happen to the last generation, but the consummation of time He did not make known to him. . . . The interpretation of [Habakkuk 2:2] concerns the Teacher of Righteousness to whom God made

known all the secrets of His servants the prophets (*1QpHab* 7:1-5).

The crucial touch point for the Qumran community is seen in the clause "all the secrets of His servants the prophets," for with this statement the history of the present community was joined with that of the past, and a prophetic continuum was established through divine revelation to the Teacher of Righteousness, the supposed founder of the Sect.[25] This fundamental principle of Jewish interpretation—of a perceived relationship between the past and the present—forms the basis of Danelic exposition, which explains the mysteries of past divine revelation with a view to historic interpretation. In other words, not until the two parts of the revelation, *pesher* and *raz,* are joined is the meaning made plain—a revelation which is predominately concerned with the last days.[26]

### Daniel's Prophetic Status at Qumran

The earliest record of Daniel's prophetic status is preserved at Qumran, where the book and its predictions played a central role in the apocalyptic views of the community, which probably had canonical status.[27] Its significance as prophecy at Qumran is attested by its frequent citation, especially of Daniel 9-12 (for example, Daniel 11-12 is cited in *4QFlorilegium);* the many pseudepigraphical imitations that have been discovered (for example, the "Prayer of Nabonidus"); and more recently, the collection of apocalyptic fragments in quasi-prophetic form known as Pseudo-Daniel *(4Q243-245).* Of special interest to our discussion is the reference in *4QFlor* 2:3, where we read that a period of tribulation is predicted "as it is written in the book of Daniel *the prophet.*" In weighing the recognition of the evidence for Daniel as a prophet, K. Koch concludes:

> There is no single witness for the exclusion of Daniel from the prophetic corpus in the first half of the first millennium A.D. In all the sources of the first century A.D.—the LXX, Qumran, Josephus, Jesus, and the New Testament writers—Daniel is reckoned among the prophets. In fact the earliest literary evidence of Daniel's inclusion among the third division of the Hebrew Bible, called K*e*tubim ("writings") is to be placed somewhere between the fifth and eighth centuries A.D.[28]

*Daniel's Influence on the Qumran Community*

The book of Daniel was no doubt used as a primary text in the early formation of the Qumran movement. As Professor Talmon states, "it (Daniel) had, without any doubt, tremendous effects."[29] One of these effects may have come through Daniel's reference to a group of "wise men" (Hebrew, *maskilim*). This elect company of the last days will understand God's mysterious plan soon to be consummated (Daniel 12:4,9-10). Their hope is for a rescue of the Jewish remnant in a time of unparalleled tribulation (Daniel 12:1-2) as well as a resurrection of the righteous (Daniel 12:3). Their special discernment of the times and their influence for righteousness will set them apart (Daniel 12:10). The writers of the Scrolls patterned themselves after these ideals, perhaps even to the point of wearing linen garments after the fashion of Daniel's "man dressed in linen" who interpreted the chronology of the end-time events (Daniel 12:6-7). Some scholars believe that Daniel's prophecy of the "seventy weeks" (Daniel 9:24-27) also may have been adapted for the Sect's chronological scheme[30] (see chapter 10). These examples give us an idea of Daniel's profound influence on the way the Sect interpreted the Scriptures.

## Old Testament Problems and the Scrolls

The Scrolls have helped to resolve problems that critical and conservative scholars have had relating to the origins and the dates of certain texts. Two of the most significant debates in this area have concerned the authorship and unity of the book of Isaiah and the authorship and date of the book of Daniel. When copies of the biblical manuscripts of Isaiah (two copies from Cave 1 and 18 fragmentary copies from Cave 4) and Daniel (eight fragmentary copies from Caves 1, 4, and 6) were found, people immediately wondered if the copies would resolve the debates about the authorship and dating of these books.

At stake in these debates is the integrity of the Scriptures. Both Isaiah and Daniel present themselves as internally consistent and as having been composed in the historical period they describe, yet some scholars have questioned those assertions. Conservative scholars say that Isaiah and Daniel's prophecies were predictive (written before they were fulfilled); critical scholars say the prophecies are reflective (written after the fulfillments). In addition, some have called into question the integrity of the witnesses to Isaiah and Daniel's prophetic testimonies, such as the New Testament, which affirms both the traditional authorship and date.

Because the consequences of these debates are so important, especially for the evangelical community, let's look at how the Scrolls have contributed new evidence that enables us to arrive at a reasonable conclusion.

## The Unity of the Book of Isaiah

The view that a single author wrote Isaiah was challenged by Jewish writers as early as the second century A.D. (Moses Ibn Gekatilla), and later by the leading medieval Jewish scholar Ibn Ezra (1092–1167). Multiple authorship was proposed by "Christian" scholars beginning in the late 1700s (J.C. Döderlein and J.G. Eichhorn) on the basis of literary-critical studies. The theory (now assumed as fact) has since enjoyed an almost universal consensus among critical scholars. It is based on the observation that the three main divisions of Isaiah significantly differ from one another in style of composition. There have been attempts to demonstrate this through stylistic statistics (a computer analysis of comparative linguistic features), though with mixed results.[31] While other linguistic divisions have been proposed, the generally accepted divisions are "First Isaiah" (chapters 1-39), dated to the eighth century B.C., and "Second Isaiah" (chapters 40-66), dated to the post-exilic period. Scholars who hold these divisions attempt to counter predictive prophecy, since the division containing Isaiah's Babylonian prophecy (chapters 40-66) was considered *vaticinium ex eventu* ("prophecy after the [fulfillment of the] event"). In response, conservative scholars have offered sufficient defenses of the book's unity on internal (similar verbal, stylistic, and conceptual structure) and external grounds (ancient textual witnesses).[32] Thus when the discovery of the *Great Isaiah Scroll* (*1QIsa*[a-b]) was announced, people of both viewpoints hoped that it held conclusive external evidence to support their position.

When the *Isaiah Scroll* was examined it revealed no break or demarcation of any sort between the contested divisions. Chapter 40 begins on the very last line of the column that includes Isaiah 38:9–39:8. The last words on the former column are "cry to her . . . " and the first words on the latter column are " . . . that her warfare is accomplished."[33] It is evident that the scribe who wrote those words was not aware of a supposed change in situation or authorship beginning with chapter 40. Four samples of *Isaiah Scrolls* subjected to carbon 14 dating produced calibrated age ranges between 335–324 B.C. and 202–107 B.C., and the paleographic date range is between 125–100 B.C. The scribal evidence in these copies indicate that they were the results of at least several generations of copying.

Therefore, even with a date sometime during the second century B.C., critical scholars can no longer assign portions of Isaiah's prophecies to the Maccabean period,[34] or claim that first-century insertions were added to the text.[35] The second-century B.C. date should also establish the *Isaiah Scroll* as an early witness in favor of the unity of Isaiah, since it (or an earlier copy from which is was generated) accorded roughly with the time the Septuagint version of the prophets was written (the Septuagint also has no indication of a textual break between chapters 39 and 40). However, critical (and many conservative) scholars disallow this early evidence in support of single authorship because it is claimed that scribal recognition of multiple authorship (along with final redaction of the book) came later than these Qumran copies.

### Reconsidering the Scroll Evidence

If we consider again the evidence of the *Great Isaiah Scroll A*, which may have been considered an early *vulgate* or common text of Isaiah,[36] we find that it does divide into two sections, but between chapters 33 and 34. This separation is the result of a seam in the skin of the Scroll and a space of three lines at the bottom of the twenty-seventh column. This "gap" in the text may indicate a scribe's awareness of an original compositional change, rather than simply a change in scribes or in manuscripts.[37] This is evidenced by the more frequent use of *plene* ("full") writing (consonants used as vowels) in chapters 34–66 than in 1–33.[38] William Brownlee has asserted that this break between the chapters was a deliberate scribal indication that the book had been copied from two separate Scrolls, balanced perfectly by the division of 33 chapters to each Scroll.[39] He noted that the midpoint of Isaiah, according to the Masoretes, occurs at Isaiah 33:20, only shortly before the end of the chapter. On this assumption he sought to see parallel relationships between these two sections with categories in one corresponding to the other.[40]

Avraham Gileadi has recently confirmed Brownlee's bifid ("twofold") structure, but with some revision of his categories.[41] Gileadi's analysis has concluded that the division is more than an ancient literary device, as Brownlee had sought to prove; it had the unique purpose of conveying a prophetic message that unifies the book. If the scribe(s) writing *1QIsa*[a] had an understanding of this bifid structure, or was copying a manuscript that did, and recognized it by inserting the three-line space in the text, then couldn't we assume that he would have recognized and indicated so significant a break as that alleged between chapters 39 and 40?

## Recognizing Distinctions in the Text

Even if this explanation for the break is rejected, we still have other evidence for scribal awareness of compositional problems. It is likely that *1QIs^a* was a study version of Isaiah because it was copied in the Qumran scribal style with the inclusion of various marginal notations. If *1QIs^a* was a study version, then that would add weight to the argument for scribal recognition and identification of textual discrepancies. Professor Tov adds to this his own observation on scribal sensitivity to the text:

> We find a few hundred of what I call scribal signs in the Scrolls. There are signs for new paragraphs, signs in order to fill up the end of the line, and signs that say "be careful, there is something in this text that I don't understand exactly what it means but I'm sure that at the time [the original authors] knew." Some of these signs are in the ancient script, [while] others are signs we don't yet understand. We see this both in the text and in the margin of the text, and in a few occasions, at least three or four, we have writing in red ink which is quite unusual. In one Scroll this marks the beginning of new paragraphs, and in a Scroll of the Psalter this is for the beginning of a new song. There are many more small details in which these scribes showed their understanding of the written text.[42]

One example of this may be seen in a textual variant in Isaiah *1QIs^a*38. In the Masoretic Text, 2 Kings 20 and Isaiah 38 present parallel accounts of the healing of King Hezekiah. Verse 7 of the account appears out of sequence because the king seems to have been healed while he is still seeking a cure. In Isaiah 38:1-8, verse 7 does not occur where it does in the King's account, but is postponed until the end of the chapter as verses 21-22. However, in *1QIs^a*, the scribe wrote in the margin of the Scroll in an attempt to insert the verse in its proper place. Unless this was an unintentional error, the scribe is demonstrating (or reflecting) a recognition of the textual difficulty. Again, if the scribes were sensitive to textual distinctions, then it seems that they would have indicated whether different portions of a manuscript had different authors. On the other hand, if the scribe had this level of awareness but didn't know of any tradition that required a break at the end of chapter 39, the text would have continued on with chapter 40, as it does. If so, he is in good company with a tradition that has recognized Isaiah's unity: Ben Sira (Ecclesiasticus) from about the same time period (early second century B.C.); Josephus

(*Antiquities* 11. 3-6.1 § 1-2), who regarded Isaiah as containing predictive prophecy; and the New Testament, where, in over 20 citations mentioning Isaiah by name, both "divisions" of the book are regarded equally. It would seem proper to add the witness of the *Isaiah Scroll* to this list.

The evidence, then, seems to point in favor of the unity of Isaiah, and therefore argues for a single author. That (*1QIs*ᵃ) is one of the oldest of the Scrolls rules out a Maccabean origin, although we cannot tell when Isaiah was originally written. However, if the biblical and extrabiblical witnesses are accepted, the author is the same eighth- or seventh-century Isaiah as its text affirms.[43]

## When Was Daniel Written?

Pre-New Testament Jewish tradition as a whole regarded the book of Daniel to be of sixth-century B.C. exilic origin, including the book within the Hebrew canon[44] and ranking its author as a biblical prophet.[45] The New Testament figures and writers held the same view, citing Daniel as a prophet and employing the book as an example of predictive prophecy (see Daniel 9:27 in Matthew 24:15; Mark 13:14; 2 Thessalonians 2:4; and numerous citations and allusions in Revelation). This is especially the case with Jesus, who does not refer to a book called Daniel, but to the agency of Daniel personally (as implied by the use of the Greek preposition *dia* ["by"] with the genitive).

The modern attack on the accepted date for Daniel came in the eighteenth century as a revival of the theory of Neoplatonist Porphyry (A.D. 233–305).[46] This view, early revived by J.D. Michaelis and J.C. Eichhorn (who also revived the Isaianic criticism),[47] maintained that the final form of Daniel was a pseudononymous product of the late post-exilic Maccabean period (165–165 B.C.). The Hebrew lexicographer S.R. Driver then championed this position in an 11-page essay, basing his arguments on the external support of philology and history—in spite of his own testimony to the superiority of internal evidence.[48] The Maccabean date likewise related Daniel to the status of *vaticinium ex eventu*, even though the New Testament writers cited in the last paragraph regarded Daniel's prophecies as predictive of future events. Even so, a date of 168 B.C. was still too late to accommodate a past fulfillment if Daniel's fourth kingdom was interpreted as Rome (which conquered Israel more than 100 years later in 63 B.C.). Critical scholars thus divided the Medo-Persian empire (the second kingdom) into two separate kingdoms (second and third), and advanced Greece to become the fourth kingdom, and the evidence for

Rome was made to fit Greece.[49] Such a progression, however, has been shown to be unlikely based on the historicity of the Persian successor to Belshazzar, "Darius the Mede."[50] Nevertheless, ever since Driver proposed a revised date, critical scholars have regarded the traditional sixth-century date as no longer defensible, while conservative scholars have accepted and defended it.[51]

## Surveying the Evidence

Among the biblical manuscripts found at Qumran are eight copies of the book of Daniel, represented by some 20 fragments. These fragments came from Caves 1, 4 and 6, and have been designated as *1QDan^{l-b} (1Q71-72)*, *4QDan^{a-e} (4Q112-116)*, and *pap6QDan (6Q7)*. Altogether, these fragments attest to chapters 1-11 in Daniel, while chapter 12 is briefly cited in the *Florilegium* (Daniel 12:10 in *4Q174* ii.3, 4).[52] The Scrolls also contain other witnesses to biblical Daniel, such as the pseudo-Daniel fragments (*4Q243-245*), pseudo-Daniel apocalypses (*4Q246, 4Q547*), related apocryphal documents (*4Q550, 4QPrNab*), and parallels in other apocalypses (for example, *4Q174*, cf. *4Q180-181*).

The fragmentary copies of Daniel date from the late second century B.C. to the middle of the first century A.D. On the basis of paleography, these fragments are comparable to the *Great Isaiah Scroll A* and the *Pesher Habakkuk*, so they cannot be dated *later* than 125 B.C.[53] Because of the copies' close proximity in time to the autograph (original manuscript), it might be thought that the Maccabean dating of Daniel would have serious difficulties because there would seem to be insufficient time for such copies to be produced. In addition, linguistic comparisons of Qumranic *midrashim* from the third-second centuries B.C. with the Aramaic and Hebrew chapters of these Daniel fragments have revealed matching traits in vocabulary, style, morphology, and syntax. This same sort of evidence for the dating of Chronicles forced Jacob Meyers to contend: "The discovery of a fragment of Chronicles at Qumran renders a Maccabean date virtually impossible for any part of Chronicles."[54] This has also been the case for the dating of Ecclesiastes, based on two Scroll copies found in Cave 4[55] and for many of the Psalms.[56] Frank Cross revised the dates of their autographs on the basis of the new Qumran evidence:

> Ecclesiastes, sometimes dated in the second, or even in the first century B.C., by older scholars, appears in one exemplar from Cave 4 (*4QQoh^a*) which dates ca. 175–150 B.C. Since the text of the manuscript reveals textual development, it is demonstrably

not the autograph, and hence the date of the composition must be pushed back into the third century. A second-century B.C. copy of the canonical Psalter (*4QPsa*), though fragmentary, indicates that the collection of canonical psalms was in the Persian period.[57]

If scholars have accepted this mitigating evidence from Qumran and abandoned a Maccabean date for other books of the Bible, could they not also do the same with Daniel?

## Is the Late Date Theory Unassailable?

Unfortunately, critical scholars have not arrived at a similar conclusion for the book of Daniel, even though the evidence is identical. While a Maccabean provenance should raise doubts that Daniel be composed during this same period,[58] rather than pose a problem, it has been heralded (in Daniel's case) as an unparalleled cause for excitement. Such was the frame of mind upon its first announcement:

> It is surprising that Daniel should have been among the manuscripts of the cave. Since the completion of the book is believed by modern scholars to have been about 165 B.C., the fragments must date within two centuries at the most from the original. Indeed, if two of them are paleographically similar to the *Isaiah Scroll*, we may say conservatively that we are less than a century from the original—something no one dared hope for in Old Testament study.[59]

This chronological distance was finally reduced to "no more than a half century younger than the autograph, ca. 168–165," by Frank Cross.[60] With this evidence against the "unassailable" Maccabean date, critical scholars have attempted to portray the pseudo-Danielic Qumran texts as being in their favor. For example, some have said that related material like the *Prayer of Nabonidus*, which apparently recounts the same story as Daniel 4, is the *older* of the two! But the differences are so extensive that no one has yet suggested a literary dependence or influence (for this or any of the other pseudo-Danielic "additions"). The prevailing view is that they are variants of a tradition on the sojourn of Nabonidus in Teima, with the *Prayer of Nabonidus* retaining the "more accurate historical remembrances."[61] However, Robert Vasholz contends that the evidence is very sparse for such a conclusion, and observes:

> It is not necessary to think of the *Prayer of Nabonidus* as a literary source of the canonical Daniel, or even to give the "Prayer" priority in terms of its written composition . . . without the *a priori* that Daniel must be second-century there is no more reason to believe that Daniel is dependent on the "Prayer" than that the "Prayer" is dependent on Daniel. We have no precedent, however, of a canonical Jewish book dependent on an intertestamental noncanonical literary source, while there is abundant evidence that the reverse is true.[62]

The fact that there are so many Danielic pseudepigraphs indicates that the book of Daniel was popular among copyists. Daniel was recognized as a prophet, and his apocalyptic writing had already been canonized, or at least considered a standard reference for apocalyptic chronology. The book of Daniel seems to have served this purpose at Qumran, as it did for a long tradition of later Danielic-style apocalypses that were written down to the Middle Ages.[63] For this reason, some critical scholars view Daniel chapters 1-6 as an older core of material, and state that the apocalyptic material in chapters 9-12, along with the pseudo-Danielic materials, form an "uncanonized" collection from the Maccabean period, some of which was finally excluded (if the canon had not yet closed at Qumran). H.H. Rowley also differed in his view, continuing to assert that all of Daniel had a Maccabean setting, and offering parallels for every story in the first half of the book.[64]

Since the book of Daniel and the cycle of Danielic literature had such important roles in the apocalyptic scheme at Qumran, and most scholars see the Qumran Sect as having its origin in the Maccabean Revolt, they conclude that Daniel and many of the Qumran compositions are products of this period. Of course, it is legitimate to say, as did the late Manchester scholar F.F. Bruce, that Daniel and the Qumran texts are "within one stream of tradition," and that the Sect "looked on their 'Unique Teacher' as successor-in-chief to the 'man greatly beloved' who is the hero of that book [Daniel]."[65] But to say this does not affect the dating of the book, it merely reflects the profound impact these texts had on the Sect. Yet, it is this very significance, tied to a Maccabean provenance, that has led other scholars—such as the Qumran patriarch John Trevor—to identify Daniel as the Sect's Teacher of Righteousness![66] Trevor seeks to make the Sect's leader and founder the same person who writes under the pseudonym of "Daniel" because of numerous similarities he observes between the Qumran Scrolls and the book of Daniel. These include a presumed common origin among the Hasidim of the early second century B.C., the use of the *pesher* method, the use of the term *maskilim* ("wise men"), reference to the *Kitti'im*, similarity in wording, apocalyptic chronology, use of visions, use of angelology, belief that the end time was at hand, and a devotion to Scripture.[67]

Most of these similarities, however, are so general that they could apply to other books of the Bible as well as to a number of intertestamental writings. Why should Daniel be singled out except that it is assumed that he lived and wrote his book at the same time that the Qumran community began? It is only upon this assumption that similarities are sought. Is Trevor's allegiance to the late date motivated by the old concern over predictive prophecy? Such may be inferred from an article in which he included a two-page excursus on "Prophecy and the Book of Daniel." There, he said, ". . . it should be clear that it is very important that the book of Daniel be understood in terms of the historical-literary ethos of the second century B.C. rather than in the usual eschatological ('end-time') sense."[68] This, of course, is "very important" because the late date and predictive prophecy cannot coexist.[69]

Keep in mind that if Daniel were instead an early inspired source for the Sect, we would still expect their literature to reflect similarities. Yet, it is the differences, not the similarities, that will define this issue for us. These differences have become evident over the last two decades from scholarly analyses of both the Hebrew and Aramaic versions of Daniel. These analyses have concluded that the evidence demands an early date for Daniel.

## Support for an Early Date

We have already noted that the early semicursive script of *4QDan*[c] (*4Q114*) has been dated to the late second century B.C., or within less than 50 years from the assumed autograph of Daniel. While this date based on scribal characteristics makes it unlikely that the original composition took place in the Maccabean period, the Hebrew version of Daniel—compared linguistically with the Hebrew of other Qumran Scrolls—makes this an impossibility. After conducting a comparative analysis of the syntax and morphology, the use of postbiblical words, postbiblical pronunciation and spelling, and words used with a postbiblical meaning, Gleason Archer concluded:

In light of all the data adduced under the four categories just reviewed, it seems abundantly clear that a second-century date for the Hebrew chapters of Daniel is no longer tenable on linguistic grounds. In view of the markedly later development exhibited by these second-century documents in the areas of syntax, word order, morphology, vocabulary, spelling and word-usage, there is absolutely no possibility of regarding Daniel as contemporary. On the contrary the indications are that centuries must have intervened between them. . . . Otherwise we must surrender linguistic evidence altogether and assert that it is completely devoid of value in the face of subjective theories derived from antisupernaturalistic bias. . . . If all of the book was written even as early as the third century (and there really is nothing in the linguistic data to militate against a late sixth-century composition by the ostensible author himself), the supernatural element of fulfilled prediction would still remain.[70]

This conclusion also seems to be supported by a comparative analysis of the Aramaic version of Daniel. H.H. Rowley had claimed in 1929 that the Aramaic Daniel was of late origin.[71] However, based on an analysis of the Elephantine Papyri from Upper Egypt, which were written in Aramaic and dated to the fifty century B.C., the Aramaist Franz Rosenthal argued in 1939 that the "old 'linguistic evidence' [for a late date] has to be laid aside."[72] Some 30 years later, on the basis of new Aramaic manuscript discoveries, as well as a reexamination of Rowley's "evidence," British Egyptologist Kenneth Kitchen demonstrated that 90 percent of Daniel's Aramaic vocabulary occurred in documents dated to the fifth century B.C. or earlier, that Persian loan words were Old Persian, and that Greek loan words also could precede the fifth century B.C.

In addition, some syntactical forms in Daniel were shown to have not survived beyond the fifth century B.C., precluding any later date.[73] He thus concluded, "The Aramaic of Daniel (and of Ezra) is simply a part of Imperial (Official) Aramaic—in itself, practically undatable with any conviction within c. 600 to 330 B.C."[74] Kitchen's view was supported (against Rowley) by his colleague at the University of Liverpool, Semiticist Alan Millard,[75] as well as by the leading Aramaist E.Y. Kutscher, who showed from Daniel's Aramaic word order that the provenance was Eastern (Babylon), not Western (Palestine), as the Maccabean date required.[76]

Most of these arguments against the late-date view were based on a comparison of Daniel's Aramaic with that of the Elephantine Papyri and the book of Ezra (dated by critical scholars to the fifth and fourth centuries B.C. respectively) because the Qumran evidence was not then fully accessible. When a comparison was able to be made with the Aramaic of the Qumran texts, they corroborated an early (pre-second century) date. Gleason Archer compared the Aramaic *Genesis Apocryphon (1Q20)*, dated to the first century B.C.,[77] with that of Daniel, and concluded that the latter was centuries later than the former.[78] When the Aramaic *Targum of Job (11QtgJob)* was published, scholars agreed that it was younger than the Aramaic Daniel, but older than the Aramaic *Genesis Apocryphon*.[79] Working from an assumed fixed date for Daniel in the Maccabean period (mid-second century B.C.), some scholars then attempted to push the date of *11QtgJob* to the first century B.C. and *1Q20* to the first century A.D. However, in a comparative study of these texts, Robert Vasholz determined that the date of *11QtgJob* was late third-early second century B.C., a century older than *1Q20*.[80] This evidence demands that Daniel, which is acknowledged as older than *11QtgJob*, be pre-Maccabean in origin.

In addition, A. York's similar study revealed that *11QtgJob* (which corresponds to Job 40:10-11) alludes to Nebuchadnezzar and indisputably reflects the vocabulary of Daniel 3:13,19; 4:33-34, and 5:20.[81] This, then, would make the Qumran *Targum of Job* dependent on some copy of Daniel older than itself. Furthermore, the Daniel fragments, especially *1Q72*, show that Daniel was used at Qumran (both in its Hebrew and Aramaic parts) without the expansions found in the Greek. This apparently was the same canonical Hebrew-Aramaic text of Daniel used by the first century A.D. Jewish writer Josephus, for his account of the story of Daniel also lacked any knowledge of these deuterocanonical additions.[82] This suggests that more than one Hebrew recension of Daniel was made prior to the LXX translation (circa 200 B.C.).

In light of all this evidence, Old Testament scholar Gerhard Hasel concluded:

> The Aramaic documents from Qumran push the date of the composition into a period earlier than the Maccabean date allows. Thus the alternative date for Daniel in the sixth or fifth century B.C. has more in its favor today from the point of view of language alone than ever before.[83]

## A Valuable Contribution

The discovery of the Dead Sea Scrolls, then, has made a contribution toward confirming the integrity of the biblical text and its own claim to predictive prophecy. Rather than support the recent theories of documentary disunity, the Scrolls have returned scholars to a time when the Bible's internal witness to its own consistency and veracity was fully accepted by its adherents.

# 8

# THE SCRIPTURES AND THE SCROLLS:
## The New Testament

*When will Christian preaching finally learn that Christianity does not live by distinguishing itself from Judaism? That the Old Testament belongs truly and completely to the canon of the Bible and that early Christianity is an intensification of certain Jewish themes and not their destruction or condescending conquest? That Jesus has something different in mind than differentiating himself from Moses? And that therefore the Judaism during the time of Jesus was not the dark background for the luminous message, but rather the larger family providing the context for early Christians?*[1]

—Prof. Klaus Berger,
University of Heidelberg

The common assumption of many people is that the Dead Sea Scrolls contribute more to our understanding of the Old Testament than the New. In actuality, the Scrolls have much to offer in our study of the New

Testament. Qumran scholar Geza Vermes says that for New Testament research, the Scrolls are "the only suitable comparative material."[2] No other documents that record similar material (such as the rabbinic writings and Palestinian Targums) preceded and were contemporaneous with first-century Jewish Christianity. Both the Qumran Scrolls and the New Testament were produced in the matrix of what is known as "Palestinian Judaism." They were both messianic and eschatological in orientation, they both shared a sectarian separatist position among Jewish movements with a unique allegiance to a central prophetic leader, and they both produced their own sectarian literature while regarding the Old Testament and divine inspiration as the authoritarian source. For these reasons Vermes declares that "comparison between the two bodies of literature is not only reasonable, but indispensable."[3]

Professor David Flusser, unique among Israeli Scroll scholars because of his expertise with the New Testament, sees the identification with a Jewish context as one of the great advances made possible by the Scrolls:

> In the light of the discovery of the Scrolls, it has been definitely established that Greek influence on early Christianity was but weak, for most of the concepts in the New Testament previously believed to stem from pagan thought are now found to originate with a Jewish Sect and in a most definitely Jewish context.[4]

In light of the above comparisons we can expect to find similarities in style, theological perspective, and vocabulary. David Flusser is representative of those who contend that the doctrinal system of Qumran enables us to discern areas of dependence by the New Testament from the Scrolls. He states:

> Comparison of the New Testament with the Scrolls confirms the subdivision of early Christianity into two streams: The first is Jesus and the Mother Church in Jerusalem; the second is the trend on which, among others, Paul and John the Evangelist based. Jesus received from the Sect, whether directly or indirectly, several socio-religious tenets: esteem of humility and poverty as religious value and the belief that the mysteries of God are not revealed to the wise and understanding, but rather to the simple. The two main passages where influence of the Sect is evident are the Beatitudes at the beginning of the Sermon on the Mount (Matthew 5:3-12) and the hymn of praise in Matthew

11:25-30. This is not, evidently, incidental for these two passages are poetic in form. Jesus did not accept the Sectarian theological system and opposed social separatism: in this connection he quite specifically mentions the "Sons of Light" (Luke 16:8-9). From an organizational standpoint, it appears that the institution of twelve apostles is derived, directly or indirectly, from the Sect.[5]

Yet even though the Qumran community and the early Jewish Christians shared the same historical context and undoubtedly were aware of each other's existence, we find no explicit statements in either the Qumran texts or the New Testament to this effect. They simply do not recognize each other via a direct statement. Thus we should be careful about trying to use parallels to establish any kind of identity or intentional interrelationship between the two. This kind of direct association—with Jesus as the founder of the Qumran Sect, equivalent to or the successor of the Righteous Teacher, or with Christianity as an offshoot of the movement—has been tried without success, even though some have tried to revive such thinking recently (see chapters 15–17). However, the Qumran group and early Jewish Christians may have made indirect statements about each other, and without a doubt their documents possess parallels that help us better interpret the New Testament. But I think from these parallels it is wholly unwarranted to suggest, as does VanderKam, that "some parts of the New Testament may have been drawn from Qumran or Essene sources and then revised and edited into their present contexts."[6]

## Noteworthy Parallels and Differences

As we survey the parallels between the Scrolls and the New Testament, we will examine four areas in which such comparisons have been traditionally made: 1) the Scrolls and John the Baptizer, 2) the Scrolls and Jesus, 3) the Scrolls and John the Apostle, and 4) the Scrolls and Paul.

### *The Scrolls and John the Baptizer*

From the beginning of comparative studies between the Scrolls and the New Testament, the figure of John the Baptizer has been prominent and connected to varying degrees with the Qumran Sect. The reasons for this are obvious: John's father was a priest (Luke 1:5,8-23), as were the core leaders of the Qumran community. John grew up in the wilderness

(Luke 1:80), perhaps near where the Qumran settlement was located. John called the Pharisees and Sadducees corrupt (Matthew 3:7-9; Luke 3:7-8), as did the Qumran Sect. John preached repentance (Matthew 3:2; Mark 1:4; Luke 3:3) and practiced water baptism in relation to repentance (Matthew 3:6,11; Luke 3:3), and the Qumran community did likewise. John regarded his mission as that of being Isaiah's pre-messianic messenger (Isaiah 40:4): "crying in the wilderness to prepare the way of the Lord" (Matthew 3:3; Mark 1:2-3; Luke 3:3-6), just as did the Qumran Sect. John wore simple apparel and ate a limited diet (Matthew 3:4-5; Mark 1:6)—similar to the members of the Qumran community. John proclaimed the imminent coming of the Messiah and a time of divine judgment (Matthew 3:10-12; Mark 1:7-8; Luke 3:16-18; John 1:19-28), a message also broadcast by the Qumran Sect.

While these similarities are striking, they are not as significant as they appear. In context, they actually appear dissimilar: John's father was a priest, but he functioned as a prophet (Matthew 11:9). John's location was north of Qumran, "in Bethany" (John 1:28) and "at Aenon near Salim" (John 3:23).[7] John indeed called the Pharisees and Sadducees corrupt, but did not likewise condemn Jewish tax-gatherers or Roman soldiers. Rather, he merely admonished them to deal justly as they continued their work (John 3:12-14). Such "compromise" with the enemy and their collaborators would have been unthinkable to the Qumran Sect. John's form of repentance, like his method of baptism, were one-time acts, unlike the Qumran membership, which daily confessed their sins and practiced multiple ritual immersions.

In fact, John's baptism was so unlike that at Qumran that it may have been seen as a polemic against it. For instance, John's baptism was mediatory and initiatory, whereas Qumran baptism was self-administered and non-initiatory.[8] John's baptism was immediate upon confession and repentance, whereas Qumran baptism came only after a two-year probationary period. John's baptism was related to the messianic purpose, whereas Qumran baptism was simply a purification ritual and not related to any eschatological figure or event. However, this comparison is with the *daily* baptisms or purification washings of the membership. If we compare John's "baptism of repentance" with the *initiatory* baptism, we find a practice of immersion that required the initiate to first give evidence of his repentance. That is what John required of the tax-gatherers and the Roman soldiers—to demonstrate the fruit (or acts) of repentance in their daily lives before they came to be baptized. Therefore, in this case there is a partial similarity.

We should also note that John's use of Isaiah 40:4 was different from that of the Qumran Sect. No Scroll reveals a member of their community saying, "I am the voice of one crying." In fact, this part of the quotation is absent from the Qumran texts.[9] The *Manual of Discipline* (8:12-15) quotes this verse only in relation to the group's move to Qumran to prepare the Lord's way through Torah study. John's camel-hair garment and highly restricted diet was in keeping with the prophets (especially Elijah), whereas the white linen robes of the Sect and dietary regimen (which included meats and breads) was in keeping with the priesthood. John (according to John the apostle) anticipated a divine Messiah with a sacrificial redemptive purpose (John 1:29-30), whose career first involved a baptism with the Spirit, and then with fire (judgment) in the Day of the Lord (see Isaiah 11:4; Malachi 3:24; 4:1).[10] While the Qumran Sect may have also looked for more than a human messiah(s), the messianic redemption was not sacrificial, but followed the messianic war (judgment).

John the Baptizer's activities and actions, then, can be explained apart from any influence by Qumran. His ascetic lifestyle was in accord with Old Testament Nazirite vows, which was in keeping with both the scriptural example of dedication (see 1 Samuel 1:11,28) and the angelic command to abstain from wine and liquor (Luke 1:15).

In addition, John's public presence among people stands in stark contrast to the isolationist practices of the Dead Sea Sect. More unusual still was the way John challenged leaders, even rebuking King Herod Antipas (Matthew 14:3-4). This was something no leader (*mebaqqer*, "overseer") in the Qumran community would have done; they were prohibited from rebuking anyone who was not a member of their own Sect. The reason for this is because they viewed rebuke as a form of instruction, and they were not to teach nonmembers.

Based on the above-stated observations, it is possible that John may have spent time with the Sect prior to his public ministry; however, nothing in the biblical account calls for this assumption. Thus the scholars who believed that John had some connection with the Qumran community admit that when he began his public ministry he must have departed from, or parted with, the Sect. Therefore, the similarities between John the Baptizer and the Qumran Sect were probably because of commonly held Old Testament distinctions rather than the Sect's direct influence on John's life. Even so, the Qumran texts reveal these common notions and practices, and so help establish John in a proper historical context and validate the integrity of the New Testament's description of him.

## The Scrolls and Jesus

Did Jesus have any connection with the Qumran Sect? We'll consider that question in detail in chapter 15, so for now I will present only some suggested parallels between Jesus and the Scrolls. These will be limited to the following topics: the Beatitudes, the Temple, Jesus' trial and crucifixion, the practices of divorce and communion, and several Gospel texts that may offer possible glimpses into Qumran practice.

### The Beatitudes of Qumran

The recently published Cave 4 text designated *4Q525*, known as *Beatitudes*,[11] includes some interesting parallels and differences with both Jesus' Sermon on the Mount (Matthew 5:3-12) and Sermon on the Plain (Luke 6:20-23). Written in Herodian script, which dates it to between 50 B.C.–A.D. 50, this fragmentary text opens a section of proverbial wisdom sayings and a personification of wisdom (as a lady, cf. Proverbs 1:20-33; 4:6-9; 9:1-6) attributed to David (or David's son Solomon). In columns 4-6, the text moves into an apocalyptic section that features harsh judgmental pronouncements. One characteristic of biblical proverbs is that they often develop into apocalyptic promises applicable to the last days or the millennial age. This is seen in the Old Testament "beatitudes" (especially in Isaiah and the Psalms) and the Gospels, where the "kingdom of heaven" or "inheriting the earth" is the eschatological setting for the righteous (see Matthew 5:3,5,10), and "mourning and weeping" is the judgment of the wicked (see Luke 6:24-26).

According to Emile Puech, who translated the Beatitudes of Qumran, the series of "blessings" or "beatitudes" (from the Latin *beatus*) in column 2 are purely wisdom-oriented with no apocalyptic overtones. In that sense, they are different from the beatitudes in the Gospels. Puech also says that the arrangement of these beatitudes confirms for the first time that the original literary form of the Gospel's beatitudes are nine in number. By contrast, modern literary analysis has separated Matthew's ninth beatitude from his first eight and put it into a new literary unit. In addition, the first eight beatitudes in both Matthew and *4Q525* were written in the third person.[12]

The subjects addressed in these beatitudes are also similar to those found in the Gospels: truth, the tongue, folly, having a pure heart and hands, walking in ways of the law, and humility. These beatitudes from Qumran help set the beatitudes of the Gospels in a common first-century context, revealing that Jesus used recognizable themes and proverbial statements in His teaching to the masses.

## Jewish "Rejection" of the Temple

One area of pronounced similarity between Jesus and the Qumran Sect was their "rejection" of the Temple in Jerusalem. We'll examine the Qumran group's attitude toward the Temple in chapter 11 as well. The *Temple Scroll* makes it evident that Jesus was not alone in His negative view of the Second Temple (the Scroll also features a positive view of restoration with a Third Temple). In fact, there is substantial evidence from historical sources that a fairly large percentage of Jews viewed the Second Temple negatively. Markus Bockmuehl cites examples from Josephus, Tacitus, and early rabbinic literature, all of which indicate there was a flourishing hermeneutical tradition before A.D. 70 that predicted the Temple's destruction. He gives a twofold reason for this tradition:[13]

1. *Theological.* The first and most important reason was that the promises of restoration, which had been given by the biblical prophets, had not been fulfilled. Prophecies about the exile and subsequent return to the Land under ideal conditions had obviously gone unfulfilled. This awareness on the part of the Jewish people is found in the pre-Maccabean book of Tobit (13:16-18; 14:5) and in Daniel 9:17,26-27. The corruption and decline of the Hasmonean dynasty and subsequent occupation by Roman forces exacerbated doubts that a full restoration, much less a liberation, of the Jewish nation would take place. In addition, there were doubts—by groups such as the Essenes and those who frequented the Jewish temple at Leontopolis—that the Maccabees had effected a complete cleansing of the Temple. Even though the Second Temple had been splendidly restored, the consensus was that if it was not the eschatological Temple, and if the purity of the Zadokite priestly line was at all a matter of concern, then the only logical conclusion was that the present corrupt system would need to give way to a new one.

2. *Social and Political.* The degeneration of the priestly aristocracy at this period in time invited comparison with the earlier prophetic oracles of judgment and destruction. Of the 28 high priests between 37 B.C. and A.D. 70, all but two came from illegitimate non-Zadokite families.[14] It became increasingly clear to most Jews that the cultic center, which regulated all of Jewish life, was in the hands of a vast network of economic

and religious oppression. The legitimate and necessary operation of the Temple was supported by a maze of intrigue, nepotism, and graft (Mishnah *Keritot* 1.7); among those involved in this were members of the well-known priestly family of the house of Kathros (see *Baraita*, B. *Pesahim* 57a). Consequently, many Jews of that era anticipated the eventual removal of the Second Temple and a future, restored Third Temple.

**Jesus and Qumran on Temple Abuses.** The nature of Jesus' "rejection" of the Temple wasn't exactly the same as that expressed in the Scrolls. Both stated similar concerns about Temple abuses, but there were also some differences.

The Qumran community rejected the Temple priesthood, calling its high priest "the Wicked Priest" (*1QpHab* 1:3; 8:9; 9:9; 11:4). They opposed the accumulation of wealth by the priesthood, whom they felt was "robbing" the people, especially the poor (*1QpHab* 8:8-12; 9:4-5; 10:1; 12:10; *CD* 6:15-16). In like manner, Jesus said that the priests oppressed the poor, especially in the areas of excessive laws (see Mark 7:9-13) and self-aggrandizing attitudes about their priestly status at the expense of the people (Mark 12:38-44). Jesus' anger about the Temple becoming a place of disadvantage for the poor was dramatized when He cleansed the Temple by driving out the money changers (Matthew 21:12-13). However, despite this shared rejection of the Temple establishment, Jesus, unlike the Sect, apparently honored the authority of the high priest's office. His response to the high priest, even after He had been beaten and accused of disrespect, reveals no depreciation (John 18:19-23).

Other Temple concerns were also shared by Jesus and the Qumran Sect. One example was the payment of the half-shekel Temple tax. Jesus, while complying with the law (Mark 12:17), questioned the practice (Matthew 17:24-27), as did those at Qumran: "As for the half-[shekel, the offering of the Lord] which they gave, each man as a ransom for his soul: only one [time] shall he give it all his days" (*4Q159* 2:6-8). Like Jesus, they paid the tax, but objected on biblical grounds (see Exodus 30:13) that it was not to be paid yearly, but once in a lifetime.

**Jesus' Denunciation of the Temple.** Jesus' life—as the life of any observant Jew—revolved around the Temple and its calendar. That sets Him apart from the Qumran community. But some people say His attitude was the same as that of the Qumran group by pointing to His predictions about the Temple's destruction (Matthew 23:37–24:2; Mark 13:2; Luke 19:42-44) and His "cleansing"[15] of the Temple, which is recorded in each of the Synoptic Gospels and the Gospel of John (Matthew

21:12-13; Mark 11:15-17; Luke 19:45-46; John 2:14-22).[16] It is significant that at His trial before the crucifixion, this event is cited by witnesses as evidence of Jesus' hostile attitude toward the Temple.

Opinions about Jesus' motive in the "cleansing" have ranged from 1) a formal declaration of opposition to the Temple's existence to 2) a symbolic enactment of Temple destruction to 3) an act of taking possession of the Temple to 4) an attack on Sadducean enterprise, and to 5) an attempt to signal the permanent cessation of the sacrificial system by the temporary interruption of daily sacrifices.[17] Still others believe that the problem addressed in the "cleansing" was not the Temple, but the behavior of the people who had assumed control and maintenance of the Temple.[18] This appears to be the position Stephen took in his comments concerning the Temple (Acts 7). His abrupt shift in verse 51 makes sense only if he was making a transition from a historical review of the rebellious attitude of the individuals who possessed the Tabernacle and First Temple (verses 44-50) to a present-day statement about the rebellious attitude of those who possessed the Second Temple (verses 51-53).

Thus, while opinions vary about Jesus' view of the Temple, we can be certain the Qumran Sect was opposed to both the behavior of the priesthood and the state of the Temple itself.

I have written elsewhere about the nature of Jesus' remarks about the Temple,[19] and it is my opinion that Jesus' words were balanced by a comparison of the presently defiled Second Temple to the restoration ideal—the eschatological Temple. Jesus not only cited what the prophets said against the Temple, but He also stated positive eschatological affirmations. One such statement is made in Mark 11:17 when Jesus cites Isaiah 56:7: "My house shall be called a house of prayer for all the nations." The phrase is appropriately applied by Jesus because the money-changer incident occurred within the Court of the Gentiles. While it may appear that Jesus is talking about universal access to the worship of God, He is actually focusing on the future Temple, as the context of Isaiah 56:1-8 confirms (cf. Zechariah 6:15; 14:16). Matthew and Luke's omission of "for all the nations" may have been to more effectively contrast "house of prayer" with "den of robbers," but their purpose was the same as Mark's—to describe what the Temple should be opposed to what it had become.[20]

Jesus' concern about the Temple is parallel to that which is expressed in the Scrolls (especially *11Q19*). Neither Jesus nor the Qumran Sect rejected the Temple in the sense of replacement, for Jesus regarded it as

"My [Father's] house" (Mark 11:17; John 2:16; cf. Matthew 23:21), and both envisioned a future restoration. Even the accusation against Jesus that He sought to "destroy the Temple" must be tempered with His claim that He would "rebuild it in three days" (Matthew 26:61; 27:40; John 2:19-20). Zechariah 6:12-13 also affirms that one of the roles of the expected Messiah was that of a Temple builder.

In Jesus' prediction of the Temple's destruction (Matthew 24:1-3; Mark 13:1-4,14; Luke 21:5-7,20-24) as well as His declaration to the Jewish nation that "your Temple is being left to you desolate" (Matthew 23:37-38) there is also a clear anticipation of restoration. In the Olivet Discourse, Jesus, like the Scrolls, places the desecration of the Temple in a future time of tribulation, during which an evil figure will arise based on Daniel's prediction (Matthew 24:15; Mark 13:14). In Luke, Jesus speaks about the Roman destruction of Jerusalem and the Temple (Luke 21:20-24), yet in all of these statements He adds the promise of the Messiah's coming to rescue, redeem, and restore Israel and judge her enemies (Matthew 24:29-31; 25:31-46; Mark 13:26-27; Luke 21:27-28). This same assurance closes Jesus' declaration of desolation in Matthew 23:39: "You shall not see Me until you say, 'Blessed is He who comes in the Name of the Lord!'" The pronouncement of desolation, then, came with a promise of restoration following Israel's repentance (Psalm 118:26; Zechariah 12:10–13:2).

The main differences between Jesus and the Sect, then, are that He remained active in the Temple's rituals and abided by its festival calendar, whereas the Sect didn't. Craig Evans affirms Jesus' attitude with these words:

> Both Jesus and the Essenes anticipated an eschatological restoration of Israel. Both apparently believed that some sort of national purification was necessary. Although critical of the Temple establishment, Jesus and the Essenes were committed to Israel and to the nation's restoration. In no wise does Jesus' criticism lay a foundation for the condemnation of Judaism or the Jewish people. Jesus' criticisms were motivated by a deep desire for Israel's best, a hope that Israel would someday attain to its God-given destiny.... [21]

## The Trial and Crucifixion of Jesus

One area in which the Scrolls have proved especially significant in helping us to understand the New Testament is in the confirmation and clarification of social customs and Jewish *halakha* of the first century. For example, Professor Otto Betz says that the *Temple Scroll* provides us with new insights about concepts related to Jesus' trial and crucifixion. Betz has written a work on this matter,[22] and I reproduce here his summary of the issues:

> The *Temple Scroll* is very important for the trial of Jesus as a historical document. For example, it has a very interesting section on Deuteronomy 21:22-23 in which the punishment of hanging a man on the tree is mentioned. This passage is interpreted in the *Temple Scroll* and related to crucifixion. In contrast to the Pharisees, we think that this is an additional punishment for a man who has been stoned—to be hung up for an hour or two on the tree. The Qumran Scrolls clearly indicate that this punishment of crucifixion is for a man who betrays the whole nation to a foreign power like the Romans. This is exemplified from an incident recorded in Josephus and the Scrolls, of the Hasmonean King Alexander Jannaeus' crucifixion of 800 Pharisees because they committed the crime of high treason. The Romans also punished high priests by crucifixion for this same charge. So here the *Temple Scroll* sheds new light on the trial of Jesus. We can no longer say that the Jews were not involved in the trial of Jesus because He was sentenced to the death sentence of crucifixion, a strictly Roman punishment [see John 18:31]. No, crucifixion was also, and especially by the Sadducees, a punishment for people who did commit the crime of high treason. The claim to be the Messiah was, in their eyes, a kind of high treason (see John 11:48-50; 18:33-37; 19-12,15,21). In John 11:49 there is especially the statement of Caiaphas that they thought Jesus would betray the whole nation and Jerusalem to the Romans. So we get from the *Temple Scroll* a confirmation that the Sadducean trial of Jesus ended up with the kind of death sentence the Sadducees, the judges, and the High Priest knew would be here carried by the Romans if Jesus was tried by the Roman prefect Pilate. When they accused Jesus of being the Messiah, which He confessed to be, they judged Him guilty for this kind of punishment. The Sadducean High Priest could then

expect to get this punishment from the Romans which would be applied to Jewish interpretation of the law.[23]

## Jesus and Qumran on Divorce and Communion

Another parallel often discussed in literature on the Dead Sea Scrolls is the strict view of divorce, held alike by Jesus (Mark 10:6; Luke 16:18) and Qumran (*11Q19* 57:17-19). This latter ruling from the *Temple Scroll* forbids both polygamy and divorce, and therefore eliminates polygamy as an option for explaining the term "unchastity" (Greek *porneia*) in Matthew's so-called "exception clause" (Matthew 5:32; 19:9). But the Qumran texts do provide some assistance in discerning the meaning of this controversial term. In the Scrolls the term is the equivalent of the Hebrew word *zenuth*, a term said to refer to one of the three deadly snares of Belial (*CD* 4:17). Chaim Rabin saw this term as a specific reference to the *zonah* ("unchaste woman") of Leviticus 21:7, whose status has been incurred by incest.[24] Therefore, as Neil Fugita concludes, "in Qumran and the Gospels, the only condition for divorce which Matthew mentions ... may well refer to the case of incest."[25]

A second parallel that is offered is that between the *Pesach* (Passover) Seder or Last Supper of Jesus, and the ongoing ordinance of the Eucharist or communion and the communal meal of the Qumran community. Both involved a priestly blessing over the bread and wine (Matthew 26:26-27; *CD* 6:2-8) and were enjoyed in view of the future messianic banquet (Matthew 26:29; *1QS* 2:11-22). However, again, the differences are too pronounced for any equation or dependence to be established. The order of seating at the Qumran meal was strictly by rank (*1QS* 2:11-12), was only for full-fledged members of at least one (for the bread) and two years (for the wine) (*1QS* 6:20; 7:20-21), and was practiced twice daily (*1QM* 2:133-138). If someone was guilty of slander he was unable to attend the meal for one year (*1QS* 7:16).

At the Lord's Supper, there is no rank or privilege prescribed for attendance, although membership in the Christian community is usually assumed. In addition, all attempts to prove that the Qumran communal meal was a ritualistic meal have failed.[26] No text reveals any words spoken in remembrance or any symbolic interpretation repeated. The meal is best patterned after the model of Pharisaical "table fellowship," as a regular non-cultic activity of the Sect where ritual purity was enforced and *halakhically* prepared foods were eaten[27] as a pre-enactment of the messianic banquet. Thus there are only slight parallels between Christian communion and the Qumran communal meal.[28]

## Did Jesus Refer to the Qumran Sect?

There is one Bible passage—the parable of the unjust steward (Luke 16:1-8)—that may offer us a brief look at the Qumran Sect. At the conclusion of this passage Jesus says, "The sons of this age are more shrewd in relation to their own than the sons of light." If Jesus' intention in this comparison was to critique a particular Jewish group who called themselves "the sons of light" as opposed to the commercially minded Jews who kept up with the world, then it is possible He could have had members of the Qumran Sect in mind. They eschewed personal wealth, and the moral of Jesus' story is to show how the proper use of such wealth can help make friends that will last for eternity (verse 9). Perhaps Jesus was subtly rebuking the Sect's vow of poverty, which members took at the time of initiation. But this is mere speculation, for "the sons of light" could just as well apply to any supposedly enlightened group that might be characterized by a lack of concern with money management, including Jesus' own followers.

Even though Luke 16:8 cannot clearly confirm for us Jesus' recognition of the Qumran Sect, we can probably assume that if He was aware of their presence He might somehow have made His awareness known. It is unreasonable to believe that Jesus would have failed to acknowledge the Qumranites at all because they lived for so long at their settlement and they were major players on the religious scene of His day. Perhaps direct statements were not included in the Gospels because Jesus never had a confrontation with the Sect. However, Jesus' awareness of the Sect may be inferred indirectly by carefully analyzing idiomatic statements in His teaching.[29] Jesus often used *halakhic* issues of the day in His teaching because they were a source of controversy and therefore practical for illustration. In one example, Jesus admonished His hearers to "not give what is holy to dogs" (Matthew 7:6). This statement can be better understood with a look at the Scrolls. We know that the Qumran Sect did not allow dogs to enter their camp because they wanted to preserve the sanctity of their community and its sacred meals. They were afraid that dogs might get to bones with meat on them, which had sacrificial symbolism, and thus defile the sanctity of the meal and the camp. This, apparently, was an issue between the Qumran Sect and the Sadducees, and being familiar to both, Jesus refers to the matter in His teaching.

In another message, Jesus referred to the *halakhic* concern over the ceremonial purity of usable vessels. According to the book of Leviticus (11:29-33), if a lizard dies and falls inside a vessel, the vessel no longer can be used because the corpse has made it impure. The Pharisees interpreted that passage to mean that if the lizard dies and falls on the *outside* of the vessel, it is still usable because the corpse did not touch the inside. The Qumranites, however, objected to this and argued that the uncleanliness would contaminate the entire vessel. Jesus had this debate in mind when He said, "Clean the inside of the cup and of the dish, so that the outside of it may become clean also" (Matthew 23:25-26; Luke 11:39-40).

In the aforementioned Bible passages and many other scriptures, we can pierce beyond the veil of the Gospel's silence concerning the Qumran Sect and see something of the common knowledge people had of this group during Jesus' day.

## The Scrolls and the Apostle John

Some of the most striking parallels between the Scrolls and the New Testament occur in the Gospel of John, which has recently been recognized as "the most Jewish Gospel in the Christian canon.[30] These parallels deal primarily with theological concepts, dualistic motifs, and terminology. For example, John will speak about light versus darkness (John 1:4-5; 3:20-21; 12:35; 1 John 1:5-7; 2:8-11), while the Scrolls will speak about "the prince of light" versus "the angel of darkness" (*1QS* 3:20-21). John will speak about "the sons of light" (John 12:36) and "the Spirit of truth" (John 14:17), just as do the Scrolls (*1QS* 3:13,18-19; *1QM*). John's theme in chapter 15-17 is unity, or that His followers would be one. The very name the Qumran Sect called itself was *Yahad* ("community"), which has to do with oneness. Both the Dead Sea Scrolls and the New Testament are unique in their belief in divine election and predestination. In the Scrolls we find evidence of this in various places (*CD* 2:7-10; *1QH* 1:7; 12:9-11; 4:29-33; 15:13-23; *1QS* 3:15-17), and in the New Testament these concepts are especially prominent in John (John 6:44-47,64-65,70; 9:1-3; 10:26-30; 12:32,37-40; 17:1-2,6-10; 18:37; 19:11). Similar eschatological ideas are also shared concerning rewards and punishments (John 5:29; *1QS* 4:12-13), with wrath to God's enemies (John 3:36; *1QS* 4:12) and eternal life/light for the righteous (John 3:16; 6:47; *1QS* 4:7-8) and the coming of Antichrist/"son of Belial"/"blasphemous king" (1 John 2:18; 4:3; *4Q385* 2:3-4, 9-10).

While John and the Qumran community may have shared similar concepts and terms, there are some definite differences in the understanding behind the concepts and terms. John's "Spirit of Truth" is God, whereas the similar figure at Qumran describes an angel. John's sense of "oneness" is a union of the individual believer with God (John 17:21-24), and on this basis, with each other in community (John 17:11). The Qumran concept was of communal oneness and all that it entailed—the sharing of property, unity of purpose, sectarian discipline, commitment to laws and rituals, and so on. John's view of his Christian "sect" is that they should remain in the world (John 17:15), not remove themselves from it, as the Qumran Sect did. Furthermore, John gives no sectarian rules; he and his fellow apostles said Christians were to love one another and their enemies as well. By contrast, the Qumran Sect had the *Zadokite Fragments*, the *Rules of the Community*, and other sets of strict regulations, in which they were told to "hate" their enemies.[31]

In summing up John's relation to Qumran teaching, James H. Charlesworth concludes: "In short, the two . . . differ from each other in their angelology, their eschatology [future versus realized], their view of predestination, and their solution to the problem of evil."[32] He further notes, "The Dead Sea Scrolls challenge us to think about the source of John's vocabulary and perspective, and clarify the uniqueness of his gospel and John's distinct Christology and theology."[33]

### The Scrolls and Paul

When we compare Paul's writings with the Qumran texts, we receive new insights into the Jewish background of Pauline doctrines and phrases. We also see confirmation that Paul's teaching was indeed rooted in the Old Testament and traditional Judaism. For instance, familiar Pauline phrases like "the righteousness of God" (Romans 1:17; 3:5; 2 Corinthians 5:21), "the works of the Law" (Romans 3:20,27-28; Galatians 2:16), and "the mystery of iniquity" have no Old Testament or even rabbinic counterparts. However, these expressions have exact Hebrew equivalents in the Scrolls: "righteousness of God"—*1QS* 11:12 (*sidqat 'El*); *1QM* 4:6 (*sedeq 'El*); "works of the Law"—*4Q174* 1-2.1:7; *4QMMT (ma'ase torah)*,[34] and "mystery of iniquity"—*1Q20* 1:2 (*raz ris'a*).

Interesting, too, is the Pauline Greek phrase "church of God" (*ekklesia tou theou*). Although an exact counterpart of this phrase is not found in the Septuagint, it appears at Qumran in its Hebrew form "assembly/congregation of God" (*qehal 'El*) as the name to be used on a standard carried into the end-times war (*1QM* 4:10).

Also, like Jesus and John, Paul uses the phrase "sons of light" as a designation for Christians, but he uniquely projects it into the eschatological context of the Day of the Lord, paralleling it with "darkness" (1 Thessalonians 5:5) in a manner similar to the Scrolls.

## The Qumran and Pauline View of Justification by Faith

One of the central teachings in Pauline theology is the doctrine of justification by faith. For many years Paul was a Pharisee and a teacher of the Law, so it should not be surprising to find this was originally a Jewish teaching. At Qumran, we find statements that offer a close parallel to the Pauline concept.[35] For instance, in the *Rule of the Community* and the *Thanksgiving Hymn* we read an admission of utter human sinfulness:

> As for me, I belong to the wicked humanity, to the assembly of perverse flesh; my iniquities, my transgressions, my sins together with the wickedness of my heart belong to the assembly doomed to worms and walking in darkness (*1QS* 11:9-10). As for me, I know that righteousness belongs not to a human being, nor perfection of the way to a son of man. . . . It is because of my transgression that I have abandoned far from Your covenant (*1QH* 4:30-33).

While there are differences about the object of faith, these statements are reminiscent of Paul's statements that "there is none righteous, not even one . . . there is none who seeks for God . . . there is none who does good . . . destruction and misery are in their paths. . . . All have sinned and fall short of the glory of God" (Romans 3:10-12,16,23). This admission of sinfulness is coupled with an acknowledgment that God alone is able to save:

> No human being sets his own path or directs his own steps, for to God alone belongs the judgment of him, and from His hand comes perfection of way. . . . And I, if I stagger, God's grace is my salvation forever. If I stumble because of a sin of the flesh, my judgment is according to the righteousness of God, which stands forever. . . . In His mercy He has drawn me close [to Him], and with His favors will He render judgment of me. In His righteous fidelity He has judged me; in His bounteous goodness He expiates all my iniquities, and in His righteousness

He cleanses me of human defilement and of human sinfulness,
that I may praise God for His righteousness and the Most High
for His majesty (*1QS* 11:11-15; cf. *1QH* 9:32-34; 14:15-16).

Even with the similarities we've noted, there are some substantial differences between the Qumran and Pauline concepts of justification. For one, Pauline justification is forensic. It is a *legal* declaration of the fact that the righteousness of the Messiah (Jesus) has been credited to the sinner's account, and that the sinner has been declared righteous by God. No such idea existed at Qumran. This is seen in the *Pesher Habakkuk* interpretation of Habakkuk 2:4: "The one who is righteous shall find life through fidelity." The Qumran commentator explains this text (upon which Paul rests his justification argument—see Romans 1:16-17), as: "The interpretation of it concerns all doers of the law in the house of Judah, whom God will rescue from the house of judgment because of their striving and their fidelity to the Teacher of Righteousness" (*1QpHab* 8:1-3). For Paul, it is not faith or fidelity that justifies, but Messiah, who alone is able to rescue the sinner from judgment (Romans 3:24-26). Neither is justification dependent upon striving and fidelity to Messiah (Romans 3:28), but rather it rests upon His own striving and fidelity (Romans 5:10).

Therefore, while we acknowledge that the Qumran Sect was repentant, scrupulous beyond all others, faithful to the Law, and conscious of their own sinfulness and of God as a sufficient Savior, they were far from Paul's understanding of grace "apart from the deeds of the Law," which is centered in the righteous work of the Messiah (Galatians 2:16,21; 3:11-13).

## *The Qumran and Pauline View of Predestination*

There is no doubt that both the Qumran texts and Paul teach the doctrine of election and predestination. Many scholars believe that because both teach these doctrines, Paul must have depended upon Qumran, which in turn depended upon Zoroastrianism or a similar post-exilic dualism. One representative of this position is Magen Broshi:

I believe that there were among the Essenes people from the
Hellenistic Diaspora whose native tongue was Greek. They were
the first people in world history that we know of who wrote about
the idea of predestination, and they were the channel through which
St. Paul got his Essene influence, and through him the idea of predestination entered into Christianity. This is why there are passages

in Corinthians and in Romans, especially chapters 8, 9, and 10, that read like quotations of Qumranic literature.[36]

What we need to determine, then, is whether Paul's teaching was influenced by Qumran or whether it was derived from another source. A brief comparison of the Qumran and Pauline teachings will help in this determination.

According to the *Rule of the Community* (*1QS*) and the *Thanksgiving Hymn* (*1QH*), Qumran predestination involves a sovereign foreknowledge by which all is predetermined (*1QH* 1:7-8). It consists of a rigid dualism of "Two [created] Spirits" whose functions are to control all things for good or evil (*1QH* 14:11-12). God assigns at His good pleasure one of these to men and their destinies are thereby determined (*1QH* 3:22; 4:21, 33). Nevertheless, the antinomy that exists in the Qumran view of predestination is between their beliefs in the freedom of will for individual responsibility and the ability to achieve a right posture before God (*1QH* 4:6; 14:26; 16:10-18).

According to Paul, predestination is not mediated through dualistic spirits or inclinations. Rather, it is a predetermined process beginning with divine foreknowledge, which leads to predestination and the issuing of a call that results in justification and the assurance of glorification (Romans 8:29-30). God works all things, both good and evil, by His sovereign will to result in His good purpose (Romans 8:28). And even though He as the divine Potter has the right to make vessels for glory or destruction, they come from the same lump of clay, which has no right to wrangle with its Maker (Romans 9:14,18-23).

Paul's view of predestination in the book of Romans does not include free will or ability (Romans 9:16), but it does emphasize human responsibility (Romans 9:19-20). Both Paul and the Scrolls teach that the purpose of God in predestination was His own glory (see Romans 11:33-36). However, in the context surrounding Paul's teachings on predestination, we find that he is largely dependent upon the Old Testament for his concepts. For example, Romans 9–11, which is heavily predestinarian, is predominately made up of quotations and allusions from the Torah and the prophets. By contrast, the source of the Qumran concept of predestination is the Teacher of Righteousness, although it is evident his concept was also rooted in the Old Testament (*1QpHab*).

Therefore, while there are some similarities owing to the common influence of the Old Testament, Paul's teaching steered away from the kind of dualism and determinism found in the Scrolls, yet both include the matter of human responsibility and state that the goal of election is the glory of God.[37]

Having evaluated the relationship between the Scrolls and the New Testament, we must finally examine the claims of an even closer association between these documents—claims that say fragments of the New Testament have been found among the Dead Sea Scrolls.

## The New Testament at Qumran?

In 1955, 19 papyrus fragments were discovered in Cave 7 adjacent to Khirbet Qumran.[38] These fragments were unusual because they were all written in Greek rather than the customary Hebrew or Aramaic. The appearance of Greek among the Scrolls is rare: Only five examples of Torah fragments that closely resembled the Septuagint text were found in Cave 4 (*4QLev*[a]; *4QLev*[b]; *4QNum*; *4QDeut*[a]; *4QDeut*[b]). Otherwise, only Greek words (such as the name of God) and letters (abbreviations or cryptograms) are found in various other Scrolls. Of course, in the later finds made far south of Qumran, much material was found in Greek.[39] But the Cave 7 find in the Qumran area provided an entire cache of Scroll fragments written exclusively in Greek; that had never happened before.

The unusual nature of this find invited immediate speculation about the identity of the documents. Two were identified as *7Q1*=Exodus 28:4-6, and *7Q2*=the apocryphal book of Baruch 6:43-44 (an appendix to Baruch, also known as the *Epistle of Jeremiah* 43-44). However, the rest of the fragments have so far defied decipherment, although Gordon Fee once suggested identifying *74Q* with Numbers, Psalms, or Isaiah.[40] The extremely fragmentary state of the texts has made identification, even with computer assistance, impossible. Another reason identification has been difficult is because some of the fragments, such as *7Q3*, which is considered fairly large by a papyrologist's standards, have no known literary correspondent. Even computer searches have been to no avail. It may be that many of these unidentifiable texts, including the contested fragments *7Q4* and *7Q5*, cannot be positively matched with an existing text because they represent presently unknown ancient texts. This is a strong possibility because the Greek text of Baruch found in Cave 7 is unattested elsewhere.

Why the Sect had possession of these Greek texts we cannot be sure. Perhaps the Sect was associated with a Hellenistic group that used these texts, or the Sect may have simply collected the Greek texts from outside sources, which was a known practice of the Essenes.[41]

## The Revolutionary Identification

This exceptional collection of Greek fragments would have quietly taken their place among other unidentifiable Scroll fragments had it not been for the revolutionary proposal of the Spanish Jesuit José O'Callaghan, then professor of Papyrology at the Biblical Institute in Rome. As a specialist on the Septuagint, he began studying the Cave 7 fragments in hopes of finding additional Greek Old Testament texts. Unable to find a concordance match, it struck one day that 7Q5 bore an uncanny resemblance to a passage in the Gospel of Mark. Before long, he had identified this fragment and others with various New Testament texts! He claimed that 7Q4 and 7Q5 were copies of Paul's first epistle to Timothy (3:16–4:3) and the Gospel of Mark (6:52-53), while less certain identifications were suggested for 7Q6=Mark 3:28; 7Q7=Acts 27:38; 7Q8=James 1:23-24; 7Q9=Romans 5:11-12; 7Q10=2 Peter 1:15; and 7Q15=Mark 6:48.[42] Most Jewish scholars scoffed at these identifications, of which Lawrence Schiffman's terse rebuff is typical:

> The claim that New Testament manuscripts were found at Qumran can be dealt with in a sentence. None was found—for a very good reason: New Testament texts are later than the Qumran texts.[43]

Many conservative Bible scholars, on the other hand, almost unreservedly embraced O'Callaghan's theory. Protestant fundamentalists in the United States showed even stronger support than conservative Catholics,[44] with the now-defunct evangelical magazine *Eternity* devoting a cover story to the topic with the byline: "Could One Small Fragment Shake the World?"[45] Perhaps some evangelicals were hasty to accept O'Callaghan's claims because they hoped this could upset higher criticism's denial that the New Testament was authored by the apostles. Yet most evangelical scholars joined with nonconservative scholars in remaining skeptical or outright rejecting O'Callaghan's theory. Foremost among these were the respected textual critic Kurt Aland[46] and New Testament scholar Gordon Fee.[47] These criticisms helped to somewhat silence scholarly concern with the theory for almost two decades, even when several evangelicals tried to revive the debate by presenting O'Callaghan's technical evidence in a more popular format.[48]

Not until the Dead Sea Scroll scandal of the late 1980s and early 1990s did we see a resurgence of interest in O'Callaghan's view, which was championed by the German literary critic Carsten P. Thiede. In his book

*The Earliest Gospel Manuscript: The Qumran Fragment 7Q5 and Its Significance for New Testament Studies,*[49] he supersedes even O'Callaghan in contending for *7Q5* as the oldest existing New Testament text. So convinced is Thiede of this identification, that he has called for its inclusion among all future listings of New Testament papyri and in the critical apparatus of new editions of the Greek New Testament.[50] And now, recent support from leading papyrologists,[51] New Testament scholars,[52] and even openmindedness from such conservative Catholic Scroll scholars as Joseph Fitzmyer,[53] and Protestant Christian Scroll scholars like James Charlesworth[54] has given a new impetus to the debate. This time around, too, sensationalists have sought to make radical claims about the assumed connection of Cave 7 with the New Testament. For instance, Australian Qumran scholar Barbara Thiering has sought, in her imaginative revision of Qumran and Christian history, to make Cave 7 the tomb of Jesus! (See chapter 17.)

Sensationalists aside, three matters are at stake in this debate: Are these fragments our oldest examples of the New Testament? Will we need to revise even the conservative dating of much of the New Testament? And, might these fragments give us a new understanding of the relationship between the Qumran community and the early Christian community? Most evangelicals, in particular, would welcome this evidence—but only if it is sufficient to prove the case.

Because the debate has centered on *7Q5* as a portion of Mark's Gospel, and it is acknowledged that other identifications hinge on this example, I will limit the presentation to this fragment as we consider a summary of the arguments both for and against this proposal. Although *7Q5* is small in size and contains a limited number of clearly discernible letters, fragment size and paucity of letters do not eliminate the possibility of identification.[55] The identification of *7Q2* with Baruch/*Letter of Jeremiah* 6:43-44 (which is undisputed) faced even greater textual difficulties, having only *one* clearly discernible letter.

## The Case for 7Q5=Mark 6:52-53

The following arguments in defense of *7Q5* as a New Testament document were made originally by O'Callaghan, but have been revised and reinforced by Thiede. To aid our understanding of this discussion, I've included the following chart (on the next page) which compares Mark 6:52-53 with *7Q5*.

# Mark 6:52-53 and *7Q5*

Translation of reconstructed text of Mark 6:52-53 based on *7Q5*

[52] . . . for they did not understand
**a**bout the loaves,                                line 1
but their hearts were hardened.              line 2
[53] **And** when they had crossed over,    line 3
(to the land) they came to Ge**nes**saret and   line 4
m**oo**red.  And when they . . .              line 5

| Greek text reconstructed on basis of *7Q5* | Comparison of *7Q5* parallel letters |
|---|---|
| **Mark 6:52-53** | **7Q5** |
| οὐ γὰρ συνῆκαν ἐπὶ τοῖς | ------ ε̣------- |
| ἄρτοις, | ? |
| ἀλλ' ἦνν αὐτῶν ἡ καρδία | ---υτων̣/ιη-- |
| πεπωρω- | |
| μένη.  [53] Καὶ διαπεράσαντες | --η̣ και τι̣-- |
| (ἐπὶ τὴν γῆν) ἦλθον εἰς Γεννησαρὲτ καὶ | -----γννησ---- |
| προσωρμίσθησαν. | -----θησα---- |

N.B. (Standard Greek text includes ἐπὶ τὴν γῆν)

---

   In the English translation of Mark 6:52-53, the bold letters correspond to the Greek letters preserved with some certainty in *7Q5*.
Words in parentheses are in the standard Greek text but are omitted
in *7Q5*. The Greek letters on the right side are based on the reconstruction of the text of *7Q5* by O'Callaghan and Theide. Letters with
dots underneath are those that *cannot* be read with certainty. The
Greek text on the left side is a reconstruction based on *7Q5*. Under-
lined letters represent those letters allegedly present in *7Q5*.

The following represents the more substantive of the arguments for the defense:

1. More than two decades of attempts, using the most elaborate Greek text computer programs (including Ibycus), which are able to search through all extant Greek literature databases to find any known text that matches the combination of letters in proximity in *7Q5*, have been unsuccessful. The only proposal that has come close is the O'Callaghan/Thiede reconstructed text of Mark 6:52-53.[56] Their argument is strengthened by the identification of the Greek letter *nu* in line 2 following the two Greek letters *to*. This almost assures a match with the Greek word *auton* ("their") in verse 52. Although this letter appears to the unaided eye as the Greek letter *iota* ("i"), an X-ray photo of *7Q5* made with the stereomicroscope at the Division of Identification and Forensic Science of Israel's National Police seems to have revealed traces of a top diagonal line, which distinguishes a *nu* from an *iota*.[57]

2. The omissions, inclusions, and transpositions[58] that occur between the hypothetical reconstruction of Mark 6:52-53 based on *7Q5* and all extant manuscript copies of Mark are comparable to those found between $P^{52}$ (A.D. 125), the oldest exemplar of John 18, and other known Greek manuscripts of John, as well as *7Q2=Letter of Jeremiah*, which assumed omissions.

3. *7Q5* has small gaps between letters, which may indicate the beginning of new words, and with larger gaps a paragraph break and the beginning of a new section of narrative. Before the only complete word in the fragment, *kai* ("and"), such a large gap occurs. In the Greek text of Mark 6:52-53 a new section of narrative begins with the word "and" in verse 53.[59]

## The Case Against 7Q5=Mark 6:52-53

The fragment under consideration, no bigger than an average commemorative postage stamp (3.9 cm × 2.7 cm.), written in the Herodian "decorated" script and dated between 50 B.C.–A.D. 50, contains only 20 Greek consonants (whole or damaged) on five lines (see chart). Of these letters, only six can be read with any certainty, and only one complete word—*kai* ("and")—can be read at all. As C.J. Hemer has cautioned, the mathematical probability of producing a hypothetical "restoration" on such meager evidence is against success.[60] Chances of success in this case are even more questionable when we consider that the identification of 7Q5 (with Mark) now rests upon the correct reading of a *single* letter not even completely visible to the unaided eye.

The following arguments against the identification of 7Q5 with Mark 6:52-53 take into account the evidence from the defense and express concern about a reconstruction based on unclear and therefore uncertain readings of letters or words:

1. That 7Q5 (and other fragments) have not been able to be identified by computer programs only proves that this text is either beyond such identification (less likely) or represents a previously unknown text (more likely). Since two of the other fragments have been identified as Old Testament canonical and apocryphal texts, as expected from this period and this community, it is more reasonable to assume that 7Q5 also fits within this lot. However, Daniel Wallace of Dallas Theological Seminary examined the Greek database via the Ibycus program and found 16 texts which could possibly fit, though admittedly none as close as Mark 6:52-53. In addition, Professor Hartmut Stegemann of the Qumran Research Department of Göttingen University believes 7Q5 is a genealogy (based on the sequence of consonants in line 4 being expanded to form the Greek word [ege]nnes[en], "he begot").[61]

Even so, the computer identification of 7Q5's letter proximity combinations with Mark 6:52-53 depends upon the validity of Thiede's reconstruction of the existing text. If the unclear letters are identified differently, or the textual changes (discussed below) are disallowed, the results are altered accordingly. This is especially true for the letter *nu* identified by Thiede from the X-ray photograph. Others who have examined the enlarged photo have come to the opposite conclusion as Thiede. R.G. Jenkins, who has been working for some time on the Cave 7 fragments, studied the new photo and believes that the faint traces may be nothing more than a shadow. T.C. Skeat, an experienced papyrologist, also examined the photo and concluded that there was not sufficient room for a *nu* in the line. He also concluded that the next letter was most likely a damaged Greek letter *alpha*, which would further eliminate the possibility of Thiede's reconstruction.[62]

Therefore, if the letter in line 2 is not a *nu*, then the fragment will not fit the text of Mark, and as longtime opponent of this position Gordon Fee, who also looked at the photo, stated, Thiede's case is totally disproved.[63]

2. The identification of *7Q5* with Mark 6:52-53 requires two textual variants, a significant amount for a short fragment. These variants are the substitution in line 2 of the Greek letter *tau* ("t") in *7Q5* for the Greek letter *delta* ("d"), and the omission in line 3 of the Greek phrase *epi ten gen* ("to land"). In the first instance, while there are examples of such letter interchanges, in the case of *tia* for *dia* in *7Q5* there is no semantic overlap (as exists in all other such cases), and in fact *tia* is not even a word.[64] While it could be an example of misspelling, the preposition *dia* is so common a word that it renders this explanation improbable.

In the second instance, the omission is made in the reconstruction because there is not enough room for it in line 4. However, to insert it there would make the line nine letters too long for the appropriate stichometric (average length of a reconstructed line) letter count. While previously unattested readings are sometimes found in New Testament manuscripts, this phrase occurs in very well known ancient Greek manuscripts of Mark, including early translations into other languages.[65]

3. The gap before the *kai* ("and") has no clear significance and may not have been an intentional space to indicate any grammatical break.[66] In addition, only one word is clearly discernible—*kai*—and only six letters are undisputed· *to* (line 2), *t* (line 3, after *kai*), *ne* (line 4), and *e* (line 5). There is also, in addition, the problem of the questionable reconstruction of the other letters, which are significantly damaged and cannot be read with any degree of certainty.

### Counsel for the Controversy

Some form of contact between the members of the Qumran community and Jewish Christians before A.D. 68 is assumed by most Qumran scholars. In addition, a significant minority of New Testament scholars date much of the New Testament before A.D. 70. And it is also possible that someone without any link to the Qumran community could have stored Scrolls in Cave 7 after A.D. 68. For these reasons it is not improbable that portions of the New Testament could have somehow ended up in a Qumran settlement cave.[67] The problem, of course, is that the Cave 7 fragments themselves do not provide us with clear evidence. Before we take sides in the debate, then, we should consider this admonition from Daniel Wallace:

> I find it disturbing that many conservatives have been so uncritically eager to accept the O'Callaghan hypothesis. *7Q5*

does not, as one conservative put it, mean "that seven tons of German scholarship may now be consigned to the flames" [cf. "Eyewitness *Mark*?" *Time* magazine, May 1, 1972, p. 54]. On the other hand, I find it equally disturbing that many liberal scholars have uncritically rejected O'Callaghan's proposal without even examining the evidence. . . . Both attitudes, in their most extreme forms, betray an arrogance, an unwillingness to learn, a fear of the truth while clinging to tradition, a fortress mentality—none of which is in the spirit of genuine biblical scholarship.[68]

At present the evidence is too tenuous to side with O'Callaghan and Thiede. Matters, however, remain inconclusive, and as Alan Johnson has poignantly stated, "The jury is still out and may be hung indefinitely."[69]

It was once hoped that new evidence might be forthcoming from Cave 7. In 1991, Dr. Yitzhak Magen, the area official in charge of all excavations in Judea and Samaria for the Israel Antiquities Authority, seemed to promise a reexamination of the site "in the near future."[70] However, archaeologists such as Hanan Eshel, who knows the area well, contends that there is not enough of Cave 7 left to warrant such an attempt. So it seems that the scholars will have to resolve the debate based on the scant fragments at hand. We can only hope that we will not have to wait another 20 years!

# PART III

## What Do the
## Scrolls Teach?

# 2

# THE DOCTRINE OF THE SCROLLS

*The Dead Sea Sect . . . was the only group within Second Temple Judaism to develop a systematic theology . . . a system which later influenced the history of all mankind.*

—Professor David Flusser

Perhaps more than any other Jewish group in their time, the members of the Dead Sea Sect were a People of the Book. The abundance of biblical manuscripts found in the 11 caves at Qumran testify to this, as well as the many commentaries on the Bible that they wrote based on their study of and reflection on Scripture. The Scrolls bear their own witness to the community's devotion to the Bible in their primary sectarian document, the *Manual of Discipline*:

> And where the ten are, there shall never lack among them one
> who shall study the Law continually, day and night, concerning
> the right conduct of a man with his companion. And the

Congregation shall watch in community a third of every night
of the year, to read the Book and to study the Law and to pray
together (*1QS* 6:6-8).

Because the people at Qumran majored on the biblical text, we can
expect that their unique society and apocalyptic expectations were built
upon concise concepts from Scripture. Professor David Flusser affirms
this when he states:

One of the major tasks of Scroll research is to study the spiritual doctrine of this wonderful Sect. A perusal shows the Sect's
doctrine to be as homogeneous as is possible. Before us is a
knowingly defined discipline of thought. . . . The Sect's religious
doctrinization is consistent also in that it represents a homogeneous philosophy, the principles of which are found in the theological chapter of the *Manual of Discipline*. From within this
particular religious outlook the Sect set up a definite theological terminology.[1]

What were the doctrines that permitted this developed theological perspective?[2] When we ask this question we must first qualify our sources
for this information, for while we have entitled this chapter "The *Doctrine
of* the Dead Sea Scrolls," this is a misnomer, for not all of the Scrolls
belonged to the Sect nor shaped their theology. In actuality, it might be
more accurate to entitle this section "The *Doctrines in* the Dead Sea
Scrolls." Professor Talmon touches on this when he says:

When one sits down and asks questions [about their leaders
and those they confronted] one comes to the conclusion that
there must have been many more diversifications even within
that movement, over half a millennia. There were those that
adjusted their ideas to the major stream of their group and to the
changing situations, and in this process there may have also been
individuals within the stream like we have in the biblical days.[3]

For this reason, scholars have refined their views to distinguish
between documents that actually may have influenced the Sect and
documents that reflected the theologies of other Jewish groups and
were simply collected by the community.

# Discerning the Doctrines
# of the Dead Sea Sect

James H. Charlesworth has offered a sevenfold caution for those who endeavor to study the doctrines of the Scrolls.[4] These guidelines are designed to help the modern student approach the Qumran literature selectively and develop a "Qumran theology" rather than a "Scroll theology," which was the approach used by earlier scholars and writers. These criteria are as follows:

1. *The Old Testament Pseudepigrapha are not from Qumran.* Although they represent the theological views of other contemporaneous Jewish groups, several were important to the formation of the Sect's beliefs: *Jubilees, 1 Enoch,* and early versions of the *Testaments of the Twelve Patriarchs.*

2. *Some Scrolls originated outside the Qumran community, but may have been edited at Qumran.* These documents may reflect ideas that antedate the founding of the community and may or may not reflect their own doctrinal views. Among these are included the *Damascus Document* and the *Temple Scroll.*

3. *Some Scrolls originated outside the community and were not edited at Qumran.* These documents should not be used in developing a Qumran theology because they may not reflect the Sect's actual beliefs. Among these are the *Pseudepigraphic Psalms (4Q380-381),* the *Prayer of Joseph (4Q371-372),* and *Second Ezekiel (4Q385-389).* Charlesworth had also included the *Copper Scroll* in this list. However, both the identification of Scrolls hidden with the *Copper Scroll* (assuming they were hidden contemporaneously) and the recent confirmation by Eshel and Broshi (see chapter 20) of trails leading from Khirbet Qumran to the area of the caves (where Cave 3 of the *Copper Scroll* is located) imply a connection with the Qumran Sect. Therefore, the *Copper Scroll* should be allowed as a witness to their views (see chapter 12).

4. *Scrolls composed at Qumran must be the focus of Qumran theology.* These are the foundational documents known as the sectarian Scrolls: The *Rule of the Community (1QS),* the *Rule of the Congregation (1QS^a), Rule of Benediction (1QS^b),* the *War Scroll (1QM),* the *Thanksgiving Hymns (1QH),* the *Angelic Liturgy*

(*4W400-407*), and the *Persharim* (especially *1QpHab, 4QpNah, 1QpPs68*).

5. *There is no single Qumran theology.* Just as many scholars now contend that there was no mainstream or normative Judaism during the Second Temple period, so also at Qumran there was no single theology that characterized all the members of the community. Although we often contrast the Sect with the rest of Judaism because they followed a solar calendar instead of a lunar one, the Sect's calendar was actually luni-solar. This is still significantly different from the strictly lunar calendar of the Jerusalem Temple, but the use of a luni-solar calendar shows that various theological views were tolerated in the community. Other examples of differences in doctrine might be seen in the expectation of a single or dual Messiah(s) and in differing explanations for double predestination.

6. *Qumran theologies held certain convictions in common.* Despite the lack of a single theology, there were doctrinal distinctives that united the Sect. Some of these were the same distinctives that united all Jews: belief in one God (Deuteronomy 6:4), the authority of the Mosaic Law (Exodus), and a messianic expectation (Deuteronomy 18:15). Other doctrinal distinctives were shared with other groups in Judaism: a cosmic dualism, a developed angelology, and belief in miracles/resurrection. Still other doctrines made the Qumran group a separatist community: an inspired prophet/Teacher, an intermittent angelic presence in the community, an eschatological imminency, and a predestinarian perspective.

7. *The coherence of Qumran theologies does not lie in disparate concepts.* Even though we will attempt to examine the community's doctrinal concepts in individual categories, the ideal method of understanding these doctrines is to consider the context in which they appear, and then look at their related expression throughout the foundational documents.

With these guidelines to help us, let us proceed to a survey of the Sect's historical origin. This will help put the group's beliefs into perspective.

# The Historical Origin of the Sect

Although in chapter 5 I concluded that there was insufficient evidence at present to precisely identify the Sect with a known historical movement, here I offer some thoughts toward a historical reconstruction of their movement. Doing this would be a contradiction if my purpose was to tie specific historical events and personages to events and unnamed figures in the Scrolls. Yet this is not the purpose, for such a practice is uncertain because we have only one text to date that actually mentions a person by name—King Jonathan (*Prayer for King Jonathan, 4Q448*). Even here we have yet another debate—whether this is Jonathan the brother of Judah the Maccabee or Alexander Jannaeus ("Jannaeus" being a shortened Greek form of the Hebrew *Yonathan*). Nevertheless, we can make some very general deductions about the historical origin of the Sect by looking first at the datable period of the Scrolls (those from the last half of the second century B.C.–first half of the first century A.D.), and then working our way back to the formative events that preceded this period.

Sectarianism, in the Second Temple period, finds its origin from the very time the Babylonian exiles began their return to Judah. From the biblical books that chronicle this return and resettlement (Ezra, Nehemiah, Haggai, Zechariah, Malachi) we learn of the deplorable spiritual conditions that existed. First, it must be remembered that only 50,000 of the most committed Jewish families (that is, "whose spirit God had stirred to go up") returned under the edict of Cyrus (Ezra 1:5; cf. 2:1-70). The majority of the Jewish exiles chose to continue living in Egypt and Babylon. For the new generations of Jews that had been born in exile, these lands were home, and the land of Israel was an unknown place—the ruined homeland of their ancestors. Much like many of the Diaspora Jews today, the exiled Jews of that time felt secure in the world they knew and weren't as eager to revive the past, a mission better left to the religious zealots and fervent Zionists.

These sentiments were experienced not only in the exilic community, but also the post-exilic community. Among the people who returned to the Land, two groups became evident: one comprised of the returnees and the resident Jewish population who had remained separate from pagan assimilation (Ezra 6:21), and one comprised of those who had not. Some of the violations committed by the latter group included idolatrous marriages (Ezra 9:1-4), Sabbath-breaking (Nehemiah 13:16), spiritual apathy and personal indulgence to the exclusion of religious obligation (Haggai 1:3-11), and various social and spiritual abominations (Malachi 1:6–2:17; 3:7-15). Life in the Land from 1,000–597 B.C. (the period of the monarchy) was a life lived in relation to the land, which was a symbol of the life of blessing (Deuteronomy 26:9). At stake was the spiritual and social quality of life (that is, blessing) which could be experienced only through a proper relationship with God through the covenant (Deuteronomy 8:6-18; cf. Jeremiah 2:7).[5] Therefore, the Temple, which enforced and regulated the terms of the covenant, was necessary to any restoration program. The fact that most of the sins committed by the post-exilic community were in relation to the Temple and its services impressed the faithful remnant with the unsettling conviction that the restoration promised by the prophets would not occur with their generation.

Although a renewal of the covenant took place after the exiles returned (Ezra 3:10; Nehemiah 9:38), that renewal was practiced only by a remnant of the people in the post-exilic community. Those who didn't practice this renewal were threatened with exclusion from the assembly of exiles (Ezra 10:8), but it is not clear if this threat was enforced to any degree. Thus, a spiritual and social crisis continued that schismatically separated those of the "renewed covenant" from the less committed people in the community. Crisis became conflict when Antiochus IV Epiphanes imposed Hellenistic policies and established a Hasmonean state where rulers usurped the high priestly office or appointed an illegitimate priesthood. During this period *Hasidic* groups began to multiply; these groups were characterized by their strict observance of the Law and apocalyptic interpretation of prophecy.[6] The internal schism that had been present from the time the exiles returned was now evidenced in external sectarianism. From the groups that broke with the established leadership in Jerusalem came those who would eventually withdraw from Jerusalem to the desert, start a settlement at Qumran, call themselves the "Community of the Renewed Covenant," and preserve and pass on to the world the Dead Sea Scrolls.

### Their Proximity to Other Groups

Moving from the historical roots of the Dead Sea movement, let us now consider some important aspects of the Qumran community to set a context for their beliefs. First, the Qumran community was not as isolated as has been often believed. Even though the settlement was situated on a remote plateau overlooking the Dead Sea, the people were still only a few hours' walk from Jericho and just one day's journey from Jerusalem. So they were somewhat secluded, but they were also able to keep in contact with the Holy City (and if they were Essenes, keep in touch with their friends and families in the Essene Quarter). This proximity to other Jewish groups and frequent contact with them affected to some degree the Sect's theological outlook. Professor Talmon, understanding the broader context of the Sect, remarks:

> I object to the term Qumran community. That community was only the spearhead of a much larger movement. They speak of what they have in towns where their families resided. So we go wrong from the beginning by presenting that settlement, which was permanent but had a changing population of about 200 men, as representing what is called the Qumran community.[7]

### Membership in the Community

Membership in the Qumran community was on a contractual and voluntary basis. The people called themselves "volunteers" (*mitnaddebim*) in a proud fashion not unlike the Zionist "Pioneers" who voluntarily resettled in Palestine in the early part of this century to reclaim it as 'Eretz-Yisrael (the "Land of Israel"). We also get an idea of how they viewed themselves as separatists by the names they used for themselves: the "Elect," the "Remnant," "the Assembly" (or "Congregation"), and the "Men of the Renewed Covenant." The principal designation they used for themselves was *Yahad*, which Professor Talmon has demonstrated is a noun, drawn from biblical usage, and used with the meaning "assembly" or "congregation," but often translated as "the community." The Hebrew root has the basic idea of "one," with a stress on "exclusive oneness" or "unity." In this sense the term may underscore the Sect's united stance as an assembly. This name was probably inspired by the passage in Deuteronomy 33:5, which contains the phrase "the tribes of Israel united" (*yahad shibte Yisra'el*).[8]

What was the size of the Qumran Sect's membership? Over the hundreds of years that the Sect existed, did it experience considerable growth from new converts or did it limit its membership to a set number? Some of these questions cannot be answered with certainty; however, the approximate size of the Sect can be determined by measuring their main places of assembly. Dr. Magen Broshi, the former curator of the Shrine of the Book, comments on this procedure:

My way of computing the number of the people living there is to compute how many people could seat in the dining hall and the refactory, as this was a central activity of the community. The room which is almost a thousand square feet could seat between 120 to 150 people. That is the maximum. If they had had more people they would have enlarged it, but they didn't need to.[9]

It was this small group of priests who daily assembled, studied, discussed, dined together, and prayed. When they met with others from the council of the community, they met in a minimum quorum of ten (a *minyan*) and always with a priest (see *1QS* 6:2-4; *CD* 13:1-2; *1QS*ᵃ 2:22). They also observed the Sabbaths, feasts, and rituals according to their unique calendar, and may have also performed secret rites unique to their Sect (see *4Q512*). They accepted new initiates, but only after a prolonged and much-supervised probationary period. Their community was communal, but not monastic, and there is evidence that some men had wives and children who lived in camps nearby.[10] The limestone caves in the cliffs were used to store goods and Scrolls, while the caves on the marl terrace of the plateau were used for living quarters. Yet despite the strict discipline exercised by the Sect and the regularity of its rituals and lifestyle, significant (and expected) changes occurred in the community during its life span, which, according to Talmon, spanned from 400 B.C.–A.D. 70-100. These changes, too, affected the doctrinal view of the Sect.

## The Catalyst for Change

The changes that took place in the Qumran community were perhaps more the result of failed expectation than of historical consequence. The one known historical consequence to the community was the earthquake of 31 B.C., which ended the first phase of settlement. However, this displacement was only temporary and soon the community rebuilt the settlement and continued as before. There is no evidence that this historical event caused any internal or interpretive change in the group. On the other hand, when the timetable of their calculated eschatology was upset, change was inevitable. Professor Talmon explains:

> In the development of the movement, I see two stages. When you look at the beginning of the *Zadokite Fragment* it seems that at first this was a quietist millenarian movement. Everything was foreseen and divinely ordained, so they sat back and let

history unfold. The expectation was that 390 years after the destruction of the Temple, as Ezekiel had foreseen, the world would change and a new world would come. But this didn't happen and they complained bitterly about it. They tell us that it [the failure of fulfillment] was their fault. They were still sinners, they had not fully repented. Then the Legitimate Teacher came along and told them why things did not change. He arose because of the internal pressure and the disillusion that took hold of them. His task was to structure this group into a community in order to survive the interval between the now and the then [the eschaton]. No structure was needed while they were awaiting the determined moment, but when the moment didn't arrive the only way to survive was by structuring the group anew. Therefore the *Zadokite Fragments* contain a wealth of new regulations that go beyond the biblical regulations, even concerning family life. This is completely different from what I would have expected in a group that says tomorrow everything is going to change.

The result was what I would describe as an anarchistic movement, which brought about a militant messianism, instead of the quietist millenarianism of before. Now they have to interfere, to take part in bringing about, or trying to bring about, the new world as with Isaiah 40:[3]: "to clear the way for God," to bring in the new age. That is why they went into the desert. So this was an active participation in helping God to unfold history as He had promised to do previously without their interference. There they remained standing on the threshold of the messianic age but never past this threshold.[11]

## The End of the Qumran Sect

From this last stage the Sect continued in stasis until it was disbanded or destroyed. The majority view among scholars is that the members of the Sect were forced to hurriedly hide their property, including the Scrolls, when the Roman army came to attack the community in A.D. 68. Unable to return to their settlement because it was turned into a Roman garrison, the remaining members joined with other Jewish refugees (Essenes, if this theory is accepted) or became exiles in other lands. In this case the Sect was, for all practical purposes, destroyed. Another view is that the Scrolls were systematically and intentionally hidden over a period of time as a means of archival storage, possibly because the community was slowly dying and felt it was necessary to preserve its documentary heritage.[12] In this case the Sect was dismantled as a result of internal changes or defections deemed too great to maintain the community.

# The Doctrinal Views at Qumran

## *Predestination*

The Qumranic teaching on predestination is considered the most distinguishing of the Sect's doctrines. This is because it cannot be traced in the same form to any other Jewish Sect except the Essenes (Josephus, *Antiquities* 13.171-173), unless it be identified with the sect, and Jewish-Christianity (if predestination is accepted in the New Testament).[13] Most scholars deny that the concept of predestination was developed from the Old Testament; thus they believe that the New Testament references to predestination were influenced by the Scrolls. However, predestination *is* found in the Old Testament, especially with respect to Israel (election) and her adversaries (divine hardening).[14] This should be seen as the common source for both the Qumranic and Christian formulation of the doctrine.

At Qumran there were strict and moderate views of predestination. The strict form, which is usually viewed as deterministic, is most prominently expressed in the *Rule of the Community*, the *War Scroll*, and the *Thanksgiving Hymns*, although other texts such as the *Ages of Creation* (*4Q180*) also speak of the ages as predestined (1.1-2; 2.10 2-4). We find the most thorough presentation on predestination in the *Thanksgiving Hymns*, and Eugene Merrill, who has done the most extensive study of the doctrine in this document, lists three principal passages for treating the subject systematically: *1QH* 1:7-31; 3:19-25; and 15:12-22.[15] In one of these we read this about man's foreordination:

> You have apportioned it to all their (mankind's) seed for eternal generations and everlasting years. . . . In the wisdom of Your knowledge You have established their destiny before ever they were. All things [exist] according to [Your will] and without You nothing is done (*1QH* 1:18-20).

### *The Strict View of Predestination*

In the *Thanksgiving Scroll* we also find the strictest view of predestination. Here we learn that man's entire existence is sovereignly governed by God (*1QH* 15:13,22), and that man is dependent upon the divine will for all his works (*1QH* 10:5-7). Free will is excluded, because God Himself determined men's thoughts (*1QH* 9:12,30) and established his activities from creation (*1QH* 1:7).

In the strict view, mankind was divided into two groups: the elect, who belonged to God and for whom there was salvation (*1QH* 2:13; 6:6); and the ungodly (*1QH* 14:21), who were allied with Belial to war against the elect (*1QH* 2:22, 5:7,9, 25). The salvation of the elect was said to be predetermined (*1QH* 2:20; 5:18): "You alone have [cre]ated the righteous and from the womb You have predestined him for the appointed time of Your choice" (*1QH* 15:14). All repentance and atonement was therefore subject to the individual's predetermined status rather than to a decisive act of the human will (*1QH* 6:8), so that only the elect were able to repent, receive forgiveness (*1QH* 12:11-13), and be cleansed of their guilt (*1QH* 3:1). Because of their status, they alone were privileged to understand something of the divine plan through the revelation of His mysteries (*1QS* 4:2-6). Only the elect received spiritual insight for discerning the times and properly sanctifying themselves as the righteous remnant (*1QH* 11:10-12; 12:20).

The final fate of the wicked was also predetermined:

> You have created the evildoers for [the periods of] Your [wr]ath, and from the womb You have set them aside for the day of slaughter, for they have walked in a path which is not good, and they have despised Yo[ur] covenant (*1QH* 15:15-18).

Thus the wicked didn't repent (nor could they repent) of their transgressions, for their lot was to follow Belial into the judgment appointed for him. This presents a form of "double predestination" (supposedly symmetrical) in which God has apportioned out the creation for an ongoing conflict to His greater glory (*1QH* 1:8-16; 11:25). This double predestination becomes even more pronounced in the doctrine of the "two spirits," found in the *Rule of the Community*. Here it is taught that God gave each of the divisions of mankind a "spirit of truth" to enable the elect to serve God, and a "spirit of iniquity" or "perversity" to dominate the desires of the evildoers and align them against God and the elect. Every transgression in the righteous is a result of this spirit (externally) as is every wickedness of the ungodly (internally). A few selections from the *Rule of the Community* help to make these perspectives clearer:

He (God) put into them two spirits that they should walk according to them until the time of His visitation: they are the spirits of truth and iniquity. The origin of truth is a fountain of light, and the origin of iniquity is a source of darkness. Dominion over all the sons of light is in the hand of the Prince of Light; they walk in paths of light. But in the hand of the Angel of Darkness is all the dominion of the sons of iniquity; they walk in paths of darkness.... By these the generations [walk] of all the sons of man; by their divisions all their hosts inherit a share from age to age. In their paths they walk, and all the reward of their deeds is according to the divisions of (these two spirits).... For God has set these (two spirits) with equal influence until the end-time and has put eternal hatred between their divisions ... that they may know good [and evil, that] lots may be cast for every creature according to his spirit within [him until the season for vis]itation (*1QS* 3:15-20; 4:26).

## The Moderate View of Predestination

The Qumran group also taught a more moderate view of predestination. With more of an emphasis on foreknowledge than foreordination and preterition rather than reprobation, we read in the *Damascus Document* concerning the destination of the wicked:

They will have no remnant nor survivor. For from the beginning God chose them not; He knew their deeds before they were ever created and hated their generations, and He hid His face from the Land until they were consumed. For He knew the years of their coming and the length and exact duration of their times for all ages to come and throughout eternity. He knew the happenings of their times throughout all the everlasting years (*CD* 2:6-10).

In a similar fashion throughout the *War Scroll*, the tenor of the text is that the outcome of the 40-year war has been foreknown and is part of the divine plan. And passages in some texts emphasize the individual's (free?) choice and responsibility: "... they became as though they had not been, through doing their own will and not keeping the commandment of the Maker" (*CD* 2:20-21). In like manner, the judgment of the pre-exilic community was brought on by their own actions—their violations against the covenant—bringing about the destruction of the First Temple:

> . . . the members of the first covenant became guilty and were given over to the sword when they forsook the covenant of God and chose their own desire and went about after the stubbornness of their hearts by doing each man his own desire (*CD* 3:10-12).

Both divine determinism and human responsibility were part of the Qumran predestination doctrine. Holding to both of these concepts required a willingness to maintain a theological tension, and this apparently was done. Thus, the doctrine of predestination, whether in its strict or moderate form, was a defining characteristic of the Sect, governing its overall theology. We will see this next as we see how predestination is related to the Sect's gift of the Spirit to perceive divine revelation and continue the inspired interpretation of the prophets, the assurance of repentance and proper sanctity leading to salvation, and the guarantee that history is proceeding toward its eschatological consummation as predicted in the Scriptures.

### The Spirit

Most scholars would agree that the idea of the Spirit as a distinct being, as implied in the Old Testament (cf. Isaiah 48:16), is not present at Qumran. Rather, the "Spirit" is seen as a power granted by God to perform a certain act or in connection with God's saving activity (but cf. *4Q521* 1.2 where the Spirit is said to "hover over the poor" in language reminiscent of Genesis 1:2). According to the *Rule of the Community* and the *Thanksgiving Hymns*, the Holy Spirit (or "Spirit of Holiness") operated in three ways at Qumran. First, it was bestowed as a divine gift from creation (*1QS* 9:12; *1QH* 9:32; 15; cf. *4Q186*). This, as we have seen earlier, is depicted as a predestined act whereby the "spirit of truth" or "spirit of iniquity" has been allotted to humanity and thus controls them respectively as "sons of righteousness" and "sons of wickedness" (*1QS* 3:13–4:26).[16] In this sense, those who have the Spirit have had it since birth. Second, the Spirit was imparted when initiates joined the community (*1QH* 13:19; 16:11; 17:17). That the Spirit was bestowed on the sectarian at birth and then also as an initiate are conflicting concepts. However, this is another example of how disparate doctrines (in this case, pneumatologies) existed together within the

Qumran community. Third, the Spirit was expected, based on the Old Testament prophets (see Joel 2:28-32), to be poured out fully during the end times (*1QS* 4:18-23). The text used in *1QS* 4:21 (cf. 3:7) to explain this eschatological outpouring is Ezekiel 36:25-26, which connects the removal of ritual desecration with the spiritual regeneration of the heart. A similar idea may be expressed in Jesus' connection of new birth by "water and the Spirit" (John 3:5), which, if it is an allusion to the Ezekiel text, may have the connotation of "cleansing Spirit."[17] There is, however, no connection between the gift of the Spirit and either the Qumran act of ritual purification or the Christian act of baptism.[18]

These three works of the Spirit, taken together, imply that the gift of the Spirit is a part of divine predestination, with a partial spiritual purification upon entrance into the Sect and a full purification poured out during the end times (*1QS* 4:20-21).

## The Spirit and Divine Inspiration

The Qumran community had as its unique claim the presence of the Spirit within its midst and especially within select individuals. This is evidenced by the use of the formula "the Spirit which You [God] placed in me" (see, for example, *1QH* 12:11; 13:19; 16:11; 17:17). Thus Arthur Sekki, who has carefully studied the function of the term *spirit* at Qumran, has concluded:

> The evidence, then, points to Qumran as an eschatologically oriented community which saw itself as the heir of God's eschatological Spirit and regarded this Spirit as the basis and source of its spirituality.[19]

According to the Qumran community, one special function of the indwelling Spirit was its service in divine inspiration. Other Jewish sects believed that the prophetic spirit had been withdrawn, and thus, divine revelation and inspiration had ceased with the destruction of the First Temple (see TB *Berakoth* 34b). The Qumran community, however, believed that because they were living in the last days, during which time prophecy was expected to be restored (see TB *Baba Metzia* 59b), this restoration had begun with some of their own leaders. The foundational documents, and especially the *Pesharim*, were believed to have been authored under the Spirit's agency. Such a conviction was acknowledged by the writer of the *Thanksgiving Hymns*:

> I have insight, I know You, my God, through the Spirit which
> You have given me, and what is sure I have heard in Your won-
> drous council. Through Your Holy Spirit You have opened to
> my innermost parts the knowledge of the mystery of Your insight
> (*1QH* 12:11-13).

The "Teacher of Righteousness" was said to have been given a more
significant presence of the Spirit to enable him to act in the role of a
prophet and to receive divine inspiration and infallible insight so he could
decisively interpret the Old Testament (*1QpHab* 2:5; 7:3-5). For this
reason, those who opposed the words of the Teacher opposed God:

> They did not believe when they heard all that which was
> hap[pening to] the last generation from the mouth of the priest
> (i.e., the Teacher) in whose [heart] God had put the [know]ledge
> to interpret all the words of His servants the prophets, [in who]se
> hands God recounted all that which was happening to His people
> and [to the nations] (*1QpHab* 2:6-10).

The Qumran Sect further believed that when God first revealed His
prophetic timetable to the prophets, they did not understand what they
had been told. The explanation of these prophecies awaited an interpreter who would be living in their time and whom God would then inspire
so he could explain the revelations. Thus the Teacher is seen as superior
to the biblical prophets because to him alone was granted the key to unlock
their mysterious prophecies. This concept is clearly set forth in the
*Habakkuk Commentary*:

> God told Habakkuk to write down the things that will happen
> to the last generation, but the end of that period He did not make
> known to him. . . . The interpretation of [Habakkuk 2:2] concerns
> the Teacher of Righteousness to whom God made known all the
> secrets of the words of His servants the prophets (*1QpHab* 7:1-5).

This divine inspiration also applied to the proper interpretation of the
Torah, by which means the authoritative *halakhic* system of the Sect was
derived. In the mind of the Sect, then, the gift of the Spirit and of prophecy
may have served to associate the Teacher with the coming Messiah. Scholar
Geza Vermes saw such an association in *1QpHab* 2:4 and *4QpPs37* based
on the Teacher's function as a representative of God.[20] Professor Talmon
has observed a similar example:

> I have a reference I have not yet published in a tenth-century
> Midrash where the *Moreh ha-Sedek* ["Teacher of Righteousness"]
> is mentioned for the first time in medieval literature. His task is
> to solve problems. It compares roughly to what is said about
> Elijah, who will come and answer all questions except the unan-
> swerable.[21]

The Teacher's function as both a prophet and priest was to serve as a messianic forerunner, after whom would come the Messiah. He would hold the position of "Interpreter of the Law" and would resolve all unsettled questions, including the unanswerable (*1QS* 9:11; cf. *CD* 7:18-21). This is seen in several texts where the Holy Spirit is associated with the Messiah either as the agent of anointing (*11QMelch* on Isaiah 52:7) or as that which rests upon Him and provides counsel and power (*4Q287* 3:13; *1QS^b* 5:25).

Thus, the Spirit was resident in the community and within leaders of the Sect, but was still to be experienced in a fuller and more extensive manner during the messianic age.

### Salvation

From the outset of the study of this doctrine in the Scrolls, scholars were impressed at the supposed departure from ancient Judaism and the affinities with Pauline Christianity.[22] The statements they examined seemed to be echoed in the Pauline epistles, especially the book of Romans.

However, as Lawrence Schiffman, a rabbi, has pointed out, "[The] notion of the lowly nature of flesh, although not emphasized in premedieval Jewish literature, was certainly present in early Jewish thought."[23] Also, it is unnecessary to seek any outside influence for the formation of the Sect's beliefs about salvation because there are abundant texts in the Old Testament that have almost identical terminology and intent.[24] Therefore, with the Scrolls we may have a window into the ancient interpretation of the Old Testament texts concerning salvation before a theological revision occurred within Judaism because of its conflict with Christianity. As we consider this doctrine, our progression of thought will start with man's condition, go on to the requirement of repentance, and finally, conclude with the divine act of justification.

## The Sinful Condition of Mankind

The *Thanksgiving Hymns* describe man in his natural frailty with a propensity to sin (*1QH* 38:29-31) and a destiny to return to the dust (*1QH* 46:31; 53:1,4; 54:4,11). Some of this language is designed to emphasize man's humble state as a created being (of "potter's clay") and to stress his inherent weakness in being so tied to the earth (see *1QH* 35:21-23; 38:29-31; 41:32; 44:3-4). Many times the contrast between human nature and the divine is made by the juxtaposition of the terms *flesh* and *spirit*.[25] However, other passages are quite forthright in their description of man, who is sinful by nature (*1QH* 1:21; 3:21), carnal (*1QH* 15:21; 18:23), has a perverted heart and spirit (*1QH* 3:21; 7:27), and has spiritually uncircumcised hearts and ears (*1QH* 18:4,20,24). He is "guilty of evil-doing from his mother's womb to old age" (*1QH* 4:27-30,35). Therefore, man cannot justify himself before God (*1QH* 1:25; 9:14-18), cannot answer God when rebuked (*1QH* 7:28), has no right before God (*1QH* 7:28; 9:14-18), cannot answer God when rebuked (*1QH* 7:28), and cannot comprehend nor proclaim God's glory (*1QH* 12:30).

## The Requirement of Repentance

This condition of man, as stated in the preceding verses, led the author of the *Thanksgiving Hymns* to confess that he had almost despaired of the hope of salvation, for "I remembered my guilt, with the iniquity of my fathers" (*1QH* 4:34; cf. 17:19). This weight of guilt that so crushed his spirit was elsewhere called "the first sin" (*1QH* 9:13). When the Sect's calculation of the 390 years of Ezekiel's prophecy failed, they identified themselves with their pre-exilic forefathers, who had also failed to experience the expected restoration, and blamed their own sinfulness. In keeping with their predestinarian perspective, the origin of their and all of humanity's transgressions is the "spirit of iniquity," the pervasive domination of the Angel of Darkness, and their ongoing struggle with the sons of light (*1QH* 3:13–4:26). The only remedy for this condition was repentance from sin, which was characterized as a dependence upon God for divine mercy in light of man's weakness and unworthiness. In the hymn that closes the *Rule of the Community* we find an example of such confession and contrition:

> As for me, I belong to wicked humanity, to the assembly of
> perverse flesh; my iniquities, my transgressions, my sins together
> with the wickedness of my heart belong to the assembly doomed

to worms and walking in darkness. No human being sets his own path or directs his own steps, for to God alone belongs the judgment of him, and from His hand comes perfection of way.... And I, if I stagger, God's grace is my salvation forever. If I stumble because of a sin of the flesh, my judgment is according to the righteousness of God, which stands forever.... In His righteous fidelity He has judged me; in His bounteous goodness He expiates all my iniquities, and in His righteousness He cleanses me of human defilement and of human sinfulness (*1QS* 11:9-14; cf. *1QH* 9:32-34).

Note here that the doctrine of predestination was the basis for the psalmist's assurance; only a God who controls and orders all things would be able to sovereignly pardon and restore His elect. Otherwise, salvation might not be forever, for if a man could determine his own destiny, nothing could be certain. Rather than being troubled that a man's will is coerced by not being free to "set his own path or direct his own steps," the psalmist takes comfort in the fact that the forgiveness he seeks does not depend on him, but on God. Despite his staggering and stumbling, God judges and expiates him on the basis of His own righteousness, not the psalmist's.

## Divine Justification for Salvation

In the last column of the *Rule of the Community* we read, "For as for me, my justification belongs to God" (*1QS* 11:2). While many of the foundational Scrolls describe justification as based on God's mercy, goodness, righteousness, and grace, other texts (if we can include them) speak of a justification through the "works of the Law." One such text, which has been considered a foundational document of the Sect, is the *Halakhic Letter* (*4QMMT*). In this document we read of the connection between "works of the Law" and "justification":

> ... we have written to you some of the *works of the Law* which we consider were good for your people, [for we have seen] that you have wisdom and knowledge of the Torah. Understand all these (matters) and seek from Him that He correct your counsel and distance from you evil thoughts and the counsel of Belial, in order that you shall rejoice in the end when you find some of our own words true. It will thus be *imputed to you as righteousness* that you did what was right and good before Him, for your own good and for the good of Israel (*4Q397* 26-32, emphasis added).

In this example, justification is forensic (legal), but it comes on the basis of a person's actions rather than solely by the grace of God, and certainly not by the Pauline concept of "faith alone." There is in the Qumran sense of justification a *halakhic* path that leads to righteousness, even though God graciously chooses to make justification available because no works are acceptable before Him due to man's condition. Schiffman softens the statement above when he translates it, "And let it be considered *right for you, and lead you to do righteousness and good*, and may it be for your benefit, and for that of Israel."[26] Nevertheless, it seems that a qualification for understanding the salvation of the elect at Qumran, of which justification was an ordained part, depended on having a special understanding of the Law and adhering to it faithfully.

## The End Times

Because we will examine the Sect's eschatological views in depth in the next five chapters, we'll concentrate here on the Sect's concept of the end-time war and the army against which it would do battle.

### The End-Time 40-Year War

According to the Sect, a great eschatological war had to occur before the conclusion of the age of wickedness and the beginning of the age of redemption. This war, called the "revenge of God" (*1QS* 1:10), would last for 40 years, the length of an average generation, during which time there would be alternating periods of respite from battle in order to observe proper ritual (*4QpIsa*[a] 7-10; 22-25; *4QIsa*[b] 2:1; *4QCantena*[b] 3:7-8). The war would be between both the cosmic powers (God and Belial [Satan]) and the terrestrial armies of the wicked ("Sons of Darkness") and the righteous ("Sons of Light").

This war, which will "shake the foundations of the universe" and be climaxed with lightning (*4Q558*) is the main theme of the *War Scroll* (which combines military tactics and spiritual warfare), the fragment known as the *War Rule* (*4Q285*), *Blessings* (*11Q14*), and the *Aramaic Apocalypse* designated as *4Q246*. The battle moves from a time of birth pangs to deliverance in the age of redemption (*1QH* 3:7-10). The battle is waged against Gog and Magog (Ezekiel 38:1–39:20)—an alliance of evildoers from the Gentile nations and the rebellious Jews, all of whom are backed by Belial and his evil spirits. Elements of Daniel's description of the evil rulers who will invade Israel are also models for the battle and its characters.

The *War Scroll* gives explicit instructions to the priests and Levites about marshalling and exhorting them in the battle (*1QM* 5:3–6:6; 7:9–9:9). The camp of the "Sons of Light" is to be arranged according to the instructions given in Numbers 2:15:4, and they are said to be led by the archangelic warriors Michael (the "Angel/Prince of Light," *1QM* 17:6-8), Raphael, and Sariel (*1QM* 9:15-16; cf. *4Q285* 1:9-10; *11Q14* 1-2, 13-14). The Scrolls speak of these angels in the camp, and supposedly this was a sign to the Sect of both angelic protection and the nearness of the approaching conflict. It was because of the angels' predicted presence in the great war that strict laws of purity were to be enforced within the military camp (see Deuteronomy 23:10-15). In the final battle, these forces would be joined by Elijah (*4Q521*) and the Davidic Messiah, the "Prince of the Congregation," who would direct the assault and finally destroy the enemy (*4Q285* 4:2-5; 5:1-5; cf. *1QM* 13:10-12).

## The End-Time Army of the Kitti'im

The Scrolls frequently refer to an end-time army called the *Kitti'im*. This term is apparently derived from the Greek word *Kition*, which was used as the name of a town located on the southeastern coast of Cyprus (modern-day Larnaka). This usage is consistent with what we find in the Old Testament prophets, where the word denotes the Gentile people of the far western Mediterranean "coasts" (Jeremiah 2:10). In 1 Maccabees (1:1; 8:5) the term is used to designate the Macedonian Greeks. However, it is the prophet Daniel who provided the word its eschatological context. Daniel makes reference to "the ships of the Kittim" that will come against a wicked oppressor of Israel (Daniel 11:30). The historical oppressor Daniel wrote of was probably Antiochus IV Epiphanes, the Greco-Syrian ruler who was thwarted in his invasion of Egypt by the Romans in 170 B.C. (see Polybius' *History* 29.27). Antiochus, angry about this encounter, returned to Israel to impose more stringent enforcement of his Hellenizing policies, an act which translated into persecution for religious Jews. Yet Daniel chapter 11 also portrays an end-time oppressor, typified by Antiochus, who will desecrate the Temple and ultimately be brought to an end himself (verses 36-45). Based on Daniel's usage of Kittim in an eschatological context, the interpreters of the end time at Qumran measured the future in light of their present circumstances. They saw the Wicked Priest—who had abandoned God for riches (*1QpHab* 8:8-11), persecuted the Qumran community, and even disrupted the Sect's own Day of Atonement (*1QpHab* 11:5-8)—as typical of those who would desecrate Jerusalem at the end of days. Thus, the Roman occupiers (as the Gentile remnant) would fulfill their eschatological role by despoiling these wicked priests through their invading army (*1QHab* 9:4-7; cf. *4QpNah* 1:11).

## From Doctrine to Prophecy

The Dead Sea Sect had a unique theology developed from the Old Testament and the Jewish apocalyptic literature and largely controlled by their overarching concern for the imminent advent of the messianic era. Now that we have seen how some of the doctrinal views of the Sect relate to the theme of prophecy, let us in the next number of chapters explore the intricate eschatology that so defined them and continues to excite biblical students as they seek to discern the nearness of the final hour.

# 10

# PROPHECY AND THE SCROLLS

*From the very beginning of the study of the Dead Sea Scrolls, it has been clear that the documents of the Qumran Sect place great emphasis on eschatology.*

—Dr. Lawrence Schiffman

Perhaps you've heard the whimsical proverb, "It is difficult to prophesy, especially about the future!" No Sect of the Second Temple period embodied this verse better than the writers of the Dead Sea Scrolls. They were first and foremost students of prophecy, laboring with difficulty to discern their days in an age of people that had lost the power to prophesy. In fact, the Qumran community bears the distinction of being classified as "the most decidedly millenarian or chiliastic movement in Second Temple Judaism and possibly in antiquity altogether, Christianity included.[1] As such, their apocalyptic literature[2] offers us an unparalleled glimpse into the eschatological perspectives of that day. The Sect's interest in prophecy is affirmed by what books they chose for commentary, the very books that formed the perspective and practice of the Sect. As Professor Shemaryahu Talmon observes:

> We have indications of the trust they put in biblical prophecy and of their preference regarding this or that prophet. For instance, we have the remnants of over ten copies of the book of Isaiah; more than any other prophet. This book obviously must have been important to them. The [book of] Ezekiel also played an important role, and on it they built their own interpretation of history. For example, the *War Scroll* clearly is based on the story of the battle of Gog of Magog in Ezekiel [38–39]. They included Daniel, not as one of the writings, but as a prophet.[3]

The emphasis on interpreting prophecy is most obvious in the sectarian writings that formed the core of the community's beliefs. In surveying the continuous commentaries, those that contain verse-by-verse interpretations of the text, 100 percent are on the biblical prophets: six on Isaiah; three on the Psalms (since they considered David a prophet, *11QPs*[a] 27.11); two each on Hosea, Micah, and Zephaniah; and one each on Nahum and Habakkuk. Isaiah was especially prominent as a prophecy text, and its marginal markings reveal how highly it was regarded as a source of messianic prophecy. Since the prophetic views of the community were so pronounced and serve to characterize them in respect to other Jewish sects, it is important that we consider them in depth. In addition, both in method and interpretation, Qumran eschatology resembles the prophetic perspectives of some Christian groups.[4] This is not surprising because the framework of Qumran eschatology is the Old Testament, and the Sect developed within Second Temple Judaism as did early Jewish Christianity. So by coming to understand the prophetic perspective of the Dead Sea Sect, we can gain insights about the eschatology of the New Testament.

## The Prophetic Perspective at Qumran

The prophetic perspective of most of the major sects of Judaism during the Second Temple period was that inspired prophetic interpretation like that of the biblical prophets was no longer possible. Only books written in Hebrew and certified to have been authored before the cessation of prophecy with the latter prophets (thought to have occurred in the late Persian period around 150 B.C.) were considered part of the biblical canon of the Hebrew Scriptures. No books written in Greek or written after the incursion of Hellenism could qualify. Books written in Hebrew which claimed pseudonymously to be ascribed to a biblical author were rejected simply because they sought candidacy into the canon after it was closed. If a book was written in Hebrew but its biblical status was uncertain, it was rejected. Even books that were written in Hebrew and ascribed to the biblical period yet were inconsistent with the rabbis' accepted *halakhic* teachings were excluded.[5]

## A Prophetic Continuity

Even though the Sect followed the prevailing belief that the gift of prophecy had been lost in their day, they did not believe that prophecy had been lost to them. At the same time that they awaited the universal renewal of prophecy as a sign of the coming age of redemption (*IQS* 9:10-11), they also maintained a prophetic continuity with the biblical prophets. This took the form, as Gershon Biran notes, of appointing themselves "as the living substitute for the defunct office of the prophet."[6] Though with the Jews of their day they awaited the return of the messianic Prophet, the Dead Sea Sect considered their own Teacher of Righteousness a present prophet whose understanding of the ages superseded that of the earlier prophets. Thus the Qumran Sect viewed itself as uniquely the recipient of men who were inspired by the Spirit to interpret the future divine program.[7] German Scroll scholar Annette Steudel[8] has pointed out that this was because they saw themselves as the Israel of the last days. As a result, Old Testament prophecies (and also some apocryphal and pseudepigraphal texts) that spoke of the last days were interpreted by the Sect as applying to them and their time.

In addition, new prophetic texts were produced by the community, and special prophetic guidance was provided by their inspired Teacher of Righteousness, who in messianic fashion was to teach righteousness at the end of days.[9] In the *Pesher Habakkuk* it is declared that the Teacher received special revelation from God concerning "all the secrets of the words of His servants, the prophets" (*1QpHab* 7.4-5). The Teacher was described as one who wore the mantle of the *maskilim* (the "wise ones" of the book of Daniel). He was especially gifted with prophetic insight to interpret accurately the hidden mysteries of the apocalyptic announcements concerning the land of Israel and the people of God (*1QpHab* 2.8-10). In fact, they perceived that the biblical prophets had lacked the insight to understand their own predictions (see 1 Peter 1:10-12). Such insight had been reserved for their Teacher, who, as God's inspired interpreter at the end of the present age, was able to unravel the agenda set for the Age to Come. There is also mention of a figure known as "the Interpreter of the Law" (*doresh hattorah*), who was raised up to assist the wise among the priests and laymen with the *halakhic* (legal) interpretations that would govern the community (*CD* 6. 2-11).

## The Method of Interpreting Prophecy

We have already seen in the *Pesharim* (commentaries of the Dead Sea Sect that the community interpreted the Bible in light of their own time. The reason for this was not arbitrary, but based on their observation of the prophetic works. When they read the prophets, they saw that in most cases the prophets intended their message for the latter days rather than for their own time. The Sect had come to believe that they were living in the latter days and that it was their responsibility to search the Scriptures, unravel the mysteries of prophets, and interpret the text for their times. Because they often applied their interpretations to historical figures of their day—figures whom they thought were fulfilling the prophet's words—they also have left us some clues about the historical situation of the community.

When the writers of the Scrolls sought to apply the prophecies of the past, they did so with the realization that they were actualizing the prophecies of certain key prophets. They especially identified with the prophet Habakkuk, who had grappled both with the spiritual declension of his day and the impending judgment of God. For example, Habakkuk wrote, "I must wait quietly for the day of distress, for the people to arise who will invade us" (Habakkuk 3:16), and the community at Qumran understood these words to refer to their own community living in the last days. However, they saw Habakkuk's revelation as imperfect next to that of their Teacher, who was "divinely inspired" to alter even the prophetic scriptures in his interpretation.[10] In the Teacher's interpretive commentary on Habakkuk, the community was pictured as the faithful remnant waiting for the day of judgment that would fall upon the idolaters and wicked of the earth (*1QpHab* 13:3-4)—a judgment that would also fall on the Roman army and the city of Jerusalem, where the Wicked Priest performed his acts of defilement (*1QpHab* 9:5-11; 12:5-13). After this would come the final age which Habakkuk had been told would come without fail (Habakkuk 2:3). In the Qumran commentary, the prophet Habakkuk is said to have been told by God "to write what was going to happen to the last generation, but He did not let him know the end of the age" (*1QpHab* 7:1-2). Rather, this knowledge was reserved for their Teacher of Righteousness, who interpreted the last days as an era extended beyond the prophets—an era that, though possibly delayed, would still come at the appointed time within the divine program (*1QpHab* 7:4-14). It was for this time that the Sect at Qumran was chosen to wait and prepare.

## The Prophetic Literature at Qumran

From about the fourth century B.C. onward,[11] the prophetic literature at Qumran takes on the genre of apocalyptic.[12] It is this genre that is characteristic of the eschatological material of the Dead Sea Scrolls.[13] Among the works discovered at Qumran are commentaries on the books of the prophets and the Psalms, which scholars refer to as *pesher* because this noun is used frequently in the Scrolls themselves for the "interpretation" of a *raz*, an Aramaic term for "mystery." The Qumran *pesher* developed through the prophetic influence of Daniel as a special means of reconstructing the hidden history revealed to the prophets concerning the end of time, but reserved in mystery form for the generation upon which the end would come. The apocalyptic vision of Qumran's *pesher* literature is derived from its understanding of human history as being built up in stages determined by God and linked together to move toward an inevitable goal, the eschaton.[14] John Collins referred to this as patterns projected into the eschatological future, which disclosed the dominance of the hostile order of Belial and the affirmation of an alternative order, at present eclipsed though practically experienced by the elect, but yet to be completely revealed in the future.[15] David Flusser argues that:

> This is not an evolutionary approach containing the concept of progress, for in this view, it is precisely before the end that the worst time will come, troubles of a kind not seen since the beginning of the world. History and its stages have been predetermined, one after another, by God. And after the final crisis (the War of Gog and Magog, or an invasion of monstrous enemies, or . . . of a terrible and wicked king, who corresponds with the Christian Antichrist), after all this, the final peace will come; men will live a thousand generations, evil will be destroyed, and an ideal world will come about.[16]

In concluding his study of the use of the Old Testament at Qumran, which primarily consisted of the Torah and the prophets,[17] George Brooke affirmed that one cannot approach this usage without presupposing that such use was guided by an overall eschatological perspective.[18]

The Scrolls depict a defined order of the ages that unfolds progressively and successively in predetermined periods of time, or in keeping with biblical usage, "generations" as in *1QS* 4:13 (see Deuteronomy 32:7; Isaiah 41:4). The order of these ages according to *4Q180* (*The Ages of Creation*) consecutively enumerates these periods, beginning with the time prior to the creation of man (*CD* 2:7; *IQS* 3:15-18; *1QH* 1:8-12). The history of mankind is traced from creation (*1QS* 4:15-17) and leads up to the eschaton or the "latter generation" or "end-time," an inverted technical term (*4Q169* 3-4 iii. 3; *173* 1, line 5), finally culminating in the "latter days" (*1QpHab* 4:1-2,7-8,10-14; cf. 2:5-7). This culminating period also looks forward in its description of this age ending the era of wickedness as "the decreed epoch of new things" (*1QS* 4:25; cf. Daniel 9:26-27; 11:35-36; Isaiah 10:23; 28:22; 43:19). The dividing point of this order of the ages is the destruction of the Temple (586 B.C.), with the ages preceding it termed "the generations of wickedness" and those that follow after (the post-destruction/post-exilic period) as "the generations of the latter days."[19]

## Prophecy and the History of the Sect

Historically we may understand how those who penned the apocalyptic literature of the Scrolls came to this portion (see chart on page 221). The First Temple had been destroyed because of Israel's unfaithfulness to the covenant—more specifically, to purification and Temple-related laws. Those who returned to Judah after the destruction and exile to rebuild the Temple expected a national restoration and spiritual revival according to that earlier predicted by Jeremiah and Ezekiel, and reinforced by the post-exilic prophets, especially Zechariah and Malachi. But the Persian authorities granted the Judean remnant only limited autonomy in the sphere of Temple-building and ritual maintenance (Ezra 1:1-4; 4:8-23; 5:3-5), an act which both reduced the status of their government and enhanced the status of their priesthood (Ezra 7:11-26). The ideal government (that is, the messianic kingdom) envisioned by the prophets combined the offices of king and priest, and such was typified at the beginning of this period by the Davidic descendant Zerubbabel and the high priest Joshua. This

# THE QUMRAN COMMUNITY'S PROPHETIC PERSPECTIVE OF ITSELF IN THE CONTEXT OF HISTORY

"... in the age of wrath. ... He remembered them and caused the root He had planted to sprout [again] from Israel and Aaron to take possession of His Land" (CD 1:5-7).

Program of progressive succession of generations or epochs (creation to latter days) CD; 1QS; 1QH; esp. 4Q180; 4Q181

## Former Wicked Age
(CD 1:16-20)

Age of Wickedness also called:

Age of Israel's sin, CD 20:23;
Age of the desolation
of the land (CD 5:20)
Age of the punishment
of the forefathers (CD 7:21)

## 390 Years
(Based on Ezekiel 4:4-5)

Beginning from
destruction of
First Temple
(CD 8:52-54)

586 - 390 = 196 B.C.
(Qumran sect begins)

## Latter Wicked Age
(CD 5:20-21; 7:14,21)

circa 162 B.C.

Rise of Wicked Priest
(= non-Zadokite [High] Priest)
(1QpHab 8:16; 9:9; 11:12; 12:8)

Conflict between the Liar/Scoffer
(= Wicked Priest) & Teacher over
millennial expectations of the Sect
(CD 6:11; 1QpHab 11:4-8)

Possibly assumed own
sinfulness resulted in
delays or postponement
of expected prophetic
fulfillment (CD 1:8-9)
but still expected 40-year
war between "Sons of Light"
(the sect) and "Sons of
Darkness" (non-sectarian
Jews, esp. followers of
Wicked Priest and all
Gentiles) (1QM 1-2)

Predestined ages ordered consecutively

40 Years of Ezekiel 4:6 (divided into two equal periods, CD 8:52-54)
(from Teacher's arrival to end of his opponents, CD 8:52-54)

## Past Predictive Failures

lead sect to cease setting
dates, wait pietistically at first,
then to adopt a more militant
stance

20 years without Teacher

20 years with Teacher
Sect retreats to desert,
organizes as community

Loss of
Teacher

Righteous
(or legitimate)
Teacher arises from
their ranks (able to
discern prophetic
puzzle)
(CD 8:10-11)

Application
of 70 years
of wrath of
Daniel 9:3?

Some
members
of sect join
Jews at
Masada
and bring
scrolls
with them

"Groped like
blind men
for their way"
(CD 1:8)

Scrolls and
treasure
of Copper
Scrolls
are
hidden

Destruction of
First Temple is
dividing point
of Qumran
history
(CD 1:8-11)

Historic period of Qumran community
(c. 196 B.C. - A.D. 70)

Romans
destroy
Qumran
settlement
A.D. 68

Romans
destroy
Qumran
settlement
A.D. 68

Destruction
of Second
Temple
(A.D. 70)

Members
of sect
die at
Masada
(A.D. 73)

History of
Israel and
all mankind
traced from
creation
(1QS 4:15-17)

Sanctuary
of Israel
that was
defiled
(4QFlor 107)

*Pure*          *Impure*

Second Temple (515 B.C.-A.D.70)

Sons of Zadok (elect of Israel =
Qumran community) True
representatives of Israel
(CD 4:4)

Applied "northern
exile to Damascus"
(Amos 5:27) to
exilic condition
of desert life at
Qumran
(CD 7:13-14)

## Ages before creation of mankind
(4Q180, 181)

## Creation    First Temple (960-596 B.C.)

First failed expected of restoration was
with first post-exilic community due to ritual
impurity; this led to founding of sect as "Holy
Members of Renewed Covenant"; sectarian
chronology ignored first exilic community
and viewed their own history as a continuation of the First Temple period; withdrew
from Second Temple because it followed
incorrect festival calendar which would
prevent the promised redemption

Write *Pesharim*, sectarian and apocalyptic documents that interpret
sect as "first Judean exiles to return [in holiness] to the land of Israel
and to be prophesied remnant that would see eschatological war and
restoration (CD 1:3-8; 12:2-22; 1QH 17:14)

union of monarchy and priesthood, guided by "a counsel of peace," was the insignia of the Messiah, who would build the ideal, eschatological Temple with the help of the Gentile nations (a sign of a complete restoration—Zechariah 6:13-15).

But this union was never realized by the post-exilic community, nor did the Temple built by Zerubbabel achieve the glory the prophet Haggai had predicted for the First Temple's successor (Haggai 2:7-9). Why did not Jeremiah's 70 years end with the restoration? The Jews who settled at Qumran answered this by observing that Ezekiel's symbolic act depicting the Judean exile (Ezekiel 6:4-6,9) represented 390 years (verses 5,9). So applying this prophecy literally, they understood that 390 years were to transpire from the captivity to the time God would end the exile and begin the restoration (*CD* 1:3-8).[20] At the conclusion of this period, in what they termed "the age of wrath" (*CD* 1:5), they believed God planted again a righteous remnant (the Qumran community). Subtracting 390 years from 586 B.C. (the beginning of the Babylonian exile), we arrive at 196 B.C. Subtracting another 20 years (which *CD* 1:8-11 reveals was a time of preestablishment preparation for the community) we arrive at 177 B.C., the approximate time for the commencement of the community at Qumran.[21] Professor Talmon explains the Sect's thinking from this point:

> So they found another prophecy—the 390 years of Ezekiel. When these 390 years passed and nothing happened, the Zadokite Fragment says, "we were," and I paraphrase this freely, "we were groping like blind men in a chimney stack, we were lost." This was because there was a pre-appointed timetable [which did not come to pass]. They groped for twenty years and then God let arise for them the Legitimate Teacher (I think this is a better term than the Righteous Teacher). He explains to them why their hope had not been realized and became their sole leader for [at least] 20 years. We have 390 + 20 + 20 = 430 years, which we have in Ezekiel and which is the length of time given for the Egyptian slavery. Symbolic figures from one stage of history are carried forward [and applied] to their own [age].[22]

From the beginning of this period they apparently interpreted the 40 days of Ezekiel 6:4 as 40 years—one generation—and expected the 40-year eschatological war (of Gog and Magog) to take place at its conclusion. Their first 20 years of "groping"—that is, searching for direction—ended when the Teacher of Righteousness arose. He was a priest (possibly a high priest) who apparently claimed to have the gift of prophecy. Under his leadership and instruction in the desert (CD 1:8-11) during the next 20 years, they applied to themselves the role of Isaiah's messianic preparer, "a voice crying in the wilderness" (Isaiah 40:3; 1QS 8:12-16). This wilderness—Egypt and Babylon in one—was probably also viewed as a typological "Damascus," since Amos 5:27 had predicted that God would take Israel into exile beyond Damascus (CD 7:13-14), and Zechariah 6:8 had said that from there they would escape in the time of God's visitation of judgment upon the wicked (CD 7:20-21).[23] This 40-year period is the same as that given for the duration of the climactic war between the "Sons of Light" and the "Sons of Darkness" (1QM 2-3). At this time they were to conquer all the nonaligned (non-New Covenant) Jews, all foreign nations (and especially the Kittim, who embodied the oppression). To explain these events within their calculated chronology, some scholars have argued that the Sect may have attempted to appropriate Daniel's "seventy weeks" prophecy, since its "seventy sevens" (490 years) are matched by the 390 years of Ezekiel + the 20 years of groping + the 40 years with the Righteous Teacher (CD 20 [b]:14-15) + the 40-year war expected after the Teacher's death = 490.[24] During this period they believed that their chronology was divinely ordained, and so waited patiently for the appointed day.[25]

When the end of this period failed to produce the expected ends, the community apparently did not attempt further calculations; however, some feel that the 70 years of wrath in Daniel 9:3 (mentioned in the *War Scroll*) could have been employed as a means to determine the end of the Roman oppression of Judea (4Q243-245).[26] Still, when the expected judgment did not come, they apparently reformulated their earlier expectations to accommodate a divine postponement or delayed judgment, and they also adopted a new militaristic posture that saw the urgent need for intervention to bring about the next age. They were expecting a messianic intervention "imminently," since the date indicated by their chronology had passed. In this we were able to see that the Sect's eschatology was developed from a literal interpretation of prophetic texts, a numerological calculation of temporal indicators in judgment pronouncements, and understood a postponement of the final age while not abandoning their hope of it.

## Prophetic Terms in the Scrolls

The eschatological perspective of the Scrolls is seen in the terms that were used to describe the expectation of the days about to arrive on the historical scene: "the latter days," "the end of days," "the appointed time," "the new Creation," and the "visitation" (divine retributive judgment, intervention). The eschatological scheme of the Scrolls (see chart on page 225) was a two-stage eschatology (*now* and *then*), with the past being the condition of exile imposed by the destruction of the First Temple, and the present characterized by a nonrestoration of the proper spiritual order in the Second Temple, or an age of wickedness that served as a time of trial and testing (that is, refining) for the elect remnant (the Qumran community—*4QCantena*ᵃ 2:9-10; *4QFlor* 2:1). This age was to see a visit from Elijah as the precursor of Messiah (*4Q521*) and the advent of the Messiah(s), who would slay the wicked (the correct interpretation of *4Q285*) in the great war of Gog and Magog (*1QM*; *4QpIsa*ᵃ 7-10; 22-25; *4QpIsa*ᵇ 2:1; *4Cantena*ᵇ 3:7-8) at the Day of the Lord (*4Q558*). This would be followed by the promised age of messianic rule and righteousness (*1QSa* 2:14; *4Q554* 11:20-22). This, however, was not the final age, for according to Daniel (12:1-2) it was held that the righteous would be resurrected (*4Q521* 1:1, line 12, cf. *1QH* 4:18-21; 11:12; *1QS* 4:7-8).

Several of these themes, especially that of the age of evil preceding the advent of the Messiah(s), needed to atone for Israel and establishment of the messianic kingdom, are important for study in relation to Judaism and for comparison with New Testament eschatology. The messianic theme is reviewed in an upcoming chapter, and the issues concerning the kingdom are discussed in the chapter "The Temple and the Scrolls." Here, then, let us examine the evil age and the expected war that would end this age.

### *The Age of Evil*

The Qumran community called the post-exilic age "epoch of wickedness" (*CD* 4:10; 12:23; 14:19; 15:7,10), "the epoch of Israel's sin" (*CD* 20:23), the "epoch of the desolation of the land [of Israel]" (*CD* 5:20), and the "epoch of the punishment of the forefathers" (*CD* 7:21ᵃ). The chief characteristic of this age is a wickedness that escalates until the final conflict between the "Sons of Darkness" and the "Sons of Light." According to the *War Scroll*, the final age was to be preceded by a period of tribulation or "birth pangs [of the Messiah]" (*1QH* 3:7-10),[27] which

# THE ESCHATOLOGY OF THE DEAD SEA SCROLLS

## Two-Stage Eschatology: This Age/Age to Come

Program of progressive succession of epochs (CD; 1QS; 1QH)

**40-year period (average generation) of Judah's (sect's) exile**
**40-year period of eschatological war(s) to bring redemption (CD 8:52-54; Ezekiel 4:6)**
First 40 years divided into two 20-year periods

Destruction of First Temple is sect's division between the days of wickedness and latter days and beginning of 390 years of Ezekiel's prophecy (based on *pesher* of Ezekiel 4:4-5)

Present age for the sect was the continuation of the First Temple period since the sect was the true Israel destined to escape from the wilderness exile and realize the eschatological restoration on earth with an undefined Jerusalem, ideal Temple, and ultimate redemption that would prevent another exile

Interim period characterized as time of *birth-pangs*; troubles ; Qumran community brings the Messiah (1QH 3:7-10)

**Advent of eschatological Messiah (or anointeds) variously called:**
Messiah of Righteousness (4QPBless 3)
Messiah of Holiness (1Q30 1:2)
Messiah(s) of Aaron and Israel (1QS 9:11; CD 12:23; 14:19; 19:10; 20:1)
King Messiah (4Q541, frags 9, 24)
Messiah of Heaven and Earth (4Q521)
High Priest (4QAaron A, frag 9)
Branch of David (4QpIsaa, 1QSa, 4QFlor 1:11)
Teacher of Righteousness (CD 6:11; 19:35-2C:1)
Interpreter of the Law (4QFlor 1:11)
Scepter/Star (of Balaam's Oracle)
Prince of the Congregation (1QSb 7.20)
The Herald (11QMelch 2:15-16)

**New Jerusalem (4Q554)**
Rectangular city (13 x 18 miles) 12 gates for each tribe; Eastern Gate in line with Temple; 1500 towers @ 100'

---

**This Age**
*Former Age of Wickedness*

**(This Age - Interim)**
*The Latter Age of Wickedness*

Pre-Messianic Period

**Age to Come**
*Age of Redemption*

---

566 B.C. - 390 years = 196 B.C. Beginning of Qumran community

Sanctuary of Israel (4QFlor 107) Zadokite Priesthood

First Temple (960-586 B.C.)

Second Temple (Begins 515 B.C.)

Non-Zadokite Priesthood
Lunar Calendar

Sanctuary that was defiled (4QFlor 107) Zadokite Priesthood

Zadokite Priesthood
Solar Calendar

War and Turmoil (4QpIsa 7:10; 22:25; 4QpIsab 2:1; 4QCantenaa 3:7-8)

Time of Testing/Refining 4QCantenaa 2:9-10; 4QFlor 2:1

Sanctuary of Men (4QFlor 107-110) after plans in Temple Scroll

40-year war (Gog and Magog) climaxed by Day of the Lord (lightning as sign) (4QS58)

Elijah precedes Messiah (4Q521)

"Time of salvation for the people of God" (1QM 1:5)

**Day of [New] Creation (11QT 29:9)**
Eschatological Temple = Sanctuary of the Lord New Temple made by God) (11QT 29:9; 4QFlor 07)

"Decreed epoch of new things" (1QS 4:25; cf. Daniel 9:27; 11:36; Isaiah 10:23; 28:22)

**Age of Messianic Rule** (not a perfect period nor end of history)
Messiah to rule over purified Israel (1QS2:14)

**Resurrection of Righteous**
"[God] will raise the dead" (4Q521 2 i, 4, line 13; 4Q385 12:2-14) based on Ezekiel 37 and Daniel 12:1-2

---

Exiles return to Judah; apathy and violation of law; Zerubbabel and Joshua serve as king and high priest; eschatological restoration does not take place; Hellenism and political appointments to high priesthood anger pious movement that becomes sect begins under Zadokite priests

Temple of Temple Scroll built in ritually purified Jerusalem before age to come); Ark of Covenant not restored to Holy of Holies

Interim King (subject to Zadokite high priest and conditional reign) (11QT 57:1-59:11)

The "Revenge of God" (1Q S 1:0)
Battle of the Sons of Light and Sons of Darkness (1QM)

Assault of the Kittim (= Romans?) (1QpHab 9:6-7)

Antichrist figure proclaims self "Son of God" (4Q 246)

Final Kingdom in which all nations serve Israel (4Q554 11:20-22)

"Time of the End" (4Q 16 3-4 iii 3; 173 1 line 5)

"shall be a time of salvation for the people of God ..." (*1QM* 1). One such reference to this time of eschatological woe appears in the third hymn of the *Thanksgiving Hymns*:

> I was in distress as a woman in travail with her firstborn child, when her pains come upon her, and violent pains upon her womb, causing writhing in the crucible of the pregnant woman. When children come to the waves of death; and the one bearing a man suffers in her travail, because in the waves of death she gives birth to a man-child; and in deadly travail (or birth-pangs of Sheol) there will break forth from the crucible of the pregnant woman, a wonderful thing; counsel in his might and the man-child will be delivered from the waves ... (*1QH* 3:7-10).

Interpreters have compared this text to the "tribulation texts" in the Old Testament (especially Isaiah 26:16-18), where Israel is described as suffering like a woman giving birth in the eschatological "Day of the Lord" (Isaiah 13:8; 25:17-18; 66:7-8; Jeremiah 22:23; 48:41; 50:37; Hosea 13:13; Zephaniah 1:14-18; Micah 4:9-10; 5:1[2]).[28] The New Testament also uses this figure to describe the unparalleled experience Israel will face in the "Great Tribulation" (Matthew 24:4-8; 1 Thessalonians 5:2-3). Such an age is also predicated on the Old Testament teaching of a period of distress in the end time (Daniel 12:1-2), also known as "the time of Jacob's trouble" (Jeremiah 30:7), from which Israel will be delivered into the messianic age. In this sense, the Qumran community, as the pure remnant of Israel, was suffering tribulations as a sign of the imminent Great Tribulation, in which the 40-year war would see them bringing forth the Messiah to wage a priestly war of righteousness (*1QM*).

Central to this coming age of conflict is the image of evil rulers and deceivers (counterparts to the true Messiah[s]. The Dead Sea Sect saw a cosmic conflict (dualism)[29] between the "Angel/Spirit of Truth/Holiness/Prince of Light" and the "Angel of Darkness/Spirit of Perversity/of the Pit." The conflict (dualism) on the human level was between the members of the Qumran Sect, characterized as the "Sons of Light" (*1QS*; *1QM*) and "sons of truth" (*1QS*; *1QH*; *1QM*), and their opponents, referred to as the "Sons of Darkness" (*1QS*; *1QM*), "sons of perversity" (*1QS*; *1QH*), and "sons of the pit" (*CD*).[30] This conflict between the forces of light (good) and darkness (evil) has been declared by J. Daniélou as "nothing else but the *leitmotif* ['main motive'] of Qumran."[31] These cosmic desecrators were mirrored by the conflict between the Sect and two figures: the "Wicked Priest/priests," and the "Man of Lies." Let's first consider this earthly dualism and then proceed to the negative element of this cosmic dualism.

## The Wicked Priest and the Man of Lies

Neither the "Wicked Priest/priests" nor the "Man of Lies" are identified by name, like the "Teacher of Righteousness" (with whom they principally contend). However, the "Wicked Priest" was apparently a non-Zadokite high priest (or a group of Hasmonean priests)[32] who was considered an illegitimate priest, while the "Man of Lies" was seemingly a traitor who was formerly an ally of the Zadokite "Teacher" (the legitimate priest) but subsequently betrayed him. J. Murphy-O'Connor has suggested that the "Man of Lies" became the opponent of the "Teacher" as the result of a schism within the Sect in Jerusalem—a schism that forced the covenantors to withdraw to Qumran.[33] As a non-Zadokite, he was not only considered an illegitimate priest, but was also said to be guilty of terrible desecrations of the Temple. According to the *Pesher Habakkuk* (*1QpHab* 8:12-13; 12:7-9) the "Wicked Priest" defiled the Temple of God (12:9) and profaned (through violence) the Land (12:9; cf. 2:17).[34]

Other censures listed for the "Wicked Priest" are his abuse of power, his drunkenness, his violence and arrogance, his greed (in the accumulation of wealth), and especially, his persecution of the "Teacher." The "Wicked Priest" also violated the divine order by substituting a strictly lunar calendar for a luni-solar one. Since the calendrical order was a rule expressive of divine creation and the preservation of the universe, regulating the festivals and normal Jewish life, altering or modifying it was a crime against Jewish worship.[35] The "Teacher" and the Qumran Sect believed that the dates on which the festivals were held at the Jerusalem Temple were "those in which all Israel was in error" (*CD* 3:14), while to them were revealed the true times of "the Sabbaths of His holiness and the festivals of His glory" (*CD* 3:15-16). Thus the "Wicked Priest," in *Pesher Habakkuk*, was basically a rebel against God—a rebel who would receive divine punishment.[36] Some scholars have busied themselves with finding the historical person behind both the Teacher and the Wicked Priest. According to Professor Talmon, this is an impossible pursuit given our present state of knowledge. Another problem is that these figures may have greater meaning:

> If we have only one *Moreh Ha-Sedeq* ["Teacher of Righ-
> teousness"] we possibly have only one specific Wicked Priest.
> This *Moreh Ha-Sedeq* is a type and so the Wicked Priest could
> be a type as well. It can be a title that applies to a specific indi-
> vidual at a specific stage or it could be a title which applies to a
> number of individuals who are more or less playing the same
> role in different stages of history. It is impossible to identify a
> historical person behind the figure because in Jewish history
> there are so many possibilities of someone in a specific situa-
> tion who could be the enemy. Much more information is needed.[37]

As Professor Talmon has noted, the Righteous Teacher and the Wicked
Priest could be types of eschatological figures. If so, they may have been
left unidentified intentionally, just like the unnamed Pharaohs of the
oppression and exodus (who were historical personages) to accommodate their cosmic counterparts around whom the predestined end-time
conflict will revolve: the "messiahs of Aaron and Israel" and "Belial"
and the "Angel of Darkness."

### The Figure of Belial

The figure of *Belial* ("worthlessness") in the New Testament has been
considered a cognomen of Satan (see 2 Corinthians 6:15; 2 Peter 2:15;
Jude 11; Revelation 2:14), and on this parallel usage the term has been
said to be used for the figure of the devil at Qumran (see *1QS* 2:19-25).
Since polluting the Temple is one of the three "nets of Belial" according
to the *Damascus Document* (column iv), this figure is as central in the
use of the desecration motif at Qumran as it was in other apocalyptic literature (for example, 3 Sibylline Oracles 63-74).

The *Rule of the Community* clearly describes the present age as the
"dominion of Belial" (*1QS* 2:19). This rule of Belial (like the influence
of the Angel of Darkness, whom we'll look at next, was in accord with
the predestined plan of God, which included his evil actions in bringing
about the sin of Israel. This is evident from the statement in *1QM* 13:9-
11: "From former times You [YHWH] appointed the Prince of Light to
help us . . . and You made Belial to corrupt." We also find that the desecration of the legitimate worship system by religious syncretism and
violations of the purification laws were the result of Belial's corruption
of the nation: "The Levites shall recite the iniquities of the sons of Israel
and all their guilty rebellions and their sins, accomplished under the

power of Belial" (*1QS* 1:22-24). Conversely, the righteous man is the one who resists the power of Belial, and he will be rewarded at the restoration. For example, we read in the *Halakhic Letter* (*4Q397-399*): "... and to keep you far from evil thoughts and the counsel of Belial. Then you will rejoice at the endtime" (lines 32-33). Thus, the desecration of the Temple, Land, and exile was part of the cosmic conflict, and there was coming an eschatological restoration at the eschaton (the day of deliverance for the righteous), yet both positively and negatively with reference to the rule of Belial.

Belial follows in the developmental progression of typical desecrators revealed in the Old Testament. For example, in the *Damascus Document* Belial is portrayed as a ruling angel in opposition to the law of God: "At the beginning Moses and Aaron arose through the hand of the prince of light, but Belial, in his wickedness, raised up Jannes and his brother" (*CD* 5:17). Notice that in this instance, Belial is equated with Pharaoh (cf. Exodus 7:11; 2 Timothy 3:8) as a type who is an oppressor of God's agents (and God Himself). And in the *Damascus Document*, we read that the "Prince of Lights" is directly opposed by Belial (see *CD* 5:18).

### The Angel of Darkness

There is still some debate about whether the "Angel of Darkness" and "Belial" are one figure or two.[38] Many scholars have assumed they both refer to one figure and have identified Belial with the devil as the Angel of Darkness, who is opposed to Michael, the "Angel of Light."[39] On the other hand, while the consensus of scholarly opinion has been that *1QS* 3:13–4:26 (the most representative text for the dualism concept, and the possible influence for other such texts) reveals an eschatological cosmic conflict of two warring spiritual forces, it has been contended that at times this dualism approaches the "psychological" arena.[40]

The arguments in favor of this position have been predicated on the use of the Hebrew term *ruah* ("spirit") in the Old Testament, where it is thought the idea of incorporeal entities is never intended. However, A.A. Anderson has correctly pointed out that in the Scrolls, *ruah* is frequently used to denote *supernatural beings* or *angels* as an apocalyptic development in comparison with the usage in the Old Testament.[41] Therefore, what approaches the "psychological" may simply be a reflection of the ethical power exerted over men by these beings—a thought certainly in harmony with the predestinarian viewpoint found in the Scrolls.[42] Also, the distinctions drawn between "angel" and "spirit," as well as statements depicting the spirits under the command of (in this case) the single Angel of Darkness (*1QS* 3:24), seem to make the equivocation of angel with spirit impossible.[43]

The Angel of Darkness was explained as one who had produced desecration historically, and it was expected that he would continue to do so until the final conflict. The language of cultic pollution, and particularly Temple pollution, runs throughout the whole of Qumran literature (for example, the *Damascus Document*), and one means of assuring the eventual restoration of the Temple and the remnant to a purified state was to see its desecration as caused by a cosmic entity rather than a cosmic conflict that was greater than any one religious Sect or political regime. It appears that the author of *1QS* 3:13–4:26 felt that the recognition of an Angel of Darkness resolved the problem of the post-exilic community's failure to attain proper purification and holiness and to receive the promised restoration: "Through the Angel of Darkness all the sons of righteousness stray and all their sins, their faults, their defilements and their acts of disobedience are caused by his rule" (*1QS* 3:22). Thus, if the problem of desecration was part of a predestined plan (under the rule of evil forces), so also must the resolution through restoration (under godly forces) be the expected climax of that plan. In this theology, then, greed, falsehood, pride, deceit, hypocrisy, lust, and all other evils in the world were seen to be caused by this entity, also called the "Spirit of Perversity." Because Belial is seen as having a similar role in seducing people to do evil, we perhaps should not distinguish the two. However, it may be possible that the Angel of Darkness functions primarily as a pervasive evil influence[44] (much like the Angels of Mastemoth) in conjunction with Belial, whose figure has supernatural proportions but is better defined as an evil adversary to the community and their Teacher of Righteousness, and ultimately Messiah.

One of the primary characteristics of Qumran dualism is the eschatological dimension, and we must always keep the figures of desecration and destruction in the eschatological perspective. Indeed, the oldest form of dualism found at Qumran is found in the *War Scroll*, which has as its emphasis the imminent last-days combat. The decisive apocalyptic intervention of God and the triumph of the "Sons of Light" was always a future act. In this context, the ultimate outcome for the Angel of Darkness, Belial, and the "Sons of Darkness" is destruction or annihilation in a final battle at the eschaton (the final judgment): "until the time of decreed judgment" (*1QS* 4:14,19b-20a; cf. *1QM* 1:4-7). This war which will take place between the tribes of Israel (assisted by the powers of light and justice and the angels appointed over them) and the enemies of Israel (at whose head is the nation called the *Kitti'im* [also, Kittim-Romans], assisted by Belial and the powers of Darkness). This war will end only when the Sons of Light and Darkness have each been the victor three times. In the seventh struggle, victory will be achieved by the Sons of Light through God's intervention. Professor Talmon summarizes this final war:

> The apocalyptic war described in the *War Scroll* will go on for forty years, a schematic figure from the Bible for one generation. This forty years is subdivided in two stages, each of twenty years. The first twenty years all the external enemies (and they enumerate them) are done away with. This is taken from the judgments against the foreign nations in the Bible. But since these people considered themselves as pious Jews, they would rest every seventh year. This is a nice arrangement because the enemy also lays down their weapons after every sixth year. The second twenty years is for fighting against other Jews, especially the followers of the Wicked Priest. After this last war, a new world of total peace will come in, as described in the Hebrew Bible.[45]

## The "Antichrist" at Qumran

While Belial may generally be equated with the image of Satan, his role as an evil spiritual influence appears in many texts to be that of an end-time human desecrator. In some texts there appears a contrasting pair of figures: "Melchizedek" and "Melkiresha," the latter of which fits the description as an evil human oppressor. Consequently, this figure has been identified by some as a depiction of the Antichrist. However, more significant comparisons appear in *Second Ezekiel* (*4Q385-389*), where reference is made to both a "son of Belial" and a "blasphemous/boastful king" who will arise and oppress the Jewish people. These terms occur in texts (both in fragmentary form) that are within a context alluding to the national regathering and restoration of Israel from the vision of the valley of dry bones in Ezekiel 37:4-6, which is immediately followed by a prayer about the time of this end-time regathering.[46] The following description of the "son of Belial" and the "blasphemous/boastful king" may tell us when this individual desecrator functions. At any rate, the description of this individual reveals significant details of his role in desecration:

> YHWH sai[d]: "A son of Belial will plan to oppress My People, but I will not allow him to do so. His rule shall not come to pass, but he will cause a multitude to be defiled [and] there will be no seed left (*4Q385* 3.2.3-4). In those [days] a blasphemous king will arise among the Gentiles, and do evil things [ . . . ] Israel from [being] a People. In his days I will break the Kingdom (*4Q385* 4-6.9-10).

From these lines we can see that a future Gentile king will seek to oppress the people of Israel, and this king will be destroyed by God. In the same context are references to Babylon, to God's hiding His face until Israel has filled up the measure of its sins, and to a period of apostasy characterized by the breaking of the Abrahamic Covenant. There is also an interesting comment about the wicked before they are taken in judgment: "Just as they will say, 'Peace and quiet is ours,' so they will say 'The Land rests quietly.'" All of this is reminiscent of passages concerning the "prince that shall come" (Daniel 9:26-27) and the deceptive security before the war of Gog and Magog (Ezekiel 38:8-16; cf. Jeremiah 6:14; 8:11; 1 Thessalonians 5:3). Eisenman and Wise suggest that these terms may have parallels in *Pseudo-Daniel* (*4Q243-245*); the terms "Kings of the Peoples" and "Kingdom of the Peoples" appear in a similar context during which time "[ev]i[l] has led astray . . . " and "the called ones will be gathered" (lines 33-34, cf. lines 51-55).[47]

Other texts at Qumran also appear to refer to this "son of Belial" using different descriptive terms. In *CD* 6:10 and *1QpHab* 5:7-8, texts that depict a period of great spiritual declension in Israel, the future apostasy is said to be spearheaded by a figure called "son/man of sin" (see *CD* 6:15; 13:14; *1QS* 9:16; 10:19). This expression is quite similar to the Greek "son of destruction," an expression found in the Pauline description of the eschatological desecrator, the Antichrist, in 2 Thessalonians 2:3. The expression is also complemented by another term: "son of iniquity" in *1QS* 3:21, which can be further compared to another phrase in this reference—"the man of lawlessness." In addition, the phrase "the mystery of lawlessness" (found only in 2 Thessalonians 2:7, the Pauline Antichrist context) has an almost identical corresponding phrase at Qumran: "mystery of iniquity" (*1QH* 5:36; 50:5).[48] Some scholars also claim to have found another parallel in the Scroll's use of "detain" (*1Q27* 1:7) with the cryptic Pauline term "restrains" (2 Thessalonians 2:6-7). Though the sense of "hold back" may not be exactly the same as that in Qumran usage, Dupont-Sommer, on the basis of this comparison, translated the complete line of the text: "And all of those who detain [unjustly] the marvelous mysteries.[49]

David Flusser[50] also claims to have identified a Qumran "Antichrist" in the Aramaic pseudo-Daniel fragment known as *4Q246*.[51] In this text, a foreign Syrian king who seems to hold universal dominion attacks Israel, usurps the place of divinity as "Son of God and Son of the Most High," and then is finally put down by the triumphant Jews (see chapter 14). If the figure in this text can be interpreted negatively (as anti-Messiah) rather than positively (as Messiah), then there may be an allusion to Daniel's fourth beast/kingdom (Daniel 8:23-27 or 9:27; or cf. 11:35-45; 12:1), which may have served as the original seedbed for an apocalyptic Antichrist imagery. It also bears several parallels with 2 Thessalonians 2:4, which portrays the deification of the "man of sin."

F. Garcia Martinez has criticized Flusser's argument that the use of Jewish apocalyptic parallels forms a Jewish Antichrist tradition in *4Q246*. Martinez complains that "the New Testament influences are so evident that it appears futile to me to search for the remnants of an ancient tradition.[52] Even so, Martinez does see the idea of an anti-Messiah as a human antagonist in the messianic *Testamonia* (*4Q175*), but with the same characteristics as other angelic antagonists (Belial, Melkiresha, Mastema, Prince of Darkness, and so on). He agrees with Flusser that the concept of Antichrist as a future opponent of Messiah is Jewish and pre-Christian, but still denies that the concept includes the New Testament elements of divine self-proclamation and is present in *4Q246*.

However, we've seen ample evidence that the Scrolls carry the roots of ideas and expressions that appear in the New Testament (which Martinez concedes). Besides, Flusser is not projecting later concepts into the ancient texts, as Martinez believes. Flusser has based his argument primarily on the text of *4Q246* and its context, which appear to depict both an apocalyptic setting and a negative figure usurping divine prerogatives (see chapter 14). We could equally argue that the predisposition to see the terms "Son of God" and "Son of the Most High" used positively (as does Martinez) is influenced by New Testament usage. Yet even though a negative usage in *4Q246* can be demonstrated apart from New Testament parallels, we must still explain where the New Testament, which was contemporaneous with the last period of the Qumran community, got its concept of Antichrist—if not from an ancient Jewish tradition informed by the Old Testament (see Daniel 8:1-14; 9:27; 11:36-45). Apparently the authors of the Scrolls used the same source to develop their concept.

## A Clear Prophetic Influence

The Sect at Qumran was clearly controlled by eschatological expectations. As Lawrence Schiffman has observed:

> The Dead Sea Sect expected that the end of days would inaugurate an era of perfection in which they would see the culmination of the rituals and regulations practiced in the present pre-messianic age. The eschatological community would be structured as a reflection of the present community.[53]

This eschatological ambition governed their daily lives, sustained them in the midst of their separation and persecution from other Jews in their society, and supported them in their purpose as a vanguard for the age to come. In summary, the Qumran group believed that God had predestined history in cycles of time, which consisted of two opposing ages: 1) the *Present Age*—"the age of evil" when wickedness would flourish, Satan (Belial) and his agents (anti-Messiah, wicked angels) would increase their attacks on the righteous (the "time of travail," or "birth pangs"), and divine intervention would come at the end of the age in the form of military and priestly messianic leader(s) who would wage a messianic 40-year war; and 2) the *Age to Come*—the messianic interregnum, which would last for 1,000 years and during which a divine dominion, a restored national Israel, and a ritual purity would be pervasive and complete.

In the next chapter, we will examine how the Sect may have planned to bring together this fervent nationalism, concern for universal purity, and prophetic perspective in their concept of the Jerusalem Temple.

# 11

# THE TEMPLE AND THE SCROLLS

*The Scrolls of Qumran make it abundantly clear that the Essenes saw themselves as a new camp in the wilderness, awaiting their rise to power and control of the Temple.*[1]

—Bruce Chilton

From the prophetic program we see outlined in the Scrolls, the Temple seems to have played a key role in structuring the eschatological order of events both in its past and future forms. Its present form was also a principal factor affecting the laws and ritual life of the Qumran community. In addition, the largest of the Scrolls, the *Temple Scroll*, deals with theological interpretations of the Torah which were probably shared by the community. Only in the Dead Sea Scrolls do we find reliable references to a Jewish theology of the Temple. One must be careful, however, not to draw incomplete inferences by deduction from this theology.[2] Let's begin by considering the Qumran Sect's attitude toward the Temple. From there we'll examine the various ideas the Scrolls present about the Temple, giving special attention to the Temple described in the *Temple Scroll*.

## The Attitude Toward the Temple

The Qumran community separated themselves from the Second Temple because of their belief that its structure and service were not according to proper ceremonial law. Its Sabbaths, rituals, and feasts followed a strictly lunar (therefore, corrupt) calendar, and its priests were of an illegitimate origin, which made them ceremonially impure. This negative attitude is seen in some texts (for example, *4QpIs*[a] and the new text *4Q285*) that bear allusions to the destruction of the Second Temple or the priesthood in references such as "the falling of the cedars of Lebanon," or "Lebanon being felled by a Mighty One."[3] This is in keeping with the Sect's rejection of certain elements of the Second Temple institution.[4] Stephen Pfann, director of the School of Early Christianity, offers this summary:

> The Temple priesthood was not of the original line that was considered acceptable from the time of David onward. During the time of the Essenes the high priesthood had been transferred from the Zadokite priests to non-Zadokite priests. The Essenes felt that these Temple priests were corrupt, did not keep the rules correctly, and were allowing impurities to come into the Temple. Therefore, this Temple would either have to be thoroughly cleansed or, as the Essenes saw it, totally replaced.[5]

## The Question of Spiritual Replacement

Given this understanding of the Sect's attitude toward the Temple, there has been considerable debate about whether this attitude meant a complete abandonment of the Second Temple and a spiritual replacement of it in the form of the Qumran community, or if the Sect continued to use the Temple, though not regarding its sanctity, and expecting its literal replacement with a Third Temple. Those who hold a complete rejection/spiritual replacement view say that when the Scroll authors called the Qumran community a "temple" they meant the community was *the* Temple.[6] However, the nomenclature of replacement, especially with reference to the Qumran community as a new temple, is questioned by E.S. Fiorenza on the grounds of the anti-cultic implications of the term *new*. He prefers rather to speak of the concept at Qumran as that of "transference" or "reinterpretation."[7] Other scholars have used terms such as a "spiritualization of temple," or a "spiritualized temple."[8] However, these terms also fail to understand the full-orbed concept of the Temple as it existed at Qumran. I prefer to speak of the community as a "symbolic" temple (see below), since, in my opinion, the Sect did not think in terms of replacing the sacred distinction held by Jerusalem and the Temple Mount, but conversely derived their own concepts of their community as a holy priesthood from the implicit sanctity of the Jerusalem Temple.

## The Question of Temple Rituals

Another question arising from the Scrolls, particularly the *Temple Scroll*, is whether or not the Sect was involved with sacrifices and other ritual functions of the Jerusalem Temple. It is clear from the *Temple Scroll* that the Sect believed sacrifices were essential in a ritually pure future Temple, for it describes in detail the installations for slaughtering the sacrifices and the laws governing their proper offering. However, texts such as *Purification Rituals* (29-32. 7:6-9; c. *1QS* 2:26–3:12), dated to the early first century B.C., reveal that the Sect practiced atoning ritual acts with an emphasis on spiritual repentance, which are thought to have been a replacement for actual Temple sacrifice. Schiffman says that "when these rituals were performed with genuine feelings of spiritual purification, they apparently served as a substitute for the sacrifices no longer being offered by the sectarians."[9] Former Shrine of the Book curator Magen Broshi also is convinced the Qumran group did not perform sacrifices at the Temple, or anywhere else:

> It seems that they might have brought presents to the Temple but it's inconceivable that they sacrificed there. They couldn't sacrifice there because they believed the place was impure according to their very strict (some may say very reactionary) *halakah*. Furthermore, I believe that they couldn't sacrifice anywhere else because in the law of Deuteronomy it states that you can sacrifice only in this particular place [Jerusalem], and Deuteronomy was one of the three most popular books at Qumran. Therefore, they did not participate in the sacrifices in Jerusalem at the Second Temple because they couldn't sacrifice outside this particular site and [consequently] they did not sacrifice at all, even though at that time not sacrificing was a

problem; it was not natural. Nevertheless, they would rather not sacrifice in an impure Temple.[10]

The passages Broshi refers to in Deuteronomy are 12:5-6,10-14,17-18. All of these passages specify a chosen place where God will cause His name to dwell. This place, though unnamed, must be Jerusalem and the Temple Mount (2 Samuel 7:10-13; 1 Kings 8:16-21; 1 Chronicles 22:6-10). Thus, a central sanctuary was to unify the tribes, and while slaughtering could take place outside Jerusalem, offerings could not (Deuteronomy 12:21-27). For Broshi, this indicates that the Sect did not offer sacrifices so that they could maintain their own laws of separation from impurity. However, this is not a solution, because *not* offering a sacrifice was a violation of the commandment to sacrifice. The law apparently did not regard the pollution of the Temple as an excuse to avoid fulfilling the required offerings—if offered humbly, obediently, and with a repentant heart (Psalm 50:7-15; Malachi 3:8-15; 6:6-8), as the prophets repeatedly pointed out (Jeremiah 7:21-23; Ezekiel 8:5-17; 22:26; Hosea 4:8-9; Micah 3:11). Stephen Pfann, arguing from the same text in Deuteronomy, believes this implies that they did offer sacrifices and perform other functions at the Temple:

> The question of purity in the Temple was a major one for them, and forced them to live outside Jerusalem and to no longer directly cooperate with the Temple priesthood. But this did not mean they totally rejected the Temple in all of its functions because there are certain commandments in the Torah that require the Temple in order to be able to fulfill them. However, being forced to use the Temple on certain occasions did not imply they accepted the *status quo*. Rather, they were all looking for a better day. Nevertheless, to think that they would have had some form of substitution [for the Temple] is certainly not the case. When you look at the site of Qumran with all its ritual immersion pools and at all the details in the Scrolls about how one should live according to Jewish law, you realize that these people were really very strict and took the law of Moses very literally and very seriously. And the Temple would have to play some role in that. [In fact,] certain *halakhic* practices required [access to] the Temple. One example is the biblical command to use the ashes of a red heifer for purifying a person who had touched a dead body. We know they were very strict about this rule and the source for these ashes. There's really no good

evidence that they would have sacrificed anywhere else but in Jerusalem, especially since the book of Deuteronomy says that is the only place for sacrifice.[11]

Some of Pfann's arguments may depend upon identifying the Sect with the Essenes, since Josephus speaks about Essene sacrifices including that of the red heifer (*Antiquities* 18.1.5 § 19).[12] In support of the view that the Sect offered sacrifices, broken pots with bones and ashes have been found at the site of the Qumran community. However, it is unclear whether these were the remains of routine meals or sacrificial offerings (probably the former). If the latter were true, it still does not imply that sacrifices were offered *at* Qumran, since that would be a clear violation of the Deuteronomic prohibition.

Some scholars have contended that the Sect continued to pay the Temple tax or that the treasure of the *Copper Scroll* was really a collection from Qumran for payment of the Temple taxes.[13] Again, if the Sect is identified with the Essenes, this continued veneration may find support in Josephus' statement that they regularly sent offerings to the Temple (*Antiquities* 18.1:5 § 19). However, there is simply not enough evidence to make a clear case. It is possible that the Sect was involved with the Temple cultus, as Pfann suggests, but it's equally possible they could have abstained from sacrifice, as Broshi argues, if they believed the Temple's replacement was imminent or that their position in the end time permitted a different course. Adding to the argument in favor of continued Temple contact is Philip Davies, who through his studies of the *Damascus Document* has concluded that "the community did not boycott the Temple," but that the Temple could "be used under the terms of its own *halakah*."[14] He contends that while the Sect believed it was "no longer the seat of the law, the Temple itself was not rejected, nor had it been defiled in some specific act."[15]

Whatever the case concerning the Sect's ritual relationship with the Temple, the Scrolls do reflect a positive view towards the Temple despite the community's disdain of its present form. One example of the community's esteem for the Second Temple is found in the *Halakhic Letter* (*4QMMT* or *4Q394-399*):

> [34]We reckon that the Temple [is "the Tent of Witness," while] Jerusale[m][35] is the "camp" outside the camp [means "outside Jerusalem"] (It refers to) the camp . . . [38][He chose] from among all the tribes of Israel, to establish His name there as a

> dwelling . . . ] . . . Because [from [67]] [68]Jerusalem is the Holy
> "camp"—the place [69]that He chose from among all the tribes of
> Israel. Thus Jerusalem is the foremost of [70]the "ca[m]ps of Israel"
> (*4Q394* 34-35,67-70).

From this text we can see that the Temple was considered to retain the distinction of sanctifying Jerusalem as the place where God's name had been caused to dwell. If this is so, then the Qumran community used the imagery of the Temple only in analogous terms to express their role as an elect remnant. It is also possible that the priests at Qumran wanted to keep channels open with the Jerusalem Temple in case future events might bring them back to the city and the Temple. Stephen Pfann observes:

> There's a possibility, as Roland deVaux asserted, that they
> went up to Jerusalem at the time that there was a time of aban-
> donment between the mid-first century B.C. and the beginning
> of the first century A.D. But they may have been endeavoring to
> make amends to change things hoping perhaps this was the time
> of their vindication and that perhaps they themselves would be
> reinstated as priests in the Temple. We do know that in the end
> they expected that an entire Temple would replace the one that
> was standing there at the time.[16]

Even with their somewhat positive attitude, the community did criticize the polluted state of the Temple and priesthood, and positioned itself *outside* Jerusalem. Also, it is clear that the community intended to construct its own purified Temple after the final battle between the "Sons of Darkness" and the "Sons of Light." However, the Sect still revered the sanctity of the Second Temple because God had chosen Jerusalem and the Temple Mount.

## The Community As a Symbolic Temple

The Qumran community used the language of the Temple to describe its own ritual life. There has been some discussion about how this symbolism is to be understood. For example, in *4QpIs*[a] 7:7-6; 9:6, the Qumran community [council] is paralleled to the Temple via spiritual imagery, for there it is referred to as a "Holy of Holies for Aaron and a Temple for Israel." John Townsend has noted that because Jewish literature from the Second Temple period used sacrificial language in reference to various nonsacrificial aspects of life, interpreters have often been tempted to argue that the Scroll authors regarded the Jerusalem cult as unnecessary.[17] However, these references include authors such as Aristeas and Ben Sira, who clearly held the Temple and its cult in high esteem.[18] We learned earlier that while the community may have regarded itself as a symbolic temple, it may have also continued to support the divine institution of the Temple. Based on the *Rule of the Community* (*1QS* 5:5-6; 8:4-10; 9:3-6) and the *Damascus Document* (*CD* 3:18–4:10),[19] the following points summarize this concept of the community as a symbolic temple:

First, the community is, by analogy, conceived of as a temple, the repository of divine truth—that is, the revealed mysteries concerning God's will (evidence of God's presence among the community) for holiness, and the means of eschatological preparation for the last days. In *1QH* 7:8f the community is portrayed as being an immovable temple-city built upon a rock. The rock probably symbolized the eternal truth and knowledge of the community, which would serve as an "everlasting foundation" for Israel. The Sect believed that by fulfilling their representative function for all Israel, the nation could become purified and realize a restored sanctity in the sanctuary.

Second, the community as a symbolic temple consisted of both priests ("the house of Aaron," or Zadokites), and non-priests (*am-Yisrael*, or "people of Israel") corresponding to the graded holiness of the Temple precincts, which stood in contrast to the non-Zadokite or unqualified priests and worshipers at the desecrated Second Temple.

Third, the sacrificial offering in this temple-community (*1QS* 9:4-5) exhibits the proper interpretation and observance of the cultus, as opposed to the ritually defiled offering performed in the Second Temple. Since obedience to the Law was symbolized by participation in the Temple sacrificial system, if this cultus was defiled, obedience to Law itself would symbolize a pure cultus apart from the inaccessible ritual. The fact that burnt offerings were not performed at Qumran, but rather "the offering of the lips," or "prayer" (*1QS* 9:5; cf. *CD* 11:8-21) is evidence both of the regard for the Jerusalem Temple as the only acceptable place of sacrifice, and the original intention of the First Temple to be a "house of prayer" (1 Kings 8:28-53; 2 Chronicles 6:19-40; Isaiah 56:7; cf. Psalm 40:6; 51:16-17). This emphasis on prayer as sacrifice also has eschatological connotations in view of the Essene desire to remove the unlawful sacrifices and restore the Temple to holiness (see Isaiah 56:7).

As the above summary implies, the primary motives for the development of the community as a symbolic temple were: 1) because of the defilement of the Jerusalem Temple, which is documented in *CD* 20:22: "Israel sinned and made the Temple unclean." The Sect's departure from Jerusalem to live at Khirbet Qumran was because of their inability to participate in a religiously and morally corrupt worship system; 2) their belief that God had established a unique covenant with them as the vanguard of the messianic era. In this regard they considered themselves a "divine planting" (*1QS* 11:8; *1QH* 6:15; 8:5); 3) that the divine Presence was dwelling in their community and constituting it as the representative eschatological Temple.

Stephen Pfann points out that these motives, based analogically on the Temple and its functions, did not replace the Temple as a vital and legitimate institution:

> This type of dissatisfaction with the Temple as it stood led Hellenistic Judaism to look for symbolism in the actions of the Temple. However, it doesn't mean that they never came to the Temple. Certainly Philo and other Hellenistic Jews came to the Temple as they were commanded. They felt that the overriding reason for the Temple and all its practices was in the symbolism, and what could actually be understood about God and his ways with man. From the books of Moses and the ways of the priests and the sacrifices they derived symbols concerning man, his psyche, and the makeup and his relationship with man and his relationship with God. Soon there was something symbolic in the Temple. The same was true for the Essenes: their prayers in themselves could become like sacrifices. But to what extent they really wanted to supplant the Temple with these practices I don't think can really be understood because we don't have everything [they wrote on this subject]. However, it seems that in the case of the Essenes, as in the case of the Hellenistic Jews who came from thousands of miles to come to Jerusalem, that even though they had other symbolic ways of carrying out Temple worship miles away from the Temple, they did believe in pilgrimage and they did believe in the importance of the Temple and in the commands of God to do sacrifices.[20]

It is also clear that any use of analogy between the Temple and the community's spiritual structure and service did not replace the hope for a literal future Temple. In the Cave 4 documents *Words of the Luminaries*, Jerusalem is elevated as the City of God, and the Temple is presented as the place to where nations will one day bring their tribute:

Jerusalem [the city which you c]hose from the whole earth for your Name to be there for ever. . . . And all the nations would see your glory. . . . And to your great Name they will carry their offerings: silver, gold, precious stones, with all the treasures of their country, to honor your people and Zion your holy city and your wonderful house (*4Q504* 4:1-4,8-12).

In this text we see a literal future Temple to which foreign nations will come after the restoration (Isaiah 56:6-7; 60:10; Zechariah 2:11; 6:15; 14:16). *The Florilegium* tells us this Temple was to be "built by men" (*4QFlor* 107-110)[21] according to the plans laid out in the *Temple Scroll*, which would itself be replaced at the end of days (that is, in the new creation) by the Temple built by God Himself (*11QTemple* 29:9; *4QFlor* 107). The gigantic dimensions of this Temple are described in *The New Jerusalem* document (*4Q554*)—a rectangular city 13 miles by 18 miles with 12 gates for the 12 tribes and guarded by 1,500 towers 100 feet high. Yet the phrase "Temple built by men" has also been given a symbolic interpretation, so let's examine the literal and symbolic interpretations in more depth.

## The Temple of Men

There has been considerable debate over the use of the phrase *miqdash 'adam* in the thematic *pesher* known as *The Florilegium* (*4Q174*). Scholars are divided over whether this key phrase should be interpreted literally to mean a "Temple (or 'Sanctuary') built by men," or symbolically to mean a "temple consisting of men or mankind." The phrase in question appears in a section of the *Florilegium* that comments on 2 Samuel 7:10-14, where we find an ambiguous reference to a "place that God will establish for His people where they will dwell securely." This is explained by the reference to a future Temple in Exodus 15:17-18. The relevant text, in context, reads:

"[And] an enemy [will trouble him no mo]re, [nor will] the son of iniquity [afflict him again] as at the beginning. From the day on which [I established judges] over my people, Israel" (2 Samuel 7:10). This (refers to) the house which [they will establish] for [him] in the last days, as is written in the book of [Moses: "A temple of the Lord] will you establish with your hands. YHWH shall reign for ever and ever" (Exodus 15:17-18). This (refers to) the house into which shall never enter [ . . . ] either the

Ammonite, or the Moabite . . . or the foreigner, or the proselyte, never, because there [he will reveal] to the holy ones; eternal [glory] will appear over it for ever; foreigners shall not again lay it waste as they laid waste, at the beginning, the tem[ple of Is]rael for its sins. And he commanded to build for himself a *temple of men*, to offer him in it, before him, the works of the Law. And as for what he said to David: "I shall obtain for you rest from all your enemies" (1 Samuel 1:11) (it refers to this,) that he will obtain for them rest from all the sons of Belial, those who make them fall, to destr[oy them for their s]ins, when they come with the plans of Belial to make the s[ons] of light fall, and to plot against them wicked plans so that they are trapped by Belial in their guilty error. . . . . And YHWH de[clares] to you that he will build you a house. I will raise up your seed after you and establish the throne of his kingdom [for ev]er. I will be a father to him and he will be a son to me" (2 Samuel 7:12-14). This (refers to the) "Branch of David," who will arise with the Interpreter of the Law who [will rise up] in Zi[on in] the last days, as it is written: "I will raise up the hut of David which has fallen," (Amos 9:11). This (refers to) "the hut of David which has fallen," who will arise to save Israel (*4Q174* i 1-12).

The view that the phrase "temple of men" indicates a *human* temple is represented by James C. VanderKam:

This section is speaking about a sanctuary of the last days that God, not humans, will construct; it will be a "sanctuary of men," that is, it will not be a building; and the sacrifices offered in it will not be animal and cereal offerings but "the works of the Law." In other words, the Lord's sanctuary will be like the Qumran community or perhaps equal to it.[22]

Those who believe that a spiritual temple made up of the community is being described here do not necessarily reject that the Sect also expected a literal Temple to be rebuilt in Jerusalem. Yet there are several reasons why a symbolic interpretation should be rejected. First, the biblical expectation of the last-days Temple was literal, not symbolic, as Ezekiel 40–48 reveals. We have already seen that this literal idea of a Third Temple is supported by the *Temple Scroll*. This idea also finds support from the *Florilegium* (*4Q174*). The commentator interprets the prophecy to Nathan in 2 Samuel 7 as having reference to three Temples. One is the eschatological Temple to be built by God Himself (*4Q174* 1-2 i 1-5), which is also mentioned in the *Temple Scroll* (*11Q19* 29:10). Another is the Second Temple, which existed at the same time as the Qumran community, for it is said to have been "built by Israel" and to have been "desecrated" (*4Q174* 1-2 i 5-6). The final reference is to our "temple of men." There is no good reason to say that two of these temples are literal, but the third is symbolic, when all three include the same explanation of the prophetic promise of a literal sanctuary promised to the house of Israel.

Second, in the context of *4Q174*, the references to the "Temple of men" relate to Israel's restoration and the revival of the Davidic dynasty (see Amos 9:11), which corresponds with the biblical expectation of a literal Temple (see Ezekiel 37:25-28). The references to a future Temple that will no longer be subjected to desecration by foreigners allude to Zechariah 14:20-21, which also refers to a literal Temple. We know that the Qumran community was not free from desecration, as *4QpPsa^a* and *4QpNah* reveal with the intrusions of the Wicked Priest, the Man of Lies, and their followers. Furthermore, the community's own members were often criticized in sectarian disciplinary texts for having proclivities toward defiling actions (for example, "he loved his bodily emissions," *4Q477*). It is hard to believe, then, that the Qumran commentator would have felt his community could have fulfilled the promise to David to be "the Lord's sanctuary."

Third, the reference to offerings of "the works of the Law" speaks of sacrifices which are made according to the Law. The Qumran community was particularly distressed over what they considered corrupted sacrifices given by illegitimate priests in a defiled Temple, because the Law was not being properly followed. This was what brought about the destruction of the First Temple and doomed the Second. They looked for a Third Temple in which proper sacrifices would be offered. They did not offer sacrifices at Qumran, most likely because they did not envision it as a place for sacrifice. That was a role reserved for the restored Jerusalem Temple.

In my opinion, the phrase "Temple of men" should be equated with the ideal Temple of the *Temple Scroll*, which the Sect believed would be built in Jerusalem during the interim of the last days (in which the community lived or expected imminently) prior to the eschaton and the advent of the "Age to Come." At that time, the eschatological Temple will be built by God.

## The Eschatological Temple

The idea that the Temple "built by human hands" (Acts 7:48) would be replaced with a divinely ordered eschatological Temple is presented in the *Book of Enoch*, a favored book of the Sect:

> ... till they covered up that old house. ... And I say till the Lord of the sheep brought a new house greater and loftier than the first, and set it up in the place of the first (*1 Enoch* 90:29).

One of the most explicit Qumran descriptions of the eschatological Temple is provided in the Aramaic work from Caves 1, 2, 4, 5, and 11 known as *The New Jerusalem* (*4Q554; 5Q15*). This text, clearly influenced by what is written about the eschatological Temple in Ezekiel 40–48, provides an extended description of the restored Jerusalem, and is comprised largely of instructions for measuring the new Temple based on Ezekiel's scheme. Michael Wise, in his Chicago University dissertation on the *Temple Scroll*, has also shown how favorably this text compares with the measurements given in *The New Jerusalem* for the Qumranic Third Temple.[23] While many details of the text remain elusive because of *hapax legomenon* (that is, words appearing only once) and multiple breaks in the manuscripts, we can discern that the author envisioned an immense rectangular city (13 x 18 miles) with a surrounding wall containing 12 gates (one for each of the 12 tribes of Israel with Gate of Levi centermost, aligned with the sacrificial altar and the Temple entrance), and with nearly 1,500 towers (100 feet tall) guarding the city. Dr. Magen Broshi, former curator of the Shrine of the Book, has observed that these dimensions clearly indicate the eschatological nature of the Temple in the *Temple Scroll* as well as help pinpoint the time that Scroll was written:

> The *New Jerusalem* document is found in Qumran in several copies in Aramaic, although we believe that everything Qumranic was composed in Hebrew. It has incredible figures for the Temple, (like the *Temple Scroll*) which must have been as big as the whole city today. I believe it would take million upon millions of hours just to level the ground before building could [commence]. Therefore, although it is almost impractical in this sense, they didn't worry because the Lord is the one who is going to build it, or enable it to be built. Jerusalem, according to *New Jerusalem*, must have been gigantic, bigger than any modern city, [yet] they were very accurate about all the architectural details. Their design shows a very good knowledge of Hellenistic architecture.

Therefore the *Temple Scroll* could not have been a product of the Persian period, it has too many Hellenistic conceptions.[24]

Another eschatological element in the *New Jerusalem* text is seen in the specific reference made concerning the Kittim[25] (see also Daniel 11:30), which appear frequently in Qumran apocalyptic literature, but here are joined in column 11 with a probable reference to the messianic kingdom.[26] If this is the proper reconstruction of the text, then the kingdom may be the same as that first introduced in Daniel 2:45 and paralleled in the collection of *pseudo-Daniel* texts (*4Q243-245*). This Temple, then, would be the eschatological Temple of the messianic age.

This understanding helps prepare us for the Sect's quest for the ideal Temple as expressed in the *Temple Scroll*. We must also remember that the Dead Sea community selected their site for a reason, and one possibility could be the location's prominence in the biblical accounts of the restoration of the final days. When the eschatological Temple is constructed, waters will flow from beneath the Holy of Holies and freshen the Dead Sea (Ezekiel 47:8-9; Zechariah 14:8). Perhaps the community was strategically placed so its members could witness the fulfillment of this eschatological event.

## A Description of the *Temple Scroll*

The complete text of the *Temple Scroll* came from Cave 11, hence its designation as *11QTemple* or *11Q19* (primary copy) and *11Q20* (fragmentary copy), although several fragments from two or three other copies have now been identified from Cave 4. The *Temple Scroll* is made up of 19 sheets, each containing three to four columns of text for an approximate length of 28.5 feet, longer than any of the previously discovered Dead Sea Scrolls (the *Isaiah Scroll* is about 4 feet shorter). Its contents include architectural plans for building the Temple as well as detailed descriptions of the Temple services and festivals, many of which are not mentioned in the Bible or elsewhere.[27] For this reason Yigael Yadin, who first found and prepared the document for publication, named it the *Temple Scroll*. In addition, a monarchial government structure, based on the law of the Torah, is described in a section that has been designated "The Law of the King" (*11Q19* 56:12–59:21). Some scholars have unsuccessfully argued for an early first-century date; however, the consensus of scholarship places the date in the second half of the second century B.C. (103–88 B.C.), and some have contended for an even earlier date (third century B.C.). If the polemics in the *Temple Scroll* are calling for a revision of the religious and political order of John Hyrcanus, then only a date after 120 B.C. is possible.[28] Although it's debatable whether Hyrcanus' reign is in view in the Scroll, the paleographic data is consistent with a date in the Hasmonean period (165–63 B.C.); however, it is still possible the original composition dates to an even earlier time.

## The Origin of the *Temple Scroll*

Some scholars believe the *Temple Scroll* contains clues that may reveal the identity of the Sect itself, but again, there is no agreement on this identity. Most scholars, beginning with Yadin, believe that there are sufficient similarities between the *Temple Scroll* and other Qumran documents to argue that the *Temple Scroll* originated at Qumran. In a similar manner, Philip Davies sees "a possible connection between events related in Ezra and Nehemiah with the formation of the *Temple Scroll* and the origin of the Qumran community represented in the *Damascus Document*."[29] The primary evidence for an origin with the Qumran community is the apparent use of a solar calendar in the *Temple Scroll* as well as affinities with the *Zadokite Fragments*.

However, the *Temple Scroll* deals with topics that are not mentioned in any of the other Scrolls, and more importantly, is silent on the topic most central to the Sect—the daily observation of ritual purity. Furthermore, there are significant incongruities with the *Zadokite Fragments* in such crucial areas as the laws of idolatry and the swearing of oaths. For these reasons, scholars such as H. Stegemann and Lawrence Schiffman have contended that the *Temple Scroll* was composed independently of the Qumran community. Stegemann argues that it was written as long as two centuries before the Sect existed and was intended for the whole of Israel as an appendix to the Torah, providing the Temple plan and an updated version of the law-code of Deuteronomy 12–26.[30] Schiffman believes that based on parallels with *4QMMT*, which he believes resemble Sadducean legal interpretation, the pre-Qumranian sources for the *Temple Scroll* probably also reflect Sadducean views. Thus, the *Temple Scroll*'s author, as well as the Qumran Sect, may have held Sadducean views or early forms of it.[31] Another variation on the theory that the *Temple Scroll* belongs outside the Sect is the view that it was written as a polemic against the Righteous Teacher of the Sect by another faction who opposed his teaching.[32]

Despite the near-consensus for a Qumranic origin, most scholars admit that the origin of the *Temple Scroll* still remains one of the unsolved mysteries of the Scrolls. Yet even though we cannot be certain about the authorship of the *Temple Scroll*, we do know that it was an important document to the Qumran Sect and that its theology and purpose reflected or was adopted as their own. For this association Yadin offered the archaeological evidence from Cave 1 of several rectangular linen sheets with an embroidered pattern in blue thread.[33] This pattern is of a rectangle surrounded by three quadrangles that become progressively squared. If these linens wrapped the Scrolls,[34] then the image on them may represent the design of the *Temple Scroll's* Temple and reveal how central a hope this rebuilding of the Temple was to the Sect.

## The *Temple Scroll* As a New Torah?

The *Temple Scroll* presents itself as a rewritten Torah that begins with the renewal of the Sinaitic covenant in Exodus 34 and then gives the instructions for the building of the Tabernacle in Exodus 35. Exodus 34 fits the Sect's idea of itself as the community of the renewed covenant, and their desert setting parallels that of the Sinai. Exodus 35 provides the divine command to build a sanctuary (verse 1), although the command in Exodus 25:8 "to build Me a Sanctuary" may have originally stood at the top of column 3 (now missing), since the *Temple Scroll's* use of Deuteronomy 12:10-11 continues this theme. Exodus 35 also presents the tribal arrangement for the Tabernacle in the desert, which provided the structural pattern for the Temple described in the *Temple Scroll.*

With this identification established, the text then follows the order of the biblical Torah in its presentation of the Temple structure, services, and national government. The alteration of divine statements in the biblical Torah from the third person ("God said ...") to the first person ("I said ...") gives the impression that the work came as direct revelation from God rather than through Moses. It also attempts (through a unique type of midrashic exegesis) to clarify ambiguous laws in order to establish a harmonious legal stance. These peculiar traits have led many to speculate on the author of the *Temple Scroll's* intentions. Some scholars believe the author may have incorporated a supposedly lost book of the Bible known as the "Book of Temple Plans," which was given by God to David and by David to Solomon. The biblical chronicler recorded the existence of such plans when he wrote, " 'All this,' said David, 'the Lord made me understand in writing by His hand upon me, all the details of this pattern. . . .' Then David gave to his son Solomon the plan [of the Temple]. . . " (1 Chronicles 28:19,11-12). The rabbis recorded in a midrash that such a document once existed, even referring to it as the *Temple Scroll*. They argued that it was received at Sinai by Moses, then from Moses to Joshua, from Joshua to the elders of Israel, from the elders to the prophets, from the prophets to David, and finally from David to Solomon.[35] Whether or not we accept this, it seems clear that the form of *11QTemple* is not a sectarian book, but a Torah-like document.[36] The Qumran community may have believed that their *Temple Scroll* was a holy book that was equally a part of the God-given Torah.

However, it is strange that only one complete copy of so central a document as the *Temple Scroll* was found in Cave 11 with several fragments from Cave 4. We would expect that a "second Torah" or "addition to the Torah" would have been considered at least as sacred as Deuteronomy upon which its laws are based. How, then, do we explain its few copies in contrast to 31 to 34 copies of the book of Deuteronomy? In addition, none of the other Scrolls quote from or make reference to any portion of the *Temple Scroll*. Furthermore, while the complete *Temple Scroll* is a single copy, its form reveals that a number of different sources were used by its author. Its sacred calendar, festivals, and sacrifices, and the laws dealing with these matters find parallels in the apocryphal *Book of Jubilees*.[37] The *Temple Scroll's* revisions of the laws related to slaughtering animals (also found in *4QMMT*) may have depended on *4QLev$^d$* (*4Q26*) as a source.[38] Its eschatology is similar to both *Jubilees* and possibly *1 Enoch*. Other parallels have been drawn between the *Temple Scroll* and the prayer of Nehemiah 10, the prayer of the pre-Qumran text *4QDibHam*, and the *Damascus Document (CD)*.[39]

## The Temple of the *Temple Scroll*

Any study of the *Temple Scroll* faces a plethora of different opinions in interpretation: 1) Was *11QTemple* a proto-Qumran document on par with the *Book of Jubilees* or an eschatological Torah, or more specifically, an eschatological Deuteronomy or an inspired holy book considered to be an additional Torah? 2) Does it present one or two eschatological Temples; and 3) Did the community actually envision the construction of this Temple by their own hands, or view it as merely a collection of interesting biblical notions for sectarian study? Let's answer these questions one by one.

First, *11QTemple* cites the same solar calendrical system that was used by the Qumran community, its contents parallel the cultic concerns of the community, its various laws are based on Deuteronomy (a book used by the Sect to critique the Jerusalem priesthood), many of its regulations for the Temple are unique (having no parallels in either biblical or rabbinic legislation), and its text is composed in divinely directed (non-mediated) style, unlike any other Jewish document. For all of these reasons, Yadin contends that *11QTemple* has a Qumran provenance.[40] Of course, we could contend that the Sect developed its theology from *11QTemple*. However, Michael O. Wise has shown that while the work is not as apocalyptic as the other Qumran Scrolls, it does derive from an apocalyptic milieu, and is comparable to the *Book of Jubilees*.[41] According to Asher Finkel, *11QTemple* picks up where *Jubilees* ends, and both share many common elements (such as solar calendar systems). He has shown that the major redactional concern of *11QTemple* was governed by what he called "canon consciousness."[42] This "canon consciousness" is rooted in a profound awareness of God's direct revelation that affects the legal interpretation of the Scroll, reshaping the Pentateuchal text to conform to the theme of God's presence. In this manner, *11QTemple* projected itself as an original Torah and pattern for the future restored Temple.

Second, Judith Wentling has successfully demonstrated that there was only one eschatological Temple apparent in both *11QTemple* (29:3-10) and the expectations of the Qumran community.[43] This eschatological Temple made use of the literary models in the Pentateuch, the writings of prophets such as Ezekiel, and *Jubilees-11QTemple*; and depended also on the Old Testament and the cycles of biblical history (possibly prophetic motifs), which reaffirmed that God would continue to act on behalf of His covenant people. To suggest that *11QTemple* mentioned two Temples would deviate from the biblical precedent of one central sanctuary—a precedent the community was careful to preserve and follow. Wentling thus concludes: "Only one eschatological temple would be built. Perhaps corresponding to the rabbinic notion of man's partnership with God in the act of creation, the future *miqdash* [sanctuary] would be built by those in whom the spirit of God already dwelled."[44]

Third, H. Stegemann has argued that the Qumran community never intended to build their Temple in Jerusalem; rather, it served as a means to secure proper *halakah* so that eschatological Israel could function according to God's covenant.[45] Stegemann sees nothing in *11QTemple* specifically designed for the Qumran community or its time; instead, it is an updated version of the law-code of Deuteronomy 12–26 and a pattern-book for the Temple, designed to help prevent Israel from a second exile by reconforming it to the ideal standard of the divine will.[46] Michael Wise appears to agree with this assessment, arguing that the how of building the Temple was not important to *11QTemple* 29:3-10 (the covenant section), but rather the restoration of the patriarchal covenant, which guaranteed God's abiding presence.[47] While there is much we can agree about in Stegemann and Wise's statements about the practical use of the *Temple Scroll*, it must be contended that the eschatological aspirations presented in the text were not simply idealistic, but flowed from the author/redactor's commitment to a biblical command to build a ritually pure Temple. The possession of the *Temple Scroll* by the Qumran community was in line with their own conviction that they were to implement the events that would accompany (or perhaps lead to) the eschaton.

## A Description of the Temple

Johann Maier of the University of Cologne has presented one of the most detailed studies to date on the architectonic structure exhibited in the Temple of *11QTemple*.[48] His conclusion was that the plan was not only an actual reflection of realistic concepts and traditions of the Jerusalem school of architecture, but that it may have served as one source of design-style for Herod's restoration of the Second Temple. Furthermore, the Scrolls themselves give the impression, as Chilton has pointed out, "that the Essenes saw themselves as a new camp in the wilderness, awaiting their rise to power and control of the Temple."[49] If this is so, then they had a detailed architectural plan in hand to complement their victory. There is still a difference of opinion, however, about whether the Sect believed that they would erect the Third Temple[50] or that the work would strictly be an act of God.[51]

The details of *11QTemple* do not match those of any Temple ever built—neither the post-exilic Second Temple of Zerubbabel (see the Mishnah tractate *Middot*) nor its Herodian enlargement, or even the eschatological pattern of Ezekiel 40–48. Rather, the *Temple Scroll* proposes a square-shaped edifice to be constructed on the Temple Mount after the polluted Jerusalem Temple was removed (see diagrams on pages 254-56). This Temple was to be surrounded by three concentric square courtyards (page 254). The innermost courtyard was to encircle the altar and sanctuary and was to be restricted to qualified priests only (*11Q19* 35:5-9) (page 255). The middle courtyard was accessible only to Israelite males over 20 years of age (*11Q19* 39:7-10), and the outer court was accessible to all ceremonially clean Israelites (*11Q19* 40:5-6). The Temple and the city of Jerusalem were to be transformed from a city with a Temple to a Temple City (that is, "the city of the Sanctuary"), and the dimensions were to encompass most of what was then the holy city (page 254). This Temple City reveals a sacred interrelationship between the concepts of Temple and city, with each being an entirely new construction and combination superseding any previous. In a functional sense, the city would serve as a hedge around the Temple, with the result being a radical elevation and change in status for Judaism.[52]

While the dimensions of this Temple are much larger than those of the Second Temple (the outer court measuring about a half-mile on one side)[53] and differ in many other respects, the design itself may reflect the idealic expectations of the Jerusalem school of architecture, and may very well evidence a plan underlying Herodian construction (page 256). Such a limited correspondence was demonstrated from its architectonic structure by Johann Maier in a study of the architectural history of the Temple based on *11QTemple*.[54] It has often been supposed that the reason that *11QTemple* presented a differently structured Temple from that of Herod's Second Temple was because the authors of *11QTemple* were opposed to the Jerusalem Temple. However, nothing in *11QTemple* gives any impression that they had anything but reverence for the Jerusalem Temple.

Interestingly, a prophecy Josephus cited about the destruction of the Temple may relate to the *Temple Scroll*'s square Temple design. In Josephus' concluding description of the Second Temple's destruction, he noted that on the eve of the Romans' assault "false prophets" attempted to persuade the people that the Temple was inviolable and that the deliverance of the Temple was imminent (*Wars of the Jews* 6.5.3 § 285-315). Of particular importance here was Josephus' statement that after the destruction of the Antonia Fortress the Jews had made the Temple platform square, even though Jewish tradition (not Scripture) had warned that when the Temple was made square it would be destroyed (*Wars of the Jews* 6.5.3 § 311). Josephus also noted the prevailing Jewish belief that the Roman attack was evidence that they were in the messianic age and that the prophesied universal Jewish rule was on its way (*Wars of the Jews* 6.5.3 § 312).[55] This places Josephus' statement about the prediction of the square Temple in an eschatological context. Since there is no biblical

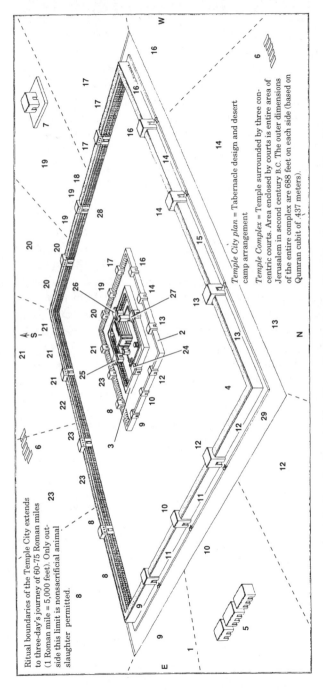

Ritual boundaries of the Temple City extends to three-day's journey of 60-75 Roman miles (12 + 4). Gates in the Middle Court area are set up in the same arrangement. The dotted lines outside the structure indicate the tribal allotments. Each tribe has its own city outside its gate and thus encircled the Temple City. 2. *Middle Court:* Gates are named after the 12 tribes of Israel. 3. *Inner Court:* Gates are named after four groups in the tribe of the Levi. The arrangement is the same as that in the Sinai desert camp (Numbers 3:14-19) and use is restricted to priests and Levites. 4. Temple platform. 5. Temporary places for the impure (defiled) located to the east of the Temple City, with three buildings for the three groups of impurities. 6. Cemeteries—one for each of the four tribal cities (at equidistant points oriented north/south). 7. Latrines—roofed houses with pits located northwest of the city. 8. Reuben 9. Judah 10. Levi 11. Aaron 12. Simeon 13. Asher 14. Naphtali 15. Merari 16. Dan 17. Gad 18. Gershon 19. Zebulun 20. Issachar 21. Benjamin 22. Kahat 23. Joseph 24. Aaronites 25. Merarites 26. Gershonites 27. Kohathites 28. 16 three-story chambers or room units with place on top for Succot (Feast of Tabernacles) 29. Moat

*Artistic Rendering of the Temple City Described in the Temple Scroll*

1. *Outer Court:* Gates (outside) are named after 12 tribes and 16 room units (inside) are allocated to 12 tribes and sons of Aaron (priests) and one of three Levitical families (12 + 4). Gates in the Middle Court area are set up in the same arrangement.

*Temple City plan* = Tabernacle design and desert camp arrangement

*Temple Complex* = Temple surrounded by three concentric courts. Area enclosed by courts is entire area of Jerusalem in second century B.C. The outer dimensions of the entire complex are 688 feet on each side (based on Qumran cubit of .437 meters).

*Drawing by Dr. Leen Ritmeyer*

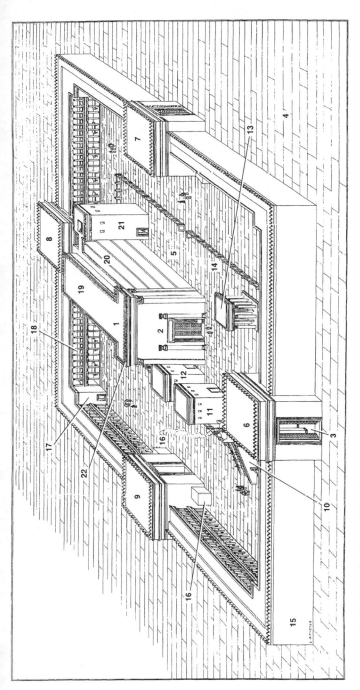

## Artistic Rendering of the Inner Court Area of the New Temple (As Described in the Temple Scroll)

1. Temple  2. Temple entrance  3. Eastern Gate  4. Temple platform (Middle Courtyard)  5. Inner Courtyard  6. Gate of Aaronites  7. Gate of Kohathites  8. Gate of Gershonites  9. Gate of Merarites  10. Great Altar  11. House of the Utensils  12. House of the Laver (ritual washbasin)  13. Slaughterhouse (with tethers for slaughtered animals)  14. The Soreg (boundary to restrict entrance to ritually qualified individuals)  15. Walls of Inner Court  16. Cooking places  17. Stove  18. Stoa (with sitting places and tables)  19. Inside of Holy Place is the Temple furniture and in the Holy of Holies is the restored Ark of the Covenant and cherubim  20. Priestly chambers  21. Gilded staircase to reach roof of the Temple (connected by elevated walkway)  22. Spires to prevent birds from perching on buildings and defiling structures

*Drawing by Dr. Leen Ritmeyer*

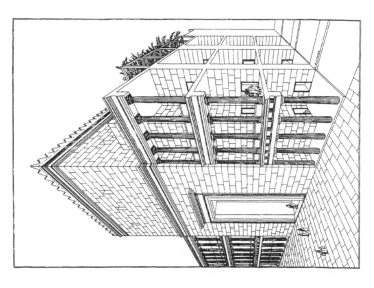

**Artistic Rendering of the
Three Stories of the Outer Court**

*Drawing by Dr. Leen Ritmeyer*

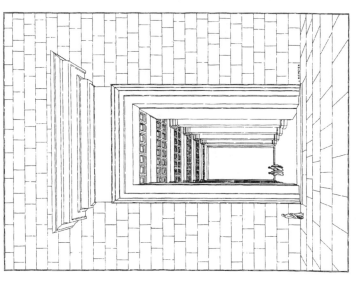

**Artistic Rendering of a
Gate of the Outer Court**

*Drawing by Dr. Leen Ritmeyer*

The Ta'amireh Bedouin shepherd Muhammed edh-Dhib (Abu-Dahoud), standing in front of Cave 1, where he found the first Dead Sea Scrolls. At the top of the picture is the hole into which he threw a stone that broke a scroll jar and led him to the discovery. (Photo by Paul Streber.)

Muhammed edh-Dhib shows where he discovered numerous storage jars (one containing four scrolls) inside Cave 1. (Photo by Paul Streber.)

Author explains the symbolism of the Shrine of the Book during filming at Israel's museum of the Dead Sea Scrolls. The white dome in the background represents the lid of a scroll jar. Inside the building (see accompanying photo) are displayed the seven scrolls found in Cave 1 (the *Great Isaiah Scroll* is at the center), the *Temple Scroll* from Cave 11, and other discoveries from the Judean desert. (Top photo by Paul Streber.)

The Wadi Qumran (right) and the author standing on a marl bluff (left). Behind the author (at the top of the picture) is Cave 4 and the Qumran plateau, on which sits the ruins of the Qumran community. (Photo by Paul Streber.)

Three views of Cave 4 (with the author on top, at entrance, and inside). In the middle picture, author points to area where over 15,000 fragments of scrolls were found. The lack of access to photos of these fragments caused the much-publicized Dead Sea Scrolls "controversy." (Photos by Paul Streber.)

Dr. Magen Broshi, Dead Sea scholar and former curator of the Shrine of the Book. Dr. Broshi joined with Dr. Hanan Eshel in excavating the newly discovered caves near Qumran in the beginning of 1996. (Photo by Paul Streber.)

Professor Hanan Eshel, pictured on location at one of the newly discovered caves where he and Dr. Broshi supervised the excavation work. Dr. Eshel also discovered in a cave near Jericho one of the oldest papyrus scrolls ever found in the Holy Land. (Photo courtesy of Hanan Eshel.)

Author with Dr. David Flusser, Hebrew University professor of Early Christianity and Judaism of the Second Temple Period. Dr. Flusser is one of the foremost scholars on the connection of the Dead Sea Scrolls with Christianity.

The author with Hebrew University professor Emanuel Tov, editor-in-chief of the Dead Sea Scrolls Project, which includes supervising the International Team of scholars who translate the Scrolls and prepare their work for publication.

Author and Israeli Scroll Team member Professor Shemaryahu Talmon view calendrical texts which Dr. Talmon is preparing for publication. (Photos by Paul Streber.)

Allegedly one of the original jars that contained Scrolls, purchased by Bethlehem antiquities dealer Kando and now in the office of his son Edmund in East Jerusalem. (Photo by Paul Streber.)

The author with one of the original jars from the Qumran caves, now in storage at the Rockefeller Museum. (Photo by Paul Streber.)

At the scene of the 1995 excavations on the Qumran plateau (across from Cave 4), drilling to reach stone-lined cavities where scrolls and other objects were indicated by ground-penetrating radar. Finds included Persian period artifacts, ostraca, and a jar handle stamped with the words "the king." (Photo by Paul Streber.)

Stone-lined pits excavated in 1992 during Operation Scroll. Similar and yet unexcavated pits in the same area may contain Scroll jars and other artifacts. (Photo by Gary Collett.)

The Temple Scroll—note the deterioration at the top of the
Scroll caused by improper storage in a shoebox by the dealer
Kando. (Photo courtesy of the Shrine of the Book of the Israel
Museum.)

View of the main block of the Qumran community. (Photo by Paul
Streber.)

Aerial view of the Qumran community. (Photo courtesy of "House
of the Scribe" Museum.)

The "Scriptorium," where it is
believed the Qumran community
wrote and copied many of the
manuscripts that became the
Dead Sea Scrolls. This work was
probably done on the second floor
of the building, which yielded
remains of ink wells and possibly
scroll tables. (Photo by Paul
Streber.)

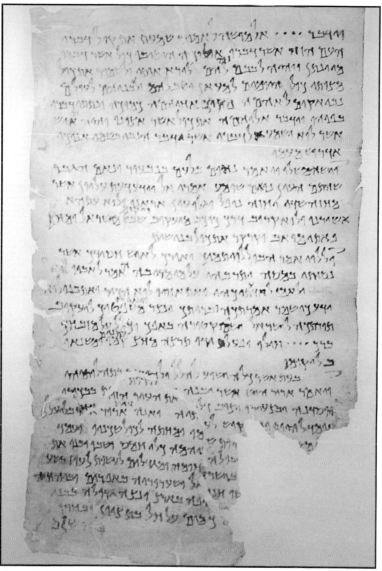

One of the newly published scroll fragments—*4Q175 (4QTest)*:
A *Messianic Testimonia* or *Anthology*, so called because it is based
on the biblical texts of Deuteronomy 18:18-19 (the prophet like
Moses) and Numbers 24:15-17 (the star and scepter of Balaam's
oracle), which are considered prophetic messianic passages. (Photo
courtesy of Bruce and Ken Zuckerman, West Semitic Research.)

A manuscript fragment of Genesis (*4Q2 Gen^b*) as it was found in Cave 4 and photographed in normal light. It is impossible to read because of the severe darkening of the leather.

The same fragment after it has been photographed in infrared (results of spectral imaging are similar). This new technology allows the text to be read for the first time. (Photos courtesy of Bruce and Ken Zuckerman, West Semitic Research.)

Father Emile Puech of the École Biblique at work on his translations of the controversial Messianic texts *4Q246* and *1Q521*. (Photo by Paul Streber.)

The famous *Isaiah Scroll (1QIsaᵃ)* from Cave 1. This is the best preserved of all the biblical manuscripts of the Dead Sea Scrolls. (Photo courtesy of Shrine of the Book of the Israel Museum.)

The author, inside Cave 3, pointing to the place where the *Copper Scroll* was discovered resting on a stone shelf. The *Copper Scroll* lists 64 places were Temple treasures may be hidden. A second copper scroll, as yet undiscovered, provides additional details about locating these treasures. (Photo by Paul Streber.)

Section of the *Copper Scroll* (cut 15) showing column 8, which describes items 34-38 (tithe jars, scrolls, and a total of 161 talents of silver and gold) hidden in the Jerusalem area.(Photo courtesy of Bruce and Ken Zuckerman, West Semitic Research.)

A partial view of the remains of Caves 7-10 as seen from Cave 4. In Cave 7, Greek papyri fragments were discovered (one of which is shown in the accompanying photo), which some scholars have claimed are portions of the New Testament. (Photo by Paul Streber.)

Greek papyri Fragment 5, which is claimed to be Mark 6:52-53.

Vendyl Jones's Cave of the Column at the Wadi Jawfet Zaben. He claims that at this site are hidden the ashes of the red heifer, the Tabernacle, the high priest's vestments, the Urim and Thummim, and the Ark of the Covenant. In a cave nearby he also claims he discovered 1,320 pounds of a reddish powdery substance in 1992 and 1994, which he identifies as *Qetorit,* or "Temple incense." (Photo courtesy of George Weiss.)

The late Rav Shlomo Goren inspects the excavation work at Vendyl Jones's Cave of the Column. (Vendyl Jones stands to Goren's upper right, wearing a vest and hat.) (Photo courtesy of George Weiss.)

or rabbinic source predicting the destruction of a square Temple platform, the source may have been the *Temple Scroll*. As Yadin conjectures:

> Perhaps Josephus—as in other instances . . . —set down something he had learned from the Essenes writings in general, and from our Scroll in particular? He may have arrived at the notion that somewhere in the writings of the Sect . . . there is a hint that before the Lord will create His Temple, the Temple must be square, as set forth in the Scroll.[56]

If this was so, then the *Temple Scroll*'s influence in Judaism may have spread beyond the Qumran community, for Josephus says it was in the Jewish records (without distinction). Also, according to Yadin's understanding of Josephus' statement, the "false prophets" were providing false assurance that the Temple's destruction was all part of a divine plan to rebuild a better Temple, and that with the destruction of the Temple would come the advent of Messiah and the destruction of the Roman army. However, this false assurance only hastened the destruction and prevented people from leaving the Temple area in order to preserve their lives. Also, the "false prophets" were basing their ill-fated counsel on a tradition that continued to be accepted in Judaism. Dr. Dan Bahat comments:

> What is this square Temple Mount? Where does it originate? How should we look at it? Should we refer to the square Temple Mount as the one which is the Maccabean one, which we believe is still underground by the water walk—I don't know the answer. But one thing I can tell you—during the Second Temple period a squarish Temple Mount played an important role in the ideology of the people, not only of the Dead Sea Scroll people, because Ezekiel represented ordinary Judaic beliefs.[57]

As Bahat notes, the tradition of a modular Temple and city goes back to the First Temple and that is the design presented for the eschatological Temple of Ezekiel (Ezekiel 40:47). It is also the preference in the Talmud (see *'Erub.* 6.10, p. 145; *Bar. b.'Erub.* 56.5)[58] and for the New Testament's New Jerusalem (see Revelation 21:16). These may have been sources for Josephus other than the *Temple Scroll*, but because he does not say the source was biblical, the *Temple Scroll* still remains a valid candidate.

## The Time of the Temple's Construction

Some individuals have wondered if the Temple in the *Temple Scroll* was to be built during the interim period of the eschatological age or in the eschatological period following the 40-year war. Either way, the Temple remains an eschatological structure because from the Sect's perspective, their present age was already part of the eschatological age. However, if it was to be built during the interim period, then we have *two* Temples presented in the *Temple Scroll*—a man-made one that will be replaced by one made by God. If it was to be built after the 40-year war, then we are looking at the divinely created Temple of the age to come. Yigael Yadin, who first published the *Temple Scroll*, believed there would be two Temples:

> The author [of the Temple Scroll] was definitely writing about the earthly man-made Temple that God commanded the Israelites to construct in the Promised Land. It was on this structure that God would settle his glory until the day of the new creation when God himself would "create my Temple . . . for all times" in accordance with his covenant "with Jacob at Bethel."[59]

Some scholars have agreed with Yadin's conclusions that the *Temple Scroll* does not refer to the final Temple, but an intermediary pre-messianic Temple. Therefore a restored Third Temple was envisioned as a replacement of the Second Temple, which was perceived to be desecrated. Its plans represented the only legitimate way to construct the Temple and legislate its cult until the divinely created sanctuary appeared. Remember, even though the Sect withdrew from the Jerusalem Temple, they never ceased to regard the Temple Mount as the only legitimate site for the Temple. If the Dead Sea Sect intended to implement the plans of *11QTemple*, then their problem was to gain control of the Temple Mount. Once this was accomplished and the site properly sanctified, they could begin to rebuild the Temple according to the restoration ideal of the pattern established at Sinai.

Other scholars have argued that only one Temple is in view in the *Temple Scroll*, since God said He would dwell among Israel at this sanctuary *forever* (Ezekiel 37:26-28). How could a temporary status "*until* the day of creation" be reconciled with a promise of permanency? The leading proponent of the one-Temple theory, Qumran scholar Ben Zion Wacholder, therefore translates the Hebrew adverb *'ad* not as "until," but as "during" or "while," with the sense that God's glory would settle on one Temple only.[60] However, if the text is read "until," it does not deny a continuity between the two Temples. Just as the *Shekinah* was "present" with the Tabernacle and then filled the First Temple without a sense of discontinuity, so also could it remain forever when the man-made Temple gives way to the divine creation.

This man-made Temple is interpreted as a rebuilt Temple during the present age for several reasons. First, the *Temple Scroll* does not discuss the end of days/age to come. This can be seen in the distinct terms its author used, which differ from the Sect's eschatological writings. An example is the use of the term *hacohen hagadol* ("the high priest")[61] rather than *cohen harosh* ("the chief priest"), which is found in the eschatological literature. There is also no mention of "the high priest" in Ezekiel's account of the eschatological Temple in chapters 40–48. Second, as Yadin has noted, "The Temple laws presented in the *[Temple] Scroll* are those conveyed by the Lord to Moses . . . as an eternal command for the Children of Israel."[62] These commands from Exodus 25–31 were understood in rabbinic Judaism to apply to any time within their age that it became possible to rebuild the holy Temple. Third, the *Temple Scroll* explicitly stated that the Temple was to be rebuilt before the end of days, even contrasting it with the new one to be built by God in the Age to Come:

> And I will consecrate My [T]emple by My Glory (*Shekinah*), (the Temple) on which I will settle / My glory, until the day of blessing (= the end of days) on which I will create My Temple/ and establish it Myself for all times, according to the covenant which I have made with Jacob at Bethel (*11QTemple* 29:8-10).

The covenant made at Bethel included the vision of the heavenly ladder (which may also have messianic connotations; see John 1:50-51). After receiving the vision, Jacob called this location "the house of God" (Hebrew, *Beth*—"house," + *el*—God") and "the gate of heaven" (Genesis 28:12-17). In the same manner, the heavenly Presence was to be restored to the Temple of *11QTemple*—the *Shekinah* glory, which would make it the legitimate "house of God."

## New Laws for the New Temple

The *Temple Scroll* also includes *halakah* that differs or is considered "new" with respect to the Mosaic legislation. For instance, the festival calendar includes several new festivals not a part of any biblical or later Jewish tradition (for example, a second New Year, two extra first fruits festivals, and the annual wood offering festival). Also, the Scroll includes extensive laws that seek to protect the sanctuary from becoming ritually defiled. That is the purpose for the large areas inside the courtyards and the placement of the Israelite tribes beyond the Temple city. Such additions might imply that the Temple was designed for the messianic age, which would be appropriate, since both pseudepigraphical and rabbinic sources indicate that in the new era there would exist new laws.[63] However, if the purpose for constructing this Temple was to make possible the conditional advent of the messianic age by demonstrating fidelity to the covenant, these premessianic elaborations would be in token of that promised period. This may contrast with other Scrolls of the Sect, which stated that their own laws were temporary. For example, the *Rule of the Community* stated that the members "shall be ruled by the first commandments with which the men of the community began to be instructed until the coming of a prophet and the anointed ones [that is, the two Messiahs] of Aaron and Israel" (*CD* 9.10-11).[64] However, while at Qumran, the Sect's laws were considered temporary; they did not believe that the Mosaic Torah would be replaced (see *Sibylline Oracles* 3.373-374, 757-758).

## The Ark of the Covenant in the *Temple Scroll*

One of the surprising features of the Temple described in the *Temple Scroll* is that it will include the Mosaic Ark of the Covenant as well as a new set of Solomonic cherubim (as in the First Temple).[65] The text reads:

> And two cherubim [you shall make at both ends of the cover, the one cherub on this end, and the othe]r end the second, spreading (their) wings [over the place of the ark, and shielding the cover with their wings] above the ark, with their faces on[e to the other . . .] (*11Q19* 7:10-12).

If this Temple was to be legitimate it had to include the Ark, as did the Tabernacle in the wilderness (and the First Temple), for only with the Ark present could the glory of God return to take its appointed place "between the wings of the cherubim" (see Ezekiel 43:1-7). The *Temple Scroll* seems to communicate that the restoration Temple would at least have included the elements of the Tabernacle and the First Temple (see Haggai 2:3-9). The rabbis noted that five things[66] from the First Temple were missing from the Second Temple, including the Ark (m. *Seqalim* 6:1-2; m. *Yoma* 5:2; t. *Yoma* 3:14; t. *Sota* 13:1; b. *Yoma* 21b; cf. *Jewish Wars* 5.5 § 5). Apparently the author of the *Temple Scroll* felt that only the Tabernacle would suffice as a pattern for his Temple, since he probably regarded the First Temple as having been improperly built, and the Second Temple, aside from being polluted, contained no Ark. This fact was stated in the extrabiblical literature (2 Maccabees 2:4-5; 2 Apoc. Bar. 6:7-10), but only as means to emphasize the Ark's return as a sign of the messianic age. In part, for the same reason, the *Temple Scroll*'s author would have included the Ark.

However, if the Ark of the Covenant disappeared with the destruction of the First Temple and was not present in the Second Temple, from where would those who were to construct this new Temple expect to recover it? The answer, undoubtedly, is to be sought in the Jewish traditions concerning the hidden Temple vessels. These traditions began sometime shortly after the return from exile and were included in the apocryphal and pseudepigraphical literature that arose in the post-exilic period— about the same time as the Scrolls were written. These traditions may have also influenced those who later hid the treasures of the *Copper Scroll*.

The traditions themselves may go back to the texts in 2 Chronicles 35:3, which the rabbis later interpreted as implying a hiding place for the Ark, and Jeremiah 3:16-17, the only text that relates both to the Ark's disappearance and Jerusalem's future restoration. While the author of the *Temple Scroll* did not base his new Temple on Ezekiel's plan, he may have been aware of Ezekiel's indirect statement about the Ark's return to the future Temple (Ezekiel 43:1-7). The Jewish versions of the traditions all tell of the Ark safely and secretly hidden (either by men or by angels) within the Temple precincts (usually in a subterranean chamber beneath the Holy of Holies).[67] The information about the actual location of the Ark was said to have been entrusted to one priestly family, and it is possible that in some way this information was conveyed to the author of the *Temple Scroll*. If so, the Sect's assumption would be that when they took possession of Jerusalem and the Temple Mount and restored its sanctity, they would also be able to restore the Ark to the new Temple.

## The Heavenly Temple at Qumran

At most, the *Temple Scroll* indicates that two Temples were expected to be built on the Temple Mount before and during the ultimate eschatological age. Other Scrolls, however, may give us glimpses of yet *another* ideal Temple. While these descriptions could be merged with the designs laid out in *11QTemple*, I believe that—along the lines of Qumran dualism and its celestial projection—the Temple described by these texts is the heavenly Temple, or the archetypal sanctuary of the divine abode. In this regard, J. Strugnell has presented a report concerning the angelology of *Serek Sirot 'Olat Hassabbat* (a document from the early stage of the development of Qumran theology), which pictures a celestial setting. In this text (*4QSl* 37-40) the Essenes imagined a heavenly sacrificial cult with angelic beings performing priestly functions.[68] In *4QpIs^d*, fragment 1, we find a restored city bejeweled with every kind of precious stone, especially those representing the 12 tribes on Aaron's breastplate (Exodus 28:17-20). The imagery is like that of Revelation 21:18-21 (with allusions to Ezekiel 48:31-34), where we read a description of the heavenly Jerusalem, which has no Temple. Since the fragmentary commentary is based on Isaiah 54:11-12, a text dealing with the age of restoration and messianic blessing, the context is eschatological. The highly symbolic nature of the text leads me to believe that it describes a heavenly rather than earthly scene, and that the Temple portrayed is celestial rather than terrestrial.

## The Eschatological Jerusalem in the Scrolls

The Qumran commentary on Isaiah (*4QpIsa^d*) offers a connection between the eschatological Jerusalem and the Dead Sea community. Based on Isaiah 54, the *pesher* interpretation relates the community's council and its 12 leaders with the imagery of the New Jerusalem—especially in relation to the precious stones found in the city and on the high priest's breastplate (*4QIsa^d* 1. 2-3). However, this imagery does not equate them, and certainly does not, as many writers have suggested, replace the Temple with a community. These writers often look for comparative New Testament texts, such as Ephesians 2:19-20 and Revelation 21, for parallel thoughts, but neither Paul nor John replaces the Temple with a community in those passages. In Ephesians 2 Paul was using the metaphor of the Temple's spiritual function to illustrate the new nature of the Christian community, while John in Revelation 21 was describing a four-square Temple (actually Holy of Holies) which has at its center God and His Messiah (verses 16-17,22).

Also on this city's wall were 12 foundation stones with the names of the 12 apostles. This may indicate the church's presence, but in light of Jesus' statement to these Jewish apostles that in the regeneration [the Millennium] they would "sit upon twelve thrones, judging the twelve tribes of Israel" (Matthew 19:28), the identification is better made with a redeemed Israel (Acts 3:19-21). Thus there is no reason to spiritualize the Israelite elements in this "Christian" context. In like manner, the Temple remained the epitome of the earthly promise to true Israel, and the Sect, believing they were such, would not have sought to replace such a concept with their community. Rather, borrowing their analogy from the Temple as Paul did in Ephesians 2, they saw their position as priests within a sanctified congregation as a spiritual temple.

## Isolated, Yet Hopeful

Even though the Dead Sea community isolated itself from most aspects of Temple life, the group members continued to carry out the spiritual aspects of Temple worship symbolically and retained a hope for the imminent rebuilding of a ritually pure Temple. They also expected a new Temple of divine design to arrive with the eschaton at the end of the age. However, there are still many secrets that remain to be understood about the Qumran conception of the Temple, and none are more mysterious than those that surround the *Copper Scroll*, which we will examine in the next chapter.

# 12

# SECRETS OF THE COPPER SCROLL

*The* Copper Scroll *is an anomaly in the inventory of Scrolls from Qumran. It does not fit into any of the categories customarily included when the Scrolls are discussed. . . . It is not in the Rockefeller Museum in Jerusalem nor in the Shrine of the Book . . . it is written in a language that is different from the language of any of the other Scrolls. It is written in a script that is not like the script of any of the other Scrolls. It is written on a material that is different . . . and its content has no parallel . . . it does not resemble any of the other Qumran Scrolls—or anything else, except pirates' treasure maps in Hollywood. It is an unusual phenomenon, an anomaly.*[1]

—P. Kyle McCarter, Jr.

As we have been finding and fitting together the pieces in this puzzle known as the Dead Sea Scrolls, we have had some success in gaining a perspective of the complete picture. However, what do we do with a piece of puzzle that not only does not seem to fit, but appears to have come from an entirely different puzzle? This puzzling piece is known as the *Copper Scroll.* Professor P. Kyle McCarter, Jr., of John Hopkins University, who has done the most recent research on the *Copper Scroll* and has published a newly revised translation, confirms this assessment, stating that it does not fit into any of the categories of the Dead Sea Scrolls except that it came out of a cave! For this reason the *Copper Scroll* has been described as "enigmatic," "mysterious," "cryptic," and "anomalous," and its contents are said to be "intriguing," "unique," "unparalleled," and "controversial." It has certainly proven to be all of these and more! What are the secrets of this strange piece of our puzzle called the *Copper Scroll?*

## The Discovery of the *Copper Scroll*

The Israeli-Arab war of 1948-1949 interrupted the professional searches for Scrolls in the Dead Sea region. Not until 1952 was a major expedition again mounted, which eventually located many more of the caves that contained Scrolls and Scroll fragments. Prior to this time, most of the discoveries had been made by the Bedouin; this time it was the archaeologists who made the finds. From March 14-25 a team of archaeologists from the École Biblique and the Albright Institute (formerly the American School of Oriental Research, led by Roland de Vaux, explored and excavated Cave 3, the northernmost cave on the high western slopes of Qumran (about one and a half miles from the Qumran settlement). Bargil Pixner relates what happened when the team initially examined the large main cave on March 20:

> I went myself several times with the experts to Cave 3 and I noticed that in that cave something special had taken place. First of all, the outside of the cave had collapsed and a little bit of the roof had fallen down and crushed jars containing different manuscripts. One large rock from the ceiling had fallen down and had covered the entrance to the cave. Behind this rock the *Copper Scroll* was hidden on a little shelf in a perfect state of preservation. The team of the École Biblique had to chip away part of the rock in order to enter from behind it to reach the *Copper Scroll.*[2]

Adding detail to Pixner's description, the roof of the main cave had collapsed in antiquity, preventing later access to the cave. This fact is important to note because it helps us determine whether the *Copper Scroll* was written by different people at a later time than the other Scrolls with which it was found. The *Copper Scroll* was set securely within a man-made shelf cut from the rock wall—a method of storage which indicates not only its uniqueness but its value. The jars found within the cave were some 40 in number and had lined the edges of the cave, including the rock shelf holding the *Copper Scroll*. Most of the jars had been crushed, but five were found still intact. Unfortunately, exposure to the elements had completely ruined the contents of the jars. However, to the north, just beyond the main cave, the excavators found two side caves blocked by fallen boulders. Within these caves the excavators made a surprising discovery Bargil Pixner relates what they found:

> They also found little side caves—just holes—where rats of the desert had made their nests. These rats had taken some of the paper and parchment that was outside [in the main cave] and had brought them inside to the cave in order to make their nests. That paper, little slips of it, showed wonderful handwriting, and must have come from the Scrolls themselves. Though the cave had collapsed, and the jars found by the excavators were empty, fortunately for us their contents had been preserved inside the rat nests, behind the area of the *Copper Scroll*.[3]

Pixner believes this cave was the most important of all the Qumran caves because it was situated the farthest away from the settlement. The distance may have been an added security measure, and may explain why the *Copper Scroll* was hidden at this site. The importance of the cave has also been affirmed by the infrared analyses of the scraps of Scrolls found in the rodents' nests. These analyses revealed that beside the *Copper Scroll* itself, the treasures this cave once contained included copies of the books of Ezekiel, Psalms, Lamentations, a Hymnal Scroll, a sectarian scroll, several apocalyptic scrolls, a beautifully written commentary on the book of Isaiah, and various undeterminable Hebrew and Aramaic scrolls.[4] Even though the remains are just blackened bits of leather and represent only a fraction of what the jars must have contained, they are sufficient to show that Cave 3 was surely one of the richest in manuscripts. The *Copper Scroll* was a part of this valuable collection, yet it was also a uniquely designed document with a special purpose of its own.

## A Description of the *Copper Scroll*

The *Copper Scroll* (designated *3Q15*) is so called because, unlike the other Scrolls made of parchment or papyrus, it is made of pure copper. The use of copper preserved the document from severe deterioration over the many centuries that it was hidden away. Also, unlike the other

Scrolls, it was not intended to be a Scroll at all! Although it was found as two separate rolls, which gave the document the appearance of being a scroll, it is apparent that it was originally one sheet that broke into two pieces at its rivet points when it was first rolled up for storage.

When the *Copper Scroll* was first found, oxidation had so corroded the copper that it had become brittle and was impossible to unroll. It took three more years to find a proper method to open it so that its contents could at last be deciphered. This was accomplished on January 16, 1956, by Dr. H. Wright Baker, a professor of mechanical engineering in the College of Science and Technology at the University of Manchester, England. Using a specially constructed high-speed circular saw originally designed to split pen nibs, the "Scroll" was cut between its 12 columns of text into 23 segments. One report said that about five percent of the text had been destroyed by the cutting procedure and another two percent rendered illegible,[5] but Baker himself declared that no letters were eliminated.[6] Finally it was opened and readable! However, both transcripting and translating the writing proved difficult for scholars. Stephen Pfann explains:

> There are some problems as far as the actual transcription because it was originally one piece of flat copper that was riveted together at certain points but ended up breaking in two back in antiquity. Because the letters are basically indented letters into the copper it's sometimes difficult to tell in certain places what letters are really there. For the most part it's clear, but from the different transcriptions that are available it is evident that there are some very strong disagreements over what the transcription should be.[7]

Transcription (the reproduction of the Hebrew script) was also made difficult by the form of the writing itself. The writer was most likely not the author, but a craftsman who may have been illiterate (which prevented him from being able to read the contents of what he was copying).[8] This is assumed from the many grammatical and orthographic lapses in the document. In addition, since he was engraving on metal rather than writing on parchment or papyrus, he could not create Hebrew characters that were precise. Therefore, certain similarly shaped letters that are normally distinguishable (for example, *kaph* and *beth*) are here completely indistinguishable. Translators have also had difficulty with the *Copper Scroll* author's predilection for Greek loanwords (most of which are not attested elsewhere), and the use of a series of cryptograms, consisting of seven sets of Greek letters, which occur at the end of content listings in columns 1-4. Thus very special care has to be exercised by anyone attempting translation, as P. Kyle McCarter, Jr., points out:

> I remind you that the problem is not always our ability to see what the scribe put here. This was an unusual scribe writing in an unusual way in what seems to be an unusual language. There are thus a number of peculiarities. Once you are certain of what you are reading then you despair of going to the standard sources and finding anything that corresponds. Very often there are aberrations in spelling and grammar. The mistakes are common enough that they tempt the interpreter to assume mistakes where there are none. Once you begin to do that, you can read anything you want.[9]

In spite of these difficulties, from the time that the *Copper Scroll* was discovered, when only the outsides of the two rolls could be read, it was proposed that the document contained a description of treasure hidden in the desert by the Qumran Sect.[10] This was confirmed when the full contents revealed a list of one geographical place after another where gold, silver, and other valuables were hidden away. The nature of this listing leads us to consider the significance of the *Copper Scroll*.

## The Significance of the *Copper Scroll*

It is difficult to exaggerate the significance of the *Copper Scroll*. Here in bookkeeping style is carefully recorded a description of treasure deposited in 64 different caches or hiding places throughout the Qumran, Jericho, and Jerusalem areas as well as other areas in northern Israel almost as far away as the Galilee and perhaps even as far as Damascus. Most of the caches include a large number of talents of gold or silver, but some also include priestly utensils and other precious items. Here are some lines that demonstrate the typical style of the text:

> In the ruin which is in the valley, pass under the steps leading to the east forth cubits . . . (there is) a chest of money and its total: the weight of seventeen talents. . . . In the sepulchral monument, in the third course: one hundred gold ingots. . . . In the hill of Kochlit, tithe-vessels of the Lord of the peoples and sacred vestments . . . (*3Q15* 1:1-5,9).

The very fact that the *Copper Scroll* mentions geographical locations, specific kinds of treasure, and does so in a colloquial Hebrew are all significant to students of this period, whether in archaeology, history, or linguistics. Although there is no dispute that this document is a catalog of treasures, there has been a long-standing controversy over whether these treasures are real. After the Scroll's contents were revealed, the *Copper Scroll* was identified with everything from a medieval fable to an end-time treasure map. One reason some scholars once doubted the integrity of the *Copper Scroll*'s treasure account was because of the conclusion reached by J.T. Milik, the scholar who published the official translation of the text. He stated that the Scroll was nothing more than Jewish religious folklore: "la réalité de ces histories" ("fictional inventions").[11] On the other hand, noted Israeli linguist Chaim Rabin disputed this view and defended the Scroll's authenticity.[12] Let's consider the arguments for these contrary positions.

## The *Copper Scroll* Treasure:
## Fact or Fiction?

### *Interpreting the Scroll As Fiction*

The argument that the *Copper Scroll* was fiction was spearheaded by Milik.[13] He based his "rejection" of the document on what he took to be parallel accounts of hidden treasure in comparative literature. His primary parallel, which he believed provided an interpretive key to the *Copper Scroll*, was a medieval Jewish midrash known as *Masseket Kelim* ("Tractate of the [Temple] Vessels"). This text records one of the traditions about the hiding of the Temple treasures in secret underground compartments. The location of these places would not be known until the coming of the Messiah ben David. This information by itself was not remarkable, since many other traditions preserved the same information.[14] What struck Milik was this document's statement that "Shimmur the Levite and his companions wrote them [that is, recorded the Temple vessels] on a copper tablet."[15] In addition, the text indicated that the number of items hidden was incredibly large—about one million.

Milik also sought to identify the uncertain place name *Kochlit* in the *Copper Scroll* with a spring mentioned in the tractate *Kelim*—a spring called *'Ein Kahal*, which, according to Milik, was located on the western slopes of Mount Carmel. Because the prophet Elijah was associated both with Mount Carmel (1 Kings 18:18-45) and the coming of the Messiah (Malachi 4:5; Matthew 17:10-1; Mark 9:11-12; Matthew 27:49; Mark 15:36; Mark 6:14-15; John 1:19-21,25), Milik concluded that the *Copper Scroll* was both apocalyptic in nature and legendary in character.

### Interpreting the Scroll As Fact

Interestingly, the opposition to Milik's view, championed initially by Chaim Rabin, also employed the tradition of the Temple treasures—but as proof that the treasures in the *Copper Scroll* were real! For Rabin, these traditions were based on a historical event, and he suggested that the reason the Scroll was written might be compared with a statement in the Babylonian Talmud: "They sought to hide away all silver and gold in the world on account of the silver and gold of Jerusalem" (*Bekhoroth* 50a). Rabin, a linguist and epigraphist, observed that the Scroll's unique use of "colloquial Mishnaic Hebrew" was evidence that it was a catalog of a priest's eyewitness account of the Temple treasure, and that its deposition had been faithfully inscribed word for word.[16] In addition, the locations of the buried treasure listed in the *Copper Scroll* matched exactly with priestly plans revealed in the Temple treasure traditions, which had Jerusalem set at the center of the hiding places. This, to Rabin, provided evidence that the treasure of the *Copper Scroll* was indeed Temple treasure, the knowledge of which had been carried by the priests who had fled from Jerusalem to Qumran in order to preserve the record of the hiding places.[17]

Milik and others view the high sum total of the *Copper Scroll*'s treasure of 4,630 talents (one talent = 25-75 pounds, for a total of 58-174 tons) to be unrealistic and a "fantastic amount." Israeli archaeologist Dan Bahat agrees with Milik, stating that the treasures of the *Copper Scroll* were probably an ideology: "I don't believe that such an enormous sum of money was in those places."[18] Some people have tried to defend some of the "excessively large" totals as coded amounts, based on the presence of Greek ciphers elsewhere in the text, but this kind of reasoning is unnecessary. The historian Josephus recorded the use of even greater sums: 10,000 talents of tribute money for Pompey from Jerusalem in 63 B.C. (*Antiquities* 14:4.5 § 78), and Crassus' later removal from the Temple of an additional 2,000 talents plus gold for 8,000 talents (*Antiquities* 14:7.1 § 105-109). In addition, A.C. Wolters has noted that the amounts in the *Copper Scroll* should not be regarded as extreme because the community was preparing for eschatological war (*1QM*) and the building of their own Temple (*11Q19*).

Another sign that the *Copper Scroll* is valid is the accuracy of its geographical descriptions, as Stephen Pfann affirms:

> These were actual places because several are names of major places, especially around the Jerusalem area, which are fully identifiable places. So they are not mythological places like in J.R. Tolkien's "Lord of the Rings" or something like this. Although some of the places are not easy to identify or find, they are real places describing actual localities where these treasures are said to have been located or deposited.[19]

Were this document a fictitious work, actual place names could have been used, but not with the same careful attention to detail. As a story there would have been no need to convince an audience that the Scroll was a real treasure map, as such details would suggest. Instead, as Bargil Pixner's studies show and excavations have demonstrated, there are enough reasonable clues to locations to identify some with certainty and most with a few reservations.

In further defense of the *Copper Scroll*'s authenticity is the fact that its author used a precious, wear-resistant metal. Al Wolters concluded that "this inventory was inscribed on copper to ensure the future recovery, by ordinary human means, of treasures which had been so carefully recorded."[20] Also, the Scroll's author wrote complex cryptic descriptions of hiding places in a factual, nonliterary, prosaic style using colloquial Mishnaic Hebrew. Furthermore, that another copy was preserved as an archival or security copy (as we'll see soon) also argues against this being simply a folkloristic composition.

In addition, the use of the seven double or triple Greek ciphers at the end of the treasure locations in columns 1-4 would make no sense nor serve any purpose if the Scroll was a legendary account. However, they make good sense and serve a special purpose if a real catalog of hidden treasure is being described. One theory for these Greek ciphers is that they stand as abbreviations for the names of those responsible for certain treasures. While not claiming that the ciphers have any relationship with the *Copper Scroll*, Pixner has shown how these abbreviations could correspond to actual Greek names of persons as recorded in Josephus' writings.[21] He does suggest that one of the ciphers in cache 7 (*3Q15* 2:3-4), θε ("*The*,") goes with the name *Yeshu* listed there, and may indicate the actual name of Yeshu's father: a priest named *The*buthi.[22] The only historical reference we have to a priestly Thebuthi is by the early church father Hegesippos, as preserved in Eusebius' *Ecclesiastical History* (1.3.11; 22.5). There we read about one who came to Christianity from one of the seven Jewish sects and later aspired to become a leader of the early church after the death of James the Just (A.D. 62). Pixner's theory has a certain appeal because both Yeshu and Thebuthi were priests, and all of the seven Greek ciphers are found only in the series of treasures hidden around Jerusalem. At any rate, this example demonstrates that the Greek ciphers had a real purpose and could represent actual people.

There is ample evidence, then, that undermines the fictional theory and argues for the veracity of the treasure account in the *Copper Scroll*. Based on the weight of this evidence, Wolters concluded:

> A scholarly consensus seems to be emerging that the *Copper Scroll* is an authentic record of ancient treasure, to be dated around 69 C.E., and that its treasure belonged either to the sectarians of Qumran or the Temple in Jerusalem.[23]

## The Date of the *Copper Scroll*

The date of the *Copper Scroll*, according to Milik's official publication, was about A.D. 100. Other scholars, such as the French scholar Laperrousaz[24] and the Israeli scholar Luria,[25] had sought an even later date during the time of the Bar Kokhba Revolt (A.D. 132–35). However, almost all Scroll scholars agree that the Scrolls were hidden within the caves at Qumran and the Wadi Jawfet Zaben sometime between the destruction of the Qumran community in A.D. 68 and the destruction of Jerusalem and the Temple in A.D. 70. Pixner has argued that any date for the deposition of the *Copper Scroll* must take into account the original shape of Cave 3 and the placement of the many Scroll jars in relation to it before the cave's ceiling collapsed.[26] De Vaux, who had reluctantly agreed with Milik about the Scroll's fictitious character, provided this evidence when he wrote that the *Copper Scroll* "was found in the outer part of the side cave, resting against the rock wall a little to one side of the mass of broken pottery and inscribed fragments of skin and papyrus."[27] This description points to a placement of the *Copper Scroll* on its special rock shelf prior to, or contemporaneous with the deposition of the Scroll jars.[28] In support of this, Frank M. Cross has paleographically dated the Scroll to about A.D. 25-75.[29]

It would have been extremely difficult to have buried so much treasure at such depths and in so many diverse locations, especially at Qumran and around Jerusalem, after A.D. 70. It's highly unlikely that such amounts of treasure would have survived the Roman pillage of Qumran and Jerusalem and other areas of Judea. No ancient sources report offerings disposed of through burial after the destruction of the Temple. Therefore, the treasure was most likely hidden prior to the Roman invasions, and if not recovered in antiquity, remains there today.

## Where Was the Treasure Hidden?

The *Copper Scroll* may have been written to serve as a memory aid for a secretive team of diggers that planned to recover the buried treasure at an appointed or opportune time. For this reason the team avoided the use of well-known geographical terms. This, unfortunately, has made it more difficult to pinpoint the exact locations, because most of the toponyms were written to keep the treasure from falling into the wrong hands. Nevertheless, Pixner believes that the *Copper Scroll* shows a systematic order in the topographical distribution of the 64 caches (see maps on pages 275-277). He observes that caches 1-17 were placed near Mount Zion on the southwestern hill of the city, a placement that suggests a special quarter also existed there. This Pixner seems to have confirmed by his rediscovery of the Essene Gate, which Josephus mentions in *Wars of the Jews* (5.4.2§145). Caches 19-34 were hidden in the Qumran area, and caches 35-47 were placed to the far north in the Yarmuk Valley (which Pixner equates with the "land of Damascus"). Finally, caches 48-60 were again located around Jerusalem, and caches 61-64 at diverse places to the north.

## From Where Did the Treasure Come?

Among the scholars who believe that the treasure of the *Copper Scroll* is real, there is still considerable disagreement over the question of its origin. A good starting point is to consider the nature of the treasure in relation to those who might have controlled it, beginning first with the Qumran Sect itself. In the sectarian documents we learn that the Sect considered the acquisition of personal property and possessions as a sin, and

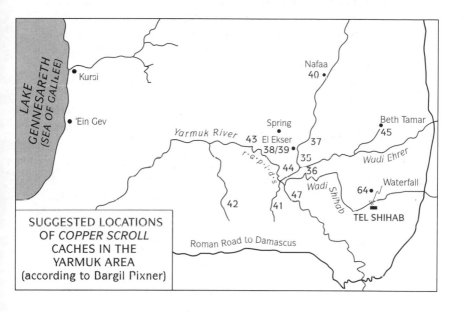

SUGGESTED LOCATIONS
OF *COPPER SCROLL*
CACHES IN THE
YARMUK AREA
(according to Bargil Pixner)

**Treasure items according to numbers**
*(Yarmuk area):*

35—tithe vessels, books
36—17 talents (gold and silver)
37—4 talents
38—66 talents
39—70 talents (silver)
40—4 double-mines of silver bars

41—22.5 talents
42—22 talents
43—much silver
44—9 talents
45—things "under the ban"
47—12 talents
64—duplicate *Copper Scroll*

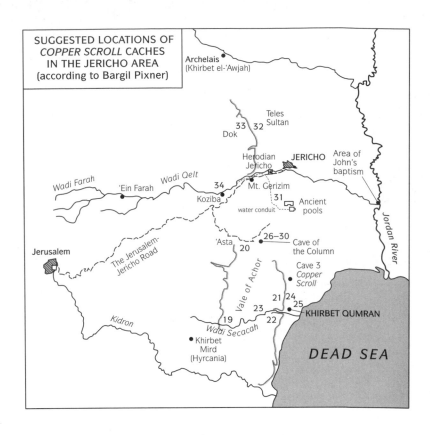

SUGGESTED LOCATIONS OF
*COPPER SCROLL* CACHES
IN THE JERICHO AREA
(according to Bargil Pixner)

---

**Treasure items according to numbers**
*(Jericho area):*

19—2 pots full of silver
20—200 talents (silver)
21—17 talents (silver)
22—12 talents (silver)
23—7 talents (silver)
24—tithe vessels
25—23 talents (silver)
26—32 talents

27—jar with scroll, 42 talents
28—21 talents
29—27 talents
30—22 talents
31—400 talents
32—6 silver pitchers
33—22 talents
34—60 talents (silver), 2 talents (gold)

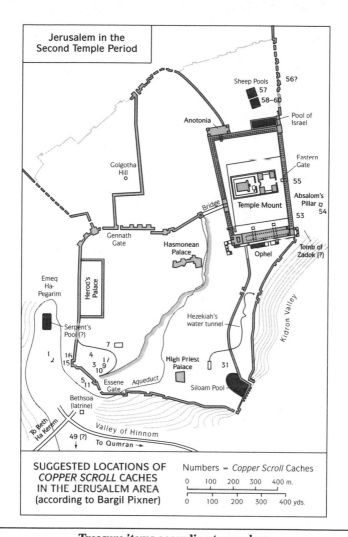

SUGGESTED LOCATIONS OF *COPPER SCROLL* CACHES IN THE JERUSALEM AREA (according to Bargil Pixner)

Numbers = *Copper Scroll* Caches

| 0 | 100 | 200 | 300 | 400 m. |
| 0 | 100 | 200 | 300 | 400 yds. |

## Treasure items according to numbers
### *(Jerusalem area):*

**1**—money chest
**2**—gold articles
**3**—900 talents
**4**—tithe vessels
**5**—40 talents (silver)
**7**—65 gold articles

**9**—vessels
**10**—10 talents
**11**—six bars (silver)
**15**—tithe vessels, sacred garments
**16**—13 talents
**17**—14 talents

**31**—400 talents
**49**—300 talents (gold), 20 vessels
**53**—tithe vessels
**54**—something "under the ban"

**55**—40 talents
**56**—tithe vessels
**57**—tithe vessels
**58**—900 talents (gold)
**59**—60 talents
**60**—42 talents

renunciation of such was a prerequisite for admission into the community. Also, the sect's commentaries frequently denounced their enemies for hoarding riches. Some scholars say that these expressions of communal poverty are in conflict with the vast accumulation of treasure displayed in the *Copper Scroll*, indicating that the Qumran community had no relation to the treasure. But this "poverty" extended only to the *individual*, not the *collective*. The required renunciation was of private possessions, not of the communal treasury. If this took the form of donations to the community or the future Temple, then the members' donations fulfilled a sectarian obligation as well (*1QS* 9:6-7).[30]

Scholars have also argued that because many of the treasure items appear to relate to the Temple, and the Qumran community shunned the Temple, they could not have been responsible for writing the *Copper Scroll*. However, as I pointed out in the previous chapter, the community's rejection of the Temple because of its corrupted priesthood and calendar does not mean that they rejected the Temple vessels, which provided an ongoing continuity between Temples (Isaiah 52:11-12; Jeremiah 27:21-22; Ezra 1:7-11), nor that they would not have assisted in preserving these items, along with the monetary treasure, because of their hopes of building a future Temple of their own design (*11Q19*). Furthermore, Pixner argues that the *Copper Scroll*'s placement in Cave 3 alongside manuscripts from Qumran clearly link it with the community:

> To me that is proof enough that the *Copper Scroll* must have been part of that larger collection. No one would have entered the cave and left all the other Scrolls in there and just put the *Copper Scroll* there, although some believe that the *Copper Scroll* was put there much later.[31]

Let's look now at the various proposals about the origin of the *Copper Scroll* treasures.

## A Communal Collection

One proposal—put forth initially by K.G. Kuhn,[32] John Allegro,[33] and Dupont-Sommer and renewed by Pixner—is that the treasure comprises the collected assets of a monastic community that rejected the Second Temple and considered their collection a substitute for the Temple treasure. Pixner is perhaps influenced in his views by his own experience in a monastic order; nevertheless, he contends that the Essenes were just such an order, "preparing ideologically for a great war to come, a war between 'the sons of light' and 'the sons of darkness,' and were storing provisions for that day."[34] With that inevitable day in mind, then, the community leaders had secured their end-time treasure by the separate concealment of the *Copper Scroll.*

Pixner's proposal is certainly possible, even probable. Although the Qumran site could only sustain about 200 men at any one time, if it maintained this number over a span of 250 years (with an average generation calculated at 50 years) the total would be 1,000 men. While a collection from this number of men probably would not have created the amounts recorded in the *Copper Scroll*, if the settlement was recognized as an Essene "monastery," it may have received additional support from the more than 4,000 Essenes who resided in various parts of the country. Stephen Pfann explains this possibility:

> It isn't totally outlandish even though a large quantity of money is mentioned, because when people came to the Essene community they surrendered everything to the community. The community center at Qumran itself was probably a gift from somebody who became an Essene, because the original buildings had to be modified by the Essenes for their purposes. It's the same with many of the Scrolls that were found. People came with Scrolls—some biblical Scrolls and some other Scrolls which were not Essene, but probably part of a possession of people who came to the community. They also brought money with them from the sales of their own lands. This is similar to the picture that we have in the Acts of the Apostles concerning the first Christians who sold their lands and brought the money and laid it at the feet of the Apostles (Acts 4:32-37). So there must have been a lot of things hidden.[35]

Dr. Pfann, while agreeing in essence with Pixner's proposal, also believes the treasures were connected with the Temple in some way. He says, " These were either Temple treasures, or items which the Essenes themselves were holding onto and were expecting to use once their Temple was built, which I think is a bit more likely."[36] This latter view, which a number of scholars hold to, is commendable for several reasons. First, it has a clear biblical precedent as the means for the people's preparation for building the earthly sanctuary. Moses had taken a similar collection among the Israelites (much of it comprised of the spoils taken from Egypt) for the Tabernacle (Exodus 35:5-9,21-29), as had King David for the First Temple (1 Chronicles 29:5-9,14-19) and the returnees from the Babylonian captivity for the Second Temple (Ezra 2:68-69). Second, this view provides a meaningful connection between the *Copper Scroll* and the *Temple Scroll*, both hidden in fairly close proximity to one another. Third, it helps explain why a community of priests, whose very purpose was for Temple service, would have felt compelled to keep such treasures.

## A Temple Connection

Yet another popular proposal is that all of the treasure belonged to the Temple in Jerusalem. It seems evident that the Dead Sea Sect envisioned furnishing a future Third Temple with the sacred artifacts and utensils that had been part of the First Temple. They believed that at some future time they would be able to return and recover their treasure for the erection and equipping of their restoration Temple. The destruction of the community in A.D. 68, followed by the destruction of the Second Temple in A.D. 70, may have made these hopes appear more realistic because the Second Temple had been cleared out of the way in preparation for the Third Temple.

Although the *Copper Scroll* has been considered as a part of the apocalyptic tradition of the Qumran community,[37] it does not necessarily fit within this literary genre. While it may not be apocalyptic like the other Scrolls, it still may convey one of the strongest apocalyptic images of the restoration motif: that of fervent hope in a Jerusalem and a Temple made according to the divine ideal.[38] Yet the author of the *Copper Scroll* may have not envisioned the work as belonging to the apocalyptic period, but to the age before the advent of Messiah (as in the *Temple Scroll*). This premise has proven attractive to a new consensus of scholars who have read the *Copper Scroll* in light of the Temple treasures. Let us consider two of the major proposals of the theory that all of the treasure belonged to the Temple.

## A Treasure Derived from Temple Taxes

One proposal by Manfred Lehmann seeks to merge Pixner's position of a communal collection with a Temple connection. He suggests that the treasure originated with the Qumran community, but represented the regular Temple tithe (or tax) that continued to be collected after the fall of the Temple in hopes of its soon rebuilding.[39] This, however, has been regarded by critics as an illogical hypothesis based on historical grounds.[40] The continued collection of a Temple tax after the Temple's destruction would have been impossible for several reasons. First, there was the so-called "vengeful tax" (*Fiscus Judaicus*) imposed by the Romans during the time of the first Jewish revolt (A.D. 66-70). This tax usurped the Temple tithe and diverted it to Rome. Second, it is unlikely that much wealth was left to be collected from the impoverished Jewish refugees and beaten populace of Jerusalem and Judea (including Qumran). Third, what Jewish monies might have available would surely have gone to ransom or relieve the suffering of the hundreds of thousands of Jewish captives. And finally, the huge sums mentioned in the Scroll seem entirely too large for a dev-astated, postwar Judea to have collected at the rate of one-half shekel per adult per year after only a few years.[41]

Despite these criticisms, P. Kyle McCarter has defended Lehmann's view, revising it in some details. First, with respect to the date, he believes these treasures were taken from the Temple's coffers and deposited before the Roman army appeared in the Galilee. This was a time well *before* the Temple's siege and destruction. Second, he speculates that most of these Temple tithes never reached the Jerusalem Temple because of fears that the public treasury was vulnerable; thus the tithes were hidden in different locations east of the city.

## A Treasure Belonging to the Temple

Another proposal links the treasure of the *Copper Scroll* directly with the Temple's ritual objects and contributed wealth. Norman Golb, who accepts this proposal, uses it in defense of his position that none of the Scrolls were produced at Qumran or by a single Sect.[42] In his connection of the Temple treasure with the *Copper Scroll* he finds proof that it could not have been written nor deposited by anyone except Jewish priests in Jerusalem officiating at the Temple. With this assumption he moves to his larger theory that the Scrolls represent the Jerusalem Temple library, of which the *Copper Scroll* was a part. However, as I pointed out in my critique of Golb's theory in chapter 5, the other Scrolls uniformly objected to the Jerusalem Temple and the conduct of its priests, so it is unlikely that they would constitute the Temple library. On the contrary, because the *Copper Scroll* was found with Qumran Scrolls in Cave 3, an associ-ation between the Sect and the *Copper Scroll*'s author seems required.

Al Wolters believes that the fairly extensive presence of cultic termi-nology in the *Copper Scroll* may indicate that the treasure belonged to the Temple. He identified 32 places where such terms occur, and all but five appear in descriptions of treasure.[43] These terms are connected with items such as priestly vestments, various kinds of vessels, incense, precious kinds of wood, tithe-jars, precious stones, and gold and silver, suggesting that at least some of the treasure may have come from the Temple.[44] He also mentioned a doctoral dissertation that demonstrated parallels between the *Copper Scroll* and genuine Greek temple inventories of sacred treasure.[45]

Perhaps the strongest case for the treasure having belonged to the Temple is made on the basis of the cultic terminology coupled with the historical traditions concerning the Temple treasures. Of the 64 caches of hidden treasure, at least 16 (25 percent) are said to have included sacred objects that were restricted to Levitical, priestly, or Temple use by *halakhic* regulations. However, we should note that the *Copper Scroll* does not mention the most sacred Temple treasures—the Tabernacle furniture, Ark of the Covenant, or the ashes of the red heifer. According to various historical traditions, the treasures of the Jerusalem Temple were removed to protect them from the Romans during the Jewish revolt of A.D. 66–70. This was not an unusual procedure, even for the Temple priests. Josephus tells us that during this time Jews frequently fled into the Judean desert to hide their property. However, P. Kyle McCarter, Jr. suggests that if these caches included Temple property, then most likely they were hidden in the wadis east of Jerusalem by Temple personnel in anticipation of the first Jewish revolt.[46] In Ezra 2:59-63 and Nehemiah 7:61-65 (cf. 1 Esdras 5:38) we read that the members of the House of Hakkoz (a priestly family of the Davidic line; see 1 Chronicles 24:10); unable to substantiate their genealogy after the return from Babylon, were reassigned to priestly duties that did not require genealogical purity. Connecting the reference in Nehemiah 3:4 of Meremoth son of Uriah son of Hakkoz to Ezra 8:33, which says the Temple treasure was entrusted to "the priest Meremoth son of Uriah," we learn that this family became the treasurers of the Temple. In 1 Maccabees 8:17 we find that Judas Maccabeus appointed a Eupolemus, son of John, son of Hakkoz, an ambassador to Rome. This suggests that the Hakkoz family remained prominent as late as the Hasmonean period. In the *Copper Scroll*, a specific reference (in cache 32) links the treasure mentioned in the Scroll to both the Temple treasury and the Hakkoz family: "In the cave that is next to the founta[in] belonging to the House of Hakkoz, dig six cubits. (There are) six bars of gold."[47] It is probable, then, that the *Copper Scroll* treasures were removed from the Temple treasury and hidden near Jerusalem, but probably also in the

Judean desert under the supervision of the sons of Hakkoz and other Temple officials.

Professor Shemaryahu Talmon also views the connection with Temple treasure traditions as the proper background for the origin of the *Copper Scroll*:

> After the destruction of the First Temple several of the implements and the riches that had been accumulated there were hidden away to await the time when there would be a reconstruction of the Temple so they could be taken there. In both Samaritan literature and from Samaritan history we know that when someone said he had discovered the implements, this caused the revolt against the Romans. Because people saw this as a sort of indication that the new time or new age had arrived. So possibly the idea that is behind the *Copper Scroll* goes together with the expectation of an [eschatological] war that will change the world, usher in the true anointed, and bring the restoration of Israel.[48]

If we further investigate the Samaritan tradition regarding the Temple treasures as mentioned by Talmon, we find a connection with the *Copper Scroll* may be implied. Josephus records that a messianic pretender proposed to reveal to the Samaritans the location of Temple vessels hidden beneath their sacred Mount Gerizim. The pretender's attempt to scale the mountain with a company of Samaritans was interpreted by Pontius Pilate as an insurrection, which his forces violently quelled (*Antiquities* 18:85-88). In the *Copper Scroll*, lot 61 is said to be located "at Mount Garizin" and that here "beneath the ascent [or entrance] of its upper ditch" is "one chest with its contents and sixty talents of silver."[49] Is it possible that this pretender had obtained knowledge of the location based on familiarity with a source common to the *Copper Scroll*?

One problem yet to be resolved about the Temple treasure theory is explaining how those in control of this treasure could successfully hide it in such a wide distribution of sites which, soon after the outbreak of the Jewish War, came into Roman possession. The answer could be, as Kyle McCarter suggested, that these treasures were systematically buried one by one during an earlier period prior to the Roman invasion. It's also possible that the Sect, which expected an end-times conflict, secretly hid the treasure in progressive burials, perhaps as a ritual, which could have begun from their inception at Qumran (usually considered to be during the Hasmonean period).

## The Controversy over the *Copper Scroll*

When the *Copper Scroll* was discovered the Qumran area was under the administration of the Hashemite Kingdom of Jordan, whose Department of Antiquities resided in Jordanian (East) Jerusalem. When the discovery was first announced in a press release on June 1, 1956, in the *New York Times*, the release said that the contents of the *Copper Scroll* "sound like something that might have been written in blood in the dark of the moon by a character in Treasure Island."[50] The widely publicized news of the find, communicated in such a romantic fashion, greatly excited the general public. The excitement grew even more after an American writer published a fiction novel built around finding the *Copper Scroll*. This type of publicity was of great concern to the Jordanian authorities, who feared a "gold rush" by untrained foreign "treasure hunters" who might find and illegally export a vast fortune from Jordanian territories. They also feared the political ramifications of any related discovery that might serve to promote "Zionist causes." This fear was aggravated by Allegro's public statement that not only was the *Copper Scroll* an authentic inventory of buried treasure, but that other Dead Sea Scrolls might contain a reference to a crucified Messiah. Such statements could not have been more ill-timed, since they collided with the intense rise in Arab nationalism being experienced at that time in Jordan. The German scholar Joachim Jeremias put the Jordanian government's concern in perspective when he wrote:

> It is to be feared that it could have negative consequences for scientific work in Palestine. At all times the natives have regarded the excavations in the Holy Land with suspicion. They find it scarcely credible that such great expenditure is made simply to uncover old walls and to find potsherds. Secretly, they suspect, treasures are being brought to light and carried away. The possibility must unfortunately be reckoned with that suspicions will receive fresh nourishment from the *Copper Scroll* from Qumran.[51]

Western scholars working in Jordan did not entertain these Arab fears, for they were either apolitical or favored the Arab cause, and had worked long and hard to dispel such notions by demonstrating that their intentions were entirely scholarly. In fact, when the British director of the Jordanian Department of Antiquities, Lankester Harding, issued the initial press release, his statements were intended to emphasize that the treasure of the *Copper Scroll* was not fact, but fiction. Whether or not the

Jordanian authorities believed the Scroll to record a genuine treasure, they reasoned that such knowledge belonged exclusively to Western scholars and gave them unwarranted access to what were assumed to be the treasure's hiding places. To Harding's chagrin, only one month after the press release, he was fired from his post and replaced by a Jordanian. Perhaps in view of such action, as well as the fear of possible restrictions on the other Scrolls, J.T. Milik, along with Roland de Vaux, restated their belief that the *Copper Scroll* was fictitious and legendary in character. Following the press release, Milik stated this conviction even more caustically:

> It goes almost without saying that the document is not a historical record of actual treasures buried in antiquity.... " The Copper Document is best understood as a summary of popular traditions circulating among the folk of Judaea, put down by a semi-literate scribe ... the work of a crank."[52]

Such statements, however, made little difference to the Jordanian authorities, for their fears of treasure hunters had not been unjustified. In the years that followed Allegro's publication of the Scroll, a number of professionally sponsored and amateur excavations took place that used the *Copper Scroll* as their map.

## Excavations Related to the *Copper Scroll*

The first excavations undertaken to identify the sites and recover objects mentioned in the *Copper Scroll* were those under the direction of John Allegro himself. Because Allegro had been present for the cutting of the Scroll at the University of Manchester and had made handwritten copies of the text as each segment was made available, he gained favor with the Jordanian authorities. He had been invited by then Director of Antiquities of the Hashemite Kingdom, Dr. Ghuraibi (and later his successors Mr. Said Durra and Dr. 'Awni Dajani), to prepare a translation of the text. When the text was published, Allegro's relationship with the Jordanian government was evident in both his dedication to King Hussein of Jordan — "With profound admiration and respect to his majesty"—and in his foreword to the published text:

> The trusteeship of these recent discoveries we call the Dead Sea Scrolls has fallen to a predominantly Muslim country, a fitting complement to their importance as a potential bridge across some of the most tragic religious divisions of mankind.[53]

While Allegro's publication caused controversy among the Scroll Team, his platitudes secured him the blessings of the Jordanian government to conduct an official search for the *Copper Scroll*'s treasures. Because no official report was published about Allegro's secretive excavations, we cannot know exactly what he recovered. However, his silence about the work may indicate that he found no real clues to any treasure or any treasure itself. Because of this, Stephen Pfann suggests another possible alternative:

> Our problem is that we have no evidence that any of the treasures are there because none have been located. They had a *Copper Scroll* excavation in the early sixties headed up by John Allegro but didn't find anything. There were also others in the archaeological community that looked and they couldn't find anything. It doesn't mean that they aren't there or that there isn't something left to be found, although I think that the more complete Scroll, mentioned at the end of the *Copper Scroll*, was probably found by someone and they followed the map and found everything.[54]

Dormition Abbey Prior Bargil Pixner has suggested modern geographical locations throughtout the land of Israel based on the ancient identifications in the *Copper Scroll* (see maps on pages 275-277):

> They had treasures hidden away and I think that those [hiding] places are the ones mentioned in the *Copper Scroll*. [I deduced that] they must have owned these areas in order to have had access to them [to hide the treasures]. These hiding places were called *Kochlit*, [the term used for] the monastic centers of the community. One *Kochlit* was in Qumran itself, although it was not called Qumran since this is an Arabic word, but was called Saccacah, a place mentioned in the Bible. A second was on Mount Zion, and a third one, in my opinion, was in an area of the Yarmuk River south of Damascus.[55]

Pixner also conducted his own excavations based on locations he had identified in the Jerusalem area (see page 277). One of these locations relates in part to his rediscovery of the Essene Gate on Mount Zion, which he believes is mentioned in the *Copper Scroll*:

> I did an excavation here on Mount Zion and rediscovered the Gate of the Essenes which had been discovered a hundred years

previous by Bliss and Dickey. However, they were unable to differentiate the layers of the gates they found. From our archaeological discoveries of coins and other [datable material] we were able to establish the respective dates for the three layers of seals found there. The lower seal is that of the Essene Gate, the middle one is one from a kind of ghetto wall around Mount Zion, and the third—the top one—is the Gate of the Byzantine time, probably built by Eudokia's [mother of Constantine] workmen around A.D. 450.[56]

In this same area, Pixner believes that he has been able to identify other structures mentioned in the *Copper Scroll*:

I have been trying to locate these areas and I found some of these locations here on Mount Zion. The *Copper Scroll* speaks of a place near the Gate of the Essenes, where a big cistern lies. Here things were said to have been hidden, as well as close by where there was said to be a kind of pillar with something inside. This Essene Gate and the large cistern can still be seen today. [In addition,] the *Copper Scroll* says that near the Gate of the Essenes, below the walls of the city, and next to a cistern, there is a rock shaped like a tooth. I [also] found it here on Mount Zion, in this area of the Essene Gate where the Essene community lived.[57]

Al Wolters was once anxious to include Joseph Patrich's excavation at the Wadi Jawfet Zaben within the sphere of *Copper Scroll* excavations because he believed a juglet that was found containing an unknown liquid (possibly balsam) represented a part of its treasure.[58] Although Patrich would welcome this association if the evidence warranted it, he admits that it does not.[59] We will learn more about this juglet in chapter 16, where we will see why it should not be connected with the Temple treasures or the *Copper Scroll* inventory.

## Other Treasures of the *Copper Scroll*

While the buried treasures of the *Copper Scroll* remain hidden, the *Copper Scroll* is still valuable to scholars and students for other reasons. For example, the *Copper Scroll* gives us insight about the nature of the Scroll jars found in the Qumran caves. Stephen Pfann observes:

One of the treasures of the *Copper Scroll* for us today is its linguistic information. For example, we call these jars in Qumran "Scroll jars"—but they're very unique. In the *Copper Scroll* it says that a couple of Scrolls were hidden in jars that were called *klei dema*, which means "tithe jars." So what we're looking at when we look at a Scroll jar is probably not truly a jar that was just made for containing Scrolls, but jars that were actually made for carrying tithes that were to be given to the priests. What better place to actually carry Scrolls in than a tithe jar? Since as purity goes, they were [ritually] acceptable.[60]

Pixner offers an additional piece of useful information hidden within the *Copper Scroll*—possible information about the identity of the Qumran community and where the Sect members lived:

It would be worthwhile for scholars to study that part [of the Scroll] which reveals that Qumran wasn't the only place where the Essenes lived, but that they lived in many, many places around the country—mostly in the villages of Judea, but also in the Galilee. I believe that by studying more deeply, more profoundly the *Copper Scroll*, much more could be known about the Essenes and especially their [geographical] distribution.[61]

The *Copper Scroll* has also proven helpful in the field of lexical studies, where new terms and forms of known words have enriched our knowledge of the Mishnaic Hebrew vocabulary. The very use of this vocabulary in the *Copper Scroll* is an important witness to the popular use of Hebrew during the Second Temple period.

For the above-stated reasons, Dr. Pfann concludes, "There are many such things in the *Copper Scroll* that still need to be tapped, and while these may not be real treasures, they are treasures nevertheless."[62]

## The "Secret" Scroll

In the closing lines of the *Copper Scroll* we find a surprise: the mention of a "secret" scroll. This scroll stands in contrast to the *Copper Scroll,* as noted by Pixner:

One Scroll is mentioned in the last part of the *Copper Scroll* which has more detailed indications where these different treasures are. The *Copper Scroll* was only something like an emergency Scroll for times when the war was coming and they wanted to be sure that these treasures wouldn't be lost. So in kind of a telegram style they put various things together, with very few words to indicate generally the place and how much is there and what sort of access there is to it.[63]

## What Is It?

This "secret" Scroll is identified in the *Copper Scroll* text as follows:

> In the tunnel which is in Sechab, to the north of *Kochlit*, which opens towards the north, and has graves in its entrance: a copy of this text and its explanation and its measurements and the inventory, [blank] item by item (*3Q15* 12:10-13).

Scholarly debate has been generated over the function of this additional *copper scroll* due to uncertainty about the words here translated "explanation," "measurements," and "inventory." As this translation appears, the three words correspond with the threefold description of every treasure in the preceding list and form a notice that an almost exact copy, a duplicate, of the *Copper Scroll* is buried in a separate location. This was what Milik understood when he made his official translation. He argued that this "duplicate copy" was in fact a longer original (probably written on a parchment scroll), and that the *Copper Scroll* was merely a shorter version containing the essential details. However, as we learned earlier, he concluded that the contents of both of these Scrolls were imaginary.

Al Wolters challenged Milik's translation of the key terms and sought to make "explication" mean "explanation."[64] Whereas Milik's "explication" had in view an expanded version of the catalog of treasures, Wolters' "explanation" understood the sense of an "interpretive key" giving the correct value to the extremely large measurements and amounts as well as more exact directions for the coded locations. He also argued that the term translated as "measurements" could mean "portions" and refer to "anointing oil" which would legitimize the succession of the Qumran/Zadokite priesthood. Finally, he saw the word translated "inventory" as the Greek loanword *protokollon*, which refers to the first sheet of a papyrus roll. According to Wolter's theory, this "protocol" or text written at the beginning of the duplicate Scroll, but omitted from the *Copper Scroll*, may have contained a secret password or official authorization granting access to the treasure.

With this reasoning, Wolters concludes that the *Copper Scroll* is tied to the Qumran priesthood because it lists sacred items dedicated for priestly service, and the Scroll's duplicate holds the final interpretive key to finding the hidden treasure caches.

As intriguing as this last possibility may be, Paul Mandel has demonstrated that Wolters' translations are not in accord with normal Mishnaic Hebrew usage.[65] He maintains that the term *prwsh*, translated as "explication" and "explanation," fits best with the former translation yet would be better understood as "specification."[66] He also argues that it is not lexically possible to make the translation "anointing oils," for the very root of the word so translated means "measure," which is attested in various forms in other Dead Sea Scroll texts, and even in the *Copper Scroll* itself.[67] Wolters himself has since changed his position on this.[68]

Furthermore, Wolters' reading of two separate words together to form what he takes as a Greek loanword is precluded on both lexical and syntactical grounds. The Hebrew word *prt*, in Mishnaic Hebrew, has the basic meaning "item, itemization." Although the form *prtwt* (assumed by Wolters to be a transliteration of the Greek word *proto*, "first") does not appear in other Mishnaic texts, it must have the same sense as its other nominal forms.[69] Thus Mandel would see this second document as a duplicate copy—not as a more expanded or detailed list, but as a more complete or definitive specification of each treasure item. In this sense, the duplicate does not include material missing from the *Copper Scroll*, as though supplementation were needed, for the *Copper Scroll* is elaborately detailed itself. The two Scrolls, then, are almost identical except for the closing lines of the *Copper Scroll*.

### Where Is It?

According to Pixner, the most likely site for Sechab, the location where the duplicate copy of the *Copper Scroll* is buried, is Tell Shihab, which lies east of the confluence of the three rivers that form the Yarmuk. On modern maps this is to the far east of the Sea of Galilee close to the remains of the old Roman road to Damascus (see map on page 275). That this duplicate was important is affirmed by the fact that it was buried in a subterranean vault in an underground passage at a site far to the north. Pixner's identification assumes that the Scrolls' references to the city of Damascus—such as the *Damascus Document* (*CD* 7:15-19)—refer to the actual city of Damascus in modern Syria and are not a code word for the Qumran community. Pixner believes there was an Essene settlement in

Damascus that was significant enough to have its own *Kochlit* (monastic center). He suggests that since robberies in that area were frequent, the people of the region may have become experts at hiding valuables in holes, cisterns, and subterranean vaults (see *Strabo* 16.26; Josephus, *Antiquities* 17.2.1 § 23).[70] Others, such as Vendyl Jones (see chapter 16), believe that the second Scroll does serve as an interpretive key, and Jones thinks that it is buried nearby his own site at Qumran (the Wadi Jawfet Zaben). However, whether or not this duplicate document is ever found will not affect the identification of the locations of the treasure caches to any degree, for many of the toponyms for these areas have changed since ancient times.

## An Enriching Discovery

The *Copper Scroll* is an important anomaly that holds some intriguing secrets yet to be resolved. It may hold out for us the possibility of one day recovering the lost treasure of the Temple, an event that would most certainly excite large numbers of people worldwide. And even if the treasures described in the *Copper Scroll* are never found, still, we have been greatly enriched by the new historical and linguistic knowledge gained from the study of this intriguing document.

# 13

# THE MESSIAH IN THE SCROLLS

*The Dead Sea Scrolls provide us with some of the oldest messianic texts in the Jewish tradition. . . . Messianic expectation is widely attested in the Scrolls, and is certainly important.*

—John J. Collins

I once heard a story about a foreign student who, never having seen a Bible, was given a copy to read for the first time. When he completed his reading of the Old Testament, he looked up at a friend and asked, "Where is He?"

"Who?" inquired the friend.

"I don't know, but someone's coming!"

That is the impression a person gets from reading the Old Testament. Someone is coming! *Coming* to rescue Isaiah's lost sheep gone astray (Isaiah 53:6), *coming* to return the hearts of Malachi's people to the faith of their fathers (Malachi 3:7; 4:6), *coming* to rebuild the Davidic dynasty according to Zechariah's vision (Zechariah 6:12-15), and *coming* to restore God's honor through the lives of His chosen people (Ezekiel 36:18-36).

This is also the impression a person can get from reading the first chapter of the Gospels in the New Testament. During that time a fervent expectation of the Messiah filled the Land. Simeon, already an old man when Jesus was born (circa 4 B.C.), was waiting "for the consolation of Israel," believing "that he would not see death before he had seen the Lord's Messiah" (Luke 2:25-26). So widespread was this messianic hope that even the "despised" Samaritans were seen to share in the expectation: "I know that Messiah is coming" (John 4:25; see also verse 29).

In previous decades, critical scholars challenged the idea of a personal Messiah, which they said was a later invention by church theologians. They assert that the expectation seen in the New Testament period was actually a Jewish nationalism that had messianic character.

That all changed with the Dead Sea Scrolls. Suddenly we had documents written by people of the Old Testament who shared the same messianic hope sounded in the New Testament. Here were Jews that looked into the Old Testament for answers about the future and found a personal Messiah. While the messianic figure they anticipated might not completely conform to the Messiah portrayed in the New Testament, their ardent messianism confirms that this age was one of common expectation.[1] In this chapter we want to consider the Qumran view of the Messiah, exploring both the scholarly consensus on well-known texts as well as the question of controversial revelations in the newly published texts.

## The Concept of the Messiah in the Old Testament

Given the Qumran Sect's allegiance to the Old Testament, we would expect that the concept of the Messiah as found in the Scrolls should not deviate in any dramatic fashion from what is found in the Old Testament. At the same time, the Scrolls, like other intertestamental literature and the New Testament, reflect a development of concepts which are expressed in the Old Testament only in the barest form. In any case, a brief survey of the use of the word *Messiah* in the Old Testament will help us better understand the Qumran concept of Messiah.

In the Old Testament, the Hebrew word *mashiach* ("Messiah") is rarely used as a technical term for the Davidic ruler promised by the prophets (for example, see Isaiah 9:7; Jeremiah 23:5-6; Ezekiel 34:23-24; 37:25;

Amos 9:11-12). The two texts where this may be the case are Psalm 2 (verses 2-9) and 89 (verses 3-4,20-29). The explicit use of the term *mashiach* in Daniel 9:25 in reference to the Messiah is perhaps the most developed usage in the Old Testament. The normal use of the term is simply to designate "one anointed" (with oil and/or the Holy Spirit). The infrequent use of this term by the Old Testament writers does not, of course, imply that they had no developed concept of the Messiah. It simply means that no such designation for this concept had crystallized until later in the Second Temple period. Because the term *mashiach* indicated someone who had been anointed and set apart by God and enabled for a special task (a prophet, priest, or king),[2] its use for the greater embodiment of these offices was to be expected. Thus, the Greater Prophet spoken of by Moses (Deuteronomy 18:15), the unending priesthood of Melchizedek (Genesis 14:18-20), and the eternally enthroned seed of David (2 Samuel 7:12-16; 23:1-3,5) all find a common connection to this term.

The connection of the term *Messiah* as applied to an anointed king appears especially strong in the Old Testament and was used in a prophetic sense of the coming Davidic ruler.[3] Both 2 Samuel and the Psalms refer to King David as the "anointed one" (*mashiach*) whose descendants will rule forever (2 Samuel 22:50-51; Psalm 18:50). In addition, the concept of a universal Messiah is seen in texts that speak of the Davidic house's dominion over foreign nations (2 Samuel 22:44-51; Psalms 2:7-9; 18:44-50). The pre-exilic prophet Isaiah combined these concepts in his depiction of the future Davidic Messiah who would rule in justice over the nations of the world (Isaiah 11:1-10). In like manner, the Chronicler spoke of a Davidic ruler-restorer who would rebuild the Temple, to whom God would be Father without the need for correction, and who would serve as regent in God's kingdom (1 Chronicles 17:11-14).

When the exiles returned to Judah, they viewed the reestablishment of the Davidic dynasty (Zechariah 4:7-10) as a prelude to national restoration (Ezekiel 36:24; 37:12) and an indication that God would also fulfill His remaining promise of spiritual restoration (Ezekiel 36:25-27; 37:14). However, the post-exilic community soon realized that the prophetic ideals of restoration had not been met. The postexilic leader and restorer of the Temple, Zerubbabel, although of Davidic descent, could not rule as king under a Persian administration (only as a governor or satrap—Haggai 1:1, 14;2:2,21). Later, when the Hasmoneans exerted rulership over the Jewish people, this dynasty of high priests at first carefully avoided assuming the title of "king" (which was reserved for the Seleucid monarchs). Alexander Jannaeus (103–76 B.C.) appears to have been the first to have assumed the title "king" in addition to that of high priest.

Despite the achievements of the Hasmoneans, some Jewish religious groups, such as the Pharisees, were opposed to them, but above all, the Qumran Sect. They understood that the Hasmonean rulers (either as kings and/or high priests) did not constitute a *legitimate* Davidic or priestly line. The failure of the post-exilic community to experience restoration, coupled with a growing apostasy in Israel (due to the influence of Hellenism and the Hasmoneans), provoked an earnest desire for a truly God-sent, anointed King and Priest who would restore the old order—a Davidic monarchy with a Zadokite priesthood. This desire became even more pronounced when the Jewish people lost their sovereignty following the Roman conquest in 63 B.C. As one writer observed, "Illegitimate Hasmonean kingship and Roman conquest had stimulated a longing for an eschatological 'anointed' king."[4]

If we continue to trace the concept of Messiah through the Old Testament without exclusive dependence on the term *mashiach*, we find that not only is there portrayed a royal "Son of David" and a redeemer/restorer of Israel, but also a heaven-sent ruler who is able to bear titles of divinity (Isaiah 9:6-7) and restore the whole of the created order (Isaiah 11:1-2). We also find references to a figure who is a combined King-Priest (Psalm 110; cf. Zechariah 6:9-13), and a Priest-Servant who cleanses the nation through priestly atonement (Isaiah 52:13-15; cf. Leviticus 4:6; Ezekiel 43:19-20). Most important of all, we see that the Messiah's coming would not take place until the last days (Jeremiah 33:14-18; Isaiah 59:16-20). The messianic advent was to come after (and in response to) a time of distress that will come upon Israel (Deuteronomy 4:30; Jeremiah 30:4-11).

## The Concept of the Messiah in Early Judaism

The messianic expectation prophesied in the Old Testament and presumed in the New was expressed in late Second Temple Judaism through sustained hopes for restoration and deliverance from the religious and political conditions of the day. The apocryphal and pseudepigraphical literature containing messianic references span a period from about 200 B.C.

to 40 B.C., a time contemporaneous with the Qumran Sect. This literature includes the Jewish reactions to the rule of Simon as high priest, the desecrations of Antiochus IV Epiphanes, and the Roman emperor Pompey's invasion and conquest of Jerusalem. All of these events fanned the fire of messianic hope. A brief survey of this literature reveals some aspects of Jewish messianic interpretation that were common to both the Dead Sea community and the later writers of the New Testament.

In the apocryphal work known as The Wisdom of Ben-Sira (or Sirach), composed around 180 B.C. by a professional scribe whose proper name was *Yeshua'* (Jesus), we find a prayer for the deliverance and restoration of Israel through divine intervention (36:1-17). In this prayer God appears to act alone, yet the expression "the Lord and His anointed" appears later (46:19) with reference to 1 Samuel 12:5 (where both figures are mentioned). Still later, Ben-Sira praises God, "who makes a horn to sprout for the house of David and elects the sons of Zadok to be priests" (51:12). These words, most likely based on Psalm 132:16-17, present one of the foundational messianic ideas seen in the Dead Sea Scrolls—that of a Davidic and priestly Messiah.

This royal priestly theme is also evident in the apocryphal book of *Jubilees* when it cites the biblical account of Isaac's blessing of Jacob's sons Levi (*Jubilees* 31:13-17) and Judah (*Jubilees* 31:18-20). Levi and his sons' descendants are depicted as judges and teachers of the Law, ministering in the sanctuary and executing righteousness (30:18). Judah, however, is said to receive power to be Jacob's help, and through his righteousness peace was to come for all Israelites. To him it is said, "A prince shall you be, you and one of your sons" (30:19-20). Later we are told this future Davidic king will rule over an Israel that is both a priestly and a royal nation (33:20).

The concept of the Messiah as a "son of man" after the figure in Daniel 7:13 is found in the apocryphal book of *1 Enoch* in a section known as the *Similitudes*. This book has been argued to go back to as early as 40 B.C.[5] While we will deal more with the "son of man" title in the next chapter, we should note that scholars[6] have found in the *Similitudes* four features for this figure:[7] 1) it refers to an individual and is not a collective symbol, 2) it is clearly identified as the Messiah, 3) the Messiah is preexistent and associated with prerogatives traditionally reserved for God, and 4) the Messiah takes an active role in the defeat of the ungodly. New Testament parallels with the *Similitudes* (for example, Matthew 19:28 with *1 Enoch* 45:3, and John 5:22 with *1 Enoch* 61:8) may affirm that both the Scroll and New Testament writers depended on a common Jewish messianic interpretation (or tradition) based on Daniel's vision.[8]

These brief examples, which reveal that the messianic concepts rooted in the Old Testament were developed in the Jewish literature written during the later Second Temple period, provide a context for the expression of the messianic ideal as seen in the Scrolls.

## The Messiah at Qumran

There is no question that the Qumran Sect expected a coming Messiah. This is affirmed in texts such as *Patriarchical Blessings* (*4QPBless* 3): "until the coming of the Righteous Messiah, the sprout of David" (see also *4QFlor* 1-2. 2:11; *4QpIsa*[a] 8–10:17). The clearly expected "coming of the Messiah of Aaron and Israel" is also found in the *Damascus Document* (*CD* 19:10; 20:1). As in the Old Testament, the use of the term *mashiach* in the Scrolls may refer to a prophet as "an anointed one" (*1QM* 11:17; *CD* 2:12; 6:1; *6Q15* 3:4). Also as in the Old Testament, messianic terminology is applied to a variety of figures (for example, "Branch of David," "Scepter," "Star").

While the expectation of Messiah is evident in the Scrolls, there are still some difficult questions that arise in our study of the messianic texts. As Lawrence Schiffman has pointed out, "Serious methodological problems—better, pitfalls—await anyone who seeks to investigate this area of Qumran studies."[9] This is because the Qumran community may not have had a uniform conception of the Messiah. For example, at times the Messiah appears as a singular "Anointed," but on other occasions we see a dual "Twin-Anointed." In most cases, the Messiah is a human being, but on occasion he may also be described with heavenly (or divine) characteristics. We find texts that speak of "God begetting the Messiah" (*1QSa* 2:12), of the Messiah as a "firstborn son" (*4Q369*), and of the Messiah as subordinate to the priests (*1QSa* 2:14-20); and yet we also have a text that may read, "The heavens and earth obey the voice of His Messiah" (*4Q521* line 1), and another that speaks of the Messiah "raising the dead" (*4Q521* line 12). It's possible that these differences indicate that the documents had different origins, with some coming from outside the Sect, and others evidencing a developing messianism within the Sect.

Let's look now at texts that portray the Qumran community's concept of Messiah, beginning with the controversial question about the number of messianic figures that were identified by the Sect.

### How Many Messiahs?

Most interpreters of the messianic figure in the Scrolls conclude that not one but *two* (or even three) messiahs may be discerned, each with his own office as King and Priest (and Prophet). This assumption rests upon a plural reference that appears in the *Community Rule* (or the *Manual of Discipline*): "the Messiahs of Aaron and Israel" (*1QS* 9:11). Although this same construction is found elsewhere only in the singular, and three times in the foundational text the *Damascus Document* (*CD* 12:23; 14:19; 19:10), some scholars argue that the singular *mashiach* ("Messiah") are defective spellings for the plural *mashiachey* ("Messiahs"), with the *yodh* = *ey* alone making the plural.[10] A different approach suggests that the singular construct applies to both modifiers, hence "two messiahs."

Similar confusion results from a problem text in *CD* 20:1, where we read, "until the rise of a Messiah from Aaron and from Israel." There are two ways we can interpret the singular *mashiach* in this phrase: Either there is only one Messiah who will represent both the priesthood and the people of Israel, or there are two Messiahs because *mashiach* is modified by both prepositional phrases.

One early explanation of the use of the singular *mashiach* came from H.W. Kuhn, who suggested that the medieval scribes who had copied the Cairo Genizah copy of the *Damascus Document* and saw the reference to dual messianism simply assumed it was a textual error and corrected the text to bring it into conformity with their own theology of a singular Messiah.[11] However, J.T. Milik, the "genius" of the original Scroll Team, claimed that the disputed passage (*1QS* 9:11) was not in the oldest extant copy of the *Community Rule* (*4QS^e*), which cites *1QS* 9:12 directly after *1QS* 8:16.[12] Lawrence Schiffman countered this assertion with the suggestion that Milik improperly connected the two fragments.[13]

Because no actual case of a defective spelling like this is to be found in either the Cairo Genizah manuscript or among any of the Dead Sea Scrolls, and many of the more recently published Cave 4 texts speak of a singular messianic figure (for example, *4Q246; 4Q521*), the case cannot be resolved based on the one expression occurring in the *Manual of Discipline*. In addition, the new Cave 4 text *4QD^b*, which corresponds to *CD* 14:19, reads, "until the rise of a Messiah of Aaron and Israel" (fragment 18, column 3.1:12). Here, the grammar permits only one Messiah. For this reason, John Collins[14] and others have proposed that a better method for determining whether dual messianism is present in the Scrolls is to consider the broader context of messianic terminology.

The document known as *Testimonia* (*4Q175*) provides a list of Old Testament passages the Sect regarded as messianic (see below). In this list many terms for the Messiah are used, oftentimes describing priestly or regal activities. In these references we find that the priestly and kingly figures are either equal to one another, or the kingly figure (that is, the Davidic Messiah = "the messiah of Israel") is subordinate to or defers to the priestly figure ("messiah of Aaron") (*4QpIsa*[a]; see Isaiah 11:3; *4Q285* line 5). One example of the latter appears in the controversial text *Messianic Rule* (*1QSa*), which Lawrence Schiffman translated as follows:

> [The priest] shall enter [at] the head of all the congregation of Israel and [all his brethren the sons of] Aaron, the priests, [who are invited] to the feast, men of renown, and they shall sit be[fore him, each] according to his importance. Afterwards, [the messiah] of Israel [shall enter] and the heads of the [thousands of Israel] shall sit before him [ea]ch according to his importance. [No] one [shall extend] his hand to the bread first (portion) of the bread and [the wine] before the priest. Fo[r he shall extend] his hand first. Afterwa[rds,] the messiah of Israel [shall exten]d his hand to the bread. . . .[15]

This passage describes the eschatological messianic banquet, and even though the priest is not explicitly referred to as a messiah, he clearly takes precedence over the "messiah of Israel." It could be argued, however, that the priest is intentionally *not* stated to be a messiah, and that a messianic identity should not be deduced from his superior position, since the "men of renown" also share this position. Are they, too, messiahs? Perhaps the reason that the priest extends his hand first to the bread and wine is because the "messiah of Israel" is simply following a ceremonial convention, in which an officiating priest enters first to preside over the ritual meal. However, other texts, such as the *Temple Scroll*, which is neither eschatological nor messianic, present a pattern of subjecting even the authority of the king to the high priest.

If a messianic dualism was taught at Qumran, it most likely would have been based on the Sect's interpretation of Zechariah 3–4 and 6. In Zechariah 3–4, the high priest Joshua and the civil leader Zerubbabel appear as prominent figures in a messianic context (3:7-9; 4:7-10). Joshua is described as "standing before the angel of the LORD, and Satan standing at his right hand to accuse him" (3:1). Then he is told to expect the coming of a God-sent figure known as "the Branch" (3:8), and that a stone set before him symbolizes the eschatological cleansing of the nation (a priestly act—verse 9). Zerubbabel is identified as the builder of the Temple (a messianic role) and told that the Spirit of the Lord will remove all earthly obstacles so that his work might be accomplished (4:6-10). He then is shown "two anointed" who are "standing by the Lord of the whole earth (4:11-14). The usual term for "anointed" (*mashiach*) is avoided here because Zechariah wants to connect these "anointed" with the oil of the olive trees—oil that fills the menorah (the sacred seven-branched candelabra). The term *bene hayyishar* ("sons of fresh oil") restricts the anointing to the two kinds of officials uniquely anointed with olive oil: priests and kings. These two offices, in context, belonged to Zerubbabel and Joshua. This messianic allusion is amplified in Zechariah 6 as Joshua the high priest is crowned and "the Branch" is identified as the Temple builder (verses 11-15). Again there is a reference in the context to "two offices": one royal and ruling, the other priestly and peaceful (verse 13). While these offices could be united in one figure, it is easy to see how the Sect could have identified them as two separate "anointeds" or messiahs. If the Sect interpreted the passage this way, the fact that Joshua the high priest is crowned (Zechariah 6:11), but *not* Zerubbabel the governor, may reveal why the Aaronic (priestly) messiah was elevated above the Davidic (ruling) messiah at Qumran.

John Collins has suggested that the use of the dual reference to a priestly and kingly messiah may have been used as a polemic against the Hasmonean ruler John Hyrcanus, who bore both of these titles.[16] There may be some support for this in a curse text based on Joshua 6:26 (as cited in the *Psalms of Joshua*), which is included in the *Testimonia* (*4Q175*). If so, the use of the two figures is a political statement against the Hasmonean rulers, who combined the priestly and kingly offices.

Therefore, despite the lack of plural references to Messiah, the Sect's messianic terminology and pattern of priestly superiority does seem to support the idea of more than one messianic figure in the Scrolls. We should not forget that the Scrolls were not all the products of the Sect, so divergent theological views may be present among the Scrolls, although the only dual reference occurs in a text thought to be written by the Sect. If dual messianism is indeed characteristic of the Sect, their view is understandable in light of how difficult it is to interpret the relevant Old Testament passages (such as the one from Zechariah). It's also possible that the Scrolls, which span the period from the mid-second century B.C. to the latter half of the first century A.D., reflect a developing theology within Second Temple sectarian messianism which may have shifted from a dual to a single messianic reference.[17]

## An Eschatological Messiah

The Messiah of the Dead Sea Scrolls is clearly eschatological. His coming is at "the end of days," and is royal (Davidic), priestly (Aaronic), and prophetic (Mosaic) in nature. At one time the number of manuscripts using the technical term for this eschatological Messiah (*mashiach*) was thought to be only four (*1QS, 1QSa, CD, 4QPBless*).[18] Today, however, that number has risen to 17 manuscripts.[19] Even so, only 11 of these contain unambiguous references, while the others are possible references (when we permit a nontechnical sense of "anointing"). This number (in my opinion)[20] could be raised to 21 if we also include messianic terminology such as "Prince," "Scepter," "Branch of David," and perhaps "First-Born."[21] All of these readings occur in eschatological or apocalyptic contexts[22] in which the overriding theme is royal messianic expectation. The support for this expectation is built upon citations or allusions from Genesis 49:10, Isaiah 11:1-4, and two of the aforementioned biblical messianic titles: "Prince" (Ezekiel 34:24; 7:25), and "Branch of David" (Jeremiah 23:5; 33:15). These terms appear in some of the fragmentary Cave 4 texts recently made available to scholars (which we'll look at in a moment). Apocalyptic scholar John J. Collins summarizes the eschatological nature of the Qumranic messiah(s), laying stress on the inclusion of the messianic terminology when he says:

> In modern, and indeed in traditional Jewish and Christian usage, "messiah" is an eschatological term, nearly always referring to the King Messiah at the end of days. In the Scrolls, the term can also refer to figures from the past, notably the prophets, and to various eschatological figures, including at least a priest as well as king, and possibly also a prophet. . . . It is of fundamental importance that figures who are called "messiahs" or "anointed ones" in the Scrolls can also be referred to in other terms. The royal messiah is simply the eschatological king, whether he is called "messiah" or "Branch of David." The priestly messiah, equally, is simply the eschatological High Priest, whether or not he is called "messiah of Aaron" in a specific text.[23]

Therefore, support for identifying the Qumranic Messiah relies not only on the usage of the term *Messiah*, but also on the use of messianic terminology. Our knowledge of messianic interpretation at Qumran has been helped significantly by the discovery of fragmentary texts that apparently served as messianic "proof texts," or collections of Old Testament passages considered by the Qumran Sect as messianic.

## Messianic Proof Texts

The expectation of the Messiah at Qumran is evidenced in a one-page text consisting of four messianic "proof texts" from the Old Testament known as *4QTestimonia* (*4Q175* [*4QTest*]) (see photo section—photo of *4Q175*). These messianic passages are strung together without commentary, but obviously represent those texts of greatest eschatological significance. Even though the term *messiah* does not appear, the text is filled with messianic terminology. According to F. Garcia Martinez, "This is an important text for the history of Qumran messianism."[24]

A similar trio of messianic characters (but in different order) occurs in the disputed *Manual of Discipline* dual messianic text (*1QS* 9:11). However, this text may include four different messianic figures: a Mosaic Prophet Messiah, a Davidic Conqueror/Ruler Messiah, a Priestly Messiah, and a Lay or Secular Messiah (unless this last is the Messiah of Israel = Davidic Messiah, as in *1QS* 9:11). To get a sense of how the Sect presented this material in the *Testimonia* we will follow its order, citing the texts (with their intended Old Testament citations supplied) then providing an explanation.

## 1. The Messiah of Moses

> [1]And [ . . . ] spoke to Moses saying: (Deuteronomy 5:28-29) You have heard the sound of the words [2]of this people, what they said to you: all they have said is right [3]If (only) it were given to me (that) they had this heart to fear me and keep all [4]my precepts all the days, so that it might go well with them and their sons for ever! [5](Deuteronomy 18:18-19) I would raise up for them a prophet from among their brothers, like you, and place my words [6]in his mouth, and he would tell them all that I command them. And it will happen that the man [7]who does not listen to my words, that the prophet will speak in my name, I [8]shall require a reckoning from him.

This text based on Deuteronomy 5:28-29 and 18:18-19 (Exodus 20:21 in the proto-Samaritan Pentateuchal tradition) promises an eschatological

Mosaic prophet who will tell the people what God commands and the consequences of disobedience. Apparently the concept is that of a Messianic prophet, but whether he is to be viewed as a distinct messianic figure separate from "the messiahs of Aaron and Israel" is unclear.

## 2. The Messiah of David

> [9]And he uttered his poem and said: (Numbers 24:15-17) Oracle of Balaam, son of Beor, and oracle of the man [10]of penetrating eye, oracle of him who listens to the words of God and knows the knowledge of the Most High, [11]of one who sees the vision of *Shaddai*, who falls and opens the eye. I see him, but not now, [12]I espy him, but not close up. A star has departed from Jacob, /and/ a sceptre /has arisen/ from Israel. He shall crush [13]the temples of Moab, and cut to pieces all the sons of Sheth.

This text from Numbers 24 is also cited in other Qumran Scrolls (*CD* 7:19; *1QM* 11:6-7) and in the *Testament of Judah* 24:1-6 (although no fragment with this text has yet been found at Qumran). The passage concerns a militant messiah who conquers the borderland of Moab and destroys the Shethites. According to other traditions, this figure relates best to the royal or Davidic Messiah. Rabbi Akiba believed this figure referred to the "King Messiah" (TJ *Ta'anit* 68d), Philo to a great "warrior" (*De Praemiis et Poenis*, 95), and the *Testament of Judah* to a "savior-judge."

## 3. The Messiah of Aaron

> [14]And about Levi he says: (Deuteronomy 33:8-11) Give to Levi your Thummim and your Urim, to your pious man, whom [15]you tested at Massah, and with whom you quarrelled about the waters of Meribah, /he who/ said to his father [...] [16][...] and to his mother "I have not known you," and did not acknowledge his brothers, and his son did not [17]know. For he observed your word and kept your covenant. They have made/ your judgments /shine/ for Jacob,[18] our law for Israel, they have placed incense before your face and a holocaust upon your altar. [19]Bless, [...], his courage and accept with pleasure the work of his hand! Crush /the loins/ of his adversaries, and those who hate him, [20]may they not rise!

This text relates the blessing of Levi to the duties of the high priest: oracular discernment, teaching of the Torah, and sacrifice. That the *Book of Jubilees* uses words from Deuteronomy 33:8-11 to exalt Levi and his priesthood may imply that the author of the *Testimonia* received his concept of a priestly messiah from Deuteronomy 33.

### 4. The Messiah of Israel

> [21]At the moment when Joshua finished praising and giving thanks with his psalms, [22]he said (Joshua 6:26): Cursed be the man who rebuilds this city! Upon his firstborn [23]will he found it, and upon (the son of) his right hand (lit. Benjamin) will he erect its gates!

Messianic passages rarely include historical events, but this passage is an exception. The text finds its explanation in the *Psalms of Joshua* (*4Q378-379*), upon which the remainder of the *Testimonia* is based.

> And behold, an accursed man, a Belial, [24]has arisen to become a fowler's snare to his people, and destruction to all his neighbors. [25]And he shall arise [ . . . ] the two of them being instruments of violence. They shall rebuild [26][the city and will] set up for it a wall and towers to make of it a refuge of ungodliness [27][a great evil] in Israel, and horror in Ephraim and in Judah. [28][ . . . They shall] cause abomination in the land, and great contempt among the sons of [Jacob], [29]and they shall shed bl[ood] like water upon the ramparts of the daughter of Zion and within the precincts of [30]Jerusalem.

According to Collins, this statement becomes intelligible if the application is made to a figure contemporary with the writer, who attempted to rebuild Jericho.[25] The excavations of Ehud Netzer at Jericho in 1987–1988 have revealed that John Hyrcanus, a Hasmonean ruler, was that man. That doesn't necessarily mean we should consider this passage as nonmessianic (as Collins does), but that we could see it as a type of messianic polemic against the Hasmoneans, who illegitimately combined the offices of king and priest. The reference then could be to "the messiah of Israel" as a parallel with "the messiah of Aaron" following the pattern of *1QS* 9:11. In addition, the writer's inclusion of one (or two) antimessianic figure(s) such as Belial reveals that negative eschatological characters played an important role in the dualistic drama of end-time events as interpreted at Qumran.

### Marking Messianic Texts

Another form of messianic proof texting occurs within a number of Dead Sea Scrolls in which various types of marginal markings appear at certain verses in a number of the Dead Sea Scrolls. One prominent example is the *Great Isaiah Scroll* (*1QIsa^a*), three types of marks are used to designate either messianic or eschatological texts. According to New Testament archaeologist Jack Finegan, who did a study of these marks in this Scroll, the paleo-Hebrew letter *Taw*, which appears as a cross mark (either + or X, used interchangeably), was one of these marks used to single out passages of messianic import.[26]

Prior to the Christian era, this mark had an early history of usage as a mystical or magical mark of protection. During the Second Temple period, the Semitic *Taw* became the Greek *Tau* and the Latin letter "T."[27] Also, because of its form it was considered equivalent to the Greek letter *Chi* (written both as + and X). The *Chi* is the first letter in the Greek word for Messiah—$\chi\rho\iota\sigma\tau\acute{o}\varsigma$ (*Christos*)—and was frequently used for its abbreviation ($\overline{x}$). This letter has also been used from the first century onward as a sign for the cross. It appears frequently on early Jewish-Christian ossuary inscriptions from tombs on the Mount of Olives. In Greek and Syriac manuscripts of the early church bishop Epiphanius (circa A.D. 315), who headed a monastery near Gaza, the cross mark appears as (+ in Greek, and X in Syriac). Epiphanius himself said the sign stood for the Messiah and was used to mark passages concerning Him.

Although this mark was used by Christians during the last period of the Qumran settlement, this doesn't necessarily mean that the marks on the *Great Isaiah Scroll* are evidence that "Essene Christians" lived at the Qumran community or that the marks represent revisions added later by Christian scribes. For the Sect, the *Taw* mark had significance as a sign of messianic salvation (in the apocalyptic sense). We find this use in the *Damascus Document* (*CD* B. 19:12) where the text cites Ezekiel 9:4:

> These [people] shall escape in the time of the visitation, but they that hesitate shall be given over to the sword when the Messiah of Aaron and Israel shall come. As it happened in the epoch of the visitation of the forefathers, which He said by the hand of Ezekiel: "to set the mark (*ha-Taw*) upon the foreheads of such as sigh and groan."

The context of Ezekiel 9:4-6 is the judgment of Jerusalem for its abominations. Those who were appointed to destroy the city were to kill everyone who did not have a "mark" on their foreheads. The *Damascus Document* interpreted this text apocalyptically for the Sect's era, expecting a messianic advent in which the unrepentant ("they that hesitate") would be destroyed, but the faithful ("such as sigh and groan") would be delivered. The sign that distinguished the faithful from the unrepentant was the *Taw* (translated "mark"). Apparently the Dead Sea Sect understood this as more than figurative, because the *Damascus Document* uses the *Taw* with the definite article (*ha*)—that is, "the mark" (the Masoretic Text lacks the definite article). This may suggest they understood that a literal mark on the forehead would serve as protection in the messianic war (Genesis 4:15). If so, the identical mark in messianic passages may likewise be understood as a "sign of salvation." While this does not presage a Christian understanding of the cross, its association with messianic deliverance from judgment makes possible an understanding in that direction.

## The Messiah as King

We now move on to consider the basic Qumranic concept of the Messiah as a ruler or king who will deliver Israel from her enemies, subjugate the "Sons of Darkness" and effect dominion for God over the Gentile nations.

The recently published fragmentary text known as *The Genesis Florilegium* (*4Q252*), in its interpretation of a cryptic Old Testament passage, may reflect just such a Second Temple-period messianic concept. Categorized as a thematic *pesher*, this interpretation appears in an exegesis of the blessing of Judah in Genesis 49:10, which says, "The scepter shall not depart from Judah, nor the ruler's staff from between his feet, until Shiloh comes, and to him shall be the obedience of the people." The text reads as follows:

> "(A) ruler shall [not] depart from the tribe of Judah (Genesis 49:10)." Whenever Israel rules there shall [not] fail to be a descendant of David upon the throne. For the [ruler's] "staff" is the Covenant of the Kingdom (or kingship), [and the leaders/clans] of Israel, they are "the feet" (referred to in Genesis 49:11), until the Messiah of Righteousness, the Branch of David comes. For to him and his seed was given the Covenant of the Kingdom (or kingship) of (or over) His people for everlasting generations ... (*4Q252* 5.1-4).

Robert Eisenman and Michael Wise translate the last line (*4Q252* 5.5) as saying, "... because he kept ... [*lacuna*] ... the Torah with the men of the community ..." in an attempt to link the observance of Torah with the Messiah and the Qumran community (to see more about Eisenman's theory of origin, see chapter 17). However, the word "kept" might not be in the text (the reading is not clear), and the *lacuna* ("gap, omission") only permits speculation about the connection between the words "Torah" and "Messiah" (line 3). What is preserved here, however, is quite significant for understanding the messianic interpretation given to certain Old Testament titles in Second Temple Judaism. Here we find that the Sect clearly identified both Jeremiah's "Branch" (Jeremiah 23:5; 33:15) and the term *Shiloh* (Genesis 49:10) with the Messiah. The Hebrew word *shiloh* is usually translated in Jewish versions of the Bible as "to whom it belongs" (taking the term as *she-lo*, lit. "that [which is] his"),[28] although some versions recognize a messianic association with the messianic age and translate it as "tranquility."[29] In many Christian Old Testaments a capitalized transliteration, "Shiloh," appears to signify a messianic appellation. This view also finds support from the Jewish Talmud (*Sanh.* 98b), *Targum Onkelos* (on Genesis 49:10), and the midrash *Bereshit* ("Genesis") *Rabbah* (99), in which *shiloh* is understood as a proper noun, the name of the Messiah.

These messianic epithets are connected with Davidic descent and the "staff" or object of rule. The eschatological picture in these epithets is that of a coming Messiah, of the tribe of Judah, of the lineage of David, who will rule over Israel for "everlasting generations." The text from *The Genesis Florilegium*, then, not only provides further evidence of the well-established notion that the Davidic Messiah was the King Messiah, but also implies by the phrase "everlasting generations" that the Qumran community's understanding of this Messiah was that he was more than simply a human religious or military figure who would act as God's agent in delivering Israel. Such an implication of the concept of a divine Messiah may also be inferred from other Dead Sea texts.

One such text is the newly published document *Messianic Apocalypse* (*4Q521*). In the opening words of the text we read this: [for the heav]ens and the earth will obey (or listen to) His Messiah" (Fragment 2, column 2.1). However, lest too much be read into this verse, we should note that the messianic figure here is depicted as a human being who is subject to the Law, and the next line of the text is based on Psalm 146, which exhorts its audience not to trust "in mortal princes ... in whom there is no [help, but] in the LORD . . . who made heaven and earth" (Psalm 146:3,6). Also, the word *Messiah* (*meshicho*) here carries the possessive suffix, and therefore should be translated as "His [that is, God's] Messiah." The same construction is found in *The Chariots of Glory* (*4Q287*), which says the "Holy Spirit rested on His Messiah." In this case, the emphasis is on God's sovereign authority over the angels and mankind. While this might portray the Messiah as a royal or kingly figure representing or delegating divine authority (which is a unique and significant attribution), it diminishes the identification that might be made directly with divinity.[30] *11QMelchizedek* (*11Q13*) is similar in its indirect implication of a divine Messiah. In this highly midrashic text the priest-king figure of Melchizedek is seen as a heavenly judge executing vengeance for God (based on Psalm 82:1). As in *4Q521*, the judgment is mediated; it is not an intrinsic attribute that might indicate a divine status. Nevertheless, both of these figures laid the groundwork for the concept of a divine Messiah in Jewish-Christianity (who could be understood to have both the attributes and titles of God) with imagery that took a human character beyond the realm of humanity. At the same time, such an understanding was an impediment for identifying Jesus with this/these Messiah(s). Jesus was not from the tribe of Levi, and therefore was not qualified to be a priest. Jesus was from the tribe of Judah and of Davidic descent, and therefore qualified to be a king. Yet Jesus, while not denying His kingship, said that His kingdom was not of this world (John 19:36), and rejected or rebuffed those who sought to make Him king by force or by faith (John 6:14-15; Acts 1:6-7). This awaited the eschatological age, at which time He would come on the clouds of heaven (Matthew 24:30; 26:64), establish His rule as a divine warrior (2 Thessalonians 1:7-8; Revelation 19:14-16), and continue it through a restoration of national Israel (Acts 3:20-21; Romans 11:26-27).

## A New Perspective

As we saw in chapter 10, the Qumran Sect had used Ezekiel's vision to attempt to calculate the arrival of the messianic age. They expected the promised restoration of Israel to take place in the Age to Come, but meanwhile, as Professor Talmon has explained, "The divine promise had not yet been fulfilled. . . . It fell to them to close the circle and assume the preordained task of the Restoration Generation."[31] Thus, they believed that God had granted to them as members of the "Renewed Covenant" the opportunity to reconstitute Israel's sovereignty, rebuild its Temple in a ritually proper manner, and usher in the King-Priest Messiah(s). When the expected event failed to materialize, they were forced to modify their messianic perspective. This changed perspective included beliefs that their own sinfulness had, in part, caused the postponement of the promised restoration (*CD* 1:8-9), and that repentance as a means of atonement would now pave the way for the arrival of the Messiah(s). Now they had to wait for the appointed and preordained messianic program to progressively unfold. As they saw it, the transition from the present age of evil to the future time of righteousness would be brought about by Messiah's arrival in the midst of an apocalyptic battle modeled on that of Gog and Magog (Ezekiel 38–39) and Daniel's end-time period of tribulation (Daniel 7–12).

This reformed messianic posture is more like the messianic concept presented in the New Testament, which portrays sinful Israel's need for atonement through Messiah (Matthew 1:21; 15:24; 18:11-14; John 1:29; cf. Acts 3:19-21; 8:28-37), and the eschatological deliverance of Israel in the "Great Tribulation" (Matthew 24:1-31; Mark 13:1-27; Luke 21:5-11,25-28; cf. 2 Thessalonians 1–2; Revelation). In fact, in the next chapter, we'll look more closely at how the Sect's concept of Messiah lined up with the New Testament's understanding of Jesus as Messiah.

# 14

# IS THE CHRISTIAN MESSIAH IN THE SCROLLS?

*These texts show a point of shared yearning between these people [of Qumran] and the New Testament community with respect to Messiah. There is a sense that there are promises that God will keep.*[1]

—Paul Hanson,
Harvard University

Having seen in the last chapter that the teaching of an eschatological Messiah(s) was central to the Qumran Sect, we will now examine select messianic texts from Qumran and especially the more controversial, recently released texts from Cave 4, with which points of comparison with the Christian concept of the Messiah in the New Testament could possibly be made. We will begin by considering whether key New Testament expressions and ideas used in reference to Jesus' person and work as Messiah are to be found in the Scrolls.

311

## The "Son of Man" in the Scrolls

In a vision, the prophet Daniel saw a "Son of Man" coming on the clouds of heaven (Daniel 7:13). Scholars generally concede[2] that Jesus and the New Testament writers understood this passage as referring to a heavenly or divine Messiah (for example, Matthew 16:27; 24:30; 26:64; Revelation 1:7 with 13; 14:14). According to Hebrew University professor David Flusser, this Old Testament figure was also accepted in ancient Judaism as divine and messianic:

> The Son of man has a superhuman, heavenly sublimity. He is the cosmic judge at the end of time; seated upon the throne of God, he will judge the whole human race with the aid of the heavenly hosts, consigning the just to blessedness and sinners to the pit of hell; and he will execute the sentence he passes. Frequently he is identified with the Messiah. . . . [3]

Flusser's statement about how Daniel 7:13 was interpreted in Judaism reflects his understanding of the use of this phrase in the Jewish intertestamental literature. In this literature, we find parallels to Daniel 7:13-14 in the *Similitudes of Enoch (1 Enoch* 37-71 and *Fourth Ezra* (4 Ezra 13). The clearest allusions are in *1 Enoch* 46:1 and 47:3, in which a figure called the "Head of Days" is substituted for Daniel's "Ancient of Days," and his companion is spoken of as "one whose face had the appearance of a man" in place of Daniel's "Son of Man." In *Enoch* 60:10 an angel calls Enoch "son of man;" however, in *1 Enoch* 70–71, which serves as an epilogue for the *Similitudes*, there are two distinct references to "Son of Man," and Enoch is clearly distinguished from this figure *(1 Enoch* 70:1; cf. 71:14). In *4 Ezra*, while the expression "Son of Man" is not used, an allusion to the figure in Daniel 7:13-14 may be found in the identification of a man in a vision "kept for ages by the Most High to deliver His creation" with the Messiah, who takes his stand on Mount Zion and burns up Israel's enemies (*4 Ezra* 12:26; 13:33-38,52).[4]

Even though the Dead Sea Scrolls were influenced by Daniel, we have not yet seen in the Scrolls any precise parallels to the Danielic title "Son of Man." The only allusion is the indefinite Aramaic *bar 'enash* ("a son of man"), which appears in the *Genesis Apocyrphon (QapGen* 21:13). In this case it is not used as a title, but as a paraphrase of Genesis 13:16, where the Aramaic phrase translates the Hebrew *'ish*—"man" (that is, a human being). But it is possible that the Qumran Sect understood Enoch's interpretation of Daniel 7 because the book was known and used by them (even though no fragment of the *Similitudes* has been yet found).[5] Also, correspondences between *4 Ezra* and the *Similitudes of Enoch* point to common assumptions about the interpretation of Daniel 7:13-14— assumptions that apparently were widely held in first-century Judaism. Thus it is possible that the Sect shared these assumptions, even though we have no direct evidence of such from the Scrolls.

## The "Son of God" in the Scrolls

### *Identifying the "Son of God"*

It had long been thought that the idea of a divine Messiah was *never* held in ancient Judaism.[6] However, such an idea may be implied in some of the Scrolls, as we observed in the previous chapter. One of the most important and controversial texts in this regard comes from the collection of fragmentary Aramaic apocalyptic texts known as *Pseudo-Daniel* (*4QpsDn*). Joseph Fitzmyer says of this text, "The importance . . . for the tenets and theology of the Qumran community cannot be underestimated."[7] In this text, which has been designated as "Son of God" (*4Q246*), we have an unidentified figure referred to in Aramaic as *bereh dî 'el* ("son of God") and *bar 'elyon* ("son of the Most High"). Regardless of who we interpret this figure to be, the context is apocalyptic with messianic overtones, and reveals that the one who adopts this title will have an exalted position and receive universal homage and servitude. Such usage links these Old Testament expressions, which are clearly divine, with the New Testament application of these terms to Jesus as a divine Messiah (see Matthew 16:15; 26:63; Luke 1:32).

Although the full text was published only recently, it has already produced an extensive quantity of interpretation and commentary. Let us first consider the translation of this text,[8] and then the various arguments concerning its interpretation. The text was originally three columns in length; however, the extant fragment preserves only two columns, each with nine lines. The important second column is better preserved than the first:

> **Column 1** [1] [. . .] dwell (or settled) [u]pon him, he fell down before the throne [2] [. . .] O King, forever! You are angry, and changed [3] [is the complexion of your face; de]pressed is your gaze. (But) [you shall rule over] everything forever! [4] [And your deeds will be g]reat. (Yet) distress shall come upon the earth; [5] [There shall

be war among the nations (or peoples)] and great carnage in the provinces (or cities) [6] [which the bands of] the king of Assyria [shall cause]. [And E]gypt [7] [shall be with them, but your son] shall be great upon the earth [8] [and all nations (or peoples) sh]all make [peace with him], and they shall all serve [9] [him, (for)] he shall be called [son of the great [God], and by his name shall he be called (or designated).

**Column 2** [1] He shall be hailed (as) "Son of God," and they shall call him "Son of the Most High." Like comets [2] that one sees, so shall be their kingdom (or rule). They shall reign for (some) years upon [3] the earth and shall trample all (or everything); one nation (or people) shall trample on another nation (or people) and one province (or city) on another province (or city) [4] [*vacat*] until there arises the people of God, and all (or everyone) shall desist (or rest) from the sword. [5] (Then) his kingdom (shall be) an everlasting kingdom, and all his (or its) ways (shall be) in truth. He shall jud[ge] [6] the earth in righteousness (or the land with truth), and everyone shall have (or make) peace. The sword shall disappear from the earth (or land), [7] and every nation (or province) will submit to (or worship) him. The great God is himself his might (or help); [8] He shall make war for him. Peoples shall he give (or put) into his power, and all of them [9] He shall cast down before him. His dominion (or rule) (shall be) an everlasting dominion (or rule), and none of the abysses of [the earth shall prevail against it]!

Several hypotheses have been offered about the identity of the primary figures and the setting of the text.

1. The central character is the Syrian king Alexander Balas (150–145 B.C.), the evil son of Antiochus IV Epiphanes (who persecuted the Jews in 167–164 B.C.). It was Balas who bestowed the high priesthood on the Jewish ruler Jonathan (Josephus, *Antiquities* 13. 2. 2 § 45). The setting is the end of the Seleucid period, and the text depicts the disastrous reign of this Syrian king being climaxed by his supreme act of blasphemy, in which he will proclaim himself "Son of God" and "Son of the Most High." The end of the Seleucid empire described here would then be followed by the eschatological rule of Israel, called in the text "the people of God." J.T. Milik,[9] who proposes this hypothesis, cites as supporting evidence coins minted during Balas' reign, which bore his image with inscriptions in Latin: *Deo Patre Natus* ("born of [or, son of] a divine father"), and in

Greek: *Theopator* ("god-begotten" or "son of god").[10] However, F. Garcia Martinez has argued that because Balas appointed Jonathan as high priest, Balas would not have been regarded as an oppressor of Israel.[11] Yet the Qumran Sect *would* have regarded Balas as an oppressor for two reasons: one, he was a foreign king who imposed his rule over Israel; and two, he further corrupted the priesthood by illegitimately appointing Jonathan, who was a Hasmonean. Milik's view is also weakened by his segregating of the apocalyptic context to column 2 alone. The same concepts of dominion and designation are also in column 1. So it, too, should be viewed as apocalyptic.

2. Another hypothesis, from F. Garcia Martinez, is that the central figure is an eschatological savior of angelic or heavenly character. He equates this character with the "Prince of Light" (also Michael and Melchizedek) who is promised to come in the end time and destroy the wicked rule of the "Prince of Darkness" (*1QM* 1:5-8). However, titles such as "Son of God" and "Son of the Most High" are never used of angelic beings in the Qumran texts (or elsewhere).[12] The intent of the text seems to be that these titles are ascribed to a human being rather than a heavenly being.

3. A popular hypothesis is that these titles, as in the New Testament, refer to an expected Messiah. This then gives the text both an eschatological and messianic interpretation. The arguments against the messianic interpretation are that these titles do not connote the Messiah in the Old Testament (although it can be argued that they do), and that the term *Messiah* does not appear in the text. These are valid arguments; however, the New Testament usage of these terms, as well as similar usage in other extrabiblical sources, implies that they were considered as messianic by the Qumran Sect's contemporaries. If so, the text may imply a messianic interpretation. Yet if this language is messianic, it may not necessarily have a direct reference to the Messiah, but to another figure who usurps these messianic titles. This is the view proposed in a final hypothesis.

4. Except in the first hypothesis (by Milik), the current opinions about the central actor in this end-time drama view him positively as a messianic deliverer rather than negatively as an antimessianic despot. We should note, however, that viewing the figure negatively as an antimessiah who assumes (or usurps) these divine titles does not remove, but rather reinforces, their application properly to the true Messiah. This negative view was championed early in the debate by Professor David Flusser of the Hebrew University. He sees the account as purely apocalyptic, and,

in fact, having common apocalyptic traits. In this light, he would see a seer, probably Daniel, interpreting for the king a mystery concerning the last days, which he has received either in a dream or a vision. The vision is of a time of wars and great distress, during which a wicked kingdom will rule over the world. This end-time condition is described as "one nation shall trample another" (*Sibylline Oracles* 635-636: "nations ravage nations"; *4 Esdras* 13:31: "city against city . . . kingdom against kingdom"; and Matthew 24:7; Mark 13:8; Luke 21:10: "nation shall rise against nation"), which sets the tone for this text of a conflict between opposing kingdoms and a militant, nationalist king who is extremely warlike.[13] This ruler will be served by all nations and he will claim to be the son of the Most High. His reign will continue until Israel ("the people of God") will be restored ("rise") (column 1, line 6; column 2, line 4). Then all war will end and universal peace will be established. In concert with biblical prophetic literature and Jewish apocalyptic literature, the wicked are deposed by divine intervention, and Israel is exalted in its messianic kingdom. Note that this peace will come only *after* the cataclysmic (messianic) war, which explains the tone of conflict that characterizes this text.

## Antichrist As "Son of God"

What Flusser sees in the "Son of God" text is the self-enthronement of a wicked ruler who is worshiped as, in some sense, divine. He argues that we should identify this figure (who either claims or demands from others that they ascribe to him the titles "Son of God" and "Son of the Most High"), as the king or leader of an oppressing kingdom.[14] Flusser's translation of the critical section is as follows:

> (7) [ ] he shall be great on earth . . . (8) [all] will worship[15] and all will serve [him] . . . great . . . (9) he shall be called[16] and by His name he shall be designated.[17] (1) He shall be named[18] son of God and they shall call him "Son of the Most High."

Flusser's translation, however, does not differ significantly from those who disagree with his interpretation. What controls Flusser's view of the text, and draws the interpretive line between scholars, is the understanding of the *vacat* in the middle of column 2 before the phrase "until there arises the people of God." If this break is taken as an indication of the beginning of a new topic which is viewed positively, then by contrast, what precedes it would be viewed negatively. Accepting this as an intentional hermeneutical key, Flusser, and Milik before him, interpreted what preceded the *vacat* as a description of the wicked ruler who brought distress and war and demanded divine worship from his subjects.

Flusser rightly observes that the text does not say this usurping figure will *be* the Son of the Most High, but that he and others will *call* him such. Flusser conjectures that the claim of this Antichrist may be even greater than the available text reveals. Because the beginning of line 9 of the first column is missing, we can only read, " . . . [g]reat . . . he shall be called, and by his name shall he be designated." The words "by his name" are enigmatic if we assume that the person will be designated by his *own* name. However, if we determine that the person will be designated by the name of God, then the words have been effectively defined. It is therefore possible to venture that the text once read, "Great [God] he shall be called and by His name he shall be designated. He shall be named son of God and they shall call him son of the Most High."

Flusser argues that this parallelism is consistent with the general nature of the text and suggests an affinity with other apocalyptic texts. Three striking parallels are adduced by Flusser: 1) the *Ascension of Isaiah* 4:2-16, which speaks of the incarnation of Belial, in whom all the peoples will believe and to whom they will sacrifice; 2) the *Oracles of Hystaspes*, which describes a king who will arise from Syria (as in *4Q246* column 1, line 6) as a destroyer of mankind, who "will constitute and call himself God and order himself to be worshiped as the Son of God";[19] and 3) the *Assumption or Testament of Moses* 8:1-5, in which an end-time king of supreme authority persecutes the Jewish people, blasphemes God, violates the Law, and desecrates the Temple by forcibly entering the Holy of Holies and offering pagan sacrifices on the altar.[20] Flusser likewise sees a parallel in the New Testament apocalyptic text of 2 Thessalonians 2:4-5, where an end-time ruler, identified as the "man of sin," demands investiture with divinity by seating himself in the Temple and proclaiming himself God in language reminiscent of Daniel 9:27 and 11:31.[21]

The chief argument in opposition to Flusser is that while the *vacat* does mark the transition to the final stage of the drama, it does not require that everything preceding it be understood as negative because repetition is a general characteristic of apocalyptic literature and would not require the assumption of sequential order, as proposed by Flusser. However, if repetition is the literary device employed in the text, we must ask why the figure identified (or identifying himself) as the Son of God appears only in column 1. John Collins, addressing this problem, answers that "the figure who is called the Son of God is the representative, or agent, of the people of God. That is why he is not mentioned again after the rise of the people of God in column 2. His career and the rise of the people of God are simply two aspects of the same event."[22]

Because both repetition and sequential order are often employed in apocalyptic literature, it is necessary to know the literary structure of the narrative before we can determine how to interpret it. However, with fragmentary texts such as this, the decision is difficult. Collins' argument depends upon the prior acceptance that "Son of God" refers to the Messiah, or at least that the phrase is used in a positive sense so that the figure can be viewed as the representative of God's people.

Fitzmyer and Collins both object that this text could not refer to the Antichrist because the Antichrist is a *Christian* concept and not found in pre-Christian Judaism.[23] However, while the concept of the figure as a "mirror-image of Christ" (Collins' words) does not appear in Judaism, nearly every trait associated with the Antichrist depicted in the New Testament has a corollary in pre-Christian apocalyptic literature, especially in the "son of Belial" text we considered earlier. Furthermore, there appears no reason why, as Flusser contends, this text might not be *the* exceptional example of such a pre-Christian anti-Messiah. This is in fact what Collins claims for this text as an example of a pre-Christian reference to the Messiah as the Son of God,[24] a concept also lacking clear parallels in Jewish apocalyptic literature. It is for this reason that Fitzmyer hesitates to make this identification.[25] While some of Flusser's exegesis and reconstruction of the text may be questionable, his argument for an Antichrist figure in this text does appear plausible.

Based on what we've examined, we can make the following observations about the nature of the Antichrist figure, who is an integral element in the desecration motif in Jewish apocalyptic literature:

1. The idea of Antichrist is "strictly Jewish and pre-Christian" (Flusser's words). We also need to recognize that while this figure may well be anti-Messiah, the Greek preposition *anti* can also mean "in place of" and indicate one who *substitutes* himself for or *counterfeits* the claims of another, (as this Qumran fragment may suggest).

2. As a Jewish apocalyptic motif, it grew and developed within the apocalyptic worldview—dualism between the cosmic and earthly forces of good and evil. The Antichrist became the human exponent of the evil forces that oppressed the people of God and desecrated the legitimate cult by which God was represented. Second Thessalonians 2:4 pictures the Antichrist seating himself in the Temple in order to proclaim his divinity,

a blasphemous act that Jesus described as the "Abomination of Desolation" (Matthew 24:15; Mark 13:14; based on Daniel 7:27, 12:11).

3. The eschatological desecration/restoration setting of this fragment suggests that the interpretation of "mystery," both in the context of Daniel 9 and, in this instance, at Qumran, was connected with a future revelation of a "mystery of lawlessness," which involved the unveiling of a human antagonist who usurps divine authority (His reign) and title (His Name). The defeat of this epitome of human arrogance and defiance will end all lesser displays of human rebellion and usher in the restored kingdom of Israel.

Thus, this important "Son of God" text may connote a divine Messiah whose prerogative of deity, expressed in the bearing of divine titles, is usurped by a wicked protagonist whose evil dominion is a dark mirror image of the Davidic Messiah.

## Is a Suffering Messiah in the Scrolls?

It is clear that a "suffering servant" motif is present in the Old Testament. This motif is presented in four sections of poetic prose in the book of Isaiah (42:1-7; 49:1-6; 50:4-9; 52:13–53:12). The last of these four depicts the servant as being despised, oppressed, rejected, afflicted, and slain. In particular, his death is seen as substitutionary, atoning for the sins of Israel (53:4-6,10). Based on this last text, Otto Betz, professor emeritus of New Testament at the University of Tübingen, believes that the Qumran community identified itself with this suffering servant of the Lord (in Isaiah 53).[26] This, of course, was not necessarily the recognition of an individual suffering servant; rather, they saw the community as fulfilling a role as "a servant of the Lord." Like Israel of old, their own persecution and suffering, and especially the persecution of their Righteous Teacher, may have been seen as a fulfillment of (or at least in unison with) the prophetic pattern in Isaiah's third servant song. If we can allow that the Old Testament's "suffering servant" was also identified (though not exclusively) with the Messiah (as in New Testament interpretation—see Luke 24:26,46; Acts 3:18; 26:23), then there exists the possibility that a suffering Messiah may also have been considered by the Sect. In this light, some scholars have suggested that a certain Qumran text may offer just such an interpretation. This extremely fragmentary text, dated to about 100 B.C., is known as *4QAaron A (4Q541)* because it refers to a sagely and priestly figure. The translation of the crucial fragments (9 and 24), often considered together, but probably not related, reads as follows:

> He will atone for all the children of his generation, and he will be sent to all the children of his [pe]ople. His word is like a word of heaven, and his teaching is in accordance with the will of God. His eternal sun will shine, and his light will be kindled in all corners of the earth, and it will shine on the darkness. Then the darkness will pass away [fro]m the earth, and thick darkness from the dry land.
>
> They will speak many words against him, and they will invent many [lie]s and fictions against him and speak shameful things about him. Evil will overthrow his generation [ . . . ] His situation will be one of lying and violence [and] the people will go astray in his days, and be confounded (*4Q451* .9).
>
> Do [not] grieve for [him] [ . . . ] God will set many things right [ . . . ] many revealed things [ . . . ] Examine and seek and know what the dove (or: Jonah?) sought (?) and do not afflict the weak by wasting or hanging [. . .] [Let] not the nail approach him. So you will establish for your father a name of joy, and for your brothers a proven foundation [. . .] You will see and rejoice in the eternal light, and you will not be an enemy (*4Q541* .24).

Fragment 9 apparently describes an eschatological high priest because he teaches (the Torah) and atones for the nation, both priestly functions, and the setting is obviously eschatological: "His eternal sun will shine . . . in all corners of the earth . . . darkness will pass away from the earth." This atoning function is not substitutionary but representative, and the atonement is not made by offering himself, but by offering a sacrifice. Therefore, even though this text does not offer a parallel with the substitutionary death seen in Isaiah 53, we still have in this fragment a messianic figure who atones for his people. While the term *messiah* is not present, we have already seen that the concept of an eschatological priestly messiah was strong at Qumran, and no other figure, except possibly the Teacher of Righteousness, could fit this description. Its application to the Teacher depends on whether he can properly be interpreted as an eschatological figure in addition to his role as the community's leader (or if he is seen as returning at the end time). The figure in fragment 9 may be analogous to the Teacher as the epitome of the true priest, yet still it is preferable to view in it a separate eschatological figure who is best identified with the Messiah.

What is relevant to our present discussion is the theme of persecution and putting to death in both fragments. It is clearly the eschatological priest who is persecuted in fragment 9, but it is not clear that he is also the one who is executed in fragment 24. More likely, this latter text is admonishing a son (in the wisdom tradition) not to dishonor his father and brothers by wrongfully killing the weak. This wrongful method of death is probably crucifixion, which both the terms *hanging* and *nails* imply. Crucifixion was a well-known practice of execution, and the Jewish priest-king Alexander Jannaeus had crucified 800 of his Jewish opponents (probably Pharisees)[27] around the time this document was written. Although a valid punishment, hanging (a form of crucifixion) was considered a curse in the Law (Deuteronomy 21:22-23; Galatians 3:13), and this, coupled with the example of Janneus, may well have turned Jews against committing their own to such a defiling death. If so, fragment 24 may be counsel to "not be an enemy" of the people by committing such an act.

Fragment 9, however, clearly presents an eschatological priestly figure who will be oppressed and suffer, even if not to the point of death. He will be persecuted because he will appear in the days of confusion and apostasy—the latter days referred to in the Old Testament as "the times of distress" (Deuteronomy 4:30; Daniel 12:1) and "the time of Jacob's trouble" (Jeremiah 30:7). It was later called by the rabbinic sages the *ch^avalim* ("birth pangs") and technically as *chelvo shel mashiach* ("pangs of the Messiah") and by Christians as "the Tribulation period." Later rabbinic teaching also put forth the interpretation of Messiah ben Joseph, who, as a national leader of the Jewish people, was expected to be slain on the eschatological battlefield.[28] However, this text does not say that the priestly messiah dies in his situation, but rather that he triumphs, putting an end to the darkness and shining forth his eternal light to all the world.

Therefore, we may conclude that while this text does not offer a parallel to the specific details of Isaiah's "suffering servant," it does generally present a messiah who suffers, atones, and reverses the condition of his people—a messiah with whom these Isaianic details may be compared (Isaiah 53:4,10-12).

## Is a Dying Messiah in the Scrolls?

The text known as *4Q Serekh Milhamah (4Q285)* was once at the center of controversy. On November 7, 1991, newspapers across the globe heralded the news that a vital link between Judaism and Christianity had appeared in the Dead Sea Scrolls—a crucified Messiah![29] Originally dubbed *The Dying* or *Pierced Messiah* text, its release by Robert Eisenman and Michael Wise came at the height of the battle to break the suppression of the Scrolls. Unfortunately, some within the evangelical community, misled by its eagerness to find New Testament parallels in the Scroll, began to talk widely of "new proof" that the Jews believed in a crucified Messiah before the time of Jesus. However, after evangelical scholars were able to study this text, they—as well as Eisenman and Wise— have agreed that they had been premature in their interpretation.[30] The translation of the part (fragment 7) of their reconstructed text which caused the controversy reads:

> [1][ . . . ] Isaiah the Prophet, ['The thickets of the forest] will be fell[ed with an axe] [2][and Lebanon shall f]all [by a mighty one. A staff shall rise from the root of Jesse, [and a Planting from his roots will bear fruit'] [3]. . . the Branch of David. They will enter into judgment with . . . [4]and they will put to death the Leader (lit. "Prince") of the Community, the Bran[ch of David] [5]and with woundings, and the (high) priest will command . . . [the sl]ai[n of the] Kitti[m]. . . . [31]

The controversy was primarily over the translation of line 4, which cites a figure called the "Prince of the Community [or Congregation]" who is clearly identified here with the "Branch of David," the royal Messiah. The problem is how to understand the Hebrew verb-form *hmytw* (from the root *hmt*, "kill"). Because the Hebrew of the Qumran texts is not pointed (has no vowels), the verb in question can be vocalized in one of two ways.[32] In the first, the "Prince" is the object of the verb: "They will kill him" (*hemitu*), making the "Prince" the one who is executed. In the second, the "Prince" is the subject of the verb: "He will kill him" (*hemito*), making the "Prince" put to death another unidentified figure. According to Marcus Bockmuehl, "Syntactically, if the sentence continues from the previous line, the third person plural might seem more likely [since the verb there is third person plural]; but in that case . . . 'the Prince of the Congregation' as the object of killing would invite (though not perhaps require) the presence of an *'et* [Hebrew sign of the direct] object marker."[33]

However, syntax alone cannot resolve this problem; context is needed. That brings us to another problem: The context is not complete, and it is uncertain whether fragment 7 actually goes before or after fragment 6. If before, the messianic figure would do the killing, but if after, the messianic figure would be alive after the events of fragment 6 and could be put to death. In addition, it is uncertain if the individual brought before the "Prince" in fragment 6 is the same one referred to as "him" in fragment 7. Even so, the context of fragment 7 alone does offer us some substantial clues for the proper interpretation of the verb *hmytw*. The *4Q285* text is based on Isaiah 10–11, and the line in question is based on Isaiah 11:4. In the Hebrew text, the messianic figure clearly is doing the killing of his enemies. The "Prince" or "Branch of David" is seen here, as in the Isaiah text, as a military figure, at war with the Kittim (Romans).

We may also compare this text with another from Qumran (*1Q28b* 5.20-26), which is based on the same chapter of Isaiah and contains a blessing for the "Prince of the Community." Here we find that the "Prince" is understood as a messiah who triumphs victoriously over the godless. If, then, the very biblical text upon which the *4Q285* midrash is based and a comparative text both have a triumphant messiah who kills rather than is killed, the translation of the questionable text should follow in the active sense: "The Prince of the Community will kill him" (the godless or the evildoer mentioned in Isaiah). This context has also been shown to most likely belong as a missing piece of the *War Scroll*, with which it has almost identical verbal affinities.[34] If so, it would align with the messianic figure in the *War Scroll*, who is clearly victorious. If this is the case, the beginning of Fragment 5, which contains the Isaiah quotation followed by the references to "killing," "strokes," and "wounds," completes the scene of Fragment 4 with the Prince killing the enemy leader and his reigning in righteousness (in fulfillment of Isaiah 11). Then the questionable text of line 4 could be translated: "by strok[e]s and by wounds. And a Priest [of renown (?)] will command [the s]lain of the Kitti[m]."[35]

While *4Q Serekh Milhamah* cannot be used as a Qumranic parallel for a dying Messiah, by its use of the term "Prince" for the Messiah it may offer an allusion to Daniel 9:25-26, where the "anointed Prince," the Messiah, is said to be "cut off and have nothing" (that is, slain). Otto Betz has demonstrated that at Qumran, the idea of being "cut off" was wholly negative. He cites a text from the *Rule of the Community*, which says, "May he be cut off from the midst of the sons of light because he swerved from following God. . . . May he place his lot in the midst of the eternally cursed" (*1QS 2:16-17*).[36] Jesus would have been regarded by the Sect as one who "swerved," and as a result should have been "cut off" by God. Therefore, this text (*4Q285*), as others, presents a persecuted messiah who slew his enemies, which contrasts significantly with Jesus, whose enemies persecuted and slew Him. As such, it may illustrate one of the "stumbling blocks" mentioned by Paul concerning faith in a crucified Messiah (1 Corinthians 1:23; 1 Peter 2:8). Nevertheless, it does accord with Jesus as the eschatological Messiah who will slay the wicked (Matthew 25:31, 46; Revelation 11:17-18; 19:12-15) at His second Advent.

## Is Messianic Resurrection in the Scrolls?

When the Dead Sea Scrolls were first studied, there was considerable debate about whether or not the Qumran Sect believed in the idea of resurrection. There were texts that implied this, but most scholars remained doubtful. We return here to the text *4Q521*, called the *Messianic Apocalypse*, but also entitled by some *On Resurrection*. The purpose for this latter title is because here we have an unambiguous statement of belief in resurrection and the possibility that it is the Messiah who will effect that resurrection. Lines 11-13 are pertinent to our theme, but let's view them in the context of lines 5-13:

> [5]Surely the Lord will seek out the pious, and will call the righteous by name. [6]His spirit will hover over the poor; he will give power to those who believe. [7]He will glorify the pious with the throne of eternal kingdom. [8]He will free the captives, open the eyes of the blind, straighten those be[nt double]. [9]For[ev]er I will cleave to [to him aga]inst the [po]werful, and [I will trust] in his lovingkindness [10][and in His goodness forever. His] holy [Messiah] will not be slow [in coming.] [11]And for the glorious things that are not the work of the Lord, when he (that is, the Messiah) [come]s [12]then he will heal the wounded, resurrect the dead, proclaim glad tidings to the poor. [13]. . . he will lead the [Ho]ly Ones, he will shepherd [th]em. . . .

The biblical text behind this thematic *pesher* is Psalm 146. The lines above are drawn from Psalm 146:6-7, which has an eschatological context focusing on changes to take place in a future state. In this case, the activities of restoration, healing, and resurrection all take place at the time of the resurrection, after which transformed bodies are no longer subject to various maladies or even death. This, then, would remove the text from direct comparison with Matthew 11:5 and Luke 7:22, in which Jesus quoted Isaiah 35:5-6 and 61:1-2 as evidence that His works were messianic in nature. However, none of these Gospel texts mention resurrection, which was certainly presented by these writers as an authenticating work of the Messiah (John 11:25-27,42,47; 12:9-11). Perhaps this is because they focus on a present age in which the "good news" is proclaimed through redemptive acts (Isaiah 61:1) rather than the eschatological Age to Come, in which the Messiah will raise all the dead (John 5:24-29). However, the text is unclear as to whether it is the Messiah in line 1 or the Lord in line 5 that performs these miracles. The translation assumes it is the Messiah of line 1, but this assumption rests on paralleling the text with New Testament references. But if it is the Lord of line 5, then how does He "bring the good news"? In the text *11Q13*, Melchizedek is a messianic figure who also "brings the good news and proclaims the great year of the divine good pleasure" (*11Q13* 2.9.18). So if comparison is made with this text, it is Messiah who does the work in line 5. We must also ask how "the good news" is to be brought in the Age to Come, for the good news will have already arrived prior to that age. The conclusion is that the passage looks at present experiences of restoration enacted by God, but also looks ahead to the consummation in the eschaton, during which the Messiah acts as God's agent (an agency which both the *11Q13* passage and line 1 of the present text reveal). Because Jesus referred to these acts of present restoration in his reply to the imprisoned John the Baptizer, some have wondered whether the disciples whom John sent to Jesus were in fact members of (or had contact with) the Qumran community.[37] If so, Jesus was responding to them with texts of Scripture that alluded to issues of importance to the Sect (see *11Q13* 2:4,6,9,13,18; *1QH* 15:15; 18:14-15), and paraphrasing these passages in a way familiar to them.

This leads us to our next question: What contact might Jesus Himself have had with the Qumran Sect? In the history of Scroll studies, scholars have proposed that these points of contact have ranged from Jesus being a member—or even the leader—of the Sect, to casual contact and influence upon its members. Let's turn now to some of the crucial concerns that have both shaken and stimulated the faith of those who have sought Jesus in the Dead Sea Scrolls.

# PART IV

A Call to

Discernment

# 15

# JESUS AND THE QUMRAN COMMUNITY

---

*It is true to say that the Scrolls add to the background of Christianity, but they add so much that we arrive at a point where the significance of similarities definitely rescues Christianity from false claims of originality in the popular sense and leads us back to a new grasp of its true foundation in the person and events of its Messiah. Only in this sense is it true to say that the difference between the two Sects is one of messianology/christology, or that it is Jesus that makes the difference. The roots, the prophecies, the concepts were the same. But different things happened.*[1]

—Krister Stendahl

---

The Dead Sea Scrolls have opened for us a window on the period of the Second Temple period, during which Jesus was born and carried out His ministry. From the time the Scrolls could first be studied, people have sought to find the figure of Jesus within the context of the Scrolls. As we have seen, the Jewish concepts of the Messiah during that era were not uniform, although those who differed in their views made reference to the same messianic texts to discern his person and the time of his coming.

329

Yet there is still a large gap between the concept of the Messiah at Qumran and finding Jesus there, either as the Sect's leader or as its expected Messiah. To be sure there are statements in the Scrolls and in the Scriptures that seem parallel or related in some way, that seem to hint at intentional comparisons to the Sect. Since both arose from the same social and religious environment at roughly the same time, it is easy to find resemblances and relationships that are generic rather than specific. But before we attempt to make direct connections between expressions of common culture and the shared source of sacred Scripture, we must carefully weigh the evidence.

## The New Testament's Concept of Messiah

While it might be said that the concept of Messiah in the Old Testament as compared with the New Testament was an outline as opposed to the finished picture, we must still ask the question, Where did the *developed* concept of Messiah in the New Testament come from? We cannot say that these details were unknown to the Old Testament authors; Jesus and the New Testament writers repeatedly state that they were "saying nothing but what was written beforehand in all the Scriptures"—that is, the Old Testament (Luke 24:27,44; John 5:46; Acts 3:18; 17:2-3; 26:22-23). At the same time, the Old Testament itself only vaguely points us to a messianic fulfillment for these texts. Consequently, conservative scholars have held the view that the Old Testament was *typically* messianic; therefore, the details developed as the antitype came to fulfillment in future events. Liberal scholars, by contrast, have contended that the New Testament's view of Messiah was new, created by Christian theologians after the church had left its Jewish roots and come under the influence of the pagan mystery religions.[2] According to this position, the New Testament's concept of Messiah was never present in the Old Testament nor any form of first-century Judaism.

The resolution to the question of development has been provided for us in the literature written during the intertestamental period, and by the Dead Sea Scrolls in particular. This literature has confirmed that Jesus and the writers of the New Testament spoke and wrote in the context of their day and that in their era many of the New Testament details about the Messiah were also present within the various forms of Judaism. Not only do the Scrolls show the development and elaborate expression of the messianic idea typical of this period, they also demonstrate the exegetical methods used in the New Testament to interpret the details from the Old Testament. The authors of the Scrolls depended on the Old Testament for their messianic views,[3] and, by example, have affirmed the conservative position that "at every point early Christians . . . used the Old Testament to prove their Christian theology and to solve Christian problems, [and that] the Old Testament provided the substructure of New Testament theology."[4]

As we move then to the Qumran Scrolls, is the concept of Jesus as the Jewish Messiah—developed in the New Testament based on the Old Testament—in agreement with what the Sect expected or what its leading figures modeled? The claim from many quarters is that Jesus either appears in the Scrolls or was embraced by the Sect (or a faction of it). Does the evidence back that claim? Let us first consider what has been said and then evaluate the evidence for these views.

## Was Jesus an Essene?

One of the almost immediate reactions to the early knowledge of unidentified figures in the Scrolls, mostly by nonevangelical Protestants or agnostics (like John Allegro), was to identify them with Jesus. And because the majority opinion has been that the Sect was Essene, many came to assume that Jesus, too, may have lived as an Essene. To some, such as the Rev. Francis Potter, this was a foregone conclusion:

> For centuries Christian students of the Bible have wondered where Jesus was and what he did during the so-called "eighteen silent years" between the ages twelve and thirty. The amazing and dramatic Scrolls of the great Essene library found in cave after cave near the Dead Sea have given us the answer at last.[5]

Other writers have said that the Essenes were primed by prophecy to accept Jesus and followed His progress from the beginning. According to Upton C. Ewing, the timing of the Sect's return to Qumran from "Damascus" was guided by their revelation of the birth of Jesus:

> It is now about the year (6–4 B.C.) or about a quarter century since the surviving members of the Qumran priesthood had come out of the land of their fathers. . . . Each night, as was their custom, several of the brethren kept watch, scanning the heavens with the hope of discovering some sort of sign which might inform them that the time was near for a return to the deserts of Judaea. . . . It was during these periods of watch that a most unusual phenomenon appeared in the night heavens. According to astronomers, a fiery conjunction of several planets appeared

in the zodiacal sign of Pisces. Strangely enough, from a calculated alignment with Damascus, Pisces appears south by south-
east, or in the direction of both the Qumran monastery and a little
town called Bethlehem. . . . According to the findings of archaeologists excavating in the ruins, the monastery could not have
been reoccupied before the year 4 B.C.[6]

Such assertions are based largely on alleged parallels sought in an
eagerness to find historical and theological origins for Christianity. These
parallels have often been based on very general similarities, such as both
Jesus and the Sect calling greater Israel to repentance, practicing hospitality and a communal lifestyle, performing ritual baptism and communal
meals, denouncing the rich while extolling the poor, opposing the Jewish
religious leadership, rejecting (apparently) the Temple and its high priest,
upholding the Mosaic Law, teaching predestination, condemning divorce,
and advocating an ideal teacher with 12 disciples.

It should be apparent to anyone that most of these parallels could be
made with any Jewish Sect of that time period. Furthermore, these parallels are frequently exaggerated. There is no evidence that either Jesus
(or His disciples) were baptized ritually other than with John's baptism
of repentance. As observant Jews they may have followed Jewish custom
and sought ceremonial purification at certain occasions and under certain conditions, but that is quite different from the daily purification rites
(baptisms) that were required by the Qumran Sect. By contrast, Jesus'
own command for baptism (Matthew 28:19) is of a singular act as an
expression of the believer's faith (see Acts 2:41).

In like manner, there is no evidence that Jesus and His disciples ate
communal meals. The Last Supper is usually given as an example, but as
the Gospels clearly state, this was a Passover Seder (Matthew 26:17-19),
an occasion that was observed only once a year. In addition, the seemingly more specific parallel to a teacher with 12 disciples becomes more
general when we consider the common source of the Old Testament, which
established the pattern of 12 tribes from the 12 sons of Jacob. In fact, the
common allegiance to the Old Testament as an authoritative source
explains most of the parallels between the Scrolls and in Scripture,
including Jesus' predestinarian views and teaching on divorce, for which
He often cited Scripture (Isaiah 6:10; 53:1 in John 12:38-40; Genesis 2:24
in Matthew 19:3-6). This explanation may account for the even closer
parallels, such as those between, for example, Jesus' statement to "believe
in the light in order that you may become sons of light" (John 12:36; Luke

16:8) and the Sect's use of the term "Sons of Light." Going back to the Old Testament, in Psalm 36:9 we read, "For with Thee is the fountain of life; in Thy light we see light," and Daniel 12:3, which promises those "who have insight" and "who lead the many to righteousness" that they will "shine brightly like the brightness of the expanse of heaven," and "like the stars forever and ever."

What these similarities *do* teach us is that Jesus was at home in His Jewish culture and not distinct from it as has been often thought. Christian theologians have often overemphasized one side of the divine/human equation by citing verses such as "He came to His own, *and those who were His own did not receive Him*" (John 1:11, emphasis added) or, "*The World became flesh*, and dwelt among us" (John 1:14, emphasis added). Held together in balance, these statements affirm Jesus as a Jew in the historical context while not diminishing His uniqueness as "the only begotten from the Father" (John 1:14).

We need to keep in mind that the rule for understanding a Sect such as that at Qumran is to focus more on the differences than the similarities. When the differences are observed, it becomes readily apparent that Jesus could not have been a member of the Sect, nor even a former or renegade member. I have provided a chart depicting the major differences between Jesus and the Sect on page 334. This chart clearly shows that at the most crucial points of definition, Jesus and the Sect part company. If the Sect believed in a future *dual* messianism, this would have separated them from Jesus, who taught a *single* messianism (Matthew 22:41-45; Mark 12:35-37; Luke 20:41-44), and said that He as the Messiah had already arrived (Matthew 16:15-17,20; John 4:25-26). The Sect might have accepted Him as one of their expected messiahs, yet apparently they expected their messiahs to arrive together. Also, the Sect was strict in matters of ceremonial purity (*11Q15* 45; *4Q174*), whereas Jesus (in their estimation) was lax, even self-defiling (Matthew 11:19; Mark 7:5; Luke 7:34), socializing with Hellenistic Jews, Roman collaborators (tax gatherers), Gentiles, and even lepers (Matthew 2:16; 8:5-13; 9:11; Mark 14:3; Luke 7:1-10). What is more, Jesus (again, in their view) had publicly taught against ceremonial purification (Mark 7:14-15) and had preached love for one's enemies (Matthew 5:43-45). This last teaching stands in stark contrast to the Sect's hatred of "men of the Lie," "false teachers," and all of "the sons of darkness," whom they cursed (*1QS* 2.5-8).

Deviation in matters of *halakah* would have been considered by the Sect as particularly serious, but none more so than with regard to improper

## Differences Between Jesus and the Essenes

| *Jesus* | *Essenes* |
|---|---|
| • Concept of Messiah as divine and singular | • Concept of Messiah as human and probably dual |
| • Claimed to be the Messiah | • "Teacher" of sect made no such claim |
| • Messiah both suffering/dying and triumphant | • Messiah only triumphant |
| • Messiah as "Son of God" | • No such concept clearly recognized |
| • Wrote no documents | • Were considered "writing sect" in Judaism |
| • Rejected swearing of oaths | • Required oaths to enter their community |
| • Quoted biblical prophets as authoritative | • Disdained biblical prophets as ignorant of the meaning of their prophecies |
| • Emphasis on Daniel's 70th week in eschatology | • No clear use of Daniel's 70th week in eschatology |
| • Revered Temple and respected priesthood | • Rejected Temple and despised priesthood |
| • Observed traditional lunar calendar | • Observed unique luni-solar calendar |
| • Had open contact with Gentiles | • Strictly forbade contact with Gentiles |
| • Socialized with and included women in His company | • Excluded women from company and community |
| • Socialized with religious leaders of Pharisees | • Rejected Pharisees and all other parties |
| • Openly fellowshiped with ritually unclean | • Fellowshiped only with ritually pure |
| • Worshiped in established synagogues | • Worshiped only with own Sect |
| • Teaching was in public and included all | • Teaching was only in private to members of Sect |
| • Missionary zeal—calling people to follow Him | • Anti-missionary—accepted only volunteers |
| • Accepted all who came to Him | • Rejected many who came to join Sect |
| • Did not oppose Roman authorities | • Opposed Romans as enemies (Kittim) |
| • Exhorted love even for enemies | • Hated and cursed enemies |
| • Messages were clear and simple | • Teachings were secretive and elaborately concealed |
| • Maintained equality among disciples | • Rigid hierarchy of rank among members |
| • Opposed veneration of human leaders | • Fanatically devoted to their human leader(s) |
| • Accepted a fixed/completed canon | • Possibly did not yet have a fixed canon |
| • Had no recognized or formal religious education | • Had to demonstrate proficiency in Essene doctrine to instructor |
| • Spoke against adding regulations to Torah | • Added many regulations to Torah |
| • Encouraged people not to practice legalistic Judaism | • Existed to promote strict legal interpretations of practices |
| • Accommodating or open sabbatarians | • Strict or closed sabbatarians |
| • Accommodating or open concept of ritual purity | • Strict or closed concept of ritual purity |
| • Accepted anointing with oil as righteous act | • Rejected anointing with oil as defilement |
| • "Kingdom of God" as central teaching | • Little mention of "Kingdom of God" |

observance of the Sabbath. That was the very sin which the Sect believed had thus far prevented Israel from receiving the promised restoration (*CD* 10:14–11:18). Jesus, according to their view, violated the Sabbath and gave license for others to do the same (Mark 2:27-28). But perhaps the most significant point of contention was that the Sect and Jesus followed different religious calendars. The Sect followed a luni-solar calendar, and Jesus followed the strictly lunar calendar of the Second Temple, observing the Sabbath and attending the feasts (including the Day of Atonement, which was very important to the Sect), with other Jews of the day, in distinction to the Qumran Sect (John 7:2-10,37; 11:55-56). This difference alone would have sufficiently disqualified Jesus from any identification or involvement with the Sect.

Addressing the question of Jesus' involvement with the Sect, Dr. Stephen Pfann, Scroll scholar and director of the Center for the Study of Early Christianity in Jerusalem, offers this verdict:

> There is no direct mention of Jesus or the disciples or any of a number of elements that we would expect to find [if there was a connection] of the Essenes with Christianity. We have no New Testament books at Qumran. Whether people want to think so or not, we've checked and there just are not! There are also conflicting ideas in the Scrolls that Jesus and the first Christians would not hold, and even though there are many parallels, such is expected between two or more groups within Judaism who would have things in common. The differences between these groups (Pharisees, Sadducees, Essenes, Jesus) were the issues of the day. And on most of these issues, Jesus and the Essenes didn't agree.[7]

## The Teacher of Righteousness and Jesus

Although it may seem superfluous, there continues to be teaching on the popular level that identifies Jesus with the Teacher of Righteousness, who was the dominant figure of the Qumran Sect.[8] The Scrolls do not give any explicit information about this figure whose title in Hebrew was *Moreh ha-Tzedeq* ("Teacher of Righteousness," or "Legitimate Teacher"), and almost as many historical identifications have been proposed as there are scholars to suggest them. What we can know is that he was a priest; in two texts he is called "the Priest" (*4Q174* 3:15; *1QpHab* 2:8), the titular sense probably indicating he was "a high priest." By contrast, Jesus was not qualified to be an Aaronic priest because He was not from the tribe of Levi (Hebrews 7:14).

Within the Dead Sea Scrolls there are no direct statements that the Teacher authored any of them. This should not surprise us because they were not written for outsiders and their primary purpose was to provide instruction for a community that believed itself poised on the edge of the end times. Given this perspective, we should not expect the Sect to have recorded historical information for the benefit of others at a future day. By contrast, the Gospels and Acts were written to inform an outside audience about historical facts (Luke 1:3; John 20:30; Acts 1:1). Although Jesus did not write any of this material, its purpose was to explain "all that *Jesus* began to do and to teach" (Acts 1:1, emphasis added). Thus, while scholars may question Jesus' interpretations and His messianic identity, there should be no question, as there is today with the Jesus Seminar, about whether the authentic proclamations of Jesus can be discerned in the New Testament.

Early in the history of Scroll study, sensationalists reported that the Teacher of Righteousness was said to have been viewed by the Sect as the Messiah, slain by the Jerusalem priests, and expected to return in the future (via a resurrection or second coming). These reports were made at a time when access to the primary documents was extremely limited, so at first the sensationalists could not be easily countered. Today there is still some debate about how the term *Messiah* was applied to the leader of the Sect, but we do know the Teacher was *not* regarded as the eschatological Messiah. Yet the Sect's regard for him as a prophet and inspired teacher of Torah (*1QpHab* 7) fit with their expectations for the messiah of Aaron. Also, the claim that the Sect viewed the Teacher as having been slain has been shown to be unlikely, although he was certainly persecuted. Likewise, any concept that the Teacher was expected to be resurrected or return eschatologically in the future is equally unfounded.

Ron Rhodes has offered a dozen arguments, summarized from various writers,[9] which confirm the impossibility of identifying Jesus with the Teacher of Righteousness. Three of the more significant points are: 1) The Teacher lived long before Jesus was born (around the second half of the second century B.C.); 2) the Teacher is never given the epithets accorded a messianic figure, such as "Son of Man," "Son of God," etc., as is Jesus in the New Testament; 3) the Teacher prepared the Sect for one greater than himself (the eschatological Messiah[s]), while Jesus pointed only to Himself as Messiah (John 4:25-26; 8:24; 9:35-38; 10:36; cf. Luke 22:70).

## Jesus' Contact with the Qumran Community

Although most scholars today have rejected any identification of Jesus with the Essenes or with a figure of the Qumran community, many do accept that Jesus may have had contact with members of the Sect at different points throughout His earthly ministry. This seems reasonable given Jesus' proximity to the Jordan region, His time of temptation in the desert, and, according to Josephus, the presence of some 4,000 sectarians in various villages, especially in the southern section of Jerusalem (if the Sect was Essene). That such contact occurred is likely; however, the question is whether the Sect exerted some kind of influence upon Jesus in some way. One proponent of such influence (and here the assumption is *Essene* influence) is Father Bargil Pixner, prior of the Dormition Abbey on Mount Zion, Jerusalem, and a respected scholar on the relationship between the Scrolls and Christianity:

> To begin with [let me make it clear that] neither Jesus nor His apostles were Essenes. However, He probably came from a family that had been Essene *influenced*. His predecessor, John, was in the "Baptist" movement of that period, and might have been connected with the Essenes as a little boy at one of the places where the Essenes lived. [If so,] he left the Essenes because they were too restrictive, and because he wanted to preach to all the people in the [region of] Jordan and beyond. Jesus may have followed in John's path, breaking with the Essenes, and probably also with His family in Nazareth. Although He formed His own group, He remained close to His family, who remained more or less in their group. At the end of His life, when He came to Jerusalem, He lived in Bethany near Jerusalem. According to the *Temple Scroll*, Bethany was one of three villages set up by the Essenes where people could go who were not clean enough to go to the Temple in Jerusalem itself. Jesus spent most of His time there during His last days with His friends Lazarus, Mary, and Martha. These people were not married, they were celibate. The Essenes had this kind of vow of abstinence, they didn't marry, they were all celibates.[10]

Father Pixner, as others who have taken monastic vows, tend to see the Essenes (and, of course, Jesus and His disciples) in light of their own traditions and experience. This was true of Father Roland de Vaux, who first excavated the site of Qumran and proposed that this was one of the earliest monastic communities.

Following this same assumption of Essene influence, Father Pixner offers the occasion of the Last Supper (which many consider a Passover Seder), as evidence of Jesus' involvement with the Essenes. How can it otherwise be explained that Jesus and His disciples ate their Passover in advance, since Jesus died the next day as the Paschal Lamb (of God) on the Jewish Passover (Hebrew, *Pesach*)? Father Pixner believes an Essene connection offers a solution to this chronological problem:

> Jesus knew that his end was near and that on the *Pesach* of the Temple [calendar] he would already be dead. The *Pesach* of the Temple was on a Saturday in A.D. 30, so I think he celebrated his *Pesach* Seder meal on Tuesday evening ([actually] the eve of Wednesday by Jewish reckoning), rather than on Thursday according to the Jewish calendar. Where could this have been done? [We believe that] the Judean Christians, the first Jews that believed in Jesus, had their community here [on Mount Zion]. I think that Jesus himself used a guest house [for the Last Supper] which was outside the [Essene] quarter, but was used by the Essenes or their guests who came to attend feasts [according to the Essene calendar]. We know that the Essenes were very hospitable, so I believe that Jesus used this guest house for his Last Supper and celebrated the *Pesach* meal according to their calendar, which was on Tuesday evening. Several things may support this [theory]. First, it is interesting that during [the preparation for] the Supper the apostles are to find a man carrying a water pitcher to lead them to the Last Supper. [Carrying a water pitcher] is something that only women would have done. Could it have been an Essene monk who had no wife and had to get water himself? It is also interesting that the room was already prepared for *Pesach* [when the disciples arrived]. This [also] indicates an earlier date [for Jesus' observance] because the Jews [normally] made their room preparations on Good Friday morning, the eve of [the Jewish] *Pesach*. Why was it prepared before? Was this another group? Had they another *Pesach*? Had they a different date? [The answer] it seems [must be] that Jesus had the Last Supper in an Essene community where he found amongst the Essenes his first believers.[11]

While this view seems to offer some intriguing solutions to the supposed problem of two Passovers in the Gospels, Dr. Stephen Pfann believes that this theory of an Essene Passover actually creates more problems than it solves. He explains:

> First of all, if Jesus was actually working on the Essene calendar, none of his days that he came up to Jerusalem for the feasts would have been on the same day [as the rest of Judaism]. Another problem is that on the Essene calendar there are only three days a year in the three-year cycle in which a Passover can be in relationship to the full moon. Since the full moon doesn't fall during that week there is no time in which an Essene Passover, which takes place on Tuesday evening, could have had a full moon toward the end of the week. There is also a problem with the conclusion that the man carrying a jar of water must have been a celibate because only women carry water. If it could be proved that there was an Essene quarter in Jerusalem, and this has not been substantiated, there would have been all kinds of men carrying water on that day. How then would the disciples have understood that one man carrying water was assigned to lead them to the Passover?[12]

According to Father Pixner, another incident, this time involving the apostles only, may indicate that the Essenes actually joined the ranks of early Jewish Christianity at its beginning:

> We find in the Acts of the Apostles in the sixth chapter, the seventh verse, that a whole group of priests joined the community and became believers. Where did these priests come from? We know that the priests were either Sadducees or Essenes. The Sadducees were the high-class authority, aristocracy, and were the sworn enemies of the primitive Church with Peter and all his clan. The Essenes were most likely to have priests in them; those would be the most likely to join the [Jewish-Christian] community.[13]

Yet another argument for Essene influence comes from the account in Acts of a communal sharing of property (Acts 2:44-45; 4:32-35), an act that apparently distinguished the early believers from others in the Jewish community (whether orthodox or Hellenistic). Father Pixner explains the evidence for this theory:

> Why would the first [Jewish-Christian] community have community goods? Nobody in the world had it except here in the first community. The Essenes were waiting for the messianic

power which they believed would be imminent, therefore, there was no reason to accumulate possessions. So they got rid of everything and lived a holy life. Jesus never commanded them to do that, but under the Apostles the first community sold their possessions and waited for the coming of the Lord in the same manner as the Essenes. The early Church was not Essene, it was Christian. It had a different ideology than the Essenes, yet they also had many things in common.[14]

Other New Testament scholars, such as Professor Otto Betz, agree with these last two proposals of Essene involvement with the Christian community. I would agree that these unidentified priests might have included Essenes (from the Essene quarter or camp), or members of the Qumran community. But then we have to explain why members of the Sect, who eschewed Hellenistic Jews, would have been in their company (Acts 6:1-6) or at the Temple area (which the Sect avoided), where the disciples met to teach about Jesus (Acts 5:42). Such contact would have been considered defiling and would have warranted temporary exclusion from the Sect's assemblies. On the other hand, Sadducean priests were comfortable with Hellenistic Jews and would have normally been present in the Temple precincts at this time. Also, in Acts 6:7, the definite article *the* before the word *priests* seems to imply that this was a recognized group of priests. Essenian or Qumranic priests probably would have not been present (the book of Acts was written circa A.D. 61) before the end of the Qumran period (A.D. 68). In my mind, these factors indicate that the priests in Acts 6:7 were probably Sadducean priests.

## Jesus' Crucifixion and the Dead Sea Scrolls

Crucifixion was considered an abhorrent and obscene punishment in both the Jewish and Gentile worlds (1 Corinthians 1:23; Galatians 5:11). This form of punishment was particularly well known to the Dead Sea Sect (and to all in Judea) because of the act of the Judean (Hasmonean) king Alexander Jannaeus (103–76 B.C.). According to Josephus, he crucified 800 Pharisees who had joined the Seleucid king Demetrius III Eucerus (95–88 B.C.) in a rebellion against him (*Antiquities* 13.14.2 §§ 379-383; *Jewish Wars* 1.4.6 §§ 96-98). This mass crucifixion took place while Alexander was feasting with his concubines. In an attempt to induce fear against future revolts, Jannaeus also slaughtered each Pharisee's family while the Pharisees were being crucified. We know that the Sect knew about this because in the *Nahum Pesher* they refer to "the Lion of Wrath who would hang men up alive" (*4QpNah* 3-4 i 7). This apparently refers to Jannaeus' murderous actions. Yigael Yadin believed that the Sect actually approved this punishment of the Pharisees because of the legal ruling in the *Temple Scrolls* (based on Deuteronomy 21:2-23) that traitors should be hung alive (*11QT* 64:6-13).[15] If this is correct, then it appears unlikely that the Qumran community could have accepted the crucifixion of Jesus as anything other than a deserved execution, a verdict which was apparently accepted by the other Jewish sects (Matthew 26:59; 27:1; Acts 2:36; 7:52; 1 Corinthians 2:8) and the general population (Matthew 27:21-25). In fact, the Jewish leadership in Jerusalem felt that only a person who could reverse his crucifixion could be a proper messianic claimant (Matthew 27:40-43,47-49; Mark 15:30-32,36).

Let us be clear, then, about how the Scrolls actually serve us in our understanding of Jesus *and* note how, at the same time, they were far from the mark. This difference is succinctly stated for us by Professor Otto Betz and Pastor Rainer Riesner when they say:

> In light of the Qumran texts it is becoming increasingly clear both how firmly rooted Jesus was in the Judaism of his time and what an unprecedented claim he made about his person. Like the pious people of Qumran, he lived by the Old Testament. But he interpreted the Old Testament with a direct divine authority and related it to himself in a way that far transcends the Essene awareness of being at the end of time. Jesus was a Jew and not the first Christian; however, he was not just any Jew, but the Christ, the Messiah of Israel and the Redeemer of the whole world.[16]

By contrast, the Old Testament messianic texts that were referenced, for the most part, in the Scrolls appear to have combined the messianic offices in one person, and this is the Jewish theology reflected in the Gospels (Matthew 2:4-6; 22:42; Mark 14:61; Luke 2:25-38; 3:15; John 6:14; 7:27,31; 12:34).[17] The New Testament clearly regards Jesus as the King Messiah after the Davidic dynasty (Matthew 1:1; Luke 1:32; 3:31; cf. Acts 2:29-31)—and as a Priest, though not Levitical, but after the order of Melchizedek (Hebrews 10:12-14).

Jesus, then, was not an Essene and cannot be identified with any figure in the Qumran community, including its Teacher. Those who do make such identifications have exaggerated the points of correspondence while minimizing the abundant differences. While Jesus probably knew of the

Qumran Sect, or at least certain members in it, He was not influenced by it nor did He have cause to follow its calendar (even for the Last Supper). The Qumran Sect, like most other Jewish sects of the time, believed that the Messiah was coming to effect national deliverance for Israel and to usher in an age of Israelite dominion and universal righteousness (in conformity with the Torah). It *is* possible that former members of the Qumran Sect were later counted among the Jewish-Christian community (Act 6:7). However, had that happened, that would have severed their association with the Sect. This might have been possible, given the Sect's messianic beliefs, if members understood and believed Jesus' promise to return as the eschatological messianic King (Matthew 24:30-31; 25:31-46; Acts 1:6-7; 3:20-26; 17:31; Hebrews 9:27-28; Revelation 11:15) or recognized that Jesus was an eschatological High Priest after the order of Melchizedek (Hebrews 5:5-10; 6:20; 7:1–8:13). Yet like the disciples and others who had so believed, they still had to reconcile Jesus' promises with His passion (Luke 24:19-21). Only the fact of Jesus' resurrection could have successfully harmonized these supposed contradictions (Luke 24:22-34). This event would have enabled them to understand two phases of resurrection (present and prophetic), and in like manner, refine all of their messianic views to include both a cross and a crown.

## Gaining a Proper Perspective

The real point of contact between the Scrolls and Jesus is that they are, as James Charlesworth has stated,

> an invaluable source for helping us understand the life and teaching of Jesus. They provide some ideological context for his thought, and they illumine the social setting and context of pre-70 A.D. Jewish life in the Land. . . . We begin to appreciate more fully the wise counsel of [Samuel] Sandmel, one of the great Jewish scholars of the last generation; he urged us to comprehend that Jesus was not only a Jew, "but a figure such as he could not have arisen in any other tradition or culture but Judaism."[18]

Only in this way, then, may we look through the ancient windows of the Scrolls and truly see Jesus.

# 16

## SENSATIONALISM AND THE SCROLLS

*In the four decades since they surfaced, the Scrolls have driven a remarkable number of scholars, mystics, seekers, Messiah theorists, and apocalypse freaks (and some who are all of the above) to make some remarkable claims about "explosive" discoveries.*[1]

—Ron Rosenbaum

I was in the checkout line at a local store when my eye caught the heading of the front page of a supermarket tabloid: "Dead Sea Scrolls' Predictions for the New Year." The article in the tabloid quoted a Dr. David Minor, who was said to be a "noted biblical historian":

> Newly released transcripts of the ancient Scrolls provide a chilling glimpse into the new year. . . . They provide a detailed description of what will occur in the final days leading up to the year 2000 and the second coming of Christ.[2]

Among the predictions: A UFO will crash-land at the U.S. Capitol, the Loch Ness monster will be caught in Florida, Elvis's grave will be found empty, the dead will begin communicating with the living via cellular phones, and scientists will discover a vaccine for the common cold and AIDS. The article concluded by stating that "all of these predictions will surely happen because they are foretold *in the Dead Sea Scrolls.*"

The Dead Sea Scrolls have always been a favorite fodder for sensationalists. Like the cryptic quatrains of Nostradamas, the Scrolls can easily be manipulated so that they appear to predict earthquakes and presidential elections with credibility.

## Sensationalist Viewpoints

For the general public the Scrolls have long been surrounded by an aura of mystery, so it has been easy for sensationalists to use the Scrolls to propagate their unorthodox views. In most cases these views have been introduced by popular figures who are limited in their access to the Scrolls and their ability to properly interpret them. We have already seen how writers such as Michael Baigent and Richard Leigh used this sense of mystery and the delay in Scroll publication to create suspicions about an international conspiracy. They claimed that religious authorities were suppressing Scroll texts that would dramatically revise traditional Christianity. However, in the years since the "suppressed" Scrolls were released, nothing has been found to support their charge. Remarkably, many fundamentalist and evangelical Christians are unaware of this and continue to promote sensationalist viewpoints.

One such popular fundamentalist Christian sensationalist is Texas-based author Texe Marrs. He has attempted to tie the Catholic deception theory of the Scrolls to a New World Order conspiracy.[3] He claims that a Vatican-Israeli plot exists to infiltrate the Christian faith with heretical doctrines and an unholy New Age Bible. He cites as evidence the facts that the Rockefeller Museum was once funded by John Rockefeller and the Israeli authorities allowed Catholics Roland de Vaux and John Strugnell to head the Scroll Team. (Marrs also implies that the Huntington College Library may have been controlled by Rockefeller as well.) All of this, he says, is part of a diabolical scheme on the part of the International Bankers, the Tri-lateralists, and the Illuminati to gain global domination. Even more incredible is his belief that the Scrolls are a hoax created as part of the hidden agenda for the last days:

I am convinced that the Dead Sea Scrolls are a hoax, and if they are not a hoax, the reason they have been kept away from us is because I believe there is a hidden agenda at work, an agenda to bring Gnostic New Age occultic teachings into the Christian church, an agenda to discredit the book of Acts, to discredit the Bible as we know it, and thus, to undermine and subvert all of Christianity; that is the true role of the Dead Sea Scrolls, and that is perhaps the reason the Rockefeller and Rothschild dynasties have been involved with these Dead Sea Scrolls.[4]

By failing to do proper research, Marrs has allowed his views to be shaped by theories of conspiracy and the unfounded speculations of Baigent and Leigh. This is unfortunate, because ironically, Marrs has aligned himself with the very people whose agenda is to discredit the Bible and subvert the Christian faith (more on this in the next chapter).

## An Archaeologist by Any Other Name...

Other popular sensationalists present themselves as "archaeologists," yet these same people have been denied archaeological credentials by the official agency of recognition—the Israel Antiquities Authority. In order to secure a permit to excavate in Israel, the person planning to do the excavating must have at least a master's degree in archaeology and be on the teaching faculty of a recognized university or its equivalent. He then must also present a written, technical proposal, which is subject to a rigorous evaluation.[5] For this reason, those sensationalists who pass themselves off as "archaeologists" but lack such credentials can only "excavate" if they do so on private land or by association in some manner with a credentialed archaeologist. In the past, money and volunteers (both desperately needed by real archaeologists), which sensationalists can often more easily produce than an academician with a busy schedule and limited contacts, have sometimes brought such associations.

Because sensationalists have a significant effect on the public's perception of the Dead Sea Scrolls and of the Christian faith in general, let's familiarize ourselves with their tactics and claims by considering one individual whose archaeological excavations in the Dead Sea region frequently make the news—Vendyl Jones.

## The Profile of a Sensationalist

Vendyl Jones is perhaps the most publicized of the Dead Sea Scroll sensationalists. The founder and director of the Vendyl Jones Research Institutes headquartered in Arlington, Texas, he boasts that the film *Raiders of the Lost Ark* and the character Indiana Jones was based on his life and work.[6] He also believes that he is destined to find the Tabernacle, the Ark of the Covenant, the ashes of the red heifer, and other treasures that will have a part in the restoration of Israel and the conversion of Gentiles to Judaism. This belief stems from his interpretation of a text that appears on a fifteenth-century A.D. woodcut of the red heifer ceremony, which he translates as saying, "There is a Gentile, who is not an idol worshiper, a Gentile who believes in the one God, and he will find the ashes. . . . And they will sweep every corner until they have found her." Jones applies this text to himself, and also frequently quotes the late Rav Shlomo Goren's statement that Gentiles will help discover the Temple vessels and restore Temple worship (based on Zechariah 6:15).

When Jones writes to supporters he regularly asserts and supports his claims in unusual ways, such as Kabbalistic numerology:

> What does 1995 or 5755 in the Jewish Year mean? There are a lot of possibilities hidden in the prophetic character of this year. . . . To examine the obvious, let's see how it is written in Hebrew and then break it into three simple grammatical parts. The year is written התשנ"ה. . . . The letter "ה" (hey) is the article "the." The letter "ת" (taf) means future third person feminine, intensive or repeated action. The word "שנה" means "year." All these meanings add up to say, "The intensive year of her return." The words "Parah Adumah" and the word "Mishkan" also occur in the feminine gender. This may suggest that the year 5755 means the year of the return of the ashes of the red heifer and the Tabernacle.[7]

Seeking to discern the prophetic character of a year in this manner is a common practice in Kabbalistic (or mystical) Judaism. Whether this esoteric method is legitimate or not is beside the point. How Jones has interpreted it is the problem. By suggesting that the year 5755 *implies* the impending discovery of the red heifer's ashes and the Tabernacle, he has subjectively interpreted the number according to his own designs. While the words *Parah Adumah* ("red heifer") and *Mishkan* ("Tabernacle") are indeed in the feminine gender, so also are *thousands* of other Hebrew words. To select these words and then associate them with the undefined sense of "return" is a contrived conclusion. But to the untrained and undiscerning such "logic" appears as a "confirmation" from the Hebrew language. In actuality, Jones's statements are irresponsible and deceptive.

Jones is using the *Copper Scroll* in his effort to find the sacred Temple treasures, according to the "correct translation" of this document made by his second wife, Zahave Cohen. Jones claims that he has identified one or more of the caves mentioned in the *Copper Scroll*, all of which are located near Cave 3, where the *Copper Scroll* was discovered. Before we examine these claims, it is necessary to look at the man who is making them. While credentials (or the lack of them) do not necessarily determine whether a person is right or wrong, they do indicate that serious attention be given to his theories and work. In the case of Vendyl Jones, are we dealing with a recognized scholar of the Scrolls, a trained and certified archaeologist, or something else?

## The Real Vendyl Jones

Vendyl Jones once wrote a book entitled *Will the Real Jesus Please Stand Up*. Taking a cue from his book, it would be well for those who have heard about him and his discoveries to ask for the real Vendyl Jones to please stand up! Undiscerning Christians are often attracted by Jones's support for Israel, his teaching of prophecy, his Jewish-flavored studies of the Bible, and especially his claims to have found or be on the verge of finding archaeological sites and hidden Temple treasures. Since he funds his "excavations" from donations and study-tour excavation programs (these are tours for which he gives a tax-deductible receipt), he is careful to keep a positive public image.

However, potential Christian volunteers should understand that Jones has publicly rejected the Christian faith and actively seeks to subvert Christianity. Although Jones was once an ordained Baptist pastor, his views of the Christian faith changed drastically during his early years in the ministry. He says that he "awakened" to "the greatest hoax of mankind—the conspiracy of Christianity over Judaism." He regards the New Testament as a fraud, which, according to Jones, is "as a whole, a concoction of books and letters that were put together in one book to replace the Old Testament."

Jones says that in this deception, "the Christian replaced the Jew as the Chosen People, the church replaced the synagogue, Sunday replaced the Sabbath, and finally Jesus replaced God." He therefore brazenly says concerning the authors of the New Testament: "What authority did these people have to come along and change anything?" For Jones, "the New Testament didn't exist until the fourth century, when monks and church fathers got twenty-seven books together and called 'em the New Testament."[8]

Jones is right about the anti-Semitic replacement theology that arose in the Gentile Byzantine Church, but this theology arose from a political structure more than 300 years *after* the New Testament was written. In addition, the vast majority of Christian scholars have recognized that the New Testament is a Jewish composition.[9] And there is now clear evidence that Jews and Christians had positive relations into the fourth and fifth centuries A.D. They built their synagogues and churches next to one another, and Christians often attended synagogue services and even joined with Jews in their fasts and festivals.[10] Though some church fathers opposed Christian involvement in Jewish synagogues, they nevertheless admitted, "[Some Christians] go to these places as though they were sacred shrines."[11] The facts, then, present a much different historical picture than the one Jones seeks to promote.

### Jones's Religious Beliefs

Jones once served Southern Baptist pastorates, and apparently it was during one of his pastorates that he made his radical shift to an anti-Christian Judaistic theology. Instead of resigning from the ministry, however, he took a new pastorate at First Baptist Church in Lynn, North Carolina, and, for the next five years, attempted to teach his anti-Christian views to this unsuspecting Christian congregation![12] He finally left his church in 1967 and moved to Israel with his first wife and five children because he believed, based on his study of Matthew 24, that "a war would begin in Israel between Passover and Pentecost," and he wanted to offer his services to the Israelis during that war. After the war he became acquainted with the renown archaeologist Pesach Bar-Adon, who would help launch Jones's "archaeological career" by virtue of their association.

Jones's anti-Christian beliefs were put into action through his founding of the *B'nai Noach* ("Children of Noah") movement.[13] This organization ostensibly seeks to teach the Torah to Gentile Christians, but in fact seeks to make church members proselytes to Judaism.[14] In the case of one congregation, which was visited by rabbis from Israel at Jones's request, the rabbis refused to "approve" them, saying they "still believed too much in Jesus"![15] The *B'nai Noach* teachings propagated by Jones and his disciples have disrupted many local churches and disillusioned many young Christians who have unwittingly participated in one of Jones's tour digs or listened to his teaching tapes.[16] In addition, his attitude toward messianic believers (Jews who accept Jesus as Messiah) is one of bitter opposition, and he has attacked them openly through the orthodox Jewish press, calling them "missionaries who steal precious Jewish souls."

Jones later divorced and married a young Moroccan Jewess from Haifa, Zahava Cohen, through whom he claimed Israeli citizenship and upon whose translation work he has depended for his interpretation of the *Copper Scroll*. With this translation and bold claims to be on the verge of discovering the ashes of the red heifer, the Tabernacle, the Ark of the Covenant, the priestly vestments, or various undiscovered Bible sites, Jones lures volunteers (at their expense) on his tour digs.

Jones often entertains his untrained participants by making fanciful historical and theological associations that have no basis in fact. For example, Jones has said that the Israelites "carried the Tabernacle in the wilderness for 33 years, the same age of Israel today, and of course, the same age Jesus Christ was when he was crucified."[17] In actuality, the Tabernacle was carried for 40 years (Numbers 14:33-34; 32:13; Deuteronomy 2:7; 8:2-4; Joshua 5:6; Acts 7:36,42), and it is pure sensationalism to draw any connection between the Tabernacle and the age of the modern state of Israel and the career of Jesus. In like manner, Jones has also taught that the Ark "is a sacred coffin that contains the souls of the Jewish people,"[18] that Mount Nebo in Jordan "is the place for the transfiguration [of Christ], not Mount Tabor,"[19] and that the Essenes at the time of the Temple's destruction substituted replica Temple furniture for the true Temple furniture and hid the latter in the valley of Achor between Beth Arava and Even Bohan.[20] In 1981 Jones predicted that "all things will be in God's place within 19 years [although] this has nothing to do with the second coming of Jesus."[21] What he was saying would be in place is everything necessary for the rebuilding of Jerusalem's Third Temple and the restoration of the sacrificial service—all of which he predicts he himself will find.[22] One of the essential items includes the ashes of the red heifer, about which Jones makes this claim: "Whoever gets these ashes will rule the world. . . . If Israel gets the ashes, Israel will rule."[23]

Jones continues to make these kinds of wild assertions today, and does so in churches and on Christian radio programs. In fact, he claims to be in a special position with God (like the prophets) and under His divine protection. In a letter to supporters, he wrote:

> The closer we come to finding those things G-D has appointed by the words of the Holy Prophets to be found *at this time*, the more the "Adversary" tries to inhibit, delay or destroy our efforts. Yet without letting any of these forces distract us from our noble objectives, HaShem has turned their foolish efforts into folly! I do, however, have the wisdom to believe in the words of Isaiah which read, *"I created the smith that bloweth the coals, I wrought the work of his hands. No weapon that is formed against you will prosper. Every tongue that shall move against you, in Judgment thou shalt condemn. This is the heritage of the servants of HaShem."* . . . So far, everything the enemies have done to destroy Vendyl Jones and IJCR [Institute for Judaic-Christian Research] has failed![24]

## Jones's Archaeological Activities

Potential volunteers should not only be aware of Jones's heretical beliefs, they should also know that the Israeli Antiquities Authority rejects *all* of Jones's archaeological claims past and present. If this is so, how can Jones carry out yearly excavations (11 so far) when he cannot personally secure a professional dig permit? A source within the Israeli Antiquities Authority explains that Jones simply has his volunteers dig sites with no recognized archaeological significance: "We can't stop them from digging in the ground any more than we could stop kids from playing in the sand!" If this were so, how could Jones continue to convince groups to join him in worthless excavations? The same Antiquities Authority source answered that it has good reason to suspect that Jones has in the past "salted" his sites with common potsherds and other valueless artifacts to give the appearance of significance to his site and keep his volunteers satisfied. Yitzhak Magen, who has in the past granted Jones temporary dig permits "for the sake of the volunteers he brings," nevertheless has ordered Jones to vacate his sites when he has made a claim to a "discovery."

Jones frequently makes claims of stupendous discoveries. Currently he has claimed to have discovered two sites from the time of Joshua (thirteenth century B.C.): a Canaanite cemetery of 200,000 graves (mainly of the inhabitants of Jericho), and the ruins of the biblical site of Gilgal, located by Jones north of the Dead Sea (there is also a present-day Gilgal). Jones says he discovered both of these sites using satellite remote-sensing radar. In typical fashion, Jones is said to have called a press conference to announce his Gilgal discovery. However, a source within the Antiquities Authority says that his "Gilgal" is actually evaporation ponds (reflected by the satellite) that were part of a British encampment in this area during the 1930s. In like manner, when Jones brought his "discovery" of the Canaanite cemetery to the attention of the Antiquities Authority, Joe Zias, a Curator in Anthropology and Archaeology at the Antiquities Authority's Rockefeller Museum, told me that he personally explained to Jones that his gravesite was well-known to archaeologists and that it was not from the time of Joshua, but from the late Second Temple period. Jones, however, has ignored the statements of the Antiquities Authority and continues to assert in his publication *The Researcher* that he has made great new discoveries. In fact, according to Gordon Franz, an American archaeologist in Israel, Jones has also called a press conference and showed as proof of his new discovery of the vast cemetery "from Joshua's time" the satellite maps of the evaporation ponds!

Our attention will now be centered on Jones's repeated assertions to have made great finds connected with the *Copper Scroll*, so let's look in greater detail at his "excavations" and the claims he has made for them.

### The Cave of the Column

Vendyl Jones began excavating a cave at the Wadi Jawfet Zaben in 1977. The cave is in the same vicinity as Caves 1, 3, and 11. Jones's excavation centered on a large double-entrance cave because of a reference in the *Copper Scroll* to "the cave of the column with two entrances facing east" (*3Q15* 4.1). Even though this cave had already been excavated down to bedrock by three archaeologists, Jones was convinced this was site of the Cave of the Column, later stating that he also believed it to be where Zadok, the high priest from King Solomon's time, was buried.

The original permit to excavate this area was granted to the late Pesach Bar-Adon, a respected Israeli archaeologist whose own finds in the Judean desert are renown. Jones had made friends with Bar-Adon and eventually began making use of the elder archaeologist's credentials to pursue his own ambitions. According to Dr. Dan Bahat, former district archaeologist of Jerusalem, Jones's professional association with Bar-Adon was questionable. He says that at the time Jones began his excavations at the Wadi Jawfet Zaben, Bar-Adon was elderly and usually slept much of the time he was at the site. Israeli archaeologist Hanan Eshel told me that because Bar-Adon had made one important discovery in the Judean desert (and become famous as a result), he expected to make yet another equally great discovery. His hope was that Jones's effort to find the treasure of the *Copper Scroll* might lead to that discovery.

In connecting the Cave of the Column with the cave mentioned in the *Copper Scroll*, the assumption was that many of the treasures listed in the Scroll would be found there. These treasures included a vessel, a Scroll, and 63 talents of silver in two different locations. Jones determined that the vessel must be a copper container with 30 eyelets that held the sacred stoneware in which were stored the ashes of the last red heifer sacrificed during Temple times. He decided this based only upon the fact that in the *Copper Scroll*, the Hebrew word used for "vessel" was *kalal*. This may be the term that was used for the vessel that stored the ashes, but it is also the common word for *vessel* and can be used to refer to the vessels of the Temple service (*kley ha-miqdash*) as well as vessels of other kinds. Standard translations of the *Copper Scroll*, such as that by F. Garcia Martinez, simply render the word as "amphora," a common classification of vessel and the kind expected at such a site. There is no way anyone could be more specific about this *kalal* based on the word alone or its context.

According to the *Copper Scroll*, this *kalal* was supposed to be buried four and a half feet down at the northern entrance. Jones also claims that there is a "specific reference in the [Copper] Scroll's mishnaic Hebrew to . . . the *mishcan ha-malak* . . . the Tabernacle of the king." [25] Yet after 19 years and the removal of tons of dirt from this northern entrance, Jones has yet to find this object or anything else of significance. Nevertheless, Jones continues to insist that deeper down inside the cave is the tombstone of Zadok, and beyond this is a large chamber housing the Tabernacle, the high priest's vestments, and the Ark of the Covenant. He bases his conviction on his assumption that the Ark and Tabernacle were removed from the First Temple by Jeremiah in the year 447 B.C., hidden on Mount Nebo in Jordan, [26] then transferred to this cave by the Essenes and buried. [27]

When I visited Jones's site with an archaeologist working at another Dead Sea location, we surveyed the entire cave and concluded that it had been completely worked (maybe more than once!). Because of this, the Cave of the Column would most likely have been abandoned if it were not for two nearby discoveries that Jones capitalized upon and now says *prove* his site was correct all along. These discoveries, from two different caves, were an oil-filled juglet and a large deposit of a reddish substance. Jones boldly announced to the press that these were the "Temple anointing oil" and the "Temple incense." He said, "We hope to find [in the new cave] a burial stone that closes the mouth of a second chamber and 40 steps that lead to a massive underground chamber. That's where everything is hidden. The incense and the anointing oil were deposited in this area to encourage you to say, 'You are on the right trail.' "[28] But do Jones's finds indeed substantiate his claim?

## The "Anointing" Oil

In 1988 Jones announced to the media that "he and his team" had discovered a 2,000-year-old juglet of oil that had been confirmed by professional testing to be none other than the *Shemen Afarsimon* ("holy anointing oil") of the Temple, which was used to consecrate the priests, kings, and prophets of ancient Israel. Jones also declared that this was one of the Temple vessels listed in the *Copper Scroll*, a sign that he was getting closer to the Temple treasures at this site. Jones's statements about the discovery made the front pages of the *New York Times*, and were prominently reported by *CNN* and the respected *National Geographic* magazine. Christian talk shows, magazines, and newsletters also spread the news to their audiences.

The facts of the discovery, however, are another story.[29] The credit for finding the juglet actually belongs to Benny Arubas, an associate of Dr. Joseph Patrich, the excavation supervisor. While Jones's Institute for Judaic-Christian Research did share jointly in the excavation with the Hebrew University's Institute of Archaeology, the original survey of these caves was begun in 1983 by the late Yigael Yadin, a legend in Dead Sea Scroll scholarship.[30] Dr. Patrich's agreement with Jones was that he would help supply volunteers for the dig and supervise them. This agreement did not place Jones in a position of archaeological representation, like that of Patrich, because Jones has no qualifications in the field. How, then, could Jones represent the find to the media—complete with official photographs of the juglet—when neither he nor any of his volunteers actually made the discovery? As for the pictures, they came from Joe Mains, one of Jones's volunteers on the dig. Joe was taking the photographs for Dr. Patrich. Jones later asked Joe for copies of the pictures, and after receiving them, called the media to publicize "his" discovery.

When the oil was officially analyzed by the Casali Institute for Applied Chemistry and Organic Chemistry at the Hebrew University, the tests proved one thing conclusively: It cannot be the "holy anointing oil of the Temple." That's because the oil in the juglet is not *olive* oil, the chief component of biblical "anointing oil." An analysis of the items suspended in the oil revealed that it is probably some sort of aromatic oil, possibly that of the now extinct balsam plant.[31] Yet Jones has continued to assert that the juglet is part of the Temple treasures of the *Copper Scroll,* even though neither the anointing oil nor balsam oil is clearly indicated there as a treasure. Meanwhile, Dr. Patrich issued to the media his own press statement concerning Jones's claim:

> What does the anointing oil have to do with the Temple artifacts? He's [Jones] just wasting money and wasting time and wasting the goodwill of people because of the place he insists on excavating.[32]

Undaunted by the criticism directed against him, Jones next set his sights on another nearby cave in which he believed was buried the long-lost explanatory copy of the *Copper Scroll.* In this cave, Jones claims to have discovered proof that he is nearing his objective.

### The "Temple Incense"

In April of 1992 Jones again called the media, this time asking them to come to his excavation site for a major archaeological announcement. And because of "his" earlier discovery of the juglet, they did come. At this new site, located adjacent to his Cave of the Column, he revealed that he had "unearthed" an estimated 900 pounds of a reddish substance from beneath the floor of the lowest chamber of the cave. The substance had been given to the "Weisman Institute of Science" for chemical analysis and they had identified elements in the mixture that proved it was the *pitum haketoret*, a specially mixed incense used in the ancient Temple service.[33] Jones even supplied copies of the report by a Dr. Marvin Antelman, allegedly a chemical consultant at the "Weisman Institute." The report was on a press release with the name of the institute appearing at the top, making Jones's claim appear credible. Jones again declared that this incense was the kind of incense listed on the *Copper Scroll* as part of the Temple treasures. He went on to say that in another part of the lowest chamber he had discovered an area of blue light, which, according to his wife's translation of the *Copper Scroll,* was mentioned in the last words of the Scroll as indicating the place where the original copy of the Scroll, with complete directions to the treasure, was stored. Jones also announced that he was close to finding the Ark of the Covenant, the Tabernacle, and the priestly garments with the Urim and Thummim.

This story, however, has another side. Marvin Antelman once worked for the Weizman Institute of Science (note the difference in spelling from the name that appeared on Jones's press release), but never as a chemical advisor, as Jones claimed. In 1992 when the Israel Antiquities Authority called the Weizman Institute to verify Antelman's position, they were informed that no one by that name worked there. Apparently, by that time he had already retired from the institute. The reason for the differences in spelling has to do with a different institute within the Weizman Institute itself (the Weisman Institute of Physical Sciences). However, a Weizman Institute spokesman said that it was not legal for anyone no longer employed at the institute to use his credentials to support an independent analysis.[34] Jones has since claimed that one of his volunteers, a paleobotanist, has further tested the "incense" and that Jones can now solve the mysteries of both the "balm" found in the spices of the "incense" and the "unidentified oil" from "our 1988 discovery."[35] He also said he knows where he can get the plants from which both the "balm" and the "oil" were extracted, and "plans to bring them to Israel and re-establish groves of them in the Valley of Achor"—"when," he adds, "we get sufficient funding."[36]

The day after Jones went to the media with his "incense" discovery, the Antiquities Authority went to Jones. They told him to close down his "excavation" and leave the site. This was not because, as Jones claimed, his find upset Israeli authorities who were afraid that any find connected with the Temple would cause a breach in the sensitive political situation in Israel. Rather, it was because Jones had claimed to have found something of archaeological significance, which now made his excavation illegal because he did not have an authorized permit. Antiquities Authority spokesman Efrat Orbach explained at that time that Jones had obtained temporary permits because of the volunteers with him but he had not received an official excavation permit.

Still, Jones returned to this site in 1994 with about 40 volunteers. They discovered an additional 300 pounds of "incense" (bringing the total to 1,320 pounds), and they attempted to locate the cave's supposedly hidden chamber by using ground-penetrating radar. Jones said that he found two hidden caverns, "both of which coincided with the descriptions in the

*Copper Scroll*." However, rather than investigate through excavation when they were so near to their goal, Jones said it was "absolutely imperative that we leave the cave excavation until we could find the location of Gilgal.... According to the Prophets, the Ark of the Covenant and the Tabernacle will first be returned to Gilgal and later to Jerusalem."[37]

## Jones's Pattern of Progress

Jones's delays and circumventions are apparently all part of a progressively developing prophetic sequence that he has contrived from his own peculiar method of biblical interpretation. Jones's sequential scheme has been given as follows: first, the anointing of the high priests Aaron and Eleazar with the anointing oil (Numbers 7); second, the holy incense offered by the true heads of the tribes (Numbers 7); third, Korah, a Levite, led a rebellion to overthrow Moses' leadership (Numbers 16); fourth, the *Haftorah* for Korah is 1 Samuel 11:14-22, which opens with Gilgal; and fifth, the next Parsha after Korah is Numbers 19, which is devoted to the ashes of the red heifer.[38] This prophetic sequence is meant to follow the events in Jones's archaeological career: first, he discovered the "anointing oil"; second he recovered over 1,000 pounds of the "holy incense"; third, he had a man attempt to take over his organization; fourth, he claims to have discovered Gilgal; and fifth—and yet to be fulfilled—he will find the long-sought-after ashes of the red heifer.

## Jones's Attempts at Credibility

The high-profile news reports portraying Jones as an archaeologist and announcing his claims about the oil and the incense were sourced out of articles that, for a time, appeared frequently in the *Jerusalem Post*.[39] Wire services picked up these reports and published them in papers throughout the world. As a result, Jones received widespread recognition and significant boosts to his reputation and donor base. However, if Jones is not a certified archaeologist, and if his work is not approved by the Antiquities Authority, then why would a respected paper like the *Jerusalem Post* repeatedly report on his work? According to the *Post* representatives, this was not an editorial decision. As they tell it, a man named Dell Griffin, who worked for Jones, was employed at the *Post*. He wrote these favorable (actually laudatory) articles about Jones, until one night he was caught in an unauthorized entry to the *Post* and was summarily dismissed. No one can say what part Jones had in this; we only know that the *Post* denies knowingly profiling Jones in the manner in which he was published in their articles.

In the fall of 1995, an Associated Press story about Jones surfaced in newspapers around the country. This time Jones received press because of his association with established Israeli archaeologists Hannan Eshel and Magen Broshi, who had just announced their discovery of new and supposedly undisturbed caves (see chapter 20 for the details on this excavation). In typical fashion, Jones told the press they were expecting a great discovery and were keeping the location a secret. However, when I spoke with Eshel and Broshi after this news story had been published and a month prior to the dig, they told me that Jones was no longer involved in any way, and freely shared the location and photographs of the caves. Eshel said that initially they considered including Jones because he had promised a large amount of money and volunteers. But when Eshel and Broshi received their own funding and volunteers, they decided not to pursue the association.

Even with the full knowledge that he was not a part of the dig, Jones went ahead and organized a study and excavation program promising volunteers an opportunity to visit the new caves. When I called his office in early November for information on the program, I was sent a support letter along with a copy of the Associated Press news article! Jones's groups started arriving in Israel in November for the promised dig. I happened to be at Kibbutz Almog (a cooperative with guest quarters on the shores of the Dead Sea) when Jones frantically called them, saying that he was bringing his first group over from Jordan but had no place for the group to stay! Apparently something else in Jones's plans had also failed.

## A Call to Discernment

Vendyl Jones is portrayed here because he is the most prominent example of the popular sensationalists who have associated themselves with the Scrolls. There are others, and there always will be others who abuse the public trust (and especially the religious community) by making unsupported archaeological claims. Those who will not submit to developing the proper qualifications for archaeological work via the required institutional study often will seek to qualify themselves by association with legitimate archaeologists and scholars. Or, they may justify themselves by inventing conspiracy theories that make the certifying institutions who require their certification appear untrustworthy. When we are confronted with amazing archaeological claims or conspiracies, we should ask for verifiable evidence and examine the credentials of the claimants as well as seek opinions from reliable authorities. But what if such claims are made by those who *have* credentials and are recognized as authorities? These are the sensationalizing scholars, and in our next chapter we'll take a close look at how to respond to their claims.

# 17

# SENSATIONALISM AND THE SCHOLARS

*Qumran scholarship both scales the heights of academic activity and plumbs its depths. There are some matters about which one would prefer to keep silent, for the sake of those concerned, but in the end truth cannot be concealed.*[1]

—Otto Betz and Rainer Riesner

The overwhelming majority of the scholars who are involved in studying the Dead Sea Scrolls are responsible individuals who actively oppose any sensationalism or sensationalizing of their research. Their writings have proved greatly beneficial for everyone who wishes to better understand the secrets of the Scrolls. However, there are a few legitimate scholars whose writings have been considered curiosities on the academic level but have caused both confusion and controversy on the popular level. These "sensationalist scholars"—whether devoid of personal faith, on a skeptical pilgrimage, or motivated by a radical revisionist agenda—each have theological or historical presuppositions that have motivated them to use the Dead Sea Scrolls to attack traditional Christianity. While differing in their methods and identifications of figures in the Scrolls, these sensationalist scholars agree on at least two fundamentals: 1) the Scrolls and those who produced them were not pre-Christian, but represent the Christian community in its original state; and 2) the Scrolls present the real historical Jesus, not the Christ of faith whom the church confesses.

## Who They Are and What They Teach

### The Father of Scroll Sensationalists

One of the first scholars to sensationalize the Scrolls was the British agnostic John Allegro. Allegro was on the original team of scholars who were responsible for publishing the translations and commentaries on the Scrolls. Though trained for the Methodist ministry, Allegro abandoned his faith and wrote a series of printed attacks on Christianity, using the Scrolls to demonstrate that the New Testament account of Jesus was fictitious (for example, he believed Jesus was made up from the Essene Teacher of Righteousness). He also declared that he had discerned the secret code of the Essenes and could unlock the true meaning of New Testament names. Thus, *Jesus* was "Essene," and *Peter* contained an Essene title.[2] Later, however, in his book *The Sacred Mushroom and the Cross* (in which he sought to show that Christianity was a disguised fertility cult based on hallucinogenic drugs derived from a sacred species of mushroom), he decided that the name *Jesus* meant "Semen, which saves," and that *Peter* meant "Mushroom."[3] In his last two books, *The Chosen People* (1972) and *The Dead Sea Scrolls and the Christian Myth* (1979), he used his theory to argue that the rituals of both Judaism and the Essenes were in fact coded to conceal the secret instructions of their fertility rites.

Allegro, then, could be called the father of Scroll sensationalists, for his influence was evident in the writings of early authors on the Scrolls who followed his anti-Christian theses.

Some of those who followed Allegro's speculations about the Scrolls and Christianity included such names as André Dupont-Sommer, A. Powell Davies, Edmund Wilson, and Rev. Francis Potter. In fact, essayist Edmund Wilson was so enamored by the writings of Allegro that in 1955 he wrote a book entitled *The Scrolls from the Dead Sea* in order to popularize Allegro's theories. Wilson's purpose was to demythologize Christian origins for the public, and he claimed that New Testament scholars were deliberately ignoring the study of the Scrolls because the Scrolls would disprove Christian teachings.

Disciples, as a rule, generally enlarge upon the extremes of their master, and these writers, building upon their radical predecessor, refined his revisions of Jesus, Christian origins, and the New Testament. The themes that usually prevail in their works are these: 1) the New Testament is not new, but a development of one branch of Judaism that, when mingled with Gentile religions, evolved into a religious system;[4] 2) Christian figures are present in the Qumran Scrolls under aliases; and 3) these new insights require a radical reinterpretation of the history of Jesus, early Christianity, and our traditional understanding of all of the New Testament.

Even today many of the books by these older sensationalists are still in print and are considered reference works for Christian pastors who want to study about the Dead Sea Scrolls. When I checked my own library for the titles I collected during my earlier years in seminary and the ministry I found those by Davies, Wilson, and Potter. It is difficult to know how much the sensationalist viewpoints in these books has affected the perceptions of the pastors who may have read them.

Today a new generation of sensationalist scholars have entered the field, and taking advantage of the advances in media, have promoted their theories about Christian origins to an even larger audience. Their written works are often reflective of scholarly ability and have made contributions to Dead Sea Scroll research, yet at the same time are marked by speculative theories and sensationalist claims. So that we can get a better idea of what these scholars say, let's look now at two of the more publicized of these sensationalist scholars: Barbara Thiering and Robert Eisenman.

### Barbara Thiering

Barbara Thiering, who teaches at the Divinity School of the University of Sydney (Australia), has long been a contributor in the field of Dead Sea Scroll studies.[5] In common with other skeptics, she approaches the texts as a rationalist, denying the possibility of the supernatural. Her book *Jesus and the Riddle of the Dead Sea Scrolls: Unlocking the Secrets of His Life Story* is a popular-style presentation of her "revelations" previously published in three academic books.[6] She contends that the New Testament is actually a coded document that has concealed for 2,000 years the secret meanings of historical events. These secret meanings, as she defines them, dramatically alter the orthodox historical accounts found in the Gospels. This is best seen in her revision of the life of Jesus.

## The Gospel According to Thiering

According to Thiering, her historical "Jesus" was born into the royal priestly line of the strictest Essene Sect. The Boethusian party (followers of the high priest Simon Boethus, circa 23-5 B.C.) viewed Jesus' birth as illegitimate because he was regarded as an extranuptial child (equivalent to an orphan). Thus he had to be born at "the Queen's House" (which Thiering interprets as "Bethlehem of Judea," according to her code), about a kilometer south of the Khirbet Qumran plateau (known as Khirbit Mird) in March of 7 B.C. The "wise men" who came to visit him were really the more liberal "Diaspora Essenes"; they sought to protect Jesus from the Boethusian priestly party, which opposed Jesus' legitimacy as a claimant to the Davidic dynasty.

Jesus, whom Thiering depicts as a sort of endomorphic midget (because Mary Magdalene thought she could "take him away," John 20:15), lived most of his life at Qumran and not in the Galilee. He was accepted as a novice Essene, received full initiation into the order in A.D. 17, and was baptized by John the Baptist—the Essene leader known as the Teacher of Righteousness—in A.D. 29.

Thiering states that Jesus never performed any miracles, but on Yom Kippur of A.D. 32 he adorned himself in the high priest's robes and sought to claim both the title of high priest and king. Because this was unacceptable to the tradition-minded Essenes, they broke away from the rest of the Sect. Along with the apostolic council of 12, Jesus sided against the nationalistic Zealot John the Baptist and championed peace with Rome. Later, however, he broke away from the peace party and became a Zealot accomplice.

In March of A.D. 33 he rode into Qumran on a mule to release the magician Simon Magus (Acts 8:9-24) from his excommunication at Qumran. Disappointed that a divine intervention had not accompanied Jesus' "triumphant entry," the community betrayed him to Pilate, who came to Qumran to arrest Jesus. These events led to his trial and "crucifixion" with Simon Magus and the Zealot Judas Iscariot in the unclean area at Qumran. Before the end of the day, however, the method of execution was changed from crucifixion to live burial in Cave 7. Therefore, Jesus, who had earlier taken poison to end his suffering, was only unconscious in the tomb, and could be rescued by friends and revived with "healing herbs." He then "ascended to heaven" by returning to the Essene place of prayer, which the Scrolls called the place "of gods and angels."

Jesus' career also included a three-year trial marriage to Mary Magdalene (September A.D. 30), and the fathering of a daughter (A.D. 36) as well as a son named Justus (A.D. 37). Bearing a son who could become a royal successor, Thiering says, was required of Jesus as a Davidic descendant. Eventually Jesus and Mary Magdalene separated, and Jesus entered into a second marriage (A.D. 50) with Lydia of Philippi, the "seller of purple [dye]" (see Acts 16:14-15). Jesus later visited Jerusalem (A.D. 58), and joined Paul on his journey to Rome (A.D. 61). After the deaths of Paul and Peter, he took refuge with his family and was last seen at age 70, living either in Rome or at a Herodian estate in southern France.

## The Method in the Madness

Thiering's outrageous reconstruction of Jesus' life is not based on any historical evidence, but upon an allegorical deciphering of the Gospels and Acts. She arrived at her conclusions by using what she calls a *"pesher* procedure." Her presuppositions include an Essenic origin of the Qumran community and an inner-Essene movement that was responsible for both the Scrolls and the New Testament Gospels and Acts.[7]

Thiering believes that the Scrolls, the Gospels, and other works of that time period can be fit together historically, but in order to do that she must import "historical data" from such later works as the *Clementine Recognitions* and *Homilies,* the writings of Epiphanius and Hegesippus, and the Gnostic Nag Hammadi writings (especially the Gospel of Philip). Her reasoning is that if the same history is being described in different places, then it might be possible to identify unknown figures in the Scrolls with the help of the New Testament, Josephus, or later Christian writings. Thus Thiering equates the foundational figures of the Qumran community (mentioned in the *Habakkuk Commentary*) with well-known individuals in the Gospels. For example, she identifies the "Teacher of Righteousness" with John the Baptist and "the Wicked Priest" (or, "the Liar") with Jesus.

Thiering's central thesis is her contention that the New Testament, using a form of Essenic exegetical technique, was written in a cryptic code with the deliberate aim of obscuring the actual historical events. This "Essene" method of textual interpretation allegedly was derived from reading the Galilean references in the Gospels using the *pesher* technique. Thiering says there is no question that the sectarian Scrolls were written for the members of the Sect; more specifically, they were designed for those with inside knowledge. This may be the reason principal figures in the Sect were not identified by name in the Scrolls, although in some cases contemporary historical figures were (as we'll soon see).

In normal *pesher* exegesis, a text is applied from the biblical context to the time of the commentary. This was the form most used when the Scroll writers wrote commentaries about the books of the Bible and when the apostles exegeted the Old Testament.[8] However, Thiering likens *pesher* exegesis to the solving of a riddle or the interpretation of a cryptogram, which is closer to *raz-pesher*, a type of mystery interpretation that refers to hidden or secret meanings. Yet this is not the normal form of *pesher* exhibited in the exegesis of the Scrolls. The mysteries of God are treated in the *Pesher Habakkuk* (*1QpHab* 7:8), but the form of the *pesher* here is the normal form of Old Testament citation followed by a contemporary application of the passage, all introduced by the standard formula ("its interpretation is . . . "). If the *Pesher Habakkuk* interpreted the Babylonians as the Romans, it is only because in the context of Habakkuk, the Romans fit the prophetic pattern described for the Babylonians. That is *analogy*, not allegory, and is a far cry from saying that the term *Babylonians* was a code hiding the true meaning "Romans."

Thiering's *pesher* interpretations assume that the Bible was written on two different levels—level one for uneducated people who would accept supernatural occurrences and find religious value in them; and level two for more educated people who would not accept the miraculous, but would look for deeper, accurate meanings.[9] According to Thiering, then, the miracles of the Gospels and Acts did not historically occur. For level one readers the accounts were written to give the appearance that miracles had occurred in order to bolster the faith of the simple. For level two readers, or the initiated, the meanings of the code words in the text became evident; these readers understood the true figures and the naturalistic events behind the symbols.

It is this method of *pesher* exegesis, peculiar to Thiering, that permits her to decipher the supposed Gospel codes and arrive at a *complete* biography of Jesus, something no historian or theologian has ever been able to accomplish. In fact, her biography is so complete that it includes detailed information about the "missing years of Jesus" and precise dates for every event in His life. Her procedure, however, is mixed with a great deal of subjectivism. For instance, she interprets the "certain man" waylaid in the Parable of the Good Samaritan as John the Baptizer simply because he was "going down from Jerusalem to Jericho" (Luke 10:30).[10] According to Thiering, "in code" this phrase referred to joining the Essene Sect, and the problems encountered by this waylaid man conceal John's experiences as leader of the Qumran community.

In like manner, the Parable of the Prodigal Son is viewed as a coded history. The father is identified as the Essene Simon (considered the same person as the righteous Simeon at Jesus' dedication, Luke 2:25!). The younger son in the parable was Theudas the Revolutionary (although Thiering claims he was not "slain" as Acts 5:36 asserts), who was also Thaddeus of the 12 apostles. The older son was Judas the Zealot, and the fatted calf was Herod's son Archelaus, who was deposed by the Romans in A.D. 6. Thiering unfolds the story around Theudas, who became the leader of an Egyptian group of Essenes called the Therapeutae. He also is said by Thiering to be later seen as the nationalist Zealot leader who preceded Judas the Galilean (mentioned in Acts 5:36). Moving from Egypt to Qumran (the "far country" of the parable), he supposedly turned the site into a Zealot fortress, influenced the Sect to include women in its communal life, and then "squandered his father's inheritance" by purchasing weapons to fight the Romans![11]

## Allegorical Insights in the New Testament?

As we can see from the examples we've looked at, Thiering's perspective is that the New Testament was written to conceal the details of the religious and political disputes within the Essene movement. Thiering says the original Essene group split into two factions—one headed by John the Baptizer, the other by Jesus. Out of this resulted the Gospels, Acts, and the rise of the early church, which was the less chauvinistic branch of the Essenes.

In her interpretive technique, Thiering argues that every proper name and most common nouns stand for something or someone unexpected from the surface reading. For instance, Lazarus, the brother of Mary and Martha, is Simon Magus (Acts 8), but also Simon the Leper and Simon the Zealot. The Sea of Galilee is really the Dead Sea, Capernaum is Mazin (a site on the shores of the Dead Sea), and Jerusalem is Qumran. In like manner, all the locations in the Gospel accounts are identified with sites at Khirbet Qumran. The Temple with its Holy of Holies was in the court area next to the round well, the Pool of Siloam was the exclusion cistern, the Mount of Olives was the Celibate House, the Garden of Gethsemane near the pillar bases, and the Kidron was the community aqueduct. In addition, well-known sites such as Jericho, Egypt, the Red Sea, and Jordan refer to caves or other ruins at Qumran.[12]

When Thiering applies her method of interpretation to a Gospel event, we come up with equally surprising results. For example, in John 11, when Jesus raised Lazarus from his grave in Bethany, Jesus was actually releasing Simon Magus, the Zealot leader, from imprisonment in Cave 4 at Qumran! Deciphering the coded text, we discover that Lazarus (Simon Magus) had "died," which meant he was excommunicated by the stricter Essenes, and been "buried," or put into confinement in Cave 4. Martha, Lazarus' sister, was actually Simon's wife, Helena. When Martha said Lazarus would stink if he was brought out of the tomb, she meant that Simon would be ceremonially unclean. When Lazarus emerged from the tomb still in his grave clothes, this was actually Simon's appearance in his high-priestly garments.

With this method of interpretation, and the use of an esoteric vocabulary that is too complex to consider here, Thiering reinterprets history and the Christian faith.

## An Evaluation of Thiering's Method

Thiering has obviously expended a lot of effort in her interpretive analyses, but her principles for interpretation are faulty and misleading. There is no evidence that the *pesharists* themselves wrote with double meanings at all times. The New Testament use of *pesher* sometimes cites the Old Testament to show that a particular prophetic event was fulfilled in the work of Jesus (See Matthew 1:20-23), although use of the word *fulfillment* (Greek, *pleroō*) and the so-called "fulfillment formula" does not always indicate fulfilled prophecy.[13] However, as Betz and Riesner point out, "nowhere in the New Testament is a word or an action of Jesus cited with the claim that it is a cryptic reference to a completely different historical event."[14] And, if secrecy was a foremost concern for the New Testament authors, then why did they sometimes use real names as well as code names? Even Thiering herself is not consistent in her application.

**Problems with Identification.** Thiering often arbitrarily assigns symbolic meanings that end up complicating the obvious meaning of simple terms. For example, she says the Greek word *epaurion* ("the next day") means the 36 hours of the changeover in an intercalation year, the words *all* and *crowds* refer to King Herod Agrippa I (as does the title "disciples of John"), while *earthquake* means the head of the Egyptian Essenes.

Thiering also does this with common titles: *Jews* means the head of the circumcised Gentiles, *elders* means James the Just (also Joseph of Arimathea), *apostles* refers to John Mark, *Pharisees* means the high priest Caiaphas, and *Zacchaeus* refers to the high priest Ananus.[15]

However, it is not necessary to decipher a nonsupernatural (and in this case, antisupernatural) history in order to force it into a coherent history; the conditions under which the Gospel events arose are easily reconstructed within the known historical settings and backgrounds. By contrast, the Qumran community which was isolationist, reactionary, and forced its own interpretation on history, would not serve as a suitable parallel. In addition, A.R.C. Laeney has observed, "A generation impressed by fulfillment in their own day of ancient scriptures would not necessarily write in a code, but rejoice to set forth plainly the actual facts."[16] The apostles Luke and John said that was their motivation for writing (Luke 1:1-4; 1 John 1:3).

To the objective reader, Thiering's strange and insupportable identifications should provoke caution. As Scroll scholar James C. VanderKam has noted, "the bizarre results of Thiering's deciphering of the code should in itself be sufficient to show either that the two-level theory is inappropriate or that she has not correctly understood the code."[17] In summary, there is nothing in the Gospels or any of the New Testament that requires an allegorical interpretation to be understood. The accounts given to us, even in the parables, are straightforward and deal with realities that are applicable to present experiences—not hidden histories of the rival factions of a secret Sect.

**Problems with Facts.** There are also factual errors or inaccurate statements in Thiering's work. For instance, her statement that Jesus presented Himself as a high priest (based on the Transfiguration account in Matthew 17:1-8; Mark 9:2-8; Luke 9:28-36) goes against the clear statements of the New Testament to the contrary: "Christ did not glorify Himself so as to become a high priest" (Hebrews 5:5). Christ's priesthood could not have been after the Aaronic order because He was not born of the tribe of Levi (Hebrews 7:14). A human priesthood is the only kind Thiering can have in mind, for the Melchizedekean priesthood required that Jesus be divine (Hebrews 5:6; 6:20; 7:3, esp. 16-17, 21-28).[18]

Another inaccuracy relates to Thiering's zeal to give historical support to her theory that Khirbet Mird was part of the Qumran Jewish-Christian organization that became westernized and Christian. In this regard she claims that "copies of some of the gospels" were found at the site. Her statement gives the impression that the site developed early as a Christian community and that copies of the Gospels were produced there. In reality, the only historical Christian presence at the site was a monastery (like many in the region) built in the fifth century A.D. Thiering's "copies of the gospels" were found at this monastery, yet they are dated 500 to 700 years after her hypothetical history at the site.

Thiering also errs when she says that the Greek emphatic negative *ou mé* ("by no means") is really a double negative that would translate as an emphatic positive ("by all means"). This not only goes against the accepted grammatical rule, but would also contradict some of Thiering's own theories. For example, Thiering contends that John the Baptizer was the leader of the strict Sect of the Essenes and therefore would not have defiled himself with alcoholic drink. But the statement in Luke 1:15 that John did *not* drink wine or liquor expresses this by use of the emphatic negative. If, as Thiering argues, it is an emphatic *positive*, then John "most emphatically" would have been a drinker, and that would contradict her theories about him.[19]

## Thiering's Pervasive Influence

Some people may wonder whether anyone actually accepts Thiering's astounding revision of the New Testament and what impact her theories have on the reading public. Her publisher HarperCollins is said to have spent over 30,000 dollars on the promotion of her book. In 1990, her views became the source for the television documentary *Riddle of the Dead Sea Scrolls* seen by millions on a nationwide broadcast in Australia on Palm Sunday! On August 23, 1992, the Discovery Channel first broadcast this same documentary in the United States, and has repeated the program several times since. How many of the people who watched this documentary will begin to question the reliability of the New Testament account as a result of this supposed scholarship?

In Israel and Europe, Thiering's book was entitled *Jesus the Man*, and I saw it prominently displayed in Israel in the popular Steimatsky's bookstore chain. What confusion will result for Israelis from this "Christian" presentation of Jesus? Recently I received a call and later a manuscript from a researcher (by profession a geologist) who had been a volunteer on one of Vendyl Jones's digs at the Wadi Jawfet Zaben. With great mathematical precision he was attempting to pinpoint the locations of the Temple treasures as listed in the *Copper Scroll*. His identifications, however, were based on Thiering's *Jesus and the Riddle of the Dead Sea*

*Scrolls*, which he referred to as "the book that started it all." At the same time, this author stated his intent was to show evidence that Jesus is the Messiah! It was sad to read in his conclusion the effect of Thiering's anti-supernaturalism:

> I have tried to answer in as brief a manner and as exact a manner as I can . . . the question of why the world is as it is, and the why of history and religion. . . . I have tried to find natural-istic answers to some of these questions and I may have. I have ended however with an enigma and a question. . . . The existence of God is a given for me, existence itself seems to otherwise be pointless. The actions of God, if they are evident, must have been through natural processes, and if they are above nature are not of significance to people because we are part of nature.[20]

In the foreword to *Jesus and the Riddle of the Dead Sea Scrolls*, Dr. Leonie Star wrote, "There is no doubt that some find difficulty in accepting her reasoning, despite its meticulous documentation, because what is being examined is a matter of faith as much as a scholarly hypothesis."[21] As evidenced above, however, the end result of adopting Thiering's thesis is an undermining of faith. Thiering herself admitted that as a result of her conclusions "the divinity of Jesus may have to be sacrificed to the humanity."[22]

## What the Experts Say

Theology aside, Thiering's meticulous documentation has not con-vinced those who know the Dead Sea Scrolls best. Dr. Florentino Garcia Martinez, one of the foremost Scroll scholars and translators, gave this verdict: "Thiering's work is a wholly artificial construction that not only disregards logic and distorts the meaning of the texts, but trespasses all reasonable boundaries of sound historical reconstruction."[23] But perhaps the best assessment concerning the publication and promotion of Thiering's book was that of *Biblical Archaeology Review* publisher Hershel Shanks:

> The real mystery is how Harper San Francisco, a sub-divi-sion of HarperCollins, generally known for solid academic books, could have decided to publish this weighty tome. Doubtless the answer has something to do with what was on the tables that Jesus overturned.[24]

## Robert Eisenman

Robert Eisenman is professor of Middle East Religions and chair of the Religious Studies Department at California State University, Long Beach. He is not an archaeologist, philologist, or even a theologian, as are most scholars in the field of Dead Sea research. Rather, he is a historian who focuses on the history of the Qumran community, especially in relation to early Jewish-Christianity. This, of course, means that before he can offer a historical interpretation of the Dead Sea texts, he should properly be dependent on a contextual identification by the archaeologist, the restoration of the text by the philologist, and to a degree, an analysis of the text by the theologian. Only after this can he as an historian begin his comparative analysis. But Eisenman dismisses all that; he prefers to have a published text without waiting in line and without having to consider the inhibitions and prejudices (as he sees them) of other disciplines. His attitude was reflected in a recent exchange with other scholars at a Dead Sea Scrolls symposium when he stated, "I don't need any of your books anyway."

Earlier in this book we saw that Eisenman was a key player in the eventual release of the Cave 4 documents that had long gone unpublished. Like Thiering, Eisenman is a maverick scholar and a religious skeptic whose views present radical reconstructions of established historical events. Unlike her, his contributions to Scroll scholarship have been late, outside the journals of the field, and written with almost total disregard to the views propounded by more seasoned Scroll scholars—especially those who differ with him.[25]

## A Survey of Eisenman's Theory

Eisenman went to Jerusalem in 1985–86 to research the relationship of the Qumran community to the Jerusalem Church. He had already published his theory that the Zealot/Zadokite movement was to be identified with the Essene movement.[26] This research, which included a study of the *Habakkuk Pesher*, led him to further develop his theory, and he now argues that the Scrolls were firsthand reports of the historical events of Jesus, the early Jewish-Christian movement, and Pauline Christianity.[27] In 1992, with University of Chicago professor Michael Wise, he wrote a controversial book of new Scroll translations that advocated his theories.[28] His latest book (1995) is *James the Brother of Jesus*, in which he makes the claim that "we have found the historical Jesus."

In this popular-audience work he presents his thesis that a very different "Christianity" than is recognized by the church through the centuries existed in the first century. This difference, he says, came about because the Gentile church departed from its Jewish roots and lost the knowledge of its true origins—knowledge that was supposedly concealed in the Scrolls. In reconstructing these "true" origins, Eisenman, like Thiering, sees two groups at Qumran: one moderate and the other reactionary. Eisenman believes the moderate group was comprised of Sadducees and Pharisees who tolerated Roman rule and collaborated with both the government and the Herodian dynasty. The latter group he believes was a "breakaway" group of Sadducees who were awaiting a warrior-Messiah to lead them against the Romans and the moderate Jews. For this reason Eisenman admits that the "eyeglasses" through which he views the Qumran community is closer (in ethos) to Islam than Christianity or rabbinic Judaism.[29] But Eisenman says he does not think there were two messianic movements in the first century with opposing ideologies. Therefore, this latter group, which Eisenman believes is to be identified with the Zealots, Zadokites, Essenes, and the early Christian movement, is considered by him as that

> messianic movement in Palestine [that] developed with the demise of the Maccabean family and the evocation of a new leadership principle, revolving about prophecies like the Star Prophecy, and some of the ones in the *Messianic Florilegium* and so on.[30]

## Eisenman's View of Christianity

We must acquaint ourselves with Eisenman's view of what is called "early Christianity" before we can understand his interpretation of its relation to the Qumran Sect. Eisenman assumes that Jewish Christianity dates to the second or third century A.D. (that is, 200-300 years after Christ). He says, "I don't think there was 'Jewish Christianity' in Palestine in the first century, I never imagined such a thing."[31] Rather, Eisenman's version of first-century Christianity is termed "Palestinian Christianity," or "Messianic Movement in Palestine," and focuses on the Jerusalem Church headed by James the Just. Therefore, he does not claim that the history of early Christianity is reflected in the Scrolls, only that there are parallels. However, he believes these parallels reveal the true precursor of Jewish Christianity (that is, Jamesian Christianity), which is faintly seen in the Gospels and Acts—works that Eisenman regards as "fictional material . . . Hellenistic romances."[32] In fact, on the dust jacket of his book *The Dead Sea Scrolls Uncovered*, Eisenman advised, "Anyone who wants to know what really happened in Palestine in the century before and after Christ should not read the Gospels but the Qumran Scrolls." Furthermore, according to Eisenman (via Baigent and Leigh), Paul created a later form of Christianity by altering the concept of Jesus as a Jew observant of the Law and transforming Him into a miracle-working god who seasonally died and arose and was a counterpart to the Hellenist deities Tammuz, Adonis, and Attis.[33] Thus, the historical Jesus was lost.

If this is Eisenman's view of Christianity, how does he interpret the New Testament in light of the Scrolls?

## Eisenman's Views of Key Figures

Eisenman identifies the chief figures in the Scrolls with New Testament personalities. The Qumran "Teacher of Righteousness" was the leader of the Jerusalem Church, James the Just. And the Teacher's opponents, the "Man of the Lie" and the "Wicked Priest," were the apostle Paul and the high priest Ananus. Let's take a careful look at Eisenman's reasoning for these identifications.

**James.** James the Just was the central figure in early Jewish-Christianity, just as the Teacher was at Qumran. Eisenman feels that because both the Teacher and James were priests, were called "righteous," and were put to death by a high priest in Jerusalem, they must be the same person. Of course, the New Testament says nothing like this about James. Eisenman's information was gleaned from sources such as Josephus and the early church writer Hegesippus. But from some of these same extrabiblical sources we learn, contrary to Eisenman, that Josephus never referred to James as a priest, that James spoke against the Temple and sacrifices,[34] and that Hegesippus only stated that James was opposed and killed by "the scribes and Pharisees," not the high priest. Eisenman's "James," then, depends on which sources a person is willing to select and then combine in order to produce a description not found in any one source alone.

**Paul.** Eisenman's identification of Paul as the "Man of Lies" also rests on a flimsy foundation. Eisenman argues that in the *Habakkuk Pesher* the "Man of the Lie" is depicted as one who rejects the laws of God and establishes "a city in bloodshed." In like manner, he says that Paul founded a city—that is, a competitive movement, Gentile Christianity—which was based on the blood of Christ and on faith "apart from the law." Because Paul defended himself against the charge of lying (2 Corinthians 11:31), Eisenman says he must have been called the "Man of Lies."

Eisenman's reasoning assumes that Paul founded Gentile Christianity, yet it was Jesus, not Paul, who first reached out to the Gentiles (Matthew 12:21; Luke 2:32) and presented many accounts of Gentile conversion and faith in contrast to Israel's rejection of His Messiahship (Matthew 8:5-13; 15:21-28; Luke 4:25-27; 10:25-37; John 4:1-42). The apostle Peter also had a vision for reaching the Gentiles, and defended their inclusion in the faith before the Jerusalem Council (Acts 15:7-11). In fact, in this very account, it is James himself who concludes the argument in favor of the Gentiles (Acts 15:12-21) and is part of the group that commissions Paul to represent the Jerusalem Council's decision to the Gentile churches (Acts 15:22).

Finally, for Eisenman to argue that Paul must be the "Man of Lies" because he told the Corinthian church he was not lying about his apostolic authority is to misunderstand Paul's use of rhetoric in 2 Corinthians 11:31 and to assume that Paul was the only religious figure in his day so accused.

**Ananus.** The identification of the "Wicked Priest" with the high priest Ananus has similar problems. Josephus tells us that Ananus assumed the high-priest's role for only a three-month period during which the province suffered a temporary loss of local Roman leadership. Eisenman places Ananus' execution of James at the start of his priestly office. But note carefully what the *Habakkuk Pesher* says: "... the Wicked Priest, who is called by the name of loyalty at the start of his office. However, when he ruled over Israel his heart became conceited, he deserted God and betrayed the laws for the sake of riches. And he stole and hoarded wealth from the brutal men who had rebelled against God" (*1QpHab* 8:8-11).

The text goes on to list other atrocities committed by the "Wicked Priest," but notice that at the beginning of his reign he was loyal. Not until later did he become corrupted. Eisenman seems to be stretching credulity when he presses all of the Wicked Priest's atrocities into a time span no longer than three months and when he has the corrupted high priest commit his greatest atrocity (the execution of James) at the beginning of this period.

**An Unlikely Scenario.** Finally, using the *Habakkuk Pesher*, Josephus, and early church tradition, Eisenman creates a scenario that has Jesus executed for being a Zealot. He also has James, as leader of the Zealots, excommunicate the moderate, Gentile-sympathizing Paul for his focus on Jesus. He then says that James was executed by members of the Sanhedrin for conspiring to take over the Temple, installing himself as a rival high priest, and "causing others to pronounce the forbidden Name of God."[35]

We can immediately raise an objection to Eisenman's interpretation based on his use of alleged parallels between the *Habakkuk Pesher* and other historical sources. For instance, his attempt to parallel Josephus' account of James' stoning under Ananus (*Antiquities* 20:9.2) with that of the Wicked Priest's pursuit of the Righteous Teacher in the *Habakkuk Pesher* (*1QpHab* 21:4-8) reveals only the most general similarity: a righteous man being persecuted by an opponent. The details, however, reveal striking inconsistencies between the passages. Furthermore, there is nothing in the Scroll account that states that the Man of Lies actually *killed* the Righteous Teacher, only that he pursued him for this purpose. In addition, some of the historical sources Eisenman cites do not support these details, such as his claim that Josephus recorded the accusation made against James in regard to pronouncing the divine Name.

### Resurrecting Old Theories

Eisenman's basic premise and identifications are not new; they have appeared elsewhere in long-refuted theories proposed by earlier writers on the Scrolls. Eisenman's Zealot theories were earlier proposed by Roth and Driver (see chapter 5), and Jacob L. Teicher of Cambridge hypothesized that Ebionite Jewish-Christians were the authors of the Scrolls, with Jesus as the Teacher of Righteousness and Paul as the Man of Lies. Others have suggested that Eisenman's historical assessment is reminiscent of a scheme that Ferdinand Christian Baur (1792–1860) of Tübingen (Germany) had developed in the middle of the last century.[36] So Eisenman's views are not entirely unique; they are a rehash of similar theories that have already been laid to rest in the past.

Like Thiering, Eisenman gives the Dead Sea Scrolls priority over the New Testament books, which he judges to be much later compositions that depended on the Scrolls for their origin and meaning. But in the end, Eisenman and Thiering's reconstructions of the Dead Sea community become as fanciful as their revisions of Christianity, and must be rejected as sensationalism even though their work is regarded as scholarly.

# The Dating Dilemma

Both the theories of Thiering and Eisenman require that founding events of the Qumran community be dated to the Herodian period because the Qumran members are used as "eyewitnesses" to the New Testament events. There are also significant problems with Eisenman's chronology of events. He has James executed in A.D. 62, but the Scrolls had to have been written and hidden by A.D. 68 when the Qumran community was destroyed. This leaves only a few years between James' death and the writing of the *Habakkuk Pesher*, which, according to Eisenman, records the events involved in his scenario. Not only does that brief time span pose a problem; there is also the problem of dating the *Habakkuk Pesher* and the other sectarian Scrolls to this time period.

## *Dating the Scrolls*

The Scrolls from Caves 1 and 11 were originally dated on the basis of archaeology, paleography, and textual analysis. In the case of archaeology, the jars and other attendant remains, such as coins, were used as an index and yielded a date in the second century B.C. In the case of paleography, an analysis based on the development of the original script (in this case, Hebrew) has led epigraphists such as Frank Cross of Harvard University and Nahman Avigad of the Hebrew University to conclude that the style of writing indicates an origin during the Hasmonean period (150-100 B.C.). The traditional view, then, places the events at Qumran in a pre-Christian period, at least a full century earlier than the Gospel events that Thiering and Eisenman attempt to connect with the Scrolls.

## *Thiering and Eisenman's Objections*

Thiering has countered that the script used in the Scrolls is actually a late form of Herodian alphabet which had been influenced by the style of Palmyrene engravers in the first century B.C.[37] Yet, as Scroll scholar Father Jerome Murphy-O'Connor has pointed out, "Thiering did not first have problems with the conclusions of the paleographers and then was forced to develop a new historical reconstruction. Her theory came first and the evidence of the scripts had to be reinterpreted in order to harmonize with it."[38]

Also, the Palmyrene letters were inscribed in stone, whereas at Qumran the letters were written on parchment or papyrus. Since the writing material influences the development of a script, and parchment would facilitate a more rapid evolution than stone, the influence of Palmyrene character-istics on the Qumran script would be unlikely. For his part, Eisenman challenged the paleographical evidence on the grounds that the paleo-graphic sequences "depend on the faulty assumption of a 'rapid' and 'straightline' development of scripts . . . a proposition that is by no means capable of proof," and that they were "too uncertain to have any real rel-evance to such a narrow chronological period."[39]

## Direct Dating of the Scrolls

Direct dating of the Scrolls by the carbon 14 method was performed soon after the Scrolls were discovered. Both the leather parchment mate-rial of the Scrolls and their linen wrappings contained carbon, so it was possible for them to be tested by this technique. The C-14 tests dated the Scrolls to between 200 B.C.–200 A.D. (with a 10 percent margin of error). These dates, however, were too broad for Eisenman, and when the advanced process of Accelerated Mass Spectrometry (AMS) became avail-able in 1989, he demanded that the Israel Antiquities Authority submit the Scrolls for testing by this technique. This was done in 1991 and again in 1994 at the Institut für Mittelenergiephysick in Zurich, and the tests were done by the same scientists who had tested samples from the famous Shroud of Turin.[40] Fourteen samples were submitted for testing—eight from Caves 1 and 11 (including the *Genesis Apocryphon*, the *Thanksgiving Scroll*, the *Habakkuk Commentary*, the complete *Isaiah Scroll*, and the *Temple Scroll*), and six from other Judean desert sites, four of which had been internally dated by the scribes who had written or copied them. The results of the tests confirmed the Hasmonean date (between 150–50 B.C.), contrary to Eisenman's hypothesis! In particular, the 1994 test revealed that the *Pesher Habakkuk*, the source document Thiering depended on for her correspondences, was written between 140–43 B.C.—again, a full century before any New Testament figure had even been born![41]

Eisenman has since protested that "the tests that were conducted were neither extensive nor secure enough to be of any real use in making defin-itive determinations."[42] While AMS carbon-14 tests can vary and conta-mination of the samples is possible, these tests fall in line with the dates already established by archaeology, paleography, and textual analysis.

On the basis of dating, then, the reconstruction theories of Thiering and Eisenman cannot be supported.

### Chronological Evidence from the Scrolls

The theory of a Herodian origin for the Scrolls has been further refuted by Eisenman's own publication[43] of new fragments from Cave 4 (for example, *Prayer for King Jonathan*, *4Q448*; *Aemilius Kills*, *4Q323-324A-B*), which mention over a dozen historical events as well as several Hasmonean rulers or high priests by name. Some of these include Salome Alexandra (76–67 B.C.), her son Hyrcanus II (67–30 B.C.), possibly John Hyrcanus (134–104 B.C.), his son Alexander Jannaeus (104–76 B.C.) and Aemilius Scaurus, Pompey's general in Syro-Palestinia (circa 31 B.C.). The *Pesher Nahum* also mentions the names of the Syrian rulers Antiochus Epiphanes and especially Demetrius, who crucified the 800 Pharisees for high treason (*4QpNah* 1:6-8; *Jewish Antiquities* 13. 377f). Among these texts, however, are no names from the Herodian period.

# A Right Perspective of the Scrolls

The imaginative revisionist theories of sensationalist scholars Barbara Thiering and Robert Eisenman are no better than the fanciful quests of sensationalist "archaeologist" Vendyl Jones. The Scrolls themselves are sensational, but sensationalism in any form, popular or professional, tends to diminish their testimony and redirect the focus from their actual importance (as discussed in chapters 5–7) to an imaginative leap beyond historical and theological boundaries. The Scrolls cannot anymore be used to fill in the missing years of Jesus, to decode the Gospels, or to revise the history of Christianity than to predict the events of the New Year, but they can and do still shed new light on old truths in the unrevisable Scriptures. Yet attacks continue to come against the Scriptures by way of the Scrolls from those outside the pale of orthodoxy. In the next chapter we will examine these attacks which come from the cults and the New Age movement.

# 18

# CULTS AND
# THE SCROLLS

*The messages of the Dead Sea Scrolls are not self-evident; their
meaning is hidden beneath layers of symbolic allusions covered
over by centuries of silence.*[1]

—Ita Sheres and Anne Kohn Blau

The Dead Sea Sect was a secretive order that carefully guarded its
sacred initiation rites and solemn rituals by sworn oaths and severe punishments. Many of today's cults and the New Age movement have drawn
parallels between themselves and Qumran doctrine and practice in order
to historicize their own beliefs. However, the antiquity of a belief does
not legitimize that belief. Ancient heresies are still heresies; as someone
has poignantly stated, "Heresy is just error grown old." Nevertheless,
when a cult is seeking justification for (or in addition to) the esoteric revelations of its founders, it frequently turns to the literature outside the
Bible. There awaits a smorgasbord of truth mixed with error for those
whose appetites are not accustomed to discernment. On this cultic menu

of literature the specialty item is, without question, the Dead Sea Scrolls. As a result, it's not unusual to see books and television documentaries that use the Scrolls as support for the most radical revisions of the historic Jesus and the Christian faith. These presentations are made by groups that say Jesus studied in Tibet or Egypt, that He was actually an Essene Teacher or an Ascended Master, and that He appeared in the Americas to teach the Indians and would later commission a restoration of His former secret society.

Most scholars do not concern themselves with such peripheral beliefs. Rather, in academic isolation, they resign themselves to nonconfrontational and sometimes socially insignificant studies. Many people in the synagogues and churches also prefer to ignore such teachings, all the while bemoaning the growing number of individuals who defect to the cults. It is not difficult to sympathize with the desire to avoid spiritual controversy, but as one Christian author has implied, avoidance may degenerate into indifference:

> It is certainly regrettable how many false and indeed slanderous theories are put forward about Jesus and earliest Christianity. But one could also put forward the view that dispute over the figure of Jesus is better than the deathly silence of complete lack of interest.[2]

It is appropriate, then, for scholars and students who are concerned about the proper use of the Scrolls to also concern themselves with the improper use of these texts. Also, those who don't know anything about the Scrolls but are hearing cultic claims about them should take time to evaluate those claims.

For the following discussion I have selected two representative cult groups: Mormonism and the New Age movement. Both share the same assumptions about the Scrolls: that they were produced by the Essenes (a view we dismissed in the previous chapter), that their doctrine is primarily esoteric, that their teachings comprise a purer stream of revelation than that which flowed into orthodox Christianity, and that their doctrine is of the same kind as their own.

Mormonism makes much of Qumran as a secret society and of the mysteries thought to characterize the Sect. New Agers embrace Jesus as an Essene mystic who mastered the cosmic secrets of the Sect. Other cultic groups such as Rosicrucianists, Theosophists, and Anthrosophists also view the Essenes as part of a mystical continuum and use the Scrolls to demonstrate comparisons with their founders and doctrines. Since all cults are attracted to the mystery element in the Scrolls, let us first briefly survey the nature of mysticism and the secret society at Qumran.

## The Nature of Qumran Mysticism

Mysticism, as seen at Qumran, was simply an attempt by the sectarians to draw closer to God. This was facilitated by means of contemplation of God's heavenly existence; the use of divination, amulets, and phylacteries; and ritualism. This mysticism does not necessarily owe its origin to pagan or foreign influences, but most likely developed within the context of Judaism. This was the trend in rabbinic and medieval times as a mystical Jewish literature developed characterized by *Hekhalot* and *Merkavah* mysticism: contemplation on God's heavenly Temple (Hebrew: *hekhal*, "Temple") and heavenly throne (Hebrew: *merkavah*, "throne"). This early form of mysticism may have influenced the development of foreign mysticism, including Gnosticism.

Although astrology, amulets, magical incantations, and divination were forbidden by the later rabbinic sages, their presence in the Judaism of this period is affirmed in the Scrolls. Also among the collection of esoteric texts are a horoscope text, a physiognomy text (discerning a person's nature from his or her physical appearance and mannerisms), a Chiromancy text (palmistry), and a Brontologion text (prediction of the future based on where thunder is heard in the heavens). From this sampling, as well as similar references throughout the sectarian literature, it is evident that the Qumran community considered these esoteric ideas and practices as a normal part of their Jewish sectarian life. It's possible that they felt special allowance was given for the use of such things because they viewed themselves as a last-days community which was predestined to draw closer to God than their contemporary Jewish brethren. That may also be the same reason that they strictly guarded their esoteric practices from outsiders.

## The Secret Society of the Scrolls

The cults have had available to them only the early sectarian, apocryphal, and pseudepigraphical documents. From these they have, with much speculation, assumed their parallels in doctrine. Until only recently (1995), very little has been known about the newly released obscure and very fragmentary esoteric texts from Cave 4, which reveal much new information about the secretive rituals of the Qumran Sect. In their book *The Truth About the Virgin*, authors Ita Sheres and Anne Kohn Blau mention ritual texts such as the "Angelic Sabbath Bath Ritual" and the "Rite of Immaculate Conception." They examined these texts for information about the role of women in the Sect and ritual sexual associations.[3] Approaching the subject with a feminist bias of uncovering "a focused ideology that promoted male exclusivity and female subordination,"[4] their conclusions were predictably radical. Despite their questionable reconstruction and interpretation of the texts, their work permits us to see that a high degree of esotericism and an equally high level of secrecy was maintained at Qumran. Some of this may have been because of the separation demanded by their strict interpretation of the purification laws. Perhaps, too, they maintained secrecy because of their desire to preserve their exclusive claims to new prophetic revelation and a revealed messianic timetable. Another possibility is that their esoteric practices would have been misunderstood and perhaps condemned by other Jewish groups. Whatever the case, the concept of a secret group, complete with coded language and punishments for revealing their mysteries, is present at Qumran.

## Mormonism and the Scrolls

When Dead Sea Scroll research was first undertaken by Latter-day Saint scholars, Brigham Young University assistant professor of religion Lewis M. Rogers suggested a tentative position be adopted by his colleagues. In a Latter-day Saint publication on archaeology he wrote an article entitled "The Significance of the Scrolls and a Word of Caution":

> Latter-day Saints have cause to rejoice with other Christians and Jews for the new light and fresh perspective brought to them by the Dead Sea Scrolls, but occasionally they need to be reminded that their hopes and emotions make them vulnerable. It is quite possible that claims for the Book of Mormon and for the L.D.S. theology will not be greatly advanced as a consequence of this discovery.[5]

Dr. Roger's attitude reflects that of Mormon academics, who often distance themselves from the more restrictive popular level of LDS missionary activities to pursue the more inclusive aims of biblical scholarship. In fact, credit should be given to these scholars for their extraordinary support and advancement of Dead Sea Scroll studies through funding translations and computer-assisted research.[5a] Yet, despite the warnings of Mormons—on the scholarly level, popular-level Mormonism has since sought to draw parallels between both the Dead Sea Scrolls and the Nag Hammadi Codices and the writings of Joseph Smith in order to establish both a prehistory for their doctrines and to claim special revelatory knowledge for their founder. In fact, Latter-day Saints scholar Eugene Seaich presents the Mormon claim as a challenge when he writes:

> We would rather challenge the reader to explain just how Joseph Smith was able to incorporate so many of antiquity's forgotten doctrines into Mormonism, preserving at the same time the authentic patterns in which they originally appeared. Even if one desired to reject these doctrines, one would be hard-pressed to account for Smith's knowledge of their existence at a time and place where nothing of the sort had been previously suspected. This remarkable fact should be pondered by all who question the relationship of Mormonism to the texts from the Dead Sea and the Egyptian desert.[6]

The argument behind this Mormon claim is twofold. First, if parallels in thought exist between ancient and modern texts, then the earlier material must have had a direct influence, at some point in history, on the development of the later doctrine. If direct influence could be established, it would provide a continuity between the ancient and the modern, supporting Mormonism's claim to be the ancient church. Joseph Smith taught that Mormonism, which finds its historical origin with Smith's vision in 1820, was simply the latest restoration of a religious movement that had been restored five times in past history. Therefore, to find parallels from the past is to "prove" the antiquity of Mormonism's doctrines.

There is, of course, a great difference between proving the antiquity of a doctrine and proving its orthodoxy. The Essene and Gnostic doctrines that Mormons cite as supporting their beliefs have universally been rejected as heretical by every form of orthodox Christianity from the time of the apostolic church. Such linkage by Mormons only forges more firmly Mormonism's connection with ancient heresies rather than the biblical doctrines of the historic Christian church (whether East or West).

Second, these ancient doctrines were not discovered until recent times (1945 for the Nag Hammadi Codices and 1947 for the Dead Sea Scrolls). Thus for Joseph Smith to promote similar teachings in the 1800s must prove that his "revelations were not imagination, but correspond to actual, historic realities."[7]

## The Mormon Claim Regarding Gnosticism

Our concern here is not with the Nag Hammadi Codices, which form a Coptic collection of mostly Gnostic writings from the fourth century A.D. Nevertheless, we must address the Mormon contention that the Gnostics "became apostates" even though their "materials are largely Christian in origin and help us determine just what the early church *actually taught*."[8] The assertion here is that Gnostics looked back on the original ideas held by the church, then later went astray from those ideas. The Mormon explanation for this departure is that it was "more the result of feeding in isolation upon their own substance than of outside influences. In other words, the Gnostics were speculative theologizers who carried the traditional doctrines to fantastic extremes, exaggerating the significance of isolated Scriptures beyond their original intent."[9]

However, when the Mormons consider the apostasy of the Gnostics, which Gnostics do they mean? Gnosticism was not a monolithic movement, but represented various sects (four are well known) and as many as 60 different teachers,[10] all of whom had significant doctrinal disagreements among themselves.[11] Furthermore, Gnosticism, as expressed in its own writings, is radically different from either Judaism or Christianity, and its roots must be traced to a variety of influences including the mythology of Persian Zoroastrianism, the ideas and imagery of Greek religion and philosophy, and the esotericism of Jewish mysticism. Apparently it existed in an early form in the first century (as reflected in the New Testament), and conflicts with both Jewish rabbis and Christian leaders radicalized it in the second century to its full form. Thus, the heresy of Gnosticism resulted from both reception of and reaction to outside influences. It wasn't simply an "exaggeration" of scriptural texts by "speculative theologizers."

There is nothing "largely Christian in origin" about Gnosticism (nor the Dead Sea Scrolls Sect or the Essenes) as the Mormons would like to believe. But the mysticism, dualism, esotericism, and apocalypticism of the Dead Sea Scrolls may have served as original Jewish sources influencing the *development* of Gnosticism (but not Gnosticism *itself*), so an examination of the Mormon claim to parallels with this material will sufficiently address the Gnostic concern as well.

## The Mormon Claim Regarding Parallels

### A Survey of the "Parallels"

In 1979 Melaine Layton published a monograph entitled *The Truth About the Dead Sea Scrolls and Nag Hammadi Writings in Reference to Mormonism*.[12] The following year, the Mormon response was issued by Eugene Seaich, entitled *Mormonism, the Dead Sea Scrolls, and the Nag Hammadi Texts*. Layton had examined a set of lecture tapes by Mormon teacher Einar Erickson (1975), and Seaich did not attempt to defend Erickson's teaching, but simply noted that he was a "popularizer" and that he taught "correctly." He also said, "Ms. Layton's criticisms are at best a criticism of Einar Erickson, not of the Mormon position."[13]

The purpose of Seaich's work, though "occasioned by the appearance of a booklet by Melaine Layton," was not to respond to Ms. Layton's criticism of Erickson, nor to defend the content of his lecture tapes. Rather, it was "to discuss the Dead Sea Scrolls and Nag Hammadi texts in a fresh light, seeking to supplement mere 'parallelmanias' with historical connections and actual line of filiation."[14] It is surprising, then, to find in Seaich's book of 147 pages only 8 pages that contain references to Dead Sea texts. These references are to *4Q Serek Shirah* (p. 15), *1QH* (pp. 15, 66, 104), *1QS* (pp. 41-43, 104), *11QT* (p. 41), *CD* (p. 43), and *Book of Giants* (p. 75). In most cases the references are part of a citation from anothe source and not the result of actually consulting the Qumran text. In all but two cases (*4Q Serek Shirah, 11QT, CD, Book of Giants*) the references are general and don't deal with any texts in particular. Given this paucity of texts, it is difficult to understand how an adequate argument can be made for the claim that Mormonism has teachings that are parallel to those found in the Scrolls. Let's consider the parallels Seaich uses in support of his argument that the Dead Sea Scrolls "agree in principle with the Book of Mormon's claim that 'Christian' doctrines were known before Christ (2 Nephi 25:24)."[15]

Seaich first attempts to find Dead Sea parallels to the Mormon doctrine of the heavenly pre-existence of the soul. He begins with Josephus' statement that the Essenes believed the human soul was "immortal and endured forever" (*Jewish Wars*, 2.8:154). This, of course, assumes that those who wrote the Scrolls were Essenes. Yet all Josephus' statement tells us is that the Essenes held to a doctrine of immortality, not preexistence. What's more, nowhere in the Scrolls themselves do we find evidence that the Sect taught a preexistence for the human soul.

Seaich next cites *4Q Serek Shirah* (today known as *Songs of the Sabbath Sacrifice* or the *Angelic Liturgy*) as teaching the concept of a *corporate* pre-existence. He says, "This 'heavenly Council' was an early form of the pre-existent community of which the sectaries at Qumran claimed to be a living part."[16] However, the context of this poetic praise clearly delineates between a present heavenly angelic order whose benedictions and blessings will come upon a present earthly community "who have laid the foundation of [true] knowledge." In his analysis of this work, Dr. Lawrence Schiffman pointed out, "The poet looks at the heavens and the angelic hosts arrayed in them. Yet although the poet witnesses this angelic drama, the text does not suggest that he joins in the process himself."[17] Also, no known Qumran text regards "heavenly angels" (also called an "angelic priesthood") in their "heavenly Temple" as preexistent souls who later find bodies on earth. On the contrary, as both the *War Scroll* and the *Damascus Document* reveal, "Holy Angels" were regarded as being in the camps with the members of the Sect. There is nothing to support Seaich's claim (which follows his reference to *4Q Serek Shirah*) that "the pre-existent community of apocalyptic became the *pre-existent Church* of Primitive Christianity." Nor can he rightly add: "This pre-existent community can further be seen in such works as the Qumran *Hymn Scroll . . . 1QH* 13:7-10." The context of *1QH* 13 will not support this interpretation, for it contrasts the temporal nature of things "newly created" and whose "outworn forms" are "done away" with the "eternal nature" of God that "endures for all time" (13:1,10-11; cf. 19-21).

Another parallel raised by Seaich is that of the Qumran community as a spiritual temple. He says: "Their idea of the Congregation as a 'temple' for the Lord's Spirit also foreshadowed the Church's belief (*1QS* 5:5ff; 8:4ff)."[18] Here he also references Bertil Gärtner's work on *The Temple and the Community in Qumran*. However, this concept, rightly understood, is also clearly taught in the New Testament (1 Corinthians 3:11; 2 Corinthians 6:16; Ephesians 2:19-22). In the Pauline epistles the Jerusalem Temple is used metaphorically of the sanctification relationships that exist for the believer (individually) and in community (corporate). Because the Holy Spirit takes residence in the lives of believers, their relationship to their flesh is like that of the physical Temple to the presence of the *Shekinah*—that is, the outer structure acquires sanctity by virtue of indwelling holiness. For this reason, believers are not to involve their now "holy bodies" in immoral acts (1 Corinthians 6:18-20).

Using the same analogy, the church—believers in community—is like the Temple in that it is comprised of those set apart to God (like priests). For this reason, those who are unholy must be separated from the church just as those who were ritually unclean had to be excluded from the Temple (2 Corinthians 6:14-17). Therefore, the idea of a sanctified community representing the spiritual concept of a temple is not an unknown or secret doctrine that requires a Qumran parallel. Seaich rightly observes that the "spiritual use" of "temple" in no way implies a substitution of the spiritual for the physical. This he uses to support the Mormon teaching of the "necessity of an earthly Temple which would serve as a ritual center for the community."[19] His parallel for this teaching is the Restoration Temple of the *Temple Scroll*. However, the restoration of the Temple is a concept central to the Old Testament and continued by all forms of Judaism, not an ancient and unknown doctrine that would support Smith's claim to revelation.

Yet another of Seaich's parallels involves the organization of the Qumran community. Citing texts in the *Damascus Document* and the *Manual of Discipline (Rule of the Community)*, he notes that there was a supervisor over every "camp," and that they were to be priests. This he equates with L.D.S. bishops, who are of the Aaronic priesthood *(Doctrine and Covenants* 107:76). While we may question whether the Qumran overseer (Hebrew, *mebaqqer*) is the equivalent of a bishop (Greek, *episkopos*), these roles are typical of the structural organization of the synagogue and the church, and again, offer no mysteries that confirm Smith's revelatory knowledge.

In this same discussion Seaich brings forth two parallels that he believes shows a historic connection between Mormonism and the ancient truths revealed at Qumran. For the first he calls attention to the well-known use of Isaiah 40:3 by the Qumran Sect to justify its presence in the Judean desert: "The Qumran community, which withdrew into the desert to 'make straight the way of the Lord' (Isaiah 40:3), a technical expression meaning 'to be instructed in the mysteries' . . . (*1QS* 9:18-20; 8:12-16)."[20] The actual references, however, do not relate to a technical expression regarding mysteries, but to a study of the Mosaic Law and the prophets for insight in discerning the times for which the Sect was preparing. This study may have involved the use of mystical methods, but these texts do not imply this. In fact, nothing of the cultic activity imagined by Seaich is suggested here.

His second parallel in this discussion is about the Mormon claim to continuing revelation. This, he says, "is also attested in the Dead Sea Scrolls, proving once and for all that prophecy did not cease with Malachai [sic]."[21] He cites *1QH* 4:5-6 as saying God still revealed Himself to the Teacher of Righteousness. The text reads, "I give thanks unto Thee, O Lord, for Thou hast illumined my face with the light of Thy covenant. [Day by day] I seek Thee, and ever Thou shinest upon me bright as the perfect dawn." It should be evident that such intimate, poetic language cannot be pressed to support a concrete theological doctrine. Seaich *is* correct in his understanding that the Teacher of Righteousness was thought to have prophetic discernment and that he was continuing in the prophetic tradition of the Old Testament. Yet the presence of this belief at Qumran does not "prove that prophecy did not cease." In this respect the Qumran community represented a departure from other Jewish sects, which believed that inspired prophecy had ended with the last of the writing prophets.[22] In the New Testament, Jesus continued the prophetic tradition, as did the apostles. However, whether the "gift of prophecy" (1 Corinthians 11:4; 12:10,28; 13:2; 14:1-40) was understood by the early church as a continuation of the prophetic tradition is debated, as is the question of historical continuation beyond the first or second century (1 Corinthians 13:8; Hebrews 2:3-4).

The final parallel drawn by Seaich is the most obvious. This concerns the Mormons' claim to secret doctrines that are not to be disclosed to outsiders. Seaich writes:

> *The Community Rule*, for instance, speaks of "those things hidden from Israel" which the founder of the Sect received for restricted use in the community (*1QS* 8:11). Every member of this esoteric group was commanded to "conceal the teaching of the Law from men of falsehood (outsiders) but shall impart true knowledge and righteous judgment to those who have chosen the way . . . and shall thus instruct them in mysteries of marvelous truth" (9:17-18).[23]

Seaich is correct in this interpretation of Qumran practice. Other Jewish sects and almost all pagan cults (especially the mystery religions) also guarded secret doctrines reserved only for initiates or an enlightened inner circle. So common was this trait in religions of the time that even the early church was mistakenly charged by the Romans with practicing secret rituals in its seclusive observance of the Lord's Supper. However, the New

Testament rejected the concept of secret revelations and rituals in its declaration of the sufficiency and perspicacity of Scripture. The knowledge of God's truth is given for doctrine and instruction to all believers so that they may mature (2 Timothy 3:16), live godly lives (2 Peter 1:2-4), and be known of all men (2 Corinthians 2:14-15; 3:2-3). The gospel is not hidden from any who believe (2 Corinthians 4:2-6), for the Spirit reveals the knowledge freely given by God (1 Corinthians 2:10-15). Furthermore, the New Testament issued a strict prohibition against those who "teach strange doctrines" (1 Timothy 1:3), and "pay attention to myths" (Titus 1:14). These caused "speculation" (1 Timothy 1:4) and argumentation (2 Timothy 2:14), rather than furthering the knowledge of God's plan through a "sincere [literally, 'unconcealed, genuine'] faith" (1 Timothy 1:4-5). If the New Testament is taken as a standard for faith and practice, as the L.D.S. Church professes, then it is difficult to see how Seaich can conclude, "Thus, secret knowledge was part and parcel of Qumran belief, and represented the same mentality which characterized early converts to the Church."[24]

### The Source of Smith's "Secrets"

If parallels do exit between the Dead Sea Scrolls and Mormon doctrines, it is not because the two had a heterodox "pre-Christian Christianity" in common. Parallels could have been just as easily transmitted through the common Judeo-Christian heritage of ritual tradition from which many different Christian and non-Christian sects have borrowed. Much of what Seaich considers as parallels can be found in the Old and New Testaments. There is no need to resort to any secrets found in the ancient mystery religions. However, in Mormon founder Joseph Smith's case, these, along with the more esoteric and unorthodox parallels, more likely came from his Masonic indoctrination.

Freemasonry is a secret society that teaches doctrines formed from an ecumenical mixture of historical pagan and esoteric religions combined with some Jewish and Christian teachings. Masonic doctrine claims to borrow from Gnosticism, the Kabbalah, Zoroastrianism, Greek philosophy, occultism, and most other world religions.[25] According to L.D.S. leader Reed C. Durham, Jr., Joseph Smith founded Mormonism upon "the true ancient Mysteries" that he found and accepted in Freemasonry:

> The philosophic and more reflective Masonic scholars have always believed that the symbols embodied in masonry were indeed the ancient Mysteries coming from remote antiquity. The

> Mysteries were said to be traced back through the Hermetic Philosophers, through Plutarch, the Cabala, the Pythagoreans, the Magi of Media, to Babylon, to Chaldea, and Egypt. And as these Mysteries came down into the modern institution of Masonry—the 12th and 13th centuries A.D.—they had experienced so many progressive alterations that there remained only an imperfect image of their original brilliancy. My assumption is that Joseph Smith believed he was restoring Masonry's original pristine brilliancy, and that he was recreating the Mysteries of the ancient Priesthood.[26]

Therefore, from Freemasonry alone Smith could have acquired every idea for which Dead Sea Scroll parallels are sought. However, in Smith's translation work, we find other claims of connections with the Scrolls.

## *The Mormon Isaiah and the* Isaiah Scroll

Seaich makes the unsupportable statement that "the Qumran versions of Isaiah (circa 200 B.C.) also agree in surprising ways with the passages quoted in the Book of Mormon.[27] This should be an important point for Mormon scholars. They claim that Joseph Smith produced an *Inspired Version of the Bible* [a revision] and that in particular, his version of the text of Isaiah in the Book of Mormon is actually a translation of an ancient copy of Isaiah which is superior to the translation found in the Bible. Evidence from the *Isaiah Scroll* of the "agreement" in "surprising ways" would have strengthened Seaich's argument for the Mormon Isaiah. Wayne Ham attempted to prove this very point in his 1961 thesis written for the department of biblical languages at Brigham Young University, entitled, "A Textual Comparison of the Isaiah Passages in the Book of Mormon with the Same Passages in the St. Mark's Isaiah Scroll of the Dead Sea Community." After completing his study, Ham reported in a *Courage* magazine article:

> Latter-day Saints were hopeful that these Isaiah Scrolls would bring some supportive evidence for the Book of Mormon.... After a thorough investigation of the matter ... this writer found no noteworthy instances of support for the Book of Mormon claims.[28]

This conclusion was also reached by Mormon apologist Dr. Sidney B. Sperry. Writing an article in the L.D.S. publication *Progress of Archaeology*, he candidly stated:

We should be especially interested in the light the *Isaiah Scroll* throws on the problem of the Isaiah text in the Book of Mormon. I have compared in some detail the text of the Scroll with its parallels in the Book of Mormon text. This tedious task has revealed that the Scroll seldom agrees with the departures of the Book of Mormon text from that of the conventional Masoretic text of Isaiah and consequently the Authorized Version. . . . The *Isaiah Scroll* is of relatively little use to Latter day Saints as showing the antiquity of the text of Isaiah in the Book of Mormon.[29]

## Alterations in the Bible?

Mormonism also claims that the original text of the Bible was significantly different than the text we find in versions today. Joseph Fielding Smith, Jr., son of the tenth president of the Mormon Church, contended that the early church fathers "altered, transplanted, or completely removed" any viewpoint that endangered their own.[30] Apostle Mark E. Petersen argued that many insertions, deletions, changes, and forgeries were made by the Catholic Church for the purpose of deliberately falsifying the translations for selfish purposes.[31]

If these Mormon claims are true, then the discovery of almost every book of the Old Testament among the Dead Sea Scrolls should have revealed this malicious practice of altering the biblical text. However, the Scrolls proved the opposite. The Scrolls revealed no substantial variations between their text and the oldest copy of the traditional (Masoretic) text. There were no evidences of changes in doctrine, nothing had been omitted or lost, nor had any insertion of new viewpoints been made. Over the more than 1,000 years separating these versions, not a single doctrine was affected in any way. This, of course, completely refutes the Mormon contention that the Bible had been corrupted by the church throughout the centuries until it was "restored" by Joseph Smith.

In light of the lack of support for connections between Mormon doctrines and the Scrolls, Mormon apologist Dr. Sidney B. Sperry was forced to concede (contrary to Seaich) that the Scrolls do not help the case for the Book of Mormon. He writes:

> After reading the Scrolls very carefully, I come to the conclusion that there is not a line in them that suggests that their

> writers knew the Gospel as understood by Latter-day Saints. In
> fact, there are a few passages that seem to prove the contrary.[32]

Despite the absence of supportive parallels and the difficulty presented to Smith's translation of Isaiah by the Dead Sea Scrolls, Mormons continue to be involved in Dead Sea Scroll research and in the attempt to secure a position within the exclusive society of Dead Sea scholarship. They have done this by sponsoring international conferences on the Scrolls (such as that held July 15-17, 1996, in Provo, Utah, at Brigham Young University). Thus they continue in their effort to use the Scrolls as a source for verifying Mormon doctrine, a task impossible to perform regardless of the academic profile maintained in the endeavor.

## The New Age Movement and the Scrolls

The New Age movement, which is now comfortably established within mainline Christian circles on almost every continent, has found in the Dead Sea Scrolls (and especially the Essenism they believe is contained in the Scrolls), the hidden essence of their spiritual masters. Seeking the Christ Consciousness, New Age practitioners understand the Essenes to have preserved an ancient form, perhaps the highest form, of this cosmic teaching. New Age popularist Shirley MacLaine regards the Essenes as a "New Age Sect," Jesus as an Essene, and finds Essenism permeating all of the world's religions.[33]

As we examine the New Age interpretations of the Scrolls, we will focus on two authorities who are respected for New Age thinking on the Scrolls: Edgar Cayce and Edmond Szekely.

### Edgar Cayce

The American psychic and medium Edgar Cayce,[34] esteemed as a seer in New Age circles, claimed that the Scrolls verified his occultic "Life Readings" about the Essenes. These Life Readings were conducted over a period of 11 years prior to the public announcement of the Dead Sea Scroll discoveries (Cayce died in 1945). In these Readings, Cayce identified Jesus and other prominent New Testament figures with the Essenes. A book written about Cayce's knowledge of the Scrolls tells us this:

> An impressive factor about the Edgar Cayce Readings is that
> so many of the details have subsequently been confirmed by the
> Qumran literature. For example, before the discovery of the Dead

Sea Scrolls, no acknowledged expert in history or religion ever put forth the possibility that Jesus, Mary, Joseph, John the Baptist, and other leading figures in the Gospels were associated in any way with the Essenes. Yet for over twenty years, the Life Readings given by Edgar Cayce had been producing information regarding this association.[35]

The information Cayce received while in trances was that the Essenes were to be identified with the Great White Brotherhood that had started in Egypt but later either assumed different names or existed as branches of the Brotherhood throughout history (for example, Nazirites, School of the Prophets, Hasidees, Therapeutae, Nazarenes). The Essenes, in particular, were an outgrowth of the teachings of Melchizedek—teachings also propagated by Samuel, Saul, Elijah, and Elisha. They were "set aside for preserving themselves in a direct line through which there might come the new or Divine Origin [the Christ]."

Cayce also said the Essenes practiced fortune-telling and studied astrology. According to Cayce, Elijah's prophets were the *first* Essenes, and the Essene headquarters was located on Mount Carmel. The Essenes were also said to have built a large temple on the mountain's eastern face. At this Essene center, Cayce said, both Jews and Gentiles were accepted as members, men and women were considered equals in their activities and abilities, and all were to be channels for souls. Mary, the mother of Jesus, was one of 12 women especially chosen and dedicated as channels for the new race, and submitted to Essene training of her own free will when she was four years old. She, like her husband Joseph, first encountered the Sect when dedicated at the Essene temple by her parents.

According to Cayce, Mary was the twin soul of Jesus (the two were one soul that split in the incarnation), and like Him, was originally born without a human father. When she was 12 the Essenes began to prepare her to become the mother of the Christ. The consecration for this event took place when either a shadow or an angel hovered above Mary on "the stairs" leading to the altar of the Essene temple. Joseph, as an Essene, already knew that the Christ would be incarnated in their Sect, but was concerned about outside Jewish opinion. Yet, as an Essene, his "soul-mind" finally accepted his role in the Divine Plan.

Later, Mary and Joseph were married at this Essene temple. Mary also had an Essene handmaiden called "the entity Josie." She had studied the messianic prophecies in Egypt, had stood beside Mary when she was consecrated at the Essene temple, and remained with her throughout Jesus' growing years.

Phinehas (a priest in the Bible, but apparently here a member of Elijah's School of the Prophets and an organizer of the Essenes) was the father of "the entity Judy." This Judy, though a daughter, received special training in the traditions of Egypt, India, and Persia. Judy was the leader of a group of Essenes who were being prepared as channels at the Essene temple. She was also the supervisor of the Brotherhood during the Herodian period. When the wise men came from the East, they came to consult with the Essenes, but especially to study with Judy.

When they were teenagers, Jesus and John the Baptizer studied under the Essenes. Jesus was under the tutelage of Judy, while John was also assisted in the temple service by a female named Sofa. Judy later sent Jesus to Persia and India to study astrology. Mary, Martha, and Lazarus were said to be Essenes, and so was the innkeeper at Bethlehem, but Nicodemus was said to have never fully accepted Essene tenets or teachings. In addition, all four Gospel writers were Essenes or influenced by Essenes.

When we consider Cayce's statements in light of the Scrolls and the archaeological record at Qumran, we find that most everything he said was nonsense. Nothing suggests an Essene establishment or temple at Mount Carmel, which is on Israel's northern Mediterranean seacoast. The ideas of male and female equality in the Sect, of women Essene leaders, and of Gentile members are all completely disproved by the Scrolls themselves.

In addition, there is no truth to the claim that Cayce was the first to connect Jesus and others with the Essenes and that such identifications had never been made by "acknowledged experts in history or religion." As Duncan Howlett, author of *The Essenes and Christianity* states, "The attempt to identify Jesus with the Essenes is not new. The discovery of the Scrolls has merely revived and strengthened an idea long familiar to Bible students."[36] In his book *The Counterfeit Christ of the New Age Movement*, Ron Rhodes provides a list of past proponents of the Jesus as Essene theory.[37] The following authors all predated Cayce's Readings: Karl Bahrdt, *An Explanation of the Plans and Aims of Jesus* (1790), Karl Venturini, *Non-Supernatural History of the Great Prophet of Nazareth* (1800), and Ernest Renan, *Life of Jesus* (1863). However, in spite of evidence to the contrary, Edgar Cayce will continue to be thought of by

New Agers as an authority on the Scrolls because his interpretations align with their esoteric philosophy.

### Edmond Bordeaux Szekely

Edmond Bordeaux Szekely, a unitarian bishop and cofounder of the International Biogenic Society, lists his academic credentials as a Ph.D. from the University of Paris and other degrees from the Universities of Vienna and Leipzig. He is also said to have held professorships of philosophy and experimental psychology at the University of Cluj. In addition, he claims to be a philologist in Sanskrit, Aramaic, Greek, and Latin, and able to speak ten modern languages. To these credits are added his own translation of the Dead Sea Scrolls and his discovery, translation, and publication of the *Essene Gospel of Peace*, which by 1977 he claimed had sold over 800,000 copies in 23 languages. Leaving aside his Dead Sea Scrolls translation, let's concentrate on his claim to have found this Essene manuscript in the secret archives of the Vatican Library in 1923–24, for it is on the basis of this document that he has developed his New Age teaching of an Essene Jesus.

In his booklet *The Discovery of the Essene Gospel of Peace: The Essenes and the Vatican*, Szekely describes his discovery of a complete and previously unknown Aramaic manuscript of Essenic teachings. This manuscript was said to have been on the locked shelves of the private study of Benedictine monk Msgr. Meracti, prefect of the Archives of the Vatican.[38] Supposedly, duplicate copies existed in fragmentary form in Hebrew at the Benedictine monastery in Cassino, Italy, and in Old Slavonic at the National Library of Vienna. Although Szekely had but a few days with this manuscript, and did not report taking photographs or even making a written copy, he was later able to produce a lengthy translation of the text. Forty years later he also produced a translation of a fragment of the *Essene Gospel of John*, hitherto unmentioned.

His tale is laced with monks who cryptically question him about finding first "the stream" (the Aramaic manuscript), and then "the source" (the Hebrew fragments), and thereby lead him to the discovery. The impression he gives is of a secret society which, knowing the way of the Essenes, cautiously initiated him into its mysteries by leading him to the manuscript. Szekely then wrote two publications: *The Essene Jesus: A Revelation from the Dead Sea Scrolls* and *The Teachings of the Essenes from Enoch to the Dead Sea Scrolls*. In the latter work Szekely explained his understanding of Essenic teaching:

> From the remote ages of antiquity a remarkable teaching has existed which is universal in its application and ageless in its wisdom. Fragments of it are found in Sumerian hieroglyphs and on tiles and stones dating back some eight or ten thousand years.... How many thousands of years previous to that the teaching existed is unknown.... Traces of this teaching have appeared in almost every country and religion. Its fundamental principles were taught in ancient Persia, Egypt, India, Tibet, China, Palestine, Greece, and many other countries. But it has been transmitted in its most pure form by the Essenes, that mysterious brotherhood which lived during the last two or three thousand years B.C. and the first century of the Christian era at the Dead Sea in Palestine and at Lake Mareotis in Egypt.... The esoteric part of their teaching is given in The Tree of Life, The Communions, and the Sevenfold Peace.... Some believe it [the Essene brotherhood] comes from Esnoch, or Enoch ... their Communion with the angelic world having first been given to him.... The Essenes'... way of life enabled them to live 120 years or more and they were said to have marvelous strength and endurance. In all their activities they expressed creative love. They sent out healers and teachers from the brotherhood, amongst whom were Elijah, John the Baptist, John the Beloved and the great Essene Master, Jesus.[39]

Szekely's Essenism is clearly of a cosmic kind. In relation to the same thoughts expressed in the Mormon interpretation of Essenism, it is intriguing that Szekely lists "the rituals of the Masons" as one of the forms in which Essene teaching exists today.[40]

In Szekley's work *The Essene Jesus*, his "Essene Jesus" is revealed. This Jesus exists in relation to the corresponding forces of the Heavenly Father and the Earthly Mother, is a vegetarian, and is a biogenic healer. His doctrines are found in nature, not Scripture, and in cosmic and natural law, not the Law. His ministers are the angels of water, the earth, air, sun, creative work, life, peace, joy, power, love, and wisdom, all sent by the Earthly Mother. These assist in cleansing the body from sin by leading the individual to practice proper diet and principles of natural healing.

What can be said about Szekely's manuscript discovery and of his Essenism? First, it should be evident to anyone acquainted with the actual Dead Sea Scrolls (and not their New Age version) that the concept of Essenism put forward by Szekely has nothing in common with the biblically oriented Jewish Sect at Qumran—whether or not the members are identified historically with the Essenes of classical literature. Szekely's Essenism is universalistic, pantheistic, monistic, esoteric, and earth-centered. Any interpretation that departs so radically from the accepted views of Qumran scholarship requires careful argumentation with thorough documentation. Szekely offers neither.

Second, no corroborating evidence of any kind was given by Szekely in support of his story about how he discovered the manuscript. In all the books in which Szekely told of the discovery and gave a translation, he published a photograph from Cave 3 of the *Copper Scroll* sitting on the shelf where it was found. Because he did not identify this photograph, the reader is left with the mistaken impression that this is a photograph of his *Essene Gospel of Peace*. But there are no photographs, no handwritten facsimiles, no notes on the text, no details about the form of the document (Scroll or codex) or of the Aramaic and Hebrew scripts— nothing. In addition, all those who have sought to retrace Szekely's meager information and recover the manuscript have failed. One such researcher, Per Beskow, published a letter from the prefect of the Vatican's archives stating that no such manuscript is housed there and that no record exists of Szekely's alleged visit.[41] Also, Szekely claimed to have been at the Vatican in connection with research for his thesis at the University of Paris, and that he presented the details of his discovery to his classmates there in 1925. He stated, however, that his thesis was lost long ago (and apparently no other copies existed).[42] Szekely's statement that an Old Slavonic copy was in the National Library of Vienna has also proven to be false.[43] (The monastery at Mount Cassino, where he supposedly saw Hebrew fragments, was destroyed in World War II, and so cannot be investigated.) After examining all the available evidence, Per Beskow concluded:

> The [Essene] *Gospel of Peace* is a sheer forgery, written entirely by Szekely himself. It is one of the strangest frauds we know of in the biblical field, as it has been carried through by stages during a whole lifetime and has been built into an entire body of research based on imagination only.[44]

Szekely's Essenism is only as strong as his sources, and these evidently were of his own making. His Jesus is, as seminary professor Douglas Groothuis has labeled him, "a mellow metaphysician and an organic physician who bears no cross, sheds no blood and startles no disciples as the resurrected Lord. Instead he, fictitious though he may be, validates the message of the New Age."[45] This, in the end, will be the reason why, regardless of Szekely's exposure as a fraud, his "message from the Scrolls" will continue to be attractive.

## The Church's Response

The cults are aberrations of the historic Christian faith. If the church is silent about what it has held for millennia as truth, it will condemn men to be enticed by lies. If the cults are permitted to raise an unchallenged voice in the marketplace of ideas, then their models of faith, philosophy, or whatever will become the orthodoxy of a new age. This theological malaise in orthodoxy is both reflected in scholarship and revealed in society. German authors Otto Betz and Rainer Riesner rightly discern the reason the cults can use pseudoscholarship, such as they do with the Scrolls, to gain the high ground for their claims:

> The controversy over the Qumran Scrolls is only one sign among many of the deep crisis in which the major churches at present find themselves. Certainly in the past, too, those who really believe were also only a minority in society. But at an earlier stage the churches to a remarkable degree succeeded in convincing large groups of the population—not through pressure but through solid information—that the New Testament account of Jesus and earliest Christianity corresponds to historical reality. Doubt about this arose at the periphery of the churches or outside them, but in the meantime it has penetrated deeply into their ranks.[46]

In order to confront the cults that are using the Dead Sea Scrolls to promote radical revisions of historic truths or to unveil an alien Christ, the church must care to know its faith and care about the faith it knows. The alternative is to lose even the influence of that believing minority in an overwhelming tide of darkness and deceit. My hope is that this chapter will have a part in offering a discernment that will equip the church to rise out of its theological lethargy and embrace more firmly a Christ worthy to be believed.

# PART V

---

A Look Ahead

# 19

# POLITICS AND
# THE SCROLLS

---

*We ask that all archaeological activity in the West Bank be stopped. There is no reason to start excavations in a land that will be turned over to us.*

—Hamdan Taha, PLO negotiator

*We have to find a balance between our deep feelings regarding our own history and respect for international law.*

—Anat Maor, member, Israeli Knesset

---

There's a well-worn Israeli joke that capitalizes on the importance of the Dead Sea. One day an American, a Frenchman, and an Israeli were talking about their family heritage. The American began to boast about his family, saying, "Have you heard of the Empire State Building? Well, my grandfather built it!"

"Oui!" said the Frenchman. "Have you heard of the Eiffel Tower? Well, *my* grandfather built it!"

The Israeli, having no similar landmarks to boast about, was nevertheless equal to the occasion. He said, "Have you heard of the Dead Sea? Well, *my* grandfather *killed* it!"

Only when something like the Dead Sea is a part of a people's history can it become a part of their humor about themselves. Take away the Dead Sea and the long history of its Jewish presence, and you have removed a vital part of Israel's heritage. Today, Israel is faced with a conflict over the control of the Dead Sea, and especially the relics along its shores. As a result, the Dead Sea is no longer a laughing matter.

## The Conflict Over Control

Today a political contest is under way for control of the biblical land of Israel (Judea and Samaria) and the archaeological treasures that continue to reveal her ancient past. Several years ago this conflict of control over the past was impressed on me by a television drama. It was the second show in the first season of the television series "SeaQuest," a fictional show about future undersea exploration. The plot was centered on the surprise discovery of the famous lost library of Alexandria, Egypt. According to history, this library was built in the third century B.C. by Ptolemy I to house one-half million papyrus scrolls containing the writings of the ancient world. These were the original classical Greek manuscripts and copies of rare documents that eventually formed the basis of all the great libraries of Europe. Destroyed in a fire during an Arab invasion, this library perished to the ages. The scriptwriters of "SeaQuest," however, created a scenario in which the library was still preserved in an air pocket on the ocean floor. The discovery of the library was followed by an instant international reaction. Representatives from various countries argued that the ancient manuscripts were each their own national treasures, and threatened to take aggressive action against the others to secure their rights. An all-out war between the nations of the world was at hand because of these long-lost scrolls.

This fictional situation may be exaggerated in proportion to the state of controversy over the Dead Sea and its Scrolls in the Middle East today; however, truth is sometimes stranger than fiction. As many people consider what is being said and done in the present peace process, they are indeed alarmed that what was once imagined as fiction is fast becoming fact. Let's see how the Dead Sea Scrolls may play a part in this modern drama, which is still in the process of being scripted.

## The Demand for Land

The Palestinian Liberation Organization's (PLO) charter, based on the Arab League Charter of 1948, did not call for "liberating" the West Bank and Gaza, as is being considered under the ongoing peace process. Rather, it called for "liberating" the *whole* of Palestine, which by definition is *everything* west of the Jordan River. I once observed (1995) an official map of the Palestinian state mounted on a wall at the Orient House, which was then being used by the PLO as their official headquarters (in violation of the Oslo Agreement). On this map, Palestine clearly included *all* this territory west of the Jordan River. In fact, *not one Israeli city* appeared on the map! The reality of this vision has been stated by Nayef Hawatmeh, leader of the Democratic Front for the Liberation of Palestine, the third largest PLO organization: "The popular revolution in Palestine will continue the struggle to expel the Zionist occupation from all Palestinian Arab soil, from the [Jordan] River to the [Mediterranean] Sea."

Evidence of the PLO's intentions was revealed in their original request for 140 square miles of land "around Jericho" in addition to the town itself. The Jericho district, as defined by Jordanian law (before its capture by the Israelis in 1967), comprised 146 square miles. The requested 140 miles was about the same as the Jericho district, and was what the PLO wanted the autonomous zone to contain. At that time (1994), Prime Minister Yitzhak Rabin pledged that "the self-rule in Jericho will not reach the Jordan or the Dead Sea and will not include any Israeli settlement."[1] When implemented, the autonomy did extend to the Jordan, but only to the inclusion of the Allenby bridge, one of two border crossings between Jordan and Israel. Even so, Israel retained the right to monitor the bridge.

## The Program of the Palestinian State

In February 1996, the PLO leadership's intentions were made known to the public.[2] On January 30, Palestinian leader Yasser Arafat went to the Stockholm Grand Hotel in Sweden to celebrate a peace prize shared by his Fatah Youth and two other organizations. His statements at this meeting were reported by one of the diplomats in attendance and relayed to Israel by the offshore radio station Arutz 7 on February 7, and to the world press via the Norwegian daily *Dagen* on February 16. Officially,

Arafat's office in Gaza called the reported contents of his talk "false and inaccurate." According to this report, Arafat is said to have declared that a Palestinian State is imminent, and with it, Israel's demise. He is quoted as saying, "We plan to eliminate the State of Israel and establish a Palestinian State." Arafat's expectation of complete control over the land of Israel, not merely the West Bank and Gaza, was also evident in his comments:

> We Palestinians will take over everything including all of Jerusalem. [Prime Minister Shimon] Peres and [Minister Yossi] Belin have already promised us half of Jerusalem. The Golan Heights, too, have already been given away, subject to just a few details. And when they are returned, at least a million rich Jews will leave Israel.

Arafat's program for bringing about the Palestinian State was also offered: "The PLO will concentrate on splitting Israel psychologically into two camps. Within five years we will have six to seven million Arabs living on the West Bank and Jerusalem." Predicting that Jews will not want to live under Palestinian sovereignty, he expressed his thoughts on a strategy for forcing Jews from the Land:

> We will make life unbearable for Jews by psychological warfare and population explosion. . . . Jews will not want to live among Arabs. . . . They will give up their dwellings and leave for the United States.

Arafat further predicted that a civil war will erupt in Israel, and said he believes Russian immigrants and Ethiopian Jews (which he feels are mostly Christian or Muslim) will fight for a "united Palestinian state." While such plans might be considered illusory, if Arafat's statements are indeed "true and accurate," they reveal the objective of the Palestinians to take over the whole of the country, including the area where the Dead Sea Scrolls were found.

## The Demand for Relics

The Palestinian demand for land has also been accompanied by a demand for all of the archaeological relics discovered in the land. In 1993, Palestinian archaeologists called for a "total transfer of archaeological sites and findings" excavated by Israel in the West Bank and Gaza since 1967.[3] There are more than 300 such sites covering the entire West Bank, which comprises most of biblical Judea and Samaria. Of course, to comply with such a demand would effectively empty the archaeological sections of every museum in Israel.

The call for this return of relics was made in a position paper presented to Palestinian peace negotiators by the Jerusalem-based Institute for Islamic Archaeology during the first phase of the Palestinian self-rule negotiations. Originally the plan was for the transfer of all objects, records, plans, and photographs to the Palestinians no later than December 1995. At that time the Israeli Antiquities Authority stated that it had not yet formulated an official position on the issues raised by the Palestinian position paper.

## An Increasingly Delicate Situation

In 1995, when the second phase of negotiations began, the Palestinian Authority added to their previous demands a call for an immediate freeze on all archaeological excavations throughout the West Bank. This demand, made at the negotiating table at the Hilton Hotel in Taba, Egypt—just a stone's throw from the Israeli border in Eliat—came in response to news reports that Israeli archaeologists were to begin excavating newly discovered caves (which might have Scrolls) in the Judean desert. Hamdan Taha, who headed the Palestinian negotiators on the issue, made this statement to the press:

> We ask that all archaeological activity in the West Bank be stopped. There is no reason to start excavations in land that will be turned over to us.[4]

In the first stage of autonomy in the Jericho region, when Prime Minister Rabin had promised not to extend control to the Dead Sea, he was referring to the water of the Dead Sea, not the archaeological site of Qumran. This can be seen in a comment made by his successor, acting Prime Minister Shimon Perez. Gary Collett, who is assisting Dr. James Strange in an excavation of the Qumran plateau (see chapter 17), appealed to Perez's office in the summer of 1995 about concerns over the possibility that Israel might give up the Qumran site. Collett reports that Perez's indignant reply was: "Let the Arabs have it!" While Perez's personal prejudice may not have made policy, the Dead Sea caves region, and perhaps the Scrolls themselves, remain as part of the many demands of the Palestinians for any promise of "peace" with Israel. Even if the Likud Party Prime Minister Benjamin Netanyahu refuses to give up more land for peace (in contrast to the policy of the previous Labor Party government), the prospect for a "Palestinian peace" will still depend on future negotiations that include the region in which Qumran and the Scroll caves are located.

Some people have felt that the site of Khirbet Qumran is secure despite the political situation because it was annexed by an Israeli settlement—Kibbutz Qalya. Rabin had promised that this kibbutz would not be included in an expansion of autonomy because it was originally established next to the Qumran site with the understanding that the entire area adjacent to the site was part of the kibbutz property. According to a representative from Kibbutz Qalya, legal ownership for the kibbutz goes back to 1937, well before the 1947 partition agreements. The kibbutz contends that in 1952–1953, when Jordan was offered the opportunity to annex the area to its own lands, the Jordanian government turned it down. Therefore, according to the kibbutz, the Palestinians cannot exert any legal claim to the area. The people at the kibbutz stated emphatically, "There will not be a giving at all of this area!"

However, the establishment of Palestinian "legal rights" has not necessarily been a deciding factor in other areas that have already been turned over to Palestinian control. If the deciding factor is the attitude of an Israeli government that may be pressured to submit to a plan for peace at any price, then the kibbutz may have reason for future concern.

## Is Palestinian Control Desirable?

Many people are concerned about what might happen if Palestine gains control of the archaeological sites in the Dead Sea region. Would the Palestinians assume archaeological responsibility for the area and send trained Palestinian archaeologists, as well as allow other qualified archaeologists, to excavate new sites? According to John Strugnell, the former editor-in-chief of the Dead Sea Publication Team, the Palestinians would be much preferred:

> Jordan . . . that's where the Scrolls were found; the Jordanian
> government collected the Scrolls. I worked with the Jordanians
> and I got to know and like them. I dislike Israel as an occupier
> of that part of Jordan.[5]

It is true that the Jordanian Department of Antiquities, which once administered the Rockefeller Museum (then the Palestine Archaeological Museum), initially helped to purchase some of the Scrolls, and cared for and provided oversight for their preservation. However, the Palestinians do not claim to be Jordanians; otherwise they would have abandoned their refugee status long ago, claimed Jordanian citizenship, and moved to Jordan. Rather, they are in competition with Jordan over the control of religious sites, including the Dome of the Rock and Al 'Aqsa Mosque in East Jerusalem. Though the protection and regulation of these sites were officially committed to the Jordanian government by Israel under the Israeli/Jordanian Peace Accord, the Palestinians have never recognized it. In fact, to demonstrate their rejection of these arrangements, they installed their own rival Mufti to regulate religious activities for the Palestinian people at the holy places.

It is the Palestinians, not the Jordanians, who are demanding the transfer of all archaeological sites, remains, and related incidentals. If we claim that the Bedouin, who discovered most of the Scrolls, are Palestinian (which they are not—historically they have been an autonomous people and respect no territorial boundaries), the case for Palestinian archaeology is not strengthened. The Bedouins' interest in the Scrolls is purely commercial, and if Jordan was unable to control their illegal looting of the caves and sales of Scrolls on the black market, why should the Palestinian Authorities expect to do better? In fact, the Palestinian Authority is presently have a difficult time operating its "government" even in the areas it controls. Also, its primary interests are in working toward the establishment of a Palestinian State; there is no history of any scientific archaeological activity in any part of the country by the Palestinians. In fact, in Jerusalem, the *only* evidence of early Islamic occupation in the city (an Ummiyad administrative building) was excavated by the Israelis!

There is no doubt that if the Dead Sea region was given over to Palestinian control the Bedouin would continue their activities. According to Abu-Dahoud (Muhammed edh-Dhib), if the territory went under Palestinian control, he and other Bedouin would immediately return to searching the caves freely and selling their finds to whomever they wished. He said that was the policy they followed when the area was under Jordanian control. Under Israeli control (and supposedly under international law), it is illegal to excavate without an authorized permit, and even then, it is illegal to remove anything of archaeological significance from a site without government sanction. Israel has enforced this policy, and as a result, the Bedouin have feared the risks involved in searching for Scrolls. They prefer to dig for coins and pottery in Arab areas outside of

Israeli scrutiny. This raises a question, however: Wouldn't we find it beneficial if the Bedouin could look for Scrolls again?

## The Best Scenario

In the past when the Bedouin had the freedom to search for Scrolls, they usually sold their finds to Arab dealers who then sought the highest bidder they could find. In 1953 the then-Palestinian Archaeological Museum and Department of Archaeology in Jordan stressed that it was necessary for their government to buy all available manuscript fragments or they would be lost to the black market in Europe and the United States. However, as manuscripts continued to surface and be offered for sale through the Bedouin and various antiquities dealers (including Kando), the Jordanian government stated that it could not afford to purchase all of the fragments. So qualified academic institutions were asked to help sponsor manuscript fragment purchases. This was somewhat successful, but it is known that private collectors and investors also got their share of fragments.

Today, however, because of enormous sums that would be necessary to purchase Scroll fragments, it is unlikely that the Israeli government would be willing to fund many such purchases, even if they had assurance that the purchases would not cause a political incident (as has happened in the past). Also, because many academic institutions are faced with financial problems, they wouldn't be able to allocate sufficient funds to bid successfully at the bargaining table. Dr. Weston Fields, executive director of the Dead Sea Scrolls Foundation, has told me the Israel Antiquities Authority was offered an opportunity to buy an already-published Scroll fragment, but the asking price was so ridiculously high that they would not even consider it.

For these reasons, if additional Scrolls were allowed to enter the market, they would most likely never be seen by scholars, much less the public. Of course we could hope that a private philanthropist might sponsor Scroll purchases (as John Rockefeller once sponsored Scroll study for six years). But in the uncertain international political arena today, the best hope for the future of the Scrolls remains with the exercise of Israeli control. Only Israel regards the Scrolls as part of their biblical and historical heritage, and cherishes them as a national treasure of the Jewish people. Only with Israeli control of the excavations and finds can we be assured that future

Scroll discoveries will be handled properly and made available to scholars and all those who are interested in the secrets they contain.

## Could Fiction Become Fact?

Whether or not the present peace process is successful, the contention over boundaries in the Dead Sea region will continue to be part of the history of Arab/Israeli conflict, and perhaps of a greater global conflict to come (see Zechariah 12:2-3; 14:2). Archaeological excavation has proved to be a major source of contention between Muslim and Israeli authorities in Jerusalem.[6] In September of 1996, the fiercest conflict in decades broke out in Jerusalem and spread to Palestinian villages of the West Bank because the Hasmonean Tunnel, which runs beneath the Western Wall, was extended. In like manner, we can be certain that the Dead Sea Scrolls have the potential to become a major point of contention between negotiating parties in the Middle East. In fact, protests have been voiced over current Israeli excavations in search of undiscovered scrolls. What if an Israeli excavation in the near future revealed another cache of ancient Scrolls? What if a huge quantity of gold and silver—one of the treasures recorded in the *Copper Scroll*—was unearthed? Could not such discoveries generate a worldwide jealousy for Israel's newfound wealth? Four Scrolls once provoked Jordan to threaten a lawsuit against Israel, even in spite of Jordan's political denial of Israel's existence! What actions could future finds provoke ... especially in the unstable Middle East, where international recognition and regional security are paramount? Could the Scrolls become a significant part of a political agenda, turning today's fiction into tomorrow's fact? In such a world, and over such a treasure as the Dead Sea Scrolls, stranger things have happened.

# 20

# New Searches for Scrolls

*There is this common understanding that there's nothing else to find, that the Bedouin went everywhere, that finding hundreds of Scrolls in Qumran was a lot, and therefore that there are no more Scrolls in this region, and that there's nothing more that you can look for.*

—Hanan Eshel

*We have high hopes to find more manuscripts. If we are right, more manuscripts are to be found.*

—Magen Broshi

Over the past 50 years our world has witnessed the discovery of priceless, ancient Scrolls and the swell of controversies that surrounded the documents that were "suppressed" from scholars and a waiting public. Throughout this book I have shared the story of the Scrolls, and perhaps as we come closer to our final chapters, it's easy to get the impression

411

that there's no more of the story to be told. However, there may be many more chapters yet unwritten, for it's possible there are more Scrolls waiting to be discovered! In this chapter I want to consider whether more Scrolls have yet to be unearthed, and introduce you to excavations that have only recently made new discoveries and promise even greater finds for the future. Let's begin with the experts who challenge the assumption that there are no more Scrolls to be discovered.

## Are There Any More Scrolls?

For many years people assumed that there were no more Scrolls to be found. Israeli archaeologist Hanan Eshel, who defied this assumption to find Scrolls near Jericho in 1979 and 1993, explains the reasoning that was behind it:

> Between 1947 and 1965 more than 1,100 texts were found in the desert. The last ones were found at Masada in 1965. From 1965 onward new texts were not discovered although some [excavation] work was done. When I went to excavate a cave in Jericho people told me, look, there is nothing left to find in the Judean desert, everything was already found by the Bedouin and you're too late. The consensus was that the Bedouin took everything and the [supposed] proof was that between 1965 and 1986 nothing [substantial] had come into the antiquity market like it had between 1947 and 1956 (when the large Scrolls of Cave 11 were found). So, since nothing after 1965 had really surfaced, the assumption was that everything was already found.[1]

Why should the Bedouin stop bringing Scrolls for sale if indeed there were more Scrolls to be found? To understand this it is necessary to consider what happened when the last batch of Scrolls entered the market in the late 1950s and early 1960s. Hanan Eshel explains:

> At the end of the 50s the Bedouin started selling Scrolls in [Jordanian] Jerusalem that were said to come from an "unknown source." Everyone knew that this "unknown source" was somewhere on the other side of the border and that the Bedouin were crossing the border and looking for documents in the northern part of the Israeli side of the border, in an area [that was then part] of Egypt. [These places turned out to be] Wadi Seiyal (Nahal Se'elim) and Wadi Khabra (Nahal Hever) and other creeks near [Ein-]Gedi. At first the archaeological authorities came to the

army and told them to stop the Bedouin from crossing the border to do illegal excavations. However, the army decided it was much cheaper to send the archaeologists to find the documents than to patrol the borders and stop the Bedouin. So in 1960–1961 the army budgeted for four camps of scholars to excavate different caves in the Judean Desert. Those were Professor [Yohanan] Aharoni, [Pesach] Bar Adon, Professor [Nahman] Avigad, and [Yigael] Yadin.[2]

From Eshel's account we can see that the Bedouin's efforts ultimately served only to inform the Israelis of potential sites, and when they took over these sites, they cut out the entrepreneurial Bedouin who marketed the Scrolls (other Bedouin helped with the excavations). After my conversation with the Bedouin Muhammed edh-Dhib I learned that the Scroll market had apparently "dried up" because the Israelis had made it too risky and unprofitable to search the caves. The Bedouin who looted the caves had taken risks enough with the Jordanian authorities, but when Israel took control of the Dead Sea region in 1967 the Bedouin basically gave up and began digging for antiquities near Arab West Bank villages. To be sure some Scrolls did enter the antiquities black market after 1967, but antiquities dealers in Jerusalem and Bethlehem have told me that such sales have been rare.

### Operation Scroll

On November 14, 1993, the Israel Antiquities Authority, under the direction of Amir Drori, launched Operation Scroll. This operation was an official attempt to survey as much of the Qumran region and its caves as possible. It was prompted not only by the belief that more Scrolls were to be found, but also the concern that one of the terms in the peace process might include Palestinian autonomy over the Qumran area and thus limit future Israeli excavations.

During Operation Scroll, 20 teams of 200 workers were headed by 46 archaeologists. Hundreds of caves were surveyed; however, these were mostly uncollapsed caves that permitted easy access as well as caves that were known to have been previously plundered by the Bedouin. At the Qumran site itself an uncharacteristically rushed excavation made use of a backhoe to uncover parts of the community structure and dig exploratory pits at other places on the plateau. It was during this sweep of the caves that Hanan Eshel found his papyrus fragments dating from the Bar Kokhba

Revolt (more on that in a moment). Other finds included objects such as ancient weapons, pottery, coins, and even the entire skeleton of a Canaanite soldier still in his armor! At Qumran it was rumored that a silver bowl had been discovered, but no published reports have confirmed such a find.

Operation Scroll was criticized as an impediment to the peace process and as an unorthodox way to explore archaeological sites; however, it demonstrated that those at the highest levels of Israeli archaeology take seriously the possibility that more Scrolls remain to be found. To understand the potential for new discoveries in the Dead Sea region, it is important to consider not only the known documents that have been recovered, but also, if possible, the unknown documents that, in a fisherman's lingo, represent the "ones that got away"!

## The Scrolls That Got Away

There are accounts of Scrolls that were discovered, then lost again. In some cases these Scrolls were retrieved by Bedouin, but lost or destroyed in the process of retrieval or transport. In other cases they were sold to private collectors or investors and are considered "lost" simply because either their location or contents are unknown. In yet other cases, Scrolls and similar artifacts have been located but were considered irretrievable because of difficulties of one kind or another.

### Kando's Buried Treasure

Former Scroll Team member John Allegro tells a tale of Scrolls that were lost in 1948 by Kando, the Bedouins' merchant, even before they could be sold.[3] According to his report, large pieces of unknown Scrolls from Cave 1 were buried by Kando in his backyard garden. The reason, Allegro claims, is that Kando became frightened after being contacted by Professor Eleazar Sukenik in Bethlehem, who gave Kando an assessment of the Scrolls' age and worth. Because Sukenik was an archaeologist, Kando feared news would leak out that he had illegal antiquities from an illegal excavation. (Similar fears later motivated Kando to hide the *Temple Scroll* beneath the floorboards of his house and other Scroll fragments behind family pictures hanging in his brother's house.)

Kando apparently felt that burying the preserved fragments in the soil of his backyard would not harm them because the Bedouin had found the fragments in the dirt of Cave 1. The pieces stayed buried for about six months, then Kando went to retrieve his treasures. Instead of the finely preserved, light-colored parchment sheets he had buried, he found worthless gooey lumps. John Trevor, who first photographed the Scrolls of Cave 1, explains that when deteriorating parchment (the condition in which all the Scrolls have been found) is exposed to high humidity or excessive moisture, the leather becomes like glue. First the parchment changes to a deep amber-colored gelatinous mass, then to a gooey chocolate mess, then it gradually evaporates into thin air.[4] Kando had learned a lesson on how not to store a Scroll: the parched dust of Qumran caves is not the same as the warm, moist soil of a garden. Evidently he learned his lesson well, for when he later buried another Scroll—the *Temple Scroll*—he did it *indoors* (see chapter 2)!

### Muhammed's Secret Scroll

According to Muhammed edh-Dhib, there are other Scrolls waiting in other caves. For example, he reports that sometime around 1950, near 'Ein Feshkha, he found a leather Scroll in a cave high in the cliffs. He called this Scroll "a Scroll for blind people," because, as he described it, it could "be read with the fingers." Muhammed edh-Dhib tells what happened:

> We were working in this cave and found this leather Scroll for blind people. We wanted to take it out but the [Jordanian] soldiers shot at us and hit one of us in the leg, so we had to run away. But the place is still untouched and there's a lot still inside. But the government will not let us dig.[5]

As Muhammed's account reveals, he was unable to get the Scroll. According to the now 80-year old Bedouin, who has kept an eye on the site for decades, no one has yet attempted to excavate the cave since he was there over 45 years ago! In 1994 he attempted to reenter the cave with Drs. Weston Fields and Stephen Pfann. With full disclosure guaranteed to the Antiquities Authority, the threesome made the arduous climb to the cave. Unfortunately, due to fatigue, a problem with equipment, and other factors, the group was unable to adequately investigate the site. So we must continue to wonder: What was this document? Was it written in some form of ancient Braille, or was it an inscribed text similar to the *Copper Scroll?* Muhammed edh-Dhib has now agreed to take me to the cave, but has added a proviso: only if I can make the climb! If I do attempt to scale the cliffs with him in the near future, who knows what might await! Perhaps we will find Muhammed's "secret Scroll"!

## Skeletons and Scrolls

In 1953 some archaeological teams explored some caves that had been revealed by Bedouin who were selling Scrolls in Jerusalem. One of the teams came to a cave called the Cave of Horrors. It had been so named because of the dozens of skeletons of women and children that were found inside—apparently Jewish refugees killed by the Romans during the Bar Kokhba Revolt. This cave was high up in the limestone cliffs and could be reached only with the help of a 300-foot rope ladder. The roof of the cave had collapsed due to an earthquake, and huge boulders were piled 20 feet high and covered with centuries of dust and bat guano. Despite these obstacles the Bedouin had already been to the cave and recovered many artifacts, as evidenced by what they left behind: jar lids, broken pieces of pottery, and woven pieces of matting.[6]

As the team members explored further, they had to tunnel beneath the immovable boulders (from the collapsed roof) in order to get into the main section of the cave. It was obvious the Bedouin had already attempted this and failed. The dig's director, Professor Aharoni, instructed team member Baruch Safrai to squeeze between the fallen boulders and survey the scene. As he did he made an amazing discovery:

> When I had penetrated down to about the length of my body, I glimpsed by the light of the flashlight, pinned under the boulders, a human skeleton lying on its side with its arms and legs asprawl. The skeleton was clothed in a white robe. Around the waist was a rope belt, knotted in front. . . . I managed to reach the middle part of the skeleton. I pulled away the robe belt and part of the robe. . . . It was a moving moment for me.[7]

This was a truly sensational find, for the first-century Jewish historian Josephus had written that the initiates in the Essene Sect were given garments of that description (*Jewish Antiquities* 15.5,2; *Jewish War* 1.15,3). This was the first material evidence of such garments and a confirmation of Josephus' account.

After emerging from the rocks Safrai gave Professor Aharoni the robe and belt, which were safely stored in a padded cardboard box. However, at some point after that the box disappeared, and to this day no one knows what happened to its contents. Safrai, who made an unsuccessful search of the Antiquity Authority's storerooms in Jerusalem, can only speculate on the whereabouts of his finds:

> It may be that they never reached Jerusalem; I recall that one of the boxes containing finds, which was carried to our base camp at Ein-Gedi by the IDF [Israel Defense Forces] soldiers who were helping us, did not get there and was either lost, stolen or forgotten on the way.[8]

Safrai is convinced that in the place where he found the skeleton there must be Scrolls. Based on the position of the skeleton, he surmises that the Essene had been trapped during the earthquake and crushed by the falling rocks. Because it is known that these limestone caves were used only for storage, it is likely that Scrolls were hidden within and the sudden earthquake prevented any from being removed. In testimony of what might still remain, the cave has yielded several Scroll fragments written in both Greek and Hebrew script, including fragments of the *Dodekapropheton Scroll (8HevXIIgr)*.[9] Indeed, Scroll fragments have been found in other similar caves with collapsed roofs. Archaeologist Pesach Bar-Adon, who found some of these fragments, noted, "Perhaps the missing part of the complete Scroll is yet pinned under these rocks."[10]

Today we have the expertise and the equipment to remove the boulders and search beneath. All that is needed is the resolve to do it and financial support. Perhaps then marvelous new Scrolls will appear, and with them an Essene robed in white, still awaiting proper burial.

### Scrolls Still for Sale

At the beginning of this chapter I mentioned Operation Scroll, which as part of its mission swept through numerous Qumran caves the Bedouin had previously plundered—including caves dating to the Bar-Kokhba Revolt. What happened to the Scrolls the Bedouin may have found in those caves? Most likely they were sold in Jordan to private collectors or investors, or perhaps are in the hands of some Bedouin or merchant in hopes of getting a higher price. That such Scrolls exist and are not among those already known is much more than probable. When Yadin and others came to these caves they found fragments of several Scrolls at the entrances and exits of the caves. Apparently these were pieces that had broken or fallen off from the intact Scrolls when the Bedouin climbed out or departed from the caves. Two fragments were from the books of Psalms and

Numbers, complete books of which have never yet been discovered. So, perhaps these exist somewhere, but it is a somewhere we may never know.

Other interesting rumors of Scrolls and Scroll-related objects are also known. A friend told me that as late as the early 1980s he knew where he could still buy an original Scroll jar from an Old City antiquities dealer for a rather paltry sum (the one presently at Edmund Kando's shop is supposedly not for sale). In like manner, the former editor-in-chief of the Dead Sea Scrolls Publication Team, Professor John Strugnell, claimed that he knew of at least four Scrolls found by Bedouin that are in private hands and have never been publicly revealed:

> I've seen, with my own eyes, two. One of the two is a complete copy of the Book of Enoch.... [Lankester] Harding, on his death bed, told me he'd seen three, only one of which I've seen—so that makes four. These Scrolls, like the *Temple Scroll*, came from Cave 11.... The manuscripts are now somewhere in Jordan. Various people own them. Several of them have been sold to big bankers. They're investments for these people.... [But] they're being kept very carefully; no need to worry about them.[11]

I also have been told of a small fragment of a Bar Kokhba letter that is still held by Edmund Kando in a bank vault in Lebanon. He offered it to the Antiquities Authority for 10,000 dollars. They refused because Magen Broshi and Elisha Qimron had already published the text. My friend Weston Fields, who serves as the executive director of the Dead Sea Scrolls Foundation, purchased an unrolled piece of parchment, which looked like a small cigar, from an antiquities dealer in the Old City as late as 1993.[12] It had been brought in by a Bedouin the very same day. When unrolled at the Israel Museum under the supervision of Magen Broshi, it turned out to be blank. (According to Professor Strugnell, a number of blank, not-yet-used pieces were found at Qumran.) Other rumors involve a copy of the *Leviticus Scroll* somewhere in France, Scrolls held by private collectors such as a Baptist minister in Louisiana, and a report from a money changer in Jerusalem's Old City that he has "seen Scrolls." The sale of Scrolls, whether real or rumored, is a fascinating hope that there is more out there, but more wonderful still are the discoveries of new caves that may hold additional Scrolls.

## New Discoveries and New Caves

While the politicians in Jerusalem have occupied themselves with the success of the peace process, archaeologists from Jerusalem have occupied themselves with the search for new Scrolls. In 1996 new caves and new discoveries have yielded exciting finds that offer new insights and confirmations about the Qumran community. One of these excavations was directed by archaeologist Hanan Eshel. Among younger archaeologists he is somewhat of a maverick, believing he can find things in places that older archaeologists have long abandoned. From 1984–1993 he proved his abilities by recovering for the first time in decades new Scrolls and fragments from the Judean desert. He recounts his thoughts concerning this period in his own words:

> In 1979 the Society for the Protection of Nature in Israel established a center and started to do surveys in different caves. From then on more and more evidence gathered. They found a horde of coins in 1980 and another huge cave that I excavated in 1987 after the first excavation in Jericho. So I became their archaeologist and every time they found shards they showed them to me. In 1984 they found a wooden comb in a cave and I had a feeling that documents might be found there as well. And sure enough we did! It was the first time I was running my own excavation and I would have to say I was shocked. I sat there for a long time just looking at the document before I could tell the volunteers what to do—like bring me a brush and to do different things. A month later, I was excavating the terrace and I found five documents—four in half an hour.[13]

In 1993 Eshel was to again repeat his previous good fortune with Scroll discovery, but this time through an unorthodox method.

### Stepping on the Scrolls

Usually the conventional method of rope ladders, lights, and generators is employed in the search for Scrolls, as in Operation Scroll. But at other times an unconventional approach may work. Hanan Eshel, who found Scrolls as a result of his ingenious and carefully thought out approach, reports that such methods are not likely to be understood or acknowledged by others:

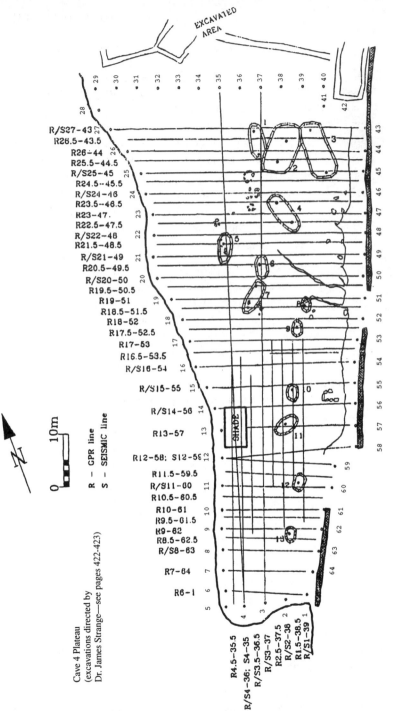

Qumran Geophysical Survey Location Map

Cave 4 Plateau
(excavations directed by
Dr. James Strange—see pages 422-423)

R — GPR line
S — SEISMIC line

0    10m

N

EXCAVATED AREA

R/S27-43
R26.5-43.5
R26-44
R25.5-44.5
R/S25-45
R24.5-45.5
R/S24-46
R23.5-46.5
R23-47.
R22.5-47.5
R/S22-48
R21.5-48.5
R/S21-49
R20.5-49.5
R/S20-50
R19.5-50.5
R19-51
R18.5-51.5
R18-52
R17.5-52.5
R17-53
R16.5-53.5
R/S16-54

R/S15-55

R/S14-56

R13-57

R12-58; S12-59

R11.5-59.5
R/S11-60
R10.5-60.5
R10-61
R9.5-61.5
R9-62
R8.5-62.5
R/S8-63

R7-64

R6-1

R4.5-35.5
R/S4-36; S4-35
R/S3.5-36.5
R/S3-37
R2.5-37.5
R/S2-38
R1.5-38.5
R/S1-39

SHADE

I was asked in 1993 to excavate in Jericho before Jericho was handed over to the Palestinians. I said I wanted to dig underneath the cave, so I was asked, "Do you need a generator and lights?" I said, "No, I don't need those things." Then they said, "Well, do you need ropes and things like that?" And I again said, "No; I'm going to excavate on a trail that hikers have walked over all the time [at least since 1967] just opposite to the monastery of Qarantal [Temptation]." Everybody thought I was crazy. They said, "You're not going to find anything in daylight and without ropes; there's no chance of finding anything!" But when I excavated, I found 15 documents from the Bar Kokhba Revolt [A.D. 132–135] just lying there underneath the cave!

The irony of discovery is sometimes amusing. While others had searched the caves high above the trail and found nothing. Eshel had literally found the Scrolls underfoot. Those who had ascended to the caves had, in fact, been stepping on the Scrolls as they did! Eshel described the reasoning that led him to the discovery and shares how he felt when Scrolls were first found:

> It took me a while to understand that I had found an upside down stratigraphy in the cave I had excavated in 1986. This meant that I had found documents from the third century B.C. lying above documents from the second century A.D. So I knew that somebody was changing the stratigraphy and had built up this [artificial] terrace in which older things were on top of newer things. It took me a while to figure out that the monks [from the monastery] who came and settled in the cave in the fourteenth century A.D. had just thrown dirt out [of the caves during housecleaning] and that if I looked underneath I might find something. I started to dig very slowly one Sunday and found some fragments. But I had to interrupt the excavation for a week to go [back to Jerusalem and] teach. On Friday I returned and found seven more documents. Again it was a very slow process and we [Eshel and his volunteers] knew that Shabbat [the Sabbath day] was approaching and it was getting late [to return home to Jerusalem]. But every time I tried to finish the dig we'd find more documents that were rolled up and fragments. Those days were very, very exciting!

## Other Monasteries ... Other Scrolls?

Monasteries like the Qarantal monastery, whose ancient monks were so helpful to Eshel, began cropping up in the Judean desert at the very beginning of the monastic movement. Around A.D. 340 the monastery of Douka was founded near Jericho by Chariton, the father of Judean desert monasticism. Today, the remains of more than 60 monasteries, mostly from the Byzantine period (fourth through seventh centuries A.D.), have been discovered by Israeli archaeologists.[14] These monks, who frequently lived in isolation, took advantage of the abundant caves that dot the limestone cliffs of the desert. Dr. Eshel's excavations have shown that when these monks cleaned these caves for rehabitation they sometimes came upon Dead Sea Scroll manuscripts. Some of the Scrolls might have been preserved, but the evidence is that they were simply swept out the cave doors as debris. At Saint Catherine monastery, located at the foot of Jebel Musa (the traditional Mount Sinai), they used ancient manuscripts as fuel to keep the monks warm during the winter![15] From this same monastery, Constantine Tishendorf (who was at Saint Catherine's from 1844 to 1859) recovered the famous fourth-century Greek manuscript containing most of the Old Testament (the Septuagint) and the New Testament—a document now known as the Codex Sinaiticus.[16] In 1975 a fire at the monastery forced the monks to open up a room abandoned for over a thousand years. In that room they discovered over 4,000 ancient manuscripts![17] In December of 1993 more than 50 Greek papyrus Scrolls some 1,400 years old were discovered beside the ruins of a Byzantine church in the Jordanian city of Petra (far south of the Dead Sea).[18]

## 1996 Qumran Plateau Excavation

A report to the Israeli Antiquities Authority in 1990 recommended excavation of the Qumran plateau opposite Cave 4.[19] The report was based on the results of molecular frequency technology applied to the site and an analysis of readings conducted from 1988–1990, which indicated significant anomalies (unnatural occurrences) beneath the ridge and adjacent to a small shelter erected for tourists. Those who examined the readings speculated that the anomalies were tunnels or collapsed caves, and that the objects in these areas were pottery jars, Scrolls, an urn, animal ashes, metals, and gemstones.[20] More conjectural was their appendix to the report, which proposed an identification of Qumran with the Wadi ha-Kippah ("wadi of the dome") mentioned in the *Copper Scroll*. The report argued that *kippah*, in Hebrew, can mean "vault," "arch," or "doorway," and that through its Aramaic nominative form as *qimron* the site of Qumran received its name.[21] The report also suggested that the marl terraces at the end of the wadi bore resemblances to the topography of Jerusalem, that Caves 4–5 symbolized aspects of the First and Second Temples, and that many of these and other details also suggested a connection with the *Copper Scroll*. In 1992 a further report issued by two scientists at Tel-Aviv University's Department of Geophysics and Planetary Sciences confirmed the presence of anomalies at the site.[22] Employing ground-penetrating radar and seismic reflection profiles, their geophysical investigation recommended more specific targets for excavation.

In the summer of 1993 exploratory trenches were made in one of the primary target areas; however, the work was stopped by Yitzhak Magen of the Antiquities Authority on the basis of technicalities. Later, in the winter of 1993–1994, the Antiquities Authority's Operation Scroll teams excavated some of the shallower anomalies and found a number of pits lined with river rocks and plastered with lime. These pits were probably used to store grains or other items. As far as is known, these pits were empty, but one excavator involved in Operation Scroll reported to me (unofficially) the discovery of a silver bowl that was said to have been made near these pits. In the spring of 1994, Dr. James Strange, who has directed the ongoing excavations at Sepphoris (in the Galilee), began formal excavations at the site.[23] Infrared TIMS Atlas scans, done by helicopter, were conducted to pinpoint the best location for a drilling probe. The actual drilling took place over the summer of 1995 and an empty space was found approximately 53 feet below ground level (see photo section). A small remote camera was lowered through the drill hole for viewing, but debris in the casing blocked the effort before the space was reached. In the fall of 1995, Resistosity tests gave confirmed readings of what appeared to be a cavern.

### Extraordinary New Finds

In the winter of 1995–1996 an excavation team reached the 53-foot level and realized that the readings they were using had taken them to a large fissure about 20 feet north of the expected cavern. Even so, by February of 1996 the excavation had revealed some unprecedented finds for the Qumran plateau. Among these were a pot handle stamped with the word *ha-melek* ("the king"), several pieces of Persian pottery including several perfume bottles, and two ostraca, one with scribal practice and another with 16 lines of Hebrew text including the word *Yahad* and a reference to the First Revolt. The Persian finds may provide the first archaeological evidence of a settlement at Qumran during the Persian period, which, in turn, could lend support to the Babylonian theory of origin. The team has since re-filed their excavation and plans to begin excavating again at the site they now feel confident will lead them to their hidden cavern. At the same time, and very close by, two other archaeologists were busy excavating newly discovered caves at Qumran.

## New Caves Found at Qumran

In the fall of 1995 newspapers announced to the public that four new caves had been discovered at Qumran and that plans were underway to excavate them beginning in December of 1995. There was, of course, immediate excitement over the news, and the location of the caves was said to be a carefully guarded secret. This news was released to the media through Vendyl Jones, who had originally planned to supply volunteers for the project (see chapter 14). The excavation itself was to be directed by Hanan Eshel and Magen Broshi, both veteran Israeli archaeologists and Scroll scholars. In November of 1995 I visited the site of the caves and spoke with the excavators about their plans and expectations for the dig. Hanan Eshel describes the site:

> The caves are somewhat hidden although they're very close to the site [of Qumran]. They're below the plateau, so nobody has noticed their existence. I found these caves because I went looking for trails that led from [nearby] Qumran. [At these four caves] nice trails lead to each cave. This proves that these are artificial caves just like Cave 4.[24]

Eshel was able to follow the trails from the settlement to the caves because the trails were well preserved. Many of these ancient trails, however, have been obliterated by army maneuvers conducted in the area. Magen Broshi provides additional details about these tracks:

> The tracks that led into these caves are preserved intact in the desert for thousands of years, unless they are disturbed by something like a tank riding over them. There were also vents in the caves, which were used [for air flow] before the invention of air conditioning. These showed us that these caves were once inhabited, which indicates there is a good possibility that these

caves once served the [Qumran] community. And [if so], these caves should contain manuscripts.[25]

Eshel expected only to find fragments, as he did in other locations. He said they would "probably be like what was found in Cave 8. If we find one piece, a nice cream [colored] one, I'll be very glad." Broshi, however, was more confident and said, "They don't have to be fragmentary. The ones he [Eshel] found were in caves that had been vandalized, but not every cave has been vandalized." As Eshel carefully examined the four caves, he found that one had been at least partially excavated by Bedouin. Eshel does not know what the Bedouin found, but among the debris they discarded from their dig he found pottery from the Second Temple period.

By January of 1996, Eshel, Broshi, and a crew of about 200 volunteers had excavated a total of nine caves. Three of the caves confirmed their belief that the caves had been inhabited by members of the Qumran Sect. Inside they found an assemblage of domestic pottery—bowls, cups, cooking pots, and storage jars—and they also found coins (the latest dating from the second year of the Jewish revolt against Rome (circa A.D. 67).[26] The next month (the last for the excavation) they had also explored two additional caves that had not been entered for over 1,000 years due to collapsed roofs. Did they find any Scrolls? They aren't sure. They did find light-colored pieces of parchment, but upon closer examination they found that the pieces had no sewing marks (as Scrolls usually do), nor any discernible signs of writing. These caves had signs of animal activity, so it is possible that the pieces of parchment may have been brought by animals from another place. Before ruling out the possibility that these are Scroll fragments, the leather will be subjected to carbon 14 testing to determine the age and to infrared photography with the hopes that some script might yet appear.

What were Eshel's thoughts about the dig?

> I wanted to excavate these caves because I happened to find things in 1986 and in 1993. It was a way of proving that if you work there is a chance you will find something. There is no rule about this. In 1987 I excavated in a huge cave, and all I found were two coins. There were no organic materials there [like Scrolls] because of the humidity. In 1990 I went to excavate in another huge cave from which I knew Bedouin had taken out at least two documents, and all I found there was one small fragment. But every time you go out and excavate a cave or a site

> you will find some important artifacts. It happened to me twice
> after people said, "Everything is gone, the Bedouin have exca-
> vated everywhere, and there's no chance to find new things!"[27]

And Eshel's team did find new things. For one, they uncovered near
their site a broad circle of stones which must have marked or secured the
location of tents. Eshel believes that these patterns of stones may finally
help locate the Qumranite residences, which up to now have been a mystery. He conjectures that the Sect would have lived in these caves during
the summer, when relief from the intense heat and protection from mos-
quitoes was most needed, but might have left the caves during winter's
rainy season because the chalky marl formations were subject to collapse (a danger Eshel's own crew faced on the dig). During the winter,
the members of the community most likely pitched their tents outside for
safety.

Another find made by Eshel's team has given new support for the
generally accepted belief that the Qumran site and Caves 1 and 11 (in the
limestone cliffs a mile to the north) were connected. Eshel's team identified the main trail between these sites just west of the present-day path
used by the Bedouin. The trail's age was established by the discovery of
60 nails (from Roman boots) and two coins from the Hasmonean period.[28]
In addition, they found clay oil lamps in every one of the new caves, which
is evidence, they say, that the Sect members borrowed Scrolls from the
main library and took them "home" for study. This, Eshel noted, gives
confirmation to the statement in the sectarian Scrolls that members were
required "to study one-third of the night."[29]

> [From the beginning] I have said that even if I don't find any
> new documents in Qumran it's still important to know where
> these people lived and how they lived. Finding new artificial
> caves that were carved by these people is very important.[30]

The new caves excavated by Eshel, because of their signs of habitation and their connection to the northern cave site, are important on a very
basic level: They add weight to the original theory that Khirbet Qumran
was the main site for the Sect and that the Scrolls were indeed their possessions. Moreover, based on their discoveries, Eshel and Broshi believe
they can reconstruct what the Sect members' daily routine might have
been like:

> Each morning ... the members of the Sect streamed out of the caves into the Qumran compound, where they prayed together facing east towards the sun rising over the mountains of Moab, their backs to Jerusalem, whose priestly guidance they rejected. Then each man turned to his assigned work. In the afternoon the members and novices immersed themselves in ritual baths and gathered for their communal meal. When they returned to their dwellings, it was not to sleep [but to study].[31]

Eshel has announced that his excavations will continue (next in the limestone caves north of Cave 3). Perhaps this in itself is the accomplishment of a goal. As Eshel said after one of his earlier discoveries:

> We have shown that it is still possible to find written documents in the caves of the Judean desert. It is our hope that the survey, exploration, and excavation of these caves will continue and that new discoveries will continue to be unearthed.[32]

## New Discoveries in Old Scrolls

While new discoveries of old Scrolls have not yet been made, new discoveries *in* old Scrolls are yet another story. By that I mean new discoveries in Scrolls which have already been unearthed. A number of Scrolls and fragments have been unreadable because of severe deterioration, and hence, for all practical purposes, "lost" to scholars. Some of the greatest finds in archaeology have come from already-discovered texts, such as the thousands of undeciphered cuneiform tablets in the basement of the British Museum, and it's possible that within the unread Scroll fragments we will find answers to our questions about the Dead Sea Sect. New advances in technology are now making it possible for us to unveil the secrets written on these formerly unreadable texts.

### Seeing the Unseen Scroll

One of the most difficult problems that scholars have encountered while working on the Dead Sea Scrolls is unreadable text. Parchment that has been heavily damaged or darkened from exposure to humidity usually cannot be read. Other problems include pieces that are stuck together (on top of one another), or script that has been written over or washed off. For many years, if a Scroll fragment had any of these problems, it had to be relegated to the unreadable category and the translation of the text marked with a *lacunae* [ . . . ] indicating missing or unknown letters or words.

Yet another problem has been Scrolls that, because of their poor condition, could not be photographed. Taking pictures of the Scrolls has enabled scholars to more effectively see and study the script written on the parchments. In fact, photographs of the Scrolls, and especially of the fragments, are usually easier to read than the originals.

For several decades, then, some Scrolls and fragments could not be read because the proper technology had yet to be developed.

## Multispectral Imaging

In 1993 a consortium of scholars from the Ancient Biblical Manuscript Center in Claremont, California, the West Semitic Research, and the Jet Propulsion Laboratory in Pasadena, California, came together to test a new form of infrared photography called multispectral imaging (MSI). This kind of imaging was originally designed for satellites and invented for espionage purposes. (Isn't it ironic that what was first used by spies to unmask a government's secrets is now used by scholars to help reveal God's Scriptures!) This technology enables us to sharpen contrasts between different parts of an image through the means of computer enhancement. Because each part of an image has its own unique spectral signature, these can be manipulated to make the script appear much darker and the parchment much lighter, even if those variables appear in the reverse to the naked eye. This gives us the ability to read text legibly down through several layers of parchment even though they are still stuck together (see photo section).

Multispectral imaging had a role in one of the more exciting Scroll discoveries in recent years. Dr. Weston Fields, executive director of the Dead Sea Scrolls Foundation, tells us about this:

> We have an example of what multispectral imaging can do in the book of Genesis. There was a manuscript fragment from Cave 4 known as the *Genesis Apocryphon b* (*4QGen B*), whose text was almost completely illegible. The work on the *4QGen B* manuscript was performed by Dr. Greg Bearman of the Jet Propulsion Laboratory in Pasadena, California, and Dr. Bruce Zuckerman of the University of Southern California. They came to Jerusalem and worked on a number of manuscripts, one of which was *4QGen B*. There were already infrared photographs of the text which were better than the dark ones, almost impossible to read, but now the text has been fully illuminated by the multispectral imaging technique.[33]

Newer imaging methods have also been used to read formerly unreadable letters on the famous *Copper Scroll*. As we learned earlier, when the *Copper Scroll* was first discovered, it was in two separate rolls. Because the copper was brittle, these two Scroll parts could not be unrolled for years. In fact, in order to read their complete texts, Scroll specialists had to cut them into strips. However, when the saw blade cut through the metal the edges became rounded and the letters distorted (see photo section). Therefore, whenever scholars attempted to reconstruct the text (the most recent effort being made by Dr. Kyle McCarter), these unreadable parts required educated guesswork. Today a new computer program has been designed that will actually "unwrap" the rounded edges of the Scroll, making it possible at last to clearly read the distorted letters.

## My Unwritten Story

It is now time to tell my own story. In the fall of 1995 I explored an unopened cave in the cliffs near 'Ein Feshkha at a slightly lower elevation than Cave 1. This was a large cave with a collapsed ceiling—damaged by an earthquake sometime in antiquity. An initial probe at the cave entrance (by scratching the sand with a pen knife) produced several pieces of a Roman cooking pot (a rim and body fragments). This provided initial proof that the cave had once been used as a dwelling place some time during the Second Temple period. Scratching a little deeper, about six inches, a small fragment of papyrus was unearthed, about an inch square and without any visible writing. No further attempt was made to dig because I had not yet applied for a survey permit, but the cave has been marked for later investigation.

Could this piece of papyrus have been part of a larger Scroll whose fragments are still buried beneath the sand? Or, like in the recent find of Hanan Eshel, could this cave have been reused—before its collapse and after Scrolls were hidden inside—with my piece of papyrus and potsherds representing scraps that were swept outside the entrance? No one can say. Yet my brief encounter has personally reinforced my conviction that there are more Scrolls to be discovered, and with them, a story yet unwritten. Presently I am pursuing an application for a permit with the Israeli Antiquities Authority. If all goes well, perhaps I may be able to join with those who strive to bring from the dust of the Judean desert new wonders for the world. It is a story I cannot wait to write!

# 21

# LESSONS FROM THE SCROLLS

*In their own time, the people of the Scrolls were unable to bring about the reign of the messiah and the establishment of the Kingdom of God. Yet in the hundreds of documents they left behind, in their hope for a world renewed by righteousness and divine order, the forgotten, radical message of the Dead Sea Scrolls—even today—lives on.*[1]

—Neil Asher Silberman

Years ago Hebrew University professor David Flusser, one of the leading experts on the relationship between first-century Judaism and Christianity, delivered a series of lectures on Israeli radio which were later published as *The Spiritual History of the Dead Sea Sect*. When he introduced his lectures, he addressed his readers about the need to measure their own lives by the life of the Sect:

> The Essene Sect was one of the strangest phenomena in Jewish history, and in the history of all mankind. . . . My main intention

431

[is] to introduce the reader to the Essenes themselves so that he can tackle the challenge of Essene ideology in the light of his own beliefs. . . . If the reader finds Essene thought limited, perhaps he will discover that his own beliefs also have limitations and unsubstantiated assumptions, and that his own philosophy and expectations, like those of the Essenes, are also "castles in the air." At any rate, it is worthwhile for the modern reader to ask himself whether he himself, like the Essenes, is not yearning for a better world, whether he thinks it a bad thing to "abstain from all evil, and hold fast to all good, that they may practice truth, righteousness and justice upon the earth" (*The Community Rule* 1:4-6).[2]

With our study of the Scrolls completed, it is both practical and profitable, as Dr. Flusser has urged, for us to consider what we can derive from the witness of the Scrolls. We will surely be poorer for having searched out their secrets if we do not seek to apply some of the lessons we can learn to our lives.

When we reflect on the Dead Sea Sect, we find that there is both much to commend and to condemn. Their devotion to God, Scripture, spirit-inspired interpretation, a prophetic hope, self-abnegation, and personal purity are all commendable. Their involvement with mysticism and tendencies toward prognostication, isolationism, and legalism are not. Yet seeing both the Sect's lighter and darker sides enables us to see our lives realistically, for we, too, have natures prone to serve and to sin (Romans 7:21). Let's look, then, at the lessons we can learn.

## The Lesson of the Dead Sea Setting

When tourists visit the Dead Sea region, every tour guide worth his salt (no pun intended) explains the spiritual analogy of the Dead Sea: The Dead Sea is called the *Dead* Sea because it *takes out* but does *not give back*. The fresh waters flowing down from Mount Hermon to the north (see Psalm 133:3), mixed with those from the Kinnert (Sea of Galilee), flow via the Jordan River and empty into the Dead Sea. But because the Dead Sea has no outlet, these once-living waters become stagnant and unable to support life.

In like manner, the Qumran Sect, which chose to live on the Dead Sea's shores, opened a secret society without an outlet. They took in only the purest of priestly volunteers, who then were trained in their exclusive doctrines. Every other spiritual center was considered defiled—the holy city of Jerusalem, the Temple, its priests, and synagogues. Because the community members did not want to defile themselves by contact with outside contamination, they restricted their fellowship. They may not have placed a sign on their clubhouse door that read "Members only," but their exclusivism was understood by all, for the historian Josephus records it as their most famous trait.

This isolationism was reinforced in the lives of the Sect members each day. Before entering the community from the outside they had to ritually purify themselves in the "living waters of the *miqveh*, and don white linen robes that symbolized their separate identity. Furthermore, the food they ate while within the compound had to come from their community kitchen. Other Jewish people outside the Sect also wore observant dress and ate kosher food, but the Sect's clothing and dietary codes were much more strict. Also, Sect members didn't see themselves as simply splitting theological hairs with other Jewish people; they believed they were to *hate* those outsiders whom they considered "the Sons of Darkness."

The Sect members kept to themselves, wrote their words of wisdom, and then hid them from the world in caves. Only by accident (if such is allowable in a God-governed universe) did we discover these ancient writings and records of the community's ways. The Qumran Sect indeed preserved for us ancient copies of the Scriptures, but they kept them buried from the sight of man for 2,000 years. Like the Dead Sea, they took in much, and like the Dead Sea, they would have returned nothing had it not been for the avarice of Bedouin or the diligence of scholars. As "the Sons of Light" they removed themselves far from "the Sons of Darkness"; evidently they had forgotten that the basic purpose of light is to illuminate the dark. Such is only possible when light is taken to those places where darkness dwells.

In bold relief stood the early Jewish believers in Jesus who took their truth to the streets and let their light shine to the world. They poured out their faith and themselves into the empty cup of a dying humanity. And though their community and its original copies of the Scriptures eventually crumbled into dust, their living Word was passed on from generation to generation and from nation to nation. The copies of the Scriptures they preached were not preserved against time in jars, but were continually copied and recopied so that they could be shared with the world. For 2,000 years, it has been the preserving force of civilization. There have, of course, been times throughout those millennia when those who professed to be Christians seemed to be anything but. At such times they behaved more like the Sect of the Scrolls in its spirit of hate that was alien to the spirit of Jesus. His life and words were never hid from others, and He stated the attitude we should have about sharing with others when He said, "From everyone who has been given much shall much be required; and to whom they entrusted much, of him they will ask all the more" (Luke 12:48).

What are you doing with what has been entrusted to you? Have you bottled up the truth and reserved it for your own private circle of friends? Have you kept secure to yourself what others have labored to pass on to you? To us has been handed the heritage of faith, which must first be seen by our families and then committed to faithful men who will teach others also (2 Timothy 2:2). Only as we carry our light into the darkness will our message be preserved for the future (see Philippians 2:15-16).

Though the Sect's isolationist lifestyle serves as a negative warning, its intent to preserve purity offers a positive witness.

## The Lesson of Uncompromised Living

The writers of the Scrolls documented for us the problem of a split in world Jewry over the question of the Jewish people's purpose in the land of Israel. This deep division is a practical reality today in the land of Israel, as reflected by the May 1996 election for the prime minister and the peace process, in which each candidate, holding opposite platforms, received almost identical numbers of votes. In separate articles in an issue of *The Jerusalem Report* magazine,[3] two opposing authors epitomized this division, as the editor described it, between those who live for "the coming redemption" and those who live for "the age of normalcy." One of the authors, a rabbi in an orthodox settlement and the head of a Temple restoration group (the Ateret Cohanim Yeshiva) argued with the biblical prophets that the relationship between Israel and the Land is like that of a bride and groom (see Isaiah 62:4-5). Such a union will not allow the Land (the bride) to be shared with others without being destroyed in the process. He defended the position that "it is permitted to fight against tearing Judea and Samaria from the land of Israel—as long as we do not damage the unity of the people of Israel."[4]

The other author, the editor-in-chief of one of Israel's leading newspapers, *Ha'aretz*, spoke humanistically about living in a post-Zionist era where the process of peace has negated the necessity for a multiplied

Jewish presence and Israel is able to become like the other nations at last. Hence, he saw no reason why the law of return should not be abolished and Israel should not adjust to "maintaining a cultural dialogue, based on equal standing, with other Jewish centers in the world."[5]

For both of these authors there exists the same problem of compromise. For the orthodox rabbi, the important issue is maintaining the Israeli people's unity. But can real unity be maintained without unanimity, especially in matters of survival and destiny? If it is the unity of "the people of Israel" that needs to be preserved, then there must be agreement about who constitutes these people. After all, at one time Reformed Jews and the Ethiopian Jews (Falasha) were not considered "the people of Israel." Today, Jewish people who believe in Jesus the Jew are not accepted as "the people of Israel." Since the assassination of Prime Minister Rabin by a member of the Jewish religious right, the Israeli media has asked whether such groups (classified as "Messianic Jews")—one of whom is the rabbi quoted above, should be considered among "the people of Israel." The rabbi, then, is left with a problematic choice: To preserve unity he must compromise peace, or to attain peace he must compromise unity.

For the newspaper editor, the problem is a compromise of that distinctiveness upon which hangs the whole question of Israel's right to exist as a state. If the land of Israel is not a defining factor for the Jewish people, then why should any Jew ever immigrate there again? But if, as the rabbi's metaphor suggests, they are wedded together, there can never be a post-Zionist era in which Jews live comfortably outside the Land.

The Israelis who separated themselves at Qumran may have been wiser than today's religious Jews, who attempt to wage a war of qualifications against a secular government that has no authoritative standards, or today's secularist Jews, who believe they can make peace with an Arab government supported by an anti-Semitic international community. The "people of Israel" at Qumran called themselves the *Yahad* ("union") because they recognized that their unity could be maintained by sharing unanimous convictions. Had they sought unity with their fellow Jews, they would have had to tolerate compromise. Had they considered Hellenism "normal," as did so many of their assimilated and collaborationist brethren, they would have had to trash their biblical concept of "remnant" as well as their place in history. They knew that if they were going to fulfill their calling to be "Sons of Light," they could not be eclipsed by the darkness.

In the same way the early Jewish-Christian community was warned by its leaders: "Do not be bound together with unbelievers; for what partnership have righteousness and lawlessness, or what fellowship has light with darkness?... 'Come out from their midst and be separate,' says the Lord" (2 Corinthians 6:14,17; cf. Isaiah 52:11). The Dead Sea Sect held fast to the faith of their fathers and dared to live for the promise of a greater day for Israel, when righteousness would reign in the Land and all the nations would be unified under God. Such a hope, though considered idealistic and doomed to defeat in a day of darkness, is the only hope that truly unites and will ultimately bring the elusive peace that Israel has sought.

Have we as Christians compromised our spirituality by trying to straddle the fence between two different worlds? Are our choices controlled by what's going on around us—doing what is popular rather than what is pure? We should care *less* what *others* think because we care *much* about what *Christ* thinks! Though we must reach out from our place of preserved purity to the world of the defiled, we must not compromise our doctrine, our convictions, our values, or our character in the process. It is only as we remain pure that we can continue to offer what others don't have. In this we have no choice, but a commandment: "Like the Holy One who called you, be holy yourselves also in all your behavior" (1 Peter 1:15).

We are to apply the Scriptures to our times and live in its light however dark our age. This requires us to separate from the world so that we can continue to have a witness to the world.

## The Lesson of Failed Figures

One of the defining features of the Qumran Sect was its practice of setting dates for end-time events. The expectations created by this practice produced an imminent hope in them that strengthened their resolve to resist the religious and political changes taking place in Israel at the time. Seeing these changes as signs of the nearness of the age of redemption, they could take confidence that the wicked age in which they lived would soon be judged and righteousness restored. Their hope also produced a religious fervency that attracted others to their Sect and encouraged them to remain separated from establishment religion. However, their date-setting practices also set them up for disillusionment and disbelief when the passage of a specific date failed to produce the expected fulfillment. As a result, they testified that "for 20 years they groped like a blind man seeking his way." That's a long time to waste recovering from failed forecasts.

Those today who seek to rightly discern the signs of the times must learn the lesson of history: "It is not for you to know the times or epochs which the Father has fixed by His own authority" (Acts 1:7). Every year, well-meaning students of prophecy mail me charts of calculations and pages of predictions. Recently one person sent me a videotape, then a series of letters, and finally—on the week of fulfillment—a postcard warning me to hurry and warn others. When the expected date came and went another postcard arrived, correcting the previous calculations by one week. Then when this date also failed, another letter followed with an apology and . . . a reworked chart! Some people never seem to learn.

Date-setting always has brought disaster and doubt. This practice was strictly condemned by the Jewish rabbis in Israel's early post-Temple period. These ancient sages were justly concerned over the misapplication of prophecy. In their days, erroneous interpretation had provoked unfounded confidence in spurious messianic claimants and incited revolutionary movements that resulted in disastrous wars.[6] But the rabbis were also concerned for a more basic spiritual reason: The Jewish scholar Moses Maimonides (Rambam) said they were concerned that if a predicted time came and went without the expected fulfillment, then those who had insufficient faith would be induced to believe that the fulfillment would *never* come. Thus people would not only lose a predictable hope, but all hope!

Judaism has its share of failed predictions to prove the point: from Simon Bar Kokhba ("Son of a Star")—proclaimed "messiah" by Rabbi Akiva, but who died in battle in A.D. 132— to Shabbetai Zvi, the seventeenth-century Jewish "messiah" who converted to Islam! It was with great foresight, then, that when the rabbis began writing down their legal instructions in the Talmud, they wrote this warning:

> If you see that a man has prophesied the advent of the Messiah, know that he is engaged either in sorcery or in dealing with devils. . . . One has to say to such a man: "Do not talk in this manner. . . . Eventually he will be the laughing stock of the whole world."[7]

Yet, while the attempt to figure out the future is foolish, an imminent expectation of God fulfilling His promise to send the Messiah, restore Israel, and reign in righteousness is not only healthy but holy (see Romans 13:11-14; 1 Timothy 6:13-15; Titus 2:11-14; John 3:1-3). In fact, both

Jews and Gentiles were explicitly told to both pray and wait for the Messiah's coming and the restoration of Israel's hope (Acts 3:19-21; 1 Thessalonians 1:10). Many pastors and teachers today have resigned completely from the study of prophecy because they view it as too divisive or too difficult. In doing so they stifle the God-ordained means of stabilizing their flock's faith, anchoring them to the one sure hope in a hopeless age! To abuse the prophetic scriptures is surely wrong, but to avoid them is even more so!

Perhaps we should not judge the Qumran date-setters too harshly, for they lived before the New Testament admonitions were written warning against this practice. It does seem that the writers of the Scrolls, or at least their predecessors, eventually learned to leave the mysteries about the end times with God, although they may never have understood *why* all of their calculations had to fail. Jesus, like the prophets, told His disciples *what* would happen, but not precisely *when* (Matthew 24:3-44; Mark 13:2-37; Luke 22:8-36). The Teacher of the Qumran Sect had taken the opposite approach: He had taken the prophets' *what* and told the community *when*. Of course the Teacher did that to help Sect members reestablish their faith after previous calculations had failed. But in doing so, he set everyone up for an even greater fall from their now higher state of confidence.

By contrast, Jesus' purpose in denying His disciples information about dates was not to leave them in doubt, but to spur them to diligence (Matthew 24:44; Mark 13:37; Luke 22:36). Certain knowledge of the *when* can lead to complacency, but limited knowledge of the *when,* combined with a certainty of the *what,* can force a person to faith and faithfulness. When we focus on the *what* and not the *when*, we will wait with a firmer faith for the unknown—but undeniable—day of His appearing.

## The Lesson of a Committed Character

I have a Christian friend, Dr. Halvor Ronning, who has lived in Israel for most of his life. He is an accomplished scholar, teacher, tour guide, husband, and father. I asked him to draw upon all of his experiences and share a lesson he has learned from the people of the Scrolls (whom he regards as Essenes). And from these resources he has offered the following.

> I like to challenge my students with the question, "Are you an Essene or are you a Christian?" You may wonder why I ask a question like

that. It's because the two share similarities in their dedication to God. Yet I always encourage students to look not only at similarities when they are studying different groups in antiquity, but to look with equal honesty at both the differences and similarities. Take for instance, the Teacher of Righteousness, the leader of the Essene Sect. He took the members of the Sect down to live at the Dead Sea as far away as possible from the influence of a pagan Greek-Roman culture. His attitude toward other groups was one of hatred, and the Essenes even pronounced curses against them. But the character of Jesus, as we read about it in the New Testament, is dramatically different. It says that, "While we were yet sinners (in Essene terms, 'Sons of Darkness'), Christ died for us" (Romans 5:8).

We also read that Jesus said we are not to isolate ourselves and go off and live away from all wickedness, but to remain where we are in the world. Jesus encouraged His followers to live right in the midst of all these other groups and taught His followers how to relate to the dominant pagan culture: living in it, but not of it. And as we reflect on that I think we see what we are faced with in today's culture—what the Jewish people were faced with in terms of the powerful impact of the pagan Greek-Roman culture— the beauty of it, the attraction of it, its philosophy, its art, its military prowess, its political power, its hierarchy. These things divided the Jewish people into opposing factions: those who accepted it completely and collaborated with it to maintain their wealth and position; and those who rejected it totally (like the Zealots) and who went off in isolation (like the Essenes).

The different responses to the dominant pagan culture caused the groups to choose different geographical retreats: Caesarea for the Herodians, Masada for the Zealots, Jerusalem for the Sadducees, and Qumran for the Essenes. Each of these places likewise represented their style of life: assimilation, rebellion, collaboration, or isolation. To follow one of those groups was easy; the greater challenge was to follow the God of Israel right in the midst of the pagan culture and still maintain a purity. That is the challenge we see in the New Testament's call to be in the world but not of the world. How is it possible? Only by the filling of the Holy Spirit of the God of Israel. That is what enabled Jewish believers to withstand their pagan background.

So I ask you to ask yourself: "Am I an Essene or am I a Christian?" Am I living a lifestyle where I pull off alone by myself in order to keep to my own ideas and not be influenced by other people? Or, am I so controlled by the Holy Spirit that I can live in the midst of a world that doesn't share my values and still live with honor and respect for the

God of Israel . . . and let the biblical revelation speak to my life and to the lives of people around me?

The spirit of that ancient age still dominates our culture today, and the Scrolls have often been an instrument to reveal this in the lives of scholars and sensationalists, even with those who call themselves Christian. They have brought rancor in the ranks of the International Team, tempted normally committed scholars to shift their priorities from publishing the texts for the good of all to withholding the texts for the gain of reputation. They have been the source of knife fights (Muhammed edh-Dhib and Kando), espionage activites, international protests, and lawsuits. Yet, they were meant to reflect a quiet and contemplative society that put personal godliness over earthly gain. The sect of the Scrolls sought to retreat from their culture, while genuine Christians sought to resist it and, at the same time, attempted to rescue it. A commitment born not of sectarianism but of the Spirit is still the old path that leads to newness of life. Let us examine our lifestyles, as Dr. Ronning has urged, and commit ourselves to living within, but not comfortably with, this world, which needs our witness.

In closing our study of the Dead Sea Scrolls it is imperative that we conclude with a focus on faith. Many groups, like the Dead Sea Sect, *profess* it, but we must be certain for ourselves that we *possess* it. Do we have the reality of a living relationship?

## The Lesson of a Living Relationship

Some scholars—and quite a few popularists—who study the Scrolls have come to the conclusion that Christianity, and even Islam, originated at Qumran. As one writer said:

> Perhaps [the Christians in the West] will finally see that the real roots of their faith are out here in the desert, with these people, and that in the beginning, Christian, Muslim, and Jew were one.
> Would only that they had seen it sooner, our history might have been far less bloody.[8]

How wonderful it would be if we could prove that the three monotheistic religions, which have been at odds with one another since their inceptions, all once had a common root at Qumran. This is an understandable sentiment, but it is without historical support. However, there *is* a common heritage in these religions, and that is the Bible. Orthodox Christianity considers the Old and New Testaments—both essentially Jewish—as divine revelation and the source and sustenance of their faith. And despite its pagan origin, Islam also acknowledges the Old and New Testaments (albeit as inferior to the Koran). Therefore, the path to peace between Jew and Christian and Muslim and all other religions is not in the Scrolls but through the Scriptures.

Peace with God cannot come through searching the desert for the faith of Qumran. Although the people at Qumran considered themselves the sole remnant of true Israel, the elect of God, the pious ones, the "Sons of Light," and those who alone preserved the knowledge of God in proper sanctity, their supposedly special position did not produce the same settled confidence of relationship known and preached by the followers of Jesus. At Qumran, whoever uttered the Divine name YHWH (even inadvertently) was to be permanently separated from the council of the community (*1QS* 7:1,3,5,16; 8:24). By contrast, those who desired to believe in Jesus as Messiah and Lord were commanded to call upon the name of the Lord (YHWH) for salvation (Acts 2:21; Romans 10:13; Joel 2:32). This verse does not have in mind the same concern about verbal pronunciation reflected at Qumran; rather, this call upon the Lord's name is an internal expression of confidence that access to God can be obtained through simple faith.

As a side note to this lesson, I want to tell you about a letter I received from a businessman who attended one of my lectures on the Dead Sea Scrolls. He wrote that he came to the lectures because he was invited by a friend and he found the subject of interest. Apparently he had become an agnostic; perhaps he was a victim of that brand of Christianity that seeks to demythologize everything sacred in order to find something believable but in the process leaves nothing in which to believe. Perhaps he had heard another lecture in which a scholar spoke of the Bible as nothing more than an evolving cultural creation produced by social phenomenon. Whatever the cause of his darkness, he arrived at my lecture prepared to hear only the facts about ancient discoveries. What occurred was far different. Instead of finding his agnosticism unmoved by archaeology, he found his faith challenged to test the truthfulness of God's Word. For as he listened to how the Scrolls had amazingly confirmed the transmission of the Bible text down through the centuries, some debris of doubt—long lodged in his mind—was unsettled, and the light broke through to his darkness. He wrote that he left that meeting having trusted in the Lord whose Word was true!

Now I must admit that I am always astonished how God can take even our most incidental remarks and use them to affect a life in ways the most crafted sermon cannot—that under His control even a lecture on the Dead Sea Scrolls maybe more powerful than the persuasive preaching of the most skilled evangelist. Here, then, in this incredible contrast, is what was missing in the Qumranites' striving for salvation: the simple truth that God can work what man cannot. The writers of the Scrolls were the most disciplined, most scrupulous, most observant Jews of their day, but it was not these things that God most wanted. In one of the favored biblical texts of the community, the book of the prophet Habakkuk, we read these words: "Behold, as for the proud one, his soul is not right within him; but the righteous will live by his faith" (Habakkuk 2:4). But when we read the Sect's own commentary on this passage we find not faith, but works:

> See, [his soul within him] is conceited and does not give way. Its interpretation: they will double [persecution] upon them [and find no mercy] at being judged. Its interpretation concerns all observing the law in the House of Judah, whom God will free from punishment on account of their deeds and their loyalty to the Teacher of Righteousness (*1QHab* 7:15–8:3).

The correction for this misdirection of discipline and devotion can be read in the writings of another who, while not a member of the Sect, once shared their passion for perfection through works of the Law. He wrote, "Where then is boasting? It is excluded. By what kind of law? Of works? No, but by a law of faith. For we maintain that a man is justified by faith apart from works of the Law" (Roman 3:27-28). This man, once a member of the sect of the Pharisees, became through faith an apostle of Jesus the Messiah. In his own striving for salvation he had also been led to that text in Habakkuk, but through the route intended—the way of faith, as his own commentary on Habakkuk 2:4 reveals:

> I am not ashamed of the gospel, for it is the power of God for salvation to everyone who believes, to the Jew first and also to the Greek [Gentile]. For in it the righteousness of God is revealed from faith to faith; as it is written, "But the righteous man shall live by faith [Habakkuk 2:4]" (Romans 1:16-17).

Paul, like those who lived at Qumran in his time, had known of Jesus and His miracles, and like them, had been unwilling to consider His claims. But one day God pierced through the darkness he thought was light and his works gave way to faith. If Jesus was true, then His gospel was true, and through it was the fulfillment of Judaism and the assurance of Israel's prophetic hope (see Romans 2:17–5:11; 11:25-29; 15:8).

Friend, I don't know what compelled you to read this study on the secrets of the Scrolls. Perhaps like my businessman friend you have an interest in this subject and did not expect it to impose upon your conscience, but it has. There are many secrets yet to be searched out from the Scrolls, but there is no secret to a personal relationship with God through faith in Jesus the Messiah. You need only to turn from your own striving and come to rest in His salvation. He has done all the work necessary on the cross, where He died for your sins. Now all you need to do is to trust Him for what He has done. Will you do that? Will you come to live by faith as the prophet Habakkuk has encouraged us to do? If so, you will find for yourself that salvation which no Scroll can hold secret.

> *It is the glory of God*
> *to conceal a matter,*
> *But the glory of kings*
> *is to search out a matter.*
> —Proverbs 25:2

# Historical Overview
## of the Second Temple Period

B.C.

*(Timeline chart, read with years B.C. across the top from 550 down to 70)*

**Foreign Rulers over Israel**

- Persian Rulers
  - Cyrus
  - Darius 1
  - Xerxes 1 & Artaxerxes
- Greek Rulers
- Ptolemic Rulers
- Seleucid Rulers
  - Antiochus III
  - Antiochus IV Epiphanes
  - Demetrius I
  - Antiochus VII Sidetes

**National Rulers in Israel**

- Zerubbabel (Governor of Judah)
- Simon II
- Judas Maccabeus
- Jonathan
- Simon
- John Hyrcanus I
- Aristobulus
- Alexander Jannaeus
- Alexandra
- Aristobulus II

**People and Events**

- Beginning of return of exiles to Jerusalem
- Second Temple is built and dedicated
- Alexander the Great conquers Israel
- Esther becomes Queen
- Nehemiah completes walls of Jerusalem
- Joshua serves as Zadokite high priest
- Ptolemy IV attempts to enter temple
- Simon II anointed high priest
- Antiochus IV desecrates Temple/Maccabean Revolt begins
- Death of Judas Maccabeus
- Simon anointed high priest, Strategos Ethnarch (Jewish autonomy)
- Jerusalem besieged by Antiochus VII Sidetes
- John Hyrcanus destroys Samaritan temple on Mt. Gerizim; forces the Judaization of Idumea
- Alexander Jannaeus in civil war with Pharisees, who are aided by Demetrius III Eucaerus

**Events at Qumran**

- Yahad movement forms from post-exile renewal covenantists(?)
- Expected end of exile and beginning of Redemption according to Ezekiel's 430-year prophecy
- Sect's sojourn in Damascus and rise of Teacher of Righteousness
- Founding of Settlement time of Hasmonean Revolt(?) (early date)
- Period Ia (founding of settlement) time of John Hyrcanus (?) (late date)
- Period Ib begins, marked by building at time of Alexander Jannaeus

**A.D.**

## Foreign Rulers over Israel

Roman Rulers

"First Triumvirate"
(Pompey, Crassus, Caesar)

Julius Caesar assassinated •

Augustus

Tiberius

Caligula

Claudius

Nero

Vespasian

## National Rulers in Israel

Aristobulus II

Hyrcanus II

Antigonus

Herod the Great

Archelaus

Philip

Herod Antipas

Pontius Pilate

Herod Agrippa I

Roman Procurators

## People and Events

• Forces of Aristobulus II besieged by Pompey on Temple Mount—Falls on Yom Kippur, loss of Jewish autonomy

Caesar comes to Syria •

• Herod, aided by Roman general Sosius, takes Jerusalem from Antigonus

Period of Herod the Great's building

• Birth of Jesus of Nazareth

• Ministry of John the Baptizer

• Crucifixion of Jesus of Nazareth
  • Conversion of Paul

• "Jewish question" in Alexandria comes to head with embassy to Gaius

• At death of Herod Agrippa I, all Palestine ruled directly by Roman procurators

Antonius Felix, procurator

• Gessius Florus robs Temple, beginning of First War with Rome
  • Josephus in Galilee

• Civil war in Jerusalem; Vespasian razes all of Judea except Herodium fortresses; thus presumably ending life of site of Qumran
  • Fall of Masada

## Events at Qumran

Period Ib ends either with Parthian invasion (40 B.C.) or earthquake (31 B.C.)

• Period I begins; approximately contemporary with Herod the Great's death

Period II, Roman military occupation

• Period II ends; destruction at hands of Roman forces during First Jewish Revolt

Period III, Roman military occupation

# A Chronological History of the Dead Sea Scrolls

## A History of the Sect, Scroll Discoveries, Research, and Excavations[1]

**c. 1406 B.C.**—First mention in the Bible of the City of Salt, one of six cities conquered by Joshua and allotted to the Tribe of Judah (Joshua 15:61). Probably the site of Qumran.

**c. 875–750 B.C.**—The Judean king Uzziah establishes "towers in the wilderness" with round cisterns (2 Chronicles 26:10). Probably the site of Qumran.

**587 B.C.**—The City of Salt is destroyed by the invading Babylonians.

**c. 196 B.C.**—Hasidic (pious) Jews of the Zadokite (priestly) line founded the *Yachad* movement, believing that the time of Israel's redemption was imminent. They based their belief on their *pesher* interpretation of Ezekiel's prophecy of 390 years, which they believed began with the destruction of the First Temple in 586 B.C.

**c. 166 B.C.**—After 20 years of searching for answers about the delay in the fulfillment of Ezekiel's prophecy, an enlightened "Teacher" arises who is able to decipher the mystery of the prophetic text. He organizes the movement into a Sect, which moves into the settlement at Qumran to wait out the 40 years of "exile" according to the Teacher's interpretation of Ezekiel 4:6. At the conclusion of this time the Sect expects to begin the 40-year war that will bring redemption (Period Ia).

**c. 146 B.C.**—After 20 years at Qumran, the Teacher dies; he was opposed by priestly leaders of establishment Judaism. The Sect continues to await the 40-year war, but no longer attempts to find precise dates for its commencement. The Sect apparently enters into a period of self-examination, believing that the postponement of the redemption is a result of their own impiety or inaction.

**c. 125–00 B.C.**—Buildings in the main block of the community are enlarged to accommodate additional members (Period Ib).

**c. 31 B.C.**—The Qumran settlement is temporarily abandoned due to an earthquake and/or possible battle with foreign foes.

**c. 4 B.C.**—The community center of the Sect is restored at Qumran (Period II).

**c. A.D. 20–35**—The Hellenistic Jewish philosopher Philo of Alexandria writes two separate accounts of the Essenes in *Quod Omnis Liber Probus Sit* ("*Every Good Man Is Free*") and *Hypothetica*, also known as *Apologia Pro Judaeis* ("*Apology for the Jews*"), which has been preserved only in Eusebius' *Praeparatio Evangelica* ("*Preparation for the Gospel*").

**A.D. 68**—The Roman assault on Jerusalem extends to Jews fleeing to the desert and settlements like Qumran, which is destroyed. Sometime before this, it is probable that members of the Sect hid the community's Scrolls in caves, and the treasure of the *Copper Scroll* in secret locations throughout the desert and Jerusalem.

**A.D. 70–90**—Roman military outpost is established on ruins of Qumran main block.

**A.D. 73**—Members of the Qumran Sect join the Jewish resisters at Masada. Their presence is attested from Scroll fragments and pottery remains (made in kilns at Qumran) at Masada.

**c. A.D. 74–94**—The Jewish historian Flavius Josephus, writing for a Roman audience, gives three separate accounts of the Essenes, with whom he professed to have lived for a time: *Bellum Judaicum* ("*History of the Jewish War*") 2.8.2-13; *Antiquities* ("*Antiquities [of the Jews]*") 13.5.9 and 18.1.5.

**c. A.D. 75**—The Roman elder Pliny records a colorful (and somewhat exaggerated) description of the Essenes in the fifth book of his *Natural History*.

**c. A.D. 132–35**—Qumran settlement is occupied during the second Jewish revolt (Bar Kokhba rebellion).

**c. 200**—The early church father Hippolytus briefly mentions the "Sect of the Essenes" in his *Refutatio* ("*Refutation of All Heresies*") 9.18-28.

**c. 217**—The Christian scholar Origen discovers Scrolls written in both Hebrew and Greek in jars in caves near Jericho. He provides no record of the contents of the Hebrew manuscripts, but among the Greek manuscripts was a version of the book of Psalms (different from the

LXX), which he incorporated into his critical edition of the Bible known as the *Hexapla*.

**c. 700**—According to one theory, the Karaites (a Jewish Sect that elevated the Written Torah and rejected the Oral Torah of the rabbis) either found or acquired copies of Dead Sea Scroll manuscripts and based some of their doctrines on sectarian texts such as the *Damascus Document*.

**c. 800**—Chance discovery of Hebrew Scrolls containing copies of Old Testament books and other Hebrew writings in a "cave near Jericho." The find was reported in a letter by Timotheus, Patriarch of the Nestorian Christians, to Sergius, Metropolitan Bishop of Elem. Possibly helped form basis of Karaite Jewish reform movement.

**c. 937**—Al Kirqisani the Karaite mentions the finding of manuscripts in caves of the Judean desert and identifies these as belonging to the literature of the Magharians (based on the Arabic word for *cave*), a pre-Christian Sect that apparently lived in caves. In his account of Jewish sects he referenced earlier writers such as David Ibn-Merwan and Al-Biruni (seventh–ninth centuries), who, in turn, cited even earlier writers concerning the "cave Sect." In Kirqisani's record he appears to place this Sect chronologically between the Sadducees (second century B.C.) and the followers of Christ (first century A.D.).

**c. 1090**—The writer Shahrastani records that the "cave Sect" flourished 400 years before the Alexandrian presbyter Arius (who died in A.D. 336). This would place the Sect in the first century B.C.

**[1935]**—According to revised 1995 account by the Bedouin shepherd Muhammed edh-Dhib (Abu-Dahoud), he discovers the first Scrolls in a cave (later to become known as Qumran Cave 1).

**[1936]**—According to 1995 account by Muhammed edh-Dhib, he returns to Cave 1 to retrieve an additional manuscript.

**1937**—The American Colt Expedition discovers two fragmentary papyrus documents dating from the seventh–eighth century A.D. at "Auja el-Hafir" (the Byzantine monastery of Nessana) in the Negev. Identified as portions of the New Testament Gospel of John and a Pauline epistle.

**[1938]**—According to Muhammed edh-Dhib's revised account, he finds additional manuscripts in Caves 4 and 11.

**[1940]**—According to Muhammed edh-Dhib's revised account, he finds intact Scroll at Wadi Murabba'at, which he sells to Kando for JD1,500 (Jordanian dinars).

**[1941]**—Muhammed edh-Dhib claims to have found hundreds of Scroll fragments at Endera (near Ein-Gedi), which he sells as lots to both Père Roland de Vaux and Kando.

**Winter 1945–46**—According to the traditional date, Muhammed edh-Dhib finds Cave 1 and, with friends Jum'a Mohammed and Khalil Musa, retrieves seven manuscripts preserved more or less in complete form (*1QIsa^a*, *1QIsa^b*, *1QpHab*, *1QS*, *1QH^a*, *1QM*, *1QapGen*).

**March 1947**—According to the traditional story, Muhammed edh-Dhib's uncle sells the Scrolls in Bethlehem to antiquities dealers. One of these dealers, Khalil Eskander Shahin (also known as Kando), becomes an agent for the Bedouin.

**April 1947**—George Isha'ya tells Metropolitan Athanasius Yeshue Samuel of St. Mark's Syrian Orthodox Monastery about Scrolls and he offers to buy them.

**May–June 1947**—According to John Trevor's account, Ta'amireh Bedouin take George Isha'ya to Cave 1, where he and Khalil Musa later recover four more Scrolls. Three are sold to Bethlehem antiquities dealer Faidi Salahi and the fourth to Kando.

**July 5, 1947**—Kando attempts to sell the four Scrolls (*1QIsa^a*, *1QpHab*, *1QS*, *1QapGen*) to the Metropolitan Samuel, but his agents are turned away by monks at the front door of the monastery and return to Kando's Bethlehem shop.

**July 19, 1947**—According to John Trevor's account, Kando buys the rest of the Scrolls and sells four to Metropolitan Samuel for £P24 ($97.20). According to Metropolitan Samuel the amount was $250.

**Late July 1947**—Father Marmardji of the École Biblique is consulted by Metropolitan Samuel about the Scrolls. Father van der Ploeg (later, the first to translate any of the Scrolls) views the Scrolls and identifies the *Isaiah Scroll*, but considers it of medieval origin.

**August 1947**—George Isha'ya takes Father Yusif of St. Mark's to Cave 1. Metropolitan Samuel continues to seek information about the Scrolls, contacting two librarians from the Hebrew University.

**September 1947**—Metropolitan Samuel and Anton Kiraz travel to Homs, Syria to show Scrolls to the Syrian Patriarch.

**October 1947**—Tovia Wechsler, an expert in Jewish antiquities, is shown Scrolls, but concludes they are of late date and little value.

**November 23, 1947**—An Armenian antiquities dealer in Jerusalem contacts Prof. Eleazar L. Sukenik of the Hebrew University about buying Scrolls from Faidi Salahi.

**November 29, 1947**—After confirming their antiquity, Prof. Sukenik buys two Scrolls (*1QH^a*, *1QM*) and several manuscript fragments from Faidi Salahi.

**December 22, 1947**—Prof. Sukenik buys another Scroll (*1QIsa^b*) and two Scroll jars from the same source. Together with the previous purchase, these three Scrolls are (*1QIsa^b*, *1QH^a*, *1QM*).

**February 4-6, 1948**—Prof. Sukenik examines the four Scrolls (*1QIsa^a*, *1QS*, *1QpHab*, *1QapGen*) lent to him by the Metropolitan Samuel through Anton Kiraz. Upon returning them on February 6, Sukenik offers to buy them.

**February 18-27, 1948**—The Metropolitan Samuel's assistant, Father Butrus Sowmy, brings three of the Scrolls to the American School of Oriental Research to seek another opinion on their antiquity. John C. Trevor, in the American School of Oriental Research director's absence, states that the Scrolls seemed to be ancient and secured permission from the Metropolitan to photograph the Scrolls. During the following weeks he was able to photograph three of the Scrolls in both color and black-and-white format. *1QapGen* had not yet been unrolled for photographic purposes.

**March 5, 1948**—Metropolitan Samuel tells the story of how he purchased the Scrolls the preceding year.

**March 6-11, 1948**—The *Great Isaiah Scroll* and *Habakkuk Pesher* are rephotographed by John Trevor for publication.

**March 12(?), 1948**—Department of Antiquities makes arrangements with the Syrian officials at St. Mark's to visit Cave 1.

**March 15, 1948**—The letter of noted Hebrew scholar and epigraphist Dr. William Foxwell Albright arrives at the American School of Oriental Research, confirming the antiquity of the Scrolls and their value as "the greatest archaeological discovery of the century."

**March 18, 1948**—American School of Oriental Research issues first local press release about the Scrolls and their value. Metropolitan

Samuel learns of Scrolls' value and, in the following month, allows the school to publish photographs of the Scrolls.

**April 11, 1948**—First international press release about Scrolls is issued.

**April 26, 1948**—Prof. Sukenik issues press release about Hebrew University's Scrolls.

**August 1948**—In the midst of the War of Independence, George Isha'ya returns to Cave 1 and recovers fragments of Daniel, the *Prayer Scroll*, and others, which are turned over to the Syrian monastery.

**September 1948**—First published articles on Scrolls with photographs are issued jointly by the American School of Oriental Research and the Hebrew University.

**November 1948**—John Trevor states that George Isha'ya, Kando, and others have returned to Cave 1 to dig for more Scrolls. They are said to have recovered numerous fragments.

**January 24, 1949**—After many unsuccessful efforts are made by others to relocate Cave 1, Captain Philippe Lippens hires members of the elite Arab Legion. They discover its location.

**January 29, 1949**—Metropolitan Samuel takes his four Scrolls (plus fragments) to the United States for exhibition and to secure a buyer.

**February 15–March 5, 1949**—Qumran Cave 1 is excavated under the direction of G. Lankester Harding and Père Roland de Vaux. Fragments of 70 Scrolls and pottery shards from some 50 jars are recovered.

**April 1949**—On behalf of the Israel Exploration Survey, B. Mazar, A. Reifenberg, and T. Dothan conduct a comprehensive survey and excavate trial soundings in the Ein-Gedi oasis.

**April 10-14, 1949**—The *Genesis Apocryphon Scroll* is opened for the first time at Fogg Museum, Harvard University.

**Summer 1949**—The Hebrew University unrolls and identifies for the first time its copy of the *Isaiah Scroll (1QIsa^b)*.

**October 1949**—The four Scrolls of St. Mark's Monastery are publicly displayed for the first time at the Library of Congress, Washington, DC.

**February 1950**—The St. Mark's Scrolls are exhibited at Duke University.

**March 1950**—First volume of Scrolls (*1QIsa^a*, and *1QpHab*) is published by American School of Oriental Research (black-and-white

453

photos accompanied by transcriptions) in Millar Burrows, *The Dead Sea Scrolls of St. Mark's Monastery*, vol. 1.

**Spring 1950**—Yusif Saad purchases the Cave 1 fragments of the book of Samuel from Kando for the Palestine Archaeological Museum.

**Fall 1950**—Carbon 14 tests are applied to some of the linen cloth used to wrap the Scrolls from Qumran Cave 1. A date of A.D. 33 200 years is given, confirming the antiquity of the Scrolls.

**November 1950**—The St. Mark's Scrolls are exhibited at the University of Chicago's Oriental Institute.

**Spring 1951**—The *Rule of the Community* Scroll (*1QS*) is published by the American School of Oriental Research (black-and-white photos with transcriptions) in *The Dead Sea Scrolls of St. Mark's Monastery*, vol. 2.

**Summer 1951**—Metropolitan Samuel removes *Genesis Apocryphon* Scroll from Fogg Museum and forbids further access to it.

**October 1951**—The Ta'amireh Bedouin discover more Scroll fragments in the Wadi Murabba'at caves and sell two leather Scroll fragments to the Palestine Archaeological Museum.

**November 3, 1951**—Dr. Awni Dajani, Inspector of Antiquities, and members of the American School of Oriental Research search new caves looking for fragments.

**November 24–December 12, 1951**—The first season of excavations at Qumran. A sounding was made by Roland de Vaux and G. Lankester Harding. The date and connection of the site with Cave 1 was confirmed by coins and pottery.

**Late November 1951**—Kando and others offer Père Roland de Vaux at the École Biblique more manuscript fragments from the Wadi Murabba'at caves. The excavations at the site of Qumran are interrupted.

**January–March 3, 1952**—Four caves at Wadi Murabba'at are excavated by R. de Vaux and L. Harding.

**February 1952**—Bedouin find Qumran Cave 2, from which they remove all *2Q* manuscript fragments.

**March 10-29, 1952**—The excavation of Cave 2 and a survey of the cliffs (8 km. long, i.e., running 4 km. north and south of Wadi Qumran), is carried out by R. de Vaux and William Reed, director of the

American School of Oriental Research (now known as the Albright Institute). In all, some 225 caves and crevices are explored.

**March 14, 1952**—Cave 3 is discovered in an expedition. The *Copper Scroll* and a few dozen leather Scroll fragments are recovered.

**July 1952**—Bedouin discover Byzantine and early Arabic manuscripts (including some Greek New Testament manuscripts) in room at ruins of Khirbet Mird (Horqania), five miles west of Qumran.

**August 1952**—Bedouin find manuscripts (including Greek text of Minor Prophets—second century A.D.) in the cave of Horrors and the Cave of the Letters in Nahal Hever. Most of the documents, represented as being from Wadi Seiyal, are offered to the Palestine Archaeological Museum.

**Early September 1952**—Qumran Caves 4 and 6 are discovered by Bedouin on marl terrace adjacent to Qumran settlement.

**September 20, 1952**—Bedouin offer for sale two lots of approximately 15,000 fragments from Cave 4, for which they receive 15,000 Jordanian dinars (then the equivalent of $842,000) from the Jordanian government early in 1953.

**September 22-29, 1952**—De Vaux and Harding excavate Cave 4 and retrieve some 40,000 fragments, including parts of 400 different manuscripts (over 100 biblical). On September 25-29, about 30 meters to the north of Cave 4, Jozef T. Milik also finds and excavates Cave 5.

**September 1952**—Bedouin discover Cave 6 and remove all *6Q* fragments.

**September 1952**—International Team of eight scholars is established to assemble and publish Scroll fragments (mostly stored at Palestine Archaeological Museum). R. de Vaux assumes position of editor-in-chief for the remainder of the texts and other finds derived from the Judean Desert (including Qumran, the caves of the Qumran region, Wadi Murabba'at, and Khirbet Mird). R. de Vaux at first limits the task of publishing the manuscripts to Wadi Murabba'at and Caves 2 and 3 to fellow members of the École Biblique.

**February 9–April 24, 1953**—The second season of excavation at Qumran is conducted. During this time, the tower and central buildings are excavated.

**February–April 1953**—Belgian scholar R. de Langhe directs excavations on behalf of the University of Louvain at Khirbet Mird.

**May 1953**—Frank Moore Cross is invited to examine all the fragments excavated by de Vaux and Harding from Cave 4. Cross, at the time a professor at McCormick Theological Seminary, was the Annual Professor at the American School of Oriental Research in Jerusalem. He assumed responsibility for most of the biblical Scrolls.

**Fall 1953**—J.T. Milik and F.M. Cross join with the scrollery to begin working on the combined lots from Cave 4. Milik's lot from Cave 4 included phylacteries, *mezuzot*, and *targumim*, as well as many non-biblical texts: pseudohistorical texts, rule books, euchologies, calendrical texts, texts written in cryptic alphabets, secular documents, and works previously entitled Apocrypha and Pseudepigrapha.

**November 1953**—The Palestine Archaeological Museum and Jordanian Department of Antiquities emphasize the importance of obtaining all available manuscript fragments before they are lost on the black market in Europe and the United States. More manuscripts do surface and become available through the Bedouin and various antiquities dealers (including Kando). When the Jordanian government cannot afford to purchase all of the fragments, an invitation is made to qualified academic institutions to sponsor purchases.

**November 1953**—A letter is issued by the Prime Minister of Jordan agreeing to allow foreign institutions to purchase Dead Sea Scroll fragments.

**December 1953**—John Marco Allegro, Assistant Lecturer at the University of Manchester, joins the International Team. He is assigned mainly parabiblical texts, commentaries, and paraphrases.

**December 23, 1953**—The Prime Minister of Jordan states that permission to export fragments bought by the sponsoring institutions would be given after completion of their processing and study at the Palestine Archaeological Museum.

**1953**—The International Team identifies the first 70 manuscripts from among the 15,000 fragments which came from the Jordanian government acquisition and the excavation of Cave 4.

**1954**—During this year, John D. Rockefeller, Jr. agrees to fund Scroll research for six years. This included funding for the scholars' expenses while in Jerusalem, secretarial staff, preservation, and photography through the Rockefeller Museum. For the most part, this excluded funds for the purchase of manuscripts. The French scholars (Milik and Starcky) were supported by funds from the Centre National de la Recherche Scientifique (CNRS) in France.

**January 1954**—Fr. Jean Starcky, a specialist in Palmyrene Aramaic texts, joins the International Team to help with nonbiblical Aramaic documents, as well as a few Hebrew documents.

**February 1954**—The Jordanian government makes a second purchase of Cave 4 documents from Bedouin.

**February 13–April 14, 1954**—The third season of excavations at Khirbet Qumran is conducted. The "refectory" and the potter's workshop are excavated.

**June 1954**—McGill University, Canada, becomes the first foreign institution to purchase Scroll fragments (a one-time purchase for $15,000; Palestine Archaeological Museum).

**June 1954**—Msgr. Patrick W. Skehan, a professor at the Catholic University of America and Annual Professor at the American School of Oriental Research in Jerusalem for the academic year 1954–55, joins the International Team. Skehan is assigned part of the biblical texts, including paleo-Hebrew and Greek texts, Isaiah, Psalms, Proverbs, and one manuscript each of Deuteronomy and the Minor Prophets.

**July 1, 1954**—The four Scrolls in the possession of Metropolitan Samuel are bought by proxy for Yigael Yadin in New York on behalf of the State of Israel for $250,000. They are added to the Hebrew University collection (making a total of seven Scrolls from Cave 1 plus fragments).

**July 1954**—John Strugnell of Jesus College, Oxford, joins the International Team and is assigned a portion of the hitherto unknown nonbiblical, Hebrew texts. These include mostly Pentateuchal paraphrases, pseudoprophetic texts, hymnic texts, liturgical and sapiential texts, and other unknown texts.

**October 1954**—The Vatican Library purchases Scroll fragments.

**October 1954**—Dr. Claus-Hunno Hunzinger joins the International Team and is assigned manuscripts of the *War Scroll* and some liturgical texts. His lot was later transferred to Baillet (1971).

**December 1954**—The University of Manchester purchases a number of Scroll fragments.

**1955**—Prof. E.L. Sukenik's *The Dead Sea Scrolls of the Hebrew University* is published posthumously (covered in the volume are Scrolls *1QIsa^b*, *1QH^a*, and *1QM*).

**February 2–April 6, 1955**—The fourth season of excavation at Qumran is conducted, and the western quarter is opened and water storage system revealed. The team investigates the sides of the marl terrace upon which the site is located and finds four additional (collapsed) caves (Caves 7-10), from which a few epigraphic fragments are removed, including the first Greek papyri fragments at Qumran (which some later theorize are portions of the New Testament).

**March 1955**—Bedouin discover a fifth cave in the vicinity of the first four at Murabba'at (5Mur) in which they find a Hebrew Minor Prophets Scroll.

**March 18-29, 1955**—The first of two seasons of the Archaeological Survey of Masada is carried out by M. Avi-Yonah, Nahman Avigad, Y. Aharoni, I. Dunayevsky, and S. Gutman on behalf of the Hebrew University, the Israel Exploration Society, and the Israel Department of Antiquities jointly. During this survey and excavation the entire mound, its visible structures and its water system were mapped and drawn. Special attention was paid to the northern palace, which was partially excavated. One ostracon, one papyrus fragment, one graffito on plaster, and 3 coins were found in this survey.

**April 1955**—Adolf Grohmann begins work on Arabic manuscripts from Khirbet Mird.

**Spring 1955**—The archaeological and manuscript remains of Cave 1, taken in controlled excavation, are published as *Discoveries in the Judean Desert I*.

**Spring 1955**—The University of Heidelberg, via Prof. K.C. Kuhn, purchases a number of Scroll fragments.

**August 1955**—By this date 330 manuscripts from Cave 4 have been identified on 420 museum plates. Fragments on 80 museum plates yet remain unidentified.

**August 8-17, 1955**—F.M. Cross and J.T. Milik direct surface explorations and soundings in the Buqe'ah southwest of Qumran.

**December 1955**—The Vatican Library purchases a number of Scroll fragments.

**1956**—McCormick Theological Seminary, Chicago, joins the institutions purchasing Scroll fragments from Cave 4.

**January 1956**—Bedouin find Cave 11 and bring it to the attention of the Jordanian Department of Antiquities in February. Well preserved, very fragmentary Scrolls from the cave are purchased by the Palestine Archaeological Museum. The longest Scroll, the *Temple Scroll (11QT)*, is purchased by Kando.

**January–February 1956**—J. Bieberkraut succeeds in completely unrolling the *Genesis Apocryphon (1QapGen)*.

**Mid-February 1956**—R. de Vaux and his team excavate Qumran Cave 11.

**March 1, 1956**—Kando pays 16,000 Jordanian dinars to the Palestine Archaeological Museum to hold in safekeeping his Cave 11 fragments.

**February 18–March 28, 1956**—The fifth season of excavation at Qumran is conducted and 18 more tombs in cemeteries are explored. A sounding at 'Ein Feshkha is also made.

**March 7-17, 1956**—The second of two seasons of archaeological survey at Masada is carried out by Y. Aharoni and S. Gutman. During this season the round tower and peristyle building of the northern palace are further excavated and their plans elucidated.

**May 19, 1956**—*11QPs^a, 11QpaleoLev^a*, and other fragments from Cave 11 are purchased by the Palestine Archaeological Museum.

**Summer 1956**—By this time, 381 manuscripts from Cave 4 have been identified on 477 museum plates with fragments on 29 museum plates yet unidentified and 13 plates of papyrus fragments not yet studied.

**June 1, 1956**—The *Copper Scroll (3Q15)* from Cave 3 is "unrolled" by being cut into strips at England's Manchester University. Its contents are revealed as a list of treasures buried at various sites.

**July 17, 1956**—Kando pays 14,000 Jordanian dinars to the Palestine Archaeological Museum to hold in safekeeping the fragments of *11QtgJob* and *11QJN* (*11QtgJob* was bought by the Koninklijke Nederlandse Akademie van Wetenschappen, Amsterdam, in 1961).

**July–August 1956**—Distribution lists for scholars and purchasing institutions are finalized. The manuscripts are divided up, both in quality and in quantity, according to the amount of their contribution.

**September 1956**—The first Suez crisis caused the dispersal of the International Team. At this time, all the manuscripts are removed to Amman, where they remain until the spring of 1957.

**Fall 1956**—Five columns of *1QapGen* are published by Y. Yadin and N. Avigad in *A Genesis Apocryphon: A Scroll from the Wilderness of Judaea*.

**July 1957**—Father Joseph Fitzmyer begins compiling the card concordance to the Dead Sea Scrolls from Cave 4. Sometime later, J. Teixidor adds the texts from the minor caves (Caves 2, 3, and 5-10).

**1958**—F.M. Cross publishes his major analysis of the scripts of the Scrolls: "The Development of the Jewish Scripts" in *The Bible and the Ancient Near East*.

**January 25–March 21, 1958**—The sixth season of excavation at Qumran is conducted. The farm installation north of 'Ein Feshkha is also excavated. Rooms for treating leather believed to be found.

**Spring 1958**—Scroll fragments from a cave near Ein-Gedi are discovered by Bedouin and brought to the attention of the Israelis.

**June 1958**—After completing his work on the manuscripts from Caves 2, 3, and 6-10Q, Maurice Baillet of the CNRS joins the International Team to work on Cave 4 manuscripts. He is assigned several documents from the lots of Starcky, Milik, and Strugnell, as well as many unassigned, unclassified papyrus fragments (40482-520).

**July 1958**—The last group of fragments from Cave 4 is made available by Kando. These are purchased by the Palestine Archaeological Museum, McCormick Theological Seminary, All Soul's Church (New York), and Oxford University.

**September 1958**—The last two documents from Wadi Murabba'at are purchased by the Palestine Archaeological Museum and the École Biblique.

**January 25–February 2, 1960**—Following news that many manuscripts sold by Bedouin in Jerusalem had come from Nahal Se'elim, a ten-day survey of the valley is conducted by Y. Aharoni. His findings result in the Judean Desert Survey of caves.

**March 23–April 6, 1960**—The first season of the Judean Desert Survey, beginning in the Ein-Gedi region. The first cave excavated is the Cave of Letters and the work is conducted by Y. Yadin. During this excavation, the Bar Kokhba letters are discovered.

**Spring 1960**—First transcription and translation of the *Copper Scroll* (*3Q15*) by J.M. Allegro is published: *The Treasure of the Copper Scroll*.

**Spring 1960**—J.M. Allegro directs the "*Copper Scroll* Expedition," which excavates various Judean wilderness sites suspected to contain items mentioned in the *Copper Scroll*. These sites included Khirbet Mird and Khirbet Mazin.

**June 1960**—Rockefeller funds that have supported the work of the International Team run out. Those team members whose work was supported by these funds leave Jerusalem. R. de Vaux notifies the contributing institutions that the work on the fragments themselves has been completed and that they will have to apply to the Jordanian government for export permits for the manuscripts.

**July 27, 1960**—Council of Ministers of Jordan rules "to keep Dead Sea Scrolls with the Department of Antiquities and to reimburse" the purchasing institutions.

**January 1-12, 1961**—The first season of excavations at Tel Goren in the Ein-Gedi region is conducted.

**March 14-27, 1961**—The second season of the Judean Desert Survey is conducted. The Cave of Horrors in Nahal Hever is excavated by Y. Aharoni. The Cave of Letters is excavated by Y. Yadin, and yields the Babatha archive with documents in Hebrew, Aramaic, Nabatean, and Greek, dating between A.D. 88–132.

**Spring 1961**—The archaeological remains and manuscripts derived from the Palestine Archaeological Museum purchases and the official excavation are published as *Discoveries in the Judean Desert II: Les Grottes de Murabba'at*.

**June 1961**—By this date, 511 manuscripts from Cave 4 have been identified on 620 museum plates with fragments on 25 plates still unidentified. The final series of photographs is completed at this time.

**September 1961**—The Scrolls at the Palestine Archaeological Museum are evaluated for insurance purposes and their commercial value is set at JD150,000.

**November 1961**—The *Psalms Scroll (11QPs$^a$)* is unrolled and editorial analysis is carried out by James A. Sanders. Thirty-seven psalms and seven non-canonical psalms are included.

**February 1962**—Ta'amireh Bedouin find about 40 Samaritan papyri and bullae in the Abu Shinjeh Cave in Wadi edh-Daliyeh (nine miles north of Jericho). These are presented to the Palestine Archaeological Museum through Kando. The American School of Oriental Research purchased the lot through a gift from Kenneth and Elizabeth Hay Bechtel. Later it was found out that the Bechtels possessed a complete set of photographs of all the Scrolls, which they had commissioned, and then donated a set of the photographs to the Huntington College Library in California.

**March 1962**—Fragments from the *Ezekiel Scroll (11QEzek)* are analyzed by Prof. W.H. Brownlee.

**March 10–April 19, 1962**—The second season of excavations at Tel-Goren is conducted.

**Fall 1962**—Archaeological finds and epigraphic remains from the minor caves at Qumran are published in *Discoveries in the Judean Desert III: Les 'petites Grottes' de Qumrân*.

**January 7-20, 1963**—The first season of excavation at Wadi edh-Daliyeh is directed by Paul W. Lapp.

**October 1963–April 1964**—Y. Yadin directs the first of two seasons of excavation at Masada on behalf of the Hebrew University, the Israel Exploration Society, and the Israel Department of Antiquities jointly. The intention of this excavation was to expose the remains at this site in their entirety. Several biblical and literary texts on leather were found as well as many coins, ostraca, and secular Roman documents on papyrus.

**January 7-20, 1964**—The second season of excavation at Wadi edh-Daliyeh is conducted.

**December 1964–March 1965**—The second season of excavation at Masada is conducted.

**1965**—The *Psalms Scroll (11QPs$^a$)* is published by J.A. Sanders as *Discoveries in the Judean Desert IV: The Psalms Scroll of Cave 11*.

**November 1966**—The Jordanian government nationalizes the Palestine Archaeological Museum.

**June 1967**—Israeli troops capture Bethlehem during the Six-Day War, and Y. Yadin finds the *Temple Scroll (11QT$^a$)* under floorboards in Kando's house. He later purchases it for the Israel Department of Antiquities and Museums. The Israeli government begins its administration of the Palestine Archaeological Museum and renames it the Rockefeller Museum.

**June 1967**—John M. Allegro's lot is published as *Discoveries in the Judean Desert V: Qumran Cave 4.1 (4Q158–186)*.

**April 1971**—Hunzinger withdraws from the International Team. His texts are given to M. Baillet.

**1972**—Spanish Jesuit scholar Father Jose O'Callaghan publishes a paper proposing to identify Greek papyri fragments from Cave 7 (in particular one fragment, *7Q5)* as portions of the New Testament Gospel of Mark, Acts, several Pauline epistles, and Peter.

**September 1975**—Father P. Benoit of the École Biblique becomes editor-in-chief of the International Team and the *Discoveries in the Judean Desert* series.

**1976**—Milik publishes part of his lot (40201-212) in *The Books of Enoch: Aramaic Fragments of Qumran Cave 4*.

**1977**—Y. Yadin publishes the *Temple Scroll (11QT$^n$)* in Hebrew. The same publication appears in English, entitled *The Temple Scroll*, in 1983 as a limited edition.

**1977**—The archaeology of Qumran Cave 4 and part of J.T. Milik's lot is published as *DJD II: Qumran Cave 4 11: 1. Archéologie II. Tefillin, Mezuzot et Targums (4Q128–4Q157)*.

**September 1977**—N.D. Freedman complains in the *Biblical Archaeologist* that the publication of Cave 4 material has not been forthcoming. His is the first official voice raised in protest against the delay in publication of this material.

**December 1980**—A second excavation is conducted at the Wadi edh-Daliyeh cave known as 'Araq en-Na'saneh. No Scrolls or fragments were discovered, but a hoard of seventeen Roman coins (Denarii and Tridrachm) are uncovered.

**1982**—M. Baillet's lot is published as *DJD VII: Qumran Cave 4 III (4Q482–4Q520)*.

**September 1984**—John Strugnell of Harvard University is appointed as editor-in-chief of the International Team and the *DJD* series. The International Team is expanded to 20 members.

**1985**—D.N. Freedman and K.A. Mathews publish *11QpaleoLev$^a$* as *The Paleo-Hebrew Leviticus Scroll (11QpaleoLev)*.

**1986**—Israel Antiquities Department director Avraham Eitan meets with Father Pierre Benoit, head of the Cave 4 Scroll Team for a progress report on the *DJD* publication schedule. There is concern that the process is taking too long because only one volume had been published with any Cave 4 material and another with only observations on the excavation of some *tefillin* and *mezuzot*.

**April–June 1986**—Hebrew University archaeologist Hanan Eshel finds numerous papyri fragments at the entrance to a cave at Ketef Jericho dated to the fourth century B.C.

**1988**—Surveys of the Cave 4 plateau are begun by Dr. Garold Collett and senior field engineer Aubrey Richardson, employing molecular frequency technology. Preliminary report (1990) to the Israel Department of Antiquities mentions what are believed to be objects (Scrolls, pottery, bronze, gemstones) in unidentified chambers (anomalies).

**March 1989**—R. Eisenman petitions J. Strugnell for access to several Cave 4 manuscript fragments of the *Damascus Document* for research he is conducting. Strugnell's refusal ignites a chain of events that draws widespread attention to the problems of access and delay in publication. The letter is published in the *Biblical Archaeology Review* in May.

**July 9, 1989**—The *New York Times* publishes an article entitled "The Vanity of Scholars," criticizing the Scroll publication schedule based on remarks previously published by Hershel Shanks in *Biblical Archaeology Review* (May/June).

**September 1989**—Colloquim on the Dead Sea Scrolls is held in Mogilany, Poland and issues a statement (known as the "Mogilany Resolution") calling for an immediate publication of all of the plates of the unpublished texts.

**October 1989**—R. Eisenman begins receiving the first of over 1,700 photographs of the Cave 4 material from an unidentified party in Jerusalem.

**1990**—Carbon 14 tests of 11 manuscripts from six sites in the Judean Desert are carried out at the Institut für Mittelenergiephysick in Zurich.

**1990**—The *Dodekapropheton Scroll* from Nahal Hever (*8HevXIIgr*) is published by Emanuel Tov as *DJD VIII: The Greek Minor Prophets Scroll from Nahal Hever (8HevXIIgr)*.

**March 1990**—*Biblical Archaeology Review* publishes its criticism of Strugnell, which induces authorities to begin investigating Strugnell's competence to head the International Team.

**June 1990**—An evening session on "Forty Years of Dead Sea Scroll Research" is held during the Second International Congress on Biblical Archaeology at the Hebrew University (Givat Ram). Joseph Baumgarten shares the initial findings from his unpublished text of the Cave 4 fragments of *Serekh ha-Yahad* (the *Damascus Document*), and several International Team members discuss with attendants the controversy over the delay in publication of the Cave 4 material.

**September 4, 1990**—The "scholarly monopoly" on the Scrolls is ended when Hebrew Union College professor Ben Zion Wacholder, and then-graduate student Martin Abegg, announce the first volume of their *A Preliminary Edition of the Unpublished Dead Sea Scrolls*, reconstructed by computer from a privately printed concordance of the texts from Caves 2–10.

**September 22, 1990**—William Moffett, director of the Huntington College Library in Southern California, ends the controversy over publication by giving "all qualified scholars" access to the library's microfilm copies of the complete Elizabeth Hays Bechtel photographic collection of the Scrolls.

**October 1990**—Hebrew University professor Emanuel Tov is told that he will be appointed to the editor-in-chief post to succeed Strugnell.

**November 9, 1990**—An interview with Strugnell in October is printed in the Israeli newspaper *Ha-Aretz* (in English in the January/February issue of *Biblical Archaeological Review*). In the interview, Strugnell criticizes the state of Israel and denounces Judaism, leading outcrys from both Israelis and the scholarly community in general.

**December 30, 1990**—John Strugnell is removed from his position and Emanuel Tov of the Hebrew University assumes post as editor-in-chief of the International Team and the *DJD* series. Emile Puech of the École Biblique, Eugene Ulrich of Notre Dame University, and Emanuel Tov are chosen as general editors. The International Team is expanded to 55 members.

**October 1991**—The Israeli Antiquities Authority makes available to the scholarly world all the photographs of the texts found in the Judean Desert.

**1992**—P.W. Skehan, E. Ulrich, and J. Sanderson published the Paleo-Hebrew and Greek biblical texts from Cave 4 as *DJD IX: Qumran Cave 4, IV: Paleo-Hebrew and Greek Biblical Manuscripts.*

**Spring 1992**—Hollow depressions (anomalies) are discovered through ground-penetrating radar and infrared surveys conducted on the Cave 4 plateau. The published report is by Prof. Zvi ben-Avraham and Uri Basson of the Department of Geophysics and Planetary Sciences at Tel-Aviv University.

**November 1992**—R. Eisenman and M. Wise publish 50 of the previously unpublished Q4 documents along with their transliterations and translations of their book *The Dead Sea Scrolls Uncovered.*

**December 1992**—Fearing an eventual loss of access to the region due to the PLO/Israeli peace process, Dr. Amir Drori, head of the Israeli Antiquities Authority, initiates "Operation Scroll"—a massive sweep of the Judean desert by 20 archaeological teams—in hopes of locating unexplored caves and retrieving new Scrolls, etc. During the same time, the Antiquities Authority excavates various sections of the Qumran site using unconventional methods (such as a backhoe), including the plateau area. No Scroll discoveries are reported; however, ancillary finds are reported, and an Arab workman in the excavation reports that a silver bowl was found.

**1993**—Fourteen of the Dead Sea Scrolls arrive in the United States for an exhibition at the Library of Congress and the New York Public Library.

**January 1993**—Sa'ar Kibbutznik Baruch Safrai reports finding a human skeleton wearing a white linen robe during an excavation in 1953 with Y. Aharoni at Nahal Hever. While the skeleton and most of the robe could not be retrieved, the sash was removed and placed in a cardboard box, which, unfortunately, was lost.

**March 1993**—Israeli court awards judgment in lawsuit to Scroll scholar Elisha Qimron over exclusive right of publication of his assigned but unpublished text of fragment *4QMMT.*

**November 1993**—Hebrew University archaeologist Hanan Eshel, working with Operation Scroll, finds fragments of a Bar-Kokhba Scroll 15 kilometers from Qumran.

**August 28-31, 1994**—International Conference on the Dead Sea Scrolls is held at University of Manchester, England.

**June–July 1995**—Dr. James Strange begins excavation of the plateau area across from Cave 4 on the basis of anomalies (possibly caverns or storage bins containing Scrolls and other objects). The preliminary phase of the excavation involves successful exploratory drilling that penetrates three of the anomalies.

**December 15, 1995**—Dr. Magen Broshi, former curator of the Shrine of the Book Museum, and Dr. Hanan Eshel, lecturer at the Hebrew University, begin excavating four new caves adjacent to the Qumran site. Because of extensive ancient trails leading to the collapsed caves, they believe that the site was used for habitation by the Qumran community. In the early excavation they removed quantities of Roman pottery.

**February 1996**—Dr. James Strange begins excavating two sites on the Qumran plateau—sites that had been penetrated by drilling probes the previous summer.

**1996**—Invitational colloquim on the *Copper Scroll* is held, with papers being presented by an international group of scholars. This is the first such conference devoted entirely to the *Copper Scroll*.

**July 15-17, 1996**—International Conference on the Dead Sea Scrolls is held at Brigham Young University, Provo, Utah.

# Glossary

**Abomination of Desolation** (Hebrew *hashiqutz meshomem*, "the abomination that makes desolate"): The expression used to describe the act of setting up an idolatrous image in the Holy Place, thus defiling or "making desolate" the Temple, and ending the offering of all sacrifices. This was done in the past by Antiochus Epiphanes IV (Daniel 11:31), whose act reflects the future defilement by the Antichrist (Daniel 9:27). Both Daniel and Jesus indicated that this future act would signal the start of the Great Tribulation (Daniel 12:11; Matthew 24:15; Mark 13:14).

**Aggadah** (adj. aggadic): The portion of rabbinic literature and tradition that consists of stories about biblical and rabbinic figures, ethical teachings, or interpretations of Scripture that teach the principles of Jewish thought and theology.

**Allegorical**: A symbolic method of interpretation which offers a different meaning of the text than what appears at first sight. In relation to Scroll interpretation, some scholars have employed a contrived form of *pesher*-exegesis to decipher or decode the Scrolls, as well as the New Testament, revealing their hidden (real) meaning.

**'Am ha-'aretz**: Literally, "people of the land," the term designates the common people in the land of Israel in Second Temple times who were not members of any specific Jewish sect.

**Amoraim** (adj. Amoraic): The teachers of the Talmud from A.D. 200–500, whose main activity was interpreting the Mishnah and tannaitic (earlier rabbinic) traditions.

**Apocalyptic**: Pertaining to a genre of literature that divulges otherwise unknown secrets about the nature of God and the heavens and the end of days. Especially prominent is the concept of divine intervention and the dualistic idea of a cosmic/earthly conflict between evil angels, their agents and God, His Messiah, and holy angels. The term is also used to describe the imminent messianism that is often part of these texts.

**Apocrypha**: Pseudobiblical books composed by Jewish authors in the Second Temple period; these were not included in the Hebrew Bible. Most of these works survive only in translation; some were included in the Septuagint and others were preserved by various Christian sects.

**Apocryphon**: Singular of Apocrypha and part of the name of an apocryphal version of the biblical book of Genesis found among the Dead Sea Scrolls of Cave 1—the *Genesis Apocryphon.*

**Aramaic**: A northwestern Semitic language used throughout the Near East in late antiquity and in which many important Jewish texts were composed.

**Bar Kokhba**: Literally "Son of the Star," it is the designation of Simeon bar Kosiba, who led the second Jewish revolt against Rome in A.D. 132–135. The discovery of the Bar-Kokhba Letters among the Scrolls at Wadi Muraba'at revealed his real name for the first time as Bar Kosiba.

**Bar Kokhba Revolt**: The second Jewish revolt against Rome, which took place in A.D. 132–135.

**Boethusians**: A Sect of Jews closely linked to the Sadducees in their ideology and interpretation of Jewish law.

**Byzantine**: The period of Roman Christian rule in Jerusalem (A.D. 313–638) during which Christianity was made the official religion of the Roman Empire, and the center of imperial power was moved to Byzantium. The Byzantine Period is divided into the early period (313–491), the great Christian architectural period, and the late period (491–638), which saw a temporary conquest by the Persians, and ended with the Islamic invasion under Caliph Omar Ibn el-Khattab.

**Canon**: A list of the books of which the Bible is composed.

**Canonization**: The process by which the contents of the Holy Scriptures, and specifically, each of the sections of the Hebrew Bible, were closed and determined to be authoritative.

**Carbon 14**: The test performed by a chemical-physical process to determine the age of organic materials.

**Chiromancy**: A type of divination that involved foretelling a person's future or determining his nature based on either the lines in the palm or other features of the hand.

**Chronology** (Greek, "study of time"): A study of the time sequence of important events. A biblical chronology is an attempt to order the various dates preserved in Scripture to arrive at a complete list of events without gaps in time.

**Codification**: The collecting and editing of a group of compositions of laws with the aim of creating a fixed text or code.

**Corpus** (pl. corpora): Referring to a body of texts or manuscripts that have been grouped together, either in antiquity or by modern scholars.

**Cryptogram**: Greek for "mysterious writing." With regard to the Scrolls, this refers to deliberately coded words in the text, which are intended to hide the meaning from all but those with special knowledge. One example: the seven sets of Greek letters found at specific places within the *Copper Scroll.*

**Cult**: In general, the term *cult* can simply refer to a religious worship system; however, it has here the more technical sense of an aberrant religious group that deviates from orthodox Christianity in its christology (doctrine of Christ) and soteriology (doctrine of salvation).

**Diaspora**: Greek for "dispersion," referring to the Jewish population outside the land of Israel. During the time of the writers of the Dead Sea Scrolls the Diaspora communities were in Babylon and Egypt.

*Discoveries in the Judean Desert (DJD)*: The title of the official 30-volume series in ongoing preparation by Oxford University Press, which publishes the research of scholars assigned to the translation and commentary of the Scrolls as well as the work of excavations and other attendant studies.

*Doreshe Chalaqot*: Literally, "those who seek smooth things," this refers to "interpreters of false laws." It was used by the Dead Sea Sect to describe the Pharisees, who, by midrashic interpretation, derived laws that the Sect believed were invalid.

**Election**: An act of God whereby He sovereignly chooses an individual for eternal salvation (see also *predestination*).

**End of days /end time** (Hebrew, *qetz ha-yammim*): A biblical term that Jewish and Christian tradition has understood to refer to the eschatological messianic era. It is inclusive of both *Yom YHWH* ("the Day of the Lord"—in which God's judgment falls upon Israel's adversaries), as well as *Yemot ha-Mashiach* ("the days of Messiah"—the period preceding the judgment). It is followed by *'olam ha-ba* ("the world to come"), the eschatological future world.

**Eschatology**: Doctrines about the end of days or the messianic era.

**Eschaton**: The final or climatic end-time event, usually associated with the advent of the Messiah and the culmination of the present age.

**Essenes**: A Sect of Jews distinguished by their withdrawal from the mainstream of society, their piety, and their ascetic ideals. Many scholars identify this group with the Dead Sea Scrolls Sect.

**Exegesis** (adj. exegetical): Used in this book primarily to refer to interpretation of the Bible.

**First Temple**: The Jerusalem Temple erected by Solomon circa 960 B.C., which was destroyed by the Babylonians in 586 B.C.

**Genizah**: A storeroom for old Hebrew books no longer used for holy purposes. The famous Cairo Genizah yielded up a treasure of manuscripts of Second Temple, rabbinic, and medieval texts.

**Gnosticism** (Greek *gnosis*, "knowledge"): A variety of religious movements of the first centuries A.D. that stressed the relation of the self to a transcendent source of being (distinct from a creator God) through secret knowledge. This knowledge offered salvation from material existence.

**Great Revolt**: The Jewish revolt against Rome in A.D. 66–73.

**Halakhah** (pl. *halakhot*, adj. *halakhic*): A Hebrew designation for Jewish law, especially the laws of the Torah.

**Hasidim**: Hebrew for "pious ones," a loosely organized group of pietists known from the Maccabean period through Mishnaic times.

**Hasmonean**: Pertaining to the dynasty of Maccabean descendants and the period of their rule (152–3 B.C.).

**Hellenism**: The amalgamation of the Greek and native Near Eastern cultures that swept over the entire Near East in the wake of Alexander the Great's conquests.

**Hellenistic culture:** The culture that arose in the Near East after its conquest by Alexander the Great. Though this culture was basically Greek, it was deeply influenced by the Oriental culture of the region.

**Hermeneutic**: Pertaining to a system of interpretation. This term often refers to specific rules for the interpretation of biblical text.

**Infrared**: A method of photography by which even the most blurred writing is made clear and legible (see *Multispectral imaging*).

**Initiation**: The rituals or rites performed during a person's admittance to a secret association or Sect.

**Josephus, Flavius**: The Roman name of a Jewish historian and military leader known in Hebrew as *Yosef ben Mattiyahu* (Mattathias). His many historical writings, apparently intended for a Roman audience, constitute the best extra-biblical sources for the study of Jewish life during the Second Temple period.

**Jubilee**: The last year in a cycle of 50 years. The Jubilee is preceded by seven units of seven years, each culminating in a Sabbatical year.

**Karaism** (Hebrew, *Kara'im*; adj. Karaite): A movement in medieval Judaism that rejected the authority of the rabbinic tradition. The Karaites claimed instead to base themselves entirely on the interpretations of the written Torah.

**Karaites**: A Jewish Sect in the Middle Ages which opposed the ruling Jewish rabbis and rejected many traditional Jewish customs and texts. It has been suggested that the Karaites derived some of their customs and ideas from the ancient Qumran Sect.

**Khirbet**: Arabic for "ruin." The term is often used in placenames in which Arabic usage preserves the name of a place that has been destroyed.

**Kingdom of God**: The manifestation of God's dominion and of divine justice on earth in a spiritual sense, and especially the literal period of God's restoration of His divine plan in history at the end of days.

**Kittim**: A placename in the Aegean Islands, perhaps Kition in Cyprus, that, in Dead Sea Scrolls texts, serves as a code word for "Romans."

*Lacunae*: A Latin word meaning "omission" or "gap," used to describe missing words or lines in the text of the Dead Sea Scrolls due to damage or deterioration and is usually indicated by use of the deletion symbol in brackets: [. . .].

**Latter days/last days** (Hebrew, *'Acharit ha-yammim*): A biblical term that can indicate a final period in history climaxed by severe judgments ("latter days"), or the final days of history prior to the end time or end of days.

*Leitmotiv*: A German term meaning the "main idea" or "principal idea" of a literary or theological composition.

**Maccabean Revolt**: The Jewish revolt led by the Maccabean family against the Seleucid rulers of Syria in 168–164 B.C. The Jewish victory is celebrated on the holiday of Hanukkah.

**Maccabee**: The surname of Judah the Maccabee (probably "the Hammer" in Hebrew), son of Mattathias, used sometimes as surname of his family (see *Hasmoneans*).

**Maccabees**: The family of Judah the Maccabee. The term is often used imprecisely to designate later members of the Hasmonean dynasty as well.

**Manichaeanism**: A dualistic religious system founded in Mesopotamia by Mani in the third century A.D. It combines elements of gnostic Christianity with Eastern religions, yielding a doctrine based on the conflict of light and darkness.

**Masada**: A site on the western shore of the Dead Sea, the destruction of which brought to an end the Jewish revolt against Rome during A.D. 66–73.

*Mashiach*: Literally, "anointed," the Hebrew word transliterated in English as "messiah." The word derives from the fact that kings and priests in ancient Israel were anointed as a sign of God's confirmation of their appointment and of His attendant blessing.

**Maskil**: A person well schooled in the doctrines of the Qumran Sect. He was expected both to communicate those doctrines to fellow sectarians and to exemplify the sectarian way of life.

**Masorah** (Masoretic Text): The "traditional" (Hebrew *mesorah*) biblical text as it was passed down through the generations. This version of the Bible was made possible by the many Jewish rabbis and scholars who labored diligently to transmit a proper, precise text in the Masoretic tradition (see *Masoretic Text*).

**Masoretes**: The group of scholars (scribes) from Tiberias, Israel who worked to establish and preserve the correct form of the consonantal text of the Hebrew Bible.

**Masoretic Text**: The traditional or received Hebrew text of the Bible, which has been considered authoritative by Jews from Mishnaic times until the present. The term derives from Hebrew *mesorah*, "tradition" (see *Masorah*).

***Merkavah* mysticism**: A form of early Jewish mysticism that emphasized speculation about the nature of God's heavenly throne (Hebrew *merkavah*, lit. "chariot" = divine throne).

**Messianism**: The belief that a messiah will come to bring redemption to the world in the end of days.

**Metropolitan**: A high office in the priesthood of the Eastern (Syrian) Orthodox Church.

***Mevaqqer***: The sectarian "examiner," an official who supervised the day-to-day life of the Dead Sea Sect and kept its legal and financial records.

**Mezuzah** (pl. *mezuzot*): A manuscript of specific Bible verses affirming God's sovereignty over the world and the obligation to observe His law. This manuscript is affixed to the doorpost of a Jewish home in accord with the command of the Torah.

**Midrash** (adj. midrashic): A Hebrew term for the method of biblical interpretation that was current in rabbinic times and earlier. The term can also designate a collection of such interpretations produced by the rabbis.

**Miqveh** (pl. *miqva'ot*): A ritual bath that may be used to fulfill the Jewish requirement of immersion after contraction of ritual impurity.

**Minyan**: A quorum of ten adult male Jews (who are past the age of bar mitzvah), which makes possible the recitation of certain public prayers, according to talmudic law.

***Mishmarot***: The 24 courses into which the Jewish priests were divided. The courses were the subject of various Qumran texts that, while setting out the schedule for officiating in the Temple, set forth the solar calendar proposed by the Sect and related groups.

**Mishnah** (adj. mishnaic): The great collection of early rabbinic law edited by Rabbi Judah the Prince, circa A.D. 200. The term can also designate a particular paragraph of that code.

***Moreh ha-Sedeq***: Hebrew for "Righteous Teacher," or some prefer "Legitimate Teacher," the leader of the Qumran community (see *Teacher of Righteousness*).

*Musaf*: An additional service recited on Sabbaths and festivals in commemoration of the additional sacrifice that was offered on those days in the Second Temple.

**Multispectral Imaging (MSI)**: An infrared photography technique that employs special computer programs to enhance contrasts between different parts of an image to make completely illegible texts readable.

*Nahal*: Hebrew word (Arabic: *wadi*) for a riverbed that is dry during the summer or flowing with water after the winter rains. Settlements were usually built near these riverbeds for access to water, hence settlements and riverbeds often share the same placename (for example, Nahal Hever).

**Numismatic**: Pertaining to coins and coinage. Numismatic evidence is often used to date archaeological finds.

**Oral Law**: A second Torah (law), consisting of interpretations of the written Torah, which was studied and passed down by oral tradition. In rabbinic Judaism, this oral Torah, believed to have been given by God at Sinai along with the written Torah, constitutes the authoritative interpretation of the written law.

**Orthodox** (Greek, "straight"): Those holding to religious views that have been traditionally accepted and taught. *Orthodox Jews* are those accepting the *Tanakh* (Old Testament) as divine revelation, and the *Talmud* as divine direction for the interpretation of the *Tanakh*, and are observant (practitioners) of Jewish law. Orthodox Christians are those who accept the cardinal doctrines of the historic faith, whether as formulated by various creeds or by personal affirmation to the basic scriptural tenets of the triune nature of the One God (Father, Son, and Holy Spirit); the deity, virgin birth, and mediatorial work of Christ as an atoning Savior; and salvation by grace through personal faith in Christ apart from works. There are many different divisions within both orthodox Judaism and Christianity today.

**Ostracon** (pl. ostraca): A piece of broken pottery (a potsherd) used in antiquity for the writing of short texts or quick notes.

**Paleo-Hebrew** (Latin, *paleo*, "old"): The name given to the Hebrew script written in letters derived from the Phoenician alphabet and used by the scribes of the Second Temple period in preservation of the national script of Israel during the First Temple period.

**Paleography**: The study of the shapes of letters and their history, usually to facilitate the dating of inscriptions and manuscripts.

**Palestine/Palestinian**: A perjorative term for the country west of the Jordan River, first coined by the Greeks and Romans after the word *Philistine*. The Philistines were enemies of Israel who inhabited the Mediterranean coastal plain. The Bible refers to the same territory as *Canaan*, after its pre-Israelite inhabitants, though Jews have always called it *'Eretz Yisrael*, the land of Israel. Often used by writers to refer to Second Temple period Judaism resident in the land of Israel, hence "Palestinian Judaism."

**Papyrus**: A writing material made of the papyrus reed that was widely used in ancient times.

**Parchment**: The skin of an animal—especially a sheep or goat—processed in ancient times as a writing material. It was of a better quality and therefore more expensive than papyrus.

**Passover**: A Jewish springtime festival commemorating the Jewish exodus from Egyptian bondage in biblical times. It is celebrated with the eating of *matzah* (unleavened bread).

**Pentateuch**: The first five books of the Bible, also termed the Torah, or the Five Books of Moses.

*Peshat*: The plain or simple meaning of the biblical text, as opposed to midrashic or aggadic interpretation, which may add layers of meaning not immediately apparent.

*Pesher* (pl. *pesharim*): The unique biblical interpretations and commentaries of the Dead Sea Sect, which understood the words of the biblical prophets as referring to the experiences of sectarians in the Second Temple period.

**Pharisees**: A group of Jews in Second Temple times who constituted the spiritual forebears of the talmudic rabbis. Led by lay teachers of the Torah, they became the dominant sect. The word derives from the Hebrew word *perushim*, which means "separate."

**Phoenician script**: The form of writing that was widely used, even by the Jews, for a long period in ancient times.

**Phylacteries**: Cubical leather compartments that contain Bible passages emphasizing God's sovereignty and the obligation of the Jew to observe His commandments. These compartments are affixed to the head and arm with leather thongs. They are known in Hebrew as *tefillin*.

**Physiognomy**: A type of divination that involves foretelling a person's future or determining his nature based on the form or features of the body or, more specifically, the face.

**Polemics, polemical** (Greek, "to make war"): An argument or refutation, usually of an idea or practice and/or the group that holds the idea or practice. In the case of the Scrolls, the manner in which other sectarian groups may be described (that is, by example in order to refute the group).

**Predestination**: The belief that the process of history and the destiny of man are determined in advance by God.

**Proselyte**: A non-Jew who formally converts to Judaism.

**Pseudepigrapha** (adj. pseudepigraphic): Literally, referring to books written during the Hellenistic age in the name of an ancient Bible figure. More generally, the term is used to designate much of the religious literature of the various groups within Second Temple Judaism.

**Ptolemies**: The rulers of Egypt and its empire; they lived in the Hellenistic era. This dynasty took its name from Ptolemy, the general who retained control of Egypt after Alexander the Great's death.

**Qumran**: A site on the western shore of the Dead Sea. The Dead Sea Scrolls were uncovered in nearby caves. Qumran itself preserves the ruins of a building complex which served as the headquarters of the Sect in the Second Temple period.

**Rabbi**: Hebrew for "my master, my teacher," referring to the Jewish teachers and judges of Palestine in the Roman and Byzantine periods. The rabbis who shaped the texts of talmudic Judaism are collectively termed "the rabbis."

*Raz*: Hebrew for "mystery," referring to the mysteries of creation and the history of the universe. The Qumran Sect believed that such secrets could be understood only with the help of divine guidance.

*Raz Pesher*: A method of interpretation combining the *pesher* and *raz* to reveal the hidden secrets of past events as being fulfilled in the present.

**Redemption**: The state of heavenly bliss and reward which will be granted to man with the establishment of God's kingdom on earth in the end of days.

**Revelation**: The process by which God is believed to have revealed His will to the people of Israel and the world.

*Rosh Hashanah*: The Jewish New Year festival, which is observed in the fall. In post-biblical Judaism, it is a time for celebration of God's kingship and for introspection and repentance.

**Sabbath**: The seventh day of the Jewish week, upon which it is forbidden to work. This day is considered holy, and there are many special prayers, customs, and ceremonies connected with it.

**Sabbatical**: The designation for every seventh year, during which the Bible commands the remission of debts and prescribes leaving the land fallow.

**Sadducees**: A sect of Second Temple period Jews, connected primarily with the priestly aristocracy, which accepted only the authority of teachings based strictly on the Bible and its interpretation. The word derives from the name *Zadok*, the high priest in the time of King Solomon.

**Samaritans**. A Jewish sect comprised of a mixed people descended from those original northern Israelites who were not exiled in 722 B.C. and the tribes introduced into the area by the Assyrians. They separated from the rest of the Jewish people early in the Second Commonwealth and set up their own religious center on Mount Gerizim, situated north of the city of Shechem (modern-day Nablus).

**Samaritan Pentateuch**: The Bible of the Samaritan community, which, as the term *pentateuch* indicates, contains only the Torah or the first five books of Moses. It was written in paleo-Hebrew script, and although the Hebrew text is usually the same as the Masoretic text, it differs in about 6,000 readings (mostly minor variants, such as spelling), most of which agree with the LXX.

**Sanhedrin**: The highest court or council of the Jews in the last years of the Second Temple.

**Second Commonwealth**: The political organization of the Jewish people in the land of Israel beginning with the return from exile in the sixth century B.C. and ending with the final dismantling of the Herodian dynasty in the first century A.D.

**Second Temple**: The Jerusalem Temple that was constructed in 515 B.C. by Zerubbabel, reconstructed by Herod the Great (beginning circa 20 B.C.), and lasted until its destruction by the Romans in A.D. 70. The term can also be used to designate the period during which the Temple stood.

**Sect** (adj. sectarian): The term designates the various groups of Jews and their particular approaches to Judaism in Second Temple times. Such usage does not imply that any one of the groups is to be considered a mainstream.

**Sectarian**: See *Sect*.

**Seleucid**: The name given to the dynasty of Macedonian rulers who ruled a large part of the Greek Empire after Alexander the Great died. This empire stretched from Syria eastward and at various times (Hellenistic times) included Palestine.

**Septuagint**: The Greek translation of the Bible, produced in Egypt in the Hellenistic period.

***Sererkh*** (pl. *serekhim*): A list of laws or regulations compiled by the Dead Sea Sect as part of their regular formal study sessions.

***Shavuot***: The Jewish holiday of Pentecost, which, in Bible times, was connected with the offering of the firstfruits of the wheat harvest. Later, *Shavuot* came to commemorate the giving of the Torah at Sinai as well.

***Shekinah***: The Hebrew term used to describe the dwelling of God's manifested presence on earth within the Tabernacle or Temple. The word is derived from the verbal form *shakan* ("to dwell") as is the word for the Tabernacle *mishkan* ("dwelling").

***Shemoneh Esreh***: The "18" benedictions (now actually 19) that constitute the central prayer in Jewish services. Known also as the Amidah.

**Sicarii**: A group of revolutionaries who fought against Rome in first-century A.D. Palestine. They were known for the dagger [Latin *sica*] they carried.

**Scriptorium**: A two-story (or second-story) room equipped with the tools the scribes needed for their work. Here the scribes wrote and copied their various texts and documents.

*Soferim*: Hebrew for "scribes," referring to the early Pharisaic sages.

**Stichometry**: Related to determining the average length of reconstructed lines produced by combinations of letter counts, this method is used in comparing unknown fragmentary texts with known manuscripts in order to identify the former.

*Succah* (pl. *Succot*): Hebrew for "booth," this term refers to the temporary shelter Jews erect in observance of the fall festival of Succot, the Jewish holiday of Tabernacles, which is connected with the fall harvest and commemorates both the exodus from Egypt and God's protection of the Israelites when they were wandering in the desert.

**Synagogue**: A Jewish house of worship. In Hellenistic usage, the term also referred to a Jewish community.

*Ta'amrieh*: The name of the seminomadic Bedouin tribe whose members found the first Dead Sea Scrolls in Cave 1 and also made most of the other significant finds in caves throughout the Judean desert region.

*Tabnit*: The Hebrew term used first in Exodus 25:8 and then repeated in commands and discussions (Exodus 25:40; 1 Chronicles 28:11-12, 19) to describe the plan or design for the earthly Temple based on the heavenly Temple as a prototype.

**Talmud** (adj. talmudic): Referring to the Mishnah and Gemara, the literary results of the rabbinic discussions of Jewish law and tradition.

**Talmud** (Hebrew, "teaching"): The entire corpus of Jewish Oral Law, including the Mishnah, together with a written compendium of discussions and commentary on the Mishnah, called the *Gemara*. The Talmud's teachings and rulings span a period from Ezra in the Old Testament (circa 450 B.C.) to the middle of the Roman period (circa A.D. 550). Because it includes rulings made by generations of scholars and jurists in many academies in both Palestine and Babylon, it exists in two versions: the Jerusalem Talmud, referred to as Talmud Yerushalmi, consisting of discussions held in the Jerusalem academies and compiled in Israel at the end of the fourth century A.D., and the Babylonian Talmud, referred to as the Talmud Babli, consisting of discussions in the Babylonian academies and edited at the end of the fifth century A.D. Talmudic Judaism is that which was defined by the rabbis in the first two centuries A.D. and further expounded until the end of the fifth century.

**Tanakh**: Term used for the Jewish Bible, comprised of the Hebrew initials for the word *Torah* ("law"), *Neveim* ("prophets"), and *Ketubim* ("writings"), the three divisions of the Old Testament.

**Tannaim** (adj. Tannaitic): The teachers of the Mishnah, Tosefta, and halakhic Midrashim, who flourished circa 50 B.C.–A.D. 200.

**Targum** (Hebrew, "translation"): The authorized Aramaic translation of the Torah by the proselyte Onkelos (circa A.D. 90). In Talmudic times, it was read along with the Torah, so that the congregation could understand what was being read (see Nehemiah 8:7-8). In many cases, the Targum renders the text homiletically rather than literally.

**Teacher of Righteousness** (Hebrew *Moreh Ha-Tzedeq*): The sectarian leader who appears to have arisen soon after the founding of the Dead Sea Sect and whose enlightened insight interpreted for the community the prophetic calculations concerning the end time. It is possible there was a series of teachers who filled this role.

***Tefillin***: Cubical compartments of leather that contain Bible passages emphasizing God's sovereignty and the Jews' obligation to observe His commandments. The compartments are affixed to the head and arm with leather thongs. They are also known as phylacteries.

**Tetragrammaton**: The four-lettered name of God, YHWH, found written in the ancient paleo-Hebrew script in some Dead Sea Scrolls. Already in late antiquity this name was not pronounced because of the great reverence in which it was held. It was therefore also called the ineffable name.

**Textual Criticism**: The name given to the technical study of ancient manuscripts and versions of texts of the Old and New Testaments in order to establish a correct reading of the text.

**Torah**: The Five Books of Moses, the Pentateuch. The Hebrew word *torah* literally means "instruction, teaching."

**Tosefta**: A collection of early rabbinic traditions that were not included in the Mishnah. The Tosefta is the earliest commentary to the Mishnah and is organized in approximately the same manner.

**Tribulation**: That period of time, according to the biblical prophets, during which Israel as a nation experiences unparalleled distress as a part of the "Day of the Lord." In Jewish theology it is the time of "messianic woes" or "messianic birthpangs" prior to the coming of the Messiah.

**Typology** (Greek *tupos*, "type"): The study of the various types found in the Bible, all of which foreshadowed later, more developed revelations of characters or figures (the antitypes), whether positive or negative. A positive example is David as a type of Christ (Psalm 22:1 > Matthew 27:46). A negative example is Antiochus as a type of Antichrist (Daniel 11:21-35 > 36-45).

**Vorlage**: A German word designating the Hebrew text that "lay before" an ancient copyist or translator of the Bible or an author who composed a text adapted from biblical material.

*Wadi* (or *Wady*): An Arabic word (Hebrew: *nahal*) for a riverbed that is dry during the summer and flowing with water after the winter rains. Most settlements were built near wadis for access to water; hence settlements and wadis often share the same placename (for example, Wadi Qumran, Khirbet Qumran).

**Wicked Priest**: A Hasmonean priestly leader seen as the Qumran Sect's arch-enemy. This priest apparently came to Qumran, where he had a confrontation with the Teacher of Righteousness.

**Wisdom literature**: A genre of literature known throughout the ancient Near East, which preaches common-sense wisdom and values designed to result in a happier and more just life.

*Yom Kippur* (Hebrew, "Day of Atonement"): The most solemn day of the Jewish year, celebrated on the ninth day of Tishri (September–October on the Julian calendar), ten days after the Jewish New Year. Considered the day of judgment and reckoning, it is a time when the Jews individually and as a nation are cleansed of sin and granted atonement. It was on this day alone that the high priest was permitted to enter the Holy of Holies in the Temple. In post-biblical tradition, the theme of the day is human repentance, which leads to divine forgiveness.

**Zadok** (adj. Zadokite): Zadok was one of King Solomon's high priests in the tenth century B.C. His Zadokite priestly line dominated the high priesthood for most of Jewish history.

**Zion** (Hebrew, "disputed"): Originally the hill area north of the City of David, the *'Ophel*, where the Tabernacle resided. Through poetic usage it became a synonym for the city of Jerusalem and Israel itself, and spiritually as the eschatological ideal of God's chosen place on earth.

**Zoroastrianism**: An Iranian religion supposedly founded around 600 B.C. Zoroastrianism is dualistic, believing in a struggle between the cosmic forces of good and evil.

# Endnotes

## Introduction

1. *The New Yorker* magazine (May 1955), pp. 45-131.

2. Edmund Wilson, *The Scrolls from the Dead Sea* (New York: Oxford University Press, 1955). This was a slightly enlarged version of the article, supplemented with information about the author's personal trip to the Dead Sea region and conversations with original participants in the Scroll discoveries.

3. Harry M. Orlinsky, "Closing Remarks," Session VI. Forty Years of Dead Sea Scroll Research, *Biblical Archaeology Today, 1990: Proceedings of the Second International Congress on Biblical Archaeology* (Jerusalem: Israel Exploration Society, 1993), p. 412.

4. Millar Burrows, *More Light on the Dead Sea Scrolls* (London: Secker & Warburg, 1958), p. 14.

## Chapter 1—The Drama of the Scrolls

1. Paul Ilton, *The Bible Was My Treasure Map* (New York: Julian Messner, Inc., 1958), p. 17.

2. Charles Pellegrino, *Return to Sodom and Gomorrah: Bible Stories from Archaeologists* (New York: Random House, 1994), p. 320.

3. The list of those killed have included many scholars and archaeologists, among them Ugaritic scholar Father Mitchell Dahood (1979) and archaeological artist and architect Marta Ritmeyer (1995) at the Wadi Qelt.

4. Roland de Vaux, "Qumran, Khirbet and 'Ein Feshkha," *The New Encyclopedia of Archaeological Excavations in the Holy Land.* Ed. Ephraim Stern (Jerusalem: The Israel Exploration Society) 4: 1235. The use of the Hebrew term *midbar* for "wilderness" indicates that the wilderness condition was regarded as so constitutive for the region that it could even provide the name for a province at this early date, cf. Ulrich Mauser, *Christ in the Wilderness. Studies in Biblical Theology 39* (Naperville, IL: Alec R. Allenson, Inc., 1963), p. 58.

5. Cf. Neil Asher Silberman, *The Hidden Scrolls* (New York: G.P. Putman's Sons, 1994), pp. 5-7.

6. Lawrence E. Stager, "Farming in the Judean Desert During the Iron Age," *Bulletin of the American School of Oriental Research* 221 (1976): 145-58.

7. Aubrey Richardson, Sr. and Garold R. Collett, "Qumran: Summary Excerpts of Research and Reports from 1988 thru 1990" (updated edition, Nov./Dec. 1990), p. 6.

8. See further W.R. Stegner, "The Self-understanding of the Qumran Community compared with the Self-understanding of the early Church" (unpublished doctoral dissertation, Drew University, 1960). Stegner argues for the Exodus motif being the primary key for self-understanding, but his parallels between the exodus generation and the Qumran community are at times excessive.

9. For the most recent defense for this interpretation see George J. Brooke, "Isaiah 40:3 and the Wilderness Community," *New Qumran Texts and Studies,* and *Studies on the Texts of the Judean Desert,* vol. 15, ed. F. Garcia Martinez and A.S. Van Der Woude (Leiden: E.J. Brill, 1994), pp. 117-32.

10. For this discussion cf. Shemaryahu Talmon, "The 'Desert Motif' in the Bible and in Qumran Literature," *Biblical Motifs: Origins and Transformations. Studies and Texts 3.* ed. Alexander Altmann (Cambridge: Harvard University Press, 1966), pp. 56-57. It may be precisely for this

negative reason that the desert motif was infrequently used in the Qumran literature, even though it was of strategic significance.

11. Ibid., pp. 57-58.

12. Yigael Yadin, *The Message of the Scrolls* (New York: Simon and Schuster, Inc., 1957), p. 14.

13. David Ben Gurion, *Rebirth and Destiny of Israel* (New York: Philosophical Library, 1954).

14. Yigael Yadin, *The Message of the Scrolls*, p. 14.

15. Cf. the ad that appeared before the Six-Day War in the *Washington Post*, May 21, 1967, announcing efforts to raise funds for rebuilding, and the article in *Time* magazine, "Should the Temple Be Rebuilt," June 30, 1967, p. 56, and the statements of Rabbi Sinai Halberstam, "The Beth Hamikdosh," in *The Jewish Press*, August 2, 1968, pp. 19-20. In addition, in 1967 orthodox groups that wanted to see the Third Temple built began organizing, although many did not become public until the beginning of the Palestinian *Intafada* in 1987. An investigation of these group's activities prior to 1987 revealed several aggressive attempts to enter the Temple Mount, but most of their activities consisted of organized study groups in yeshivot (seminaries), synagogues, or private homes.

### Chapter 2—The Story of the Scrolls

1. "The Shepherd Boy Who Discovered the Scrolls" (unpublished paper, 1993), p. 20.

2. Some accounts make Jum'a Muhammed (Muhammed edh-Dhib's older cousin) responsible for the initial find—see Harry Thomas Frank, "How the Dead Sea Scrolls Were Found," *Biblical Archaeology Review* 1:4 (December, 1975), p. 1.

3. This theory is most fervently defended by Solomon Zeitlin in a series of articles in his *Jewish Quarterly Review*—"The Alleged Antiquity of the Scrolls," *Jewish Quarterly Review* 40 (1949-50): 57-72.

4. William Brownlee reported the rumor of a murder in *Revue de Qumran* 3 (1961-62): 493, n. 28.

5. For a secondary source for this story see Edward M. Cook, *Solving the Mysteries of the Dead Sea Scrolls: New Light on the Bible* (Grand Rapids, MI: Zondervan Publishing Co., 1994), p. 29, n. 1.

6. G. Lancaster Harding in *Discoveries in the Judean Desert I*. Edited by D. Barthélemy and J.T. Milik (Oxford, 1955), p. 5.

7. Direct interviews with the original participants would have helped resolve contradictions in the history of the early discoveries. As it is, Metropolitan Bishop Mar Athanasius Samuel died in 1994 in Hackensack, New Jersey, and the Bethlehem dealer Kando died in 1995 in East Jerusalem. Unfortunately, neither the present successor to Mar Samuel at St. Mark's Monastery, nor Kando's son Edmund (both of whom I spoke with) have any exact knowledge of the events.

8. The report was made by the Rev. Dr. R. North, S.J., former director of the Pontifical Biblical Institutes at Rome and Jerusalem, and published in "Extracts from an illustrated lecture given by Rev. Dr. R. North, S.J.," *An Account of a Three-day School on The Dead Sea Scrolls Held At St. Andrew's College, on May 20–22, 1963* (Department of Semitic Studies, University of Sydney, 1964), p. 80.

9. William H. Brownlee, "Muhammad Ed-Deeb's Own Story of His Scroll Discovery," *Journal of Near Eastern Studies* 16:4 (October, 1957): 236–39.

10. Dr. R. North, *An Account of a Three-day School*, p.80.

11. This account was published as Appendix I in John Trevor's *The Untold Story of Qumran* (Old Tappan, NJ: Fleming H. Revell Company, 1965), pp. 169-71.

12. Perhaps the reason this account was told was because Jum'a was more directly involved with the discovery of Cave 4. However, in my own interviews with Muhammed edh-Dhib I had difficulty with his sometimes confusing these two accounts. Only when interrupted and asked which cave he was speaking about could the proper identification be made. This might be understood of a

man nearly 80 years of age, but not of one in his fifties. The only remaining explanation seems to be that the Cave 4 discovery was being described in 1961. Either there were conflations from the original story or perhaps the discrepancies came in response to the questions, which did not specifically differentiate the time or location of the discoveries because the questioners believed that only one time and one cave was being considered.

13. Abu-Dahoud's son David, at the time of this writing, is 35 years old. This son was not born to Abu-Dahoud's first wife (who was barren), but to his second wife. He married his second wife 20 years after his first, and had David two years later.

14. There was also the assumption held by Kando (and his son Edmund) that Muhammed had died, since it had been over 30 years since they had had contact. This assumption may have been passed on to those who interviewed Kando and asked about Muhammed.

15. On two separate occasions Abu-Dahoud told me he was 27 and 35 when he first discovered the Scrolls; however, he told Weston Fields that he was 18. He said in 1993 that he had gotten married at age 20 and had been married for 55 years, which would have made him 75 at the time. Yet in 1995 he told me he was 80 years old. He told Dr. Fields that he had discovered 45 jars in Cave 1, but he told me 47. By contrast, the first report in 1947 had been of eight jars. He told me that he found five Scrolls in Cave 1 and that two were damaged and disposed of; however, he told Dr. Fields that four Scrolls had been discovered and one damaged. He had said in 1957 that the Scrolls remained in his tent for two years, but in 1993 he said it was six months to a year. In 1993 he led Drs. Fields and Pfann to a different cave than that which is recognized as Cave 1, and mockingly rejected the traditional Cave 1. But in 1995 when we arrived at the traditional Cave 1 he was at first confused, but then excitedly recognized it as "the cave," and described it in pre-excavation detail, re-enacting his discovery of the Scrolls there. The most serious problems yet to be resolved are the chronological inconsistencies in Abu-Dahoud's accounts.

16. It was suggested to me that an enterprising Bedouin would not hesitate to make the claim to have been the discoverer of the Scrolls if tourists and reporters would pay money for his picture or an interview. Therefore, in seeking to confirm the identity of Abu-Dahoud as Muhammed edh-Dhib, we 1) had the assurance of David Bar Levav, whose reputation as a professional antiquities dealer requires him to certify his sources, 2) found that according to Steve Pfann and Weston Fields that they were aware of a large number of Abu-Dahoud's relatives living in Bethlehem, who all confirmed his connection with the Scrolls, 3) compared an old photograph of Muhammed with present photos of Abu-Dahoud and there is sufficient resemblance to establish identity, although one of the most popularly published photos captioned as Muhammed is, according to Abu-Dahoud, actually his friend Jamal, and 4) tested Abu-Dahoud concerning details of the caves, the other names of the Bedouin known to have been involved, and the transactions with Kando, and we were satisfied that he showed a correct knowledge of known facts. His own explanations of the sites and the Scroll transactions fit well within this known context. Where else could he have learned these things? He has no education, can neither read nor write, and speaks little to no English or Hebrew. And even if he could read, hardly any literature about the Scrolls is available in Arabic.

17. I understand that Abu-Dahoud has been filmed before in an interview setting, but never on location at the original caves. For our film entitled *Secrets of the Dead Sea Scrolls*, contact: World of the Bible Ministries, Inc., 110 Easy Street, San Marcos, Texas 78666-7326, or call (512) 396-3799.

18. "The Shepherd Boy Who Discovered the Scrolls" (unpublished paper, 1993).

19. Abu-Dahoud says that of this group he only knows that Juma'a is alive (at the age of 90) and living in Bethlehem.

20. For example, Yigael Yadin had several jars in his private collection. Edmund Kando, the son of the famous Jalil Iskandar Shalim Kando, today has one jar (with a lid) in his souvenir shop office (see photo section). And Manchester University professor John Allegro was rumored to have one in his living room!

21. Abu-Dahoud does not know the numerical designations for the caves, but as we went together to Caves 1, 4, and 11, he explained what Scrolls he had found and where and when he had found them.

22. Nevertheless, based on the known dates of 1947 for the first recorded appearance of the seven Scrolls to interested parties, Kando must have kept the Scrolls together.

23. Mar Athanasius Samuel, *Treasure of Qumran: My Story of the Dead Sea Scrolls* (Philadelphia: Westminster Press, 1966), p. 149.

24. Edward M. Cook, *Solving the Mysteries of the Dead Sea Scrolls:* p.14.

25. Interview with Rev. Shemun Can, Syrian Orthodox Monastery of Saint Mark, November 11, 1995.

26. According to Sukenik, when Feidi Salahi was originally offered the seven Scrolls for £20, he refused, stating that the price was too high! However, he later bought the three Scrolls, which eventually went to Sukenik. See E.L. Sukenik, "The Isaiah Scrolls," *Israel Life and Letters* (May/June, 1953), p. 31.

27. Yigael Yadin, *The Message of the Scrolls* (New York: Simon and Schuster, 1957), p. 19.

28. Ibid., p. 24.

29. John C. Trevor, *The Untold Story of Qumran*, p. 27.

30. Millar Burrows, *Palestine Is Our Business* (Philadelphia: Westminster Press, 1949).

31. Yigael Yadin, "The Temple Scroll—the Longest and Most Recently Discovered Scroll," *Biblical Archaeology Review* 10:5 (Sept./Oct. 1984), p. 33.

32. Harry Orlinsky, "The Mysterious Mr. Green," *Reform Judaism* 20:3 (Spring, 1992): 47-48.

33. Yadin, *The Message of the Scrolls*, pp. 44, 49.

34. *The Temple Scroll*, ed. Yigael Yadin (Jerusalem: The Israel Exploration Society, 1983), 1:1. Yadin died the next year.

35. See Florentino Garcia Martinez, "*11QTemple*ᵇ. A Preliminary Publication," *The Madrid Qumran Congress*, 2. eds. Julio Trenolle Barrera, Luis Vegas Montaner. *Studies on the Texts of the Desert of Judah*. 11:2. eds. F. Garcia Martinez, A.S. Van der Woude (Leiden: E.J. Brill, 1992), pp. 363-391.

36. The account of Rev. Joseph Uhrig's involvement was first reported by Hershel Shanks, "Intrigue and the Scroll: Behind the Scenes of Israel's Acquisition of the Temple Scroll," *Biblical Archaeology Review* 13:6 (November/December, 1987), pp. 23-27.

37. Ibid., p. 25.

38. *The Temple Scroll*, 1:4.

## Chapter 3—The Scandal of the Scrolls

1. Michael Baigent and Richard Leigh, *The Dead Sea Scrolls Deception* (New York: Summit Books, 1991), p. 129.

2. Not all the Cave 4 fragments were brought to the Palestine Archaeological Museum by Kando in 1952. Apparently they were brought in by lots, with the last lot purchased in 1958.

3. Origen probably never used the term *Hexapla*, which refers to the work based on its form of presentation in six parallel columns. However, it is believed that some portions contained seven (*Heptapla*) and eight (*Octapla*) columns, incorporating three versions in addition to those in the main body of the work.

4. The most recent edition of the Hexaplaric remains is that by Frederick Fields, *Origenis Hexaplorum quae supersunt*, 2 vols. (Oxford: University Press, 1875).

5. *The Dead Sea Scriptures*, trans. and ed. by Theodor H. Gaster (Garden City, NY: Anchor Books/Doubleday).

6. Just as the first seven Scrolls from Cave 1 were published by non-International Team members, so also were other Scrolls that had been committed to institutions or reserved in a museum safe published by nonmembers. These included the publication of the *Psalms Scroll (11QPsa)* by American James Sanders (1965), the *Targum of Job (11QtgJob)* by the two Dutch scholars J.P.M. van der Ploeg and A.S. van der Woude (1971), the *Temple Scroll (11Q19)* by Israeli Yigael Yadin (1977), and the *Leviticus Scroll (11QpaleoLev)* by American D.N. Freedman (1985).

7. John M. Allegro, *Qumran Cave 4:I (4Q158–4Q186), Discoveries in the Judean Desert V* (Oxford University Press, 1968).

8. Baigent and Leigh, *The Dead Sea Scrolls Deception*, p. 235.

9. This statement appeared on the book flap of the German edition of the book by Betz and Reisner, *Jesus, Qumran and the Vatican*, as the authors note on page 11.

10. Baigent and Leigh, *The Dead Sea Scrolls Deception*, pp. 136-37.

11. "This volume will probably be remembered mainly for Eisenman's attempt further to support his thesis that the Dead Sea Scrolls (or at least some of them) reflect Jewish Christianity," Philip S. Alexander, "Reviews," *Journal of Jewish Studies* (1993): 139.

12. Jonas C. Greenfield, "Deception Afoot," Book Review section, *Jerusalem Post Magazine* (February 19, 1993), p. 26.

13. Interview with Emanuel Tov, Hebrew University, Jerusalem, November 7, 1995.

14. Joseph A. Fizmyer, *Responses to 101 Questions on the Dead Sea Scrolls* (New York: Paulist Press, 1992), p. 169.

15. Geza Vermes, *The Dead Sea Scrolls: Qumran in Perspective* (London, 1973), p. 23.

16. Klaus Berger, *Jesus and the Dead Sea Scrolls: The Truth Under Lock and Key?* trans. by James S. Currie (Louisville, KY: Westminster John Knox Press, 1995), pp. 6-10.

17. See Menahem Kister, "Notes on Some New Texts from Qumran," *Journal of Jewish Studies* 44:2 (Autumn, 1993), pp. 282-86.

18. Roland de Vaux did have to acquiesce in one of the Antiquity Authority's demands: the *DJD* series had to drop the last two words from its former title: *Discoveries in the Judean Desert* of Jordan.

19. Interview with Emanuel Tov, November 7, 1995.

20. See Lawrence Schiffman, *Reclaiming the Dead Sea Scrolls* (New York: Doubleday, 1994), p. 11. This is contrary to the statement of Joseph Fitzmyer that "the exclusion of Jews from the International Team was not because of anti-Semitism; it was dictated by the political situation of the time." *Responses to 101 Questions on the Dead Sea Scrolls* (New York: Paulist Press, 1992), p. 151.

21. Interview with Dr. Weston Fields, Jerusalem, November 9, 1995.

22. Interview with Emanuel Tov, Hebrew University, Jerusalem, November 7, 1995.

23. David Noel Freedman, "Letter to the Readers," *Biblical Archaeology Review* 40:2 (September/October 1977), pp. 96- 97.

24. Interview with Weston Fields, Jerusalem, November 9, 1995.

25. Interview with Emanuel Tov, Hebrew University, Jerusalem, November 7, 1995.

26. Karlheinz Müller, "Die Handschriften und Editonen der ausserbiblischen Qumranliteratur," in J. Schreiner, *Einführung in die Methoden der biblischen Exegese* (Würzburg, 1971), p. 310, as cited in Betz and Reisner, *Jesus, Qumran and the Vatican*, p. 11.

27. The report is currently being translated, revised, and prepared for publication by Dr. Stephen Pfann.

28. Interview with Dr. Dan Bahat, Meveseret Tzion, November 12, 1995.

29. Interview with Frank Moore Cross on the Australian Broadcasting Network, as reported in *Biblical Archaeology Review* 16:2 (March/April 1990), p. 22.

486

30. John M. Allegro, *The Sacred Mushroom and the Cross* (Garden City, NY: Doubleday and Co., 1970), and *The Dead Sea Scrolls and the Christian Myth* (Buffalo, NY: Prometheus Books, 1984). For additional details on Allegro's strange diversions and views, see Edward M. Cook, *Solving the Mysteries of the Dead Sea Scrolls: New Light on the Bible* (Grand Rapids, MI: Zondervan Publishing Co., 1994), pp. 47-50.

31. Interview with Emanuel Tov, Hebrew University, Jerusalem, November 7, 1995.

32. The *Los Angeles Times*, September 23-24, 1991.

33. Ibid.

34. Ibid.

35. Ibid.

36. Interview with Dr. Weston Fields, Jerusalem, November 9, 1995.

**Chapter 4—A Survey of the Scrolls**

1. Although no copy of the book of Nehemiah has been found, it is assumed that it was considered by the Qumran community to be one book with Ezra, which was present. The inclusion of Esther may be assumed by the many Aramaic fragments from Cave 4 called *Proto-Esther (4Q550),* and the presence of terms unique to Esther in some Scrolls.

2. Hellenistic practice involved the formation of libraries, which, in contrast to Pharisaic Judaism, only preserved the biblical books and sought to perpetuate an oral Torah. They considered library collections, which included apocryphal and secular historical books, as heretical. The Sadducees did accept apocryphal books, and such were included among the Dead Sea Scrolls; however, in contrast to Hellenistic Judaism, no fragment of a historical book has ever been found. For more, see also Yaacov Shavit, "The 'Qumran Library' in Light of the Attitude Towards Books and Libraries in the Second Temple Period," *Methods of Investigation of the Dead Sea Scrolls and the Khirbet Qumran Site: Present Realities and Future Prospects,* eds. M. Wise, N. Golb, J.J. Collins, and D. Pardee (New York: New York Academy of Sciences, 1994), pp. 299-317.

3. See Lawrence Schiffman, "The Significance of the Scrolls," *Bible Review* 6:5 (October 1990), p. 23.

4. Interview with Emanuel Tov, Hebrew University, November 7, 1995.

5. See Shemaryahu Talmon, *The World of Qumran from Within* (Jerusalem: The Magnes Press, 1989, pp. 274-75; for more comprehensive surveys see F.M. Cross, *The Ancient Library of Qumran and Biblical Studies* (New York: Doubleday, 1961); and Geza Vermes, *The Dead Sea Scrolls: Qumran in Perspective* (London: SCM Press, 1982).

6. See Dodo Joseph Shenhav, "Saving the Dead Sea Scrolls for the Next 2000 Years," *Biblical Archaeology Review* 7:4 (July/August 1981), p. 47.

7. "Conservators Race Against Time to Save the Scrolls," *Biblical Archaeology Review* (July/August 1992), p. 70.

8. See James A. Sanders, *The Dead Sea Psalms Scroll* (Ithaca, NY: Cornell University, 1967).

9. For more on the tefillin, see Yigael Yadin, *Tefillin from Qumran (XQPhyl 1-4)* (Jerusalem: The Israel Exploration Society and the Shrine of the Book, 1969).

10. The term is used once in the Bible (Ecclesiastes 8:1) to introduce the interpretation of a biblical text, although it may be related to the Hebrew root *ptr* ("solve, interpret"), which was used in Genesis to speak of the interpretation of dreams. Its use is also attested by Akkadian *pisru* and Aramaic *psr,*' cf. I. Rabinowitz, "Pesher/Pittaron," *Revue de Qumran* 8 (1973): 219-32.

11. The Hebrew phrases are *pisro 'al* ("the interpretation of it [is] about . . ."), *pisro 'asher* ("the interpretation of it [is] what . . ."), and *pesher haddabar 'asher* ("the interpretation of the word/matter [is] what . . .").

12. *Anchor Bible Dictionary,* s.v. "Qumran Pesher," by Devorah Dimant (New York: Doubleday, 1992), 5:250.

13. A fourth form has been classified as *miscellaneous forms of pesharim*. Some of these function in the form of epithets that serve as cryptograms for pesher-type interpretations of biblical passages such as "the Teacher of Righteousness" which is based on Hosea 10:12 and Joel 2:18-27 (especially verse 23). Others function as interpretation by allusion (i.e., without explicit citation), such as in the *Pesher Habakkuk (1QpHab* 11:12-14) on Habakkuk 2:16 to Deuteronomy 10:16; Jeremiah 4:4.

14. For more on this, see John J. Collins, *The Scepter and the Star: The Messiahs of the Dead Sea Scrolls and Other Ancient Literature*, The Anchor Bible Reference Library (New York: Doubleday, 1995), pp. 61-63.

15. Interview with Shemaryahu Talmon, Jerusalem, November 12, 1995.

16. A survey of these works can be found in any Catholic commentary, e.g., *The Jerome Biblical Commentary*. eds. Raymond Brown, Joseph Fitzmeyer, Roland Murphy (New Jersey: Prentice-Hall, Inc., 1968), or the older and more technical work by R.H. Charles, *The Apocrypha and Pseudepigrapha of the Old Testament*, Volume 1: Apocrypha (Oxford: Clarendon Press, 1913).

17. Interview with Dr. Shemaryahu Talmon, Jerusalem, November 12, 1995.

**Chapter 5—The Scribes of the Scrolls**

1. Interview with Emanuel Tov, Hebrew University, November 7, 1995.

2. Interview with Shemaryahu Talmon, Jerusalem, November 12, 1995.

3. Joseph Blenkinsopp, "Interpretation and the Tendency to Sectarianism: An Aspect of Second Temple History," *Aspects of Judaism in the Graeco-Roman Period in Jewish* in *Christian Self-Definition*, ed. E.P. Sanders (Philadelphia: Fortress Press, 1981), 2:1-2.

4. Interview with Magen Broshi, Shrine of the Book, Jerusalem, November 12, 1995.

5. The principal ancient sources for the Essenes are Flavius Josephus (*Jewish Wars* 1.3.5 § 78-80; 2.7.3 § 113; 2.8.2-13 § 119-61; 2.20.4 § 567; 3.2.1 § 11; 5.4.2 § 145; *Life* [of Josephus] 2 § 7-12; *Antiquities of the Jews* 13.5.9 § 171-72; 15.10.4-5 § 371-79; 18.1.5 § 18-22), Pliny the Elder (*Natural History* 5.17.4 § 73), and also Philo of Alexandria [if his Essenes are the same Essenes as Josephus and Pliny describe] (*Quod omnis prob. liber* 12-13 § 75-91; *Hypothetica* 11.1-18 in Eusebius, *Praepartio evangelium* 8.6-7; on the Egyptian Therapeutae cf. *De vita contemp* 1 § 1-2; 2-4 § 11-40; 8-11 § 63-90). Other ancient sources, mainly the writings of early church fathers, may also present details about the Essenes; cf. for listing, Geza Vermes, *The Essenes According to the Classical Sources*. Oxford Centre Textbooks 1 (Sheffield: Journal for the Study of the Old Testament, 1989).

6. Frank Moore Cross, "The Early History of the Qumran Community," *New Directions in Biblical Archaeology*, eds. David Noel Freedman, Jonas C. Greenfield (Garden City, NJ: Doubleday, 1971), p. 77.

7. Todd S. Beall, *Josephus' Description of the Essenes Illustrated by the Dead Sea Scrolls*, Society for New Testament Studies Monograph Series 58 (Cambridge: University Press, 1988).

8. He also found 21 probable parallels, 10 cases where there were no known parallels, and 6 discrepancies between the Scrolls and the Essenes (however, in two of the six instances the Scrolls disagree with themselves). Ibid., pp. 123-24.

9. One of the earliest studies reviewing these problems was that by the famous Jewish scholar M.H. Gottstein, "Anti-Essene Traits in the Dead Sea Scrolls," *Vetus Testamentum* 4 (April 1954): 141-47.

10. This etymology was first proposed by Dupont-Sommer, *The Essene Writings from Qumran* (Glouchester, MA: Peter Smith, 1973), p. 43. The Hebrew term *'asa* ("to do, bear, bring forth") has also been proposed with the idea that the Essenes sought to do the will of God in order to "bring forth" His redemption, although the reason for the Sect using this name is unsupportable; see S. Goranson, " 'Essenes': Etymology from *'sh*," *Revue de Qumran* 11 (1982-4), pp. 488-98.

11. Interview with Shemaryahu Talmon, Jerusalem, November 12, 1995.

488

12. See Menahem Stern, "Aspects of Jewish Society: The Priesthood and Other Classes" in *The Jewish People in the First Century*, eds. S. Safrai, M. Stern, *Compendia rerum judaicarum and novum testamentum* 1/2 (Assen and Philadelphia, 1976), 2:561, 567.

13. *Encyclopedia Judaica* s.v. "Sadducees," by Menahem Mansoor (Jerusalem: Keter Publishing House, 1972), 14:622.

14. *Anchor Bible Dictionary* s.v. "Sadducees," by Gary G. Porton (New York: Doubleday, 1992), 5:892, 894.

15. Lawrence Schiffman, "The New Halakhic Letter *(4QMMT)* and the Origins of the Dead Sea Sect," *Biblical Archaeologist* (June 1990): 70.

16. Lawrence Schiffman, *Sectarian Law in the Dead Sea Scrolls: Courts, Testimony, and Penal Code* (Chico, CA: Scholars Press, 1983), pp. 20-21.

17. Lawrence Schiffman, *Reclaiming the Dead Sea Scrolls* (New York: Doubleday, 1994), p. 95.

18. Kenneth Hanson, "Reflections of Early Halakha in the Dead Sea Scrolls" (Ph.D. dissertation, University of Texas at Austin, 1991).

19. J.T. Milik, *Ten Years of Discovery in the Wilderness of Judaea*, trans. John Strugnell, *Studies in Biblical Theology* 26 (Naperville, IL: Alec Allenson Publishers, 1959), pp. 95-97.

20. G.R. Driver, *The Judean Scrolls: A Problem and a Solution* (Oxford: Blackwell, 1965).

21. Cecil Roth, *The Dead Sea Scrolls: A Historical Approach* (New York: W. W. Norton & Co., 1965).

22. S.G.F. Brandon, *Jesus and the Zealots: A Study of the Political Factor in Primitive Christianity* (New York: Charles Scribner & Sons, 1967).

23. None of the 26 graves excavated have contained any weapons; however, since there are still so many graves unexcavated, the possibility remains. Arrowheads were discovered in the destruction (ash) layer, but these could have come from the Romans who attacked the settlement.

24. Interview with Dan Bahat, Meveseret Tzion, November 12, 1995.

25. As cited in Edward M. Cook, *Solving the Mysteries of the Dead Sea Scrolls*, p. 121.

26. Norman Golb, *Who Wrote the Dead Sea Scrolls: The Search for the Secret of Qumran* (New York: Charles Scribner & Sons, 1995).

27. Interview with Shemaryahu Talmon, Jerusalem, November 12, 1995.

28. Interview with Magen Broshi, Shrine of the Book, Jerusalem, November 12, 1995.

29. Interview with Shemaryahu Talmon, Jerusalem, November 12, 1995.

30. Ibid.

31. Ibid.

32. Shemaryahu Talmon, "The New Covenanters of Qumran," *Scientific American* 225:5 (1971): 72-81; "Between the Bible and Mishna," "The Calendar of the Covenanters of the Judean Desert," and "Waiting for the Messiah—the Conceptual Universe of the Qumran Covenanters" in *The World of Qumran from Within* (Jerusalem: The Magnes Press, 1989), pp. 11-52, 147-85, 274-301.

33. For the supporting arguments for this new proposal see Raymond L. Edge, "The Use of Paleo-Hebrew in the Dead Sea Scrolls: Paleography and Historiography" (Ph.D. dissertation: The University of Texas at Austin, December 1995). Dr. Edge has also developed an impressive chronology of this period in support of his theory.

34. At the time of this writing Dr. Edge's dissertation is planned for publication in the *Society of Biblical Literature Dissertation Series*. Those who are interested in his detailed defense of this issue will need to refer to the University of Texas dissertation (see above) or the forthcoming work.

35. Dr. Hartmut Stegemann's argument is also based on his hypothesis that the *Temple Scroll* represented a sixth book of the Torah to a community of 5th-3rd century B.C. Jews who were pious.

For the details of this hypothesis, see "Is the Temple Scroll a Sixth Book of the Torah—Lost for 2,500 Years?" *Biblical Archaeology Review* 12:6 (November/December 1987), pp. 28-35.

## Chapter 6—The Significance of the Scrolls

1. Neil S. Fujita, *A Crack in the Jar: What Ancient Jewish Documents Tell Us About the New Testament* (New York: Paulist Press, 1986), p. 201.

2. The difference in time span is a matter of how a person dates the last written book of the Old Testament and the first written book of the New Testament. Less conservative scholars would see Daniel as the last Old Testament book (circa 159 B.C.) and the first epistle to the Thessalonians as the first New Testament book (circa A.D. 40). More conservative scholars would see Daniel as written during the Babylonian/Persian captivity (circa 537 B.C.), and would see Nehemiah or 1 and 2 Chronicles as the last Old Testament books (445-425 B.C.) along with Malachi (450-400 B.C.), with the first New Testament book usually thought to be James (circa A.D. 45).

3. James H. Charlesworth, "What Has the Old Testament to Do with the New?" in *The Old and New Testaments: Their Relationship and the "Intertestamental" Literature*, eds. James H. Charlesworth and Walter P. Weaver (Valley Forge, PA: Trinity Press International, 1993), pp. 60-61.

4. The reasons for this neglect range from simple unconcern or unfamiliarity with the content to prejudice against the use of non-canonical writings and the fear of aligning themselves with critical scholars who have used these sources to buttress their attacks on evangelical doctrines.

5. J. Julius Scott, Jr., "On the Value of Intertestamental Jewish Literature for New Testament Theology," *Journal of the Evangelical Theological Society* 23:4 (December 1980): 316.

6. Interview with Hanan Eshel, Jerusalem, November 11, 1995.

7. The oldest biblical manuscripts are those of Exod*us (4QEx^b), Samuel (4QSam^b),* and Jeremiah *(4QJer^a),* all dated to the end of the third century B.C.

8. Interview with Dr. Weston Fields, Jerusalem, November 10, 1995.

9. See E.Y. Kutscher, *The Language and Linguistic Background of the Isaiah Scroll (1QIsa^a)* (Leiden: E.J. Brill, 1974), and Elisha Qimron, *Indices and Corrections* (1979).

10. Interview with Dr. Halvor Ronning, Jerusalem, November 9, 1995.

11. Interview with Dr. Emanuel Tov, Hebrew University, Jerusalem, November 7, 1995.

12. James A. Sanders, "The Dead Sea Scrolls and Biblical Studies," *"Sha'arei Talmon": Studies in the Bible, Qumran, and the Ancient Near East Presented to Shemaryahu Talmon*, eds. Michael Fishbane, Emanuel Tov (Winona Lake, IN: Eisenbrauns, 1992), pp. 327-28.

13. F.F. Bruce, *The Canon of Scripture* (Downers Grove, IL: InterVarsity Press, 1988), p. 40.

14. For a helpful sevenfold criteria for identifying allusions (in the Pauline corpus) see Richard B. Hays, "Criteria for Identifying Allusions and Echoes of the Text of Isaiah in the Letters of Paul," paper for the International Colloquy on Isaiah 53 and Christian Origins (Waco, TX: Baylor University, February 23-25, 1996), pp. 6-13.

15. Interview with Dr. Emanuel Tov, Hebrew University, Jerusalem, November 7, 1995.

16. See Bernard Spolsky, "Jewish Multilingualism in the First Century: An Essay in Historical Sociolinguistics," *Readings in the Sociology of Jewish Languages* in *Contributions to the Sociology of Jewish Languages*, ed. Joshua A. Fishman (Leiden: E.J. Brill, 1985) 1:36-50.

17. Greek was not treated with the same disdain because it existed in a translation of the sacred scriptures (LXX).

18. See Joseph Fitzmeyer, "The Languages of Palestine in the First Century A.D.," *Catholic Biblical Quarterly* 32 (1970): 501-31, Pinchas Lapide, "Insights from Qumran into the Languages of Jesus," *Revue de Qumran* 8 (1975): 483-501.

19. The Dead Sea Scrolls represent a usage probably from the Persian period up through the Second Temple period. The last Jewish use appears to be during the Bar Kokhba revolt (A.D. 132-135),

where it occurs on nationalistic coinage. However, among the Samaritan community, whose descendants never experienced the exile, it still continues in use today.

20. See Raymond L. Edge, "The Use of Paleo-Hebrew in the Dead Sea Scrolls: Paleography and Historiography" (Ph.D. dissertation: The University of Texas at Austin, December 1995).

21. For a detailed study see Elisha Qimron, "Observations on the History of Early Hebrew (1000 B.C.E.–200 C.E.) in the Light of the Dead Sea Documents," *The Dead Sea Scrolls: Forty Years of Research*, eds. Devorah Dimant, Uriel Rappaport, *Studies on Texts of the Desert of Judah*, vol. 10, eds. F. Garcia Martinez, A.A. Van Der Woude (Leiden: E.J. Brill, 1992), pp. 349-61.

22. See J. Emerton, "The Problem of Vernacular Hebrew in the First Century A.D. and the Language of Jesus," *Journal of Theological Studies* 29 (1973): 1-23.

23. Chaim Rabin, "The Historical Background of Qumran Hebrew," *Scripta Hierosolymitana* 4 (Hebrew University: Magnes Press, 1958): 144-61.

24. See Frank Moore Cross, "The Development of the Jewish Scripts," *The Bible in the Ancient Near East*, ed. G.E. Wright (Winona Lake, IN: Eisenbrauns, 1979) pp. 170-264.

25. Three sects (Pharisees, Sadducees, Essenes) are identified in *Jewish Wars* 2.8.2 §119, and the fourth (Zealots) in §117.

26. Emil Schürer, *A History of the Jewish People in the Time of Jesus Christ*, trans. John MacPherson, 5 vols. (Edinburgh: T. & T. Clark, 1890). Schürer's work was revised and updated in four volumes to incorporate the newest material, including the Dead Sea Scrolls, by Geza Vermes and Fergus Millar in the 1970s and 1980s.

27. George Foot Moore, *Judaism in the First Centuries of the Christian Era*, 3 vols. (Cambridge: Harvard University Press, 1966).

28. Edersheim's works include *The Life and Times of Jesus the Messiah, Prophecy and History in Relation to the Messiah, History of the Jewish Nation, Jewish Social Life*, and *The Temple: Its Ministry and Services* (the last two works were recently updated, but *without* the incorporation of new sources).

29. Already at this time some works were becoming available, although their publication cost usually made them prohibitive for student purchase. Gafni himself, along with various other scholars, attempted to present a more modern treatment of these times in their publication of the three-volume *Compendia Rerum Iudaicarum ad Novum Testamentum* (1974-1986). However, the approach of rabbinic dependence in volume 1 of this series is essentially no different than its predecessors. Volume 2 at least sought to survey the Dead Sea literature, but a historical integration of the material was not attempted.

30. Examples of this are most notably Hermann Strack and Paul Billerbeck's *Kommentar zum Neuen Testament*, which illustrated New Testament texts largely in light of the rabbinic material. This, however, was *not* the purpose of Moore's work, which was one of the first works by a "Christian" to employ the rabbinic literature for an understanding of Judaism rather than to simply illustrate Christianity.

31. *Anchor Bible Dictionary*, s.v. "Dead Sea Scrolls," by John J. Collins (New York: Doubleday and Co., 1992), 2:100.

32. Interview with Hanan Eshel, Jerusalem, November 11, 1995.

33. One early attempt at this was the dissertation by William Sanford LaSor, "A Preliminary Reconstruction of Judaism in the Time of the Second Temple in Light of the Published Qumran Materials" (1956).

34. Lawrence Schiffman, "The Significance of the Scrolls," *Bible Review* 6:5 (October 1990): 26.

35. Lawrence Schiffman, *Reclaiming the Dead Sea Scrolls* (New York: Doubleday, 1994) pp. 75-76, 83-126.

36. See James Vanderkam, "The Origin, Character, and Early History of the 364-Day Calendar: A Reassessment of Jaubert's Hypotheses," *Catholic Biblical Quarterly* 41 (1979): 390-411.

37. Interview with Dr. Dan Bahat, Meveseret Tzion, November 12, 1995.

38. Interview with Stephen J. Pfann, Jerusalem, November 10, 1995.

### Chapter 7—The Scriptures and the Scrolls: *Old Testament*

1. J. Julius Scott, Jr., "The Jewish Backgrounds of the New Testament: Second Commonwealth Judaism in Recent Study," *Archaeology in the Biblical World* 1:2 (Fall 1991): 40.

2. William Sanford LaSor, *The Dead Sea Scrolls and the Christian Faith* (Chicago: Moody Press, 1962), pp. 217-20.

3. For a similar conclusion see Robert H. Gundry, *The Use of the Old Testament in St. Matthew's Gospel* (Leiden: E.J. Brill, 1975), pp. 205-08.

4. James H. Charlesworth, "The Dead Sea Scrolls and the Historical Jesus," *Jesus and the Dead Sea Scrolls* (New York: Doubleday, 1993), p. 38.

5. For a discussion of the proper understanding of preservation in light of the English text and its textual authorities, see James R. White, *The King James Only Controversy: Can You Trust the Modern Translations?* (Minneapolis, MN: Bethany House Publishers, 1995), pp. 47-48.

6. Cf. such a statement by Charles C. Ryrie in his note entitled: "Is Our Present Text Reliable?" in *The Ryrie Study Bible* (Chicago: Moody Press, 1978), p. 1926.

7. James VanderKam, *The Dead Sea Scrolls Today* (Grand Rapids, MI: Eerdmans Publishing Co., 1994), p. 123.

8. For a complete listing of these see Eugene Ulrich, "An Index of the Passages in the Biblical Manuscripts from the Judean Desert (Genesis-Kings)," *Dead Sea Scroll Discoveries* 1:1 (April 1994): 113-29, and "Part 2: Isaiah-Chronicles," *Dead Sea Scroll Discoveries* 2:1 (April 1995): 86-107.

9. For a survey of modern translations employing Qumran readings, see Harold Scalin, *The Dead Sea Scrolls and Modern Translations of the Old Testament* (Wheaton, IL: Tyndale House Publishers, Inc., 1993).

10. For a complete listing and discussion of these variants, see Ibid., pp. 108-38.

11. Emanuel Tov, "A Modern Textual Outlook Based on the Qumran Scrolls," *Hebrew Union College Annual* 53 (1982: 11-27, and *Textual Criticism of the Hebrew Bible* (Minneapolis, MN: Fortress Press, 1992), pp. 114-17, sees only a 60 percent agreement, however, he excludes from this count (20 percent) of the scrolls he considers uniquely Qumranic because of grammatical differences, such as *1QIs^a*. If we rather include these because of their textual alignment to the Masoretic Text we arrive at our figure of 80 percent.

12. Interview with Emanuel Tov, Hebrew University, Jerusalem, November 7, 1995.

13. Emanuel Tov, "The Contribution of the Qumran Scrolls to the Understanding of the LXX," *Septuagint, Scrolls and Cognate Writings: Papers Presented to the International Symposium on the Septuagint and Its Relations to the Dead Sea Scrolls and Other Writings (Manchester, 1990)*, ed. George J. Brooke, Barnabas Lindars, Society of Biblical Literature Septuagint and Cognate Studies Series 33, ed. Leonard J. Greenspoon (Atlanta, GA: Scholars Press, 1992), pp. 21, 28-29.

14. James C. VanderKam, *The Dead Sea Scrolls Today* (Grand Rapids, MI: Eerdmans Publishing Co., 1994), pp. 131-32.

15. Interview with Emanuel Tov, Hebrew University, Jerusalem, November 7, 1995.

16. Ibid.

17. Lawrence H. Schiffman, *Reclaiming the Dead Sea Scrolls* (New York: Doubleday, 1995), p. 175.

18. Interview with Emanuel Tov, Hebrew University, Jerusalem, November 7, 1995.

19. This is because they lack the characteristic features associated with the Qumran scribal school, namely *pesharim*, which may be considered an alternative to the rewritten or rephrased text. See Emanuel Tov, "Biblical Texts as Reworked in Some Qumran Manuscripts with Special Attention

to *4QRP* and *4QParaGen-Exod*," *The Community of the Renewed Covenant: The Notre Dame Symposium on the Dead Sea Scrolls*; eds. E. Ulrich, J. VanderKam (Indiana: University of Notre Dame Press, 1994), pp. 111-12.

20. See Moshe Weinfield, "Sarah and Abimelech (Genesis 20) Against the Background of an Assyrian Law and the Genesis Apocryphon," *Mélanges bibliques et orientaux en l'honneur de M. Mathias Delcor*, eds. A. Caquot, S. Légasse, M. Tardieu; *Alter Orient und Altes Testament*, eds. K. Bergerhof, M. Dietrich, O. Loretz (Verlag Butzon & Bercker Kevelaer, 1985), pp. 433-37.

21. See Timothy H. Lim, "The Chronology of the Flood Story in a Qumran Text (4Q252)," *Journal of Jewish Studies* 43:2 (Autumn 1992): 288-98.

22. N.D. Freedman, "The Flowering of Apocalyptic," in *Apocalypticism*, ed. Robert W. Funk, *Journal of Textual Criticism* 6 (New York: Herder and Herder, 1969), p. 170.

23. In Daniel, several Hebrew words—*nagid* ("leader/prince"), *sekel* ("sense"), *yadah* ("knowledge"), and *bîn* ("insight/understanding")—are also used to convey the same notion as *pesher*. The noun only appears once in Hebrew, in Ecclesiastes 8:21: "Who knows the *interpretation* of a matter?"

24. For a discussion of this perspective among the community, see F.F. Bruce, *Biblical Exegesis in the Qumran Texts*, revised ed. (Grand Rapids, MI: Eerdmans Publishing Co., 1959), pp. 27, 63-67, 70.

25. See Kurt Elliger, *Studien zum Habakkuk-Kommentar vom Toten Meer* (Tübingen: Mohr-Siebeck, 1953), pp. 118-64.

26. See George W.E. Nickelsburg, "Reading the Hebrew Scriptures in the First Century: Christian Interpretations in Their Jewish Context," *W & W* 3:3 (Summer 1983): 238-50, esp. 239-46.

27. See G.W. Anderson, "Daniel," *The Cambridge History of the Bible*, eds. P.R. Ackroyd, et. al. (New York: Cambridge University Press, 1984): 1:151.

28. Klaus Koch, "Is Daniel Also Among the Prophets?" *Interpretation* 39:2 (April 1985): 125.

29. Interview with Shemaryahu Talmon, Jerusalem, November 12, 1995.

30. F.F. Bruce, *Biblical Exegesis in the Qumran Texts* (London: The Tyndale Press, 1960), pp. 68-71; Annette Steudel, "[The End of the Days] in the Texts from Qumran," *Revue de Qumran* 62:16:2 (December 1993): 238.

31. Two such studies, employing different divisions for comparison, arrived at multiple authorship. See Yehuda Radday, *The Unity of Isaiah in the Light of Statistical Linguistics*, Collection Massorah Series 2 (Hildersheim: Gerstenberg, 1973), and A. Kasher, "The Book of Isaiah: Characterization of Authors by Morphological Data Processing," *Revue de l'Organizations Internationales pour l'Etude des Langues anci par Ordinateur* 3 (1972): 1-62, while another concluded in favor of unitary composition: L.L. Adams and A.C. Rincher, "The Popular View of the Isaiah Problem in Light of Statistical Style Analysis," *Computer Studies* 4 (1973): 149-57. For a review of the inherent problems in utilizing the statistical approach, see R. Posner, "The Use and Abuse of Stylistic Statistics," *Archivum Linguisticum* 15 (1963): 111-39.

32. For summaries of these arguments from the Jewish perspective, see Rachel Margalioth *The Indivisible Isaiah* (New York: Yeshiva University, 1964); Israel Slotki, *Isaiah: Soncino Books of the Bible* (London: Soncino Press, Ltd., 1959), p. x; and Avraham Giledai, *The Literary Message of Isaiah* (New York: Hebraeus Press, 1994), pp. 35-43. From the Christian perspective, J.J. Lias, "The Unity of the Book of Isaiah," *Bibliotheca Sacra* 72 (1915): 560-91, 75 (1918): 267-74; O.T. Allis, *The Unity of Isaiah: A Study in Prophecy* (Tyndale Press, 1951); E.J. Young, *Who Wrote Isaiah?* (Grand Rapids, MI: Eerdmans Publishing Co., 1958); J. Alec Motyer, *The Prophecy of Isaiah: An Introduction and Commentary* (Downers Grove, IL: InterVarsity Press, 1993), pp. 25-26; J. Barton Payne, "The Eighth Century Israelitish Background of Isaiah 40-66," *Westminster Theological Journal* 29 (1967): 179-90; 30 (1968): 50-58, 185-203; John N. Oswalt, *The Book of Isaiah Chapters 1-39*, The New International Commentary on the Old Testament (Grand Rapids, MI: Eerdmans Publishing Co., 1986), pp. 17-23; Gleason Archer, *Encyclopedia of Bible Difficulties* (Grand Rapids, MI: Zondervan Publishing House, 1982), pp. 263-66; Herbert M. Wolf, "The Relationship Between Isaiah's Final Servant Song (52:13–53:12) and Chapters 1-6," *A Tribute to*

*Gleason Archer: Essays on the Old Testament*, eds. W.C. Kaiser, R.F. Youngblood (Chicago: Moody Press, 1986), pp. 251-58; *Interpreting Isaiah* (Grand Rapids, MI: Zondervan Publishing House, 1985), pp. 27-38. We may also include R.K. Harrison, *Introduction to the Old Testament* (Grand Rapids, MI: Eerdmans Publishing Co., 1969), pp. 247-59, who argues for unity, but in a compromised manner based on a supposed bifid ("two-part") form composed in 630 B.C.

33. See E.Y. Kutscher, *The Language and Linguistic Background of the Isaiah Scroll (1QIsᵃ)*, Studies in the Texts of the Desert of Judah 4 (Leiden: E.J. Brill, 1974).

34. See G.B. Gray, *The Book of the Prophet Isaiah*, International Critical Commentary (Edinburgh: T. & T. Clark, 1912), 1:lvi, 332, 392.

35. See B. Duhm, *Das Buch Jesaja*, Hand-Kommentar zum Alten Testament (Göttingen: Vandenhoeck & Ruprecht, 1892).

36. This is because it is written in the Qumran scribal style and was thought to be a copy intended for study rather than for worship. Thus, it better fits the category of a *vulgate* (Latin, *vulgar*="common") text, cf. J.P. Siegel, *The Severus Scroll and 1QIsᵃ*, Society of Biblical Literature Masoretic Studies 2 (Missoula, MO: Scholars Press, 1975).

37. See R.K. Harrison, *The Dead Sea Scrolls: An Introduction* (New York: Harper & Brothers, 1961), p. 63.

38. The *Great Isaiah Scroll*'s use of *plene* writing is somewhat more pronounced than other copies of Isaiah, employing the Hebrew consonants for vowels as follows: *waw* for "ou," *he* for "aeo," *aleph* for "a," and *yodh* for "I" and "e." This form represented the official phoneticized style of the "organizational" or "foundational" texts of the Qumran community discovered in Cave 1. However, *1QIsᵃ* is considered to be the oldest of this lot, cf. Malachi Martin, *The Scribal Character of the Dead Sea Scrolls*, Bibliothèque du Muséon 45 (Louvain: Publications Universitaires/Institut Orientaliste, 1958) 2: 712-13. The use of *matres lectionis* cannot (solely) be an indication of late date, since this phenomenon was an artificial addition as a result of the Babylonian captivity. An early date for the text is indicated by its preservation (as compared with the MT) of Assyrian names in the ancient form. The explanation for the shift between chapters 33 and 34 thus cannot be simply a change is scribes, but must reflect some textual difference that the scribes could only compensate for, or indicate, in this manner.

39. William H. Brownlee, "The Manuscripts of Isaiah from Which *QISᵃ* Was Copied," *Bulletin of the American School of Oriental Research* 127 (October 1952): 16-21.

40. William H. Brownlee, *The Meaning of the Qumran Scrolls for the Bible* (New York: Oxford University Press, 1964), pp. 247-49, 253-54.

41. Avraham Gileadi, *The Literary Message of Isaiah* (New York: Hebraeus Press, 1994), pp. 37-43.

42. Interview with Emanuel Tov, Hebrew University, Jerusalem, November 7, 1995.

43. See Isaiah 1:1-2; 7:3; 13:1; 20:2-3; 37:2,5-6,21; 38:1,4; 39:3,5,8; 2 Kings 19:2,5-6; 20:1,4,7-9,11,14,16,19; 2 Chronicles 26:22; 32:20,32.

44. Although today Daniel is included in the Hebrew Bible in the division *Kethubim* ("Writings"), which might indicate a late origin and inclusion after the first century A.D., Josephus, in *Contra Apion* 1.8, wrote of the canon at his time having 22 books (5 books of Moses + 13 books of the prophets who succeeded Moses + 4 of hymns and practical precepts), all "justly believed in," and written "of events that occurred in their own time." Daniel must have originally been included in the 13 books, a fact apparently attested by the early church fathers Origen (A.D. 250) and Jerome (A.D. 400), both of whom were instructed by rabbis, and all the Greek uncials, in the placement of Daniel with the prophets, separate from the historical books.

45. This followed upon recognition that the "Daniel" of Ezekiel 14:20 (cf. 28.3) ranked with Job and Noah and help up as a model of righteousness and wisdom to the exilic community was the biblical Daniel. While neither Job nor Noah were technically "prophets" in the later sense of that word, they both functioned in the prophetic role as intercessors to their people (Job 1:5; 42:8-9; Genesis 6:8-9,14; cf. 2 Peter 2:5). The arguments that this "Daniel" was not the biblical character, but the much distant figure of Dan'el, the ancient mythical ruler who practiced magical wisdom

in the Ugaritic *Aqhat* epic (*Ancient Near Eastern Text* 153-154a), cf. J. Day, "The Daniel of Ugarit and Ezekiel and the Hero of the Book of Daniel," *Vetus Testamentum* 30 (1980): 174-84, are not convincing. The literary links between the accounts are unclear, and verbal parallels are missing, as also with the angel "Daniel" in *1 Enoch*, cf. John E. Goldingay, *Daniel. Word Biblical Commentary* 30 (Waco, TX: Word Books, 1989), pp. 7, 274, who notes the intercessory role of Daniel for "his people," "his city," and "his sanctuary" (Daniel 9:15-20) as agreeing with that portrayed for the Daniel in Ezekiel 14:20, and the comparable historicity of further references to Daniel's companions in exile as part of the leadership of the post-exilic community (Nehemiah 8:4,7; 10:2), although admittedly these could be either descendants or unrelated figures who adopted famous names.

46. For a complete survey and critique of these critical arguments, see Robert Dick Wilson, *Studies in the Book of Daniel*, reprint (Grand Rapids, MI: Baker Book House, 1972), 2:9-280; and Josh McDowell, *Daniel in the Critics' Den: Historical Evidence for the Authenticity of the Book of Daniel* (San Bernardino, CA: Here's Life Publishers, Inc., 1979), pp. 33-128.

47. S.R. Driver, *An Introduction to the Literature of the Old Testament* (Edinburgh: T. & T. Clark, 1898), pp. 497-516.

48. Driver's statement was: "The age and authorship of the books of the Old Testament can be determined (so far as this is possible) only upon the basis of the internal evidence supplied by the books themselves . . . no external evidence worthy of credit exists," ibid., p. xi; cf. for a critique of Driver's position, Stephen M. Clinton, "S.R. Driver and the Date of Daniel," *The Journal of Church and Society* 5:2 (Fall 1969): 30-41.

49. See H.H. Rowley, *Darius the Mede and the Four World Empires in the Book of Daniel* (Cardiff: University of Wales Press Board, 1964); N. Porteous, *Daniel* (Philadelphia: Westminster Press, 1965); L.F. Hartman and A. Di Lella, *The Book of Daniel*. Anchor Bible (Garden City: Doubleday, 1978); David Flusser, "The Four Empires in the Fourth Sibyl and in the Book of Daniel," *Israel Oriental Studies* 2 (1972): 148-75.

50. For the evidence against dividing the Medo-Persian empire and for support of Rome as the fourth kingdom, see John C. Whitcomb, Jr., *Darius the Mede*, Biblical and Theological Study Series, ed. J. Marcellus Kik (Phillipsburg, NJ: Presbyterian and Reformed Pub. Co., 1974); Donald J. Wiseman, "Some Historical Problems in the Book of Daniel," *Notes on Some Problems in the Book of Daniel* (London: Tyndale Press, 1965), pp. 12-16; Gerhard F. Hasel, "The Four World Empires of Daniel 2 Against Its Near Eastern Environment," *Journal for the Study of the Old Testament* 12 (1979): 17-30; William H. Shea, "Darius the Mede: An Update," *Andrews University Seminary Studies* 20 (1982): 229-48; and summary discussions: Edwin Yamauchi, *Persia and the Bible* (Grand Rapids, MI: Baker Book House, 1990), pp. 57-59; Gleason Archer, *Encyclopedia of Bible Difficulties*, pp. 286-89.

51. See, for example, Gordon J. Wenham, "Daniel: The Basic Issues," *Themelios* 2 (1977): 49-52; Edwin M. Yamauchi, "Daniel and Contacts Between the Aegean and the Near East Before Alexander," *Evangelical Quarterly* 53 (1981): 37-47; Arthur Ferch, "The Book of Daniel and the Maccabean Thesis," *Andrews University Studies* 21 (1983): 129-41; Eugene E. Carpenter, "The Eschatology of Daniel Compared with the Eschatology of Selected Intertestamental Documents" (Ph.D. dissertation: Fuller Theological Seminary, 1978), pp. 97-109; Donald J. Wiseman, et. al., *Notes on Some Problems in the Book of Daniel* (London: The Tyndale Press, 1970); Bruce K. Waltke, "The Date of the Book of Daniel," *Bibliotheca Sacra* 133:532 (October-December 1976): 319-29; Gleason Archer, "The Aramaic of the 'Genesis Apocryphon' Compared with the Aramaic of Daniel," *New Perspectives on the Old Testament*, ed. J. Barton Payne (Waco, TX: Word Publishers, 1970), pp. 160-69.

52. See Eugene Ulrich, "Daniel Manuscripts from Qumran, Part 1: A P reliminary Edition of *4QDanᵃ*," *Bulletin of the American School of Oriental Research* 268 (November 1987): 18.

53. On the discovery of the fragments themselves, see Dupont-Sommer's announcement in *Apercus preliminaries* as cited by H.H. Rowley, *The Zadokite Fragments and the Dead Sea Scrolls* (Oxford: Basil Blackwell, 1956), p. 7.

54. Jacob M. Meyers, *I Chronicles*, Anchor Bible (Garden City, NY: Doubleday & Co., 1965), p. 165.

55. See J. Muilenburg, "A Qoheleth Scroll from Qumrân," *Bulletin of the American School of Oriental Research* 135 (October 1954): 20-28.

56. See also the statement of William H. Brownlee, *The Meaning of the Qumran Scrolls for the Bible* (New York: Oxford University Press, 1964), pp. 29-30: ". . . one of the Psalms manuscripts from Cave 4 attests so-called Maccabean psalms at a period which is roughly contemporary with their supposed composition. If this is true, it would seem that we should abandon the idea of any of the canonical psalms being of Maccabean date, for each song had to win its way into the esteem of the people before it could be included in the sacred compilation of the Psalter. Immediate entry for any of them is highly improbable."

57. Frank M. Cross, Jr., *The Ancient Library of Qumran and Modern Biblical Studies*, revised ed. (Grand Rapids, MI: Baker Book House, 1980), p. 165.

58. Ibid., p. 36.

59. Announcement: "Fragments of the Book of Daniel Found," *The Biblical Archaeologist* 12:2 (1949): 33.

60. Frank M. Cross, *The Ancient Library of Qumran and Modern Biblical Studies* (Grand Rapids, MI: Baker Book House, 1961), p. 43.

61. John J. Collins, *The Apocalyptic Vision of the Book of Daniel*, Harvard Semitic Monographs 16, ed. F.M. Cross (MT: Scholars Press, 1977), pp. 4-5.

62. Robert I. Vasholz, "Qumran and the Dating of Daniel," *Journal of the Evangelical Theological Society* 21:4 (December 1978): 321.

63. See F. Macler, "Les Apocalypses Apocryphes de Daniel," *Revue de l'histoire des religions* 33 (1896): 37-53, 163-76, 288-319; P.J. Alexander, "Medieval Apocalypses as Historical Sources," *Ancient History Review* 73 (1968): 997-1018.

64. H.H. Rowley, "The Unity of the Book of Daniel," *The Servant of the Lord and Other Essays on the Old Testament* (London: Lutterworth, 1952), pp. 264-67.

65. F.F. Bruce, "The Book of Daniel and the Qumran Community," *Neotestamentica et Semitica*, ed. Max Wilcox (Edinburgh: T. & T. Clark, 1969), pp. 221-22.

66. John C. Trevor, "The Book of Daniel and the Origin of the Qumran Community," *Biblical Archaeologist* 48:2 (June 1985): 89-102.

67. Ibid., pp. 95-100.

68. Ibid., p. 92.

69. H.H. Rowley implied that the issue of predictive prophecy was not the concern of critical scholars when he wrote with conservatives in mind: "Moreover, while those who belong to the 'orthodox' school are fond of supposing that they hold the monopoly of faith . . . every 'critic' is not a Porphyry . . . and all such prejudices may be laid aside," *Darius the Mede*, vii. This may have been the case at the beginning of the debate in the last century when comparative evidence was less than today, but when scholars continue to hold to a late date for Daniel, and even a Qumran provenance, when the evidence applied to other Maccabean-dated books has forced a revision, little else remains as a ground for contention.

70. Gleason L. Archer, "The Hebrew of Daniel Compared with the Qumran Sectarian Documents," *The Law and the Prophets: Old Testament Essays in Honor of Oswalt T. Allis*, ed. John H. Skilton (Phillipsburg, NJ: Presbyterian and Reformed Publishing Co., 1974), pp. 470-81.

71. H.H. Rowley, *The Aramaic of Daniel* (Oxford: University Press, 1929).

72. Franz Rosenthal, *Die Aramäistische Forschung* (1939; reprint, Leiden: E.J. Brill, 1964), p. 70. In this conclusion he followed the earlier conclusions of German scholars H.H. Schaeder (1930) and J. Lidner (1935).

73. Examples are the preposition *lᵉ* before a king's name in dates and the word order of the Assur ostracon (seventh century B.C.) Which agrees with Daniel. See Robert I. Vasholz, "Qumran and

the Dating of Daniel," *Journal of the Evangelical Theological Society* 21:4 (December 1978): 318-19.

74. K.A. Kitchen, "The Aramaic of Daniel" in *Notes on Some Problems in the Book of Daniel* (London: Tyndale Press, 1965), p. 75. Kitchen reasserts this conclusion in *The Bible in Its World: The Bible and Archaeology Today* (Downers Grove, IL: InterVarsity Press, 1978), p. 152, n. 10.

75. A.R. Millard, "Daniel 1-6 and History," *Evangelical Quarterly* 49:2 (1977): 67-73.

76. E.Y. Kutscher, "HaAramit HaMikrait-Aramit Mizrahit hi o Maaravit?" *First World Congress of Jewish Studies* I (Jerusalem: Magnes Press, 1952), pp. 123-27.

77. The carbon 14 date for *1Q20* yielded the range of 73 B.C.–A.D. 14, which accorded roughly with the paleographic dating in the late first century B.C., See the chart in *Biblical Archaeology Review* 17 (November/December 1991), p. 72.

78. Gleason L. Archer, Jr. "The Aramaic of the 'Genesis Apocryphon' Compared with the Aramaic of Daniel," *New Perspectives on the Old Testament*, ed. J. Barton Payne (Waco, TX: Word Books, 1970), pp. 160-69; *Zondervan Pictorial Encyclopedia of the Bible*, ed. M.C. Tenney (Grand Rapids, MI: Zondervan Publishing House, 1975), s.v. "Aramaic," 1:255.

79. See J.M.P. van der Ploeg and A.S. van der Woude, eds. *Le Targum de Job de la grotte XI de Qumrân* (Leiden: E.J. Brill, 1971), pp. 3-5; T. Muraoka, "The Aramaic of the Old Targum of Job from Qumran Cave XI," *Journal of Jewish Studies* 25 (1974): 442; Stephen A. Kaufman, "The Job Targum from Qumran," *Journal of the American Oriental Society* 93 (1973): 327.

80. Robert Vasholz, "A Philological Comparison of the Qumran Job Targum and Its Implications for the Dating of Daniel" (Ph.D. dissertation, University of Stellenbosch, 1976); cf. T. Muraoka, "The Aramaic of the Old Targum of Job from Qumran Cave XI," *Journal of Jewish Studies* 25 (1974): 425-33.

81. A. York, "A Philological and Textual Analysis of the Qumran Job Targum (*11QtgJob*)" (Ph.D. dissertation, Cornell University, 1973), pp. 306-32.

82. See F.F. Bruce, "Josephus and Daniel," *Annual of the Swedish Theological Institute*, ed. Hans Kosmala (Leiden: E.J. Brill), 4: 148-62.

83. Gerhard Hasel, "Is the Aramaic of Daniel Early or Late?," *Ministry* (January 1980), p. 13.

**Chapter 8—The Scriptures and the Scrolls: *New Testament***

1. Klaus Berger, *Jesus and the Dead Sea Scrolls: The Truth Under Lock and Key*? trans. James S. Currie (Louisville, KY: Westminster John Knox Press, 1995), pp. 8-9.

2. Geza Vermes, "The Impact of the Dead Sea Scrolls on the Study of the New Testament," *Journal of Jewish Studies* 27 (1976): 116.

3. Ibid., p. 107.

4. David Flusser, "The Judean Desert Scrolls and the Beginning of Christianity," p. 2.

5. Ibid., p. 1.

6. James VanderKam, "The Dead Sea Scrolls and Early Christianity: How Are They Related? (Part One)," *Bible Review* (December 1991): 19-20.

7. It has sometimes been thought that the Greek term *eremos* ("wilderness") in Luke 1:80, with reference to John's abode, is a technical term for the Qumran settlement. However, this is disproved by the fact that the term is used of other individuals in places other than Qumran, such as with Jesus' temptation by Satan in the "wilderness" (Matthew 4:1).

8. For a thorough treatment of this matter, although without resolution, see Leonard F. Badia, *The Qumran Baptism and John the Baptist's Baptism* (University Press of America, 1980).

9. See William Sanford LaSor, *The Dead Sea Scrolls and the New Testament* (Grand Rapids, MI: Eerdmans Publishing Co., 1972), p. 147.

10. I have included Isaiah 11:4 on the strength of the article by Richard Bauckham, "The Messianic Interpretation of Isaiah 10:34 in the Dead Sea Scrolls, 2 Baruch and the Preaching of John the Baptist," *Dead Sea Discoveries* 2:2 (1995): 214-16.

11. Emile Puech, "4Q525 et les péricopes des Béatitudes en Ben Shira et Matthieu," *Revue biblique* 138 (1991): 80-106.

12. See Benedict T. Viviano, "Beatitudes Found Among Dead Sea Scrolls," *Biblical Archaeology Review* 18:6 (November/December 1992): 66.

13. Markus Bockmuehl, "Why Did Jesus Predict the Destruction of the Temple?" *Crux* 25:3 (September 1989), pp. 11-17. Holding to the same interpretation for Jesus' predictions, yet without the element of judgment, is E.P. Sanders, *Jesus and Judaism* (London: SCM Press, 1985), pp. 85-88, who notes "the naturalness of the connection between expecting a new temple and supposing that the old one will be destroyed" (p. 85).

14. Joachim Jeremias, *Jerusalem in the Time of Jesus*, trans. by F.H. & C.H. Cave (London: SCM Press, 1969), pp. 193-94, 377-78.

15. The term *cleansing* that has traditionally described this account is not an appropriate choice since it suggests purification rites or some ritual of sanctifying a de-sanctified site. Since neither Jesus' actions nor words imply any such thing, the term *clearing* would be a better substitute for the event. I have retained the customary terminology because of its universal recognition, but have indicated my reservations by using quotation marks.

16. In the Synoptic Gospels the event is cited as the last public act of Jesus in order to use it to explain the Sanhedrin's plot to arrest Jesus, while in John it is used to introduce Jesus' public ministry in the Temple. The different positionings of the account are apparently a result of authorial purpose, which governs the selection and placement of historical material for theological or dramatic emphasis. There are, however, significant differences between the Synoptic and Johannine accounts, which have led many to adopt the position that there were actually *two* "cleansings." See D.A. Carson, *Matthew, Expositor's Bible Commentary* (Grand Rapids, MI: Eerdmans Publishing Co., 1984), p. 441; Leon Morris, *The Gospel According to John*, New International Commentary on the New Testament (Grand Rapids, MI: Eerdmans Publishing Co., 1971), pp. 190-92.

17. See Jacob Neusner, "Money-Changers in the Temple: The Mishnah's Explanation," *NTS* 35 (1989): 287-90, and recently, Jostein Adna, "The Attitude of Jesus to the Temple: A Critical Examination of How Jesus' Relationship to the Temple Is Evaluated Within Israeli Scholarship, with Particular Regard to the Jerusalem School [of Synoptic Research]," *Mishkan* 17-18 (2/1992–1/1993): 65-81.

18. See David Flusser, "Jesu Prozess und Tod," *Entdeckungenim Neuen Testament*, Band 1: *Jesusworte und ihre Uberlieferung* (Neukirchen-Vluyn, 1987), p. 145; Benjamin Mazar, *The Mountain of the Lord* (New York: Doubleday & Co., 1975), p. 126; "The Royal Stoa in the Southern Part of the Temple Mount," *Recent Archaeology in the Land of Israel*, edited by Herschel Shanks (Washington, DC: Biblical Archaeology Society, 1985), p. 147; and Shmuel Safrai, *Die Wallfahrt im Zeitalter des Zweiten Tempels* (Neukirchen-Vluyn, 1981), p. 185.

19. J. Randall Price, *The Desecration and Restoration of the Temple as an Eschatological Motif in the Tanach, Jewish Apocalyptic Literature and the New Testament* (Ann Arbor, MI: UMI Dissertation Services, 1994), pp. 478-510.

20. For these eschatological observations, see Kenneth A. Matthews, "John, Jesus and the Essenes: Trouble at the Temple," *Criswell Theological Review* 3:1 (Fall 1988): 101-26.

21. Craig A. Evans, "Opposition to the Temple: Jesus and the Dead Sea Scrolls," in *Jesus and the Dead Sea Scrolls*, ed. James H. Charlesworth (New York: Doubleday, 1993), p. 250.

22. Otto Betz, "Jesus and the Temple Scroll," in *Jesus and the Dead Sea Scrolls*, ed. James H. Charlesworth (New York: Doubleday, 1993), pp. 75-103 (esp. 79-90).

23. Interview with Otto Betz, Baylor University, Waco, Texas, February 27, 1995.

24. Chaim Rabin, *The Zadokite Fragments* (Oxford: Claredon Press, 1958), p. 17. John Kampen argues that it has to do with violations of "group allegiance" and is used to define the outer boundaries

of acceptable behavior at Qumran; see "The Matthean Divorce Texts Reexamined," *New Qumran Texts and Studies* (1994): 149-67.

25. Neil S. Fugita, *A Crack in the Jar: What Ancient Jewish Documents Tell Us About the New Testament* (New York: Paulist Press, 1986), pp. 130-31.

26. See Lawrence H. Schiffman, "Communal Meals at Qumran," *Revue de Qumran* 10 (1979): 45-56, and *Sectarian Law in the Dead Sea Scrolls: Courts, Testimony and Penal Code* (Chico, CA: Scholars Press, 1983), pp. 191-210.

27. Jacob Neusner, *The Rabbinic Traditions about the Pharisees Before 70* (Leiden: E.J. Brill, 1971), 3:88.

28. For additional details and arguments against identity, see I. Howard Marchall, *Last Supper and Lord's Supper* (Grand Rapids, MI: Eerdmans Publishing Co., 1980), pp. 57-75.

29. I am grateful to Dr. Steve Pfann, director of the Center for the Study of Early Christianity, who shared the following two examples with me during a visit to his Jerusalem home, November 10, 1995. For those interested in learning from Dr. Pfann at his school in the Holy Land, please write him for information at: P.O. Box 24084, Jerusalem, Israel, or fax 972-2-731730.

30. James H. Charlesworth, "Reinterpreting John: How the Dead Sea Scrolls Have Revolutionized Our Understanding of the Gospel of John," *Bible Review* 9:1 (February 1993): 24.

31. These distinctions were adapted from Howard M. Teeple, "Qumran and the Fourth Gospel," *Novum Testamentum* 4 (January 1960): 12-14.

32. James H. Charlesworth, *John and Qumran* (London: Geoffrey Chapman Publishers, 1972), p. 99.

33. James H. Charlesworth, "Reinterpreting John," p. 54.

34. See Martin Abegg, "Paul, 'Works of the Law' and *MMT,*" *Biblical Archaeology Review* 20:6 (November/December 1994): 52-55, 82.

35. Joseph A. Fitzmyer, "The Qumran Scrolls and the New Testament after Forty Years," *Revue de Qumran* 13 (1988): 613-15, *Responses to 101 Questions on the Dead Sea Scrolls* (New York: Paulist Press, 1992), pp. 125-30.

36. Interview with Magen Broshi, Shrine of the Book Museum, Jerusalem, November 12, 1995.

37. For more details concerning predestination in the Scrolls, see Eugene Merrill, *Qumran and Predestination: A Theological Study of the Thanksgiving Hymns*, Studies on the Texts of the Desert of Judah VIII, ed. J. Van der Ploeg (Leiden: E.J. Brill, 1975).

38. Some counts list only 18 fragments. I am counting among this number *7Q19,* which is known only from the imprint left by its text on three clumps of soil.

39. Among the Dead Sea Scrolls found at Wadi Muraba'at were 68 Greek manuscripts (19 parchment and 49 papyri). Of these only five were literary texts, the rest being correspondence, etc., although one was a Christian liturgical prayer. Further south at Nahal Hever a Greek *Scroll of the Twelve Prophets* was also found. The dates for these documents are A.D. 132-135, and are therefore too late to be considered with the Qumran texts of Cave 7, whose *terminus post quem* is put at A.D. 68.

40. Gordon Fee, "Some Dissenting Notes on *7Q5*=Mark 6:52-53," *Journal of Biblical Literature* 92 (1973): 109-12.

41. Emanuel Tov, "Hebrew Biblical Manuscripts from the Judean Desert: Their Contribution to Textual Criticism," *Journal of Jewish Studies* 39 (1988): 5-37, esp. p. 19.

42. José O'Callaghan, "New Testament Papyri in Qumran Cave 7?" and Carlo M. Martini, "Notes on the Papyri of Qumran Cave 7," supplement to the *Journal of Biblical Literature* 91:2 (1972): 1-14.

43. Lawrence Schiffman, "The Significance of the Scrolls," *Bible Review* 6:5 (October 1990): 27. Schiffman's logic here is flawed in two ways. First, he assumes that "New Testament texts are later than the Qumran texts," although conservative dating of the Gospels, and by some the whole New Testament, is prior to A.D. 70, the same date for some Qumran texts (John A.T. Robinson, *Redating the New Testament*, London: SCM Press, 1976), and presumably the time during which

all the Scrolls were hidden at Qumran. Second, even with a later dating of the New Testament, and though the Romans had a garrison at the Qumran settlement from A.D. 68-75, there is nothing that would have prevented a subsequent Christian burial of texts in Cave 7.

44. One conservative Catholic scholar supporting O'Callaghan was his colleague at the Biblical Institute of Rome, Professor L. Alonso Schökel.

45. *Eternity* 23:6 (1972): 1-14.

46. "Neue neutestamentliche Papyri III," *New Testament Studies* 20 (1974): 357-81; "Über die Möglichkeit der Identifikation kleiner Fragmente neutestamentlicher Handschriften mit Hilfe des Computers," in J.K. Elliot, *Studies in the New Testament Language and Text*, F.S.G. Kilpatrick (Leiden, 1976), pp 14-38.

47. Gordon Fee, "Some Dissenting Notes on 7Q5=Mark 6:52-53," 109-12.

48. D. Estrada and W. White, *The First New Testament* (Nashville, TN: Thomas Nelson Publishers, 1978), and W. Pickering, *The Identity of the New Testament Text* (Nashville, TN: Thomas Nelson Publishers, 1980).

49. Carsten P. Thiede, *The Earliest Gospel Manuscript: The Qumran Fragment 7Q5 and Its Significance for New Testament Studies* (London: The Paternoster Press, 1992).

50. Alan F. Johnson, "Are There New Testament Fragments Among the Dead Sea Scrolls?" *Archaeology in the Biblical World* 3:1 (Summer 1995): 22.

51. Some of the papyrologists in support of the O'Callaghan/Thiede theory are papyrologists Orsolina Montevecchi, author of the standard introductory manual to papyrology; Sergio Daris, honorary president of the International Papyrologists' Association; and Herbert Hunger, the Viennese papyrologist who wrote "7Q5: Markus 6,52-53—oder? Die Meinung des Papyrologen," in *Christen und Christliches in Qumran*? ed. B. Mayer (Regensburg: Puset, 1992), pp. 33-56.

52. Two of the New Testament scholars in support of the O'Callaghan/Thiede theory are Harald Risenfeld of Uppsala, and Eugen Ruckstuhl of Lucerne.

53. Fitzmyer says, "The issue cannot be simply dismissed," while also adding that O'Callaghan (via Thiede), "has not yet proved his case." *The Dead Sea Scrolls: Major Publications and Tools for Study* (Atlanta, GA: Scholars Press, 1990), p. 168.

54. James Charlesworth has only revised his original opinion of "impossible" to "conceivable," based on the fact that no other text has been suggested for 7Q5. See "Sense or Sensationalism?: The Dead Sea Scroll Controversy," *Christian Century* (January 29, 1992): 96-97.

55. As Thiede points out, smaller fragments with more severe problems (for example, the Oxyrhynchus Menander papyrus) have been identified in the past without any concern being raised over size or substance. Thiede, "7Q5—Facts or Fiction?" (response to Wallace's review article), *Westminster Theological Journal* 57 (1995): 473.

56. Thiede, *The Earliest Gospel Manuscript?* pp. 40-41, n. 31; "7Q5—Facts or Fiction?" p. 473 (top).

57. The X-ray photograph was first made in Jerusalem on April 12, 1992, and published in Thiede's article "Bericht uber die kriminaltechnische Untersuchung des Fragments 7Q5 in Jerusalem," in *Eichstaetter Studien* 32 (1992): 239-45.

58. Thiede notes that letter switching can be observed in other New Testament papyri (for example, P⁴ and Luke 3:22; P⁷⁵ and Luke 11:39; 12:28), and 18 examples of the substitution of *tau* for *delta* (the transposition suggested for 7Q5 can be demonstrated in the Septuagint.

59. The peculiar feature of beginning a new section with "and" is a well-known characteristic of Mark's Gospel.

60. C.J. Hemer, "New Testament Fragments at Qumran?" *Tyndale Bulletin* 23 (1972): 125-28.

## 500

61. "Ein neues Bild des Judentums zur Zeit Jesu? Zum gegenwärtigen Stand der Qumran- und Essener-Forschung," *Herder-Korrespondenz* 4 (1992): 175-80, and letter to R. Riesner, January 20, 1993, as cited in Otto Betz and R. Riesner, *Jesus, Qumran and the Vatican*, pp. 123, 185, n. 32.

62. For the evaluation of both Jenkins and Skeat, see Graham Stanton, "A Gospel Among the Scrolls?" *Bible Review* 11:6 (December 1995): 41.

63. Private conversation between Gordon Fee and Alan Johnson, Washington, D.C., November 20, 1993, as recorded in Johnson's article, "Are There New Testament Fragments Among the Dead Sea Scrolls? p. 25, n. 14.

64. Daniel B. Wallace, "*7Q5*: The Earliest NT Papyrus?" (review of Carsten Peter Thiede, *The Earliest Gospel Manuscript? The Qumran Fragment 7Q5 and Its Significance for New Testament Studies), Westminster Theological Journal* 56 (1994): 176.

65. S.R. Pickering and R.R.E. Cook, *Has a Fragment of Mark Been Found At Qumran?* (Sydney, Australia: The Ancient History Documentary Research Centre, Macquarie University, 1989), pp. 12-13.

66. This objection has been raised by Rosenbaum and Focant. For their arguments see *Eichstatter Studien* 32 (1992): pp. 18-19 and the bibliography in Johnson, "Are There New Testament Fragments Among the Dead Sea Scrolls?" p. 25, n. 26.

67. One explanation that has been offered by Qumran scholar Hans Burgmann is that Cave 7 was a *geniza* for heretical documents. This might explain the presence of the fragments in Cave 7, but it still does not explain how they came to be in the possession of those who put them there. Thiede, however, following a suggestion by Fitzmyer, interprets a jar inscription from Cave 7 with the letters *rwm'* as an attempt to write Rome in Hebrew letters. He thus connects the jar with the Christian community in Rome, the same community to which the Gospel of Mark may have been addressed. However, Graham Stanton believes it is better to read the inscription as a proper name of some individual rather than propose it as a reference to the origin of the Scrolls in Rome, cf. "A Gospel Among the Scrolls," p. 42.

68. Daniel B. Wallace, "*7Q5*: The Earliest NT Papyrus?" p. 180.

69. Alan F. Johnson, "Are There New Testament Fragments Among the Dead Sea Scrolls?" p. 23.

70. Letter from Yitzhak Magen dated November 12, 1991, in response to request from attendees at the International Conference of New Testament Scholars and Papyrologists at the Catholic University, Eichstatt, Germany, October 1991.

### Chapter 9—The Doctrine of the Scrolls

1. David Flusser, "The Dead Sea Scrolls and Christian Beginnings," paper distributed in class at Hebrew University of Jerusalem, 1978, p. 1.

2. There are few actual studies that seek to comprehensively treat this subject. The standard treatment (though outdated and unrevised in the new expanded edition) is Helmer Ringgren, *The Faith of Qumran: Theology of the Dead Sea Scrolls*, trans. Emilie T. Sander (New York: Crossroad Publishing Co., 1995), pp. xv-xxi. Most books on the Scrolls also provide a cursory treatment. One dissertation, though also dated, is Charles L. Wood, "An Investigation of the Teachings of the Qumran Sect as Reflected in the Dead Sea Scrolls" (Th.D. dissertation, Fort Worth, TX: Southwestern Baptist Theological Seminary, 1961).

3. Interview with Shemaryahu Talmon, Jerusalem, November 12, 1995.

4. James H. Charlesworth, "The Theologies in the Dead Sea Scrolls," introduction to the expanded edition of Helmer Ringgren, *The Faith of Qumran: Theology of the Dead Sea Scrolls*, pp. xv-xxi.

5. On the social-ethical level this life was governed through *hokmah* ("wisdom," or "a skill in living") which took the legal outline of the cult and made it practical for life (Israel's Wisdom Literature, but especially Proverbs 1–9).

6. For a list of such groups, see Marcel Simon, *Jewish Sects At the Time of Jesus* (Philadelphia: Fortress Press, 1967). For a comprehensive list of groups stressing apocalyptic (and especially

messianic) interpretation, see Eugene J. Mayhew, "Current Trends Concerning the Messianic Idea in Judaism" (paper delivered at the annual meeting of the Evangelical Theological Society, November 18, 1995), appendix.

7. Interview with Shemaryahu Talmon, Jerusalem, November 12, 1995.

8. For a further study of this term and its meaning for the Sect, see Martin Hengel, *Judaism and Hellenism* (Philadelphia: Fortress Press, 1981), 1:243f; and Frank Moore Cross, *The Ancient Library of Qumran & Modern Biblical Studies* (Grand Rapids, MI: Baker Book House, 1961), p. 79f.

9. Interview with Magen Broshi, Shrine of the Book, Jerusalem, November 12, 1995.

10. There is the evidence of the women in the graves in the Qumran cemetery, the marriage text *4Q502*, and the prohibitions against nonprocreative intercourse with wives (*4Q477*).

11. Interview with Shemaryahu Talmon, Jerusalem, November 12, 1995.

12. See Paul E. Kahle, *The Cairo Geniza* (Oxford: Basil Blackwell, 1959).

13. See, for example, in the Gospels: Matthew 26:24; John 6:22-40; 9:1-3; 10:26-27; 12:37-40; and the Pauline epistles, especially Ephesians 1; Romans 9–11.

14. For examples of divine hardening or divine deceit (as a retributive judgment), see Exodus 4–14; Deuteronomy 2:30; Joshua 11:20; 2 Samuel 12:11-12 with 16:20-23; 16:5-11; 17:14; 24:1,7 with 1 Chronicles 21:1; 1 Kings 12:15; 21:19; 22:21-23; 1 Chronicles 10:14; Isaiah 6:9-10; 29:13 (cf. Acts 28:27); 63:17. There are also examples of negative divine foreordination (reprobation)— Genesis 37:26-28 with 45:8 and 50:20; Numbers 21:23; Judges 3:8 with 9:23,56; 1 Samuel 15:26 with 18:10; 19:9-10; 20:30-33 and 16:14-16,23; Psalm 106:7 with Deuteronomy 29:4. See Robert B. Chisholm, Jr., "Divine Hardening in the Old Testament" (paper presented at the annual meeting of the Evangelical Theological Society, Philadelphia, November 15-18, 1995), p. 30; J. Randall Price, "Reprobation Reconsidered: An Introduction to the Theology of Rejection" (paper presented to the sixteenth annual Sovereign Grace Fellowship, Salado, TX, October 6-8, 1989), p. 18. For an overall treatment, see Gordon Clark, *Predestination and the Old Testament* (Pennsylvania: Presbyterian and Reformed Publishing Co., 1979).

15. Eugene H. Merrill, *Qumran and Predestination: A Theological Study of the Thanksgiving Hymns*, Studies on the Texts of the Desert of Judah 8, ed. J. Van der Ploeg (Leiden: E.J. Brill, 1975), p. 16. For his exegesis of these texts, see pp. 17-23.

16. According to Ringgren, "In *1QS* iv.21 and *1QH* ix.32 and to a certain extent also in *1QS* ix.3 truth or the spirit of truth and the holy spirit are juxtaposed in such a way that they must be understood as practically identical." *The Faith of Qumran*, p. 89.

17. See J. Randall Price, "Theocratic Theodicy: An Exegetical and Theological Study of Ezekiel 36:18-36" (Th.M. thesis: Dallas Theological Seminary, 1981).

18. Otto Betz, *Offenbarung und Schriftforschung in der Qumransekte*, Wissenschaftliche Untersuchungen zum Neuen Testament 6 (Tübingen, 1960): 133-34.

19. Arthur E. Sekki, *The Meaning of Ruah at Qumran*, Society of Biblical Literature Dissertation Series 110, eds. J.J.M. Roberts, C. Talbert (Atlanta: Scholars Press, 1989), p. 223.

20. Geza Vermes, *The Dead Sea Scrolls in English* (Baltimore, MD: Penguin Books, 1966), pp. 49-50.

21. Interview with Shemaryahu Talmon, Jerusalem, November 12, 1995.

22. See the statements of various scholars on this connection in Walter Grundmann, "The Teacher of Righteousness of Qumran and the Question of Justification by Faith in the Theology of the Apostle Paul," *Paul and the Dead Sea Scrolls*, eds. J. Murphy O'Connor, James H. Charlesworth (New York: Crossroad Publishing Co., 1990), pp. 85-114.

23. Lawrence H. Schiffman, *Reclaiming the Dead Sea Scrolls* (New York: Doubleday, 1995), p. 151.

24. See Deuteronomy 10:16; 30:6; Psalms 14:2-3; 58:3; Jeremiah 13:23; 17:9; Ezekiel 36:25-26,31; and Isaiah 53:6.

25. See W.D. Davies, "Paul and the Dead Sea Scrolls: Flesh and Spirit," *The Scrolls and the New Testament*, ed. Krister Stendahl (New York: Harper & Brothers Publishers, 1957), pp. 157-82.

26. Lawrence H. Schiffman, *Reclaiming the Dead Sea Scrolls*, p. 86.

**Chapter 10—Prophecy and the Scrolls**

1. Shemaryahu Talmon, *The World of Qumran from Within* (Jerusalem: The Magnes Press, 1989), p. 278.

2. For a list of the foundational documents of the Sect which are apocalyptic in nature, see chapter 3. The following Qumranic texts represent the Sect's apocalyptic literature as found primarily in the newly published Cave 4 material: 1) Hebrew Pseudepigrapha: *Jubilees (4Q176:*19-20; *4Q216; 4Q218-224; 1Q17-18; 2Q19-20; 3Q5; 11Q12;* cf. *4Q482-483), Pseudo-Jubilees (4Q217; 4Q225-227), Testament of Naphtali (4Q215), Words of Moses (1Q22), Moses Apocrypha (2Q22), Pseudo-Ezekiel (4Q385-388;4Q391), Pseudo-Moses (4Q385ᵃ; 4Q387ᵃ; 4Q388ᵃ; 4Q389-390), Pseudepigraphic Work (4Q459-460), Prophetic Fragments (4Q522; 1Q25; 2Q23; 6Q10),* 2) Aramaic Texts: *Book of Giants (4Q203; 4Q530-532; 4Q533*[?]; *1Q23; 1Q24*[?]; *2Q26*[?]; *6Q8), New Jerusalem (4Q554-555; 1Q32; 2Q24; 5Q15; 11Q18), Visions of Amram (4Q543-548), Aramaic Levi (4Q537; 4Q540-541), Testament of Qahat (4Q542), Patriarchical Pseudepigrapha (4Q538-539), Aramaic Apocalypse (4Q246), Prayer of Nabonidus (4Q242), Proto-Esther*[?] *(4Q550), Daniel-Susana (4Q551),* [?] *Elect of God (4Q534), Four Kingdoms Apocalypse (4Q552-553), Vision* [?] *(4Q556-558, Words of Michael (4Q529), Tobit (4Q196-199), Genesis Apocryphon (1Q20), 1 Enoch (4Q201-202; 4Q204-207; 4Q212), Astronomical Book* [related to *1 Enoch*] *(4Q208-211), Miscellaneous (4Q535-536; 4Q549).* For a general discussion of these texts cf. Devorah Dimant, "Apocalyptic Texts at Qumran," *The Community of the Renewed Covenant: The Notre Dame Symposium on the Dead Sea Scrolls;* ed. E. Ulrich, J. VanderKam, *Christianity and Judaism in Antiquity Series* 10, ed. G.E. Sterling (IN: University of Notre Dame Press, 1994), pp. 175-90.

3. Interview with Shemaryahu Talmon, Jerusalem, November 12, 1995.

4. The prophetic position which is most similar in evangelicalism is premillennialism.

5. For further study of the relationship of the early canon to prophetic interpretation see Sid Z. Leiman, "Inspiration and Canonicity: Reflections on the Formation of the Biblical Canon, "*Aspects of Judaism in the Graeco-Roman Period* in *Jewish and Christian Self-Definition*, ed. E.P. Sanders (Philadelphia: Fortress Press, 1981), 2:56-63.

6. Gershon Biran, "Biblical Prophecy in the Qumran Scrolls" [Hebrew], *Sha'arei Talmon: Studies in the Bible, Qumran and the Ancient Near East Presented to Shemaryahu Talmon*, ed. M. Fishbane, E. Tov, with W. Fields (Winona Lake, IN: Eisenbrauns, 1992), pp. 101-12.

7. If the Essenes are to be rightly connected with the authors of the Scrolls, then Josephus in his account of the prophetic character of the Essenes (*Antiquities* 13. 171-73; 18. 12-15) even offers us names of some of their leading prophets: Judas (*Jewish Wars* 1. 78-80; *Ant.* 13. 311-13), Menahem (*Ant.* 25. 371-79), Simon (*Wars* 2. 111-13; *Ant.* 27. 345-48).

8. A. Steudel, "'ᵃchrit hayyamim in the Texts from Qumran (1)," *Revue de Qumran* 62:16:2 (December 1993): 225-46.

9. See John J. Collins, "Teacher and Messiah? The One Who Will Teach Righteousness At the End of Days," in *The Community of the Renewed Covenant*, pp. 193-211.

10. See Timothy H. Lim, "Eschatological Orientation and the Alteration of Scripture in the Habakkuk Pesher," *Journal of Near Eastern Studies* 49:2 (1990): 185-94. Nevertheless, George Brooke, based on his study of *4QFlorilegium*, has cautioned that "one cannot approach the use of the bible at Qumran presupposing that such was guided, for instance, by an overall eschatological perspective." "Exegesis at Qumran: 4QFlorilegium in its Jewish Context," *Journal for the Study of the Old Testament Supplement Series* 29. *The Dead Sea Scrolls Project of the Institute for Antiquity and Christianity* 2 (Sheffield: JSOT Press, 1989), p. 356.

11. Research into the development of apocalyptic literature has provided evidence of its developmental link with prophetic eschatology. Edwards has concluded: "What, then, marks the transition from prophecy to apocalyptic?...It is the combination of spiritual readiness and historical events. So the visions of the prophets become extended, elaborate and literary, as their symbolic acts are turned into symbols. The close relationship of these writers is seen in their concentration on the two focal points of time: the historical event of the fall of Jerusalem and the despair it brought; the historical fall of Babylon and the hope it brought. And between, the picture of the reactions of a displaced people." Grace Edwards, "The Historical Background of Early Apocalyptic Thought," *Scripture in History & Theology: Essays in Honor of J. Coert Rylaarsdam*, edited by A.L. Merrill and T.W. Overhold (Pennsylvania: The Pickwick Press, 1977), p. 202.

12. The term *apocalyptic* is used commonly to signify the sudden catastrophic intervention of God in the affairs of earth to right all wrongs and terminate human history. In general, the term has come to designate a literary genre "apocalypse" (derived from Greek *apocalypsis*, "revelation, disclosure"), and the special type of eschatology contained therein, separating from prophetic literature in only minor respects. See H.H. Rowley, *The Relevance of Apocalyptic: A Study of Jewish and Christian Apocalypses from Daniel to the Revelation* (New York: Association Press, 1963), p. 23.

13. A.D. Crown, "The Eschatology of the Qumran Sectaries," The Dead Sea Scrolls; symposium at St. Andrew's College, May 20-21, 1963 (Surry Hills: The Wentworth Press, 1967), pp. 49-50.

14. For discussion, see O. Betz, "Past Events and Last Events in the Qumran Interpretation of History," *Proceedings of the Sixth Worth Congress on Jewish Studies in Jerusalem 1976* (Jerusalem: The World Union of Jewish Studies, 1977) 1: 27-34.

15. John J. Collins, "Patterns of Eschatology at Qumran," *Traditions in Transformation*, edited by Baruch Halpern and Jon Levenson (Winona Lake, IN: Eisenbrauns, 1981), p. 375.

16. David Flusser, *The Spiritual History of the Dead Sea Sect*, trans. Carol Glucker (Tel-Aviv: MOD Books, 1989), p. 75.

17. *CD* 16:2 speaks of the Torah as that wherein "all things are strictly defined," and *1QS* 1:1-3 outlines the aim of the covenantors as "to seek God with a whole heart and soul, and to do what is good and right before Him, as He commanded by the hand of Moses and all His servants the prophets." We have also seen how *1QpHab* 7:4-5 declares that the "Teacher of Righteousness" can interpret all the words of the prophets.

18. See George J. Brooke, "Exegesis at Qumran: *4QFlorilegium* in its Jewish Context," *Journal for the Study of the Old Testament Supplement Series* 29 (Sheffield: JSOT Press, 1989), p. 356.

19. This division is similar to that of the biblical post-exilic era, cf. Zechariah 1:4; 7:7,12, where the prophets of this era are called "the latter prophets" and Haggai 2:3-9; cf. Ezra 3:12, which refers to the Second Temple (of Zerubbabel) as "the latter Temple."

20. Ezekiel's prophecy took on the same meaning as had Jeremiah's and was regarded by Talmon as an example of "millenarian arithmetics" or "messianic numerology." *The World of Qumran from Within*, p. 282 (text) and n. 18.

21. So Ben Zion Wacholder has reasoned; see *The Dawn of Qumran: The Sectarian Torah and the Teacher of Righteousness*, Monographs of the Hebrew Union College 8 (Cincinnati, OH: Hebrew Union College, 1983), pp. 177ff; see also James C. VanderKam, *The Dead Sea Scrolls Today* (Grand Rapids, MI: Eerdmans Publishing Co., 1994), p. 100.

22. Interview with Shemaryahu Talmon, Jerusalem, November 12, 1995.

23. Damascus is also taken literally as the capital city of Syria, to which the disillusioned members of the Sect fled. This is possible, but since Qumran is also viewed as Egypt in the same sense of exile, Damascus could also have this typological sense.

24. See F.F. Bruce, *Biblical Exegesis in the Qumran Texts* (London: The Tyndale Press, 1960), p. 68.

25. On the predestinarian position of the community in relation to eschatology, see Eugene H. Merrill, *Predestination at Qumran: A Theological Study of the Thanksgiving Hymns* (Leiden: E.J. Brill, 1975), pp. 51-54.

26. Eisenman and Wise suggest that they applied this figure to the first outbreak of revolutionary activity at the time of Herod's death in 4 B.C. and looked for the end in A.D. 66, the time of the Jewish uprising, which they believed would usher in the final battle of the end of days. Eisenman and Wise, *The Dead Sea Scrolls Uncovered* (MA: Element, 1992), p. 64.

27. This expression appears also in the New Testament (Matthew 24:8; Mark 13:8) and especially in rabbinic literature, in which it became a technical term for the tribulation (e.g., Babylonian Talmud, tractate *Sanhedrin* 97a). The origin of the phrase is the Old Testament prophetic teaching on the judgment of Israel (see Isaiah 13:8; 26:17; 66:7-9; Jeremiah 4:31; 22:23; 49:22; 50:43; Hosea 13:13; Micah 4:9-10). For a study of this phrase and the related concept see the author's "Old Testament Tribulation Terms," in *When the Trumpet Sounds* (Eugene, OR: Harvest House Publishers, 1995), chapter 3.

28. See John Pryke, "Eschatology in the Dead Sea Scrolls," in *The Scrolls and Christianity: Historical and Theological Significance*, ed. Matthew Black (London: SPCK, 1969), pp. 50-51; Dale C. Allison, "The End of the Ages Has Come," *Studies of the New Testament and Its World*, ed. John Riches (Edinburgh: T. & T. Clark, 1985), pp. 8-10.

29. This dualism most likely may be traced to the division of light from darkness in Genesis 1:3-5.

30. The terminology in this light-versus-darkness motif has long been considered synonymous and interchangeable; see G.R. Driver, *The Judean Scrolls, The Problem and a Solution* (Oxford: Blackwell, 1965), p. 545; F. Nötscher, "Geist und Geister in den Texten von Qumran," *Mélanges bibliques: rédigés en l'honneur de André Robert*, Trauvaux de l'Institut Catholique de Paris 4 (Paris, 1956): 305-16. James Charlesworth, "A Critical Comparison of the Dualism in *1QS* 3:13–4:26 and the 'Dualism' Contained in the Gospel of John," *New Testament Studies* 15 (1968-1969): 400, observes that the probability of these terms being synonymous is strengthened by the fact that YHWH is also given various names. He also notes that "light" and "darkness" denote origin and qualify the actions of the respective beings.

31. J. Daniélou, *The Dead Sea Scrolls and Primitive Christianity* (Baltimore, MD: Helicon, 1963), p. 107. This motif, however, is a unique paradigm to Qumran, and its contrast with other sects of Judaism, e.g. Christianity, has been demonstrated by H. Kosmala, "The Parable of the Unjust Steward in the Light of Qumran," *Annual of the Swedish Theological Institute*, edited by H. Kosmala (Leiden: E.J. Brill, 1964) 3:114-21.

32. The Wicked Priest might not be a single individual. See A.S. van der Woude, "Wicked Priest or Wicked Priests? Reflections on the Identification of the Wicked Priest in the Habakkuk Commentary," *Journal of Jewish Studies* 33 (1982); 349-59, and W.H. Brownlee, "The Wicked Priest, the Man of Lies, and the Righteous Teacher—The Problem of Identity," *Jewish Quarterly Review* 83 (1982): 4, argue that there six different individuals called by the name "Wicked Priest" in the text of the Habakkuk Commentary, probably revealing a series of conflicts between the Qumran Sect and the Hasmonean rulers.

33. See J. Murphy-O'Connor, "The Essenes and Their History," *Revue Biblique* 81 (1974): 215-44; "The Essenes in Palestine," *Revue Biblique* 40 (1977): 94-124.

34. See text and comments, George Wesley Buchanan, *Revue de Qumran* 53:14.1 (June 1989): 44-45, and "Eschatology and the 'End of Days,'" *Journal of Near Eastern Studies* 20 (1961): 188-93.

35. Shemaryahu Talmon, "The Calendar Reckoning of the Sect from the Judean Desert," *Scripta Hierosolymitana* IV (Jerusalem: Magnes Press, 1965), p. 167; for studies on the origin of the sectarian calendar, see A. Jaubert, "Le Calendrier des Jubilés et de la Secte Qumrân: Ses origines bibliques," *Vetus Testamentum* 3 (1955): 250-64; J.C. VanderKam, "2 Maccabees 6, 7a and Calendrical Change in Jerusalem," *Journal for the Study of Judaism* 12 (1981): 52-74; "The Origin, Character, and Early History of the 364-Day Calendar: A Reassessment of Jaubert's Hypothesis," *CBQ* 41 (1979): 390-411; P.R. Davies, "Calendrical Change and Qumran Origin: An Assessment of VanderKam's Theory," *CBQ* 45 (1983): 80-89. For a general overview of the problem, see Neil

S. Fujita, *A Crack in the Jar: What Ancient Jewish Documents Tell Us About the New Testament* (New York: Paulist Press, 1986), pp. 45-46.

36. On the verdict of divine punishment for calendrical offense in the Habakkuk Commentary, see Lawrence H. Schiffman, *The Halakha at Qumran, and Sectarian Law in the Dead Sea Scrolls: Courts, Testimony and the Penal Codes* (Scholars Press, 1983).

37. Interview with Shemaryahu Talmon, Jerusalem, November 12, 1995.

38. The noun *Belial* is entirely absent from early compositions such as the *Hodayot*, though it is peculiar to later texts. For example, "Belial" occurs as a *nomen proprium* in the *Damascus Document* six times, and since this Scroll was composed later than the earliest portion of the rule, it is thought that "Belial" is a substitute for "Angel of Darkness." In the *War Scroll*, the term appears 12 times, and since it is the latest of the major sectarian Scrolls, it strengthens the probability of the term becoming a surrogate for "Angel of Darkness." Further, "Belial" is found only in the preface (*1QS* 1:18,24; 2:5,19) and the concluding hymn (*1QS* 10:21) of the Rule, again, sections probably added at a later date.

39. The primary motive for this association has been the Christian tradition of Lucifer as the leader of the fallen angels and the archangel Michael as the leader of the elect angels, although this idea was certainly influenced by Tanach (see Daniel 10:13,21; 12:1) and the apocalyptic literate (*1 Enoch* 6:1-6; 7:1, 10:8-9; *Jubilees* 5:1-2).

40. See P. Wernberg-Møller, "A Reconsideration of the Two Spirits in the Rule of the Community (*1QSerek* 3:13-4:26, *RQ* 11 (1961): 423, who argues entirely for the psychological interpretation. In this case, the two spirits are equivalent to the rabbinic notion of the "good inclination" and the "evil inclination."

41. See A.A. Anderson, "The Use of '*Ruah*' in *1QA, 1QH* and *1QM*," *Journal of Jewish Studies* 7 (1962): 298. He argues that where this terminology differs, it is the result of differences in authorship, date, and nature of the writings. It also appears that the Johannine meaning of the terms "Spirit of Truth" (John 14:17; 15:26; 16:13) and "sons of light" (John 12:36), have been read back into the Qumran text. Frank Moore Cross, Jr., *The Ancient Library of Qumran & Modern Studies* (New York: Doubleday & Co., 1961), p. 213, has noted: "The 'Spirit of Truth' in *1QS* is an angelic creature who is at a greater distance from God than the 'Spirit of Truth,' who in John is God's own Spirit."

42. The source of evil in *1QS* is *external* to men and not as Wernberg-Møller has suggested "created by God to dwell in man." Rather, in *1QS* 3:18 the text says that God "allotted the spirits unto man." Furthermore, *1QS* suggests that men are divided into two mutually exclusive camps ("Sons of Light" or "Sons of Darkness"). W.D. Davies, "The Dead Sea Scrolls and Christian Origins," *RL* 26 (1957): 246-64, has pointed this out saying "that [these spirits] are not merely inherent properties of man, as such, emerges from the use of the term "angel" to describe the two spirits: this preserves the 'otherness' of the two spirits even when they appear to be immanent." Therefore, U. Simon, *Heaven in the Christian Tradition* (London, 1958), p. 173, concludes, "The struggle in the heart of man is inseparable from the cosmic array of powers (*1QS* 4:18)."

43. A.R.C. Leaney, *The Rule of Qumran and Its Meaning* (Philadelphia: Fortress Press, 1966): 43 notes: "The Tendency to personify as angels the powers which control the stars and to identify God himself with the *Urlicht* may be paralleled by the identification of the two spirits with personal supernatural beings."

44. However, if these two are one entity, then the Angel of Darkness may be construed as the deceptive functioning of Satan, much as in the New Testament, cf. Satan "appearing as an angel of light" (2 Corinthians 11:14) and "deceiving the whole world" (Revelation 12:9; 13:14; 20:3).

45. Interview with Shemaryahu Talmon, Jerusalem, November 12, 1995.

46. This is certainly the case for the term "son of Belial" (the more significant term), which occurs immediately following this context in column 3, while the term "blasphemous king" occurs in fragments, which are thought to follow this context.

47. Eisenman and Wise, *The Dead Sea Scrolls Uncovered,* p. 65.

48. See Joseph Coppens, " 'Mystery' in the Theology of Saint Paul and its Parallels at Qumran," *Paul and the Dead Sea Scrolls*, eds. Jerome Murphy-O'Connor and James H. Charlesworth (New York: Crossroad, 1990), p. 141.

49. A. Dupont-Sommer, *The Essene Writings from Qumran*, trans. Geza Vermes (Oxford: Blackwell, 1961), p. 327.

50. David Flusser, "The Hubris of the Antichrist in a Fragment from Qumran," *Immanuel* 10 (Spring 1980): 31-37.

51. This fragment from Cave 4 was bought from Kando the antiquities dealer on July 9, 1958, and officially assigned to J.T. Milik of Harvard. Milik's failure to publish the text or his translation motivated the Jesuit priest Joseph A. Fitzmyer to publish an unauthorized translation of part of the text in "The Contribution of Qumran Aramaic to the Study of the New Testament," *New Testament Studies* 20 (1973-1974): 391-94. First credit for full publication goes to Emilé Peuch, "Fragment d'une apocalypse en arameén (*4Q246* = pseudo-Dan$^d$) et le 'royaume de Dieu,' " *RB* 99 (1992): 98-131, who succeeded Milik as the officially designated editor. Following the release of a photograph of the text by the Huntington Library of San Marino, California, Fitzmyer published his own complete translation with commentary, cf. "*4Q246*: The 'Son of God' Document from Qumran," *Biblica* 74:2 (1993), pp. 153-74. It was originally entitled *Pseudo-Daniel,* with the sigla *4QpsDanA$^a$* or *Dan$^d$* 209, because of the mention of "Daniel" in column 1, line 2, although this Daniel only appeared as a man falling before the throne, yet there was also an allusion to the eternal kingdom of Daniel 2:44, which warranted this signification. However, the exceptional appearance of the term "S/son of God" and the interpretation of this text as an allusion to Daniel 7:13 has become the basis for the title and sigla.

52. F. Garcia Martinez, *Qumran and Apocalyptic: Studies on the Aramaic Texts from Qumran, Studies on the Texts of the Desert of Judah IX*, eds. F. Garcia Martinez and A.S. van der Woude (Leiden: E.J. Brill, 1992), p. 172.

53. Lawrence H. Schiffman, *The Eschatological Community of the Dead Sea Scrolls: A Study of the Rule of the Congregation*, Society of Biblical Literature Monograph Series 38, eds. A.Y. Collins and E.F. Campbell, Jr. (Atlanta, GA: Scholars Press, 1989), p. 68.

**Chapter 11—The Temple and the Scrolls**

1. Bruce Chilton, *The Temple of Jesus: His Sacrificial Program Within a Cultural History of Sacrifice* (University Park, PA: The Pennsylvania State University Press, 1992), p. 83.

2. For example, Ernest L. Martin, based on the Temple rejection texts and their historical situation in the Hasmonean period, especially with reference to Simon, argues that the Temple of Solomon was originally built on Ophel, and that the Hasmoneans destroyed the site and much of Jerusalem for their own building projects, including a new Temple in the wrong place. It is for this reason that the Sect's Teacher of Righteousness opposed Simon (the Wicked Priest = the Man of the Lies = Scoffer) and the use of this misplaced Temple. His evidence is drawn from Josephus' statements that the Essenes "offered their sacrifices by themselves"—evidence that came from apocryphal (Maccabees) and pseudepigraphical (Enoch) sources, and negative statements about the Temple in *Pesher Habakkuk* (on 2:17), and especially *CD* about "removing the landmark," which he equated with changing the location of the Temple. In my opinion, the Qumran Temple references cannot be interpreted in this manner to support such a hypothesis. See "Where did Solomon Build His Temple?" *An A.S.K. Historical Report* #00078 (Portland, OR: Associates for Scriptural Knowledge, 1996).

3. The Lebanon allusion for the Temple is drawn from the "whitening" imagery implicit in the root *lbn*. This is played upon to produce the exegesis, either to the Temple (because the priests wore white linen there) or to the community council (presumably for the same reason). This is similar to the rabbinic interpretation (*Gittin* 56a) of Isaiah 10:33-34, which tied this metaphor to the A.D. 70 fall of the Temple.

4. This negative attitude toward the Temple was also shared by other Jewish sects of the time. For them the Temple had failed to meet the prophetic restoration ideal, or else it was seen as having

served more as a symbol of unlawful complicity [whether with Persians, Syrians, Greeks, Hasmoneans, or Romans] than a symbol of Jewish independence.

5. Interview with Stephen J. Pfann, School of Early Christianity, Jerusalem, November 10, 1995.

6. See Bertil Gärtner, *The Temple and the Community in Qumran and the New Testament* (Cambridge: At the University Press, 1965), pp. 4-46, interprets such passages as *1QS* 5:6; 8:8,11 in this manner. Cf. R. J. Mckelvey, *The New Temple: The Church in the New Testament, Oxford Theological Monographs* (London: Oxford University Press, 1969), as an example of those who use the concept at Qumran to argue for the church as replacing the Temple from the New Testament metaphor.

7. E.S. Fiorenza, "Cultic Language in Qumran and in the New Testament," *CBQ* 38 (1976): 159-77.

8. For example, H Wenschkewitz, *Die Spiritualisierung der Kultusbegriffe Tempel, Priester, und Opfer im Neuen Testament, Angelos*, Beiheft 4 (Leipzig: Pfeiffer, 1932), and Yves M.J. Congar, *The Mystery of the Temple or the Manner of God's Presence to His Creatures from Genesis to the Apocalypse*, trans. by R. E. Trevett (Newman, 1962).

9. Lawrence Schiffman, *Reclaiming the Dead Sea Scrolls*, p. 299.

10. Interview with Magen Broshi, Shrine of the Book Museum, Jerusalem, November 12, 1995.

11. Interview with Stephen J. Pfann, Jerusalem, November 10, 1995.

12. A.I. Baumgarten, "Josephus on Essene Sacrifice," *Journal of Jewish Studies* 45:2 (Autumn 1994): 169-83.

13. A hoard of Tyrian silver tetradrachmas, precisely the type used for the half-shekel Temple contribution, was found in locus 120. While *4Q159* records collection of this payment, it does not explicitly state that they were delivered to the Jerusalem Temple. I can see no objection for believing, as does Stephen Goranson, "Sectarianism, Geography, and the Copper Scroll," *Journal of Jewish Studies* 43:2 (1992): 285, that they were so delivered. If not, however, perhaps they were being held in store for the purified Third Temple that was expected to replace the Second Temple.

14. Philip R. Davies, *The Damascus Covenant: An Interpretation of the "Damascus Document*," Journal for the Study of the Old Testament Supplement Series 25 (Sheffield: JSOT Press, 1983): 202.

15. Philip R. Davies, "The Idealogy of the Temple in the Damascus Document," *Journal of Jewish Studies* 33:1-2 (Spring-Autumn 1982): 300-01.

16. Interview with Stephen Pfann, Jerusalem, November 10, 1995.

17. John T. Townsend, "The Jerusalem Temple in the First Century," *God and His Temple: Reflections on Samuel Terrien's The Elusive Presence: Toward a New Biblical Theology*, edited by Lawrence E. Frizzell (New Jersey: Department of Judeo-Christian Studies, Seton Hall University, 1979), p. 49. Some of these references in Second Temple literature included living a virtuous life (Philo, *Special Laws* 1:50 (272); *Sacrifices* 12 (5); *Life of Moses* 2:22 (108); *1QS* 9:5; cf. Micah 6:7-9), martyrdom (IV Maccabees 6:27-29); prayer (*CD* 11:21); praise (*1QS* 9:4).

18. Ben Sira uses such references with regard to observing Torah (*Sira* 35:1-3, cf. 32:1-5), and Aristeas of the ransoming of slaves (*Epistle of Aristeas* 19, 37).

19. Some students of the Scrolls also include the passage in *4QFlorilegium* 6:1, which has the expression "the sanctuary of man." This has been interpreted to refer to a temple-community, cf. Gärtner, *The Temple and the Community in Qumran* (pp. 30-42). However, the text most likely refers to the future sanctuary to be built "among men," rather than having any symbolic sense. For the arguments in support of this, especially for the comparative evidence from the *Temple Scroll*, see Yigael Yadin, *The Temple Scroll* (Jerusalem: The Israel Exploration Society, 1977) [Hebrew], 1:143f; "A Midrash on 2 Sam. 7 and Ps. 1-11 (*4QFlorilegium*)," *Israel Exploration Journal* 9 (1959). 95-98.

20. Interview with Stephen Pfann, Jerusalem, November 10, 1995.

21. Some would translate the key phrase "a sanctuary of men" as "a sanctuary *consisting* of men"; however, this symbolic interpretation is unnatural, and the natural "a sanctuary of men," [that is, built by them] is preferred.

22. James C. VanderKam, *The Dead Sea Scrolls Today* (Eerdmans Publishing Co., 1994), p. 51.

23. Michael O. Wise, *A Critical Study of the Temple Scroll from Qumran Cave 11, Studies in Ancient Oriental Civilizations* 49 (Chicago: The Oriental Institute of the University of Chicago, 1990), pp. 64-86.

24. Interview with Magen Broshi, Shrine of the Book, Jerusalem, November 10, 1995.

25. The Kittim are usually considered to be the Romans, whose ships in Daniel 11:30 came from the west past Cyprus (= *Kittim*) to defeat the army of Antiochus IV Epiphanes in Egypt. However, 1 Maccabees 1:1 equates them with the forces of Alexander the Great.

26. The text (according to the reconstruction by Eisenman and Wise, *The Dead Sea Scrolls Uncovered,* p. 43) reads: "the Kittim after him, all of them after another . . . among all nations, the] kingdom . . . and the nations shall ser[ve] them," column 11 [or later], 16, 21, 22.

27. The designation for this document is *11Q19* or *11QT*. The numeral 11 indicates that the Scroll is from Cave 11, the letters *QT* stand for either *11Q Temple* or *11Q Torah*. This later designation is based on the premise that the Scroll was considered by the Qumran community as a supplementary sixth book of the Torah, or as the second half of a Scroll considered an eschatological Torah. On this latter issue there is debate, however, as to whether the Temple conceived in the Scroll is an *eschatological* Temple or a model of an *earthly* Temple that was intended to be replaced by a later eschatological and eternal Temple.

28. See Yigael Yadin, *The Temple Scroll* (Israel Exploration Society, 1983) 1:386-90; Lawrence Schiffman, *Reclaiming the Dead Sea Scrolls*, p. 257.

29. Philip R. Davies, "The Scroll and the Damascus Document," *Temple Scroll Studies*, p. 209.

30. H. Stegemann, "The Literary Composition of the Scroll," *Temple Scroll Studies* (papers presented at the International Symposium on the Temple Scroll, Manchester, December 1987); ed. George J. Brooke, *Journal for the Study of the Pseudepigrapha Supplement Series* 7 (Sheffield: JSOT Press, 1989), pp. 143-45, and "The Origins of the Temple Scroll," *Proceedings of the World Congress of Jewish Studies in Jerusalem 1986*, ed. J. Emereton (Leiden: E.J. Brill, 1988), pp. 235-56.

31. Lawrence Schiffman, "The *Temple Scroll* and the Nature of Its Law: The Status of the Question," *The Community of the Renewed Covenant* (The Notre Dame Symposium on the Dead Sea Scrolls), eds. E. Ulrich and J. VanderKam; *Christianity and Judaism in Antiquity Series* 10 (Notre Dame: University Press, 1994), pp. 37-55.

32. See Dwight D. Swanson, " 'A Covenant Just Like Jacob's' the Covenant of *11QT* 29 and Jeremiah's New Covenant," *New Qumran Texts and Studies: Proceedings of the First Meeting of the International Organization for Qumran Studies, Paris 1992*, eds. George J. Brooke and F.G. Martínez. *Studies on the Texts of the Desert of Judah* 15 (Leiden: E.J. Brill, 1994): 273-86. Swanson argues that the idea of a new covenant as a break (discontinuity) with the old covenant (presented in Jeremiah 31) was rejected by the *Temple Scroll*, which held to a renewed covenant (continuity).

33. Yigael Yadin, *The Temple Scroll* (1983), 1:198-200.

34. Such patterned wrappings for Scrolls are mentioned in the Mishnah (*Kelim* 28:4).

35. Rabbinic literature, and especially the midrash, was anxious to resolve questions that arose from the text. In this case the question was, How did David know how to build the Temple; when and from whence did he receive the *written* plans for the Temple mentioned in 1 Chronicles 28:19? The rabbis concluded that this must have been a part of the received Torah, like the instructions given for the building of the Tabernacle in Exodus 25–27. Therefore, they produced this midrash explaining that a "Temple Scroll" was transmitted through the leadership of Israel to Solomon. There may, however, be some support for this argument, since *11QT* appears to be a copy from an *earlier* original, for fragments of other copies of *11QT* manuscripts have been found in other caves.

36. One evidence for this is the way the text presents itself as direct revelation from God. In Old Testament parallel passages using the introductory formula "Moses said," where the Bible means that God gave Moses revelation, *11QT* read, "I said," meaning that God Himself is speaking.

37. James C. VanderKam, "The Temple Scroll and the Book of Jubilees," *Temple Scroll Studies*, pp. 211-35.

38. Esther Eshel, "4QLev$^d$: A Possible Source for the Temple Scroll and *Misqat Ma'ase Ha-Torah*," *Dead Sea Discoveries* 2:1 (April 1995): 1-13.

39. Philip R. Davies, "The Ideology of the Temple in the Damascus Document," pp. 287-301.

40. See also Jacob Milgrom, " 'Sabbath' and 'Temple City' in the Temple Scroll," *Bulletin of the American School of Oriental Research* 232 (1978). 25-27, and J. Kampen, "The Temple Scroll, the Torah of Qumran?" *Proceedings of the Eastern Great Lakes Biblical Society* 1 (1981), pp. 37-54. It may be that *11QT* was composed in the late Persian or early Hellenistic period (c. 200 B.C.). Knowing about this gap of knowledge, and influenced by the need to supply what was missing, the writers may have simply composed this new document based on their contemporary understanding of the Second Temple and colored by their fascination with the eschatological Temple of Ezekiel 40–48.

41. Michael O. Wise, "The Eschatological Vision of the Temple Scroll," *Journal of Near Eastern Studies* 49:2 (1990): 155-72.

42. Asher Finkel, "The Theme of God's Presence and the Qumran Temple Scroll," *God and His Temple: Reflections on Professor Samuel Terrien's The Elusive Presence: Toward a New Biblical Theology*, ed. Lawrence E. Frizzell (New Jersey: Department of Judeo-Christian Studies, 1979), pp. 39-47.

43. Judith L. Wentling, "Unraveling the Relationship between *11QT*, the Eschatological Temple, and the Qumran Community," *Revue de Qumran* 53:14:1 (June 1989): 61-74.

44. Ibid., p. 74.

45. H. Stegemann, "The Literary Composition of the Scroll," *Temple Scroll Studies: Papers Presented at the International Symposium on the Temple Scroll*, ed. George J. Brooke, *Journal for the Study of Pseudepigrapha Supplement* 7 (Sheffield: JSOT Press, 1989), pp. 144-45.

46. H. Stegemann, "Is the Temple Scroll a Sixth Book of the Torah—Lost for 2,500 Years?" *Biblical Archaeology Review* 13:6 (1987): 28-35.

47. Michael O. Wise, "The Covenant of Temple Scroll XXIX, 3-10," *RQ* 53:14:1 (June 1989): 59-60.

48. Johann Maier, "The Architectural History of the Temple in Jerusalem in Light of the Temple Scroll," in *Temple Scroll Studies*, ed. George J. Brooke (Journal for the Study of the Pseudepigrapha Supplement Series 7, 1987), pp. 23-62.

49. Bruce Chilton, *The Temple of Jesus: His Sacrificial Program Within a Cultural History of Sacrifice* (PA: The Pennsylvania State University Press, 1992), p. 83.

50. See arguments for a Temple built with human hands by Yigael Yadin, *The Temple Scroll*, 1.184, 2:125; and P. Callaway, "Exegetische Erwägungen zur Tempelrolle XXIX, 7-10," *RQ* 12 (1985-1987), p. 97, n. 5.

51. See arguments for a Temple created by God Himself, Ben Zion Wacholder, *The Dawn of Qumran: The Sectarian Torah and the Teacher of Righteousness* (Cincinnati, OH: Hebrew Union College Press, 1983), p. 23.

52. Wayne O. McCready, "Temple and Temple Scroll: A Sectarian Alternative," *Proceedings of the Tenth World Congress of Jewish Studies in Jerusalem, August 16-24, 1989*, Division A: *The Bible and Its World* (Jerusalem: The World Union of Jewish Studies, 1990): 203-04.

53. See Magen Broshi, "The Gigantic Dimensions of the Visionary Temple in the Temple Scroll," *Biblical Archaeology Review* (November-December 1987), pp. 36-37.

54. Johann Maier, "The Architectural History of the Temple," pp. 23, 50-52.

55. See Gaalya Cornfield's commentary in *Josephus—the Jewish War*, eds. G. Cornfield, B. Mazar, Paul Maier (Grand Rapids, MI: Zondervan Publishing House, 1982), p. 428.

56. Yigael Yadin, *The Temple Scroll* 1:198.

57. Interview with Dan Bahat, Meveseret Tzion, November 12, 1995.

58. See Michael Chyutin, "The New Jerusalem: Ideal City," *Dead Sea Scroll Discoveries* 1:1 (April 1994): 95 (top).

59. Yigael Yadin, *The Temple Scroll: The Hidden Law of the Dead Sea Sect* (New York: Random House, 1985), p. 113.

60. Ben Zion Wacholder, *The Dawn of Qumran: The Sectarian Torah and the Teacher of Righteousness* (Cincinnati, OH: Hebrew Union College Press, 1983), pp. 22-30.

61. *11QT* 15:15; 25:16.

62. Yigael Yadin, *The Temple Scroll*, 1:182.

63. For references, see W.D. Davies, *Torah in the Messianic Age and/or the Age to Come*, Journal of Biblical Literature Monograph Series 7 (Philadelphia: Society of Biblical Literature, 1952), pp. 73-91; and Howard M. Teeple, "The Future of the Law in Judaism: New Law and the Abrogation of the Torah," in *The Mosaic Eschatological Prophet*, Journal of Biblical Literature Monograph Series 10 (Philadelphia: Society for Biblical Literature, 1957), pp. 23-27.

64. Similar assertions are made in the *Damascus Document* (4.8-9; 6.14).

65. Lawrence Schiffman, "The Furnishings of the Temple According to the Temple Scroll," *The Madrid Qumran Congress* 2 (1992), pp. 622-23; Yigael Yadin, *The Temple Scroll*, 1:180.

66. These were 1) the Ark, 2) the Holy Spirit (of prophecy), 3) the Urim and Thummim, 4) the holy fire, and 5) the Shekinah glory.

67. For details and references, see my book *In Search of Temple Treasures* (Eugene, OR: Harvest House Publishers, 1994), pp. 102-07, 157-85, 189-94.

68. See John Strugnell, "The Angelic Liturgy at Qumran—*4Q Serek Sirot 'Olat Hassabat*," *Supplements to Vetus Testamentum* 7 (1959): 318-45.

### Chapter 12—Secrets of the *Copper Scroll*

1. See P. Kyle McCarter, Jr., " The Mystery of the *Copper Scroll*," *The Dead Sea Scrolls After Forty Years: Papers Presented at a Symposium at the Smithsonian Institution*, October 27, 1990 (Washington, DC: The Biblical Archaeology Society, 1991, 1992), pp. 41, 45.

2. Interview with Bargil Pixner, Dormition Abbey, November 14, 1995.

3. Ibid.

4. This list was first published by M. Baillet in *Discoveries in the Judean Desert of Jordan III*, eds. M. Baillet, J.T. Milik, and R. de Vaux (Oxford University Press, 1962), pp. 94-104.

5. *Encyclopedia Judaica*, s.v. "*Copper Scroll*," by F.F. Bruce, 5:957.

6. H. Wright Baker, "Notes on the Opening of the 'Bronze' Scrolls from Qumran," *Bulletin of the John Rylands Library*, 39 (1956-57): 56; A.C. Wolters, "History and the Copper Scroll," *Methods of Investigation of the Dead Sea Scrolls and the Khirbet Qumran Site: Present Realities and Future Prospects*, ed. Michael O. Wise (New York: Academy of Sciences, 1994), "Discussion of Paper," p. 296.

7. Interview with Stephen Pfann, Jerusalem, November 10, 1995.

8. See Y. Thorion, Beiträge zur Erforschung der Sprache der Kupferrolle," *Revue de Qumran* 12 (1985): 163-76.

9. P. Kyle McCarter, Jr., "*Copper Scroll* Treasure as an Accumulation of Religious Offerings," *Methods of Investigation of the Dead Sea Scrolls and the Khirbet Qumran Site*, "Discussion of the Paper," p. 143.

511

10. The first proposal was that of the German professor K.G. Kuhn, who on a visit to Jerusalem was allowed to see the copper rolls. Although not permitted to touch them in any way, he peered through the glass case for hours until he was able to decipher the words "cubits," "buried," "gold," and "silver," and concluded that this was an inventory of "Essene treasure." K.G. Kuhn, "Les Rouleaux de cuivre de Qumrân," *Revue Biblique* 16 (1954): 193-205.

11. See J.T. Milik, "The Copper Document from Cave III, Qumran," *Biblical Archaeologist* 19 (1956): 60, 62.

12. See Chaim Rabin, "The *Copper Scroll*," *The Jewish Chronicle* (June 15, 1956), p. 19.

13. Other scholars that independently advanced the legendary hypothesis (using the same source as Milik) were Sigmund Mowinkel, "The *Copper Scroll*—An Apocryphon?" *Journal of Biblical Literature* 76 (1957). 261-65; L.H. Silberman, "A Note on the *Copper Scroll*," *Vetus Testamentum* 10 (1960): 77-79; and Frank Moore Cross, Jr., *The Ancient Library of Qumran and Modern Biblical Studies* (Garden City, NY: Doubleday, 1958), pp. 16-18. It appears that Yigael Yadin had also made a connection between the *Copper Scroll* and tractate *Kelim* in a March 1958 lecture, R. Noth, "Biblical and Archaeological News," *Catholic Biblical Quarterly* 20 (1958): 356.

14. For example, 2 Maccabees 2:4-8; 2 Baruch 6:5-9; 4 Baruch, *Paralipomena of Jeremiah* 3:5-19; Mishnah tractate *Shekalim* 6:1-2. For a survey of these traditions see chapter 1 of my book *In Search of Temple Treasures* (Eugene, OR: Harvest House Publishers, 1994), pp. 23-35.

15. See J.T. Milik, "Notes d'épigraphie et de topographie palestinennes," *Revue Biblique* 66 (1959): 567-75.

16. Chaim Rabin, "The Historical Background of Qumran Hebrew," *Scripta Hierosolymitana* 4: Aspects of the Dead Sea Scrolls (Jerusalem: Magnes Press, 1958): 146.

17. See Chaim Rabin, "The *Copper Scroll*," *The Jewish Chronicle* (June 15, 1956), p. 19.

18. Interview with Dan Bahat, Meveseret Tzion, November 12, 1995.

19. Interview with Stephen Pfann, Jerusalem, November 10, 1995.

20. Al Wolters, "Apocalyptic and the *Copper Scroll*," *Journal of Near Eastern Studies* 49:2 (1990): 154.

21. Bargil Pixner, "Unravelling the *Copper Scroll* Code: A Study on the Topography of *3Q15*, "*Revue de Qumran* 11:3:43 (December 1983): 335, n. 32.

22. Ibid., "Translation of the *Copper Scroll*," pp. 344-45, n. 11.

23. Al Wolters, "History and the *Copper Scroll*," *Methods of Investigation of the Dead Sea Scrolls and the Khirbet Qumran Site*, p. 291.

24. E.M. Laperrousaz, "Remarques sur l'origine des Rouleaux de Cuivre découverts dans la Grotte 3 de Qumrân," *Revue de l'historie des religions* 159 (Paris, 1961): 157-72.

25. B.Z. Luria, *Megillat han-Nahoshet mem-Midbar Yehudah*, Publications of the Israel Bible Research Society 14 (Jerusalem, 1963) (Hebrew).

26. See *Anchor Bible Dictionary*, s.v. "*Copper Scroll (3Q15)*," by Bargil Pixner (New York: Doubleday, 1992): 1:1133.

27. Roland de Vaux, *Archaeology and the Dead Sea Scrolls* (Oxford University Press, 1973), p. 108.

28. Although Joseph Patrich, who also excavated the cave, states that "as much as I could judge from the cave, there is nothing against the possibility that the *Copper Scroll* was deposited later than the parchment Scrolls." "Discussion of the Paper," Wolters, "History and the *Copper Scroll*," p. 296.

29. See M. Baillet, J.T. Milik, and R. de Vaux, *Discoveries in the Judean Desert of Jordan III: Les "Petites Grottes" de Qumrân* (Oxford University Press, 1962), pp. 217-21.

30. See Ben Zion Wacholder, *The Dawn of Qumran: The Sectarian Torah and the Teacher of Righteousness*. Monographs of the Hebrew Union College 8 (Cincinnati, OH: Hebrew Union College Press, 1983), p. 95.

31. Interview with Bargil Pixner, Dormition Abbey, November 14, 1995.

32. K.G. Kuhn, "Les Rouleaux de cuivre de Qumrân," *Revue Biblique* 61 (1954): 193-205.

512

33. John M. Allegro, *The Treasure of the Copper Scroll* (Garden City, NY: Doubleday, 1964).

34. Interview with Bargil Pixner, Dormition Abbey, November 14, 1995.

35. Interview with Stephan Pfann, Jerusalem, November 10, 1995.

36. Ibid.

37. See Al Wolters, "Apocalyptic and the *Copper Scroll*," *Journal of Near Eastern Studies* 49:2 (1990): 145-54.

38. For a complete discussion of apocalypticism at Qumran, see George Wesley Buchanan, "The Eschatological Expectations of the Qumran Community" (Ph.D. dissertation: Drew University, 1959).

39. See Manfred R. Lehmann, "Identification of the *Copper Scroll* Based on Its Technical Terms," *Revue de Qumran* 5:17:1 (October 1964): 97-105; "Where the Temple Tax Was Buried," *Biblical Archaeology Review* 19:4 (November/December 1993): 38-43.

40. See Jonathan A. Herbst, "*Copper Scroll*: History Contradicts Fanciful Hypothesis," in "Queries and Comments," *Biblical Archaeology Review* 20:2 (March/April 1994): 20, 73.

41. However, as McCarter contends, it would have easily been possible to amass this kind of fortune during the period between the two revolts. "The Mysterious *Copper Scroll*," *Biblical Archaeology Review*, p. 64.

42. Norman Golb, *Who Wrote the Dead Sea Scrolls?: The Search for the Secret of Qumran* (New York: Scribner, 1995), pp. 117-50.

43. See Al Wolters, "The Last Treasure of the *Copper Scroll*," *Journal of Biblical Literature* 107:3 (September 1988): 423-24; "Cultic Terminology in the *Copper Scroll*," *Festschrift in Honor of J.T. Milik* 2 (1994).

44. See *Encyclopedia Judaica*, s.v. "*Copper Scroll*," by F.F. Bruce, 5:957.

45. See abstract of dissertation at the University of Chicago by David Wilmot in *Abstracts, American Academy of Religion / Society of Biblical Literature* (1984), p. 214.

46. P. Kyle McCarter, Jr., "The Copper Scroll Treasure," p. 140.

47. Translation by P. Kyle McCarter, Jr., in "The Mysterious *Copper Scroll*: Clues to Hidden Treasure?" *Bible Review* 8:4 (August 1992): 41.

48. Interview with Shemaryahu Talmon, Jerusalem, November 12, 1995.

49. The reading *bhr gryzyn* is contested. An alternate location is suggested as a hill in the vicinity of Jericho. Others argue for Mount Gerizim seeing also the presence of Essenes among the Samaritans. See Pixner, "Translation of the *Copper Scroll*" in "Unravelling the *Copper Scroll* Code: A Study on the Topography of *3Q15*," *Revue de Qumran* 11:3:43 (December 1983): 357, n. 49.

50. *New York Times*, June 1, 1956, p. 4.

51. Joachim Jeremias, "The *Copper Scroll* from Qumran," *Expository Times* 71 (1959-60): 228.

52. J.T. Milik, "The Copper Document from Cave III, Qumran," *Biblical Archaeologist* 19 (1956): 63.

53. John Marco Allegro, *The Treasure of the* Copper Scroll (New York: Doubleday & Co., Inc., 1960), pp. 6-7.

54. Interview with Stephen Pfann, Jerusalem, November 10, 1995.

55. Interview with Bargil Pixner, Dormition Abbey, November 14, 1995.

56. Ibid.

57. Ibid.

58. A.C. Wolters, "History and the Copper Scroll," pp. 293-95.

59. "Discussion of the Paper" (of Wolters), Ibid., p. 296.

60. Interview with Stephen Pfann, Jerusalem, November 10, 1995.

61. Interview with Bargil Pixner, Dormition Abbey, Jerusalem, November 13, 1995.

62. Interview with Stephen Pfann, Jerusalem, November 10, 1995.

63. Interview with Bargil Pixner, Dormition Abbey, Jerusalem, November 14, 1995.

64. Al Wolters, "The Last Treasure of the *Copper Scroll*," 419-29.

65. Paul Mandel, "On the 'Duplicate Copy' of the *Copper Scroll (3Q15)*," *Revue de Qumran* 61:1 (September 1993): 69-76.

66. For a discussion, see Ibid., pp. 73-76.

67. Ibid., pp. 71-72.

68. Al Wolters, "The Copper Scroll and the Vocabulary of Mishnaic Hebrew," *Revue de Qumran* 55:3 (January 1990): 492-93.

69. Ibid., pp. 72-73.

70. Bargil Pixner, "Translation of the *Copper Scroll*," 358, n. 52.

**Chapter 13—The Messiah in the Scrolls**

1. See Lawrence H. Schiffman, "The Concept of the Messiah in Second Temple and Rabbinic Literature," *Review and Expositor* 84 (1987): 235-46.

2. See the list of J.A. Fitzmyer, *Responses to 101 Questions on the Dead Sea Scrolls*, p. 55, of *kings* (Saul): 1 Samuel 24:7,11; 26:9,11,16,23; 2 Samuel 1:14,16 (cf. 1 Samuel 2:10,35; 12:3,5; 16:6; Psalm 28:8), (David): 2 Samuel 19:22; 22:51; 23:1; Psalm 2:2; 20:7; 84:10; 89:39,52; 132:10,17 (cf. 18:51), (Solomon): 2 Chronicles 6:42, (Zedekiah): Lamentations 4:20; of *patriarchs:* Psalm 105:15; 1 Chronicles 16:22 (?); of *foreign rulers*—Cyrus, the Persian king: Isaiah 45:1; of *Israel* (?): Habakkuk 3:3 (cf. Psalm 28:8); of *priests:* Leviticus 4:3,5,16; 16:15; of *prophets* (perhaps): Psalm 105:15; 1 Chronicles 16:22 (?).

3. See Shemaryahu Talmon, "The Concepts of *Masiah* and Messianism in Early Judaism," *The Messiah*, p. 81, and "Kingship and the Ideology of the State," *King, Cult and Calendar in Ancient Israel* (Jerusalem: Magnes Press, 1986), pp. 9-38.

4. See Richard A. Horsley, "Popular Messianic Movements Around the Time of Jesus," *Essential Papers on Messianic Movements and Personalities in Jewish History*, ed. Marc Saperstein (New York: New York University Press, 1992), pp. 92-94.

5. See M.G. Reddish, ed. *Apocalyptic Literature: A Reader* (Nashville, TN: Abingdon, 1990), pp. 164-65. Even though J.T. Milik, *The Books of Enoch: Aramaic Fragments from Qumran Cave 4* (Oxford: Clarendon Press, 1976), pp. 4-135, argued for a much later date (A.D. 270) based on the apparent absence of Similitudes in the Scroll's copy of *1 Enoch*. This dating has been generally rejected; see S. Uhlig, *Das äthiopische Henochbuch*, Jüdische Schriften aus hellenistischrömischer Zeitschrift 5:6, ed. W.G. Kummel, et. al. (Gütersloh, 1984); and Joseph Copens, *Le Fils d'Homme vétéro-et intertestamentaire* (Leuven, 1982); and J.H. Charlesworth, "The Society for New Testament Study Pseudepigrapha Seminars at Tübingen and Paris on the Books of Enoch," *New Testament Studies* 25 (1978-79): 315-23. Reddish argues for an early date based on internal chronological evidence such as the reference to the Parthian attack (56:5-7), but no mention of the Jewish War of A.D. 66-70, and the mention of healing hot springs, which might refer to those at Callirhoe, at which Herod sought relief prior to his death in 4 B.C.

6. See John J. Collins, "The Son of Man in First-Century Judaism," *New Testament Studies* 38 (1992): 448-66.

7. See this summary, following Collins' study (above) by Thomas Slater, "One Like a Son of Man in First-Century C.E. Judaism," *New Testament Studies* 41:2 (April 1995): 191.

8. See Matthew Black, "The Messianism of the Parabales of Enoch: Their Date and Contribution to Christological Origins," *The Messiah*, pp. 145-68.

9. Lawrence H. Schiffman, "Messianic Figures and Ideas in the Qumran Scrolls," *The Messiah: Developments in Earliest Judaism and Christianity*, The First Princeton Symposium on Judaism

and Christian Origins, ed. James H. Charlesworth (Minneapolis, MN: Fortress Press, 1992), p. 116.

10. The theory was first proposed by Louis Ginzburg in 1922 in his German publication *Eine Unbekannte Jüdische Sekte*, later translated in English as *An Unknown Jewish Sect* (New York: The Jewish Theological Seminary of America, 1976), pp. 257-73.

11. W.-H. Kuhn, "The Two Messiahs of Aaron and Israel," in *The Scrolls and the New Testament*, ed. Kristal Stendahl (New York: Harper & Row, 1957), pp. 54-64. This is at least as reasonable an argument as that of Ginzburg, who, seeing affinities between *CD* and the pseudepigraphical *Testaments of the Twelve Patriarchs*, and recognizing later Christian redaction from earlier two-Messiah versions, determined that *CD* also maintained a two-Messiah theology.

12. J.T. Milik, *Ten Years of Discovery in the Wilderness of Judaea* (London: SCM Press, 1959), p. 123; and see his review of P. Wernberg-Møller's *The Manual of Discipline Translated and Annotated, with an Introduction*, in *Revue Biblique* 67 (1960): 411.

13. As stated by James H. Charlesworth without reference in his chapter "From Messianology to Christology: Problems and Prospects," in *The Messiah: Developments in Earliest Judaism and Christianity*, pp. 26-27. In Collins' work (cited below), we read that Charlesworth changed his mind about Schiffman's view at a meeting of the Studiorum Novi Testament Societies in Chicago in August of 1993, and agreed with Milik (p. 97, n. 39).

14. John C. Collins, *The Scepter and the Star: The Messiahs of the Dead Sea Scrolls and Other Ancient Literature*, The Anchor Bible Reference Library (New York: Doubleday, 1995), pp. 75-83.

15. Lawrence Schiffman, *The Eschatological Community of the Dead Sea Scrolls*, Society of Biblical Literature Monograph Series 38 (Atlanta, GA: Scholars Press, 1989), pp. 54-55.

16. John C. Collins, *The Scepter and the Star*, pp. 94-95.

17. The Karaite commentators on the Twelve Prophets—Daniel al-Qumisi and Yefeth ben 'Ali—revealed that they understood Zechariah and Malachi to teach two Messiahs (Davidic and priestly). Their affinities with the Essenes may indicate that their interpretations reflect a Qumran two-Messiah theology, or it may simply reflect the development of the messianic concept that may have become an imposition that affected the Hasidean division that gave rise to the sects of both the Pharisees and the Essenes. See Emile Puech, "Messianism, Resurrection, and Eschatology," *The Community of the Renewed Covenant*, eds. Eugene Ulrich and James VanderKam, Christianity and Judaism in Antiquity Series 10 (IN: University of Notre Dame Press, 1993), pp. 237-40.

18. See Charlesworth, *The Messiah: Developments in Earliest Judaism and Christianity*, pp. 25-26.

19. *CD* 2:12; 6:1; 12:23; 14:19; 19:10; 20:1; *1QS* 9:11; *1QSa* 2:12,14,20; *1QM* 11:17; *1Q30* 1 2; *4Q252* 1 v. 3; *4Q266* (Da) 18 iii. 12; *4Q267* (Db) 26; *4Q270* (De) 9 ii. 14; *4Q287* 10 13; *4Q375* 1 i. 9; *4Q376* 1 i. 1; *4Q377* 2 ii. 5; *4Q381* 15 7; *4Q458* 2 ii. 6; *4Q521* 2 ii. 41; 89; 93; *6Q15* (D) 34; *11QMel* 2:18.

20. Some would include *4Q246* ("Son of God") and *4Q534* 1 i. 10 ("Elect of God"), however, I do not believe these are messianic. In the first instance I identify the figure with an evil eschatological ruler (Antichrist), and in the second the reference to Noah.

21. *1QSb* 5:20,27; *4Q161* 5-6 3; *4Q174* 1:11; *4Q175* 12; *4Q285* 42, 53, 4; *4Q369*.

22. For a detailed study of these terms in their contexts, see John J. Collins, *The Scepter and the Star: The Messiahs of the Dead Sea Scrolls and Other Ancient Literature*.

23. John J. Collins, "Messiahs in Context: Method in the Study of Messianism in the Dead Sea Scrolls," *Methods of Investigation of the Dead Sea Scrolls and the Khirbet Qumran Site: Present Realities and Future Prospects*, eds. M. Wise, N. Golb, J.J. Collins, D. Pardee (New York: New York Academy of Sciences, 1994), p. 214.

24. Florentino Garcia Martinez, *Qumran and Apocalyptic: Studies on the Aramaic Texts from Qumran*, Studies on the Texts of the Desert of Judah 9, eds. F.G. Martinez, A.S. van der Woude (Leiden: E.J. Brill, 1992), p. 174.

25. John J. Collins, *The Scepter and the Star*, pp. 94-95.

26. Jack Finegan, "Crosses in the Dead Sea Scrolls," *Biblical Archaeology Review* 5:6 (November/December 1979), pp. 40-49.

27. For additional details on the equivalence of the *Taw* and *Chi*, see Saul Lieberman, *Greek in Jewish Palestine* (New York: P. Feldheim, 1965).

28. See Targum; LXX, Bereshit Rabbah 99. It has also been taken as the two words *shai lo* ("a gift/tribute to him"). See commentaries by Jewish scholars Rashi, Lekach Tov, and the Jewish Publication Society's *Torah* and *Notes on the New Translation of the Torah*, ed. Harry M. Orlinsky (Philadelphia: JPS, 1969), p. 142. See for survey of views, S.R. Driver, *Genesis*, Westminster Commentaries, 12th ed. (London: Metheun & Co., Ltd., 1954), pp. 385-86, and esp. Excursus II (pp. 410-15). Another view is that *shiloh* comes from the root *nsl* and the phrase should be rendered "until *the exile* comes"; see Sh'muel ben Chofni.

29. See Sforno; *Torah Sh'lemah* 157; Rabbi Aryeh Kaplan, *The Living Torah* (Jerusalem: Maznaim Publishing Corp., 1981), p. 135.

30. However, see the arguments by James Tabor and Michael Wise, "The Messiah at Qumran," *Biblical Archaeology Review* 18:6 (November/December 1992), pp. 60-63.

31. Shemaryahu Talmon, "The Concepts of *Masiah* and Messianism in Early Judaism," *The Messiah*, p. 108.

## Chapter 14—Is the Christian Messiah in the Scrolls?

1. Interview with Dr. Paul Hanson, Baylor University, Waco, Texas, February 23, 1996.

2. However, see Barnabas Lindars, *Jesus Son of Man: A Fresh Examination of the Son of Man Sayings in the Gospels* (Grand Rapids, MI: Eerdmans Publishing Co., 1983), argues that by going back to the Aramaic phrase *bar enash* behind the Hebrew expression *ben adam*, that the humanity, not the divinity, of the figure is meant. However, his interaction with the Qumran literature is negligible at best, and he, of course, did not have access to such recently published fragments as *4Q521* or *4Q246*.

3. David Flusser, *Jesus*, translated by Ronald Walls (New York: Herder and Herder, Inc., 1968), p. 102.

4. See Michael Stone, *Features of the Eschatology of 4 Ezra*, Harvard Semitic Studies 35 (Atlanta, GA: Scholars Press, 1989), pp. 123-25.

5. The reasons most often suggested for this is that either the work was produced in a different community and late in the life of the Qumran Sect, thus it would not have reached the Sect, or, if it had Christian influence it would have been rejected, or, perhaps it was known but rejected because chapter 41 of the *Similitudes* places the sun and moon in near equality, an idea unacceptable to the Sect.

6. For a further study of this question see the author's work *The Concept of a Divine Messiah in Early Jewish-Christianity* (San Marcos, TX: World of the Bible Publications, 1989) available from World of the Bible Ministries, Inc., 110 Easy Street, San Marcos, Texas 78666-7326.

7. Joseph A. Fitzmyer, "*4Q246*: The 'Son of God' Document from Qumran," *Biblica* 74:2 (1993): 166.

8. The translation basically follows that of Joseph A. Fitzmyer, "*4Q246*: The 'Son of God' Document from Qumran," pp. 155-57 based on the fully published text by Emile Puech, "Fragment d'une apocalypse an arameén (*4Q246* = pseudo-Dan$^d$) et le 'royaume e de Dieu,'" *Revue Biblique* 99 (1992): 98-131. I have especially followed Fitzmyer's reconstruction of the first column, but in the second column have supplied alternate readings from the translation by F. Garcia Martinez, "The Eschatological Figure of *4Q246*," *Qumran and Apocalyptic*, p 164. For an example of how presuppositions can produce different translations of the same text, see the translation and reconstruction of Eisenman and Wise, *The Dead Sea Scrolls Uncovered*, pp. 70-71.

9. "Les modèles araméens du livre d'Esther dans la grotte 4 de Qumran," *Revue de Qumran* 15:3 (1992): 383; cf. Joseph A. Fitzmyer, "The Contribution of Qumran Aramaic to the Study of the New Testament," *New Testament Studies* 20 (1974) as reprinted in J.A. Fitzmyer, *A Wandering*

*Aramean, Collected Essays*, Society of Biblical Literature Monograph Series 25 (Missoula, MT: Scholars Press, 1979), pp. 92-111.

10. See F. Imhoof-Blumer, *Monnaies grecques*, Koninklijke Nederlandse Akademie van Wetenschappen, Afdeeling Letterkunde, Verhandelingen 14 (Amsterdam, 1883), pp. 433-34 (§ 102, pl. H 13).

11. See F. Garcia Martinez, "*4Q246*: ¿Tipo del Anticristo o Libertador escatólogico?" *El mistero de la Palabra: Homenaje a L. Alonso Schökel*, ed. V. Collado E. Zurro (Madrid, 1983), p. 235; [in English: "The Eschatological Figure of *4Q246*," in *Qumran and Apocalyptic: Studies on the Aramaic Texts from Qumran*, STDJ 9 (Leiden: E.J. Brill, 1992), p. 169.

12. Angelic beings are, of course, referred to in company as *bene 'elohim* ("sons of God") in the Bible, but this is different than ascribing such a title to an individual. However, those who see the "Son of Man" in Daniel 7:13-14 as an angelic being could argue otherwise.

13. See Eisenman and Wise, *The Dead Sea Scrolls Uncovered*, p. 69.

14. There is, however, ambiguity in the Aramaic wording as to whether he is self-designated or designated by others. In 2 Thessalonians 2:4 the Antichrist figure designates himself, but in Revelation 13:4 his worshipers so designate him. As Flusser (p. 33) points out, the difference is minimal: "If others 'shall call him son of the Most High' they will do it at his behest." Perhaps both could be understood in this manner: He designates himself by his actions (in 2 Thessalonians 2:4 by seating himself in the Temple), and his worshipers designate him by their acclaim (by "crowning" his actions with the self-sought title).

15. Read *y'bdwn* as a Hebraism meaning "worship" and not according to the usual Aramaic definition "they will make."

16. Or: "he shall call himself."

17. Or: "he shall designate himself."

18. Or: "he shall name himself."

19. Preserved in Lactantius, *Divinae Institutiones* 7. 17. 2-4 in *CSEL* 19: 638-39.

20. The term oJ lovgo" = *y'bdwn*, which in Mishnaic Hebrew (for example, *TJ* Shabbat 7:10a) and Aramaic signifies "the Person of God," thus, the blasphemy was directed toward God. See R.H. Charles, *APOT* 2:420, n. 5. Charles also suggest that "the innermost sanctuary" referred to may be that "of the heathen temples which the Jews were compelled to build (cf. I Macc. i. 47; Joseph. Ant. xv. 5.4)," while J.H. Charlesworth, *OTP* 1:931, translates it neutrally as "secret place." It seems preferable in light of the references to the Person of God, the Law, and the altar to see here the Holy of Holies, which Charles lists as an alternative.

21. See chapter 7 for a discussion of this text in relation to apocalyptic literature and Daniel 9:27.

22. John J. Collins, "A Pre-Christian 'Son of God' Among the Dead Sea Scrolls," *BR* 9:3 (June 1993): 36.

23. See Fitzmyer, "The 'Son of God' Document from Qumran," p. 169; Collins, "A Pre-Christian 'Son of God,'" p. 57, n. 5.

24. Ibid., p. 35. Collins notes (p. 57, n. 4) that the messianic interpretation was first proposed by Frank Moore Cross.

25. Ibid., pp. 170-73.

26. Otto Betz, "The Servant Tradition of Isaiah at Qumran," unpublished paper delivered at The Dead Sea Scrolls: Isaiah and Its Interpretation (symposium, University of Texas at Austin, February 23-25, 1993).

27. See Flavius Josephus, *Antiquities of the Jews* 13.377-79 and *Jewish War* 1.92-95.

28. See Geza Vermes, *Jesus the Jew* (1973), pp. 139-40.

29. For example, the *New York Times* read: "Messianic Link to Christianity Found in the Scrolls"; *Chicago Tribune*: "Scrolls Suggest Early Jewish-Christian Link"; *Washington Post*: "Messiah-

Like Leader Mentioned in the Scrolls."

30. See *Biblical Archaeology Review* (January/February 1993): 66.

31. Eisenman and Wise, *The Dead Sea Scrolls Uncovered*, p. 29.

32. Actually, in the Scrolls some consonants do serve as vowels called *matres lectionis* ("mothers of reading"). In the verb form *hmytw*, the *y* and *w* can be viewed as vowels, but the form still requires vocalization.

33. Marcus Bockmuehl, "A 'Slain Messiah' in *4Q* Serek Milhamah (*4Q285*)?" *Tyndale Bulletin* 43:1 (1992), p. 165.

34. See Martin Abegg, Jr., "Messianic Hope and *4Q285*: A Reassessment," *Journal of Biblical Literature* 113·1 (1994): 82-83. He list five reasons in favor of the active vocalization; see pp. 88-91.

35. Ibid., p. 86; see also Ayala Sussman and Ruth Peled, *Scrolls from the Dead Sea* (New York: George Braziller, 1993), p. 81.

36. Otto Betz, "The Dichotomized Servant and the End of Judas Iscariot [Light on the Dark Passages: Matthew 24, 51 and Parallel; Acts 1, 18]," *Revue de Qumran* 5 (1964): 56.

37. See Craig A. Evans, "The Recently Published Dead Sea Scrolls and the Historical Jesus," *Studying the Historical Jesus: Evaluation of the State of Current Research*, eds. Bruce Chilton, Craig Evans, in New Testament Tools and Studies, vol. 19, ed. Bruce M. Metzger, B.D. Ehrman (Leiden: E.J. Brill, 1994): 553.

## Chapter 15—Jesus and the Qumran Community

1. Krister Stendahl, "The Scrolls and the New Testament: An Introduction and a Perspective," *The Scrolls and the New Testament*, ed. Krister Stendahl (New York: Harper & Brothers, 1957), pp. 16-17.

2. An example of this kind of thinking is represented by one of liberal Christianity's greatest thinkers, Rudolf Bultmann, in his work *Essays: Philosophical and Theological*, trans. J.C.G. Greig (London: 1955), p. 279.

3. While many of their messianic views may have come through apocryphal works such as *Jubilees, Enoch,* and the *Testaments of Levi* and *Naphtali,* these works presented themselves as consonant with the theology of the Old Testament writers with whom they claimed company.

4. Klyne Snodgrass, "The Use of the Old Testament in the New," *New Testament Criticism & Interpretation*, eds. David A. Black and David S. Dockery (Grand Rapids, MI: Zondervan Publishing House, 1991), p. 409.

5. *The Lost Years of Jesus Revealed* (Greenwich, CT: Fawcett Publications, Inc., 1958).

6. Upton Clary Ewing, *The Prophet of the Dead Sea Scrolls* (Philosophical Library, n.d.), pp. 8-11.

7. Interview with Stephen Pfann, Jerusalem, November 10, 1995.

8. For one such popular presentation, see André Dupont-Sommer, *The Dead Sea Scrolls: A Preliminary Survey* (Oxford: Blackwell, 1952), esp. p. 99.

9. Ron Rhodes, *The Counterfeit Christ of the New Age Movement* (Grand Rapids, MI: Baker Book House, 1990), pp. 75-76.

10. Interview with Father Bargil Pixner, Dormition Abbey, Mount Zion, Jerusalem, November 15, 1995.

11. Ibid.

12. Interview with Stephen Pfann, Jerusalem, November 10, 1995.

13. Interview with Father Bargil Pixner, Dormition Abbey, Mount Zion, Jerusalem, November 15, 1995.

14. Ibid.

15. *The Temple Scroll*, ed. Yigael Yadin (Jerusalem: The Israel Exploration Society, 1983) 1:378; see also his earlier statement in his article "Pesher Nahum (*4QpNahum*) Reconsidered," *Israel Exploration Journal* 21 (1971): 1-12.

16. Otto Betz and Rainer Riesner, *Jesus, Qumran and the Vatican: Clarifications*, trans. John Bowden (London: SCM Press, 1994), p. 159.

17. For a further study of this issue, see Martin G. Abegg, Jr., "The Messiah at Qumran: Are We Still Seeing Double?" *Dead Sea Discoveries* 2:2 (June 1995): 125-44.

18. James H. Charlesworth, "The Dead Sea Scrolls and the Historical Jesus," *Jesus and the Dead Sea Scrolls* (New York: Doubleday, 1993), p. 38. The citation is from Samuel Sandmel, *Judaism and Christian Beginnings* (New York: Oxford University Press, 1978), p. 305.

### Chapter 16—Sensationalism and the Scrolls

1. Ron Rosenbaum, "The Riddle of the Scrolls," *Vanity Fair* magazine (November 1992), p. 225.

2. *Sun* (December 29, 1993).

3. Texe Marrs, "Beware of the Dead Sea Scrolls," tape copy of Marrs's prophecy radio broadcast (1995).

4. Ibid., side 1.

5. Inquiries concerning any sensationalist's claims or credentials may be submitted to the Israel Antiquities Authority for computer search or verification. Write them at: Rockefeller Museum Building, P.O. Box 586, Jerusalem, Israel, 91004.

6. Jones's claim is that the author of the script, Michael French, was in some way involved in one of his digs and so got the inspiration from him. This claim is denied by the film's producers, Spielberg and Lucas, who claim that Lucas's dog "Indiana" was the source of the name, and that Jones was completely unknown to them.

7. IJCR [Institute for Judaic-Christian Research] *Research Letter* [to supporters] (December 1994), p. 2.

8. Mark Segal, "Masquerader of the Lost Ark: Is a Renegade Texas Archaeologist the Real Indiana Jones?" *Texas Monthly* 20:8 (August 1992): 140.

9. See Donald A. Hagner, *The Jewish Reclamation of Jesus: An Analysis and Critique of the Modern Jewish Study of Jesus* (Grand Rapids, MI: Zondervan Publishing House, 1984); James H. Charlesworth, *Jesus Within Judaism: New Light from Exciting Archaeological Discoveries* (New York: Doubleday, 1988); Marvin R. Wilson, *Our Father Abraham: Jewish Roots of the Christian Faith* (Grand Rapids, MI: Eerdmans Publishing Co., 1989); Brad H. Young, *Jesus the Jewish Theologian* (Peabody, MA: 1995).

10. See Eric Meyers and L. Michael White, "Jews and Christians in a Roman World," *Archaeology* 42:2 (March/April 1989): 27-33; James H. Charlesworth, "Christians and Jews in the First Six Centuries," *Christianity and Rabbinic Judaism: A Parallel History of Their Origins and Early Development*, ed. Hershel Shanks (Washington DC: The Biblical Archaeology Society, 1992), pp. 305-25 (esp. 320-25).

11. John Chrysostom, *Homily Against the Jews* 48.847.

12. Segal, "Masquerader of the Lost Ark," p. 140. My own knowledge of Jones's religious beliefs comes from personal interaction with him in Israel while on tour. When publicly challenged about his beliefs, he denied the deity of Christ, the Messiahship of Jesus, and ended by swearing in Yiddish. The last detail was provided by my guide at the time, Avner Bosky, who is fluent in Yiddish and had also joined in the interaction with Jones.

13. Ibid., p. 141.

14. Ibid. My experience with Jones's *B'nai Noach* groups comes from discussions with Tel-Aviv journalist Yitzhak Oked, who has worked with Jones to further his *B'nai Noach* organization in the States, and with Chaim Richman of the Temple Institute, Jerusalem, who is involved with such a

group in Israel.

15. Interview with Yitzhak Oked, Tel-Aviv, June 1992.

16. Through my years as a pastor in Texas I received many calls from distressed parents whose teens had begun questioning their Christian upbringing because of involvement with Jones.

17. Marvin Ellis, "Ark of the Covenant: 'Mystical Powers'," United Press International (UPI) story, Tyler, Texas, October 14, 1981.

18. Ibid.

19. Ibid.

20. Dell Griffin, "Vendyl Jones and the Treasures of the Temple," *Jerusalem Post* (Sunday, May 28, 1989), p. 5.

21. Ellis, UPI story.

22. Dell Griffin, *Jerusalem Post*, p. 5.

23. Marvin Ellis, "Ashes of Red Heifer Site Believed Located," *Tyler Courier-Times-Telegraph* (October 12, 1981).

24. Segal, "Masquerader of the Lost Ark," pp. 1, 3.

25. Dell Griffin, *Jerusalem Post*, p. 5.

26. Marvin Ellis, "Tylerite Hunts Ark of the Covenant," *Tyler Courier-Times-Telegraph* (October 11, 1981).

27. Dell Griffin, *Jerusalem Post*, p. 5.

28. Reuters News Service article, "Man Says He's Close to Finding Lost Ark," *San Antonio Express-News* (May 16, 1992).

29. Aside from the printed reports, accounts of Jones's actions during the excavation were related to me by Dr. Nathan Meyer, who was one of Jones's volunteers on the dig.

30. For the official report of the excavation and discovery, see Joseph Patrich and Benny Arubas, "A Juglet Containing Balsam Oil(?) from a Cave Near Qumran," *Israel Exploration Journal* 39:1-2 (1989): 43-59.

31. J. Patrich and B. Arubas, "A Juglet Containing Balsam Oil," pp. 58-59.

32. Segal, "Masquerader of the Lost Ark," p. 163.

33. Marvin Antelman is a "chemical consultant" who lives in Rehovot. He claimed to have found evidence of 12 of the 15 ingredients that comprised the sacred Temple incense, including myrrh, saffron, and galbanum, and said the bulk density, pH, ash content, and reaction with acid all compare favorably with what would be expected of the ritual incense (*pitum haketoret*). Suspicious, however, was the statement that a "random sample" weighed "exactly 26.0 grams," an inappropriate manner of description in technical scientific reporting.

34. For the published report of this discrepancy see Ron Rosenbaum, "The Riddle of the Scrolls," *Vanity Fair* magazine (November 1992), pp. 227, 286.

35. IJCR research letter to supporters (December 1994), p. 3.

36. Ibid.

37. Ibid.

38. Vendyl Jones Research Institutes *Researcher* prerelease information for supporters (Fall 1995).

39. For example: Dell Griffin, "Christian Group May Have Found Temple Incense," *The Jerusalem Post International Edition* (May 9, 1992), p. 28; "Incense from the Temple found in dig near Kumran, Texas Bible scholar claims," *Jerusalem Post* (May 10, 1992); and "Was Incense Near Kumran Really for Temple Use?: Real-Life 'Indiana' Jones Looking for Ark of the Covenant," *Jerusalem Post International edition* (May 23, 1992).

### Chapter 17—Sensationalism and the Scholars

1. Otto Betz and Rainer Riesner, *Jesus, Qumran and the Vatican* (London: SCM Press, Ltd., 1994), ix.

2. John Marco Allegro, "The Untold Story of the Dead Sea Scrolls," *Harper's Magazine* 232 (August 1966), pp. 46-64.

3. *The Sacred Mushroom and the Cross* (Garden City, NY: Doubleday, 1970).

4. A. Powell Davis, *The Meaning of the Dead Sea Scrolls* (New York: A Mentor Book from the New American Library, 1956), p. 120.

5. Two of Thiering's articles on ritual purity at Qumran as compared with the New Testament are noted contributions to the study of this problem: "Inner and Outer Cleansing at Qumran as a Background to New Testament Baptism," *New Testament Studies* 26 (1980): 266-77, and "Qumran Initiation and New Testament Baptism," *New Testament Studies* 27 (1981): 615-31.

6. See *Redating the Teacher of Righteousness*, Australian and New Zealand Studies in Theology and Religion 1 (Sydney: Theological Explorations, 1979); *The Gospels and Qumran: A New Hypothesis*, Australian and New Zealand Studies in Theology and Religion (Sydney: Theological Explorations, 1981); *The Qumran Origins of the Christian Church*, Australian and New Zealand Studies in Theology and Religion (Sydney: Theological Explorations, 1983).

7. Concerning this identification Thiering argues that since they describe the same events from different standpoints, and share the same assumptions, therefore they are "two histories that fit together." Barbara Thiering, *The Qumran Origins of the Christian Church*, p. 13.

8. See Richard Longenecker, *Biblical Exegesis in the Apostolic Period* (Grand Rapids, MI: Eerdmans Publishing Co., 1975), p. 78; E. Earl Ellis, *The Old Testament in Early Christianity: Canon and Interpretation in the Light of Modern Research* (Grand Rapids, MI: Baker Book House, 1992), pp. 121, 130-38.

9. See *The Qumran Origins of the Christian Church*, p. 11; *Jesus and the Riddle of the Dead Sea Scrolls*, pp. 21-22.

10. Thiering, *Jesus and the Riddle of the Dead Sea Scrolls*, p. 98.

11. Ibid., pp. 81-82.

12. Ibid., pp. 284-331.

13. See Charles H. Dyer, "Biblical Meaning of 'Fulfillment,' " *Issues in Dispensationalism*, eds. Wesley R. Willis, John R. Master, Charles C. Ryrie (Chicago: Moody Press, 1994), pp. 51-72.

14. Otto Betz and Rainer Riesner, *Jesus and the Vatican*, trans. John Bowden (London: SCM Press, 1994), p. 111.

15. Ibid., pp. 384-98.

16. Review of *The Gospels and Qumran: A New Hypothesis* in the *Journal of the Evangelical Theological Society* 34 (1983): 236.

17. Review of *The Gospels and Qumran: A New Hypothesis* in *The Catholic Biblical Quarterly* 45 (1983): 513.

18. Christ, of course, *was* a high priest, but after the eternal order of Melchizedek, which predated the Levitical priesthood (Hebrews 7:9-10), has a uniquely combined office of King-Priest (Genesis 14:18; cf. Zechariah 6:12-13), and is superior to the Aaronic priesthood because its sacrifice saved forever, while the former only sanctified temporarily (Hebrews 7:11; 9:9-14).

19. For this example, see Edward M. Cook, *Solving the Mysteries of the Dead Sea Scrolls* (Grand Rapids, MI: Zondervan Publishing Co., 1994), pp. 144-45.

20. Jim Stone (pseudonym), *Yes!* (Part II), p. 120.

21. *Jesus and the Riddle of the Dead Sea Scrolls*, foreword, x.

22. Ibid., xi.

23. *Review of the Gospels and Qumran: A New Hypothesis* in *Journal for the Study of Judaism* 14:1 (1983): 99.

24. Hershel Shanks, "Book Reviews," *Biblical Archaeology Review* 18:5 (September/October 1992): 70.

25. Eisenman once told a group of scholars while arguing his own views that he "never read what they wrote."

26. *Maccabees, Zadokites, Christians and Qumran* (Leiden: E.J. Brill, 1983).

27. *James the Just in the Habakkuk Pesher* (Leiden: E.J. Brill, 1986).

28. *The Dead Sea Scrolls Uncovered* (with Michael Wise) (Rockport, MA: Element, 1992).

29. Eisenman's response to Lawrence Schiffman in "Discussion of the Paper" of Robert Eisenman, "Theory of Judeo-Christian Origins: The Last Column of the *Damascus Document*," in *Methods of Investigation of the Dead Sea Scrolls and the Khirbet Qumran Site: Present Realities and Future Prospects*, eds. Michael O. Wise, Norman Golb, John J. Collins, Dennis G. Pardee, *Annals of the New York Academy of Sciences* 722 (New York: The New York Academy of Sciences, 1994), p. 368.

30. Response to Ephraim Isaac, Ibid., p. 369.

31. Ibid.

32. Ibid., p. 370.

33. Michael Baigent and Richard Leigh, *The Dead Sea Scrolls Deception* (New York: Summit Books, 1991), p. 267.

34. See the third-century Ebionite work *Ascents of James* in *The Writings of Paul*, ed. Wayne Meeks (New York: Norton, 1972), p. 177.

35. *James the Just*, p. 62.

36. Betz and Riesner, *Jesus, Qumran and the Vatican*, p. 73.

37. For Thiering's various discussions of the paleographic problem, see *Redating the Teacher of Righteousness*, p. 47; *The Gospels and Qumran*, pp. 8-9; *Jesus and the Riddle of the Dead Sea Scrolls*, p. 15.

38. Review of *Redating the Teacher of Righteousness* in *Revue Biblique* 87 (1980), p. 428.

39. Robert Eisenman and Michael Wise, *The Dead Sea Scrolls Uncovered*, p. 12.

40. See Bonani, et. al., "Radiocarbon Dating of the Dead Sea Scrolls," *'Atiqot* 20 (1991): 27-32, and "Carbon-14 Tests Substantiate Scroll Dates," *Biblical Archaeology Review* (November/December 1991). For an overview of the process see Thomas C. Lynn, "Dating Papyrus Manuscripts by the AMS Carbon-14 Method," *Biblical Archaeologist* (September 1988): 141-42; "New Carbon-14 Tests on the Dead Sea Scrolls," *Biblical Archaeology Review* (March/April 1993).

41. Torleif Elgvin, "News from Qumran—On Scrolls and Messiahs," *Mishkan* 23:2 (1995): 74.

42. *The Dead Sea Scrolls Uncovered*, p. 13.

43. See Eisenman's and Wise's statements in *The Dead Sea Scrolls Uncovered*, pp. 119-22.

**Chapter 18—Cults and the Scrolls**

1. Ita Sheres and Anne Kohn Blau, *The Truth About the Virgin: Sex and Ritual In the Dead Sea Scrolls* (New York: The Continuum Publishing Co., 1995).

2. Otto Betz and Rainer Riesner, *Jesus, Qumran and the Vatican: Clarifications*, trans. John Bowden (London: SCM Press Ltd., 1994), p. 159.

3. Ita Sheres and Anne Kohn Blau, *The Truth about the Virgin*.

4. Ibid., p. 3.

5. Lewis M. Rogers, *Progress in Archaeology* (Provo, UT: Brigham Young University, 1963), pp. 46-47.

522

5a. For information on the research being conducted by Mormon scholars, contact Dr. Noel Reynolds at the Foundation for Ancient Research and Mormon Studies, P.O. Box 7113, University Station, Provo, Utah 84602.

6. Eugene Seaich, *Mormonism, the Dead Sea Scrolls, and the Nag Hammadi Texts* (Midvale, UT: Sounds of Zion, 1980), p. vii.

7. Ibid., p. 1; cf. p. 128.

8. Ibid., p. 122.

9. Ibid., p. 120.

10. The best-known sects of the Gnostics were the Valentinians, Basilidians, Encratites, and the Ophites. The 60 teachers were mentioned by Epiphanius, Bishop of Constantia in Cyprus (circa A.D. 375).

11. For examples of the inconsistencies in Gnostic teachings, see Irenaeus, *Against Heresies* I. 11. 1 in *The Anti-Nicene Fathers*, eds. Alexander Roberts and James Donaldson (Peabody, MA: Hendrickson Publishers, 1994), 1: 206-24.

12. Melaine Layton, *The Truth About the Dead Sea Scrolls and Nag Hammadi Writings In Reference to Mormonism* (Wheeling, IL: 1979).

13. Ibid., p. 3.

14. Ibid., p. iii.

15. Ibid., p. 44.

16. Ibid., p. 15.

17. Lawrence H. Schiffman, *Reclaiming the Dead Sea Scrolls*, p. 357.

18. Ibid., p. 41.

19. Ibid.

20. Ibid., p. 42.

21. Ibid., pp. 43-44.

22. See 1 Maccabees 9:27; TB *Baba Bathra* 121b; *Yoma* 9b; *Sotah* 48b; *Sanhedrin* 11a; Midrash *Horayoth* 3:5; Mishnah *Sotah* 9:12; *Song of Songs Rabbah* 8:11; Tosefta *Sotah* 13:2.

23. Eugene Seaich, *Mormonism, the Dead Sea Scrolls, and the Nag Hammadi Texts*, pp. 103-04.

24. Ibid., p. 104.

25. See Albert Pike, *Morals and Dogma of the Ancient and Accepted Scottish Rite of Freemasonry* (Washington, DC, 1958), pp. 104-05, 210-19, 277, 321; [Albert G.] *Mackey's Revised Encyclopedia of Freemasonry*, rev. and enlarg. by Robert I. Clegg, 3 vols. (Richmond, VA: Macoy, 1966), 2: 618-19.

26. Reed C. Durham, Jr., *No Help for the Widow's Son* (Nauvoo, IL: Martin Publishing Co., 1980), p. 23.

27. Ibid., pp. 44-45.

28. *Courage* 1:1 (September 1970), p. 20.

29. Sidney B. Sperry, *The Progress of Archaeology* (Provo, UT: Brigham Young University, 1963), pp. 52-54.

30. Joseph Fielding Smith, Jr., *Religious Truths Defined* (Salt Lake City, UT: Book Craft 1959), p. 175.

31. Mark E. Petersen, *As Translated Correctly* (Salt Lake City, UT: Deseret, 1966), pp. 4, 14.

32. Sidney B. Sperry, *The Progress of Archaeology*, p. 52.

33. See Shirley MacLaine, *Going Within* (New York: Bantam Books, 1989), pp. 178-81.

34. Edgar Cayce was called the "sleeping prophet" because while resting he would enter into a trance state. In this state he offered cures for various physical problems, gave information to people about past lives (reincarnation), predicted future events, and provided unknown details about biblical,

historic, and occultic subjects. His comments about the Dead Sea Scrolls fall into this latter category.

35. Glenn D. Kittler with Hugh Lynn Cayce, *Edgar Cayce on the Dead Sea Scrolls* (New York: Warner Books, Inc., 1970), p. 201.

36. Duncan Howlett, *The Essenes and Christianity* (New York: Harper & Brothers, 1957), p. 163.

37. Ron Rhodes, *The Counterfeit Christ of the New Age Movement* (Grand Rapids, MI: Baker Book House, 1990), pp. 61-62.

38. Edmond Bordeaux Szekely, *The Discovery of the Essene Gospel of Peace: The Essenes and the Vatican* (San Diego, CA: International Biogenic Society, 1977), pp. 53-54.

39. Edmond Bordeaux Szekely, *The Teachings of the Essenes from Enoch to the Dead Sea Scrolls* (England: C.W. Daniel Company Ltd., n.d.), pp. 11-12.

40. Ibid., p. 14.

41. Per Beskow, *Strange Tales About Jesus* (Philadelphia: Fortress Press, 1985), p. 129; cf. p. 89.

42. Szekely, The *Discovery of the Essene Gospel of Peace*, p. 45.

43. Per Beskow, *Strange Tales About Jesus*, pp. 88-89.

44. Ibid., p. 89.

45. Douglas Groothuis, *Revealing the New Age Jesus* (Downers Grove, IL: InterVarsity Press, 1990), p. 191.

46. Otto Betz and Rainer Riesner, *Jesus, Qumran and the Vatican: Clarifications*, p. 158.

### Chapter 19—Politics and the Scrolls

1. *The Jerusalem Post* (Friday, January 21, 1994), p.1.

2. Internet report from *The Jerusalem Post* (February 23, 1996).

3. Felice Maranz, "Palestinians Demand All West Bank Relics," *The Jerusalem Report* (December 1993), p. 5.

4. Associated Press story: "Israel, PLO Wrangle Over Right to Dig for Historical Dead Sea Scrolls," *San Antonio Express & News*, September 19, 1995.

5. Interview with John Strugnell by Avi Katzman for *Ha-Aretz* on November 9, 1990, reprinted in *Biblical Archaeology Review* 17:1 (January/February 1991), p. 65.

6. The contention was over the Israeli Antiquities Authority's excavation (under the supervision of Ronny Reich) of a section of the Herodian street adjacent to the southern extension of the Western Wall. In uncovering the street in honor of Jerusalem's 3000th-anniversary celebrations, the archaeologists had to dismantle the remains of an Umiyyad (early Muslim period) administration building. The Muslim Wakf (the Supreme Council that has jurisdiction of the Temple Mount area) protested that the Israeli government was deliberately trying to erase all traces of Arab history in Jerusalem. The Israelis, who were responsible for revealing this first (and only) evidence of early Muslim presence (seventh century A.D.) in an earlier excavation under Professor Benjamin Mazar, contended that they were only relocating the structure a short distance away at the same site. However, the late Rabbi Getz, the Chief Rabbi of the Western Wall, countered that the stones that the Muslims had used to construct the building originally came from the Temple's Western Wall. Hence, they should be returned there rather than be reused to re-assemble an Arab artifact. As a result of this encounter the Arabs called for an international boycott of the Jerusalem 3000 festivities.

### Chapter 20—New Searches for Scrolls

1. Interview with Hanan Eshel, Jerusalem, November 10, 1995.

2. Ibid.

3. John Allegro, *The Mystery of the Dead Sea Scrolls Revealed* (New York: Gramercy Publishing Co., 1981), p. 21.

4. John Trevor, "The Future of the Qumran Scrolls," *A Light Unto My Path: Old Testament Studies in Honor of Jacob M. Myers*, Gettysburg Theological Studies IV, eds. H.N. Bream, R.D. Heim, C.A. Moore (Philadelphia: Temple University Press, 1974), p. 466. Trevor also tells Allegro's story on p. 467.

5. Interview with Abu-Dahoud (alias Muhammed edh-Dhib), Dead Sea region, November 11, 1995.

6. See Y. Aharoni, *Israel Exploration Journal* 5 (1955): 272-73; *Atiqot* 3 (1961): 155-59.

7. Baruch Safrai, "Recollections from 40 Years Ago—More Scrolls Lie Buried," *Biblical Archaeology Review* 19:1 (January/February 1993): 54.

8. Ibid., p. 55.

9. These were found by Professor Aharoni at a later excavation (1961); see his report in *Israel Exploration Journal* 12 (1962): 186-99.

10. Pesach Bar-Adon, "Excavations in the Judean Desert," *Atiqot* 9 (1989) (Hebrew series).

11. Interview with John Strugnell by Avi Katzman, reprinted in *Biblical Archaeology Review* 17:1 (January/February 1991): 70.

12. Weston W. Fields, "The Shepherd Boy Who Discovered the Scrolls, Part V" (unpublished paper, 1993), pp. 21-24.

13. Interview with Hanan Eshel, Jerusalem, November 10, 1995.

14. See Yizhar Hirschfeld, "Spirituality in the Desert: Judean Wilderness Monasteries," *Biblical Archaeology Review* 21:5 (September/October 1995): 28-37, 70.

15. Such accounts were passed along by outsiders who stayed in these monasteries. One unforgettable tale at Saint Catherine's is told by Constantine von Tischendorf, who, rather than use the manuscripts provided him for warmth, examined them and found one of the oldest New Testament manuscripts, the Codex Sinaiticus.

16. See Constantine Tishendorf, *Codex Sinaiticus: The Ancient Biblical Manuscript Now in the British Museum* (London: The Lutterworth Press, 1934), and Bruce M. Metzger, "Codex Sinaiticus," *Manuscripts of the Greek Bible* (Oxford: University Press, 1981) pp. 76-79.

17. See James H. Charlesworth with G.T. Zervos, *The New Discoveries in St. Catherine's Monastery: A Preliminary Report on the Manuscripts*, American Schools of Oriental Research Monograph Series 3 (Winona Lake, IN: 1981). For a popular account of the discovery see James Bentley, *Secrets of Mount Sinai: The Story of Finding the World's Oldest Bible—Codex Sinaiticus* (London: Orbis Publishing Ltd., 1985), pp. 197-208.

18. See American Center for Oriental Research Bulletin (Amman, Jordan, February 1994).

19. Aubrey L. Richardson, Sr., and Garold R. Collett, "Qumran: Summary Excerpts of Research and Reports from 1988 thru 1990" (updated edition, November/December 1990). Aubrey Richardson, Sr., is a senior field engineer and Dr. Garold Collett is an ordained minister and the head of a Christian ministry based in Jerusalem.

20. Ibid., p. 12 (attachment B).

21. Ibid., p. 7.

22. Zvi ben-Avraham and Uri Basson, "Geophysical Investigation of the Qumran Plateau Using Ground-Penetrating Radar and Seismic Reflection Profiles" (Tel-Aviv University: Department of Geophysics and Planetary Sciences, 1992), pp. 3-5.

23. Dr. Strange also was present when Larry Blaser attempted to find the Ark at Ein-Gedi. His willingness to lend his credentials for Collett's dig may reveal his longstanding interest in uncovering such treasure, surely every archaeologist's dream.

24. Interview with Professor Hanan Eshel, Jerusalem, November 10, 1995.

25. Interview with Dr. Magen Broshi, Museum of the Shrine of the Book, Jerusalem, November 12, 1995.

26. For this report, see "So Far No Cigar," *Biblical Archaeology Review* 22:2 (March/April 1996), pp. 10, 12.

27. Interview with Hanan Eshel, Jerusalem, November 10, 1995.

28. Phone interview with Hanan Eshel, March 19, 1996.

29. Abraham Rabinovich, "Qumran: First Western Monastery," *Jerusalem Post* international edition (May 11, 1996), p. 19.

30. Interview with Hanan Eshel, Jerusalem, November 10, 1995.

31. Abraham Rabinovich, "Qumran: First Western Monastery," p. 19.

32. Hanan Eshel, "How I Found a Fourth-Century B.C. Papyrus Scroll on My First Time Out!" *Biblical Archaeology Review* 15:5 (September/October 1989): 53.

33. Interview with Dr. Weston Fields, Jerusalem, November 9, 1995.

### Chapter 21—Lessons from the Scrolls

1. Neil Asher Silberman, *The Hidden Scrolls: Christianity, Judaism, and the War for the Dead Sea Scrolls* (New York: G.P. Putnam's Sons, 1994), p. 266.

2. David Flusser, *The Spiritual History of the Dead Sea Sect*, trans. Carol Glucker (Tel-Aviv: MOD Books, 1989), p. 8.

3. *The Jerusalem Report* (February 8, 1996), pp. 54-55.

4. R. Shlomo Aviner, "These Are the Pangs of Birth," *The Jerusalem Report* (February 8, 1996), p. 54.

5. Hanoch Marmari, "Life After Zionism," *The Jerusalem Report* (February 8, 1996), p. 55.

6. See Flavius Josephus, *Wars of the Jews* (Book IV): "But what more than anything else incited them to war was an ambiguous oracle [probably Daniel 7:13-14 or 9:26], likewise found in their sacred scriptures, to the effect that at that time one from their country would become ruler of the world. This they understood to mean someone of their own race, and many of their wise men went astray in their interpretation of it. The oracle, however, in reality signified the sovereignty of Vespasian, who was proclaimed Emperor on Jewish soil."

7. *Sefer Hasidim*, edited by J. Wistinetzki (1924), 76-77, no. 212.

8. Charles Pellegrino, *Return to Sodom and Gomorrah: Bible Stories from Archaeologists* (New York: Random House, 1994), p. 330.

### A Chronological History of the Dead Sea Scrolls

1. This account is indebted to Stephen J. Pfann's "History of the Judean Desert Discoveries" and "Sites in the Judean Desert Where Texts Have Been Found," which appeared in the supplementary volume to *The Dead Sea Scrolls on Microfiche* (Leiden: E.J. Brill, 1993). Used by permission of the author. It also has consulted parts of John C. Trevor's "Outline of the Dead Sea Scroll Story," Appendix II in his *The Untold Story of Qumran* (Old Tappan, NJ: Fleming H. Revell Co., 1955), pp. 173-80.

# Additional Reading

## TRANSLATIONS

Robert Eisenman and Michael O. Wise, *The Dead Sea Scrolls Uncovered* (Shaftesburg: Element, 1972). Translation of several previously unpublished controversial texts, which must be used with caution due to premature translations and historical/theological viewpoints.

Theodor H. Gaster, *The Dead Sea Scriptures* (Garden City, NY: Anchor Books/Doubleday, 1960). Inexpensive translations of the foundational texts.

Florentino García Martínez, *The Dead Sea Scrolls Translated: The Qumran Texts in English,* 2d ed. (Grand Rapids: Eerdmans Pub. Co., 1996). The most comprehensive one-volume edition of the Scrolls available (270 texts translated).

Yigael Yadin, ed., *The Temple Scroll* (Jerusalem: The Israel Exploration Society, 1983).

## GENERAL REFERENCE

Otto Betz and Rainer Riesner, *Jesus, Qumran and the Vatican: Clarifications,* trans. John Bowden (London: SCM Press, 1994).

Edward M. Cook, *Solving the Mysteries of the Dead Sea Scrolls: New Light on the Bible* (Grand Rapids: Zondervan, 1994).

Frank Moore Cruss, *The Ancient Library of Qumran and Modern Biblical Studies,* rev. ed. (Grand Rapids: Baker Books, 1980).

Roland de Vaux, *Archaeology and the Dead Sea Scrolls* (Oxford University Press, 1973).

Joseph A. Fitzmyer, *Responses to 101 Questions on the Dead Sea Scrolls* (New York: Paulist Press, 1992).

R.K. Harrison, *The Dead Sea Scrolls: An Introduction* (New York: Harper & Brothers, 1961).

Mar Athanasius Samuel, *Treasure of Qumran: Mystery of the Dead Sea Scrolls* (Philadelphia: Westminster Press, 1966).

Lawrence Schiffman, *Reclaiming the Dead Sea Scrolls* (New York: Doubleday, 1994).

Hershel Shanks, *Understanding the Dead Sea Scrolls* (New York: Random House, 1992).

Shemaryahu Talmon, *The Word of Qumran from Within* (Jerusalem: The Magnes Press, 1989).

James VanderKam, *The Dead Sea Scrolls Today* (Grand Rapids: Eerdmans Pub. Co., 1994).

Geza Vermes, *The Dead Sea Scrolls: Qumran in Perspective* (London: SCM Press, 1982).

Yigael Yadin, ed., *The Message of the Dead Sea Scrolls* (New York: Simon & Schuster, 1957).

## SPECIAL REFERENCE

### Dead Sea Scrolls and Christianity

Klaus Berger, *Jesus and the Dead Sea Scrolls: The Truth Under Lock and Key?* trans. James S. Currie (Louisville: Westminster John Knox Press, 1995).

Matthew Black, ed., *The Scrolls and Christianity: Historical and Theological Significance* (London: SPCK, 1969).

James H. Charlesworth, ed., *Jesus and the Dead Sea Scrolls* (New York: Doubleday, 1993).

James H. Charlesworth, ed., *John and Qumran* (London: Geoffrey Chapman Pub., 1972).

Neil S. Fujita, *A Crack in the Jar: What Ancient Jewish Documents Tell Us About the New Testament* (New York: Paulist Press, 1986).

William Sanford LaSor, *The Dead Sea Scrolls and the Christian Faith* (Chicago: Moody Press, 1962).

William Sanford LaSor, *The Dead Sea Scrolls and the New Testament* (Grand Rapids: Eerdmans Pub. Co., 1972).

Krister Stendahl, ed., *The Scrolls and the New Testament* (New York: Harper & Bros., 1957).

### Beliefs of the Dead Sea Sect

John C. Collins, *The Scepter and the Star. The Messiahs of the Dead Sea Scrolls and Other Ancient Literature,* Anchor Bible Reference Library (New York: Doubleday, 1975).

David Flusser, *The Spiritual History of the Dead Sea Sect,* trans. Carol Glucker (Tel-Aviv: MOD Books, 1989).

Eugene Merrill, *Qumran and Predestination: A Theological Study of the Thanksgiving Hymns,* Studies on the Texts of the Desert of Judah (Leiden: E.J. Brill, 1975).

Helmer Ringgnen, *The Faith of Qumran: Theology of the Dead Sea Scrolls,* trans. Emilie Sander (New York: Crossroad Pub. Co., 1995).

## SPECIALIZED STUDIES

Todd S. Beall, *Josephus' Description of the Essenes Illustrated by the Dead Sea Scrolls,* Society for New Testament Studies Monograph Series 58 (Cambridge: University Press, 1988).

George J. Brooke, ed., *Temple Scroll Studies Journal for the Study of Pseudepigrapha,* Supplement 7 (Sheffield: JSOT Press, 1989).

F.F. Bruce, *Biblical Exegesis in the Qumran Texts* (London: Tyndale Press, 1960).

Devorah Dimant and Uriel Rappapart, eds., *The Dead Sea Scrolls: Forty Years of Research, Studies on Texts of the Desert of Judah,* vol. 10 (Leiden: E.J. Brill, 1992).

George Wesley Buchanan, "The Eschatalogical Expectations of the Qumran Community" (Ph.D. dissertation: Drew University, 1959).

Raymond L. Edge, "The Use of Paleo-Hebrew in the Dead Sea Scrolls: Paleography and Historiography" (Ph.D. dissertation: The University of Texas at Austin, 1995).

Joseph A. Fitzmyer, *The Dead Sea Scrolls: Major Publications and Tools for Study* (Atlanta: Scholars Press, 1990).

F. García Martínez and A.S. Van Der Woude, eds., *New Qumran Texts and Studies,* Studies on the Texts of the Judean Desert, vol. 15 (Leiden: E.J. Brill, 1994).

Harold Scalin, *The Dead Sea Scrolls and Modern Translations of the Old Testament* (Wheaton: Tyndale House Publishers, 1993).

Eugene Ulrich, *An Index of the Passages in the Biblical Manuscripts from the Judean Desert,* Dead Sea Discoveries 1.1 (Apr. 1994): 113-29; 2:1 (Apr. 1995); 86-107.

M. Wise, N. Bolb, J.J. Collins, D. Pardee, eds., *Methods of Investigation of the Dead Sea Scrolls and the Khirbet Qumran Site: Present Realities and Future Prospects* (New York Academy of Sciences, 1994).

# Index

## Author/Person

Abegg, M.G., 68
Abu-Dahoud, see Muhammed edh-Dhib
Abu-Hashaba, Juma'a, 35
Aharoni, Yohanan, 413, 416
Aland, Kurt, 184
Albright, William F., 30, 43, 125
Allegro, John, 53-54, 57, 65, 67, 278, 284-86, 331, 360-61, 414
Ananus, 373-374
Anderson, A.A., 229
Ansalam, Dahoud, 36
Antelman, Marvin, 354
Antiochus Ephiphanes IV, 23, 81, 92, 151, 198, 212, 297, 314, 377
Arafat, Yassar, 403-04
Archer, Gleason, 161, 163
Aristeas, 241
Arubas, Benny, 353
Avigad, Nahman, 375, 413
Awad, Michail, 31

Bahat, Dan, 66, 115, 139, 257, 271, 351
Baigent, Michael and Leigh, Richard, 51, 53-58, 344-45, 372
Baker, H. Wright, 268
Bar-Adon, Pesach, 351, 413, 417
Bar Levav, David, 33
Baur, Ferdinand C., 374
Beall, Todd, 107, 109
Bearman, Greg, 428
Ben Gurion, David, 26, 49
Ben Sira, 130, 156, 241, 297
Blenkinsopp, Joseph, 105
Berger, Klaus, 57, 165
Beskow, Per, 397
Betz, Otto, 57, 175, 323, 340-41, 359, 366, 398
Biran, Gershon, 217
Blau, Anne Kohn, 379, 382
Bockmuehl, Markus, 171, 322
Brooke, George, 220
Broshi, Magen, 105, 118, 181, 195, 199, 237-39, 246, 357, 411, 418, 424-26
Brownlee, William H., 155
Bruce, F.F., 130, 160
Burrows, Millar, 13, 42

Can, Shemun, Rev., 39
Cayce, Edgar, 392-94
Charlesworth, James H., 124, 145, 185, 195, 342
Chilton, Bruce, 235
Cohen, Zahava, 347
Collett, Gary, 405
Collins, John, 136, 219, 293, 299, 301-02, 305, 317-18
Cross, Frank M., 57, 59, 63, 66, 106, 125, 158-59, 274, 375

Dajani, Awni, 285
Daniélou, J., 226
Davies, A. Powell, 360-61
Davies, Philip, 239
Demetrius III, Eukerus, 91-92
Dhib, Muhammed edh-, see edh-Dhib, Muhammed
Dimant, Devorah, 90
Dio Chrysostom, 106
Driver, G.R., 113, 374
Drori, Amir, 413
Dupont-Sommer, A., 232, 278, 360
Durham, Jr., Reed C., 389
Durra, Said, 285

Edersheim, Alfred, 135, 370
Edge, Raymond, 121
edh-Dhib, Muhammed, 30-38, 47, 407, 413, 415-16
Eichhorn, J.C., 157
Eisenman, Robert, 53-57, 68-69, 232, 308, 321, 370-77
Epiphanius, 306, 363
Erickson, Einar, 385
Eshel, Hannan, 33, 119, 125, 136, 195, 352, 357, 411-13, 419, 421-22, 424-27, 429
Eusebius, 273
Ewing, Upton C., 331

Falwell, Jerry, 47
Fee, Gordon, 184, 188
Fields, Weston, 29, 32, 34, 63-65, 71, 126, 408, 415, 418, 428
Finegan, Jack, 306
Fiorenza, Elisabeth S., 236

528

# Subject

# About the Author

Dr. Randall Price is president of *World of the Bible Ministries, Inc.,* a nonprofit organization serving local churches and the Christian community as an educational equipping facility. His ministry provides a clearer understanding of the Bible and biblical issues through information on the ancient and modern Middle East; Bible prophecy; and historical, cultural, and archaeological studies. He holds a master's degree in Old Testament and Semitic Languages from Dallas Theological Seminary, and a Ph.D. in Hebrew Literature and Middle Eastern Languages, Literature, and Cultures from the University of Texas at Austin, where he also taught courses in biblical archaeology and the history and culture of modern Israel. He has done graduate studies at the Hebrew University in Jerusalem, has conducted archaeological excavations in Jerusalem and the region of Galilee, and is a certified tour guide to the State of Israel. He has authored several books on the subject of biblical prophecy, including *Ready to Rebuild: The Imminent Plan to Rebuild the Last Days Temple* and *In Search of Temple Treasures,* has appeared nationwide on the CBS television special "Ancient Secrets of the Bible," and was the focus of a series about the Temple and its treasures on the nationally acclaimed Christian program *The John Ankerberg Show.*

# Acknowledgments

With each book I write it seems that the list of those to whom I am indebted grows—which is cause for thanks in itself, for each book has also produced an ever-widening circle of friends. Thanks must first be given to the editorial staff of Harvest House Publishers—to Terry Glaspey, who first conceived the idea for this book. Also, thanks to Steve Miller, who labored patiently to get it just right; Betty Fletcher, who directed the course; and Bob Hawkins, Jr. and Carolyn McCready, whose encouragement and support for the project as well as for my own life exemplify the best of what Christian publishing should be.

I am also most grateful to Dr. Weston Fields for writing the foreword. Despite a busy year divided between a fishing business in the remote parts of Alaska and duties in Israel as executive director of the Dead Sea Scrolls Foundation, he was generous with his time during both jobs to share with me his knowledge and contacts with David Bar-Levav and Abu-Dahoud, as well as his pizza during a memorable night in the Old City!

My special thanks to Jack and Kay Arthur, for their friendship, godly example, and enthusiasm for the things I do. Thanks to you both for the generous use of your flat in Jerusalem during the research stage of this book—it made all the difference! My gratitude also goes to Mr. and Mrs. Paul Streber (who also are honored on the dedication page). Paul's faithfulness in serving the Lord and keeping company with me all over (and under) Jerusalem and through the Dead Sea caves is a constant testimony to my life and his faith! Most of the photographs reproduced in this book are credited to Paul.

I am also most grateful to my friends Dr. Gary and Debra Collett (and Jeremy), whose friendship and repeated ministry to me in Israel is deeply appreciated. The hospitality of my dear friends Meno and Anat Kalisher is always a cause for praise, and especially so on this last adventure when Meno "came to the rescue"! My thanks also go to Mr. Ken Stanford, whose labors to make my labors better have helped this book immensely. I am also thankful for the kind research assistance provided by my friends Dr. Gordon Franz and Dr. Leen Ritymeyer, with special thanks to Leen for the use of his fine drawings of the Qumran settlement reconstructions and of the Temple described in the *Temple Scroll.* Sincere thanks and appreciation must also be given to Ms. Hazel Perry for her patient and professional assistance in the transcription of seemingly endless tapes.

I am also most appreciative of those who kindly granted interviews despite difficult schedules and especially during those difficult days of mourning Prime Minister Rabin: Dr. Emanuel Tov, Dr. Shemaryahu Talmon, Dr. David Flusser, Father Emile Puech, Dr. Magen Broshi, Dr. Hanan Eshel, Dr. Dan Bahat, Dr. Stephen Pfann, Dr. Halvor Ronning, and Father Bargil Pixner. Thanks are also given to those outside Israel who granted interviews: Dr. Otto Betz, Dr. Paul Hanson, Dr. N.T. Wright, and Dr. Ronald Clements.

My thanks must also go to the faithful supporters of my work with World of the Bible Ministries, Inc., who have a significant part in making this book possible. Worthy of special mention are: Dr. G. Harry Leafe, Bruce and Barbara Horan, Jesse and Kathlene Stence, Sandy and Sheri Claus, and the saints at Grace Bible Church (Houston, Texas). In addition, I am very conscious that no work could be done without prayer, and I am most grateful for my prayer partner Rev. Steve Sullivan and the saints at Faith Bible Church (Spring, Texas), as well as my own congregation at Grace Bible Church (San Marcos, Texas).

Last in this list (but first in my affections), my love to my wife Beverlee, and my children Elisabeth, Eleisha, Erin, Jonathan, and Emilee, who always seem to understand my strange labors and trust the Lord that they will be used for His glory, and to my mother Maurine Price, who, though recently widowed, forgot her own needs to help shoulder my ministry responsibilities so this book could be written.

## Secrets of the Dead Sea Scrolls Video

Join author Dr. Randall Price on a fascinating journey through the Dead Sea caves and community of Qumran! This film version of *Secrets of the Dead Sea Scrolls* includes *material not found in the book* and the first-ever film re-creation of the discovery of the Scrolls in Cave 1 by the Bedouin shepherd who found those very Scrolls, Muhammed edh-Dhib. Also featured are leading Dead Sea Scroll scholars including Emanuel Tov, Shemaryahu Talmon, Magen Broshi, Hanan Eshel, David Flusser, Bargil Pixner, Otto Betz, Weston Fields, Emile Puech, and Stephen Pfann. In addition, the film takes you on location to excavations in search of new Scrolls.

$19.99
(plus $3.95 shipping & handling)

Order your copy today from:
WORLD OF THE BIBLE
MINISTRIES, INC.
110 Easy Street
San Marcos, TX 78666-7326
(512) 396-3799 / FAX (512) 396-1012

---

# The Dead Sea Scrolls Foundation

Would you like to have a part in helping yet-unpublished Dead Sea Scrolls reach publication? Assisting scholars using the latest technology to restore and read damaged Dead Sea Scroll texts? Preserving the Scrolls for future generations? Supporting new explorations and excavations for Dead Sea Scrolls? If so, you can do so through *The Dead Sea Scrolls Foundation*. The foundation is a tax-exempt United States corporation that was formed by the International Team of the Dead Sea Scrolls Committee and is supported by Scroll scholars to receive gifts and disburse funds for the publication and preservation of the Scrolls. For more information, contact Dr. Weston W. Fields, executive director, at one of the addresses below:

### The Dead Sea Scrolls Foundation

| | |
|---|---|
| 5 Mevo Dakkar #14 | P.O. Box 1775 |
| Jerusalem, Israel | Warsaw, IN 46581-1775 |
| Tel: 972-2-819-337 | Tel: 219-269-5223 |
| Fax: 972-2-829-704 | Fax: 219-269-2824 |